RUNNING STEEL,
RUNNING
AMERICA

RUNNING
RUNNING
STEEL, AMERICA

Race,
Economic
Policy,
and the
Decline of
Liberalism

The
University
of North
Carolina
Press

Chapel Hill
and London

JUDITH STEIN

This book was set in Minion by G & S Typesetters, Inc.

Book design by April Leidig-Higgins

The paper in this book meets the guidelines for perma-
nence and durability of the Committee on Production
Guidelines for Book Longevity of the Council on Library
Resources.

Library of Congress Cataloging-in-Publication Data

Stein, Judith, 1940–   Running steel, running America:
race, economic policy and the decline of Liberalism / by
Judith Stein.

p.   cm.   Includes bibliographical references and index.

ISBN 0-8078-2414-3 (cloth: alk. paper)

ISBN 0-8078-4727-5 (pbk. : alk. paper)

1. Steel industry and trade—United States—History.

2. United States—Economic conditions—1945–

3. United States—Social conditions—1945–   4. United
States—Race relations. I. Title.

HD515.S734   1998   97-32600

338.4′7669142′097309045—dc21   CIP

Portions of Chapters 2, 9, and 10 appeared, in somewhat
different form, in two essays previously published by
the author: "Southern Workers in National Unions:
Birmingham Steelworkers, 1936–1951," in *Organized Labor
in the Twentieth-Century South*, ed. Robert H. Zieger
(Knoxville: University of Tennessee Press, 1991); and
"The Locomotive Loses Power: The Trade and Industrial
Policies of Jimmy Carter," in *The Carter Presidency: Policy
Choices in the Post–New Deal Era*, ed. Gary M. Fink and
Hugh Davis Graham (Lawrence: University Press of
Kansas, 1998). They are are reprinted here by permission
of the publishers.

02 01 00 99 98   5 4 3 2 1

For Anne S. Stein
friend and mother

CONTENTS

ILLUSTRATIONS

While researching and writing this book, I have incurred a hefty debt to many institutions and individuals. I wish to thank the National Endowment for the Humanities, the American Council of Learned Societies, the Fund for the Study of Labor Relations Studies, the Lyndon B. Johnson Library, the City University Research Foundation, and the Eisner Fund at City College for providing the financial support and time off from teaching that allowed me to travel and write.

Presidential libraries are essential mines for every aspect of postwar history, but making good use of them requires expert guidance. The archivists at the Lyndon B. Johnson and Jimmy Carter libraries were especially helpful to me. President Richard M. Nixon's papers are at the National Archives repository in College Park, Maryland. I used them when they were in Alexandria, Virginia, where the staff, working under difficult circumstances, gave me knowledgeable, essential advice.

The National Archives was a crucial repository. Its collections of the records of the Department of Labor and the Office of Management and Budget were critical for tracking general policy as well as particular employment discrimination cases. Bill Creech was an expert guide to this material. Still, much material documenting the recent past remains in individual government departments, not in the Archives. Nelson Hermilla and Richard Ugelow at the Justice Department located critical files on the steel consent decrees of 1974. Elaine Bloomfield, a lawyer at the Equal Employment Opportunity Commission (EEOC), sent me a statistical breakdown of the impact of the consent decrees. Historian Hugh Graham generously gave me a copy of EEOC minutes, which had disappeared from the agency files. (Thanks to both of us, EEOC now has a copy.) Unfortunately, EEOC records are unorganized and difficult to use. Thomas J. Schlageter somehow located EEOC files on the steel industry for me.

Although the relevant records of steel companies are unavailable, the minutes of the board of director's meetings of the American Iron and Steel Institute, the industry's trade association, have recently been made available at the Hagley Museum and Library in Wilmington, Delaware. Corporate documents and opinion turn up in congressional hearings and the records of all branches of the government, the union, and civil rights organizations. In addition, articles in the business and trade press were essential, especially those in *Iron Age*, *American Metal Market*, the *Wall Street Journal*,

ACKNOWLEDGMENTS

Fortune, Business Week, and various publications of the American Iron and Steel Institute. I also made extensive use of the 51-volume transcript of *United States v. U.S. Steel et al.* 271 F. Supp. 1045 (N.D. Ala., 1973) at the National Archives in East Pointe, Georgia, a treasure trove of company policy at U.S. Steel's Fairfield Works.

The records of the United Steelworkers of America (USWA) are deposited in the Historical Collections and Labor Archives of Pattee Library at Penn State. First Peter Gottlieb and then Diana Shenk and Denise Conklin made this vast collection, and other related ones, accessible to me. Union officials have been uniquely generous in permitting me to use materials still in their possession. E. B. Rich, at the time subdistrict director of District 36 in Fairfield, Alabama, gave me full access to all the records in his office. Few historians of recent history have had such unfiltered access to the relevant documents. The union's secretaries and staff not only tolerated my presence in the office but helped me find sources and shared with me their own experiences. Jerome Cooper, the lawyer for the USWA in Birmingham, kindly allowed me to use his files and spent many hours talking with me. Bernard Kleiman, the lawyer for the international, retrieved the civil rights files of the USWA Legal Department, which were stored in a defunct coal mine outside of Pittsburgh. John Sheehan allowed me to use the records of the Legislation Department at the USWA's office in Washington, D.C. (Since then they have been deposited with the other USWA records at Penn State.)

James Seay sent me the papers of his friend Clarence Duncan, an early leader in the black caucus in Fairfield, Alabama. I have Fred Shepherd, a union staffperson, to thank for this gift, and I am grateful to both men. Mike Locker of Locker Associates not only spoke to me about his role with the union in the 1980s, but gave me copies of the economic studies he has made for the union since the 1980s.

It goes without saying that the labor files of the National Association for the Advancement of Colored People (NAACP) and the National Urban League and the civil rights files of the AFL-CIO (American Federation of Labor–Congress of Industrial Organizations) were indispensable. Linda DeLoach and the staff at the George Meany Archives helped by processing ahead of schedule some key civil rights files that I needed. Napoleon Bonaparte Williams III guided my search for NAACP Legal and Educational Defense Fund papers. Marvin Y. Whiting, director of Special Collections, was an unusually friendly guide to the rich resources of the Birmingham Public Library.

Oral history is not everything, but this book could not have been written without the help of participants. The following people not only answered my questions and gave me the benefit of their reflections but also gave me leads to other people to interview. I offer a collection thank-you to them all: Jim

Balanoff, Edgar Ball, Leonard Bierman, John C. Bird, Alfred Blumrosen, Paul Bowron Jr., A. C. Burtramm, U. W. Clemon, Jerome Cooper, Christopher Dixie, John Feild, David Feller, Ben Fischer, Michael R. Fontham, James C. Forman Jr., Iva Watts Goodwin, Joshua Gotbaum, Michael Gottesman, Jack Greenberg, Erwin Griswold, Robert Fowler Hall, Asbury Howard Jr., William Kilberg, Bernard Kleiman, Michael Locker, Robert C. Lynn, Luther McKinstry, Marion Martin, Jared Meyer, Robert Moore, R. B. Murphee, Winn Newman, Demetrius Newton, Virgil L. Pearson, Thermon Phillips, Willie George Phillips, Samuel C. Pointer, N. Thompson Powers, Tater Reed, E. B. Rich, Freddie Rogers, Richard Schubert, James Seay, John Sheehan, Fred Shepherd, Laurence Silberman, Jim Smith, Earl Spence, Howard Strevel, James Swindle, Edward Sylvester Jr., Bruce Thrasher, James Ward, Bennie Whitfield, Jimmie Lee Williams, Charles H. Wilson, W. Willard Wirtz, and Sylvester Wright.

Historians are still important in the writing of history, and this manuscript has been lucky to have had the benefit of readings by Eric Arnesen, David Brody, and Robert H. Zieger. They know that I have not always followed their advice, but I tried to respond to their suggestions. Lizabeth Cohen, Eric Foner, Nelson Lichtenstein, and Adolph L. Reed Jr. sharpened individual chapters and ideas. Readers will appreciate the work of Barbara Probst Solomon, who improved the entire manuscript. Mitchell Harris, my graduate assistant at the City University of New York, did some important checking for me, and I thank Barbara Brooks for translating the Japanese posters in the illustration in Chapter 8. Finally, Lewis Bateman, at the University of North Carolina Press, was enthusiastic from the beginning. He and assistant editor Mary E. Laur always offered wise and friendly counsel. I was very fortunate that Katherine Malin copyedited the manuscript.

The following abbreviations are used in the text. Those used in the notes appear at the beginning of the Notes section.

NAACP	National Association for the Advancement of Colored People
NAM	National Association of Manufacturers
NIC	newly industrializing country
NLRB	National Labor Relations Board
OECD	Organization for Economic Cooperation and Development
OFCC	Office of Contract Compliance
OMB	Office of Management and Budget
OPEC	Organization of Petroleum Exporting Countries
PCEEO	President's Committee on Equal Employment Opportunity
STAC	Steel Tripartite Advisory Committee
STR	Special Trade Representative
SUB	supplementary unemployment benefit
TAA	trade adjustment assistance
TCI	Tennessee, Coal, Iron and Railroad Company
TPM	trigger-price mechanism
UAW	United Autoworkers of America
UMW	United Mine Workers of America
USWA	United Steelworkers of America
VRA	voluntary restraint agreement
WOP	War on Poverty

RUNNING RUNNING STEEL, AMERICA

I deposited my Alamo rental car at the Ramada Inn. The driver who shuttled me to the Birmingham airport for my return trip to New York was an African American man about nineteen or twenty years old. He told me that he had been a student at a local community college but that his real ambition was to work at USX's Fairfield steelworks. The mill, outside of Birmingham, had employed 27,000 workers during World War II. About 2,400 men and women worked there now.

I learned that he had grown up in Ishkooda, a nearby town adjacent to the U.S. Steel ore mines, which had employed his grandfather. Substituting Venezuelan ore for Alabaman, the corporation had closed its mines in the state in 1962. The United Steelworkers of America (USWA), which also represented the miners, had obtained jobs for the unemployed workers in the steel mills. His grandfather had transferred to Fairfield Steel, and his father now worked in the pipe mill, built in the 1980s to supply the booming oil business. He was biding his time with minimum-wage work, like the job with Alamo, until USX started hiring again. When I asked about the likelihood of his getting a job at the mill, he replied pensively, "Well, there are a lot of men on layoff."

Perhaps he will work for USX, train for something else, or remain a driver at Alamo. But his family's history is a variation of the story of many Alabama families, white as well as black. Other versions reach the newspapers in the form of crime statistics. Parents and grandparents in Birmingham puzzle over both the behavior and the futures of the current generation. Some of the sons and daughters of industrial Birmingham are lawyers, doctors, and business managers, but they are a select few. For the majority, job prospects have shrunk. When Trico, a new steel minimill, began hiring in North Alabama, thousands sought the few hundred jobs. Applications for work at a new Mercedes auto plant near Tuscaloosa are as lengthy as any submitted to an Ivy League college. All workers find that the rules of the game have changed: health insurance, pensions, unions, and permanent work are novelties, not givens.

My driver's story straddles two histories: that of a changing economy and that of changing race relations. The two narratives usually feature different sets of actors and appear in separate books or separate chapters. The first emphasizes the state, industry, and unions; the second, the state and civil rights organizations. The first is about economic policy, the second about social policy. The first is populated by ethnics and whites; the second by blacks and sometimes recent immigrants. But real lives lived cannot be split into the historians' categories. One problem of writing the history of post–New Deal America is that the subject appears near enough in time to be seen through the narrow lens of contemporary politics.

Presidential biographies have now become surrogates for histories of the era. But biography is not history. The inevitable concentration on the individual presidents, fenced in by the calendar of presidential terms, makes it impossible to capture broad trends. Take trade. Though every biographer of John F. Kennedy discusses his legislative priority of 1962, passing the Trade Expansion Act of 1962, which aimed to reverse the U.S. balance of payments deficit, none evaluates the results of the law, because the negotiations launched by the legislation ended in 1967, during Lyndon B. Johnson's presidency. Johnson's biographers do not talk about trade because they track primarily his big decisions, of which there were many in 1967.[1] The issue of globalization in the 1960s is addressed only in specialized books on trade.

Monographs on trade and others on labor, business, civil rights, and politics also serve to keep history in discrete channels. It is not that historians are tunnel-visioned, but that sources for twentieth-century history are so voluminous. As more and more players, each with an enormous paper trail, participate in any significant event, even historians, the most hard-working researchers in the academic world, often throw up their hands. Increasingly historians are relying upon the sources generated by the subjects of their research, which means that they, like the presidential biographers, assimilate the worldview and experiences of their sources but not of others. Many contemporary histories convey little sense of options and alternatives and contain few independent evaluations of major events and decisions. Connections are lost. History is impoverished.

This state of affairs has produced five distinct narratives of the postwar world, all of them tales of the declension of New Deal liberalism.[2] The first narrative ends the story before this book begins, arguing that by 1945 the reforming impulse of the New Deal had ended.[3] The second claims that the excesses of the 1960s produced a reaction that undid the political coalition sustaining liberalism.[4] The third inverts the second; that is, defenders of the social movements of the 1960s argue that the conservatism and racism of the populace, both predating the 1960s, produced the reaction against liberalism.[5] A fourth asserts that the political culture of the 1950s and 1960s faltered when faced with the stagflation of the mid-1970s.[6] The fifth concludes that imperial overreaching downed the postwar order.[7] Each view offers insight, and many surveys tender a judicious eclecticism.[8] However, the empirical work that in the end must inform overarching interpretations consists of studies of different people, institutions, places, and times. Because the interpretive narratives are supported by narrow empirical studies, they cannot engage the other interpretations.

This book assesses these narratives by examining the history of the industry that attracted three generations of my driver's family. Although the postwar world was not only built of steel, the steel companies, the steelworkers union, and steelworkers were at the center of the New Deal compact between capital and labor, the racial changes in the 1950s and 1960s, and the economic crises and reconstructions of the 1970s and 1980s. These three historical experiences encompass key elements of current interpretations of mid-century U.S. history. Analyzing them in one industry over time offers a way to consider the merits of each.

The social welfare legacy of the New Deal is well-known, but its economic legacy has been mired in a debate over national planning.[9] Whether or not there was a potential for more extensive state planning has displaced a discussion of how the state actually did shape the economy. During the period covered in this book, most steel-producing nations owned or financed their industries according to national goals. The United States seemed to be an exception. However, both Democrats and Republicans believed that an adequate supply of cheap steel was a public matter. That they did not directly manage the industry does not mean that government policies did not shape the market for steel, define industrial options, and influence the quantity and site of investment. The state intervened on a wide range of issues—capacity, prices, wages, industrial structure, and employment practices. It acted to fulfill traditional goals like regional dispersal and competition, the post-New Deal objective of high employment, and later the fair employment mandate of the 1960s. Because the steel industry was judged to be fundamental, affecting the whole economy, the government often used the industry as a lever to effect changes in the macroeconomy. Presidents of both parties jawboned industry leaders and marshaled public opinion to keep prices down, assuming that rising steel prices caused inflation.

Foreign policy was treated as a separate sphere. At the outset of the Cold War, reconstructing or creating steel industries abroad was a keystone of U.S. strategic policy, and encouraging steel imports became a tool for maintaining vital alliances. The nation's leaders by and large ignored the resulting conflict between Cold War and domestic goals. Reminiscing about elite thinking in that era, former Federal Reserve Board chairman Paul A. Volcker recalled that "the strength and prosperity of the American economy was too evident to engender concern about the costs" of the new foreign policy.[10] I would add that there was also little concern about what was needed to maintain the marriage between modernization and working-class progress, the essence of New Deal liberalism. Foreign economic policy did not create that problem; it only made it more difficult to resolve.

I begin by discussing the stormy history of implementing the New Deal changes in the steel industry up until 1964, when many of the conflicts seemed to be resolved by the Keynesian tax cut signed by Lyndon Johnson. In the short run, the resulting boom ended the conflicts between labor and industry over wages and between the state and industry over prices. Fostering modernization in the steel industry and the economy as a whole, the tax cut and the subsequent economic expansion strengthened the notion of affluence accepted by those on the left and right during the 1960s. This complacency about the engine of progress shaped the goals, rhetoric, and methods of the government and reformers alike.

The mid-1960s boom framed the way the culture addressed the major social issue of the decade, civil rights, which emerged first in South. Examining the situation at U.S. Steel's mill outside of Birmingham, Alabama, reveals how the notion of affluence shaped the government's understanding of black unemployment and underemployment. By attributing them to bigotry, an extra-economic factor, the formulation led policymakers to overlook the radical changes transforming the South—agricultural and industrial mechanization.

The notion of affluence informed both Title VII of the Civil Rights Act of 1964, which prohibited employment discrimination, and the "War on Poverty," which provided various kinds of youth training. The former ignored the broader economic forces that diminished the work of current steelworkers and potential ones, refugees from the farms who in the past had found employment in the mills; the latter ignored the diminished supply and changing character of work in the cities—in Birmingham, Alabama, but also in Gary, Indiana. Although a diverse group of politicians, activists, and academics advocated more active labor market policies, they were overwhelmed by the dominant policymakers. The neo-Keynesian consensus accepted the idea that the pricing system in the aggregate was imperfect, yielding sluggish growth and high unemployment; thus, they were interventionist in the macroeconomy. But because they believed that labor markets performed adequately, they were laissez-faire in the microeconomy. The market, not government, would redeploy labor, they argued. Prohibiting bigotry was in harmony with this project because prejudice interfered with the proper functioning of the labor market.

However, the policies arising from this formulation did not produce sufficient black jobs in the critical cities. After big riots in Newark and Detroit in 1967, government and business leaders broadened their definition of discrimination and realized that solutions to the problem had to include providing for more black employment. Redrawing the national political landscape according to the covalent dualisms white/black, suburbs/slums, and affluent/poor made it impossible to resolve working-class questions, as we shall see in the histories of two Bethlehem steel mills, one in Lackawanna, New York, the other in Sparrows Point, Maryland. Nevertheless, in 1974 the union, government, and industry produced consent decrees that answered the question, what is fair employment in the steel industry? The settlement, which rejected previous solutions that assumed a unique black experience, addressed a present reality of declining work as well as a past reality of racially discriminatory hiring. By the mid-1970s, the state and society had fashioned the basic formulas for fair employment.

However, social policy—in the form of fair employment, education, or welfare—was not a surrogate for economic policy. Just as the Keynesian boom and the declining, aggregate unemployment rates obscured labor market questions, the rising economic growth rates camouflaged trends in different sectors. The final chapters of the book discuss how U.S. foreign policy combined with Keynesian economic policies taxed the steel industry and manufacturing in general.

In 1975, one year after the consent decrees were signed, the nation experienced a sharp recession in the wake of soaring OPEC oil prices. This contraction pressed on every weakness afflicting the U.S. economy. The stagflation of the 1970s exacerbated conflicts between domestic and international economic goals, which had been manageable during the years of global economic growth. The agenda now was to restore American affluence, which had been taken for granted earlier.

During the 1970s and 1980s, steel became the center of a national debate on industrial policy and trade. As the nation decided what to do about the steel industry, it was forced to confront the question it had ignored after the war: how do you sustain a high-wage, technologically modern industry? Democrats had assumed that the key to growth was aggregate demand, ignoring the role of public investment in R&D, the ties industry enjoyed with the technical and scientific culture of universities, relations between labor and management, and the link between profit and innovation. This Democratic tradition shaped President Jimmy Carter's response to two steel crises. In the end, Carter rejected the sectoral measures needed to restore growth and made matters worse by opting for international objectives at the expense of domestic ones. His choices not only cost Carter the election in 1980 but permitted Democratic constituencies to shop about for other solutions, candidates, and parties.

From the ruins of the old order, a new one was constructed. President Ronald Reagan propped up sectors that had been outside New Deal relationships and undermined industries, like steel, that had been at their center. Without the weight of industries like steel, market ideologies reflecting favored sectors filled the vacuum. The nation replaced the assumption of the earlier era that capital and labor would prosper together with an ethic that postulated that promoting capital would eventually benefit labor, a very different way of running a nation.

The final chapter uses the story of steel to present an alternative narrative of the postwar era. Because history is not a detective story, I will state my conclusion here: it was the foreign commitments and economic policies of liberalism, not the excesses of racial reformers or the racism of the culture, that transformed American politics in the postwar era. The New Deal was a democratic and modernizing project. Strained and stretched during the 1960s, New Deal liberalism nevertheless proved capacious enough to include African Americans and women and to sustain the shock of the Vietnam war. It fell apart in 1980 because Democratic elites did not devise a modernization project compatible with the interests of their working-class base. That failure continues today.

I hope that my argument about how we got to this point will encourage those who may not agree with my final judgments about the contemporary world to attend to the genuine problems that lead to my conclusions. The young man who drove me to the Birmingham airport was intelligent and hardworking, possessed reasonable goals, and carried the values of his family, yet he was still having trouble in the new economy. He deserves a better future.

The Politics of Steel
Fundamentalism:
The Long 1950s

I n 1951 Benjamin F. Fairless, chairman and CEO of U.S. Steel, proclaimed that the American steel industry "is bigger than those of *all* the other nations on earth put together." Fairless praised workers and managers, saying their joint achievement "stands as a glorious tribute to the men who make steel and the men who built steel in America." The causes were not as self-evident as the chairman implied, and his arithmetic was imperfect, but the supremacy was real. In that year, for the first time the industry produced over 100 million tons of steel, about 45 percent of the world's total output. Measured by technology, size, and efficiency, the United States was the leading global producer. Fairless, like the nation, had feared a return to the economic stagnation of the 1930s after World War II. But buoyant consumer demand and later the military spending that accompanied the Korean War dramatically altered gloomy forecasts, allowing the normally dour chairman to express the pride of the industry.[1]

U.S. Steel itself accounted for nearly 30 percent of the nation's output, a sizable figure but lower than the two-thirds share it held earlier in the century. Over 250 companies made steel, but twelve controlled 80 percent of the capacity. These twelve, and other integrated firms, performed three operations: made pig-iron in blast furnaces, turned the iron into steel in open-hearth furnaces, and cast or rolled the steel into different shapes, such as sheets, plates, structural beams, rails, bars, and pipes. The execution of these three main operations on one site was the most efficient means of production. Some of the largest companies, especially U.S. Steel and number-two Bethlehem Steel, also owned ore and coal mines, limestone quarries, and other raw materials necessary to produce steel. At the other end of the cycle, they fabricated products like bridges and ships. But in the main, the companies sold steel to other manufacturers.[2]

The steel they made reflected the growth of new markets. Workers cooked and poured, dipped and bathed, rolled and coiled rivers of steel for the automobile, appliance, and food-processing industries. They made structural beams to gird new office towers and steel sidings for houses and warehouses. They pressed and welded steel plate into huge arteries of oil and natural gas, which were rapidly replacing coal throughout the economy. They made steel for earth-moving equipment and urban infrastructure as well as for newer computers and household gadgets. The industry's downstream additions tapped new consumer markets. In 1944, U.S. Steel acquired an interest in Gunning Housing Corporation, a pioneer in prefabricated homes. It subsequently sold its subsidiary Federal Shipbuilding and Dry Dock Company to the Navy, and later did the same with its steamship company. In the new America, houses were in, ships were out.[3]

The twentieth-century trend that shifted production from Pennsylvania to the Midwest, the industrial core of the nation, continued. But steel output increased in every region. West coast facilities, constructed during the war to produce plates for ships, now supplied steel for the region's growing cities and canning industries. New mills in Texas supplied the oil and gas industry. Older ones in Alabama were supermarkets for an industrializing South.

Fairless's optimism, matched by that of many other industrialists, added up to a utopian vision of the American, even the global, future. In 1955, the decade's peak year for steel production, a group of British industrialists spent several weeks studying American steel foundries and returned singing the praises of the industry's use of technology, manpower, and time. The magazine *Fortune* believed their appraisal heralded a social and cultural revolution:

> Man-made abundance is making the average man wealthy by the standards of fifty years ago, swiftly eliminating poverty and distress, stamping out disease, prolonging life, undermining useless or obsolete institutions, building up useful ones, helping other nations to struggle up the difficult and often disappointing road to efficiency, creating more and more leisure, and changing swiftly and radically the tastes and habits of the people world over. Nothing, perhaps, has altered the world more in all the history of Western civilization than rising American productivity has in the last half century.[4]

Fortune's giddy projections were exaggerated, but they were not invented. Recall the situation of the typical steelworker on the eve of Pearl Harbor. His income reached 80 percent of the cost of maintaining the following modest standard of living for a family of four or five: a new coat for each parent every six years, a new pair of shoes every two, two-and-a-half shirts for the husband and two dresses for the wife each year, a rented apartment of five or six rooms, and an old used car. In 1942, 15 percent of steelworkers had lived in homes without running water and 30 percent had no indoor bathroom.[5]

During the fifteen years after the war, rising productivity advanced the GNP 37 percent in real terms, and the wage component of national income rose slightly. Disposable income increased 15 percent in real dollars. Three-fifths of all families had discretionary income. Steelworkers obtained paid vacations, holidays, pensions, and health insurance, which became norms of working-class life. For the generation that had lived through the Great Depression these improvements and the low unemployment seemed miraculous. During the 1930s, jobless rates ranged from 14 to 25 percent; in the 1950s the average was 4.6 percent.[6]

Many workers now were homeowners living outside of the cities. *Fortune* called blue-collar suburbanites "the new masses." By 1960 the number of suburbanites equaled the number of city dwellers. Fourteen of fifteen cities with more than 1 million people lost population during the 1950s. The migrations were made possible by higher wages, thirty-year GI mortgages, the application of mass-production techniques to home-building, federal highway construction, and corporate decisions to locate operations away from cities. Young, large families provided a ready market for all sorts of household goods that had been out of the reach of their parents. The washing machine, refrigerator, and vacuum cleaner had come to the working class, along with novelties that some made the signature of the era: color TV in 1953, all-transistor radios and polyurethane foams in 1955, synthetic diamonds in 1957, and stereophonic records in 1958. The automobile became the vehicle of choice. Americans owned 40 million cars in 1950, 62 million by 1960. They would eventually travel on 41,000 miles of fast roads—turnpikes, freeways, thruways—planned by the Interstate Highway Act of 1956.[7]

The academy added an approving voice. "Convergence theory" was based upon economist Simon Kuznets's argument that earning disparities declined as productivity increased. In plain language, class would no longer be a salient division in American life. Many liberals agreed and abandoned the union movement that no longer seemed to be the underdog.[8] Left-wingers sometimes disposed of workers along with their Marxism. The ex-Socialist Daniel Bell, then a writer at *Fortune*, sympathized with the "unorganized middle-class" and "petits rentiers."[9]

Intellectuals discovered new afflictions. Rising living standards transformed the mass political and economic opposition of the 1930s and 1940s into elite psychological and aesthetic dissent. The young African American novelist Paule Marshall and white anthropologist Eleanor Leacock complained that they felt "isolated, . . . powerless to direct our own lives; and increasingly threatened with becoming objects." [10] Others decried banal mass culture, the conformity of "the lonely crowd," and the bureaucratic monotony and status seeking of the corporate world. John Kenneth Galbraith's *The Affluent Society* (1958) lamented the impoverishment of the nation's public sector and exhorted Americans to pursue values more noble than productivity. But Galbraith, like his contemporaries, believed that America had eliminated most of the "uncertainties of economic life." [11]

The German émigré Herbert Marcuse was more critical than Galbraith, but he agreed that western culture had solved the age-old scarcity problem. Marcuse's *Eros and Civilization* (1955) argued only that abundance would not usher in *Fortune*'s utopia. While the technology that produced affluence eliminated the necessity for social and sexual repression, he claimed, the practices and values of the era of scarcity remained. Humans would achieve happiness, Eros would be liberated, only if the organization of production, now termed "surplus repression," ended. How this could be done was another question. [12]

The men who made steel probably never heard of Marcuse, but they agreed that the steel industry was not dedicated to Eros. Still, unlike the philosopher, they were not so certain about the permanence of affluence, despite their public oratory. They worried about markets, labor, and capital, all altered after the war. The health of the steel industry depended on the volatile consumer and producer durable market. Thus, the industry had an unusually strong interest in effective management of business cycles and growth. And although *Fortune* and Kuznets did not credit the birth of mass unionism with working-class progress, others did. The steelmen learned that unlike in the past, wages could not be reduced and work intensified to compensate for downturns or to accumulate investment capital. Finally, to meet increased demand, compete with new materials, and make the kind of steel required by new products, the industry had to expand and modernize, which was expensive, as the capital component of output rose. For the nation, it boiled down to a question of whether the pairing of efficient production and a thriving working class was an enduring or a contingent marriage.

Directly and indirectly, the state shaped the answer. But only in 1964 did the government explicitly intervene to maintain what the celebrants and critics of affluence had assumed was self-generating prosperity. In the short run, the huge Kennedy-Johnson tax cuts did the trick, producing the celebrated prosperity of the decade. But the questions the steel industry had faced from the beginning of the postwar years did not go away.

State and Industry

In the nineteenth century, state intervention in the steel industry was nurturing. During and after the Civil War, the government expanded markets by constructing railroads and legislating tariffs and guaranteed sufficient labor by encouraging immigration. Still, the nation's legal traditions blocked the resolution of the industry's major problem at the end of the century—competition. Steel companies incurred large capital costs and produced a homogeneous product, whose demand was inelastic. During economic downturns, firms cut prices to dispose of their surplus steel. As they did, many firms went under and the others saw the value of their assets decline. American culture and courts frowned upon the prophylactic cartel and other cooperative devices used in other nations.[13] Mergers became the American alternative. After a nasty depression during the 1890s, the steel industry effected a series of combinations, capped by the formation of the United States Steel Corporation, the nation's first billion-dollar company, in 1901.[14]

Mergers created problems for other Americans and inaugurated the nation's regulatory tradition—keeping the market free of the distortions arising from uncompetitive behavior. Many believed that the large corporation was an illegitimate predator, which swallowed rivals, pushed aside traditional suppliers, degraded labor, manipulated the financial system, and corrupted democratic institutions. In 1890, before the creation of U.S. Steel, the Sherman Anti-Trust Act registered popular opposition to big business.[15] In 1914, Congress added the Clayton Act, which targeted specific business practices that promoted concentration and supplemented Justice Department policing by creating the Federal Trade Commission (FTC).

The laws raised as many questions as they answered. As with many economic controversies in the United States, lawyers and the judiciary decided most of them. Courts came down hard on acts like market sharing or price fixing but not on size per se. In 1920, the Supreme Court declared that the attorney general had failed to demonstrate that U.S. Steel engaged in predatory behavior. Bigness itself was not illegal so long as there was "no adventitious interference . . . to either fix or maintain prices."[16] But the threat of prosecutions surely ended any ambition of U.S. Steel to increase its market share, which had fallen from 66 to 40 percent at the time of the court decision. Shortly afterwards, the FTC concluded that the industry's method of quoting prices and freight as if all steel sold originated in Pittsburgh, was monopolistic and put an end to the practice.[17]

Critics who accused the steel industry of monopoly had not followed industrial developments. In fact, the size and dynamics of the economy fostered newcomers. Eyeing Pittsburgh, the center of the U.S. Steel empire, such critics ignored the growing Midwest, where Armco, Inland, Youngstown Sheet and Tube, and Republic grew quickly. At the time of the Supreme Court decision, Charles Schwab had already taken Bethlehem to the front ranks of steelmakers, dominating the markets in the Middle Atlantic region. Subsequent critics necessarily attacked the market behavior of oligopolists, not monopolists.

These early regulatory acts, reflecting the interests of smaller businessmen and farmers, focused on corporate structure. New Dealers targeted mainly the industry's labor relations, especially after workers, aided by the new Congress of Industrial Organization (CIO), began to act on their own. The National Labor Relations Act of 1935 prevented employers from interfering with workers' seeking union organization. Two years later, the Supreme Court ruled the law constitutional in a case involving a Jones and Laughlin steel mill in Aliquippa, Pennsylvania. Just before the decision, U.S. Steel acceded to a new order when it recognized the Steel Workers Organizing Committee, which in 1942 became the United Steelworkers of America (USWA). By the end of World War II, all of the significant companies had come around and negotiated with unions.[18]

The government's endorsement of unions was motivated as much by economics as by social justice and politics. Because unions enabled workers to obtain more of the fruits of their labor than would be unilaterally distributed by management, they helped maintain purchasing power. The growing influence of the British economist John Maynard Keynes, who had turned his profession upside down by attributing the Great Depression to a deficiency in demand, married expertise and politics.

State regulation expanded further during World War II. The government took more of an interest in the specific wage packages produced by collective bargaining. To restrain inflation, the National War Labor Board limited wages in a series of steel cases in 1942. The War Manpower Commission trained and deployed labor. On the other side of the negotiating table, the Office of Price Administration kept the lid on prices, especially steel prices. Going one step further, the Defense Plants Corporation and the Reconstruction Finance Corporation (RFC) financed most of the nation's new investment, fostered industrial growth in the West and South, and promoted competition by funding new companies in steel, aluminum, and other sectors.[19]

After V-J Day, these developmental agencies were dismantled as quickly as possible. However, reflecting the widespread fear that the depression would return, legislation introduced by senators James E. Murray and Robert F. Wagner in 1945 proposed to achieve full employment through compensatory state investment, if necessary. The diluted Employment Act of 1946, which was passed the following year, registered the power of the opponents of the new government authority. The law eliminated Keynesian theory and talk about government investment and retreated from the goal of full employment to one of "maximum employment." It created the Council of Economic Advisers (CEA) to analyze trends and report to the president and the Joint Economic Committee (JEC) of the Congress. But the council was only an advisory body, unconnected to operating agencies and departments, and its obligations were stated so feebly and implemented so traditionally that the commitment lost its bite.[20]

This conventional story of postwar retreat is incomplete. Although the legal mandate was weaker than some had wished, the state did possess considerable power. It is true that except for agriculture, housing, and oil, the government kept its hands off individual sectors. But a plentiful supply of cheap steel was considered a legitimate concern for a government charged with maximizing employment. The debate over steel capacity in the late 1940s better revealed American economic policy than did the symbolic employment legislation. The question was heated because it was laced with talk of nationalization, punctuated by bitter fights over prices and wages, and driven by competing memories: President Harry S. Truman and the Democrats recalled the industry's reluctance to expand at the onset of World War II; steelmakers remembered operating at 20 percent of capacity in the early 1930s.

Steel capacity had declined from 1945 to 1947, largely due to the retirement of older plants that had been brought into service during the war. When domestic orders continued strong and the demands of foreign nations with war-damaged plants taxed supply, government officials urged more steel capacity. The industry began to expand, but in 1949, Truman, responding to temporary shortages, urged Congress to study the availability of "materials in critically short supply, such as steel." The president proposed loaning money to existing firms or constructing facilities "if action by private industry fails to meet our needs." Congressman Wright Patman and Senator Murray introduced the Economic Expansion Bill, authorizing government plants in critical industrial sectors, especially steel. Truman did not back the legislation; he dropped the subject in the middle of the year, when the economy weakened. But hearings before the Joint Economic Committee and a House subcommittee on monopoly power threatened to break up U.S. Steel, require government approval of price increases, and the like.[21]

Louis H. Bean, speaking for the government, acknowledged that steel production was at an all-time high, but unlike Fairless, Bean believed the figure was a sign of inadequacy, not success. He assumed that "changes in steel output and changes in gross national product . . . tend to be closely matched." Going one step further, he asserted that steel production drove the economy. For a government seeking full employment, it seemed logical to demand more steel capacity.[22]

That Bean was an agricultural economist and that many of the other government spokesmen lacked knowledge of the industry increased the steelmen's skepticism. From their perspective, U.S. demand was uncertain and the future of the European steel industries unresolved. Moreover, the industry's conversion of facilities that had produced military products to mills making civilian items did not alter total capacity, but it did increase the industry's capacity to serve the civilian market, which was the government's key concern. Expansion involved a host of issues—transportation, raw materials, product, and location—that the government ignored. The weakness of the postwar planning impulse, and of economic policymaking in general, stemmed from its macroeconomic approach to microeconomic, sectoral problems.[23]

The outbreak of the Korean War in June 1950 ended the government-industry conflict without resolving underlying issues. To meet its military needs, the government offered carrots, not sticks. As in World War II, the goal was competition and regional dispersal as well as increased tonnage for military goods. Smaller mills obtained RFC loans. But the main spur for the big ones was accelerated depreciation. Increased taxation during World War II gave the government new power to use the incentives and penalties of the tax code to obtain the goods the nation needed. Approved new plants and equipment related to defense needs could be written off in five years as opposed to the standard twenty to twenty-five.

As a result, from 1950 to 1954 steel capacity increased 24 percent. U.S. Steel built a new integrated mill on the Delaware River near Philadelphia, poised to challenge Bethlehem in the East Coast market. The mill was well situated to receive ore from its new Venezuelan holdings and to ship steel via the Panama Canal to the growing western market. National Steel announced plans to enter the eastern market with a plant near Fairless, and Bethlehem expanded capacity at its mill in Sparrows Point, Maryland. Bethlehem hoped to merge with Youngstown Sheet and Tube to compete with U.S. Steel in the Midwest. But in 1950, mergers were made more difficult by a tough new amendment to the Clayton Act, sponsored by Senator Estes Kefauver and Congressman Emanuel Celler. A federal court rejected the proposed marriage and Bethlehem instead began building a new mill at Burns Harbor, Indiana, in 1962.[24]

The government's aims were realized. Capacity grew nearly 50 percent during the decade, new companies entered the market, and the big ones seemed to be competing against each other.[25] The American way of doing business worked. What was its essence? U.S. industrial policy was effected through tax incentives, usually granted to meet defense needs. But there were other goals. All three branches of government implemented policy according to principles of antimonopolism and regional dispersal, continuing the twentieth-century regulatory tradition that assumed the steel industry was healthy, but what was good for the steel industry was not necessarily good for the economy. When facts demonstrated that steel growth not only did not drive the GNP but lagged behind it, the nation came to believe that steel prices and wages determined the inflation rate. The government assumed that the steel industry's actions affected the macroeconomy, not the other way around. Moreover, Keynesians were experts on aggregates, not on their composition. The CEA began gathering and analyzing data on industrial sectors only in 1975. Such willed ignorance resulted from the conclusion that the information was unnecessary. Because the steel industry often disagreed with the state's analysis and expressed its dissent in ideological language—championing free enterprise as opposed to socialism—conflicts, especially with Democratic presidents, were frequent and high-profile.

The Union

Philip Murray, like Fairless, had much to be proud of after the war. In 1936, John L. Lewis, president of the United Mineworkers of America (UMW), selected Murray to head the campaign to organize steelworkers. Overshadowed by the larger-than-life Lewis, Murray and numerous dedicated men and women organized an industry that had operated without unions ever since Andrew Carnegie had eliminated the Amalgamated Association of Iron, Steel, and Tin Workers from his mill in Homestead, Pennsylvania, in 1892.[26] Murray and Lewis worked together well until Lewis refused to support Roosevelt's reelection in 1940. Promising to resign his presidency of the CIO if FDR won, Lewis was true to his word. Murray became president of the CIO and then president of the USWA at its founding convention in 1942.[27] Where Lewis was regal and imperious, Murray was modest and plainspoken. With his thick Scottish brogue, he never let anyone forget that the mission of unions was, in the end, to "eliminate those hovels and slums in steel districts."[28]

The USWA represented workers in nearly all of the integrated companies, in many steel fabricators, and in ore mines. Adding aluminum workers in 1944, the union saw its membership rise to well over 1 million. During World War II, the union jockeyed between the restrictions of war and the needs of its members, between an incipient social democracy and the traditional voluntarism of the labor movement. Murray had proposed tripartite councils composed of representatives from labor, business, and government to plan wartime production, but Roosevelt dispatched labor leaders to advisory bodies and cast them in trouble-shooting roles. Many unionists believed that the National War Labor Board unduly limited steel wages. Hourly wages for steelworkers rose 40 percent, compared to a 55 percent increase for all manufacturing workers. These statistics and the bureaucracy of the new order led USWA vice president

Van Bittner and others to welcome the return of "old fashioned unionism." It was not to be.[29]

Murray would have preferred a general CIO bargaining strategy with employers after the war, but a Truman-sponsored labor-management conference failed to reach a consensus. Business preferred to go it alone, believing it had more to gain from autonomy. A key issue was wages, because ending the war had also ended overtime, which reduced average worker income by 30 percent. The big three metals unions—the USWA, the United Automobile Workers (UAW), and the United Electrical, Radio and Machine Workers (UE)—had to pull 1 million workers off the job in 1946, leading to the largest strike wave in U.S. history, to convince the companies that union workers were here to stay and merited wage increases of between 15 and 20 percent.

Steel strikes in 1949, 1952, 1955, 1956, and 1959 were signs that hard issues were unresolved. But real hourly earnings increased by 50 percent during the 1950s. In 1949, workers had obtained company-financed pensions and health insurance. In 1956, at the height of the decade's prosperity, they won supplementary unemployment benefits (SUBS) to preserve income during steel's cyclical layoffs and a cost-of-living adjustment (COLA) to protect wages from inflation.[30]

Obtaining "fringe benefits" through collective bargaining was a sign of the political weakness of the labor movement, which contemporaries barely noticed. Murray told his executive board in 1947, a year after Republican election victories, that Congress "is not going to improve federal social security legislation." Rank-and-file demands for pensions, health insurance, and better protection from unemployment meant that social welfare became an obligation of industry, not of the state. Union leaders believed that the costs of the benefits would force companies to support public provisioning. Unfortunately, they were wrong and simply gave unorganized industries other reasons to oppose unions. Collective bargaining carried the burden of social welfare and eventually those of technological change and industrial restructuring as well.[31]

It was not that the USWA was uninterested in politics. But unions were a lot stronger in the plants than in Congress. Lee Pressman, chief counsel to the USWA and CIO in 1946, observed that the recent strike wave had convinced industry that it "can't meet our organization on an economic front. . . . So they have shifted [to the political] arenas where admittedly we are weak."[32] He was correct. Labor seemed potent. Union members composed about one-third of the nonagricultural labor force. Two of every three manufacturing workers were in a union. But the labor movement was divided ideologically, limited geographically, and excluded from real influence in the Democratic party.

First, the American Federation of Labor (AFL), the older union organization, was as opposed as business was to collaboration with the state. AFL head

William Green and the independent John L. Lewis accused Murray of seeking a "corporate state." The AFL's constituent unions were better able to rely upon market power to achieve their goals. But they distrusted the state also because New Dealers usually preferred the CIO to the AFL. In 1945, the AFL's voluntarism was backed up by 7 million members, which exceeded the CIO's 5 million. AFL unions grew faster than those of the CIO because the postwar economy produced more work in construction, transportation, and service employment than in manufacturing.[33]

Moreover, political power required union density throughout the nation, given the system of territorial representation. But unions were concentrated in the manufacturing belts of the North, Midwest, and West Coast. More than two-thirds of union members lived in ten states. Industrialization and unionization proceeded rapidly in the South during World War II. However, the ending of wartime regulations permitted southern elites, eager to attract industry, to reassert their traditional antiunionism. The USWA had unionized the southern steel industry, beginning with the U.S. Steel mill outside of Birmingham, Alabama, in 1937. But in the South as a whole, the rate of unionization was half that in the nation. In 1946, the CIO launched Operation Dixie to organize the South. To Van Bittner, the head of the campaign, success would not only change the region but achieve "greater control for labor and the common people all over America." The drive, in the main, failed, producing no political breakthrough in either the South or the nation.[34]

But it was not simply the weight of southern Democrats that undermined union efforts. The CIO reached an arrangement with the Democrats, but it was more a shotgun marriage than a love match. Truman had disappointed the USWA, as well as many liberals. But Republican victories in 1946 gave the GOP control of both houses of Congress for the first time since 1931. Legislators, coached by business groups across the country, translated the public displeasure with the strike wave into a crusade to trim union power. The Taft-Hartley Act of 1947 did not directly affect big unions like the USWA, but by strengthening employers' rights, regulating and limiting the scope of strikes and interunion solidarity, and allowing states to deny protections like the union shop, the law made it more difficult to organize new workers and to maintain small unions. In the long run, the law affected the entire labor movement. Casting aside qualms about Truman, the CIO backed him because he had vetoed the legislation. To obtain the two-thirds vote to override the promised Truman veto, proponents were forced to write a bill that was less restrictive than a majority wanted.[35]

The CIO was stymied by the party as well as by the president. The Democratic party structure, organized around city, county, and state organizations, predated the unions. George L. P. Weaver, a black CIO official, complained that "the policy-making body of the Party" was dominated by "the big city organizations," while labor was forced to argue in "public forums," not "party councils." Weaver and other CIO leaders envisioned a variation of a labor party. This is not to argue that the aim was realistic, only to document the CIO's frustration with the Democrats, which cast it in the role of pressure group. If the unions relied on collective bargaining, it was because political options were meager.[36]

Some historians have concluded that the expulsion of Communist-led unions in 1949 and 1950 was the cause of subsequent labor weakness.[37] That judgment gives Communists a greater role in the labor movement than the record justifies. The significant benchmarks of conservative resurgence—the still-born extensions of the New Deal and the Taft-Hartley retreat—preceded the ouster. The politics of business and agriculture and the structure of the party were more important factors. And although union fratricide undoubtedly weakened labor, the more significant division was between the AFL and CIO. The merger of the two rival bodies in 1955 was an attempt to end these conflicts. Even then, the former CIO unions did not act as a cohesive block because of the bad relations between UAW head Walter Reuther and the USWA's new president, David J. McDonald.

The unexpected death of Philip Murray in 1952 had elevated McDonald, his former secretary. Murray's deep-seated suspicions of corporate power and sympathy for working-class life found no echo in McDonald's personality and lifestyle. Skilled at political maneuvering, McDonald lacked the intellect and fortitude to lead and ceded much of the negotiating to Arthur J. Goldberg, the union's astute lawyer.[38] Where Murray used steel strength to empower the CIO, McDonald lived off the steel boom of the mid-1950s. It was Reuther who replaced Murray at the CIO in 1952. After the merger, McDonald paid dues to the AFL-CIO but not much more. Still, there was a host of talented officers and technicians beneath the president. The union's history was shaped more by the burdens the economy placed on collective bargaining from 1958 through 1964 than by McDonald's limitations.[39]

The Practice of Steel Fundamentalism

Because the celebrants of U.S. affluence had assumed that the traditional problems plaguing capitalist societies had been tamed, troubling signs cried out for explanations. The critics of the "affluent society" had no answers either, because they also assumed that capitalism had been fixed. Both had declared economic victory prematurely. They were at a loss when the 1955–56 boom turned into a deep recession in 1957–58, followed by a brief recovery, succeeded by another downturn from 1960–61, which depressed employment through the end of 1962. The era of postwar growth had stalled or slowed, especially when compared with the fast-growing European and Soviet economies. As meager orders dried up profits, the steel industry tried to restore them in the old-fashioned way, by "taxing" labor in 1959 and consumers in 1962.[40]

Such were the ironic results of the Eisenhower years, which the steel industry initially had welcomed. Anticipating warm relations after the stormy Truman era, Arthur B. Homer, president of Bethlehem Steel, stated that "the basic economic philosophy of the Eisenhower regime is that the country should rely on free enterprise to continue prosperity and high living standards and that the government should act only as a stabilizer of desirable conditions—with a minimum of interference."[41] The recipe simply required the president, Congress, and the Federal Reserve Board to act wisely to moderate business cycles.

But economic orthodoxy was carried further than the steelmakers wanted. Eisenhower ended the rapid depreciation program of the Korean War and rejected any significant tax reduction, as federal expenditures kept rising. Then, the administration ended its silence on steel prices in 1956, a year that crowded in a steel strike, a presidential election, and rising public concern about inflation.

Today, economists look back on this period as one of low inflation. But, despite the low numbers, the United States worried about inflation more than other nations did. From 1950 to 1959, the U.S. rate was 2.1 percent, while it was 4.6 in Sweden, 4.0 in Japan, and 5.6 in France. American growth rates also were lower than those of all industrial countries but the United Kingdom. Leaders of both parties assumed that rising steel prices were a prime cause of the inflation they feared and believed the government should have some say in the matter. Republican senator Ralph Flanders stated, "in an industry as fundamental as steel, there are public questions involved as well as questions of private business policy. Any rise in prices . . . has to be defended on public grounds as well as for business reasons."[42]

The Consumer Price Index (CPI) had risen 7 percent from 1953 to 1956, while finished steel prices rose 18.6 percent. What did the numbers mean? The 7 percent increase over four years could mean that the country had no inflation problem. Rising steel prices could be attributed to the strong demand and higher costs of raw materials. The industry operated at over 90 percent capacity during 1955 and 1956, reflecting an unusual demand for automobiles and producer goods. Indeed, Yale economist Richard Ruggles concluded that there was no relationship between steel prices and inflation because the higher steel price rise had been transmitted neither to the CPI nor to the wholesale price index, which rose only 3.8 percent. Analyzing the weighted components of the CPI, Ruggles found that the CPI rises came from the service industries: public transportation rose 34 percent; medical care, 22 percent; fuels, 20 percent; household operation and rent, 15 percent.[43] In 1963, Arnold Chase of the Bureau of Labor Statistics confirmed Ruggles's findings. The reasons were not mysterious. Rising demand and low productivity translated into higher prices. But the assorted services were not good political targets.[44]

The *Economic Report of the President*, published in January 1957, singled out steel prices as a major cause of inflation, but Eisenhower prescribed macroeconomic medicine. He reduced government spending and called for tighter credit, which the Federal Reserve effected, contributing to the 1957–58 recession. Managing business cycles was no more of a science than determining optimum steel capacity.[45]

Although small, steel price increases during the recession in 1958 brought in the Democrats, who were less restrained than the GOP. In August 1957, Senator Estes Kefauver began two years of hearings, which culminated in Senator Joseph O'Mahoney's proposed bill to require government approval of price rises in large industries. The legislation reflected the continuing influence of the ideas of the New Deal planner, Gardiner Means.[46] Means had accounted for the economic stagnation of the 1930s on the basis of the administered prices of oligopolies. He believed prices then had not fallen enough to create sufficient purchasing power. Now he claimed that rigid prices insulated companies from the effects of falling demand or the lower volume of money in circulation and thus triggered inflation before the economy reached full employment. The words of one of his New Deal critics were still relevant: the discovery of price rigidity was "no more important and no less ridiculous than the discovery by Moliere's bourgeois gentilhomme that he had been speaking prose all his life."[47]

Most industries, from steel to bread, possess some form of price control. Oligopolistic industries did not necessarily raise prices. The container industry, for example, more concentrated than steel and paying the same USWA wages, reduced prices during the 1958 recession. Also, what were the alternatives? As he had argued in the 1930s, Means thought that ending administrative prices would impair "productive efficiency," producing a "lower standard of living." His approach boiled down to moderating steel prices. Means and O'Mahoney were convinced that requiring public hearings before the FTC would inhibit the industry and thus produce lower prices.[48]

The real question, however, was not about some essential quality of oligopoly but about what were the causes of the industry's price policy. The industry asserted that low prices had inhibited needed investment. From 1940 through 1952 steel prices had increased less than the prices of other industrial goods.[49] Roger Blough, the new head of U.S. Steel, attributed the low rate of return on new investment (3.14 percent) to the government's policy of cheap steel. The capital/output ratio for steel was high and growing higher through the decade. In 1960, the figure was 125 percent more than for manufacturing in general. The most rabid modernizer, National Steel, was also the industry hawk on high prices.[50] Rising productivity did not come cheap. While critics argued that its low profits were the results of inefficiency, U.S. Steel claimed they stemmed from the costs of its modern new Fairless mill. The government's preference for competition and low prices left little room for investment.[51]

Most countries during the postwar years directly socialized the costs of steel production by owning or financing their steel industries according to goals hammered out by the government, industry, and often labor (see Chapter 8). Neither the legacy of the past nor an acute crisis forced the U.S to adopt either course. Democrats and Republicans both assumed the industry had sufficient capital. The industry asserted it did not and attempted to socialize costs through prices. Conflicts were inevitable.[52]

The price disputes uncovered fissures within postwar liberalism and within the USWA. The most devoted antimonopolists in the Congress—O'Mahoney, Murray, Kefauver, and Patman—were from the West and the South. Some of them, like Patman of Texas were simply spokesmen for their region's aspiring businessmen, whose virtues did not come unalloyed. During the Korean War expansion, Patman's patronage yielded RFC loans to Lone Star Steel, a mill headed by the bitterly antiunion Eugene B. Germany, whose premodern labor ideas precipitated a bitter strike in 1957.[53] Means and many of the planners of the 1930s never integrated the new unionism into their thinking. They embraced the supposedly disinterested wisdom of experts representing the public interest, not social democracy. They preferred the FTC to tripartite management, the consumer to the worker. These divisions would become daggers in postwar liberalism.

The union lived with the conflicts for the moment, maintaining good ties with antimonopolists in Congress and society. USWA research director Otis Brubaker agreed that "steel price increases have been the most important medium for increasing profits—administered profits achieved through administered prices." The industry's insistence on the right to manage ensured that workers discounted its view of costs and profits. But the union was not willing to go to the mat on price rises. McDonald told the Kefauver committee that inflation "is but one of the economic problems which beset the Nation.... Recessions, unemployment, and inadequate growth are of equal concern."[54]

The Joint Economic Committee agreed. The report it issued after conducting hearings on steel prices in 1959 ignored inflation and oligopoly as reasons for the recession, which it blamed on poor fiscal and monetary policy: "[W]hereas private industry was making large investments during 1956 and 1957 in order to meet high anticipated levels of output, these anticipations turned out to be overly optimistic primarily because the Government stepped too hard on the fiscal and monetary brakes." The combination of defense cuts and rising interest rates in 1958 was an exercise in overkill. The downturn was most severe in the core of industrial America—the steel and auto industries. The men responsible for industry investment and labor contracts in 1956 assumed growth but obtained recession. From 1956 to 1959, steel capacity increased by 20 million tons while production fell by 22 million tons. The utilization rate plunged from 90 to 63 percent. The national unemployment rate hit 7.7 percent in 1958. Two hundred thousand steelworkers (one-third of the total) were out of work; 300,000 more were working short hours.[55] From this angle, the economic performance of the mid-1950s was anything but impressive. From 1949 to 1953, economic growth had been 4.5 percent a year; in the years from 1953 to 1958, which included two recessions, it averaged out to −0.1 percent.[56]

When the Soviet Union launched the space satellite Sputnik in 1957, low growth became a problem of national security, not domestic policy. Although there was no necessary connection between Soviet economic prowess and the scientific breakthrough of Sputnik, the academy and government made the link, which influenced public opinion. In 1958, a Rockefeller Brothers Fund report advocated more rapid economic expansion to catch up to supposed Soviet military superiority. Eisenhower had assimilated some Keynesian theory and considered a tax reduction, but he was immobilized by conflicting advice, the old-time religion's warnings of "fiscal irresponsibility" and inflation, and the risk of losing control of the process. Yielding would open a class fissure, a debate about whose taxes should be cut. Or, as the president put it, any tax cut would be assaulted "by amendment . . . [from] political demagogues and selfish interests." Faced with such a fight, he retreated in 1958.[57]

So did Senate majority leader Lyndon B. Johnson, who voted against Paul Douglas's bill to cut taxes temporarily during the recession. Senator John F. Kennedy voted no on a first vote, but yes on a second, converted by economists who would later influence his presidency. Most liberals were more interested in plugging tax loopholes, a virtuous, if deflationary, errand. The Democrats were no more committed than Eisenhower. Without government action, the steel industry attempted to restore profits through labor intensification, which turned ugly.[58]

The 1959 Strike

The steel industry's new hard line was abetted by the avalanche of favorable propaganda produced by the McClellan Committee hearings on organized crime and corruption in unions. Although the investigation targeted the

Teamsters and corruption was more prevalent in the former AFL than in the CIO unions, the public was less discriminating. Business leaders attempted to use the hearings to reduce union strength both within and outside of the plants. Congress passed the Landrum-Griffin Act in 1959, which required the Department of Labor to monitor union finances and permitted individuals to appeal directly to the secretary of labor. The law conveyed the message that there was a conflict between workers and their unions. The lesson of the movie *On the Waterfront* (1954) had been enacted into law. Popular approval of unions plummeted.[59]

New leaders at many steel companies attempted to profit from the anti-union climate. McDonald observed unhappily that the older generation, like "Fairless, Grace [Bethlehem], Randall [Inland] . . . whom it took us years to educate," had been replaced with new and very different adversaries.[60] In 1956 the parties switched from company-based to industrywide negotiations, headed by Roger M. Blough, the new chairman of U.S. Steel. Blough, a hard-nosed lawyer, had cut his eyeteeth in 1938 when he defended the corporation before a congressional investigation of monopolistic practices, a dress rehearsal for his appearance before the Kefauver committee. He brought in a team of tough labor negotiators, led by R. Conrad Cooper. Cooper was an engineering consultant identified with the Bedaux system of measuring work or, as workers called it, implementing speed-up. Blough informed McDonald that if the union insisted upon improvements in 1959, it could look forward to a long strike.[61]

The industry demanded a wage freeze and abolition of the cost-of-living adjustment (COLA). Its major objective was not money, but elimination of Section 2B of the contract, which protected existing work practices, including rules on manning. Arbitrators interpreted the section to mean that managers could alter existing work rules only when technology changed. If a new process replaced an old one, the union did not have the right to continue the same manning, called featherbedding. The clause simply protected workers when technology was stable. In other words, it guaranteed that work intensification could not be used to increase productivity.[62]

In a period of meager profits, intensification had its attractions, and abolishing 2B won the support of managers down the line. Never comfortable with the changes in the everyday life of a mill in the union era, many managers yearned for the control they had once enjoyed. The clause was both concrete and symbolic for workers, too. The abolition of 2B threatened a return to the time when foremen's barking orders moved men. The industry misjudged the situation and produced a working-class solidarity that no other issue could have achieved.[63]

Over half a million workers walked out on July 15. Eisenhower, unwilling to

Roger M. Blough (left)
chairman of the board and
CEO of U.S. Steel, shakes
hands with his predecessor
Benjamin F. Fairless, who
resigned in May 1955.
(Courtesy of AP/Wide
World Photos)

supplement steel's cash flow from the government well, supported the industry's labor objectives. He had rejected the union's request for a fact-finding
board and after 116 days obtained a Taft-Hartley injunction, claiming the strike
threatened the national interest. The union challenged the injunction, but on
November 7 the Supreme Court ordered workers to return to the mills. Nevertheless, the combination of working-class solidarity and government mediation forced the industry to yield on 2B.[64]

The package was modest. In the first year, labor costs per hour rose only
0.6 percent; the industry did not raise prices. The retention of 2B was a union
victory, even if a defensive one. But Blough told an audience in Miami, Florida,
that he had only agreed to an "armistice. The war wasn't over." Cooper, speaking at Harvard, said the industry had gained a cheap contract and won the public relations battle. U.S. Steel's bravado masked the fact that the six-month
strike had resolved nothing.[65] After-strike operating rates of 95 percent plummeted to 46 percent by the end of 1960. Coming on the heels of the 1957–58 recession, the downturn canceled the savings achieved by the cheap contract.[66]

The slump ended whatever satisfaction the union had derived from its victory, and there was a new problem—technological unemployment. Each time
the recessions of the 1950s ended, fewer workers returned to work. Brubaker
told the executive board that steelworkers faced a "serious *loss* of *job opportu-*

nity." Steel output in 1963 fell short of the 1957 total by only 3.1 percent, but production and maintenance employment fell 23 percent.[67]

As early as 1949, the union perceived that improved wages for common labor had reached the point where corporations had an incentive to mechanize handling facilities, eliminating not only much heavy labor in the mill but also substantial numbers of unskilled workers. Operatives were affected, too. The latest open hearths were larger, requiring fewer furnaces and fewer men. In 1937, it took 25.7 man-hours to produce a ton of shipped product; in 1960, it took only 12.1. Between 1937 and 1960 blue-collar employment in steel fell by 10 percent, despite the doubling of production. The industry registered a 2.5 percent rise in employment only because of increases in white-collar jobs.[68]

Many of these changes were the jewels and engines of the affluent society. One of the many virtues of higher wages is that they force industry to replace labor-intensive methods, which are possible only with low wages. The elimination of back-breaking work is a social gain. Technological change would have been manageable if steel consumption had kept pace with the rise in GNP, which was the Democratic assumption of the late 1940s. But the presumed relationship was not evident by the end of the decade. GNP grew by a little less than 3 percent each year. Steel consumption increased about 0.4 percent, while steel capacity rose 4 percent. It was not that steel was less useful, only less weighty. The thin-gauge, lighter steel with its greater strength per pound was competitive with new materials. But girding a skyscraper now required fewer tons of steel. The relative decline in tonnage, combined with technological change, reduced the number of steelworkers. The USWA urged faster economic growth because an expanded market could compensate for these changes.[69]

The unemployed steelworkers joined the ranks of workers displaced earlier in the decade. The fast-growing industries that increased employment in the 1950s were the new ones—aircraft, electronics, and industrial chemicals. Lumber, textile, and leather grew slowly, but employment fell because of automation. Declining demand for coal and rapid mechanization made miners an endangered species. By the middle of the decade, employment in goods-producing activities fell below 50 percent of the civilian labor force. Jobs in the service sector, including government, grew faster than those in manufacturing, mining, and transportation, which together managed only slight increases. The rising unemployment rate was a sign that the new jobs were not compensating for lost ones. In the early 1950s, unemployment at the peak of the business cycle was 3 percent; by the mid-1950s it was at 4; by the end of the decade it had risen to 5 percent.

Most economists, including Keynesians, believed that if the demand for labor was vigorous, the market would absorb the unemployed. But Charles C. Killingsworth, an economist at Michigan State University, argued that this neoclassical portrait of the labor market was flawed. Although white-collar work was growing, there was no guarantee that a former steelworker would be hired as a clerk or technician. Unemployment would remain in some sectors of the economy, while others suffered labor shortages. Moreover, for the first time in American history, the demand for unskilled workers fell. Labor arbitrator George Taylor, who helped end the 1959 steel strike, agreed with Killingsworth and warned that "handling technological changes was badly messed up in the agriculture industry and we must not do the same in manufacturing." As we shall see in the next chapter, the "mess" in agriculture would have profound effects on the steel industry and the nation. But the poststrike stalemate was a sign that collective bargaining could not tackle automation, and certainly not the new recession.[70]

Kennedy and the Economy

Although the presidential election of 1960 was a squeaker, John F. Kennedy's victory seemed to promise that the USWA would get more help from the government. In his state of the union address, Kennedy indicted seven months of recession, three and a half years of "slack," and seven years of inadequate growth and pledged not "to stand helplessly by." He chose Arthur Goldberg, counsel to the CIO as well as the USWA, to be secretary of labor. Goldberg promised to bring to the presidential table the numerous issues that collective bargaining did not reach. He convinced Kennedy to create the President's Advisory Committee on Labor-Management Policy. Composed of leading businessmen, labor leaders, and public figures, it was charged with effecting a consensus on key issues—recession, automation, structural unemployment, foreign investment. But business and labor clashed sharply on these issues, and Kennedy kept policymaking in his own hands, although there was little action from the White House.

Kennedy's inspiring inaugural address unleashed an idealism among the young, educated middle class, but his "ask not what your country can do for you" was a fair description of his initial economic policy.[71] The modest legislation passed in 1961 and 1962 was more the work of urban liberals in Congress than of the White House. Their numbers had increased as a result of the elections in 1958, when the Democrats attained commanding majorities in both houses.[72] Representing recession-plagued cities and states, they brought to the fore the interests of industrial workers, absent from the western and southern liberalism of the Patmans and Kefauvers. The urban liberals had forced Senate majority leader Lyndon Johnson to appoint the Special Committee on Unemployment in 1959. The committee, chaired by Senator Eugene McCarthy, included freshman Joseph S. Clark from Pennsylvania, which had a 10 percent unemployment rate. Clark, not the more diffident McCarthy, would carry the ball on unemployment.[73]

The Area Redevelopment Act (ARA), the renamed "depressed areas" legislation promoted by Senator Paul Douglas of Illinois during the 1950s, made cheap loans available to urban communities with at least 6 percent unemployment and to rural counties with low farm incomes. It offered little to steelworkers and other workers. Small sums were thinly spread over 100 urban and 662 rural labor markets. All but $94 million of the $394 million were repayable loans, not grants or tax incentives. A USWA district director complained that there were fifteen requests from southern states to establish rod and bar mills, despite the market glut. Provisions that would have relocated workers displaced by technological change were eliminated by legislators unwilling to finance the removal of their electors. ARA was a series of projects; it was never conceived of or funded as a way to address structural change or recession.[74]

The loans offered by ARA did not increase government spending, a Kennedy priority in 1961. Despite Goldberg's advocacy and a May unemployment rate of 7 percent, the president refused to support Senator Clark's public works bill, preferring "to hold tightly to prudent fiscal standards." Goldberg warned that "unemployment among youth, particularly Negro youth, constitutes 'social dynamite.'" Both Eisenhower's and Kennedy's inflation priorities had unacknowledged racial casualties, but nothing budged the president.[75] Kennedy was forced to yield in 1962, mainly because the AFL-CIO and urban Democrats became more intolerant of 6.5 percent unemployment and the fall elections were coming up. The Accelerated Public Works Act made $900 million available in grants, not loans. The backlog of city projects assured that the money would be spent more quickly than the ARA loans. But in the larger picture it was a drop in the bucket and ended after the money ran out.[76]

Addressing technological unemployment proved even more difficult. Meyer Bernstein, the USWA's international affairs representative, noted that the European Coal and Steel Community provided generous retraining and relocation allowances for redundant workers. The U.S. government simply offered unemployment benefits, which were extended in 1961. Many workers would never regain their jobs and often needed literacy and computational education as well as job training. Because the recipients of unemployment payments had to be available for work, they could not enroll in training programs.[77]

The Manpower Development and Training Act (MDTA), passed in 1962, was the first government offer of training to adults in peacetime. To obtain it, Clark was forced to delete proposals to reform the state-controlled U.S. Employment Service (USES), the gatekeeper to the program.[78] The USES was better at filling the needs of local employers than at seeking out jobs for workers. The best jobs continued to be controlled by private fee-for-service agencies. MDTA was popular across the political spectrum because it left undisturbed the various interests in the employment field. The price was that manpower programs remained fragmented and partial. The problem of workers displaced by technological change continued to be the responsibility of unions.[79] Moreover, training programs worked best when the demand for labor was high, as in World War II. A union leader quipped, if you train "on a loose labor market you are just raising the educational level of the unemployed." Kennedy did not try to tighten the labor market.[80]

How does one square Kennedy's passivity with his spirited criticism of the Eisenhower economic record? Paul Samuelson, one of the president's informal economic advisers, recalled that "although candidate Kennedy talked about getting the country moving again, . . . neither he nor his staff had really thought through at that point just what it was that it would take to get the country moving again."[81] Some have argued that he was stymied by congressional control by Southern Democrats and Republicans. But we have seen that Kennedy was uninterested in manpower legislation and complacent about unemployment. He told all who would listen that a 7 percent jobless rate meant that 93 percent were content.[82] Others claim that Kennedy was simply pro-business. But Kennedy had a fundamental distrust of businessmen. He acted in their interest only when it served his.[83]

Kennedy was concerned with growth, but the economy was a handmaiden to the Cold War, his principal interest. Like the Rockefeller report in the wake of Sputnik, Kennedy found it intolerable that the United States had "the lowest rate of economic growth of any major industrialized society in the world," not because he was concerned about unemployment but because growth to him meant "strength and vitality," the ability "to sustain our defenses." He turned to Walt W. Rostow, a philosophical economist, who shared his strategic concerns. The steel industry became the prime candidate for their experiment.[84]

Rostow possessed the expertise and optimism that appealed to Kennedy, who appointed him deputy to McGeorge Bundy on the National Security Council. His book *The Stages of Economic Growth: A Non-Communist Manifesto*, published in 1960, was the first popular treatment of the economics of growth and a rationale and recipe for increasing the U.S. rate. Shortly after the election, Rostow warned Kennedy that "without a strong economy, we shall not have the federal revenues to give extra needed thrust in military and foreign policy. If we do not evoke American effort and sacrifice for communal goals at home, we run the danger of being forced by the balance of payments position and inflation into substituting rhetoric for action abroad." These sentiments ended up in Kennedy's inaugural address.[85]

Rostow claimed that there was an "institutional basis for creeping inflation, notably in the key steel and automobile industries," a more even-handed version of the ideas of Gardiner Means.[86] Kennedy, in turn, told the National Industrial Conference Board on February 13, 1961, that "concern over the resumption of inflationary pressures hangs over all our efforts to restore the economy, to stimulate its growth, and to maintain our competitive status abroad."[87] The worry seems odd given that inflation averaged only 1.5 percent a year from 1957 to 1961. The president was embracing policies appropriate for a boom at a time when unemployment was 7 percent, demand was depressed, and prices were stable. But Rostow and Secretary of the Treasury C. Douglas Dillon believed that inflation had caused the balance of payments deficit, a threat to American foreign policy.[88]

The steel industry was on everyone's mind. In 1957, steel exports exceeded imports by $825 million. In 1960, the surplus was only $152 million. The key word was "only." Had the surplus of 1957 been maintained in 1960, the balance of payments accounts would have been better, undoubtedly. But the United States was still a net exporter of steel.[89]

In theory, any item in the accounts balance could have been singled out. Between 1958 and 1960, short-term private capital going abroad jumped from $311 million to $1.3 billion, a far heftier change than the steel balance. It was to counteract this flow that the Federal Reserve kept interest rates high, despite the drag on the economy. American long-term foreign investment had increased, too, and Kennedy admitted that "no other country would permit that kind of movement of capital. But we do it as a free society." Two years later, in 1963, Secretary Dillon stated clearly that U.S. military and foreign expenditures and capital outflows were the "primary" causes of the deficit. Dillon was forced to agree with Senator Jacob Javits's conclusion that the imbalance was "the penalty we pay for being the world leader." Kennedy spoke of responsibilities, not penalties.[90]

These obligations explained why the examination of declining steel exports excluded solutions whose implementation would jeopardize Cold War alliances. The strong dollar, aid to foreign steel companies, European tariffs double those in the United States, and international shipping rates all disadvantaged U.S. exports, but all were considered essential to American foreign policy. I discuss later how foreign economic policies deployed to solidify strategic goals affected steel exports and imports. For now, it is sufficient to conclude that the reasons for declining steel exports were more complicated than the president made them out to be. Because there were numerous items off the table, deflation—or, in the Kennedy language, sacrifice for communal goals—was the only option. The United States would generate a larger trade surplus by lowering prices and wages. Frugal budgets and wage and price restraint were the order of the day.[91]

In 1961, the administration acted informally, as the occasion arose. When a reporter from the *Washington Post* asked Kennedy what Americans could do for their country, he said, off the record, that they could moderate their wage demands. Kennedy dispatched Rostow on a mission to convince Goldberg and Walter Reuther to accept a wage freeze in the upcoming auto contract. Both resisted. As it turned out, the auto settlement was modest and prices remained stable. But the results were due more to slumping auto sales and unemployment than to government advocacy.[92]

Steel Fundamentalism, Restraint, and Economic Growth

After the auto contract was signed in August 1961, CEA head Walter Heller sent Kennedy an S.O.S., warning that the key economic danger he faced was a possible steel strike or a rise in wages and prices after the contract expired the following year, on June 30. The president even contemplated asking the union to forgo the final increase under the 1959 settlement.[93]

Kennedy's incomes policy was a presidential assertion of the national interest, not a consensual agreement with labor and business. To be effective, he would have to win over the public by making steel the totem of the American economy, a task made easier by the earlier postwar conflicts. Steel became his domestic Berlin when the Organization for Economic Cooperation and Development (OECD) warned that the labor negotiations would be the most important factor determining future American economic trends. European bankers worried about U.S. inflation rates, despite the actual figures. The bankers influenced Kennedy's actions because they held large amounts of dollars that they could legally exchange for U.S. gold.[94]

The CEA's annual economic report for 1962 began by asserting that "[c]reeping inflation in the years 1955–57 weakened our international competitive position. We cannot afford to allow a repetition of that experience." National productivity changes would be the "benchmark" for evaluating wage and price decisions in "those sectors where both companies and unions possess substantial market power, [where] the interplay of price and wage decisions could set off a movement toward a higher price level."[95] Why national, not steel, productivity changes? Heller, an expert on macroeconomics, did not know what the steel figures were, but he instructed Goldberg to employ whichever rate was lower. Actually, the national rate, between 3.1 and 3.4 percent, was lower than the 5.1 percent rate steel achieved in 1962.[96] Heller believed that "labor surpluses in steel producing centers suggests the desirability of some decline in relative wages of steel workers." And the logic of steel fundamentalism meant that a low package would limit all wage bargains.[97]

But the truth was that just as steel prices did not lead the others, for most of the period from 1940 to 1962 steel wages lagged behind those of other industries. From 1940 until 1957, the rise in steel wages was less than the increase in wages in the nonfarm economy as a whole.[98] This situation was reversed in the recession year 1958, the result of the 1956 contract. Then, from 1958 to 1962, the rate of increase in steel (0.6 percent) was lower that in other industries (1.2 percent). A study made by Eisenhower's secretary of labor after the 1959 strike concluded that steel was "conforming to, rather than establishing, major wage trends in the economy."[99]

In the end, Heller took his cue from Bob Eggert, a vice president of Ford Motors, who told him that businessmen believed the president was favoring labor and foresaw, wrongly, "a whopping wage request by McDonald." Eggert believed that a 2.5–3.0 percent increase would satisfy business, and that became Heller's goal."[100] The cabinet and the president himself worked overtime. Goldberg, a good team player, informed his former colleagues in labor that they would get no help from him. Still fatigued from the 1959 strike, McDonald and most workers had no stomach for a fight against both industry and the government. The settlement, announced on April 6, contained no general wage increase and ended the COLA. A ten-cent-an-hour raise was dedicated to the costs of creating a seniority pool for displaced workers, liberalizing interplant transfers, funding moving allowances for workers seeking employment in other company plants, underwriting early retirement incentives, and implementing a nondiscrimination clause. Although the president and the public trumpeted the noninflationary cost of the package, these other clauses, as we shall see in the next chapter, had more national significance than the modest ten-cent-an-hour raise. In the end, active workers financed the casualties of technological change.[101]

Kennedy was delighted with the outcome. "Terrific, Arthur. Terrific job," he congratulated Goldberg.[102] The 2.5 percent package, at the low end of the target, was a full percentage point less than the auto settlement of 1961.[103] It, too, reflected the depressed industry: capacity utilization in steel was at 64 percent, and 150,000 steelworkers were unemployed.[104]

The White House euphoria rested upon the assumption that the settlement precluded a price rise. Blough had told Kennedy that U.S. Steel did not have immediate plans to raise prices, but he reminded him that the industry faced cost pressures. These did not stem from wages. *Iron Age* accurately concluded that the agreement came "closer to the company position than any recent settlement," adding that the steel industry would not risk "the wrath of White House" by raising prices.[105] The nation soon learned that cheap labor contracts were simply one way the industry tried to raise profits, which had reached a postwar low of 4 percent in 1962. In theory, the CEA accepted price rises if profit rates were low, and steel prices had been flat since 1958. But Kennedy, with macroeconomic rather than sectoral purposes, wanted stable steel prices, just as he wanted stable wages. The industry calculated differently.[106]

Roger Blough informed the president on April 10, four days after the contract was signed, that U.S. Steel would raise its prices 3.5 percent, or $6 a ton. Bethlehem and four other companies followed suit. Kennedy and Goldberg felt betrayed. The president told the nation that it was unacceptable that "a tiny handful of steel executives whose pursuit of private power and profit exceeds their sense of public responsibility can show such utter contempt for the interests of 185 million Americans." Nearly every member of the administration and its allies in Congress labored to reverse the rise. The legislative and antitrust arsenal of the 1950s was readied. Finally, after Inland, and then Kaiser, Armco, and finally Bethlehem decided to maintain prices, U.S. Steel rescinded its increases.[107]

The corporation had planned the increase months before, despite sales department warnings that demand was too puny. The question was timing. Raising prices before the completion of the labor negotiations would have given the union license to demand more. The industry had not promised to maintain existing prices, but it knew that the White House had leaned upon the union to produce a cheap contract. Claiming autonomy for itself, it had been perfectly happy to benefit from government pressure on labor.[108] The industry's conflict with the government in 1962 was like its conflict with the union in 1959. Pressed by a poor market, steelmen tried to obtain a marginal improvement that violated implicit compacts. They were frustrated both times.[109]

Kennedy could not afford to gloat. Businessmen and much of the press had responded to the steel drama with a chorus of antigovernment rhetoric. The president of the Chamber of Commerce warned that "dictators in other lands usually come to power under accepted constitutional procedures."[110] And symbolic politics had its limits. Kennedy patched things up with Blough, and a week after indicting the pursuit of profit he told the press that he was not "unmindful of the steel industry's needs for profits, modernization and investment capital." A speech to the Chamber of Commerce repeated the theme and recited his record of tough action against labor—wage restraint, use of Taft-Hartley, and condemnation of featherbedding. But he defended the antitrust laws, which both Heller and Rostow wanted to use against U.S. Steel, and reminded his audience that the nation required more exports to finance the $3 billion annual cost of maintaining the American defense system.[111]

Events overcame intentions. The stock market collapse in May, which many attributed to the steel crisis, and the subsequent stalling of the recovery forced the president to change gears. Heller had used the steel crisis to promote an across-the-board tax cut "to bring about the levels of total production, employment and profits which will reconcile the interest of government and business in the most painless and constructive way." [112] Kennedy became open to the advice because he had run out of options. He had tried wage-price guideposts, budgetary prudence, and minor international currency reforms. In May the steel industry was operating at only 55 percent of capacity, and the whole industrial sector faced surplus capacity and pressure on prices.[113] Many were even predicting a recession. The AFL-CIO had warned in November 1961 that the pickup was not powerful enough to sustain the economy through 1962, but Kennedy, still worried about inflation, disagreed. He changed his mind as the CEA's optimistic forecasts of January vanished in June. A slower growth rate was one thing, but a potential Kennedy recession demanded action. Federal Reserve Board chairman William Martin helped by declaring that inflation was nowhere in sight. The president now informed business press editors that since 1959, U.S. wage increases had been lower than every industrial country but Canada. The president's fear of a recession forced him to articulate truths he had ignored when inflation held center stage.[114]

The pragmatic president turned to Keynesian theory. At a press conference on June 7, he promised to reduce personal and corporate income tax rates, which were choking off recoveries. He admitted that he had not formulated the specifics, but by proposing a revenue-losing law, Kennedy apparently bought Heller's ideas about planned deficits. But first there were other measures.[115]

Number one was the investment tax credit. The credit was part of the treasury's package of tax reform of 1961, which was still mired in committee. Combined with ending the tax advantages enjoyed by transnationals, it was a sensible program to promote investment at home. But businessmen initially viewed tax relief targeted for investment as government dictation. They preferred general tax relief and speedier depreciation, which kept decision making in their own hands. Roger Blough initially opposed the credit, even though his staff told him that it would benefit U.S. Steel, which was undergoing extensive modernization. By the summer of 1962 Blough and the business community had come around and after the credit was passed, learned to love it dearly.[116]

The president, in turn, came around on liberalized depreciation schedules, which was the steel industry's chief aim. Kennedy, noting that European nations allowed speedier write-offs, explained that the codes, based on older technology, inhibited modernization. The Treasury Department had been slow in creating new schedules, which replaced ones dating from 1942. But on July 12, the new schedules were announced with a fanfare rarely extended to the work of accountants.[117]

Because the July indicators demonstrated some improvement, Kennedy drew back some, rejecting the "quickie" temporary tax cut advocated by

Heller, a majority of economists, the Chamber of Commerce, the AFL-CIO, and major newspapers. But businessmen were lining up behind a permanent cut. The OECD, so influential in setting government policy in the steel negotiations the year before, did a 180-degree turn. It urged "a greater stimulus from the Federal budget . . . by tax reductions, by higher Federal expenditures, or by a combination of the two." Now, it argued, "confidence in the dollar" depended upon "a strong domestic economy; it is unlikely to be fostered . . . by policies which keep the level of activity low." What a difference a year makes.[118]

Businessmen would have preferred a cut dedicated completely to capital formation, one reducing both the corporate and the top personal rates, but most recognized that such a program violated the postwar compact of class equity. Thus, across-the-board reductions in individual and corporate rates, which necessarily produced a deficit, became inevitable. The rates of each income group fell. The top marginal tax rate on individuals fell from 91 to 70 percent; the rate on the lowest bracket, from 20 to 14 percent. Spread out over three years and pruned of the liberals' "loophole" reforms, the tax law had already passed the House at the time of the president's assassination in November. The Senate approved in early February, and Kennedy's successor, Lyndon B. Johnson, signed it into law on February 26, 1964. The reductions totaled $11.6 billion in 1965.[119]

When Johnson signed the law, unemployment had been 5.5 percent. By December 1965, the rate had fallen to 4.1 percent, and *Time* magazine named John Maynard Keynes man of the year. Two months later, the Joint Economic Committee hosted a public symposium celebrating the twentieth anniversary of the Employment Act of 1946.[120] Gerhard Colm, chief economist of the National Planning Association, concluded that the reduction was "the first deliberate application of fiscal policy not to counteract a recession but to reinforce an upswing and thereby to sustain economic growth." He was right. The feared recession had not materialized in 1962. Even though unemployment had stabilized around 5.7 percent, the GNP rose 4 percent, the beginning of an upturn. Fiscal policy was being used to promote growth, not to moderate business cycles.[121]

But the broad cuts reinforced the past in other ways. It is true that the investment credit and depreciation changes of 1962 privileged capital-intensive sectors, such as steel. But the AFL-CIO noted that 22 percent of the benefits would go to various commercial ventures, "which presumably includes bowling alleys, beauty parlors, chain stores, racetracks and the like." It was untargeted and inefficient in another way. Dillon believed that the steel industry's cash flow was inadequate, but most businesses had sufficient funds. Indeed, the vice president of Westinghouse Electric, which had spent $200 million in the past five years on new facilities, said that what his industry needed was market growth.[122] Nonetheless, benefits went to rich Westinghouse and GM as well as to poor U.S. Steel. Walter Reuther denounced the tax cut, predicting that it would merely generate "pools of stagnant savings." The leaders of the USWA did not praise it but did not condemn it either. Neither Reuther nor the nation asked what would happen if the pools did not stagnate at home but instead traveled abroad. The leading overseas investors were producers of motor vehicles, machinery, and chemicals. In 1964, investment abroad rose 26 percent, at home 16 percent.[123]

These unaddressed questions were buried by the 5 percent growth rates during the mid-1960s. The investment credit and depreciation changes of 1962 propelled and the tax cuts of 1964 sustained a powerful expansion. Business fixed investment exceeded 10 percent of GNP only four times between 1929 and 1965: in 1929, 1947–48, 1956–57, and 1964–65. The mid-1960s rates of 16 and 17 percent equaled the boom of the mid-1950s.[124] If Kennedy had worried about whether economic growth would be sufficient to fund an active foreign policy, Johnson had no doubt that the nation could have both guns and butter.

For the steel industry, the tax changes opened up the possibility of profitability based upon technological efficiency, not labor intensification, lower wages, or higher prices. Even before the credit was passed, stymied on the price and labor front, the big companies cut dividends and stepped up spending to reduce the costs of making steel.[125] The additional funds and growth rates of the mid-1960s launched a huge investment program, 25 percent higher than outlays during the 1950s. But it still was not enough. Departing from past practices, the industry borrowed heavily. In 1965, the industry invested $1.9 billion, the largest amount yet in any postwar year. Whereas the investment of the 1950s increased capacity, the outlays of the 1960s were dedicated to modernization. Not quite understanding the difference, Heller told President Johnson that the industry is "very much expansion- and modernization-minded." [126]

Because the increased investment did not come at the expense of wages, the industry's relations with the union took a turn for the better. Just before the 1964 election, Conrad Cooper assured McDonald that if Republican Barry M. Goldwater won, the industry would not try to eliminate the union. In 1965, a top steel executive predicted that "if new mills, furnaces, and other more efficient equipment can be installed in steel plants quickly enough, higher wages and employment costs can be partially, or even completely offset." Wages in steel, and in manufacturing in general, rose less than in any previous boom, but the ending of the persistent unemployment of the recent past seemed to moderate discontent. The number of production workers in basic steel was fewer than the 600,000 of 1957, but the 541,000 employed in 1965 was higher than the figure in any year from 1958 to 1964.[127]

The industry's relationship with government improved, too. The tax cut acknowledged the industry's low profits. Steel fundamentalism did not end. Government jawboning still kept prices and wages lower than those in other sectors. Blough continued to complain about "miserable profits"; he felt hemmed in by Kennedy's victory with public opinion, "so that anybody on a street corner can repeat the phrase that steel is basic to the whole economy and that any increase in steel prices automatically means inflation." But he subsequently recalled that "of all the Presidents that I've known since Hoover, he [Johnson] understood the business problems better than any one of the other presidents." [128]

The nation seemed to have found the formula for industrial efficiency and working-class prosperity. Added to the older tradition of competition and regional dispersal, the new economic policy searched for the right mix of spending and taxes to effect the macroeconomy. Political debates now addressed the distribution of the largess to the poor, elderly, and blacks, those inadvertently left out. These issues became moral ones, debated in an economic vacuum, because the consensus was that markets allocated capital correctly and extraneous workers would be absorbed by growth.

Even before the tax cut was signed, displaced agricultural, lumber, ore, coal, and steel workers in the South challenged each tenet. Because many workers were black and also fighting to dismantle Jim Crow, the nation discovered it had a race problem. The upsurge revealed the shortcomings of the economy of the 1950s as well as the injustices of segregation, as we shall see in the next chapter on steelworkers in Birmingham, Alabama. The nation's response to the new civil rights movement, the subject of the succeeding chapter, illustrated the deficiencies of the Keynesian solutions of 1963 and 1964.

Birmingham

Before and After King:

Racial Change in Steel

D-Day—May 2, 1963—had begun. Police vans and sheriff's cars were carrying arrested black children away from the streets of downtown Birmingham. The steady numbers and cheerful determination of youngsters befuddled the police. But on the next day Commissioner Eugene "Bull" Connor revealed his true colors: dramatic photographs of beefy men hurling K-9 dogs and aiming fire hoses at the marchers fixed world attention on the city. Rev. Martin Luther King Jr.'s bold decision to use children, when adults held back, transformed a beleaguered campaign into a brilliant triumph.

As the confrontation crested, three men—Howard Strevel, Reuben Farr, and C. Thomas Spivey—occasionally gazed down from the Steiner building downtown, overlooking the tumult. Strevel and Farr represented the United Steelworkers; Spivey, U.S. Steel. They were completing an agreement to end the racial division of labor at the city's huge steel facility. The clashes below caused Farr to hesitate. He suggested that they "back off" for a bit because there would be "hell to pay." Strevel firmly told him, "if we back off now, we are through." A week later, Strevel secretly delivered $40,000 in bail money that the union had pledged to release demonstrators from Birmingham's jails.[1]

Despite the timing, the events on the street and those in the building were unconnected. King had come to Birmingham at the request of Rev. Fred L. Shuttlesworth of the Bethel Baptist Church to revive flagging demonstrations to desegregate downtown Birmingham. Except for Shuttlesworth, the tacticians of the march were outsiders, and even he at that time lived in Cincinnati, Ohio. After the march, King monitored events in the city and the Southern Christian Leadership Conference (SCLC) continued to play a significant role in the city, but black Birmingham's traditional leaders, who had distanced themselves from King and Shuttlesworth, returned to center stage.

The men in the Steiner building were long-term actors in the city's past and future. They were responding to a new movement among black workers to end employment discrimination. The workers acted because the jobs they held were being mechanized and they were threatened by unemployment. Farr hesitated not simply because of the racial tension on the streets but because only seven of seventeen open hearth furnaces were in operation in the steel mill in 1963. For the next decade, the union attempted to foster racial progress even as recession and technological change reduced the number of jobs at the mill.

Although the civil rights movement had finally captured the nation's attention after nearly a decade of struggle, work issues remained invisible. In the decade of *Brown v. Board of Education*, the race question was perceived as a civil liberties issue—the right to equal schooling, to vote, to serve on juries in the South—not an economic one. The word "Negro" did not appear in the index of Galbraith's *The Affluent Society*. Harold Vatter's *The U.S. Economy in the 1950s*, published the year of the Birmingham demonstrations, omitted any discussion of black labor. The Keynesian school of economics addressed the volume, not the distribution, of employment.

Nevertheless, black unemployment rose first in the recession of 1954, reaching 8.9 percent, when it had been 4.1 percent the year before. It barely improved in the brief recovery that followed, then in the recession of 1957–58 shot up to 12.6 percent, double the white rate and higher than at any time during the previous eleven years, the period since the Census Bureau had begun reporting unemployment figures by race.[2] Even though work in the industrial North was scarce and the South's economic growth outpaced the nation's, southern blacks were still leaving for northern cities like Gary and Detroit.[3]

The pattern of the region's development goes a long way toward explaining the drama on Birmingham's streets and in its mills, as well as the subsequent changes in northern cities. Southern economic dynamism reflected Dallas and Atlanta more than Birmingham. But the national ideology that emerged from the streets of Birmingham turned a blind eye to the economic trends. The nation concluded that American institutions worked well but for the obstacles of bigotry. Much future trouble resulted from this shallow understanding.

The South

After World War II, southern elites built a new economy with new people and, eventually, new racial policies. Leaders fostered economic growth with little working-class input. Historian Bruce J. Schulman has called this a "Whig" strategy of development.[4] First, planters either mechanized cotton production or switched to growing new crops, like soybeans, fruits, and vegetables, or to raising poultry or livestock. During the 1950s, the farm population declined from 10 million to 6 million, falling to 3 million in 1970. Put another way, farmers made up 73.1 percent of the southern population in 1940 but only 6.8 percent in 1970.[5] Along with new crops, the South obtained new aircraft, machinery, and electronics industries, often connected to the defense industries that the region's senators and congressmen carefully nurtured for home consumption. Southern governors welcomed manufacturing of all types.

The new economic mix expelled some and attracted others. During the 1950s more than 3 million southerners, including 15 percent of the region's black population, migrated to other parts of the nation. Blacks and whites with little education left for the North and were replaced by highly educated northern whites. The median educational level of black migrants to the North was 6.6 years, whereas 35 percent of southerners possessing five or more years of college were white male migrants from the North. Southern states worked to ensure that college-bound whites remained at home, spending more per capita and per student on higher education than the rest of the nation. However, spending on elementary and secondary schools in the South fell far short of the national average.[6]

The decline in low-wage work, especially in agriculture, the anchor of the region's racial proscription, made it possible for the civil rights movement to succeed. But if the new industries in the South had little stake in segregation, they also had little incentive to upgrade black skills or employment, given the inmigration of the educated labor supply they needed, which was supplemented by native whites. It was not until the fall of 1961 that the first blacks worked on the assembly line in the General Motors plant in Atlanta, Georgia, a breakthrough that was the result of political, not market, pressures. As a GM manager explained: "When we moved into the South [in 1957], we agreed to abide by local custom and not hire Negroes for production work."[7] Although each city and industry had its particular racial division of labor, southern industrialization could proceed without upgrading blacks, who generally occupied the bottom rungs of occupational ladders.

But the issue was not simply racial hierarchy. The number of new manufacturing jobs did not compensate for the simultaneous loss of jobs in traditional industries and agriculture. Industrial mechanization was as rapid as the changes in agriculture. Unskilled factory work, the traditional outlet for farm labor, actually declined by 58.9 percent from 1950 to 1970. Over two-thirds of the new southern jobs required high school diplomas or more, but in 1960, 92.8 percent of black farmers had less than a high school education, 82.2 percent had less than eight years of schooling, and 53.3 percent had less than five.[8]

Alabama was a case study in southern economic development. On the one hand, the space program had turned the sleepy textile town of Huntsville into a high-tech metropolis. The Marshall Space Flight Center opened in 1960, followed by a research center, industrial parks, and a first-class university. The majority of Huntsville's workers had moved there from out of state.[9] Two hundred miles south of Huntsville it was a different story. The Black Belt around Montgomery and Selma experienced the brunt of declining cotton production. In 1949, Ernest E. Neal of Tuskegee Institute told Senator John Sparkman, who was holding hearings on poor farm families, that "the Old South is in the midst of a Revolution," a revolution in agriculture, not civil rights.[10] The state's farm population fell from 960,000 to 519,000 between 1950 and 1960. In 1955, William H. Nicholls of Vanderbilt University noted that the situation would have been even worse if the "safety-valve of outmigration" had not existed. But the safety valve needed repair. Farm refugees used to find work in Birmingham. Not anymore.[11]

Located between Huntsville and Montgomery, Birmingham once attracted whites from the northern hill country and blacks from the southern Black Belt. During the 1950s, 29,980 blacks, about 15 percent, left Birmingham and the small cities composing Jefferson County. And it was not simply a black exodus: 81.7 percent of the 110,988 people who left adjacent counties were white. The population decline continued. During the 1960s, Birmingham's black population fell from 135,113 to 126,388, a drop accompanied by a decline in the white population, from 205,620 to 173,911. It was the only major urban area in the nation that reported a declining birth rate, the result of the exodus of people of child-bearing age.[12]

Even with outmigration, unemployment was 10 percent in June 1961. From the beginning of the recession in 1957 to mid-1962, the city had lost 10 percent of its jobs. The South's new plants usually located in rural nonfarm areas, not in cities, but Birmingham's manufacturing growth was low even for southern cities; in 1960, it ranked forty-sixth in a list of fifty-two. The Labor Department classified Birmingham as "an area of severe and chronic unemployment."[13]

Between 1953 and 1965, the number of coal miners in the Birmingham area fell from 17,100 to 4,300. Republic Steel suspended iron ore production in 1956, and U.S. Steel closed all of its mines by 1962, when it began substituting Venezuelan ore for local Red Mountain ore. The old iron industry in the city's center and North Birmingham struggled to survive. Sloss-Sheffield's City Furnaces, a symbol of the once proud industry, closed in 1970. The situation at the U.S. Steel mill outside of Birmingham was more salient because throughout the twentieth century it had absorbed displaced industrial workers as well as farm laborers.

The Fairfield Works of U.S. Steel

U.S. Steel, the largest employer in Jefferson County, dominated the western perimeter of the city of Birmingham. Clouds of smoke drew eyes to the impressive skyline of a modern steelworks but veiled the thousands of workers who made steel. Virginia Durr, typical of the city's white upper class, recalled that before World War II "the industrial side of Birmingham . . . was a foreign country, and the people who lived there might as well not have existed." It was perhaps even truer after the war, when the white middle and upper classes migrated over Red Mountain to nests of suburban comfort. On the other side of the color line, Geraldine Moore considered "the steelworker and the miner . . . the aristocrats of Negro labor," but she nevertheless failed to mention any of their leaders in her "Who's Who" of black Birmingham, published in 1961.[14]

The steel complex grew from the Sewanee Mining Company, established in 1852 deep in the Cumberland Mountains between Nashville and Chattanooga, Tennessee. In 1886, after many mergers and reorganizations, it moved to Birmingham, the center of Alabama's rich mineral beds, under the name of the Tennessee, Coal, Iron, and Railroad Company (TCI). Even after it was purchased by U.S. Steel in 1907, locals called the facility TCI, reminding all that the mill was no northern transplant. Managers boasted that they "did not need U.S. Steel to tell us how to run our business."[15] TCI produced seventeen major product lines, more than any single company in the corporation. Its open hearth furnaces had an annual capacity of nearly 4 million tons. Its prowess trickled down. Herman Taylor, a black worker at TCI's Ensley mill, recalled that people "had a tendency to look up to the folk that worked for the big Tennessee company. . . . TCI was the big boy on the block."[16]

The Ensley mill had produced TCI's first steel in 1899. The finely made Ensley rails were still a valued commodity, but a declining railroad industry needed fewer of them. In 1963, slightly less than 2,000 men worked at Ensley, half the workforce of ten years earlier. The year before, slowing operations had led TCI to retire some furnaces and transfer the machine, forge, and electric shops one mile west to the Fairfield Steel Works, the hub of company steelmaking.

Begun in 1909, Fairfield Steel grew spectacularly during World War I, producing plates for U.S. Steel's shipbuilding corporation. It now supplied primary steel to the TCI finishing mills and independents in the region. In 1963, it

Industrial map of the Birmingham area in 1960, showing U.S. Steel's Fairfield works on the western edge. (Courtesy of U.S. Steel Group)

employed 5,000. A wire mill completed in 1914 produced everything from barbed and high-tensile wire to wire fabric. The sheet mill came on line in 1926 to supply growing consumer markets. The tin mill, built in 1937, produced metal for the food processing industry. Eight miles southeast, in Bessemer, an antique rolling mill made small shapes used in the manufacture of railroad cars for nearby Pullman-Standard. TCI also operated coke and ore conditioning plants, coal and ore mines, and a railroad to shuttle products through this vast complex. Numerous ancillary industries—brick refractories, slag processing plants, and fabricators—completed the industrial landscape.

TCI was in and out of Birmingham. Its offices were originally located in the downtown, but TCI moved them in 1951 to Fairfield, an independent city adjacent to the Ensley section of Birmingham. The new city had been created with the new steelworks in 1909 to attract a skilled and stable workforce, but TCI's top officers and managers now lived in another suburban city, Mountain Brook, a well-named exclusive retreat. Steelworkers lived in Birmingham, Fairfield, Bessemer, and many other cities of the county. Jefferson County contained fourteen municipalities within a ten- to twenty-minute drive from downtown, each with its own school system and police department.

Political power accompanied TCI's economic weight. To avoid unwanted taxes, the steel mills had been built outside of any city jurisdiction, and many believed the corporation had used its power after World War II to prevent the Ford Motor Co. and other new industries from locating in the city.[17] Alabama had the lowest taxes on coal and ore in the country. TCI had learned to live with the political dominance of rural Alabama. One-third of the voters of the state, the whites of the Black Belt counties south of Birmingham, elected the majority of the state legislature. Rural white Alabamians dominated politics until 1964, when the Supreme Court mandated the one-person, one-vote rule in the state.[18]

Along with the rest of the industry, TCI had opposed unions, but anti-unionism in Birmingham often took a violent form, especially when workers allied across the color line. The creation of durable, biracial steel, coal, and ore unions in the 1930s was a unique achievement here and in the South as a whole. When the AFL, spurred on by competition from the new CIO, organized blacks, it placed them in Jim Crow unions. The key to the Birmingham successes was the judgment by CIO leaders Lewis and Murray that organizing the southern region was central to national success in coal and steel. Without such strategic interest, and the resulting deployment of people and money, other CIO unions in the South had a tougher time. Unlike that of Northern industrialists, the hostility of southern elites—or Big Mules, as they were called—did not wane after the war. Supported by the middle class and rural elites, they kept unions on the defensive.[19]

The first goal of the CIO unions in Birmingham was to bring wages up to northern standards, a challenge to the cheap labor regime. The southern wage differential in the steel industry, which had been 17.5 cents an hour, ended in 1954. Raising wages had a racial twist because of discrimination. Blacks doing skilled work often earned only the common labor rate.[20] The union's work classification program, which set up standardized rates and job content, ended such conditions. Elmer Maloy, the international's technician who aided the unions at TCI, recalled, "we found some of these colored boys who were getting job class 4 when they should have been 14, and just because they were colored." Each job had a numerical classification, ranging from JC-1 to JC-30, which determined hourly pay rates. Blacks had been performing work that rated higher pay. A black worker put it another way: the union forced the company to pay "the job not the man."[21]

The USWA also reduced the authoritarianism of the mill. In 1951, Clyde Burks, a black laborer at Fairfield Steel, used his ingenuity to complete his work, rather than follow his foreman's literal instructions, and was suspended for insubordination. He filed a grievance, and at one meeting the plant superintendent growled, "If this had happened in 1911, this grievance wouldn't have happened. I would have taken a pick handle and made a good worker out of him." But it was not 1911, and Burks was vindicated. The union was the one institution in Birmingham where blacks had rights to equal treatment.[22] Voting made them an inevitable factor in union politics. They were elected grievance-men, often in mixed departments. When they sat at the negotiating table with managers, they were equals.

If wage inequities and dignity were the principal issues of the 1930s and 1940s, seniority became the key issue in the 1950s. After the initial hiring, se-niority governed most elements of mill work—training, promotion, layoffs, shift and vacation preferences, etc. But first there was the hiring system, which launched seniority. Southern hiring was a variation of the national pattern. Northern steel managers, confronting a polyglot workforce, minimized per-sonnel costs by adopting ideas such as Croats are good for blast furnace work, Welsh for the tin mill, Serbs for general labor work, and white Americans for the roll shop. These initial judgments were perpetuated through the informal job referrals of current workers, who recommended family, friends, and lodge brothers. After a while it appeared the Serbs really were best suited for general labor. But ethnic generalizations were rarely uniform. Two different compa-nies might assign Italians to different kinds of work, each certain that its judg-ment was valid. Family/ethnic hiring was a cheap way of sorting out workers.

The northern pattern concentrated blacks and immigrants from southeast-ern Europe in departments that were dirtier and hotter and required more manual than mental labor, although there were many variations and excep-tions to this pattern. Some dirty jobs had high incentive rates, which made them desirable. Workers often preferred the blast furnaces, even though the wages did not rise as high as those in the finishing end, because the work was steadier and less subject to the instabilities of product markets. Although hir-ing was a management prerogative, many local unions attempted to alter the racial/ethnic selections, with mixed results. The union's wage classification program moderated the economic consequences of such hiring by raising the rates of jobs with unpleasant work environments.

In southern mills, blacks held jobs that both the foreign-born and blacks worked at in the North. They were not so concentrated by department but were dispersed widely throughout the plant, although their movement upward was limited. Actual manning patterns in each TCI mill varied. More than a third of TCI's workers were black, but each mill had different statistics. There were some jobs that were "black" in one mill and "white" in another. This sit-uation prevailed because several, uncoordinated employment offices served the various mills located in different cities of Jefferson County until 1964.

The arguments for excluding black workers from skilled and supervisory positions had not changed very much during the twentieth century. In 1942, the owner of Stockham Pipe Fittings stated flatly that "Negroes as a rule can-not have first class skills."[23] In the early 1960s, such judgments were not uttered with such certitude, but most managers concluded that black workers "did not possess the necessary educational background and knowledge."[24]

There was a racial difference in educational levels, although steelworkers as a group were better educated than the typical Alabamian. The mean educational level for TCI's blacks was 7.6 years, for whites 11.3.[25] Both rates were higher than respective levels in the state as a whole—6.5 for blacks and 10.2 for whites.[26] But where racial populations differ in education and skill, the most efficient hiring policy may be to reject all members of one group, rather than incur the costs of more thoroughgoing evaluations.[27] Thus, even if managers accepted the fact that some blacks could do skilled work, they had no incentive to sift through the black population for the suitable. The conventional wisdom of the 1960s that discrimination was uneconomic stemmed more from ideology and theory than from observing the behavior of businessmen.

Left alone, managers changed their racial evaluations when traditional labor sources were unavailable. Faced with a labor shortage during and after World War I, northern managers discovered that the foreign-born could perform semiskilled work and that blacks could work in factories. The tight labor markets of World War II likewise had produced some upgrading of jobs for blacks in southern mills. But the technological change and recessions of the 1950s and early 1960s offered no market incentives for changing race- and ethnicity-based hiring practices. The managers' training methods erected still other barriers.

A basic steel mill is a series of shops and departments. Unlike work in an assembly plant, mill jobs are independent of each other, even though they are linked by a flow from raw materials to finished products. Handling material, which is never the same, at different stages of the process always requires skill. But men who roll hot steel possess skills different from those of workers who load furnaces or fabricate nails. A steel mill is like an airline, where janitors and mechanics could not easily work in the cockpit.[28] An individual was hired into a line of progression (LOP), a series of job and skill sequences in a shop or department. Entry to the bottom job on each line usually was based upon a manager's assessment of the worker's ability to progress to the top. If the top job on a line required computational skills, the company did not hire an illiterate for the entry job, even though it required no mathematics. Ideally, the training required for any job was learned informally by the worker on the rung below. When an opening arose, workers bid for it, and generally the person with the greatest time, or seniority, on the job below, the whole line, or even the department was selected, although in theory the company could take merit into account. Layoffs reversed the process.

The diverse and specialized character of steel work encouraged narrow seniority districts. Managers had no interest in facilitating the transfer of a man from one line to another, which involved additional training costs, because the jobs were so different.[29] Transfers were prohibited in most mills; where they were permitted, the worker gave up his old seniority when he transferred.

If the company considered the LOP as a way to train, workers viewed it as a system of promotion and security, which ensured opportunity and tenure to long-serving workers. They agreed that those who had put in many years possessed more skill. Given the dangers of handling steel, workers also had an interest in ability. But there was more to it than safety. Because steel skills were not easily transferable to other industries, the worker's investment of time in the enterprise made seniority the foundation of a moral economy.

Managers viewed this moral economy as an unwelcome restraint. Dennis F. Hooten Jr., in charge of labor relations at TCI during the 1960s and 1970s, put it well: "Seniority is a restriction on management rather than a guarantee you will always get the best qualified men to any vacancy." If managers lacked incentives to strengthen seniority or alter hiring practices, the union had many. Both blacks and whites were dissatisfied with TCI's seniority system, which the local union leadership had been unable to change during the 1940s.

Part of the problem was District 36's first and current director, Reuben Farr. Like many steelworkers, Farr had previously worked on the farm and in coal and ore mines. Embodying Alabama unionism, he had been a member of the UMW, Mine Mill (International Union of Mine, Mill, and Smelter Workers), and a farmer's union before he came to work in the open hearth department at TCI. But Farr and his staff of old organizers were no match for TCI managers. In 1951, in the face of mounting dissatisfaction among union members, Philip Murray appointed thirty-five-year-old Howard Strevel, an outsider from Tennessee, to the staff.[30] Strevel's great-grandfather had fought with other Germans on the Union side during the Civil War. Strevel had headed his union at Alcoa and had been president of the Tennessee State CIO Council. Almost as soon as he came, he led the first strike in TCI history that addressed mainly black issues in the coke plant.[31]

Everyone noticed the difference, but Farr was popular among blacks and whites and wielded the loyalty that founders of unions often possess. James Swindle, a white worker, welcomed Strevel but would not judge Farr harshly, saying the union needed "new blood and ideas." Robert Washington, a black worker, expressed the same thought: Farr was a "very loyal union man," he said, but Strevel was "more forceful." This was certainly true on racial issues. Instead of attending the various race relations conferences that the USWA participated in during the 1950s, Farr sent Strevel, who recalled that Farr usually "took the road of least resistance" on racial matters but "supported me 100 percent."[32]

In 1952, after threatening a strike, Strevel forced the company to allow each

Howard Strevel, a few years before 1951, when Philip Murray transferred the Tennessean to Birmingham to inject "new blood" into the USWA. (Courtesy of Howard Strevel)

mill to determine its own seniority rules, ending the stranglehold of the first 1939 agreement, which offered workers minimal protection. Under that agreement, a worker held rights only on jobs he had actually performed, not on a line of related jobs, which was the way seniority was computed in northern mills. Also, many jobs in southern mills were not connected to others in an LOP, so managers could choose whom they pleased. Given the racial ethos of managers, connecting jobs and rationalizing rules of promotion benefited black workers especially as well as workers in general. Southern seniority systems were weaker than those of the North because southern managers from the beginning possessed more control over the labor force. Making the situation more difficult, the TCI contract required that any change in the way seniority was computed had to be companywide. Because it was impossible to obtain agreement on any one seniority system, Strevel was forced first to negotiate an end to the companywide requirement. Then, he proceeded to work with those local unions (there were twelve at TCI) where change was most promising."[33]

The most radical change occurred in the wire mill, as a result of favorable technology, astute black leadership, and white support. Unlike the other mills, the wire mill approximated a mass production facility. Base rates of pay were lower, but they were supplemented by good incentives. Only a few departments employed the crew method of production, where workers were dependent upon each other and learned skills incrementally. The jobs also required less skill than did other steel work. Thus, both the organization and content of the work made it feasible for men to perform many different jobs. The tight labor markets of World War II had enabled many blacks to move into formerly white jobs.[34]

But the seniority arrangement put the brakes on further black progress. In 1946, the union had demanded the selection of either Mark Harris, a black, or Emanuel Lucia, an Italian American, as a machine adjuster in the barbed wire department. The position was filled, however, by a white from the outside. Management argued, correctly, that machine adjuster was not in the line of promotion for either Harris or Lucia; the job was unconnected to any other one, which gave the company complete freedom in filling it.[35] Other lines contained only a few jobs and were separated from skilled jobs that in a northern plant would be joined. The bifurcation was often a racial division.

The blacks "were in control" of the wire mill, recalled international representative Bruce Thrasher, and their goals were concrete, not symbolic. They elected whites to the highest offices, believing that a white would gain a better hearing from management. Only after the promotion of several friendly white chairmen of the grievance committee to foreman in the late 1940s did they decide to elect a black, again for practical reasons. Willie George Phillips, who spent his working life in the wire mill, explained: "Every time we get a white fellow, the company gets him. At that time they wouldn't make a black foreman." In 1949, the black workers decided to elect Ernest McLin, who had "a lot of good common sense." Thrasher agreed, finding McLin "very bright, very articulate, very proud."[36]

Nonetheless there were racial customs that blacks themselves were reluctant to challenge. The chairman of the grievance committee presented the union's case at the fourth-step meeting, the time when the union met the assistant head of labor relations of the company, Paul Bowron Jr. Bowron, the son of a founder of TCI and the husband of a daughter of the Comer textile family, represented Birmingham's industrial aristocracy. McLin was reluctant to tangle with Bowron, but Strevel insisted upon it. Nowhere else in the Birmingham of the 1950s would a McLin confront a Bowron on the basis of equality.

Strevel and McLin planned and plotted to change the lines, eliminating the racial designations of jobs, merging short lines to provide more opportunity, and creating a liberal system of departmental transfers. There was broad support for the seniority changes because whites too had been locked into lines of promotion. But at the time of the formal signing, one white committeeman, Archie Thompson, representing the machine shop, failed to appear. TCI often used the slightest white opposition as an excuse for inaction. This time, however, the superintendent, who initially had said he could not agree without the signatures of every committeeman, took Strevel's threat to "shut down the whole wire mill" seriously and signed.[37]

Changes in the other mills were less comprehensive. Often lines were lengthened without crossing the racial divide. Certain key jobs like roller remained white, even in the wire mill. The company continued to hire blacks and whites into separate lines. But there was enough change to convince blacks that there would be more. The much more restrictive racial practices of the city inevitably moderated black demands. Birmingham managers at other companies referred to the racial and labor system at U.S. Steel as the "Fairless" system.[38] On the other side of the color line, Strevel's simultaneous strengthening of seniority everywhere convinced whites that black gains were not being made at their expense.

Rising steel production after the 1953–54 recession lubricated race relations. In 1955, TCI produced a record 3.7 million tons. Both blacks and whites prospered. The following year, when Martin Luther King Jr. was having difficulty acquiring autos to ferry boycotting Montgomery blacks to their jobs, labor leader A. Philip Randolph told King: "Go to Birmingham, where the steelworkers are making enough to afford two cars. Ask them to donate their second car."[39]

The changes of 1954 were the industrial equivalents of Jim Folsom's gubernatorial victory of the same year, when he defeated hard-line segregationists by stressing the congruity of interest between black and white workers.[40] Subsequent Alabama politics took a turn for the worse when the militant segregationist John Patterson was elected governor in 1958. The white mobilization in the wake of *Brown v. Board of Education* blunted every progressive element in southern society. Although the AFL-CIO embraced the ruling, many white unionists did not. A representative of the USWA sent to survey conditions in every southern state in 1956 said that "the possibility of the formation of an all white Southern Federation of Labor [in Alabama] should not be taken lightly because the White Citizens Councils are no doubt behind the move." Nevertheless, it usually took a local community conflict to make civil rights issues a factor in union affairs. Black and white staff reported that neither the Montgomery boycott nor Autherine Lucy's attempt to attend the University of Alabama affected relationships in the mills in 1956. It certainly did not affect a group of black and white miners at U.S. Steel's Dolonah rock quarry, near Birmingham. All the quarry workers struck in 1956 when the company furnished rain suits for whites, but not blacks. The company subsequently issued them to all.[41]

The white mobilization against *Brown* made organizing unions more diffi-

cult, but there were many variables that entered into any union election. Southern blacks and whites usually joined unions for economic reasons. The white
labor federation never materialized. In 1957, the USWA won an NLRB election
in a large steel fabricating plant in New Orleans and inserted an antidiscrimination clause into the contract.[42] Whether it could have pulled it off three
years later when New Orleans had its school desegregation crisis is another
question.

The new civil rights movement that emerged to meet the white mobilization
affected southern unions in other ways. As direct action like the Montgomery
bus boycott superseded alliances with white liberals, tactics enhancing black
mobilization replaced those geared to eliciting white southern support. The
new southern black movement sought white allies in the North, altering the
older New Deal strategy of union-based progress in the South. But these
changes had not yet affected Birmingham. It was the recession and technological changes of the late 1950s that called a halt to black and white expectations.

Seniority Changes: 1961–1963

As in the industry as a whole, employment at TCI peaked in 1953. The subsequent decline was greatest in the southern steel district, particularly at TCI.[43]
From 1953 to 1966, employment fell from 17,000 to slightly under 10,000. Business picked up in 1965, but employment increased only modestly. During the
late 1950s and early 1960s, the sheet and tin mills, producing light, flat-rolled
products, had been completely modernized and mechanized. Larger open
hearths, a new generation of blast furnaces, faster finishing processes, and
a virtual revolution in the handling of material were only a few of the labor-
saving changes. During the 1960s and early 1970s, the mill would confront
computerization and the new oxygen furnace that truly revolutionized steel-
making.[44]

Wage equalization had encouraged TCI to rationalize and mechanize unskilled labor. As we have seen, this trend was not simply southern, but the impact was greater at TCI than in the North because the South's abundant cheap
labor had encouraged more labor-intensive methods. Mechanization especially threatened blacks because they were concentrated in unskilled work.

The recession affected all workers, as it mocked the narrow seniority systems, which had worked well during the period of rising or stable employment.[45] Rights to jobs and benefits extended for two years, a rule that reflected
the fact that unemployment had been cyclical and thus brief. The current
downturn endangered thousands of whites and blacks who remained out after
twenty-four months. Because layoffs and shutdowns were often department-
wide, older men walked the streets as young ones worked.[46]

For instance, work at the Ensley mill was slowing during the late 1950s. The company had transferred the maintenance crafts to the Fairfield Works, under the jurisdiction of a different local. The Ensley workers were given priority over new hires to jobs at Fairfield, but their seniority was eliminated. In other words, the seniority lists were not merged. Attempting to rearrange jobs would have met the opposition of both Fairfield management and workers. But W. A. Lavett, a white welder from Ensley who had not been needed at Fairfield, said "I am to [sic] old to start over. It is hard to get a good job at my age anywhere else. . . . I cannot hold out much longer hoping something will be done so the oldest man with the most seniority will have a job." [47] Lavett might have been the "oldest" measured by company service, but not by Fairfield service, the way seniority was measured at TCI. Who was the oldest was determined by specific rules, not calendars. Now, the old rules and the new recession collided with the essence of seniority, protecting workers with the longest service. Because these problems were not unique to TCI, the local union got some help from the international in 1962.

The 1962 Contract

Kennedy had heralded the 1962 contract as a bellwether on inflation and had ignored other key provisions that were to have a greater effect on the nation than the wage package did. Forced to struggle with technological unemployment without state help, the international concluded that it would ration work according to seniority. Because seniority systems differed so widely, the international had left them to the locals until the 1962 contract, which included the first industrywide provision. [48] Workers would be demoted through the jobs they had held until they reached the pool, which now included unskilled jobs in the lowest three classifications and most of those in the fourth. A person whose job or department disappeared would have security in the pool. Layoffs would take place from the pool according to length of mill service. [49]

Another provision, the one on nondiscrimination, was equally ignored and equally important. The Kennedy administration's actions on employment discrimination were no bolder than those on unemployment. To be fair, liberals themselves considered other racial issues more important. In 1961 and 1962, the priority of the Leadership Conference on Civil Rights, the lobbying arm of the civil rights movement, was a law to implement school desegregation. Bill Oliver, from the UAW, objected to the low priority that NAACP lobbyist Clarence Mitchell placed on employment, but Oliver's was a lonely voice. [50]

Kennedy did continue the postwar tradition of demanding nondiscrimination from federal contractors. On March 6, 1961, he issued Executive Order 10925, which required government contractors to hire, promote, recruit, upgrade, transfer, lay off, pay, and train without consideration of race, creed, color or national origin. He created the President's Committee on Equal Employment Opportunity (PCEEO) to enforce it.

On May 3, at a meeting with Kennedy, Johnson, and Goldberg, the USWA had pledged to support the executive order. The union informed international officers, district directors, department heads, staff representatives, and local union recording secretaries of the requirements of the executive order and began to gather its own data on compliance.[51]

But company cooperation was necessary as well. Francis C. Shane, head of the union's civil rights committee, told Edward C. Myers, U.S. Steel's vice president for personnel, that the corporation and union should issue a joint public endorsement. Myers agreed only to discussions in the Human Relations Committee, created after the 1959 strike to address work practices. He added that the corporation was about to revise its supervisors' manual. Myers did not enlist the union's help in the revision. He also refused to set up joint committees at each mill to consider steps for implementation, the only way to effect genuine change.

To put pressure on the companies, McDonald sent a public letter to the heads of the seventeen basic steel and aluminum corporations, requesting a joint statement of principles and implementation. Similar letters were sent to each of the almost 2,000 other companies with which the union held collective bargaining agreements. In a typical response, one steel executive replied, "We don't discriminate in hiring a worker." By the middle of December all had responded, but only Inland Steel signed. Most simply denied that they discriminated.[52]

Confronted with a legislative roadblock and corporate inaction, the union attempted to meet the new racial situation as it had confronted technological change and unemployment, through collective bargaining. The issues were related. In January 1962, McDonald told a House subcommittee that the rapid "technological changes . . . in the steel industry" required swift passage of a law banning employment discrimination. Displaced from jobs "eliminated by automation," blacks were often barred from training and other work.[53]

The nondiscrimination clause gave the union and workers the right to use the grievance process to end racially restricted jobs wherever they existed. It is not clear why the industry eventually accepted the clause when it had not even acknowledged that discrimination was an issue. What is clear is that all of the companies opposed it until U.S. Steel reversed its position. Shane believed that potential PCEEO pressure was a factor in the turnabout; he acknowledged, too, that there were "several officials" who "have more than a casual degree of social consciousness." Whatever the motivation, only after the signing of the 1962 contract did U.S. Steel assemble managers from all its mills to inform them of their obligations under the executive order. Union enforcement of the order was more likely than government action.[54]

Back to Birmingham

Strevel married both provisions of the new contract. He set up the pool to protect the older workers and to end the consequences of racial hiring. Workers who were demoted to the pool could bid to enter any line of progression on the basis of mill service. If the worker was black, he could now bid into a "white" line. When hiring resumed, all new workers would begin in the pool and they too could bid into any line of promotion. Managers could no longer hire workers into black or white lines.

But protecting the old and creating a better future collided with the present—young blacks in the tin mill, which had changed least during the 1950s. Because blacks composed only 20 percent of the mill's workers, the white majority had not been forced to accommodate black demands as they had elsewhere. The whites were "tight," concluded James Seay, a black who worked in the mill until he was laid off in 1962. The company complained that the workers ran the mill. James Swindle, a white operator in the hot strip mill, agreed. "We knew more about the strip mill than the plant managers or the Mesta engineers who built the machines."[55] Although blacks enthusiastically backed the frequent mill strikes, the racial attitudes of most whites were unreconstructed. Blacks in other mills held skilled jobs, but in the tin mill they rarely rose beyond JC-5.

Widening the racial gulf was the fact that most blacks came from Westfield Village, originally a black company town within walking distance of the tin mill. Most of Westfield's residents came straight from the farms, and any job in steel was an improvement over their previous lot. During the organizing drives of the 1930s, company control of the village had made it difficult for organizers to contact Westfield workers; although once they joined, they had become loyal unionists. TCI no longer owned the houses, stores, and the church, but the paternalism continued in the community and in the mill. The combination of a highly organized, skilled, white majority plus a small number of relatively passive blacks produced a mill with a class-conscious, but white, work culture.[56]

In 1959, TCI installed a new, highly mechanized temper mill. In the past, using hammers and chisels, blacks had primed the coils, which were fed into the old mill for rolling tin plate, which required unique surface finishes, flatness, and desired metallurgical properties such as temper. In the new mill, this work not only was mechanized but would be going to whites. In the old mill, the manual preparatory work had led to mill operating jobs, so it was not simply a

An example of the industry's increasing mechanization: double-stand, four-high temper mill at TCI's tin mill in Birmingham. Temper rolling imparted surface finish and improved flatness and metallurgical properties in the manufacture of tin plate. Steel coils are fed from the right, uncoiled, tempered, and then recoiled at the other end. (Courtesy of U.S. Steel Group)

job but a series of jobs. It was clear that the manual operation would eventually be shut down and its workers demoted to the pool or laid off.[57]

Clarence Duncan, whose position was threatened, was typical of a new breed of black steel worker at the tin mill. Duncan lived in the city of Fairfield, not Westfield. Born in 1930, he graduated from Fairfield Industrial High School and began working at TCI in 1947. He was a member of First Baptist Church of Fairfield, which was attended by many of the black leaders of other mills, and served as superintendent of its Sunday school. There were many jackleg preachers who worked in the mills and many evangelical churches in Birmingham, but First Baptist was not one of them. Pastored by an educated if apolitical minister, its rationalistic religion attracted men whose response to discrimination would be deliberate.

Virgil L. Pearson met Duncan at church. Pearson had graduated from Parker High School in Birmingham and started work at the American Cast Iron and Pipe Company in January 1945. After six months, he was drafted and spent thirty days at Fort Benning. Although his mother, whose husband had died when Virgil was three or four months old, wanted him to return to the pipe company because it paid "big money, 62 or 65 cents" an hour, he looked elsewhere. Pearson found a job at Fairfield Steel in 1948, first as a laborer renovating the sheet mill and then in the mill itself. An accident that crushed his leg made it impossible for him to work for twenty-six months. When he came back, he went to the tin mill as a yard laborer. TCI moved him to the rollshop where he worked as a crane hooker, then to the machine shop as a cleanup man, and finally to the bathhouse as a laborer.[58]

Pearson met Freddy Rogers at the tin mill. Rogers was born in Sumpter County near Tuscaloosa. His father had been a sharecropper who left to work in the TCI coal mines. His mother permitted a wealthy white family to take young Rogers with them to Chattanooga, Tennessee. (At the time, it was not uncommon for rich whites to raise their sons with black boys as companions.) Rogers remembers the experience warmly, but after graduating from high school, he returned to Birmingham. He found work in the TCI coal mines near Docena before he was drafted into the Navy during the Korean build-up. Returning home, Rogers did not want to return to the mines, so he opened up a dry cleaning business and then a night club. While operating the club, he found work at the tin mill in 1951. Rogers was president of a small chapter of the National Association for the Advancement of Colored People (NAACP) in the Roosevelt section of Birmingham, until the state effectively banned it after 1954.[59]

Pearson and Rogers attempted to move up in the tin mill but were rebuffed with explanations like "that job is out of your line of promotion." Their efforts to move beyond what Rogers called "the 38th parallel," attracted the attention of a foreman who told them they would "ruin the other men [blacks]." Rogers agreed that he and Pearson were a "different breed from what they had been accustomed to dealing with." The company separated the two "troublemakers," assigning Rogers to work at the black bathhouse, Pearson to the white.

Every insurgency is a civil war, as well as a war against an adversary. Pearson considered black grievanceman James Davis a "flunky." Davis, the minister of the Westfield church as well as a worker in the mill, represented an older generation. Duncan, Rogers, and Pearson, all men in their twenties or early thirties, had greater expectations than the older blacks who worked with them. The younger workers were more likely to have been born in the city, not the country; many were high school graduates. They measured their prospects by what whites could do, not by what the cotton fields had offered. And they knew they were not confronting a monolithic system. The wire mill's Ernest McLin, a member of the Fairfield church, was initially skeptical. In his no-nonsense manner, he told them "if you want to act, I'll help, if you want to talk, don't waste my time."[60]

Throughout 1959, the group met with union officials from the tin mill. They wrote to David McDonald, who referred the complaint to Farr. Nothing happened. Given these experiences, the blacks had no faith that the new pool agreement of the 1962 contract would be implemented in the tin mill. They wrote to the NLRB and the international leaders of the union in May and to the new government contract committee, PCEEO, in June 1962.

In July, PCEEO sent Emile Bourg and John Rayburn to Birmingham, where they joined Julian Campbell of the Tennessee Valley Authority (TVA), who had been selected to monitor TCI. The government agency holding the largest contract with a firm was the one responsible for enforcing the executive order. The trio first met with TCI's president, Arthur V. Wiebel, and C. Thomas Spivey, the new director of personnel services, who had just arrived on June 25. Spivey was the first outsider to head labor relations at TCI. However U.S. Steel interpreted the nondiscrimination clause, it knew that it needed its own man to implement it.[61]

Wiebel and Spivey admitted that blacks and whites were hired into different lines of promotion and that company facilities and employment offices were segregated. Although they had resisted Strevel's integrated pool arrangements, they embraced it now, claiming that it would eventually integrate the jobs. A better clue to TCI's intentions was Spivey's admission that the new instructions had been disseminated to plant supervisors only. For the system to work, the foremen would have to be informed.[62]

PCEEO representatives next met with the tin mill group and Jimmie Lee Williams, the black vice president of the coke plant local. Clarence Duncan told the investigators that the key problem was that the jobs held by Negroes were being eliminated; unless they could advance to higher classifications, they would be out. The pool would not help young men like himself. The investigators agreed. They asked Williams whether the union would accept a plan to eliminate dual lines through merger of the lines, meaning joining black and white lines that were functionally related. He said the USWA would if the company accepted it in a "forceful manner."

The investigators met next with William Mitch Jr. and Jerome A. "Buddy" Cooper, partners in the only labor law firm in Birmingham. Mitch, the son of the legendary head of District 20 of the mine workers, handled UMW work. Cooper, Justice Hugo Black's first law clerk and the lawyer for Operation Dixie, represented the USWA. The attorneys promised union help to obtain "bona fide company compliance" with the executive order.

Having won union support, Rayburn brought USWA international representative Bruce Thrasher with him to meet again with Wiebel and Spivey. However, both rejected the merger plan, insisting that the pool approach would be sufficient. Elimination of the dual lines would produce a "wildcat" strike, they predicted. The investigators concluded that the company was resisting. But TCI altered its position the next day. It is likely that the about-face was mandated from Pittsburgh, as Wiebel had been hostile from the beginning. Rayburn had to remind him that he had come to Birmingham "to implement executive order 10925, not negotiate it." Wiebel now promised to work with the union to merge the LOPs and disseminate the nondiscrimination policy down the line, including to first-line foremen. Everyone, including Duncan and the tin mill blacks, agreed that desegregating the bathhouses should wait until the job questions were resolved.[63]

The investigators also postponed seeking compliance with nondiscrimination in white-collar, professional, technical, and clerical hiring. Spivey acknowledged that blacks not been employed in those categories and that those who were qualified did not apply because they "probably knew there would be no use." But he was not optimistic about the future. One hundred workers were on layoff and new hiring was unlikely because of office automation, including the replacement of stenographers with dictation machines. He promised to interview at Negro colleges and universities when the company resumed hiring.[64]

Having completed their task, Rayburn, Bourg, and Campbell left Birmingham. The black *Birmingham World* announced in front-page banner headlines that "separate queues" in the employment office and benefits office had ended and that 63 percent of the complaints had been resolved.[65] Public understanding of labor issues was always imperfect, yet the newspaper accurately conveyed the sense that something important had happened.

The union began first to create the pools. The tin mill continued to be a trouble spot. "We will hate to fight our Union when we are already losing members and jobs on every hand, but we have no other choice unless we are relieved of this unfairness in our ranks," wrote Duncan in October. In November, Ben Fischer, the head of the international's contract department, came down to Birmingham. He discovered that the local union could not check pool movements because the company had not made seniority lists available. But blacks did not trust the union grievancemen in the tin mill. Also, although the pool provided protection and potential mobility for some, others worked in low-paying, dead-end lines of promotion.[66]

Fischer convinced the company to start merging the lines immediately. E. B. Rich, then chairman of the grievance committee at the big Fairfield Steel local, recalled that the international instructed "us to get as many dead-end jobs [as] we could tied into lines of promotion, especially to enhance black promotional opportunity." This was the work completed during the King demonstrations. Although Farr had hesitated at the moment of crisis, he proudly informed McDonald that under the new system all jobs "are open, regardless of race or color." It was now possible, he claimed, "for the colored to be promoted to Rollers or any of the top jobs." [67]

Organized resistance did not materialize. It is true that someone fired shots into Howard Strevel's home, many telephoned threats to Bruce Thrasher, a group hung grievance chairman Ralph Gurley in effigy in front of the machine shop at the coke plant, and several slashed E. B. Rich's car tires. But there was no wildcat strike or disruption in a mill known for both on other issues. While there would be pockets of resistance, whites accepted the legitimacy of the change, even if some did not like it. Virgil Pearson recalled that some of the tin mill's white workers, whom he suspected of membership in the Klan, extended a grudging respect. Others would come up and tell him, "I can't support you publicly but you did the right thing." Such unheroic approvals began to alter mill culture.[68]

However, race relations were not everything in the tin mill. "We really had a big layoff," recalled Dennis Hooten. Orders vanished. Employment descended from 2,300 in 1962 to a low of 170 in November 1965. A pickup in 1966 brought the total back up to 975, but the recovery was not fast enough for Virgil Pearson, who transferred to Fairfield Steel. Rogers left the mill to work fulltime at his night club and eventually entered politics. Another member of the group, James Seay, on layoff from 1962, accepted a transfer to U.S. Steel's Gary mill in 1964.[69]

By September 1964, the Gary Works had finally exhausted the layoff rolls that had accumulated from the 1957 recession. Unlike conditions at Fairfield, business at Gary was booming. According to the another provision of the 1962 contract, workers could enter pools anywhere in the U.S. Steel system with their seniority intact. Fifty Fairfield workers, including Seay, took up the offer. They were not only tin mill workers and not only blacks. Between 1962 and 1966 employment at TCI fell from 13,000 to 10,000. A white, Joseph Van Diver, was laid off in March 1960 after working fifteen years at Fairfield Steel. He was working as a delivery man for a Birmingham drug store, a job paying a fraction of the wages of steelworkers, when he transferred to Gary in 1964.[70]

There was not much to do when the tin mill was barely operating. The young men were the first to be laid off, leaving a predominantly older and less militant black workforce. When work became more plentiful after 1966, changes would be made in the tin mill. Clarence Duncan would get a good job, but for the moment the tin mill was a quiet place, and blacks elsewhere awaited the results of the pool and merger arrangements.

King and Birmingham

These events explain why black steelworkers were more interested in the merger negotiations going on in the Steiner building than in events on the street. Duncan had put the job issues ahead of the integration of mill facilities at TCI, and if asked, he probably would have reversed the priorities of the downtown demonstrators. Ore miners had their own problems. The day before King began the children's march, the union petitioned the U.S. Tariff Commission to obtain relief for the laid-off workers under the injury clause of the Trade Expansion Act of 1962. The USWA was trying to make the case that the Wenonah and Ishkooda mines had closed because of an earlier trade agreement that had permitted U.S. Steel to develop mines in Venezuela and thus were entitled to additional unemployment benefits. The government eventually rejected the claim.[71]

Although steelworkers and ore miners were uniquely preoccupied, most of black Birmingham also distanced itself from the King demonstrations for other reasons—until the day of police dogs and hoses arrived. Birmingham was not Montgomery, where direct action had united the black community. In 1963, politics seemed to be more potent than direct action. Less than 20 percent of black Birmingham voted, but their ballots were crucial to ridding the city of its infamous police commissioner, Eugene "Bull" Connor.

The white mobilization against *Brown* had halted Birmingham's movement for racial change in 1956, when an interracial committee planning to hire black policemen and modestly improve black life, even create a "Negro Mountain Brook," was hounded out of existence by the White Citizens Council.[72] Connor rode the segregationist wave back to power in 1957. First elected commissioner in 1937, pledging to turn back the CIO/integrationist challenge, Connor ended his long tenure in 1953 after a sexual scandal forced him out of office.[73] Connor not only refused to take any steps toward integration, but his tolerance of violence against protesters attracted the most extreme segregationists to the city—not only the Klan, but the neo-Nazi National States Rights party.

Connor's resurrection coincided with the recession, which led some businessmen to conclude that Birmingham's economy required economic diversification. Realtors, bankers, public utilities executives, and retailers planned to lure "clean" (nonpolluting) businesses to the central business district and displace the black workers living adjacent to it. In 1957, they created the Birmingham Downtown Improvement Association to plan a modern, postindustrial city. Many, like lawyer Charles Morgan Jr., saw the city's future in facilities like Birmingham's new medical center, "the city's hope, an enterprise other than steel and coal and railroads."[74] Unlike most of the other business planners, who were segregationists, Morgan was a racial liberal. He was probably unaware that his plans consigned many black workers to the unemployment lines.

On February 21, 1961, to better govern the city and perhaps incorporate the affluent suburbs surrounding it, Chamber of Commerce head Sydney Smyer, a realtor with impeccable Dixiecrat and segregationist credentials, created a blue-ribbon committee to reform the structure of city government, which consisted of a commission of three.[75] The need for reform was documented in the May municipal elections. Two weeks after the Freedom Riders came to Birmingham, Tom King, the liberal law partner of Charles Morgan, ran on a platform of economic development but was defeated by White Citizens Council organizer Arthur Hanes. Connor was reelected, as was James Waggoner, the third commissioner. City government was now completely in the hands of the extreme segregationist camp. The trio was not against economic development, but its first principle was maintaining segregation.

Business leaders did not oppose segregation, but they believed that a militant defense of it hurt economic development. They had learned the Little Rock lesson. Talk of shutting down public services kept industry out of the city, they believed. Thus, nearly every major business and civic association opposed the commissioners' decision on January 1, 1962, to close the city's parks, playgrounds, and golf courses rather than obey a federal court order to integrate them. Both city newspapers also opposed it, ending seven years of inflammatory support of segregation. The Chamber now concluded that Connor's methods were "playing into [the] hands of the NAACP." In the eyes of the businessmen, the Klan and the NAACP were equivalents. Although they had few ideas on improving race relations, the elites sought a more diplomatic, certainly a less violent, approach, following the pattern of other southern cities, like Atlanta, that had weathered the storm.[76] The closing of the parks convinced them that reorganizing city government, substituting a mayor and city council for the three commissioners, would both modernize city government and get rid of the Connor group. With the support of the Chamber and the Birmingham Labor Council, a petition drive gathered 12,000 names. A judge ordered a November referendum.

While civic elites were busy with municipal reform, Reverend Shuttlesworth and students from Miles College, a black college located in Ensley, conducted sporadic boycotts of downtown businesses. The elites feared that the demonstrations would hand Connor a victory in the referendum, as the Freedom Rides had in the elections the year before. So in September 1962, shortly before the SCLC convention in Birmingham, the white merchants agreed to remove racially restrictive signs over drinking fountains and restrooms, hire and upgrade black employees in the downtown stores, and treat black consumers more courteously.[77] They created a biracial Senior Citizens Committee. The blacks included A. G. Gaston, a millionaire businessman, the Reverend J. L. Ware, and Lucius Pitts, the new president of Miles College. SCLC's assumption that businessmen were the keys to progress seemed to be confirmed.

But the politicians struck back. Building inspectors threatened to besiege the merchants to the point of condemnation. All but one backed down. Shuttlesworth wanted to begin new demonstrations, but King, after the failure of his campaign in Albany, Georgia, was cautious. Black Birmingham admired Shuttlesworth's personal bravery, but most found him egotistical. He won the support of a few ministers but the animosity of most of them.[78]

In November, a majority voted for the new form of city governance. Local black leaders convinced Shuttlesworth and King to again delay demonstrations until after elections, which were scheduled for March 5. Connor was running for mayor against Tom King and Albert Boutwell, a moderate segregationist. When the votes were tallied, King, who had been attacked as a tool of the NAACP and the unions, came in third. A runoff election was scheduled for April 2 between Boutwell and Connor. Martin Luther King Jr. and Shuttlesworth agreed again to postpone the demonstrations until after the contest. Neither viewed direct action as a substitute for the ballot, and Shuttlesworth had always urged his followers to vote for the most liberal candidate in municipal elections.[79]

Connor lost, but he and the old city commissioners now refused to leave office, claiming that their terms did not expire until 1965. Unwilling to delay any more and pressed by the personal and organizational imperative to act, King launched the Birmingham demonstrations the day after the election on April 3. Throughout, the Connor regime held de facto power while the two governments battled in state courts to determine which was legitimate.[80]

Most of the black community, all white liberals, the city's elites, and the national government and press had opposed King's decision, arguing that Boutwell should be given a chance. To the black *Birmingham World*, King's "direct action" seemed "both wasteful and worthless." The assistant attorney general for civil rights, Burke Marshall, asked King to wait.[81] *Time* magazine called the demonstrations a "poorly timed protest"; to the *Washington Post*, they were engineered more by "leadership rivalry" than necessity; and the *New York Times* nearly canonized the vacillating Boutwell.[82] For almost a month, the protests attracted few and threatened to end in failure, which was why King's lieutenants decided to recruit the children. Only the dogs and hoses turned on the children corralled the city's blacks and the nation behind the demonstrations. Burke Marshall then hurried to Birmingham to conduct the shuttle diplomacy that effected an agreement on May 10 to integrate the downtown facilities and to hire more blacks. However, the vagueness of the promises, the reluctance of the businessmen, and the intermittent violence succeeding it did not chart a clear future.[83]

Progress was uneven. On May 23, the Alabama Supreme Court ordered the commissioners to vacate their offices. On June 19, all Alabama congressmen as well as the governor condemned new civil rights legislation announced by President Kennedy, but on the same day the new Birmingham parks board voted to reopen its golf courses on a desegregated basis. By the end of July, the new city council repealed all segregation ordinances, before civil rights legislation was even crafted. Two black youths were arrested for trespassing as they attempted to buy tickets to the Alabama Theater on July 26, but four days later, six lunch counters were desegregated without incident.

USWA leaders invariably took public positions on the left end of the possible. They and the Birmingham Labor Council endorsed the most liberal candidates on the ballot: Tom King in 1961 and in the first election of 1963 and Boutwell in the runoff with Connor. But the union's political weight in the city elections was minimized by political geography. The center of steel voting was the independent city of Fairfield. Although steelworkers were scattered throughout Birmingham, the only significant concentration was in the Ensley section, whose decline mirrored the steel mill on its edge. Its combination of black slums, black inmigration, and a white working class in decline was not the chemistry for white liberalism, even under more favorable conditions.

Local union leaders sympathized with King's objectives. At one point, civic leaders had asked Bruce Thrasher and Buddy Cooper to help stop the demonstrations. Thrasher told them, "You must be insane. We agree with what they are doing." He recalled, "They thought that we could stop it all. It was a sign of how out of touch they were."[84] The businessmen knew that blacks were fervent unionists; they thought or hoped or imagined that white union leaders could influence King. However incredible the request seems today, it must be remembered that the whites were desperate and only tourists in black affairs.

In the city council elections of 1963, accompanying those for mayor, Thrasher ran and lost on a platform of retaining the public schools, at a time when Connor was urging closure and most candidates were silent. But you could not win elections on such a platform in 1963. Thrasher made it past the first round of 75 candidates, but not the second round of 18.[85]

The international offered more public support in 1963 than it had in the past. At the time of the Freedom Rides in 1961, Farr, understanding that his own situation was not the same as the international's, nonetheless advised, "if there should be any donation made by the Steelworkers Union [to CORE or the freedom riders], I certainly hope and pray that there will be no publicity on

USWA international representative Bruce Thrasher (second from left) and three officers of TCI's sheet mill on the boardwalk in Atlantic City, New Jersey, en route to one of the USWA conventions of the 1960s. (Courtesy of Bruce Thrasher)

it." McDonald had not contributed, but assured Farr "we will of course be guided by your advice before taking action of any sort regarding this issue." But in 1963, when some white steelworkers questioned the use of union funds to bail out civil rights demonstrators, McDonald did not trim sails. "We would be shirking our responsibilities if we did not carry out our union's stated policies on civil rights," he told them.[86]

Nevertheless, the union priority was the mills. The broad purposes and antiunionism of the white actors intent on creating a postindustrial Birmingham were ones the union could not embrace warmly. The Senior Citizens Committee that conducted the negotiations was in essence the Chamber of Commerce. Moreover, black goals were propelled by ministers and businessmen whose targets, associations, and rhetoric did not mesh with the work issues that preoccupied the USWA. But, most of all, the union was involved in reforms of its own, which were threatened by the hurricane of racism that accompanied the Freedom Rides, demonstrations, and elections of the early 1960s. Politically, it played defense. Strevel forbade all but union-endorsed candidates from speaking before union locals, to keep out segregationist politicians. Undemocratic perhaps, but necessary in the Birmingham of the early 1960s. E. B. Rich, chairman of the grievance committee at Fairfield Steel, struck a bargain with a few white local presidents who mimicked outside politicians. Rich told them "I will not interfere with you, but you better not interfere with me." They did not.[87]

The acquiescence was secured partly because the justice of the work issues, which involved men they knew, was clearer to most white workers than the city issues, which many believed were generated from the outside by strangers, defined by the press, culture, and neighbors as "agitators." Alabama, which had spurned the Bilbos and the Talmadges in the past, elected George C. Wallace governor in 1962. Wallace kept the pot boiling.

His early career as a Jim Folsom supporter and subsequent career as a populist has muddied Wallace's role in the 1960s. Before, he had been moderate on race. Even after his racist campaign in 1962, Virginia Durr, one of the last popular front liberals in Alabama, thought Wallace redeemable. Durr informed her friend Lyndon Johnson, "He is smart, and pleasant to meet, not like Patterson [the former governor] who is stupid and unpleasant." Jimmie Lee Williams judged Wallace "an opportunist," in contrast to Connor, whom he characterized as "from Dallas County," the heart of Alabama's Black Belt and its most virulent white racism. Williams, who was active in black politics as well as in the union, added that although they "will not admit it to you," many black schoolteachers voted for Wallace because he expanded the school system and raised teachers' salaries.[88]

Wallace had worked with the USWA before he was governor, and the white steelworker became a staple in his populist oratory. His uncle was an elected officer in the black-controlled wire mill local at TCI. "Not a bad guy," Strevel recalled. But Wallace worked overtime to manufacture steelworker support. When he ran in the presidential primaries in 1964, he traveled with a group of white tin mill workers, who were paid for their efforts. And he sought out the approval of union leaders. Addressing a rally in Ensley, Wallace noticed Bruce Thrasher at the edge of the crowd. Thrasher, whose office was near the gathering, had decided to see what was going on. The keen governor had spotted him immediately and publicly invited him to the platform. Thrasher refused, but Wallace's desire to maintain the union ties of his past even while he embarked upon his new course was constant. In another instance, the state of Alabama threatened to request extradition of a black prison runaway, who had become a steelworker in Ohio. The USWA's Cleveland director asked Strevel to intervene with Wallace. Strevel did, and the man, who had been living a law-abiding life for nearly twenty years, was left alone. The governor told Strevel: "I am doing this just for you, Howard." E. B. Rich was not impressed with Wallace's past or present. Rich believed that he supported the union because of the power it had, not because of any commitment to workers or unions.[89]

When the union's lawyer Buddy Cooper ran in a countywide race for state senate in 1966, Wallace was a more visible opponent than John Hawkins, the man Cooper was challenging. Cooper openly supported the Civil Rights Act and the national Democratic party. In turn, Wallace, no longer race-baiting, accused him of being a "pointy-headed liberal," part of the "Washington gang." Nevertheless, it was Cooper, not Wallace's man, who swept the working-class districts of Jefferson County. White, upper-class Mountain Brook voted with Wallace. Although Cooper won the black vote, at the time he rued the fact that "not enough blacks were registered." Still, Cooper believed that it was the governor's potent patronage threats more than anything else that caused his defeat.[90]

Wallace himself was the greatest promoter of Wallace the populist. He told Stephan Lesher in 1987 that the settlement integrating the downtown allowed "the businessmen of Mountain Brook . . . [to] avoid all this [eating with black patrons at lunch counters], but the steelworkers and the [white] working people couldn't." A small truth. The class character of elite liberalism would always be fodder for demagogues. However, although the implication that Mountain Brook had planned it this way may have fit Wallace's subsequent ideology, it did not fit the facts. The agenda was set by blacks, not whites. As white realtor Sidney W. Smyer explained his purposes a week after the settlement, "I'm still a segregationist, but I hope I'm not a damn fool."[91]

Wallace did everything in his power to block change, including consorting with the National States Rights party. He encouraged violence to prevent integration of the city's schools, under the theory that if there was enough disorder, he could win.[92] But the governor's initial defense of keeping the University of Alabama for whites only and his subsequent strategic withdrawal demonstrated that he was no damn fool either. His stand at the university, however contrived and cynical, aimed at elite, not mass, support. His unwillingness to risk violence there reflected a sensitivity to an elite institution, which he lacked when it came to Birmingham's public schools. Wallace played to the classes as well as the masses. Mountain Brook and TCI management supported him even as they were forced to yield because they were concerned with a lot more than dining companions, as were African Americans.

Focusing on the lunch counters fit Wallace's demagoguery, but it minimized the challenges to racial discrimination, which took place on many fronts. If in retrospect elite fears seem exaggerated, that does not make them less real. The businessmen planned to bulldoze black slums to create a clean, white central city served by minimal public transportation, which would help to keep it so. How the demonstrations would affect such dreams was not clear in 1963. Black politics was a work in progress.

For now the ball returned to the court of the city's traditional, black leaders. The demonstrations had not thrown up an identifiable new group of local leaders, because they had been led by outsiders. As the city's black elite worked out the implications of the settlement, they joined the old Downtown Improvement Association, reborn as Operation New Birmingham. Inadvertently, they adopted the businessmen's postindustrial strategy.[93] Like Charles Morgan's, their economic and racial agendas conflicted.

If local leaders ignored the key manufacturing sector, the Kennedy administration, which had marshaled considerable resources to produce the settlement, did not. It created its own Operation Birmingham, led by PCEEO, to ensure compliance with the executive order. The Birmingham region had thirty government contractors, representing thirty-seven establishments and employing 18,215 workers.[94]

But PCEEO discovered that without corporate and union cooperation the executive order was a slim reed. Opportunities for delays were endless, as they were at U.S. Pipe and Foundry, which had purchased the Sloss-Sheffield iron works in 1951.[95] U.S. Pipe's president, R. E. Garrett, was an avid Wallace supporter; its workers belonged to the conservative molders union. Garrett responded to a complaint by denying the committee's jurisdiction, then questioning the Navy's right to investigate and refusing to permit an on-site investigation. PCEEO gave up.

Hayes International Corporation, engaged in rebuilding aircraft and missiles, was vulnerable to government pressure. But Hayes did not agree to eliminate racial job placement until the Air Force threatened to cancel its contracts. Its president was a prominent segregationist and its white workers were no better. This UAW local was well out of control of the international and had been the center of the movement to create a white labor federation in the mid-1950s. According to a union veteran at TCI, "it was never much of a union." The combination of antagonistic corporate and union leaders ensured that the agreement on paper changed little in the workplace.[96]

PCEEO had better luck with Connors Steel, a small, efficient producer of electric arc steel. The USWA decision to merge lines at TCI in 1962 was extended throughout the district. The lines of promotion had been merged at Connors in October 1962, but changes were not automatic. Maple Copeland, who had completed two years of college and two years of theology school, failed a test for a promotion. When he complained, PCEEO referred the case to the AFL-CIO, which forwarded it to the USWA. Copeland got his job.[97]

In the short run, the city crisis had hardened the opposition of TCI's top management, as it did throughout industrial Birmingham. Twenty-five years after the event, Paul Bowron's white-hot anger toward King and Shuttlesworth had not cooled.[98] His successor, the moderate Thomas Spivey, was no match for TCI's president Arthur Wiebel. Originally from the North, Wiebel regarded TCI as "his plantation," observed Bruce Thrasher. When Buddy Cooper urged him to work with the union on race issues, Wiebel told him "no nigger will tell me how to run this steel plant." Chairman Roger Blough had to pressure him to support the agreement ending the demonstrations. Wiebel protested, "My responsibility is to run this steel plant and keep people working, and not run City Hall."[99]

But part of this responsibility was to implement the executive order. PCEEO staff continued to find Wiebel openly antagonistic to it. In July 1963, the monitoring of TCI was transferred from TVA to the Army because of the greater size of its contracts. The military examiners acknowledged the significance of the company's merging of racially separate lines of promotion and filing of compliance reports. They also recognized that the company had not hired any blue-collar workers since 1960 and that the number of clerical employees had been reduced. However, they also pointed out that the company had taken no action on desegregating its facilities, its white-collar employment, college recruitment, and apprenticeships.[100] Even though some of these areas were pinched by the poor economy, PCEEO's Tom Powers judged that "the whole approach of the company appears to be negative rather than affirmative. . . . [T]he company would not accept the idea that it had an obligation to interview graduates of Tuskegee (although Mr. Wiebel was on its board of trustees) or the graduates of Negro business schools."[101] TCI had promised it would do so in 1962.

Despite the mixed assessment by the PCEEO and the military examiners, the press portrayed U.S. Steel as an enlightened corporation making progress toward ending bigotry. After the merging of the lines at TCI, the *New York Times* declared that it had made "significant strides in opening up Negro job opportunities in its Alabama plants." The *Times* concluded that hard times in Birmingham would ensure white compliance because "jobs aren't so easy to get any more."[102] This analysis, which ignored the role of the USWA, implied that the problem was the bigotry of white workers, that corporations would do the right thing, and that a poor economy was good for ending discrimination. There was plenty of bigotry in Birmingham. But in November 1962 the union's Ben Fischer predicted that "a considerable increase in business would be required" for a significant amount of integration to take place at TCI.[103] As a guide for tackling employment problems at TCI, the *Times* analysis left much to be desired.

Similarly, President Kennedy's eloquent June 11 speech, given after the Alabama crises, alerted the nation to "a moral issue . . . as old as the scriptures and . . . as clear as the American Constitution." [104] But Kennedy ignored the newer issues of the agricultural revolution, modernization of the mills, and high unemployment. The classic civil rights ideology—blending morality, constitutionalism, and equality—produced broad support and comported well with the general thrust of the movement so far. The nation had opened its eyes to prejudice, but the ideology of the affluent society held. The flaw was viewed as something outside of the changing southern economy, which remained invisible, as the nation crafted new legislation to meet the challenge of the Birmingham demonstrations.

The Strange Career of Title VII
of the Civil Rights Act of 1964:
The Segregation of Racial and
Economic Policies

The nation responded to the Alabama events with the Civil Rights Act, introduced in 1963 and signed into law in 1964. Implementing Title VII, the provision banning employment discrimination, would preoccupy the USWA and the steel industry for the next ten years.[1] The union had been a constant champion; the industry, with the rest of the business community, thought Title VII was unnecessary, but did not actively oppose it. Thus, it was ironic that the law bedeviled the union as well as the company. The source of the problem was that Title VII was intellectually thin and its enforcement instrument, the Economic Employment Opportunity Commission (EEOC), powerless. Title VII prohibited employment discrimination but did not tackle the structural sources of black unemployment. The EEOC could talk, but not act. Title VII was enforced by private lawsuits, which prolonged and hardened conflicts. In 1972, when EEOC obtained the power to file lawsuits, it simply followed paths laid out earlier.

Those paths had returned the ignored structural issues to the agenda under the guise of an expanded definition of racial discrimination. Litigation in steel addressed situations where, despite the abolition of racial rules, modernization and shrinking employment had combined to produce less change than reformers had originally envisioned. To meet this situation, civil rights lawyers expanded the idea of racial discrimination to justify policies designed to protect blacks from the results of automation, poor education, and structural change. The legal rationale was to remedy the discrimination of the past, but the trigger was the current loss of jobs. This redefinition was accepted by the courts after the urban riots in 1967 and 1968, but it set off new waves of conflicts among black and white workers, many of whom faced similar situations.

Title VII translated labor issues into discourses about a bias unrelated to the changing economy. Joined with the War on Poverty, it produced new dualisms—affluence vs. poverty, suburbs vs. slum, and white vs. black—that simplified social reality and reconfigured American politics. But this dualistic outlook was not inevitable. Some in 1963 viewed the issues of race, labor, and poverty as interrelated.

Employment and Civil Rights

Kennedy responded to the contentious issues in Birmingham and Alabama by empowering the federal government to act directly to desegregate schools and public facilities, and his successor, Lyndon Johnson, followed the same script to enroll black voters. Employment was addressed differently. To the disappointment of the civil rights and labor movements, Kennedy had not included a fair employment practices commission (FEPC) in his original package. Still, the legislative proposals he sent to Congress on June 19 tackled "job opportunities" as well as civil rights, and its longest section was entitled "Full and Fair Employment," a phrase pilfered from the left-wing of his party.[2]

Kennedy's advisers had told him that for every percentage point decline in the general unemployment rate, black unemployment would fall two points.[3] He urged "prompt and substantial tax reduction" because "Negro unemployment will not be noticeably diminished in the country until the total demand for labor is effectively increased and the whole economy is headed toward a level of full employment."[4]

But just as Keynesianism was better at measuring aggregate trends than the progress of individual sectors like steel, the CEA was better at tracking the volume of employment than its composition or distribution; its professional bias produced flabby analysis when it came to microeconomic questions like labor markets, a backwater of the economics profession. Walter Heller believed that the combination of the tax cut and business leadership would adequately address black unemployment. The PCEEO, he argued, was sufficient because once "the major defense contractors, comprising the Nation's industrial firms . . . are diligently following a non-discrimination policy, the impact on the Nation's employment practices will be dramatic and widespread." The record in Birmingham did not support such confidence.[5]

The Labor Department, more attuned to structural unemployment than the CEA, offered Kennedy other advice. It was now headed by W. Willard Wirtz, who had moved up from the post of undersecretary of labor after Kennedy named Arthur Goldberg to the Supreme Court in 1962. Wirtz had worked on the NWLB during World War II and taught labor law at Northwestern before coming to Washington. His views were similar to Goldberg's, even though he lacked his predecessor's political savvy. At Wirtz's urging, the president requested $400 million more in educational and training funds, which Congress eventually appropriated. Kennedy explained that many black unemployed were "refugees from farm automation . . . equipped to work only in those occupations where technology and other changes have reduced the need for manpower."

These refugees, however, were the least likely to benefit from training. The programs under the Manpower Development and Training Act (MDTA) and the Area Redevelopment Act enrolled blacks in numbers equal to their proportion of the unemployed, even though there were slots for only 65,000 persons when 4 million were out of work. Most of the 13,000 blacks admitted were training for work in the growing white-collar and skilled fields where nonwhites had not been employed in numbers. Evidence showed that they were finding work. But blacks at the lowest levels of literacy were untouched by the training programs or by the demand for white-collar work.[6] Wirtz thought that public works jobs would be necessary for them. Kennedy's rationale for training reflected the impact of the changing economy on blacks, but he did not follow the logic of the analysis to Wirtz's conclusion.

"The Manpower Revolution" vs. the War on Poverty

Senator Joseph S. Clark of Pennsylvania embraced the conclusion and teased out the full implications of the thinking. Before the Birmingham crisis, Clark planned hearings on new fair employment practices (FEP) legislation, part of a broad effort to reform U.S. manpower policy.[7] He presided over eight months of hearings, which were rooted in the particulars of 1963—a time of economic recovery with 5.7 percent unemployment. Addressing Clark's Senate subcommittee on employment and manpower, 150 persons—from labor, the academy, and government—explored the impact of automation and cybernetics, "the marriage of the assembly line and the computer." It was clear that the resulting productivity rises and technological change were consigning millions to idleness. Excerpts from the hearings and its report, *The Manpower Revolution*, reached a wide audience when reprinted by a commercial publisher in 1965.[8]

The consensus attributed the nation's employment and social problems to the technological revolutions in agriculture and industry. Nearly everyone believed that both structural and cyclical elements were at work and supported demand measures—public spending or a tax cut or some combination—to stimulate the economy. But most reached for a comprehensive approach and believed that more active manpower policies and training were required to address the unemployment of the changing economy.[9]

The major dissenter was CEA head Walter Heller, speaking for the administration, who repeated the rationale for the tax cut—insufficient demand. Heller told the committee that automation was only "the most recent aspect of a continuing process of technological advance that dates back to the beginning of the industrial revolution." In his view, these constants in human history required no special measures.[10]

Clark's manpower report differed from Kennedy's thinking in two respects. First, it asserted that economic policy should be determined by employment goals. It set an unemployment target of 3 percent, in place of the president's 4, to be achieved by 1968. The committee had heard how manpower policies in Europe and Japan, both of which were enjoying unemployment rates below 3 percent, could squeeze more jobs out of growth without triggering inflation. Second, it predicted that the tax cut would not produce enough jobs to reach the government's 4 percent target. The report proposed a $5-billion-a-year public works program for "the more disadvantaged portions of the labor force."[11] For the record, Clark was a better predictor than Heller and the president. The tax cut brought unemployment down to 5 percent, but by late 1964, even the CEA agreed that it would be difficult to bring it down further.[12] It was Ho Chi Minh, not Keynes, who brought it down to 4 percent.[13]

Even so, the employment of the less educated actually decreased. If jobs generated by the tax cut would not absorb their labor and if their age and functional illiteracy made classroom training unrealistic, how would "the hard-core unemployed" live and support their families? A public works program was a better solution than any kind of welfare.[14]

Clark did not stop at the margins. As we saw at TCI, technological change threatened broad sectors of the work force, not simply the hard-core unemployed. It was not that automation threatened to create a jobless future, as some predicted. Technological change disrupted entire industrial cultures, patterns of employment and training. Manpower policies were a necessary complement to Keynesian stimulation of the economy and direct creation of jobs. Clark proposed to increase the capacity of government to respond to unemployment, coordinate training, and disseminate information about available jobs, skilled and white-collar, as well as unskilled.[15]

American manpower programs were varied and uncoordinated—unemployment compensation, retraining under MDTA, trade adjustment assistance, and vocational education.[16] Many new programs were created after the public had become alarmed about a social problem. After Sputnik, the nation had focused on shortages of skilled manpower; in 1962, on adult victims of technology; and now on youth, "social dynamite," in the words of one of the many warnings in the summer of 1963.[17]

The unemployment rate for married men fell to 3.2 percent in July 1963, but the general level was still close to 6 percent because teenage unemployment rose to 17 percent. The coming of age of the "war babies" plus rapid technological change meant that current rates of economic growth were not absorbing the young. Experts predicted that during the 1960s, 40 percent more youth would enter the labor force than had entered in the 1950s. Congress modified MDTA guidelines to enroll younger workers and provide literacy training where needed. But given the level of appropriations, it was robbing Peter to pay Paul. And Paul was not getting that much, either.[18]

Clark supported incremental changes. But he wanted to free training from the vagaries of public opinion and changing unemployment categories. Only by strengthening the Labor Department's capacities to plan and guide the nation's diverse training programs, reforming the archaic U.S. Employment Service, and making employment the principal goal of economic policy could the nation successfully meet the challenge of the "manpower revolution."

Clark believed that "all the elements for a frontal assault on retarded economic growth and sluggish employment are here. . . . All that is missing is that layer of coordination and continuity at the top." Only a president could initiate such a program. Kennedy had rejected Clark's proposal to place a National Manpower Planning Commission in the White House. The senator met with President Johnson shortly after he assumed office, on December 10, 1963. Johnson was uninterested in manpower reforms and told Clark he would consider a public works program only if the tax cut passed and the economy faltered. The most he would do is create a National Commission on Automation and Technological Progress, the traditional solution to unwanted problems. Given presidential disinterest, Clark's report, which came out in April 1964, could not compete with Johnson's proposed War on Poverty (WOP).[19]

Johnson had moved what had been the germ of an idea to the top of his own agenda, and eventually the nation's. The WOP had many parents. But unlike other ideas to reduce inequality, this one assumed that the poor lacked the motivation to take advantage of genuine opportunity. Heller asserted that "the poor inhabit a world scarcely recognizable . . . by the majority of their fellow Americans."[20] He was paraphrasing Michael Harrington's *The Other America*, which had alerted the president and public opinion to the existence of U.S. poverty. It is ironic that Harrington, a socialist, borrowed his analysis from studies of the poor in Mexico, not the United States.

Instead of a manpower commission, Johnson placed an Office of Economic Opportunity (OEO) in the executive office. He shepherded the Economic Opportunity Act through the Congress in August 1964, after the tax cut and civil rights legislation had been passed. Although there was some Republican carping, the president's appealing rhetoric, conventional goals, and modest financing carried the day. The war on poverty would be a limited one: $462.5 million of the $962.5 million appropriation was extracted from other parts of the budget. By dividing training programs among OEO, the Labor Department, and the Department of Health, Education, and Welfare (HEW), and then contracting agendas out to local community action programs (CAPs), the WOP program ended the possibility of addressing manpower issues systematically.[21] Adults took a back seat to youngsters. Nearly half the money was allotted to various youth programs—the Job Corps, a boarding school for the poor, work-training, and work-study. One of Senator Hubert H. Humphrey's aides observed that "[l]earning how to swing a pick and shovel or to plant trees [in the Job Corps] does not equip a man to compete in a technological society." But Johnson had targeted "those who . . . have no motivation to reach for something better because the sum total of their lives is losing." If the problem was motivation, the aide's objection was irrelevant.[22]

Nonetheless, others believed that these "unmotivated" poor could liberate themselves. One-third of OEO's budget went to the CAPs. The community action boards set up to devise local programs were mandated to have "maximum feasible participation" of the poor, reflecting the view that grassroots persons knew their needs better than corrupted bureaucrats. Although the theory seemed radical, its effects were conservative. It was always easy to find poor people to sit on poverty boards, as the law required. The boards received money, but they had no formal role in the planning process. OEO agendas came from Washington and inevitably enhanced some demands and ignored others.

The critical difference between the OEO and manpower approaches was revealed in Mississippi. A group of blacks took over an unused Air Force base near Greenville in January 1966 because, they explained, "we are hungry and cold and we have no jobs or land." Insisting they did not want charity, they said, "We are willing to work for ourselves if given a chance." Their words and deeds were a telling critique of the cultural theory of poverty. OEO had no answers for adults. In the summer of 1965 it had funded a Head Start program in Mississippi, and today preschool training remains the symbolic legacy of the WOP. But in April 1967, Marion Wright, then a lawyer for the NAACP, told Clark's Subcommittee on Employment, Manpower, and Poverty that "the poverty program has done nothing to change the basic economic structure, which needs to be changed." But OEO had not aimed at the economic structure, and activists had simply gone along with the programs or moved on to other projects and places. Moreover, youth programs appealed to radicalized individuals from the middle class, who possessed unending faith in education's ability to empower and transform.[23] After the assumption that child education could be the basis of community organizing was proved wrong, Wright, too late, discovered the economics of poverty.

Wirtz had warned Johnson that the Clark report made "the Poverty proposals look inadequate."[24] OEO head Sargent Shriver believed that a public employment policy was the quickest way to help the poor. However, party loyalty muted the skepticism with which Wirtz, Clark, Humphrey, Shriver, and many other Democrats viewed the war on poverty. It was difficult for liberals to criticize a program to help the poor. The head of the AFL-CIO in Boston worried about the impact that the city's new training program, involving 3,100 youths, would have on the jobs of his members. No one from labor was consulted about the program. Yet he felt constrained in his criticism because, as he put it, "we do not want to oppose any program designed to aid disadvantaged people."[25]

Leon Keyserling, who had been a member of President Truman's CEA, felt no restraint. It was not "the personal characteristics of the poor," he wrote, but "the high volume of idle manpower and plant" that caused poverty. "Saying [that] these characteristics are the major cause of poverty tends to blame individuals, not the malfunctioning of the economy." Although Johnson and Heller did not "blame the victim," they had separated poverty from the functioning of the economy. As Keyserling predicted, when the OEO did not end poverty, the program's critics blamed the victim.[26]

Johnson's conception of poverty was impoverished because, unlike Keyserling, he was an uncritical admirer of the nation's economic performance. Johnson congratulated a business group during the 1964 campaign for producing an American affluence that "has never been equaled before in the annals of history of this country." He credited the tax cut but offered Reaganite, not Keynesian, logic. "We put some of the money back for the people to spend instead of letting the government spend it for them. We put some of the money back for business to invest in new enterprise instead of the government investing it for them."[27]

Johnson said much the same at the USWA convention in September. He contrasted conditions then with the USWA situation at the time of their first contract in 1937. Taking his cue from Heller, the president celebrated the tax cuts that were "expanding and modernizing" the industry. He offered workers nothing, but asked them to support his efforts to extend the "hand of a just nation to the poor and to the helpless and to the oppressed."[28] To Johnson, social and economic arrangements worked for all but those at the margins, who would be aided by the sense of social obligation of the well-to-do, extending now to the working class. His speech was a perfect expression of the new politics he fostered. Johnson's measures, dubbed the Great Society, were in one sense extensions of the Democrats' distributional agenda of the 1930s. But they were embedded in self-satisfaction, lacking a critical component. They lived in a political economy that was decidedly un–New Dealish.

S. 1937, the Humphrey Bill

Like the analysis of poverty, the causes of black unemployment were first joined to the economy, in 1963, and then divorced from it in the legislation of 1964. The experiences of blacks had percolated through the Clark hearings and report. Discussions of teenage unemployment noted that the figures for black youth were higher than those for whites due to the higher black birthrate and the expulsion of young blacks from agricultural work. Many of the victims of automation in industry were recent black hires or unskilled blacks, as was true at TCI. A disproportionate number of blacks were functionally illiterate and needed public jobs.[29]

Situating black unemployment in national trends implicitly placed less emphasis on discrimination per se. Joseph P. Lyford, who had written a book on poor blacks in New York, testified that "the civil rights groups which are demonstrating against the craft unions, continuing their ancient campaign for FEPC, and trying to get more action in the enforcement of antidiscrimination laws, are not hitting at the base of the Negro's employment problem." Such measures, he wrote, may help blacks with educational and professional qualifications who are seeking entry into "financial institutions, publishing, and many other professional areas," but "the majority of low-income Negroes never get far enough in the hiring process to find out if discriminatory considerations are at work, simply because jobs are getting scarcer."[30]

Responding to such analyses, Whitney Young, head of the National Urban League, told Clark's committee that he was "disturbed about the notion that we have got to have full employment in this country, which I do not think is possible in the immediate future, before the problem of Negro unemployment is resolved." His remarks came after A. Philip Randolph urged the establishment of an FEPC, but linked fair employment with full employment. Young was attacking a straw man. Those most concerned with full employment were the leaders in the fight for an FEPC. The multicausal analysis of black unemployment was not an argument against an FEPC, only against the kind of FEPC being offered.[31]

On July 17, Senator Humphrey told Clark that he would propose an FEPC law "geared to an economy vastly different from the one existing in the late 1940s when the initial State FEP commissions were created. . . . The combination of

vast technological changes in industry and agriculture and rising unemployment presents a challenge significantly different than existed when the first FEP
proposals were drawn up."[32] In early July, Humphrey, shepherded by Walter
Reuther, had met with European social democrats and unionists. Like Clark,
both were impressed with the Swedish program of labor planning and training.[33] John G. Feild, the director of PCEEO in 1961 and 1962, clothed the Swedish
model in American garb.

Feild believed that as long as the economy was expanding, FEPC machinery
in the form of "adjudicating" individual complaints of bias was satisfactory.
But after the Korean war, those conditions were no longer were operative.[34]
The decline of blue-collar jobs in the cities, the source of previous gains, meant
that black workers would have to shift to other sectors. Neither the labor market nor the traditional FEPC could effect the change. Labor markets perpetuate
the past. Black networks often did not reach growing sectors. The record of
state FEPCs and Feild's own experiences at PCEEO revealed that the number and
saliency of complaints did not necessarily reflect broad barriers in the employment market. The campaign for an FEPC dramatized the issue, but supporters did not systematically address questions of work, training, and discrimination. They stressed the morality of nondiscrimination and the benefits
the nation would obtain from full utilization of the labor force. Most assumed
that an FEPC would increase black employment, though equivalents in the
states had failed to change the statistics.

Feild's analysis was becoming more common among the knowledgeable.
Civil rights leaders A. Philip Randolph, James Farmer of CORE, Roy Wilkins,
and even Whitney Young now linked the black situation with mechanization
in the South and automation in the North.[35] Wirtz, closer to Clark than the
president's other advisers, adopted this analysis, which had filtered into President Kennedy's speeches.

Feild simply devised a mechanism to fit the new analysis. S. 1937 gave the
government the same power the new civil rights law would grant the attorney
general with regard to public accommodations and school desegregation, but
the means of enforcement would not be litigation. The Humphrey bill placed
an administrator, an assistant secretary, in the Labor Department because, it
argued, "discrimination—both present and inherited from the past—can be
dealt with only by coordinating antidiscrimination with the employment,
training, manpower, and apprenticeship programs in the Department." In
this view, discrimination was "one facet of the manpower and employment
problems."[36]

Under the proposed law, the secretary could receive complaints but would
have discretion over whether to investigate them, so that he, not the com-

plainants, determined the agenda of enforcement. If the secretary found that blacks lacked a particular skill in demand, whether the lack was caused by discrimination or lack of information, he could act to end the bias or use MDTA or other programs to train the workers.[37] This procedure differed from the traditional FEPC, embodied in James Roosevelt's bill reported out of the House labor committee, which he chaired. Under the Roosevelt bill, action was triggered by individual complaints, and remedies were limited to proscribing discriminatory practices.[38]

S. 1937 sent an intellectual message that black unemployment was not simply a problem of human relations, where morality and democracy demanded the abolition of actions based upon prejudice, but was a function of the changing labor market. The decision to set up an administrative procedure, permitting courts to review but not decide, acknowledged that "laws directed against complex problems which must necessarily be written in general terms require adjudication by an expert body which can fill in the general policy declared by the Congress."[39]

Anticipating Republican objections, Feild created an independent review process. If an employer resisted, the administrator could initiate hearings before a five-member Equal Employment Opportunity Board, analogous to Tax Court reviews of the decisions of the Commissioner of Internal Revenue. The board itself would be uninvolved with mediation and conciliation. The prosecutorial and judicial functions would be separated, a prerequisite for Republican support. A federal appeals court would be the final arbiter, if necessary.

The ideas for the Humphrey bill emerged from the social democratic wing of the Democratic party, but the bill's thirteen cosponsors included key Republicans and enjoyed the support of Erwin Griswold, head of the Commission on Civil Rights. Griswold, a Republican, had been a tax lawyer before becoming dean of the Harvard Law School and was familiar with the proposed enforcement structure. Speaking for the commission, he said, "we like very much the concept of the Administrator in the Labor Department who will thus have available the other resources of the Labor Department." He agreed that the idea of prejudice was an inadequate analytic tool and that "the program and direction of the agency should not be determined by individual complainants." The government, he wrote, must have the power to direct the resources of the agency "to those fields and to those problems which careful study and research have indicated are of prime importance." Ideally, it would concentrate on those growing sectors that would produce the most black employment.[40] Republican Senator Jacob Javits of New York found the Humphrey bill intellectually compelling, but the departure from the traditional FEPC model troubled him. Griswold's enthusiasm erased these doubts, which ensured that S. 1937 became the Senate labor committee's bill.[41]

The Humphrey bill labored under two disadvantages. First, the omnibus civil rights bill was fashioned in the House, which privileged the House version, the familiar FEPC, renamed the Equal Employment Opportunity Commission (EEOC). Second, the joining of the House version to the omnibus civil rights legislation, a short-term victory, made retention of an FEPC, any FEPC, the key issue for supporters. Substance took a back seat to the politics necessary to pass the package. Future controversies over the meaning of the law followed from these shallow, instrumental origins.

The assumption that FEP legislation was unlikely to be enacted meant that the writing of the Humphrey bill was delayed until late June and reported out of the Senate labor committee only in January 1964. Experienced persons—the heads of significant state FEPCs, economist Eli Ginzburg, Walter Reuther, and Griswold—enthusiastically supported it, but many FEPC supporters had not read it and simply supported the need for legislation. More concerned with other parts of the civil rights package, the NAACP's Roy Wilkins was sympathetic, if general. Whitney Young sensed that the Humphrey bill was "more affirmative" than the traditional one, but he stressed the need to act and did not address specifics. Because the White House backed legislative authority for PCEEO only, Wirtz did not comment on either version. Eventually, the Labor Department preferred the Humphrey bill.[42] George Meany and David McDonald again gave their support, but neither had examined S. 1937. McDonald simply said that by responding only to the integration issues "in the headlines," the nation would be addressing "symptoms, not . . . the underlying disease, . . . the failure of our American economy to fully integrate the Negro into the productive apparatus of our society."[43]

Even so, there seemed to be plenty of time to inform the civil rights coalition about the provisions of the bill, because during the summer of 1963 nobody thought it possible to include any kind of FEPC in the omnibus legislation. On September 11, McDonald urged Celler to include an FEPC in his omnibus bill: "The problem of combating discrimination in employment has grown out of proportion to the means which exist for fighting this evil."[44] But Clarence Mitchell, the NAACP lobbyist and leader of the civil rights forces, told Adam Clayton Powell Jr. and Roosevelt that there was "no way we can mount two major civil rights efforts in this session of Congress." Moreover, legislation to establish the FEPC was still subordinate to the other elements of the civil rights package.[45]

The March on Washington on August 28 kept the jobs question alive, but an FEPC was not its principal objective either. The original march, a project of Randolph's Negro American Labor Council, was an attempt to inject an eco-

In July 1963, USWA president David J. McDonald (center) urged the establishment of a fair employment practices commission in his testimony before the Subcommittee on Employment and Manpower of the Senate Committee on Labor and Public Welfare. On the left is David Feller, chief counsel for the USWA; on the right, Frank "Nordy" Hoffmann, head of the USWA's legislation department in Washington, D.C. (Courtesy of HCLA, Penn State)

nomic component into the civil rights agenda after the southern issues had catapulted to the top. Like McDonald, the council warned that the "integration in the fields of education, housing, transportation and public accommodations will be of limited extent and duration so long as fundamental economic inequality along racial lines persists." The NALC named automation as the main source of unemployment and sought "massive works and training programs that puts all unemployed back to work," a rise in the minimum wage to $2.00 an hour, and a federal FEPC.[46]

The employment focus of the march had been diluted to obtain the support of Martin Luther King Jr., other civil rights leaders, and an array of clerics. It became a March for Jobs and Freedom. As it turned out, supporting the civil rights package eclipsed adding to it. Insofar as there was criticism, it was over the government's commitment to civil rights, not over omissions from the proposed law. Thus, a wrangle over a speech by Student Non-Violent Coordinating Committee's John Lewis concerned his use of such phrases as "too little, and too late," rhetorical flourishes like "scorched earth" policies, and attacks on "cheap political leaders."[47] Only Randolph and Reuther raised work issues, but many of the 200,000-plus marchers were from unions and carried placards urging "Jobs For All Now," "An FEPC Now," "Civil Rights Plus Full Employment Equals Freedom," and "Higher Minimum Wages," which somewhat made up for the paucity of words coming from the speaker's platform.[48]

The march movement had been more intent upon creating public awareness than on crafting legislation. Randolph had named Bayard Rustin to organize the march. Rustin, King's brilliant political tutor in Montgomery, demonstrated his talent once again. But Rustin was consumed by logistics. Five days before the march, one of his key aides said that "we are going, all of us, to have to familiarize ourselves more intimately with . . . the legislation proposals now before Congress."[49]

It was more violence in Birmingham that brought an FEPC into the package. The final decision-making on the House omnibus bill took place in the aftermath of the September 13 bombing of the Sixteenth Street Baptist Church, which killed four little girls. The subsequent national anguish facilitated Congressman Emanuel Celler's surprise substitution of the House FEP bill for Title VII's PCEEO on September 25. Despite Robert Kennedy's angry objection (he believed the addition would sink the ship), the president's men constructed another compromise.[50] EEOC was retained, but at the Republican price of removing its power to issue cease-and-desist orders. The only legal tool it retained was the ability to sue in a federal district court, which meant a full-blown trial, not an appeals review.[51] The bill was in the unfriendly hands of Howard Smith, the Bourbon chairman of the rules committee, when the president was assassinated in November.

As happened throughout much of its history, the civil rights bill benefited from tragedy. Initially, liberals were suspicious of Lyndon Johnson's compromising past, fearing that he would give up the employment title for the public accommodations section.[52] But President Johnson had more reasons to push the package than had Vice President or Majority Leader Johnson. He assured Clarence Mitchell that he supported it all.[53] Johnson subsequently explained to historian Doris Kearns how he felt: if he failed to pass the legislation, he said, the liberals would "get me. . . . I'd be dead before I could even begin."[54] With presidential backing, a bipartisan coalition behind the bill, and the odor of the Dallas killing still in the air, Smith could not forever bottle up the bill in rules committee hearings. After ten days of debate, on February 20, the law, including the new Title VII, passed the House, 290–110.

The Humphrey bill had been reported out of the Senate Labor Committee on January 9, the day Smith began his rules committee hearings. At the onset, the happy outcome was not so apparent. Celler acknowledged the virtues of S. 1937 but was not prepared to champion it. James Roosevelt warned Clark on January 16 "not to complicate matters by interjecting the bill into the Senate debate." Clark planned to substitute S. 1937 for the House version; he did not get the chance.[55]

The strategy in the Senate was to make an end run around James Eastland's judiciary committee by offering the House package and attracting enough Republican support to obtain the 67 votes necessary to cut off a southern filibuster. By early May, Johnson concluded that there would be no cloture without the help of Minority Leader Everett Dirksen, who had strong objections to Title VII.[56] When he was finished, Dirksen had removed EEOC's only power, to sue in federal courts.

Dirksen made good use of an attack by Senator Lister Hill of Alabama and a ruling by the Illinois FEPC, which kept the civil rights forces on the defensive throughout the negotiations. Whatever discussion there was about employment discrimination now took place on the terrain of opponents of the legislation. On January 15, 1964, Hill had charged that Title VII was "a blow to labor union freedom," that it would "undermine . . . the seniority system," require black preference and "racial balance," and deprive unions of representation before the NLRB. Hill was speaking for the South, not the labor movement. Like most of the Alabama delegation sent to Congress after the New Deal, he was a liberal on economic issues. He held orthodox, but not extreme, views on segregation. But the senator had nearly lost his seat in 1962 because his opponent, James Martin, a harbinger of the new race-baiting southern GOP, waged a campaign worthy of George Wallace. Although Hill had more credibility with labor than most, many southern Bourbons suddenly became champions of unions to defeat Title VII.[57]

No labor leader or spokesperson for a civil rights organization had argued that Title VII permitted preferences or altered seniority. Clark rebutted Hill's charges on the Senate floor on February 8, and he and Republican Senator Clifford Case of New Jersey produced a confirmation from the Justice Department. Reuther wrote the Alabama senator a widely publicized letter dismissing his interpretation. Andrew J. Biemiller, head of the legislation department of the AFL-CIO, sent a four-page critique to all affiliates, telling them that the law did not require "racial balance" in the workforce or "preferential" hiring, "did not change the seniority rights of any employee, and did not remove skill as a qualification for hiring or promotion." Unions and employers, the letter explained, are simply "forbidden to judge a man by the color of his skin, or the faith he professes." That was a fair statement of the congressional, public, and liberal interpretation of discrimination. It is true that some activists advocated some form of compensatory treatment. But in 1963 and 1964, these ideas were asserted, not argued, and were not the official positions of the civil rights organizations.[58]

Dirksen found Hill's attack useful, but he was more concerned with business than with labor. John G. Stewart, Humphrey's chief of staff, present at the negotiations, recalled that Dirksen "appeared to base most of his judgment on the parochial experiences of Illinois," a reference to a ruling by the state's FEPC. To Dirksen and many northern businessmen, the experiences were not parochial.[59]

The Motorola Corporation in Chicago had refused to hire a black man, Leon Myart, after he failed a five-minute ability test, a gatekeeper to further testing for a job inspecting radios, TVs, and stereos coming off the assembly line. The FEPC examiner, a black lawyer, ruled on March 5, 1964, that Myart had passed the test but had been rejected because he was black, and ordered Motorola to hire Myart and cease using the test because it ignored the social environment of "culturally deprived and disadvantaged groups."

The luck of timing now went against the civil rights forces. *New York Times* columnist Arthur Krock warned that Title VII threatened "to project the rationale of the Illinois F.E.P.C. ruling throughout the free enterprise system of the United States."[60] The assertion of a controversial rationale by a minor black official of a state FEPC was not the best way to introduce the testing issue, a common subject in unionized plants. The charge that the FEPC was assuming "dictatorial" power gained credence by the narrative. The examiner had ordered Myart hired on the grounds that he had been a victim of discrimination, but then on his own ruled that the test was invalid. Myart had not claimed that the test was unfair, only that he had passed the test and had been rejected because of discrimination. Motorola had a record of a failing score but not the test itself, so it was difficult to reach a definitive conclusion.[61]

Later in the year the full Illinois FEPC restored the testing on the technicality that Myart had not raised the issue. But the FEPC reserved the right to consider "the possibility that tests of this nature are inherently discriminatory against persons alien to the predominant middle class white culture in this society." The commission did confirm the finding of discrimination after Myart passed the test, which he took under its auspices. It ordered the company to pay Myart $1,000 in damages. Motorola challenged the testing procedure and fought the judgment through the court system, arguing that its normal practice was to destroy tests after a period of time and transfer the results to a computer data card. Finally, three years later, in 1966, the Illinois Supreme Court exonerated Motorola, arguing that proof, not merely "suspicion," was needed to conclude that the recorded score was deliberately falsified. However, it rejected Motorola's contention that aspects of the FEPC law were unconstitutional.[62]

Coming in early March as Dirksen was formulating his objections to Title VII, the examiner's ruling made what would have been an abstract argument concrete. In essence, Dirksen was saying that any federal agency would end up espousing doctrines like the Illinois FEPC. He not only refused to give the proposed agency "cease-and-desist" power but withdrew its power to litigate, the compromise from the House. The revised bill would leave it to individuals to enforce Title VII by filing lawsuits. Although diluting the power of the commission was his key revision, Dirksen, Republican senator John Tower of Texas, and others insisted upon what became Section 703(h), which stated that the act did not prohibit bona fide seniority, merit systems, or tests, if they were not constructed with an intention to discriminate. Similarly, Section 703(j) informed employers that they were not required to grant preferential treatment to blacks, and Section 703(g) required individuals to demonstrate discriminatory intent to prove a violation.[63]

If Dirksen used the Motorola case as the poster child of an FEPC gone wild, it was also a preview of the protracted nature of court decision making, the winnowing out of key substantive issues on the basis of the technicalities, the legal hurdles of proof, and the rapid escalation to absolutist arguments—in this instance, unconstitutionality. The courts were not good forums for addressing labor matters.

The Humphrey-Clark group had initially believed that Dirksen's objections would be technical, motivated more by ego than substance. Therefore, when Dirksen revealed these and some thirty-odd other amendments on April 7, the civil rights forces were surprised and dismayed. Republican Senator Keating of New York told reporters that Dirksen's amendments would "seriously weaken the effectiveness of the bill." A good number of Republicans as well as northern Democrats in the Senate and House said they could not vote for such a bill.

Thomas Harris, the lawyer for the AFL-CIO, summed up the objections with a hypothetical case: "A Negro job applicant who was refused employment in Arkansas by, say the Aluminum Company of America, would first have to be sufficiently courageous to file a charge himself, and then sufficiently prosperous to hire his own lawyer to sue in a federal district court in Arkansas, knowing that he cannot get reinstatement even if he wins, and knowing that if he loses, court costs, including Alcoa's legal costs, will be assessed against him. Anyone who is that brave and that rich doesn't need FEPC."[64] (The relief provision was restored. A court could reinstate the worker and award him back pay if he won.)

Having committed themselves to the Dirksen negotiations, the Democratic leaders could not just walk away. But the government's negotiators, Justice's Nicholas Katzenbach and Burke Marshall, believed that the government must have some power. On May 7, one of Dirksen's aides came up with a compromise formula that gave the attorney general, not the EEOC, the power to sue after finding a "pattern or practice of resistance" to the rights guaranteed in Title VII.[65] Dirksen assumed, accurately, that the Justice Department selected its cases conservatively. Consumed with voting and school desegregation cases and about to assume responsibility for enforcing of the new legislation, the civil rights division also lacked lawyers versed in labor matters. This meant, in effect, that individuals, not the government, would enforce the law.

Harris believed that the amendments were "deliberately designed to gut the FEPC title." The Leadership Conference on Civil Rights concluded that most of Dirksen's amendments did not change the bill "except for Title VII. It is now virtually meaningless. Indeed, it would be surprising if men of stature could be found to serve on the Commission." McDonald telegraphed Robert Kennedy to say that the compromise was a "disaster," adding, "If anything, Title VII should be strengthened so as to be as effective as present NLRB procedures." Clark told senators, "This has become the Dirksen bill! I deplore it but that's it."[66]

It became Dirksen's bill not simply because his influence was needed for cloture. The only significant opposition to the civil rights package, including Title VII, was southern. Privately, businessmen worried about the vagueness of the term "discrimination." But business lobbyists were more interested in the pending tax bill than the civil rights law. A midwestern Republican observed, "There's been a lot of talk about the bill infringing on property rights, but as far as I can tell the people who own the property don't seem to think so."[67] Clark could cite only three corporate heads willing to endorse the legislation, but business remained on the sidelines.

This gave politicians a certain amount of leeway, which they chose to use conservatively, acting as if it were 1957 and 1960, not 1963 and 1964. Clarence Mitchell agreed that it was necessary to obtain Dirksen's support but in 1967 reported that Katzenbach and Marshall were not "as tough in adhering to their position . . . as they could have been." True, but both men were less committed to and knowledgeable about Title VII than other parts of the law. Humphrey was not a legislative craftsman and allowed Justice to do the negotiating. When Johnson made Humphrey floor manager for the bill, strategy became everything. Johnson, perhaps recollecting past civil rights fights, stressed Dirksen's power and not the changed national climate that the Republican minority leader himself recognized.[68]

Clark best understood the issues, but he was unsuited for the political work necessary to effect the reforms. Reserved and aloof, the patrician intellectual who had reformed city government in Philadelphia was a strange champion of labor and blacks. He was not the kind of politician who flattered to persuade, as Humphrey had wooed Dirksen.[69] Clark was not one to rally the troops, either.[70] He had planned to offer S. 1937 as a substitute to the House version, but on June 15, two days after another unfriendly amendment passed, the leadership concluded that it could not both defend the bill from further assaults and fight to strengthen it. Clark saw no way out. "Unhappily we are not in a parliamentary situation to approve [S. 1937]."[71]

Had the parliamentary situation been different would Dirksen and moderate Republicans have accepted the Humphrey bill? Dirksen might have considered the administrator in the Labor Department an advocate. But would he have so viewed the independent board? Unlike the original House FEPC and the much-hated NLRB, the judging entity in S. 1937 was outside what Dirksen might have considered an advocacy agency. But this is an academic question, because the politics preempted the discussion.

Still, politics is ultimately rooted in substance. Dirksen succeeded because the Kennedy-Johnson team lacked an analysis and an argument to counter the Illinois senator's negative project. Labor issues had been placed on the presidential plate late, and they remained half-digested. Both Kennedy and Johnson, tutored by their Keynesian advisers, exaggerated the employment dividends of the tax cut and scoffed at the structural analysis of unemployment, believing that economic growth would absorb the jobless, black as well as white. This underlying belief was at the root of all of the compromises they accepted.

Weak entities addressing genuine problems can make matters worse. This was the judgment across the political spectrum. Humphrey complained that EEOC was a "Federal Mediation and Conciliation Service. [It has] no authority of law."[72] The vice president for industrial relations of the National Association of Manufacturers agreed, saying that the EEOC "will operate more like the Federal Mediation and Conciliation Service than the NLRB." He added that the new law could well "become another full employment act for lawyers."[73]

Sensing this future, former Florida governor Leroy Collins, head of the Community Relations Service, observed that "the filing of lawsuits after horns have been locked in a locality does little to stimulate good human relations." The CEA and the Bureau of the Budget wondered whether Title VII might "suffer from a fatal flaw of providing a legal solution for what is essentially a social and economic problem." Both predicted disappointments arising from the protracted legal process.[74]

The duplication and fragmentation of authority dismayed all charged with enforcement. When FEPC prospects were unpromising, Kennedy had used his executive power to create the PCEEO to oversee government contractors. The PCEEO was now renamed the Office of Contract Compliance (OFCC) and was part of the Labor Department, but enforcement was the responsibility of the contracting agencies.[75] There was the new EEOC to mediate and conciliate, the

Justice Department, which had responsibility to bring "pattern or practice" suits, and, down the road, the various federal courts.[76]

After Title VII was passed, Humphrey tried to convince Johnson that discrimination was an inadequate concept, arguing that "the problems require much more than simply eliminating overt racial discrimination."[77] He urged the president to coordinate efforts among the OFCC, EEOC, and the Justice Department to permit strategic interventions in fields "with high potential for new jobs for Negroes."[78] Johnson was uninterested, and Humphrey gave up. His decision to be a loyal vice president drew him from his old associates and ideas, as he strenuously rowed Johnson's boat. Clark "was confident" that the nation would return to the Humphrey bill. In 1966, after every weakness detailed by the critics of the EEOC had proven true, Clark tried to abolish it and substitute the solution offered by S. 1937. In 1967 Senator Javits tried to amend the law to provide more coordination with the Labor Department, but it was too late. In 1963 and 1964, when other priorities were more pressing, black leaders had had no reason to prefer the EEOC version. Those most knowledgeable had in fact preferred Humphrey's bill. But once the EEOC was established, black leaders, viewing it as their own, preferred to strengthen rather than replace it.[79]

Thus, the critical edge of 1963 was blunted in the legislation of 1964, as the causes of both poverty and black unemployment were separated from the workings of the economy. The War on Poverty redirected both its own and the Labor Department's manpower programs from the skilled to the unskilled, from adults to young people, and from whites to blacks. Discussions of unemployment, underemployment, and low wages were replaced by discourses on inadequate motivation, education, and culture, factors limiting a person's ability to take advantage of opportunity. Instead of using the discovery of teenage unemployment as an additional argument for a comprehensive manpower policy, the government narrowed its scope to target "disadvantaged" youngsters. Manpower policies would focus on the bottom end of the labor market. This shift not only increased the political vulnerability of the program, but made it difficult to meet skill shortages when the economy picked up. When this happened, the government responded by putting the brakes on the economy, which hurt most those at the bottom end of the labor market. Manpower policy was crucial to maintaining low rates of unemployment without inflation.[80]

Title VII would affect every industry, but it remained contentious because it separated the notion of discrimination from the more powerful causes of black unemployment. When growth slowed after 1969 and supplementary measures such as the War on Poverty proved puny or disposable, discrimination became the only legal basis for attempts to increase black employment. Attempts to expand its meaning produced another round of racial conflict, and when the idea reached its limits, affirmative action replaced it.

Contemporary critics of affirmative action are correct when they argue that the classic meaning of civil rights was color-blindness. But civil rights advocates did not believe that nondiscrimination was sufficient. What produced the Humphrey bill was the judgment that bigotry was not the key problem. Humphrey did not propose affirmative action, in the contemporary sense. Today, administrators or businessmen make affirmative action decisions for their own purposes. They accept existing training and labor institutions as they are and selectively choose to give some of the graduates a break. The Humphrey bill proposed to reform those institutions and intervene strategically to train and channel black workers, and workers in general, to employment opportunities. It was formulated to serve the many, not the few. At the same time, Clark and Humphrey did not imagine their project as a zero-sum game. With the initiative in the hands of the government, they would labor to prevent racial conflict.

But the future history of Title vII was not so obvious in 1964. Since the recession in 1958 the AFL-CIO and civil rights groups, especially those representing the young, had been at each other's throats.[81] But in 1963 and 1964 the common struggle to pass the civil rights law brought them together. Union leaders worked tirelessly for the bill. When Clark asked Roy Wilkins about discrimination in unions, he said even unions where blacks had little representation "are improving." Mentioning some problems among unions in structural steel, he was quick to add "not the work covered by the United Steelworkers Union." The head of the civil rights department of the AFL-CIO, Boris Shishkin, observed that the NAACP no longer engaged in the "unwarranted attacks on unions of the kind perpetrated repeatedly in the past six years." For the first time in several years, Shishkin was invited to and attended the annual NAACP meeting and dinner. Relations with the Urban League and the Congress of Racial Equality (CORE) also improved. Working together to pass Title vII and the entire civil rights package smoothed the rough edges bonding labor and the civil rights organizations.[82]

Title VII in the Mills,

Agencies, and Courts:

Theories and Practices

Even though Title VII and the government offered little guidance, the USWA believed that labor and civil rights leaders, continuing the relationships that effected the civil rights law, could devise strategies to enhance black employment. Immediately after the Senate passed the Civil Rights Act and before President Johnson signed the law on July 2, 1964, David McDonald sent letters to the heads of the major civil rights organizations, urging them to meet with the union and the AFL-CIO to develop "a joint program for the implementation of Title VII." None replied, so the USWA acted alone, sponsoring training sessions for its members and conferences with other unions and representatives from government agencies. The silence reflected the strategic crisis of the civil rights movement at that time.[1] The resolution of that crisis was structured by the legislation passed in 1964, especially Title VII and the War on Poverty. Joint efforts were a casualty of the new outcomes.

In the spring of 1964, A. Philip Randolph had warned Martin Luther King Jr. that "the civil rights revolution has been caught up in a crisis of victory, a crisis that may involve great opportunity or great danger to its future fulfillment." Because official segregation, the target of the recent past, was about to end, black politics required new direction.[2] Randolph convened a "State of the Race" conference in New York on January 30 and 31, 1965. King did not attend but sent his aide, Andrew Young, who urged more direct action. (As it turned out, SCLC's then current direct-action campaign in Selma, Alabama, which led to the passage of the Voting Rights Act in early August, would be the last big southern battle.) Roy Wilkins of the NAACP stressed enforcement of the new legislation. The Urban League's Whitney Young spoke about the need for jobs. Kenneth Clark, the psychologist whose work had informed the *Brown* decision, thought blacks should consolidate their achievement and take advantage of integration to attain middle-class status. James Forman of the Student Nonviolent Coordinating Committee (SNCC) criticized the bourgeois mentality of the others, saying he believed that "the movement must now meet the black poor on their own terms."[3]

The news conference following the New York summit was harmonious, but revealed no consensus on tactics or targets. Leaders endorsed both politics and demonstrations, black initiatives and coalition work. This would be the last inclusive meeting. Each organization was undergoing its own metamorphosis. Criticized by younger militants, who believed he was too close to the AFL-CIO, Randolph resigned as president of the Negro American Labor Council in 1964.[4] In the spring of 1965, together with Bayard Rustin, he created the A. Philip Randolph Institute, funded by the AFL-CIO. CORE and SNCC embraced forms of black power in the North and the South. SCLC remained a regional organization, influential mainly where it had won victories, like Alabama. King's failure in Chicago in 1966 demonstrated that the direct action that had ended legal segregation did not work so well in the North.[5] Although King subsequently engaged both northern and national issues, he did so from a southern base. The older NAACP and Urban League, both of which possessed the membership and financial base the newer organizations lacked, rolled with the punches.[6]

The most comprehensive and strategic analysis offered at the summit had been Bayard Rustin's. Rustin acknowledged that the civil rights movement had much work that it alone must undertake, like registering blacks in the South. He also saw the virtue of some direct action campaigns. But he felt that the movement also needed a jobs strategy. Even though the changing economy affected whites as well as blacks, he argued that "enlightened self-interest dictates that we come up with some far-reaching answers or find ourselves stymied. For in a modern, automating society, there are limits to self-help." He endorsed the Clark committee's $5 billion program for jobs and slum elimination. Despite his best efforts, however, Rustin failed to focus a diffuse White House Conference on Civil Rights in 1965 on economic issues.[7]

Rustin's suggestions came a year too late. The tax bill, the War on Poverty, and Title VII preempted his issues and reconfigured the political landscape. Tax cuts had addressed growth and unemployment and had reduced the dollars available for a significant urban initiative. The local politics fostered by the

War on Poverty's Community Action Program (CAP) made coalition work difficult. Although the new racial politics had independent sources, it was propelled by and often emerged from the forms of organization created by the laws of 1964. Placed outside of regular electoral institutions, the CAPs prolonged the protest mode, which in the end undercut Rustin's social democratic model. The politics of Title VII enforcement followed a similar course.

The USWA assumed that the law "for the first time provides a Federal right to equality of employment opportunity in unorganized as well as organized plants." Unions had machinery to implement Title VII; the challenge lay in plants "where there is no union organization, no negotiated seniority plan, and no agreed upon grievance procedure." But as civil rights organizations were becoming racially assertive, rhetorically oriented to the black poor, and openly suspicious of enduring coalitions, such distinctions became irrelevant. Reinforced by New Left thinking that unions were part of the problem, the categories "union" and "nonunion" seemed irrelevant to the newest civil rights organizations, particularly those dominated by youth.[8]

No representative of the NAACP Legal Defense and Educational Fund (LDF) had attended the race summit, but its director, Jack Greenberg, was equally uninterested in union collaborations. Greenberg was determined to do for employment discrimination what the LDF had done for segregated education. Aided by a $500,000 grant from the Rockefeller Foundation, he sent an army of students, community workers, and staff into the South to gather complaints to present to the EEOC on July 2, 1965, the day the law came into effect. (The law thus gave employers and unions one year to end discriminatory practices.) As it turned out, the strategy the LDF eventually pursued clashed with USWA thinking. Like the advocates of the Humphrey bill, the LDF recognized that bigotry was an inadequate intellectual framework and that racial rules were ending. But instead of reforming labor markets, promoting training, and expanding the supply of jobs, the LDF extended the meaning of discrimination, thereby sharply distinguishing the interests of black and white workers. The acceptance of the LDF position by the courts in 1968 and later by the regulatory agencies undermined USWA strategy.[9]

The USWA and Title VII

As the civil rights organizations were changing, so was the USWA, which actually strengthened its civil rights work. President Johnson's speech to the USWA convention in 1964 placed steelworkers in the affluent camp. He promised them nothing, but asked them to support his programs for the poor. There was no dissent then because of the priority to defeat the Republican Barry Goldwater, who threatened to repeal much of the New Deal. But after Johnson's victory, the wraps were off. In early 1965, after a bitterly contested, close election, David McDonald was replaced by I. W. Abel.

The decision of his peers on the executive board to challenge McDonald included reasons ranging from the personal to the political. McDonald was becoming more and more aloof from union affairs, and his high living, patronage, and bullying offended many. Rank-and-file discontent was rising as well. Workers had not received a wage increase since 1961; at the same time, technological change was increasing fears of job displacement and generating grievances over the rates and positions at modernized facilities. McDonald seemed to be accepting wage restraint and also bypassing regular union structures. Created after the 1959 steel strike, the Human Relations Research Committee, including appointed union and management representatives, was ignoring and supplanting the elected Wage Policy Committee. When the economy and the steel industry took off in 1964 and 1965 and other unions, like the UAW, began reaping the gains of growth, dissatisfaction grew. The democratic and economic issues proved to be a potent brew.[10]

The election of a president of the USWA was an event of national significance in 1965. The two men's appearance on the television program *Meet the Press* offered visible proof of the challenger's characterization of the incumbent regime as "tuxedo unionism." Abel's plain demeanor was a perfect foil to McDonald's manicured good looks. In this case, the covers were true guides to the books. McDonald had risen in the USWA as Murray's secretary. Abel, the son of a blacksmith, had lost a steel job at the onset of the Great Depression. During the 1930s, he fired kilns in a brickyard and attended a small college but was often without work. He finally had obtained a job at Timken Roller Bearings, a bitterly antiunion and Republican firm in Ohio. He was Timken's local union president and became a district director before being elected secretary-treasurer of the USWA. Abel was a unionist of the old school. He identified the USWA's interests with those of the whole labor movement and society, whereas McDonald had forged a separate identity based on steel strength. In the words of an AFL-CIO official, Abel's election ensured that "the United Steelworkers is now an active participant, not just a dues-paying member."[11]

With Abel's election, the USWA became more visible in national politics. Up until then, the Washington office, headed by Frank "Nordy" Hoffmann, had been a passive player in legislative matters. Union technicians in Pittsburgh— Otis Brubaker, Meyer Bernstein, and David Feller—had tracked the manpower and social legislation of the early 1960s, but now John J. Sheehan, the son of a Bronx truck driver, directed the office. Sheehan, with an activist's bent, believed that "the collective strength of working people can bring about a change in society."[12]

Civil rights leader Bayard Rustin (left) and USWA president I. W. Abel at a luncheon at the A. Philip Randolph Institute in May of 1973. (Courtesy of HCLA, Penn State)

McDonald had done the right things when prodded by his aides, but he rarely took the initiative on civil rights any more than he had on other social issues. Abel, not McDonald, had addressed the founding convention of Randolph's Negro American Labor Council in 1960.[13] Now President Abel delivered the main address at a dinner of the League for Industrial Democracy, which gave Randolph its top award. In his own speech, UAW president Walter Reuther predicted that "when USW and UAW are marching arm in arm, there is no power that can halt the American labor movement." Abel reciprocated, saying of Reuther: "We supped at the same ideological table." The McDonald-Reuther animosity no longer braked joint action, but achieving programmatic unity would not be easy in the tumult of 1960s politics. Equally important, the continuing economic problems in the steel industry, which the auto industry would not face for fifteen years, required Abel to keep close to union business.[14]

Abel upgraded the Civil Rights Department, created in 1948, by placing an international officer, Vice President Joseph P. Molony, at its head. Molony, an Irish immigrant who came to Buffalo in the 1920s, viewed the civil rights movement as a descendant of the CIO: "I have witnessed two great social revolutions in my day—because the CIO was more than a union, it was a great revolution.

I have also witnessed the great social revolution as the Negro seeks to capture and obtain the rights which are given to all other citizens. And they too sing, that we shall overcome." [15]

Abel named Alex Fuller executive director of the civil rights committee. Fuller had been a leader of the Abel forces in Detroit, where he had been active in labor and civil rights circles, and he had served on Michigan's FEPC, but his race was key to his appointment. In 1965, when African Americans were pressing for more representation, it was time for a black director. Fuller lubricated relationships with the civil rights organizations but was less interested in the job issues.[16]

The USWA responded more directly to the newest black militants when it brought international representative Curtis Strong to its Pittsburgh headquarters. Strong, who had worked at the coke plant in the Gary Works, had created black caucuses beginning in the late 1940s, and was one of the founders of the national Ad Hoc Committee in 1964. Strong's appointment acknowledged not only the committee but the new generation of black militants emerging from the postwar period.[17]

The new regime instructed locals to process discrimination cases as grievances. But it also informed workers about options with state or federal agencies under Title VII. Molony and Fuller ordered each district to assign one staffperson to coordinate civil rights work.[18] Given the diversity of the black situations in various mills, there was no simple recipe, but they urged locals to act vigorously to root out barriers to black progress. With Maloney at its head, the civil rights department now had access to the full range of union expertise.

If the union had new men in Pittsburgh, its de facto leadership in Birmingham became de jure in 1964 when Reuben Farr retired and Howard Strevel was elected director of District 36 in 1964. But the McDonald-Abel contest the next year confused issues in the South. The issues contested in the North often did not resonate in the South. Strevel supported McDonald, who carried the district 13,115 to 7,585.[19]

Civil rights issues inevitably percolated through the elections. Ironically, Abel won the support of militant blacks and militant white racists, each for different reasons, of course. The original black dissidents at TCI were part of the Ad Hoc Committee. Both the national and local groups had endorsed Abel. The head of Abel's campaign in District 36 was Cecil Robertson, a white liberal from Gadsden. But in Birmingham, a vocal Abel advocate was Johnny Nichols, a white whom George Wallace had appointed an assistant to the state labor secretary, although he still was formally a member of Local 1013 at TCI. Tin mill worker Ed Ward, one of the steelworkers paid by Wallace to travel about with him in his presidential bid in 1964, also supported Abel. Thus, McDonald's false whispering campaign portraying Abel as a racist was believed by some blacks. At the same time, whites supporting racial change backed McDonald. E. B. Rich, chairman of the grievance committee at TCI's largest and most important local, 1013, supported McDonald because the incumbent's white critics in Birmingham were racists. Rich, acting to preserve the USWA's racial policies, recalled later that if he had known then what now he knew he would have supported Abel.[20]

Given the confused lineup of the southern vote, the new leadership in Pittsburgh was slow in figuring out Birmingham politics. The Abel team, like most northern liberals, assumed that all white southerners were racists. Bernard Kleiman, who replaced David Feller as the union's new lawyer, recalled that he initially considered all of the TCI whites "Kluxers."[21] The electoral divisions overrode efforts to sort things out. Jimmie Lee Williams, the black vice president of the coke plant, was named to the USWA staff. That he had supported Abel was as important as his race. Rich's appointment was delayed because of his leadership of the McDonald forces.[22]

But the politics at the top floated above the work in the mills, which went on uninterrupted. Strevel continued to rely upon Bruce Thrasher and Rich to implement the changes in the mills. Thrasher, it will be recalled, had been active in the attempt to overthrow Bull Connor. Born in Birmingham, the son of a railroad worker, he had started working as a weight clerk in the open hearth in 1949 after graduating from Birmingham Southern College. At the time he went on staff in 1955, he was working in the TCI comptroller's office.[23]

Originally a heater in the open hearth, Rich had become chairman of the grievance committee of Local 1013 in 1963. He was one of the five grievancemen Strevel selected from each of the major mills to implement the new transfer provisions and merged lines of promotion. A Korean War veteran, who had three semesters of college, Rich's quiet, verging on shy, manner masked a man of iron determination. He was known as the "Pied Piper" because of his frequent unofficial walkouts. He saw civil rights as a union issue; he learned from and worked closely with the black caucus at TCI. Though he was threatened with violence many times, he refused to be intimidated. Rich retained the respect of all but the most dogged racists because he was a tough bargainer on all union issues.[24]

Whatever the legal meaning of Title VII, Thrasher and Rich believed that the merger of the lines, the pool, the contract's nondiscrimination clause, and an industry-union agreement to promote opportunity gave the union legal as well as moral authority to change things at TCI. The Bureau of National Affairs, which published a handbook on the Civil Rights Act, agreed: "The enforcement procedures of the federal law promise to be ponderous and time-consuming, the

USWA international
representative E. B. Rich,
photographed in the early
1980s. (Courtesy of
E. B. Rich, photograph
by Olan Mills)

enforcement of contractual no-discrimination pledges can be relatively speedy
and direct." It cited the USWA's contract as the model. *Iron Age*, too, viewed the
union as the most likely instrument to "obtain employment equality." [25]

No clause is self-enforcing. The union did not attempt to define the term
"discrimination" but only to identify practices that impeded black mobility.
Filling temporary vacancies was the steel industry's method of training. The
USWA concluded that a key barrier was the foremen's reluctance to assign blacks
temporary vacancies in a job on the next rung of a line of promotion or on the
first rung of a new line of promotion. Foremen were working incumbents
overtime and choosing whites for temporary assignments, instead of training
other men.[26] Because the company often used the "ability clause" as an excuse,
Rich urged the international's leaders to add a clause to the contract that required senior employees to have the ability to learn the job, not the ability to
do it. Rich did not wait for contractual changes, which came in 1968. He contested the TCI process of selection all the way up through arbitration and won.

Changing Managers: Seniority, Black Training, and Promotion

The management that the union was criticizing was not the old Wiebel regime.
In the course of a general corporate reorganization in 1964, TCI was placed

more securely within the U.S. Steel organizational structure.[27] Blough replaced the intransigent Wiebel with Earl W. Mallick in July 1964. Mallick was willing to speak directly with civil rights leaders and took a more active role in facilitating the changes in the city. At the same time, Hiram Bullard was named superintendent of the works. Bullard, an industrial engineer who had been with the company since 1937, was a hard-nosed manager but not a racist. He prepared a slide show-lecture on civil rights to show to the managers of TCI and other industries in the city. TCI actively recruited and hired black technical and managerial persons. The old southern order had ended. But the corporation's interpretation of Title VII was not identical with that of the union, black workers, and the new regulatory bodies—but then, no one ever accused a steel manager of possessing a social worker's mentality. TCI's style remained authoritarian.[28]

A. F. Walker, a black, had worked for seventeen years in Fairfield Steel's blast furnace department. On October 7, 1964, a permanent vacancy in the job of motor inspector helper was posted. (The helper aided the motor inspector, who repaired, adjusted, and maintained machinery.) Although it had a job classification of only JC-16, it led to jobs classified JC-11 to JC-18. Walker bid for the job, but it was awarded to a white man named Eddins, who had only five months of service at Fairfield Steel.[29]

Eddins was no youngster. He had worked as an electrician, a job rated JC-16, at the company ore mines since 1939 and had studied electrical engineering. After the mines closed in 1962, he obtained a job at Fairfield Steel. Like all new men, he began in the pool as a laborer. Under pool rules, bids into lines of promotion were to be determined by mill seniority if the person was able to do the job. Measured in this way, Walker, who also worked in the pool, had more seniority than Eddins.[30]

The company argued that Eddins was chosen because he was able to "progress up through the line of promotion," to motor inspector. He certainly could. A motor inspector is a partly trained electrician. The selection seemed to be an open-and-shut case because rarely did "experienced Electricians bid on Motor Inspector Helper jobs." Why did the union choose to contest what appeared to be a simple case of selection based on merit and ability?

The union wanted temporary vacancies to be assigned on the basis of seniority. In his five months at the mill, Eddins had obtained 68 opportunities to work as a temporary motor inspector helper, while Walker had been refused all requests. The new seniority rules would work for blacks only if they were selected for the temporary vacancies. Many foreman made temporary assignments on the basis of favoritism or race. The union claimed Eddins's advantage came from his having been given the temporary assignments, not from his earlier experience as an electrician. If the company could simply override seniority and choose the man who acquired "ability" by obtaining temporary vacancies in violation of seniority, black promotion would be hard to achieve.

Rich also aimed to limit management's use of the ability clause, a testing issue like the one raised in the Motorola case. The issue here was movement after the initial hire. The company defined ability as competence to "progress up the line," making the test for entering a line equivalent to the ability to do the top job. To the union, the ability clause simply meant having the potential ability to learn the jobs on the line after a reasonable period of training. If two men were equal according to this calculus, seniority must hold. Using that standard, the job should have been Walker's. Given the current skills of the black workforce, if the company definition of ability became the rule, it would be very difficult for blacks to take advantage of the ending of racial barriers.

At the same time, the union was convinced that Walker was rejected because he would have integrated a formerly all-white seniority unit. At the grievance committee meeting, R. L. Lee, the white committeeman, claimed that Tom Segrest, the supervisor, had boasted that he was not going to permit a black to enter the unit. Segrest denied saying that, but admitted that he spoke to Walker and implied that he could not train for the job. The case was not so simple after all. It involved issues of management authority, seniority, training, and race.

The union took the Walker case to arbitration. In December 1965, the arbitrator, Sylvester Garrett, concluded that although the union did not establish definitively that Walker was denied the job on the basis of race, it had been a factor. Garrett acknowledged that "many Negroes have been promoted to formerly 'white' jobs" but concluded that Eddins's advantage was rooted in the temporary assignments that Walker had been denied. The arbitrator awarded Walker the job. Did this principle cost the company anything? It is unlikely. Eddins continued to work as a motor inspector helper, but with less seniority than Walker.[31] After Garrett's ruling, Bullard demoted Segrest back to foreman, an implicit acknowledgment of the accuracy of the union's charge of racism. It reinforced Bullard's words to managers that such behavior would cost them their jobs.[32]

The union successfully convinced arbitrators that formal testing did not relieve the company of the responsibility to abide by the contractual provision concerning ability. The decision made it clear that tests must be related to the job in question and were not definitive. Even if he failed the test, a worker could demonstrate that he was qualified on the basis of other evidence. The USWA placed the results of the Walker case into its contract in 1968, adding what by then had become a boilerplate provision requiring tests to be free of cultural, racial, or ethnic bias. When testing bias was raised in the Motorola case in 1963, few accepted the idea. By 1968, civil rights organizations and liberal political and even some business elites embraced the notion that many tests were culturally biased. Nevertheless, cultural neutrality was window dressing in the steel industry. The operative, contractual provision required tests to be related to the specific job, which included the ability to absorb training.[33]

Changing Work Cultures

The issue of temporary vacancies was crucial everywhere, but history and simple justice required the alteration of specific employment patterns. The millwright helper was a good example. A millwright is a partially trained machinist. The job did not require the ability to read blueprints, because a millwright specialized in a particular machine or related ones. At TCI the millwright had been white and the helper usually black, until the changes of 1962–63. The international had elevated the millwright position to a craft job in the 1965 contract and thought the helpers at TCI should have the opportunity to move up. These persons with many years of practical experience, if not formal training, were now permitted to become millwrights. But some foremen searched for ways around the new order.

For example, one black helper named Cook bid for a job as millwright in the blooming mill, but the company disqualified him on the basis of his size—he weighed over 300 pounds. The case was taken through the grievance process to arbitration. Bruce Thrasher argued that Cook had been rejected because he was black and demonstrated that Cook had worked more overtime than any one in the mill. The arbitrator awarded Cook the job. At TCI, all but one black helper, a man who could not read or write, became millwrights. Even some illiterates were promoted. Howard Strevel recalled that one man had "helped" on a machine for many years and out of that experience could have assembled and disassembled it. No amount of regulations on testing could deal with situations such as this one. Actually, these cases were anachronisms, the results of an era when illiterates were hired because they were not promotable. After many years of work, some became skilled.[34]

To alter mill culture, the union concentrated upon other jobs that broke historic manning patterns. Henry Finely, a black with thirty years of experience, sought a job as assigned labor leader in one of the pools when the white incumbent retired. The traditional work pattern was a variant of southern labor gangs: a white leader directing black workers. Managers chose the leader, even though the job was part of an LOP. Finely's grievanceman tried but could not get the job posted, the beginning of the process of bidding. He told Finely to go to Rich, who promised he would get the job posted, which he did. After checking his record and "age," Rich made sure Finely obtained it.[35]

Promoting blacks to the job of craneman revealed the diversity of race relations at TCI. Cranes were essential to move everything from small wire bundles to sixty-ton ladles of molten metal. The safety of the men who worked below depended upon the skill of the elite cranemen who carried the heaviest and hottest material. After the mergers in 1963, many black jobs were connected to the craneman's and thus they were eligible to bid and obtain such jobs. One learns to operate a crane by accompanying an operator in the cab for a couple of weeks. At TCI, whites had operated the biggest cranes. In parts of the mill, some whites either refused to accept a black trainee in the cab with them or did so reluctantly, seeking to sabotage the learning process. "I'll retire before I'll train" said one. Willie Phillips, a black in the wire mill, faced such a situation but found a white in another part of the mill willing to teach him, although he was never comfortable operating cranes and eventually obtained other work.[36] In the blooming mill, however, Fred Shepherd had no trouble. Shepherd, a hooker, had worked with his craneman, who gladly instructed him after he bid successfully for the job. In the open hearth department, E. B. Rich simply informed all white cranemen that blacks would be trained, and they were.[37]

Some white committeemen could not accept the new order and did not effectively transmit black grievances. Some black committeemen did no better. Leo Bryant, a black grievance chairman at Ensley, would not forward black grievances. Incompetent as well as duplicitous, he would rabble rouse among the blacks and then refuse to forward grievances, claiming that whites had rejected the claim. There were enough racist whites around TCI to lend credence to his self-serving explanation.[38]

Some blacks did not take advantage of the changes because they did not understand the seniority system. James Hubbard had never heard of a line of promotion until 1963. Rules were complicated, particularly after the creation of the pool and the mergers of 1962 and 1963. Thrasher addressed a different local union each night to explain the procedures. Nevertheless, the process was slow. An all-white unit could look like it barred blacks when in fact it remained all-white because there were no vacancies. A man could have a bad experience with a white grievanceman, and tell his friends that the union would do nothing for them. Community culture, the repository of the past, could function as a brake. A black minister told Luther McKinstry, a hooker at the plate mill, that "you ain't going to change anything." But these problems were not insoluble. They would simply take time to work out.[39]

Union leaders used various techniques to bring about a new order at TCI. "Spud" Darden, the president of the ore conditioning local, employed the discursive approach. When the bathhouses of the plant were integrated, one white worker haltingly asked Darden what he was going to do. The question was not academic because after a day's work at the plant, everyone was coated with a reddish layer of dust. Darden, scratched his head, and said slowly, "My Rita [his wife] won't let me in the house dirty." That settled it.[40]

Rich's approach was more direct: "It is the law, it is right, it is fair," he often said. Perhaps this firmness was required in Local 1013, encompassing all of Fairfield Steel. Rich recalled that part of the plate mill had "the strongest little group of Ku Kluxers in our organization." It was the one area where he knew that Grand Dragon Robert Shelton had attempted to intervene in mill matters. Rich informed the superintendent of the mill, who contacted the FBI. But Rich preferred to act, not wait for the law. He thought that Bob Jones, a grievance-man in the plate mill, was in the Klan. When Jones had refused to sign the new lines of promotion in 1963, Rich signed instead and superseded his authority by directly taking up the black grievances Jones ignored. Jones told several blacks that "no nigger is going to operate a crane at TCI." Blacks did come to operate cranes in the plate mill, but confronted with the Klan, Darden's indirection would have been inadequate.[41]

The union could facilitate black progress, but the individual characteristics of the worker—age, work preferences, education, and ambition—were key elements to advancement. Entry into a new LOP sometimes required a cut in pay. Under these circumstances, would blacks move to lines with more promotional opportunities? Would older blacks leave familiar circumstances to assume greater responsibilities? Again, would the fear of white resistance, genuine or not, deter older blacks? One needed assertive blacks, committed union leaders, and job vacancies. TCI possessed the first two but, unfortunately, not the third. Government enforcement at TCI centered upon implementing Title VII when jobs were declining.

Government and TCI

The first agency to confront the situation was the new Equal Employment Opportunity Commission (EEOC). Of all the parties, EEOC had the most trouble figuring out its role. Possessing little power and expertise, it became a sub-committee of the NAACP. President Johnson's choices for the five commissioners were ready only on April 29, 1965, two months before the law went into effect. Finding a chairman had been difficult. As the civil rights forces had predicted, an agency possessing little power did not attract persons of stature. Johnson eventually chose Franklin D. Roosevelt Jr., not to be confused with his brother, James, author of the House FEPC bill. Franklin Jr. was at that time serving as under secretary of commerce, a reward for the aid he had given Kennedy in the West Virginia primaries. But Roosevelt had his eye on other opportunities, intending to run for governor of New York in 1966.[42]

The other four appointments fulfilled mandated bipartisanship and desirable ethnic and gender diversity. Johnson named an ally, Luther Holcomb, a white Baptist minister who was chairman of the Texas advisory committee to the U.S. Civil Rights Commission. Another Democratic spot went to Aileen C. Hernandez, whose parents were Jamaican and husband Hispanic. She had been educational director for the International Ladies' Garment Workers Union in California and assistant head of the California FEPC. Johnson passed up Fred K. Koehler Jr., a professor of labor relations at the University of Michigan, who was backed by the AFL-CIO. The two Republicans appointed were Richard A. Graham, a white business executive at that time heading the Peace Corps in Tunisia, and Samuel C. Jackson, a black lawyer employed in the welfare department of Kansas who headed the NAACP branch in Topeka. The EEOC had the proper mix: a businessman; two blacks, one associated with unions, the other with the NAACP; two white males, one southern, one northern; and a black woman, with links through her husband to Hispanics. But Clarence Mitchell worried about the absence of "experienced" people on it.[43]

The EEOC commissioners' ignorance of labor relations and specific industries made it difficult for the commission to file its own complaints, which was the only power it had to shape priorities. Samuel Jackson concluded he did not know enough "to intelligently file a complaint at the present time" in the area of apprenticeship training. Deputy General Counsel Richard Berg wanted to forward a testing case to the Justice Department, but then he opted for conciliation, "until we know exactly what it is we want. . . . Certainly the company might reasonably complain if we refer the case to the Attorney General without first telling the company what we want them to do."[44]

Even though they lacked the power to sue, the commissioners possessed a litigious bent from the beginning. They complained that the staff was not suggesting suits. The staff in turn was overwhelmed by the numbers of complaints it received; expecting 2,000, they received nearly 9,000 in its first year, most generated by the NAACP and the LDF. EEOC processed none within the statutory limit of sixty days and quickly accumulated a backlog of 3,000 cases. Only one third of the EEOC budget was devoted to its major statutory function, investigating and conciliating complaints. EEOC employed only five conciliators. More than half of its resources were spent in its Washington headquarters because of the inexperience of the investigators in the field and the commissioners' reluctance to delegate authority.[45]

EEOC's intellectual and administrative weakness created a vacuum, which the NAACP and LDF eagerly filled. The commissioners and staff met frequently with NAACP personnel. LDF director Jack Greenberg told General Counsel Charles Duncan on October 19 that his lawyers could do EEOC's investigatory work. Greenberg was less concerned with improving agency fact-finding and conciliation than with getting the cases to court. He required only a pro forma run through the process—an investigation, a ruling of reasonable cause, and a failure to conciliate. Then, he could sue. Understandably, Roosevelt was less happy with this solution, which would reflect badly on EEOC. Hernandez insisted that EEOC must try to conciliate complaints. "We cannot just let them ride." But EEOC ineffectiveness ensured that private lawsuits would be the principal means of enforcement. The sheer volume of complaints filed by the NAACP, the only organization encouraging them, guaranteed that its agenda would be EEOC's.[46] EEOC was reluctant to work with unions, which were kept at arm's length.[47]

The history of EEOC's conduct at TCI documented each of these general characteristics—ignorance, poor investigation, preference for litigation, and collaboration with the NAACP but not the union. The NAACP had gathered forty-four complaints on September 15, 1965, after the organization's convention in Birmingham. Unable to assess their import, EEOC made them the highest priority because of the significance of the mill. TCI, the commissioners decided, would "become a national symbol for the success or failure of Title VII . . . in the South." Steel now assumed another totemic role. Jackson and Roosevelt sparred for the prestige of filing a commissioner's complaint against U.S. Steel. Eventually, both concluded they lacked enough information to proceed.[48]

On October 6, the commission assembled representatives from every government agency that had investigated the mill. Michael Gottesman, a lawyer in the Washington firm used by the USWA, had not been invited to attend but heard about the meeting from Winn Newman. EEOC had hired Newman from the brewery workers union after realizing that it needed someone with collective bargaining experience on its staff. Gottesman asked Newman if he could attend, and Newman got EEOC to agree. But Gottesman was unable to comment because the union had not been receiving copies of the complaints; he thought the union could help if it was kept informed.[49]

EEOC decided it needed to know more and authorized Commissioner Graham and Alfred Blumrosen, a law professor from Rutgers University, to visit TCI. The pair discovered that the TCI files lacked the facts necessary to document violations. Each of the twelve local unions had different rules, and EEOC's investigators were amateurs. Graham, who had planned "to straighten out U.S. Steel," was impressed with the company's progress and told the other commissioners once again that EEOC investigators were "poorly informed and prepared." Pressed by the NAACP, Jackson wanted to refer the cases to the Justice Department, but as he lacked a factual record and a violation, he could not. The investigation was suspended in 1966, when Blumrosen, the more knowledgeable of the two investigators, was off working on a conciliation at a shipbuilding company in Newport News, Virginia.[50]

While EEOC was away, the old presidential committee monitoring government contracts, operating under the new name of the Office of Contract Compliance (OFCC), returned. When Blumrosen and Graham had visited the plant in September, they had bumped into David Sawyer, an Army officer conducting an investigation for OFCC. Girard Clark, the new head of Army compliance, complained that EEOC investigators had simply gone over ground the OFCC had been plowing over the past two years. OFCC was stymied by some of the same limitations EEOC faced, but it too wanted to keep its hands in TCI. Clark proposed a division of labor whereby OFCC would monitor contractors and EEOC would handle noncontracting businesses. Even without a division of labor, Clark thought there should be "uniformity of government posture . . . in implementing the equal opportunity programs." In his view, there was "a need for collecting and disseminating information that would describe patterns of discrimination as well as the patterns of equal employment opportunity for certain industries, regions and localities."[51]

The government had passed Title VII without assessing industrial patterns. A year later, in September 1966, the Ford Foundation awarded a large grant to Herbert R. Northrup of the University of Pennsylvania's Wharton School to do precisely that. Northrup believed that studying the racial employment policies of industries and analyzing the labor market trends would permit a "more rational attack on discrimination in employment in terms of potential results for effort expended." The absence of government data on labor markets was a result both of Kennedy's aggregate approach to the economy and of the politics that had created EEOC. Because the law defined the problem as one of individual bias, knowledge about particular industries became irrelevant. The first Northrup monographs came out in 1968. But by that time government policy already had a dynamic of its own.[52]

The duplicate investigations being conducted by OFCC and EEOC convinced U.S. Steel's vice president J. Warren Shaver that Fairfield was being prejudged, not evaluated. There was some truth to his conclusion. Shaver believed that the corporation was fulfilling its legal obligations and then some. TCI had actively recruited potential managers, included engineering students. It was training black foremen and now employed thirty-eight blacks in clerical and technical positions. Over 1,000 blacks occupied formerly white jobs, and 46 percent of line-of-promotion entry positions had been filled by blacks since the mergers, despite declining employment.[53]

Government incompetence frittered away considerable goodwill among employers. In December 1966, the vice president of the American Iron and Steel Institute told Stephen N. Shulman, the new chairman of EEOC, that "the companies do not need further exhortation, but would appreciate guidance and . . . suggestions for avoiding getting involved with inspections, complaints, and investigations by a variety of government agencies, frequently over the same issue which has previously been investigated and resolved." The tone was petu

lant. Some of U.S. Steel's subsequent rigidity can be traced to these early experiences with government regulators.[54]

Black workers, unaware of the goings-on at the top, knew only that they had
filed EEOC complaints that were unresolved. Many concerned the operation of
the seniority system—sometimes involving the award of a specific job, at other
times provision for training—and still others the placement of a job or a series
of jobs in or out of a particular line of progression. It was difficult to locate a
pattern here because seniority disputes composed the overwhelming number
of white grievances, too. But the black grievances were transmitted simultaneously to EEOC.

The workers believed that the primary barrier was TCI. In advance of Roger
Blough's visit to Birmingham for the opening of the new continuous paint line
at Fairfield Steel, the Ad Hoc Committee compiled and publicized a list of
charges against TCI and other corporations in the city. The committee, now led
by Virgil Pearson and Thomas Johnson, the president of the wire mill, operated
as the Labor and Industry Committee of the Birmingham NAACP.[55]

Blough used his speech at the ceremonies on May 5 to answer the NAACP. He
was determined to "conform to both the letter and the spirit of the law." He
warned his critics that "the failure on the part of those who speak for the
Negroes . . . to brush it [the progress] aside while they launch a broadside of
alleged complaints can only tend to hurt the generally good climate of employment, frighten away new capital investment, and in the end, to foreclose
thousands of job opportunities."[56]

That night the NAACP called a meeting at Miles College to plan action to resolve the 171 complaints at TCI, which EEOC had not investigated. NAACP head
Dr. John Nixon preferred to avoid the demonstration that the workers proposed. Nixon was impressed with progress at TCI, but he was in regular contact
with Commissioner Jackson and the NAACP's national labor secretary, Herbert
Hill. Hill told Nixon that EEOC would shortly find for the complainants, and at
that point the NAACP would initiate litigation.[57]

But EEOC did not act. On June 1, a local black lawyer, Oscar Adams Jr., working with Nixon, filed a lawsuit against U.S. Steel involving two workers in the
plate mill. But the workers had less faith in EEOC and litigation than did Nixon,
Hill, and Adams. To pressure U.S. Steel, Pearson and Johnson staged a march
in Birmingham on June 6, fortified by simultaneous marches in Pittsburgh
and Los Angeles. National NAACP leaders appreciated the symbolism of the target. Roy Wilkins asserted "if we can make an impression on U.S. Steel to expand
its opportunities for Negroes, then this will raise the rate of acceptance and
promotion for Negroes in smaller companies."[58]

Some in the NAACP had wanted to demonstrate against the union too.

Grover Smith Jr., a worker in the coke plant and a member of the NAACP's Labor and Industry Committee, kept up steady criticism against the union as well as against TCI. There was a more personal story behind Smith's attacks. Earlier in January, he had resigned his NAACP post, announcing that he would be working for the union, because an EEOC official had informed him that he would be put on the staff. Union leaders were horrified that the government thought "it could pick union officials," and did not in fact hire him. When it became clear that the union had no plans to hire him, his attacks on the union increased. Eventually Herbert Hill made Smith his southern labor liaison.[59]

Hill, who was white, had initially worked closely with CIO unions, including the USWA. In 1958, in response to the recession and the growing militance of northern black workers, Hill began criticizing the civil rights policies of the AFL-CIO. At first, he aimed his fire at the old AFL unions, but then his attacks broadened to the entire labor movement. Although Hill's charges, often undocumented, caused Roy Wilkins some anguish and embarrassment, the championing of black workers served the interests of the NAACP, whose legalism was under increasing criticism from the more militant civil rights groups.[60]

In the end, politics in Birmingham did not allow small differences to develop into larger ones. Black steelworkers found no equivalent of the northern white liberal to replace the USWA as an ally. Despite Smith's advocacy, the Ad Hoc committee at TCI convinced the national NAACP to target the corporation only, just as the lawsuit charged the company, not the union. Thus, the June 6 march was supported by the USWA.[61]

The union was happy to see the extra pressure put on TCI. Rich and Thrasher believed that the company was requiring the union to fight too many issues, nonracial as well as racial, via the grievance process. The slowness of the process made it more likely that workers would seek aid from the government or outside groups like the NAACP. On the other hand, the union did not accept the validity of every complaint. USWA lawyer Michael Gottesman told Blumrosen that "if we don't stick to our guns when we're right, employees will come to view the EEOC as a convenient vehicle for seniority changes totally unrelated to discrimination. This, we think, would be an unfortunate misuse of an already overburdened agency, and would undermine our status as bargaining agent to negotiate good-faith, non-discriminatory seniority arrangements."[62]

The union and workers conceived of the march more as a vehicle to pressure U.S. Steel than to get EEOC to act. Only twenty-seven black steelworkers assembled at Miles College, but they picked up more support as they proceeded through the neighborhoods of Fairfield. The words on the posters revealed the moderation of the objectives: "Big Business Close Doors to Bigotry," "Job Discrimination Must Go," and "Bigots Must Go."[63] When the march approached Fairfield headquarters, Superintendent Bullard came out and agreed to see

Virgil L. Pearson (left) and Fred Shepherd at a District 36 staff seminar for union representatives in 1977. Pearson joined the USWA staff in 1967, Shepherd in 1977. (Courtesy of Virgil L. Pearson)

Nixon and Virgil Pearson. But Pearson refused to talk to Bullard without his committee, a standard principle of demonstrators in the 1960s, so no meeting took place. However, over the weekend Bullard phoned Nixon, who convinced Pearson to meet with the superintendent on Monday morning. The meeting did not advance matters. Bullard offered Pearson a supervisory job. Strategic black hiring was a common TCI tactic. U.S. Steel had added the grandson of black millionaire A. G. Gaston to its legal staff. Other men in the Ad Hoc caucus accepted supervisory positions, but Pearson refused.[64]

Pearson was as pragmatic as he was principled. At the time, he had a good job in the metallurgical inspection department at Fairfield Steel. He believed that if he accepted a supervisor's job, which lacked union protection, the company would get rid of him. He had recently been disciplined for a minor infraction which he considered harassment. The union filed a successful grievance on his behalf. He was put on the union staff in 1967.[65]

Even after the march, EEOC did not act. Feeling the heat from the NAACP, Jackson told his colleagues that it was imperative to "prevent criticism of the Commission" and himself. Roosevelt, as expected, resigned on May 11 to run for governor of New York. Jackson thought that resolving the steel cases was the road to obtaining the chairmanship. But George Holland, head of EEOC compliance, wanted to act as "captain of conciliation" at TCI. Holland told his fellow commissioners that he believed that it was the "most complex issue that you will ever have to confront as a Commission," but said, "I will stake my reputation that I can bring it off."[66]

Others preferred to send the cases to the Justice Department. EEOC was currently trying to obtain cease-and-desist powers from the Congress. If it forwarded the cases, EEOC could argue that it had used all of its current powers and needed more. For all of these extraneous reasons, the TCI cases had been placed on an emergency basis of priority.[67]

Race and Automation

Everyone at EEOC believed that the cases were important and would play a role in the agency's public profile, but no one knew enough to articulate a violation. EEOC faced a practical and theoretical dilemma. All of the parties acknowledged that work was dwindling even though the business pickup was finally reaching TCI. In 1965, it hired 550 new people, the first significant additions in ten years. Still, in the large Fairfield Works the number of workers declined from 13,000 in 1962 to 10,000 in 1966. In the tin mill, employment was down from 2,308 to 975 workers.[68]

No longer was automation simply a union fear. On September 16, 1966, the *Wall Street Journal* ran a front-page article predicting the loss of more than 100,000 steel jobs in the next ten years. While the computer became an element in the popular imagination during the 1980s, it was a fact of life for the steelworker two decades earlier. Computerization had come to the finishing mills. At TCI, computers controlled the new tandem cold mill, which had begun operating in 1963. Computers, not the skilled heater, would determine just when a reheated ingot was ready for rolling. The company began automating the skip cars feeding the blast furnace too. In a few years, remote-controlled cranes would mean that a person did not need to ride in the cab to direct it. In 1971, Fairfield obtained a Q-BOF, a variant on the new oxygen steel-making process, which eliminated twelve open hearth furnaces. The most traditional blast furnace department was scheduled for automation. This did not involve simply fancy new machines. The use of better bricks, lasting for 600 rather than 300 heats, cut down on the need for brickmasons; combining machine shops reduced the number of maintenance workers; contracting out work, formerly performed by the construction department, meant TCI required fewer craftsmen. Promotions still depended upon vacancies, and the number of jobs at TCI declined throughout the 1960s and 1970s.[69]

No amount of union effort could stem that tide. Many steelworkers and their children would need other work. Union lawyer Buddy Cooper was part of a small group that applied for Jefferson County's first poverty grant in 1965. Cooper was impelled by what was happening to Birmingham. "Changes in our basic industry, mechanization of coal and automation of steel and almost total elimination of ore mining have created large numbers of families whose bread-winner is unemployed or unemployable and whose children are not being given the opportunities they need to make themselves truly employable in this modern age." Cooper did not forget about adults. When Burke Marshall, a former IBM executive, was in Birmingham, negotiating the 1963 settlement, Cooper had urged him to try to get the computer company to set up a facility in Birmingham—naïve perhaps, but closer to the mark than many of the other ideas coming out of Alabama and Washington.[70]

NAACP head John Nixon agreed that "automation is the problem. . . . As an unskilled laborer, the Negro is no longer needed." Privately, if not publicly, Herbert Hill stated that because of "the rapid introduction of new steel making processes based upon automated equipment, Negro workers with many years of seniority in the all-Negro seniority line will be forced back into the lowest job categories as a result of the reclassification of jobs and eventually forced out of employment entirely." But Hill had not got the process right. With sufficient seniority, the man would not be forced out but would be protected in the pool. Hill accurately stated black fears, but automation was color-blind. Blumrosen acknowledged that the "basic dilemma [was] too many people and too few jobs in Birmingham." He thought that the problem could be solved through interplant transfers, perhaps to Houston, where U.S. Steel was building a new mill. While the analyses were remarkably similar, the new laws on the book would magnify the effects of the different constituencies and eventually lead them to seek different solutions.[71]

EEOC commissioners recognized that the union was vigorously using existing machinery to further black promotion. If TCI had been a small and insignificant plant, that might have been the end of it. But this was U.S. Steel and Birmingham. Although EEOC found some of the union's solutions to particular problems reasonable, Blumrosen told the commissioners on June 7, "if the Commission approves the position taken by the Union and the Company, it is unlikely that a Federal District Court will order any more extensive affirmative action than was taken here, and the *Whitfield* principle will become engrafted into Title VII."

Whitfield v. United Steelworkers Local 2798, decided by the Fifth Circuit in 1959, had established the principle of prospective relief. The USWA had ended the racial division of work in this Houston mill of Armco Steel before it had acted in Birmingham. Despite the fact that the company had resisted every step of the way, Benny Whitfield filed the suit against the union, because the peculiarities of the legal system then required only unions to treat blacks fairly.[72]

Whitfield wanted to alter the seniority system, rearranging workers on the basis of mill tenure, not years on a rung or line. If a black transferred to a previously all-white line, he would thus get "credit" for his time in the black line. The Fifth Circuit had rejected Whitfield's claim, concluding that "angels could do no more" than the union did at Armco. The court judged that the rules were nondiscriminatory and methods of transfer reasonable, given Armco's legitimate need to operate efficiently and safely. Finally, the court concluded that the contract embodied norms superior to those governing most southern enterprises, which at the time were governed by racial assignments. The Supreme Court seemed to agree, refusing to hear an appeal.

With jobs declining, the prospective relief offered in Whitfield seemed inadequate.[73] EEOC had no idea about how to go beyond *Whitfield*. On July 1, 1966, it issued a commissioner complaint, a holding action. EEOC claimed that the pool, whose purpose was to protect jobs of long-serving persons and provide black workers access to new lines, prevented blacks, who occupied most of the lower job categories that ended up in the pool, from gaining seniority in existing lines. The charge was racial discrimination, the only legal basis for the action. The EEOC complaint did not originate from Fairfield workers. Leading blacks there believed the pool both protected their jobs and provided mobility.[74] EEOC did not suggest a solution, offer a principle, or articulate what was really on its mind. But it threatened to send the case to the attorney general if the union and company did not come up with a new plan in a week.[75]

Instead of the Justice Department suing, one week later the LDF filed the first steel suit—against both the company and the union. LDF's Jack Greenberg announced, "it is the most important employment suit now in the Federal courts. Steel is a basic industry. Its employment patterns are extremely influential in the South and across the country." Greenberg's knowledge of TCI was even thinner than EEOC's. One week later, he asked the Justice Department to intervene, arguing that it "needs no demonstration that a law suit against the United States Steel Corporation and the Steelworkers Union will require more legal manpower than against any other possible set of defendants." Ignoring EEOC's attack on the pool, Greenberg simply charged that racially segregated seniority lines existed, that the EEOC found cause, and that efforts to conciliate had failed.[76] In the wake of the Birmingham demonstrations, bombings, and the ravings of George Wallace, who could doubt that the charge was correct?

Remaking the Past: The New Errand of Title VII

Despite the charge of segregation, it was the absence of discrimination at TCI that produced the suit. The legal question it posed was "whether Title VII can remedy the effects of past discrimination." The issue was raised in order to protect blacks from the effects of declining jobs. Blumrosen believed that "where promotional opportunities were frequent, the opportunity to enter the bottom would usually be a significant element of settlement; but where promotional opportunities were scarce, . . . additional measures [were] necessary." Moving along this track, EEOC and the LDF now concentrated upon plants with declining work opportunities but great legal opportunities. The peculiarities of the law made unionized plants prime targets.[77]

The law went into effect on July 2, 1965, meaning that individuals could file complaints arising on that date and after. It seemed reasonable. How could you correct action that was not illegal at the time? But past hiring decisions were alive in seniority systems. If one recalculated seniority on the basis of mill tenure, long-serving blacks would presumably have an edge on younger whites who were holding jobs from which blacks, at the time they had been hired, had been excluded. EEOC devoted most of its intellectual energy in the early years to seniority, because that was the only vehicle to reach the past.[78] But that option was available only in union plants; if a company lacked a contractual seniority system, no one, black or white, had rights to anything. The strategy had two problems: first, there was Title VII's protection of "bona fide seniority systems" and second, the hypothesis that changing seniority was a panacea for blacks was flawed.

In 1966, to help resolve the U.S. Steel complaints, EEOC tried to formulate seniority guidelines. Winn Newman insisted that they hear from the unions as well as from civil rights groups, but instead of trying to reach a consensus among the unions and civil rights groups, EEOC held separate meetings. It met with a diverse group of union officials, including the USWA's Ben Fischer, Alex Fuller, and Michael Gottesman on May 5. Though they all believed that the law prohibited changes in seniority except where the system had been established for racial purposes, there was a consensus that more should be done, and so they supported affirmative action. Current employees should obtain the right to seek transfers and/or upgrading before a company hired new people. Where rules required workers who transferred to new lines of promotion to yield their old seniority, they should retain rights to their old jobs.[79]

Thus, they supported *Whitfield*, which was subsequently modified by the USWA's negotiation of "bump-back" rights (whereby a worker would retain his seniority in his old line of promotion). When workers transferred to a new line, they sometimes had to take a pay cut. Many thought that in these cases blacks should get "red-circled" rates—that is, their old wages—until promotions in the new line equaled their previous remuneration. Some believed that whites, too, should obtain this income protection. Members of many ethnic minority groups in the North had faced a similar situation, and workers everywhere were being forced to start in new lines because of automation. The union officials agreed that the law did not require remedies for past discrimination but believed that unions had an obligation to practice affirmative action—to enhance promotional opportunities and cushion the risks of movement.

A second meeting, held on June 10, included representatives from the major civil rights groups, law schools, NLRB, the Department of Justice, and OFCC. The opinions were more varied than those of the unionists because of the diversity of the group, whose members had little collective bargaining experience. Jack Greenberg believed that the EEOC guidelines on seniority would be helpful; Carl Rachlin of CORE opposed them, believing that they would be produced through "political negotiations." Greenberg thought that the experience gained in school segregation cases was relevant. The NAACP's Robert C. Carter, feuding with Greenberg on other issues, disagreed.[80]

Most took an instrumental view of seniority and concluded that despite the seniority protections in Title VII, its broad intent permitted whatever changes were necessary to speed black promotion. Herbert Hill wanted EEOC to "challenge collective bargaining agreements." Hill's judgment that plant seniority was a universal remedy was challenged by Yale law professor Clyde Summer, who warned that guidelines mandating plant seniority might help older blacks, but would disadvantage recently hired blacks. Seniority, he warned, always involved trade-offs.[81]

Winn Newman, who presided over the discussion, politely thanked the participants, but told them that he "did not think that a clear consensus . . . had been realized." Although the civil rights leaders possessed more of an adversarial bent and were less familiar with the specifics of seniority, they and the unionists agreed that it was desirable to move beyond prospective remedies. What the law required was unclear. Shortly after this meeting the LDF filed its TCI suit, but both the LDF and EEOC were still groping in the dark.

EEOC endorsed the suit, but it still wanted to formulate its own guidelines and sought help from other experts. The lawyers had little definitive to say, but Harvard economist Peter B. Doeringer analyzed seniority change on the basis of equities, not the legal requirements of Title VII. He concluded that any prospective solution—that is, one offering blacks equal opportunity in the future—placed the costs of past discrimination on black workers, in terms of lost wages and work opportunities. Retrospective policies—ones in which blacks would be permitted to advance under new rules that eroded the rights of white incumbents—meant that black advance would come at the expense of whites. Remedies in which qualifications were relaxed, entailing special training, would require employers to share some of the remedial costs. Affecting the weight of these costs was the pattern of discrimination and growth prospects in each plant—the increase or attrition of the formerly white classifications, the ratio of formerly black to white jobs, the gap between the current skills of blacks and the requirements of the formerly white jobs. Because of the salience of these industrial particulars, Doeringer urged EEOC to permit parties to exercise wide discretion in fashioning remedies and to create a twenty-person advisory committee made up of representatives from management, labor, and civil rights groups as well as public members with experience in industrial relations. However, such a consensual approach, even one less unwieldy, did not fit the developing politics of EEOC.[82]

The EEOC commissioners chose instead to pursue retrospective solutions and to obtain them through litigation, not negotiation. Blumrosen acknowledged that "there does seem to be a national mood to resolve these matters [discriminatory practices] without litigation." But not so for the issue of seniority. Blumrosen thought "most Federal District Courts today are hospitable to civil rights matters, and the higher courts, which in the first years count most, are generally sympathetic." Winn Newman dissented, believing that a court strategy, would "tend to make adversaries out of some people whose commitment to civil rights is beyond challenge." Newman left the agency at the end of 1966.[83]

The unforeseen consequence of the court strategy was that it fostered conflict and perpetuated EEOC inadequacies. Refusing to pursue conciliation kept controversies alive. Subcontracting work to the LDF and the courts, EEOC had no motive to improve its own expertise. EEOC routinely and mechanically found reasonable cause in the TCI cases, but acknowledged that the "investigative files in all the cases against U.S. Steel in Birmingham are disappointing" and that "specific charges are rarely investigated and general patterns are seldom specifically noted and documented." Newman found the investigators ignorant of the basic concepts of seniority. The inadequate records inevitably led the Justice Department to reject the steel cases referred to it by EEOC.[84]

The private litigation strategy was not so promising, either. After filing the TCI lawsuit in 1966, the LDF did not invest its time in the case. Two months later, LDF's Robert Belton told Buddy Cooper that he would wait to see how much of a change was being achieved under the existing system. Instead of handling the cases themselves, Greenberg and Belton gave them to cooperating attorneys in Birmingham. One of them, Demetrius Newton, recalled that none of the lawyers were "anxious to touch" them.

The lead plaintiff, William Hardy, worked in the Ensley stockhouse, which fed raw material to the blast furnace. Between 1960 and 1962, three of the six blast furnaces were shut down permanently, reducing work in the stockhouse. The question was whether the failure to merge a formerly black and white line was fair to blacks and necessary for the proper operation of the furnace. The plaintiffs claimed that if the lines had been completely merged, the blacks would have brought their previous seniority into the formerly white line of skip car operators and moved ahead of the whites. But in the real world the change would have no such effect. Hardy himself actually benefited from the current arrangement. Merging the two lines would have given the whites access to the black jobs because the whites in the stockhouse had more "age" than Hardy and some of the other blacks did. These "black jobs" were now more desirable because of the automation of the formerly white line of skip car operators.[85] Indeed, had the lines been merged as he preferred, a white man would have had Hardy's job. The ideology of seniority reform conflicted with its reality.[86]

"Rightful Place": Quarles and Crown

The courts eventually bought the notion that Title VII required remaking the past, but not at TCI. Steel was not so fundamental after all. Judges were more willing to break new ground where companies and unions had made only minimal efforts to comply or had been openly antagonistic to Title VII. In 1968 and 1969, courts accepted the principle of retrospective remedies in cases involving a southern tobacco company and a southern paper company. Both industries had been organized by the AFL in the late 1930s and 1940s and had set up separate locals for blacks and whites. Tobacco had been hit by mechanization in the late 1940s, paper in the early 1960s. The companies had no interest in racial reform, and neither union had protected black interests. There were other plants in both industries that had addressed these issues through collective bargaining. But lawsuits emerge from the intractable, not the typical.[87]

The courts relied on a new framework formulated in an anonymous student note published in the *Harvard Law Review* in 1967. The note focused on hierarchy and asked whether Title VII should "be read as requiring the elimination of differences in competitive standing between white and Negro workers attributable to past discrimination." The answer, the author argued, was yes, because a seniority system created in an era of discriminatory hiring was contaminated, even if the rules were not motivated by racial purpose. Such a system thus was not the "bona fide" seniority system protected by Title VII. By defining the goal as one of competitive standing, the concept could improve the black situation without creating jobs, which of course the courts could not do.[88] The note opted for what it called a "rightful place" solution to redress past hiring discrimination. Incumbent blacks should be allowed to bid for formerly white jobs on the basis of their full length of service with the employer, not the existing seniority system based upon job, line of promotion, or department tenure.[89]

If the goal is "rightful place," then someone must be in a wrongful place. To communicate this morality, the note called white workers "illegitimate occupants" of jobs. The passive voice in the phrase "the employee improperly preferred" focused attention on white workers, ignoring the company's role in controlling hiring policies. The responsibility for the remedy was lifted from the perpetrator. Doeringer had spoken of equities and costs among white and black workers and business. The note narrowed the conflict to one between white and black workers and denied that whites had any equity in the matter.

But after laying out a broad statement of black workers' rights, the note proceeded to introduce the actual world, where blacks and whites were not interchangeable. All of the complications Doeringer had noted in his analysis of seniority suddenly came into play. Recognizing these actualities, the note urged that management be allowed much discretion. "Employers may set such requirements at whatever level they consider appropriate and there appears to be no basis for requiring them to provide special training facilities to enable Negro workers to meet these standards." Thus, the note concluded, the law did not require "affirmative action" or "preferential hiring." Blacks ended up with rights but management with great power to modify those rights and no obligation to contribute anything.[90]

Moreover, the note acknowledged that even if whites held illegitimate positions, they might not agree with the new morality and could create tensions and resist. Since training for white jobs required white cooperation, it asked, how forthcoming would it be under these circumstances? Given the number of worksites in the nation, implementation depended to a great extent on voluntary compliance. "Considerations of prudence" might dictate something less than "rightful place." A note that began boldly ended up concluding that it was not so easy to remake the world. Yet the morality of the note framed court and social thinking.

Judge John D. Butzner Jr.'s decision in *Quarles v. Philip Morris*, decided in January 1968, acknowledged and reproduced the analysis of the note. The tobacco union, responding to black workers and the AFL-CIO, had ended separate unions in 1963, but in the words of an EEOC investigator, the union in this Richmond, Virginia, plant was "extremely namby pamby." Prodded by government contract committees, the company had begun hiring blacks in its manufacturing division, which was geographically separate from the other departments, in the late 1950s. The question was whether blacks working in prefabrication could use their plant seniority in the manufacturing department.[91]

Judge Butzner disposed of the apparent endorsement and protection of seniority systems in the law and legislative debate. Like the note, Butzner defined "a 'bona fide' seniority system" as "one that lacks discriminatory effect," concluding that, "present differences in departmental seniority of Negroes and whites that result from the company's intentional racially discriminatory hiring policy before January 1, 1966 are not validated" by the language of the law, memorandum, and debates.

Whatever the merits of the judge's conclusion, the debates did not address "effect." The legislators' examples of the discrimination were explicit racial rules, like "no blacks need apply" or "blacks are the first to go." Sensing the weight of this evidence, Butzner advanced his solution rhetorically: "Congress did not intend to freeze an entire generation of Negro employees into discriminatory patterns that existed before the act." This phrase would subsequently be cited in court decisions governing seniority. But there is no evidence that Congress addressed the question of patterns, in the sense of hierarchy.

The *Quarles* decision narrowed thinking toward fashioning remedies for an "affected class," whose previous hiring into segregated units continued to affect their future prospects.[92] A jubilant Jack Greenberg informed UAW counsel Joseph Rauh that accommodation with the labor movement was now unnecessary and that even strengthening the EEOC through cease-and-desist powers was secondary.[93]

The same judicial conclusion emerged from a case at the Crown Zellerbach paper mill in Bogalusa, Louisiana.[94] The paper industry had been hard hit by the recession of 1958. Company plans to modernize the Bogalusa mill in 1961 were met with a seven-month, interracial strike, an action that failed to prevent the displacement of 500 of 2,500 workers. This turbulent history and the paucity of jobs made Crown cautious on the racial front. Simultaneous white resistance to the public accommodation features of the Civil Rights Act transformed Bogalusa into a boiling cauldron, attracting civil rights groups, the Klan, EEOC, OFCC, and the Justice Department.[95]

Because national attention focused on Bogalusa in 1965, each agency saw the paper mill as an opportunity for a big breakthrough. EEOC tried and failed to implement a plan to help blacks. Then, Leonard Bierman, who headed the effort at OFCC, was determined "to fix the industry." OFCC, like EEOC, had been under heavy pressure from the civil rights groups not to compromise on seniority. Jack Greenberg was currently litigating another paper case and warned OFCC's Edward Sylvester that failing to demand plant seniority, would make "[our] work more difficult." The Virginia court had not yet ruled on *Quarles*.[96]

Feeling the pressure, OFCC used its threat of debarment to force Crown to impose a plan that when put into effect ended up, the company reported, "promoting Negro over Negro, white over white, or white over Negro." Because of this unforeseen result, Justice scrapped OFCC's plan and proposed its own. The new remedy, formulated in the wake of *Quarles*, proposed an "affected class" solution, limited to blacks employed prior to the January 16, 1966, the date when hiring discrimination ended.[97] On March 26, 1968, a federal district court accepted it, ruling that when the "affected class" was involved in promotions, demotions, and layoffs, mill seniority, rather than job seniority, would be decisive.[98]

The court ruling was a victory in principle only. The advantages accrued to the oldest blacks, who had plant ages greater than whites in the paper mill lines. Because there had not been much hiring in recent years, there was not a group of obviously younger whites against which black seniority could be decisive. Those with the most plant seniority, elderly black workers, were among the most poorly educated of all black workers, and the company's crash literacy program was not very effective. While on paper the plan, and future ones, promised upgrading, it did not do so in practice.[99] Thirty-five years later, Leonard Bierman mused: "we didn't help the blacks."[100]

As in *Quarles*, black rights were modified by enhancing corporate power. Judge John Minor Wisdom, in his Fifth Circuit affirmation of the district court decision, granted Crown great power in selecting candidates, testing, and providing training. Wisdom underscored the legality of practices "*conceived out of business necessity . . .* [and] safety and efficiency." Extra training, he ruled, was permissible, not mandatory. He explicitly upheld *Whitfield*, arguing that the plan would not place untrained or unqualified blacks in mill jobs.[101]

Some issues, like testing, would be modified by subsequent court cases. But this was the problem of addressing the problem through litigation. Judges moved cautiously and incrementally. Government agencies and civil rights lawyers, assuming that seniority was the key issue, were less concerned with the others at first. So no one ever analyzed the plant comprehensively. A civil rights model of universal rights of citizenship fit poorly into the more contingent world of work. But once litigation started, it continued to be the preferred mode of resolution. What legally could be done was the question asked: not what was possible or needed to be done.[102]

The multiple enforcement agencies also impeded resolution of the issues. Three government bodies, in competition with each other, devised three different plans that allegedly defined Title VII and executive order compliance. Many bureaucrats, anxious to do good, viewed factory work through the lens of their own class background. Because they assumed that all blue-collar work was simple, they underestimated the importance of training. Their middle-class faith in education led them to believe that a sixty-year-old illiterate who already had a good job would want to learn to read and calculate. Armed with righteousness and a determination to overcome the "rednecks," they lacked the empathy necessary to acknowledge the genuine fears among whites.

That Bogalusa was a one-industry town increased the heat. In 1965 Crown had recognized that the community "faces the prospect of a declining rate of employment." It promised to support efforts to attract new industry. But two years earlier in 1963, it had invested $40 million to expand a pulp and paper mill at St. Francisville, on the Mississippi River north of Baton Rouge, not in Bogalusa. There are some situations where failure is overdetermined; Bogalusa was one example. Yet the law extracts universal rules, not social knowledge from court decisions. The principle won in *Crown* was that Title VII required seniority modification.[103]

EEOC policy at TCI in 1967 was shaped by the array of government and LDF plans proposed in tobacco and paper. But for all the time EEOC had put into TCI, it had not examined the mill. EEOC proposed that the actual plan be determined by an unnamed "expert." This was at best a naive proposition to put before the industry and at worst a cover for ignorance. U.S. Steel was willing to negotiate with EEOC officials over individual cases. The corporation was totally opposed to mill seniority, which it viewed as a system of "preferential rights" for blacks, one that would disrupt the operations of TCI and produce "a major reshuffle of people and downgrade hundreds of qualified employees who have every right to expect to retain their present position." It pointed to the progress made since 1962—30 percent of black employees had been promoted, despite losses in the overall number of jobs. It asserted that each problem could be resolved within the parameters of the current seniority system.[104]

Then EEOC interest in TCI abruptly ceased. A new chairman, Clifford Alexander, took over when Stephen Shulman resigned on July 1.[105] A close Johnson aide and the first black to chair the EEOC, Alexander refocused EEOC attention toward the expanding service industries, such as banks; white-collar employment in general; and industries such as southern textiles, which had only recently begun to hire blacks and had no unions through which workers could express grievances. However, EEOC policy on seniority did not change, and reforms for the "affected class" were still treated as "not negotiable." By 1969, though, EEOC realized it needed "detailed information about the conditions of the company, labor data, turnover rates, seniority lists, industrial economics, and other factors that will determine how a hypothetical system will work." The history of EEOC in steel guaranteed it would not obtain that expertise.[106]

Back to Birmingham

Many complaints, those not involving the seniority question, were conciliated at the Birmingham office of the EEOC. Neither the local lawyers nor the LDF pursued the lawsuits filed in 1966. After a brief investigation, the Justice Department again refused to take them up. Individual litigants continued to demand what they considered their rights, but their numbers were dwindling.[107]

Despite the rationale, to remedy past discrimination, workers evaluated seniority issues on the basis of how they effected their current situation. At TCI these varied because of the changes that had taken place over the past thirty years. The USWA, unlike the tobacco and paper unions, had not been segregated, and its local leaders were always influenced by national, as well as southern, customs. Unlike the union at Philip Morris, the steelworkers' had not been passive. Unlike the situation at Crown, the Klan had been neutralized. Unlike the tobacco and paper mill plants, blacks had always been part of the manufacturing process.

As a result, the black situation with regard to seniority was more diverse in the steel industry. Reformulating seniority might help some blacks, as well as some whites, but it was not in the interest of a black who transferred after 1963 according to the old rules to have to compete with another black of greater plant seniority who had stayed put. Older blacks did not always want to transfer. Moreover, as the Hardy case revealed, there were plenty of older whites at TCI who would benefit from seniority change. In short, even though the unresolved issue of seniority caused tensions everywhere, it was incapable of uniting significant numbers of blacks because of the uncertainty and necessary rhetoric propelling it. In some instances, broader seniority protection for all was stopped. At the sheet mill, an agreement to move from job to line-of-progression seniority was halted because of white fears that the change was the beginning of job displacement. An inevitable result of lawsuits was hardening of positions.[108]

The union continued to facilitate black promotion through the contract. It opposed "affected class" solutions because it believed that universal solutions were more workable, but it was willing to consider additional measures. Unlike racial advocacy groups, a biracial union could not disregard white workers. Moreover, any seniority change throws many workers' lives in disarray. Taking action without legal sanction would disrupt lives, but the disruption would not necessarily be permanent. The absence of clear judicial principles in the court decisions, thus, paralyzed the union. The Supreme Court had not ruled on the issue. *Quarles* was decided by a federal district court and was not appealed by the union or company. The whites at Crown appealed the Fifth Circuit decision to the Supreme Court, but it refused to hear the case and did not say why. Other courts had come to different conclusions.

Not acting had its costs, too. Ben Fischer was frustrated with the policy of waiting for "court decisions, Department of Labor findings, results of law suits or EEOC charges." He told President Abel on August 18, 1969 that the union ought to put forth its own ideas instead of waiting for governmental approval. "Government agencies," he wrote, "viewed civil rights groups as their clients and therefore hesitated to make decisions unless the groups approved. It would be better to approach the groups directly." Fischer thought that perhaps a top-level conference with civil rights leaders—Wilkins, Young, Abernathy, Greenberg, and Rustin—could produce a consensus. "Delay disadvantaged black members and kept the plants in turmoil. The Negro discontent with inaction and the white fears seem more serious than a sound program being put into effect bringing wide benefits not only to Negroes but to many white members as well."[109]

Fischer's proposal confronted three obstacles. First, civil rights lawyers had faith in litigation, even though they too were frustrated by the legal process. At an American Bar Association meeting on August 5, 1968, Jack Greenberg complained that a badly crafted statute had slowed the pace of litigation. Nevertheless, *Brown* had been a long struggle too, and the courts had proved to be allies. Second, the steel industry was dead set against additional changes. Finally, the USWA's leaders did not share Fischer's sense of urgency. Top officials still identified the problem with Birmingham. Only when the courts applied southern solutions in the North did the union conclude that it had to act independently of complainants and the government.[110]

Tales of Lackawanna and Sparrows Point: Implementing the Kerner Commission Report

I n December 1967, the Justice Department filed a Title VII "pattern or practice" suit against the Bethlehem Steel mill in Lackawanna, New York. Six months later, the Office of Contract Compliance (OFCC) threatened to debar Bethlehem's Sparrows Point, Maryland, facility from bidding on government contracts under Executive Order 11246. By 1973, the prestigious Second Circuit Court of Appeals, ruling on the Lackawanna suit, and a Republican secretary of labor, deciding the case at Sparrows Point, agreed that southern remedies were necessary in the North.

The consensus reflected the extraordinary impact of the urban riots on elite sensibilities. The judgment that the United States was a racist society became widely accepted, certified by the blue-ribbon National Advisory Commission on Civil Disorders (Kerner Commission), which President Johnson created in July 1967 in the wake of insurrections in Newark and Detroit. The corollary of the judgment was that the nation's institutions were exemplary and worked for others, if not for blacks. Pressed to act, elites transported solutions fashioned in the South to the North. With racism as its sole critical category, riot-impelled solutions attempted to provide more jobs for blacks while leaving to the market and industry the task of supplying more work.[1]

Racial conflict was an inevitable result of such solutions. Though blacks and whites, according to aggregate statistics, occupied different social and economic positions, people's lives do not always mesh with statistics. Many black and white steelworkers shared similar work and life opportunities. Thus, white workers lacked the sense of personal privilege that motivated the solutions proposed by upper-status whites. Compensatory schemes effected at their expense struck them as unfair. The government plans polarized the plants and brought numbers of white workers into the anti-civil rights camp. Nor did these solutions offer security for blacks. Lackawanna and Sparrows Point are both stories of the gap between elites and workers of all complexions that characterized the late Johnson and Nixon years.

Riots, Disorders, Rebellions

Historian James T. Patterson's phrase "the Biggest Boom Yet" characterized much, but not all, about the economy of the late 1960s.[2] Vietnam, the last American war fought with the weapons of the steel age, reduced unemployment by removing nearly 600,000 young men from the labor market and boosted economic activity, preventing the recession some had predicted for 1966. It also masked the economic changes that would haunt the nation during the 1970s and 1980s: the globalization of manufacturing and the application of labor-saving technology within mass-production industries. These changes were already altering the economy during the 1960s. Because the economic transformations disproportionately affected blacks—especially those migrating to cities that once offered manufacturing work—they were called racial problems during the "Biggest Boom." But it was not blacks in general but blacks in the manufacturing cities of the North who registered the highest rates of unemployment: Detroit (11.6 percent), St. Louis (12.0), Newark (12.0), Pittsburgh (16.0), and Cleveland (15.0).[3]

The CEA had predicted in early 1966 that by the end of the year the overall unemployment rate would drop to 3.5 percent and the black rate would fall below 7 percent, lower than the 2:1 ratio visible since 1954. But that never happened; the actual aggregate rate was 3.7 percent and the black rate about 8 percent. Even worse, black teenage unemployment, which was 22.7 percent in the first quarter of 1964, rose to 23.5 percent in the fourth quarter of 1966. The Bureau of Labor Statistics reported that "the supply of lower skill job seekers continued to exceed the number of available job openings."[4]

When it became clear that the 1966 forecast had been overly optimistic, the chairman of the CEA stated that the nation needed "structural" remedies. But the fear of inflation, which was then the government's economic priority, ruled out increased expenditures for manpower training. When the Bureau of the Budget received a study from a worried Willard Wirtz, demonstrating a 10 percent unemployment rate in ten black slums plus a 30 percent "subemployment" rate, its experts, unlike Wirtz, "were surprised by the *lack* of problem uncovered."[5]

If concerns about inflation led economic policymakers to minimize the problem until after the riots of 1967, liberals did no better. Senator Robert Kennedy of New York proposed a series of subsidies to businesses locating and hiring in the ghettos. But the problem was not jobs in the ghettos themselves but jobs in the city and immediate areas surrounding the city. Most ghetto residents, like most residents anywhere, do not work where they live.[6] Should the society work with market forces, accept the loss of manufacturing and retail jobs in the cities, spend money on fast public mass transportation to the new locations, build some decent housing, but stress population dispersal?[7] Or, should it seek to reverse these trends? There was no single answer. But most planners were blissfully ignorant of social and economic trends, unrecognized until the early 1970s. Whether they stressed helping the people or the place, none of the urban planners identified the urban crisis with the problems faced by their city's core industries.

The affected people were not only blacks. In the ethnic stockyard district of Chicago, predominantly the home of Eastern European immigrants, the unemployment rate was 20 percent. Although these Eastern Europeans and their descendants were now called white, they could hardly take comfort knowing that Chicago's white unemployment rate was 3.4 percent in 1967. Nor did they view an 8 percent black unemployment rate with the same anguish that white elites did. Comparisons in black and white were useful beginnings, but they erased the tangle of issues stemming from the migration of blacks from south to north, automation, suburbanization, and globalization. Occasionally, however, some of these issues seeped through. In 1966, after meeting with a group of business leaders in St. Louis, Ted Curtis, an OFCC official, proposed a mild form of Luddism for a genuine problem: "Business should be willing to delay automation and other labor-saving, cost-reducing projects on a *temporary*, *short-range* basis in order to utilize more unskilled labor." But the War on Poverty ideology held: the greatest need, Curtis concluded, was more "*education, training*, and, *motivation*."[8]

Time was running out. The black unemployed were situated strategically in large cities and enjoyed a moral claim on the nation's resources and conscience. Although civil rights rhetoric drew upon the past, many grievances were quite recent. The Hough section of Cleveland, for example, had been simply a run-down black neighborhood, but it became a true slum after about 1,200 low-income black families moved in. The newcomers had been displaced by an urban renewal project in the early 1960s. Had they held good jobs, they could have moved to more desirable neighborhoods; because they were not rehoused and were poor, many moved to Hough. The resulting congestion transformed Hough into a place of misery.[9] Many other cities had their counterparts to the Hough neighborhood.

Sensing their new moral and strategic power, sharpened by the white-heat words of new leaders, blacks demonstrated, protested, and rioted. In 1967, disturbances of some sort took place in more than 164 cities, topped by huge insurrections in Newark and Detroit in July. Although most riots began with inflammatory incidents involving the police, the consensus that unemployment and underemployment were the underlying causes produced feverish efforts to employ the jobless, who were believed to be the sources of the disturbances. The political backlash and the president's own inclinations ruled out a public jobs program. Once again, Johnson opposed Joseph Clark's legislation, the Emergency Employment Act of 1967, which was quietly supported by Labor Secretary Willard Wirtz and Sargent Shriver, head of the War on Poverty. All three agreed that the poverty program was not working.[10]

President Johnson turned instead to voluntarism. Urging big business to hire the "hard-core" unemployed, he proposed the JOBS program on January 24, 1968. The government organized the National Alliance of Businessmen (NAB), headed by Henry Ford II, to persuade companies to employ 100,000 hard-core unemployed by June 1969 and a total of 500,000 by January of 1971. William G. Caples, vice president of Inland Steel, believed it was "naive to expect that industry can accept large numbers of individuals for hard-core employment without subsidy and incentive." The JOBS program reimbursed employers for extra training costs.[11]

Up until this point, employers had not touched the "hard core." Driven by demonstrations and a changed public opinion, business had accepted the obligation first of fair employment and then of affirmative action. In the beginning managers had been able to obtain overqualified blacks for many jobs. As the demand rose, less qualified but easily trained blacks were hired. But in 1965 a study of 1,000 companies in Ohio and Michigan found only 6 percent willing to consider hiring high school dropouts and only 16 percent willing to hire young people immediately after high school.[12] Hiring specifications had risen during the years of high unemployment. But now industrialists from riot-torn cities, like Henry Ford II, believed they could do more. They acted out of equal measures of guilt, concern, and self-interest. "It is no longer solely a matter of justice and the principles of democracy," Ford admitted. "After the tragic events of the past few summers we just finally recognize—if we did not do so before—that our national unity and the peace of our cities are at stake." The president of Western Electric Company stated bluntly: "If the cities continue to deteriorate, our investment will inevitably deteriorate with them." Herbert Northrup of the Wharton School warned, "Industry in this country cannot survive with an unintegrated, angry minority." U.S. Steel's Roger Blough agreed. He told the American Iron and Steel Institute (AISI) that if steelmakers did nothing "business will experience a serious degradation of the climate which allows it to operate."[13]

The corporations most involved with JOBS were those with a significant stake in a city—banks, utilities, large retailers. The concerned businessmen altered the composition of their own workforce but did not change their corporate blueprints or address their city's job loss. Continuing its strategy of globalization, Ford added 50,000 workers to its overseas workforce between 1967 and 1971 while its domestic workforce fell by 8,000.[14]

The cities where the problems were greatest were the ones that lost the most work during the 1960s. In Cleveland, the numbers of jobs in the city declined from 354,200 in 1948 to 305,600 in 1958, a recession year. But despite the high national growth rates during the 1960s, the numbers continued to fall, dropping to 283,200 in 1967. Home to Republic and Jones and Laughlin steel mills, Cleveland lost manufacturing jobs, inevitably followed by corresponding losses in the wholesale and retail trades. The only category to rise was services, like health care, education, and other professional occupations. The new jobs did not compensate for the lost ones and were filled by a different population of workers.[15]

In the face of these trends, it was not surprising that only 99,000 of the 500,000 positions promised by JOBS materialized. By March 1970, only 39,000 remained. The economy had slowed in 1969 and 1970. In Detroit, automakers laid off JOBS workers as well as regular ones in 1969. The protest-driven urgencies of 1967 and 1968 waned. Guilt and concern became perishable commodities, at least with respect to the hard-core unemployed.[16]

The ethic was more durable, though practiced unevenly, when it came to hiring white-collar blacks, especially in politically sensitive sectors like communications and public utilities. The argument for the new morality was double-edged. The director of personnel of a large insurance firm stated that blacks "need an extra boost because they have been injured." The employment director at Alcoa urged a review of standards to remove "middle class bias." The rationales for racial preferences carried a therapeutic diagnosis of the black situation and new stereotypes. On the other hand, some of the onus was removed from African Americans when many corporations instituted sensitivity training for white managers.[17]

The riot-induced urgencies of 1967 affected those in charge of enforcing Title VII and the executive order as well as corporate elites. Government regulators attempted to take up the slack when the market faltered. Historian Hugh Graham has portrayed the bureaucrats at EEOC and OFCC as stealth operators, implementing a results-oriented agenda of their own.[18] But whatever their goals, their ability to act was made possible by business certification after the summer riots of 1967. Earlier, in February 1967, Edward C. Sylvester Jr., head of OFCC, concluded that "there seems to be a general consensus among responsible civil rights leaders that the more obvious barriers to minority employment are down."[19] But by late 1967, impelled by demonstrations, riots, lawsuits, a supportive elite culture, and an unpromising political climate, the regulatory agencies determined that they could do more. Sylvester took over a Department of Defense investigation at the Bethlehem mill at Sparrows Point, and demanded the southern changes that he had earlier thought unnecessary. Those in charge of civil rights enforcement could not create jobs, but they could create new rules to effect the desired results. They began to act without the hesitation and uncertainty they had exhibited for three years.[20]

They were joined by an invigorated Justice Department, which entered the employment field late. Its priorities remained school desegregation, voting rights, and ending discrimination in federally funded state programs. Most of the employment cases its civil rights division litigated in 1966 and 1967 emerged from social conflicts, not its own initiative. The suit at Crown Zellerbach was typical.[21] After Crown, Justice began to tackle employment, but it was not until after the summer riots that government lawyers planned campaigns in the North. In July, the civil rights division hired a former senior lawyer with the NLRB, Benjamin Mintz, to train its attorneys in labor law. After the Detroit riot, Clark shifted resources and staff from the South to other regions. Stephen Pollak, the new head of the civil rights division, lacked enough knowledge to carve out an area of his own, so he embraced the OFCC and EEOC priority, seniority. The Lackawanna suit announced in December was the fruit of the new policy.[22]

Lackawanna

Bethlehem Steel's Lackawanna mills were located outside of Buffalo, New York, the nation's largest inland port and second largest railroad center. In 1950, half of the area's workforce, 225,000, was employed in manufacturing. Although the city was the world's leading flour milling center, its character was stamped by the making of metal and the assembly of metal products. The Lackawanna steel mill, a big Republic facility, and hundreds of smaller foundries and finishers combined to make the Buffalo region the nation's third largest steel center. Ford and Chevrolet plants in the area bought steel and spawned numerous parts companies, the satellites of auto assembly.[23]

From its beginnings in 1901, workers at Lackawanna were a diverse lot. Some were American and Anglo-American refugees from Pennsylvania's mine, iron, and steel closings, but many were foreigners from eastern and southern Europe. In the wake of President William McKinley's assassination in Buffalo by an anarchist of Polish descent, the Poles were judged to be violent radicals. To the native-born, Italians seemed equally violent, although their lawlessness, it was believed, was rooted in village loyalties and rivalries. Small numbers of blacks were among the pioneers at Lackawanna; other African Americans entered the mill as strikebreakers during the 1919 strike. Even larger numbers came during and after World War II, and by the 1960s they composed about 13 percent of the workforce.

In the South, blacks were widely dispersed but were hired for unskilled work; in the North, and at Lackawanna, eastern European and black workers were concentrated in specific departments. In the beginning, white Americans and British immigrants worked in departments requiring the greatest skill, foreigners and blacks in sections where mechanization permitted novices to work, often the dirtiest and hottest places. The placement reflected white nativism, to be sure, but also the fact that at the time the Anglo-American group already possessed the steel-making skills. Over time, the concentrations were not so stark, but they were still visible.[24]

Ethnic hiring patterns were the least of workers' concerns. Bethlehem's decision in 1962 to build a new plant in Burns Harbor, Indiana, thirty miles east of Chicago, threatened everyone's jobs. The corporation first constructed finishing facilities, which meant that Lackawanna would supply steel to Burns Harbor throughout the 1960s, until the new mill was fully operative. Thus, steel production at Lackawanna actually expanded during the late 1960s, because of this temporary boost as well as the stimulus of Vietnam. But a union official noted in 1970, as the new facility began operating: "The Burns Harbor plant still has bugs in it, but once they're ironed out . . . [t]he automated, sophisticated Burns Harbor plant [will siphon] more and more production away from other, older mills in the company system." He was right. The decision to build Burns Harbor, combined with the increase in steel imports, became Lackawanna's death sentence.

Even during the boom of the 1960s, Lackawanna's employment declined because of mechanization, led by the introduction of the basic oxygen furnace in 1964. Despite record production, 21,500 men worked there in 1965, only 16,500 in 1969. Then, the shift to Burns Harbor had its effect. Employment fell to 12,000 in 1973, 8,500 in 1977. In 1983, confronted with a flood of imports and the Reagan recession, Bethlehem shut down most parts of the mill.

From the beginning, Bethlehem's labor relations had been poor. In 1941, *Fortune* observed that "in terms of the social responsibilities of modern American industry, Bethlehem's management is provincial. Socially, they are like characters in a majestic Gotterdammerung." Although the company was forced to accept the USWA, *Fortune*'s observation was equally applicable at the beginning of the civil rights era. Journalist John Strohmeyer recounts a telling story.[25]

On March 17, 1964, Philip B. Woodroofe, a Bethlehem manager in the corporation's hometown, Bethlehem, Pennsylvania, was fired. Woodroofe had taken to heart the Episcopal Church's urging of parishioners to improve race relations in their own communities and became a founder of the Community Civic League, a group of religious leaders and public officials dedicated to improving race relations in Bethlehem. But when Russell Branscom, the vice president of industrial and public relations at Bethlehem, found out about Woodroofe's extracurricular activity, he fired him. Woodroofe had broken two company rules: he had not cleared his civic work with the company and he had entered Branscom's domain, community affairs. Whether the firing was triggered by Branscom's racial prejudice, petty jealousy, or the sin of bureaucratic disobedience, the incident revealed a rigidity that precluded a creative response to civil rights. Founder Charles Schwab's policy of internal promotions, requirement of absolute loyalty to the company, and prohibitions against outside business activities and politics made Bethlehem managers the most insular lot in the industry.

Earlier, in 1961, when David McDonald requested meetings with the heads of the major steel companies to implement the Kennedy executive order, Branscom told McDonald, "It is a pleasure . . . to reaffirm Bethlehem's long-established policy that employment opportunity must be based upon merit, without discrimination because of race, creed, color or national origin." The policy affected all employment relations, including "placement." As we shall see, Lackawanna ended discriminatory hiring policies only in 1967, six years after Branscom affirmed Bethlehem's corporate virtue.[26]

The Justice Department entered the picture in Lackawanna in 1967 when a worker in the personnel office complained that summer replacements were monopolized by "superintendents' kids, all the general managers' kids, and all the foremen's kids." The Justice Department transformed a class question into a civil rights investigation. In the words of Bethlehem officer George Moore, "the Justice Department came in like a herd of turtles, and the next thing we know this thing has expanded way beyond the summer bit to all our employment practices and suddenly we have the first major civil rights case." It was not simply Justice. CORE sent a caravan of buses to Bethlehem's main office. Moore recalled, "you would think we're under attack."[27]

The man who had contacted Justice about the summer hiring was George Williamson, the black chairman of the Joint Civil Rights Committee, which consisted of representatives of each of the five locals. Williamson was also president of his local union, 2602. As a result of the government's prodding, the mill radically changed its personnel system. It centralized hiring and assignment, removing the power of mill managers to pick and choose and, presumably, discriminate. Bethlehem appointed an affirmative action coordinator, recruited at black educational institutions and churches, and advertised in black publications. Newly hired blacks were to be assigned on the same basis as whites; each applicant would be informed of all job openings; employment tests would be validated. It joined a local program to hire "hard core unemployables." Bethlehem refused, however, to institute the government demand for plant seniority. Stephen Pollak decided to proceed with the lawsuit and informed union lawyer Michael Gottesman in May 1968 that the USWA would be charged as well. Until then, the government had been dealing only with the corporation.[28]

By the time the trial began in December 1968, the government had the benefit of the *Quarles* and *Crown* rulings. The Justice Department adopted the *Quarles* reasoning and remedy arguing that in the eleven departments where the greatest number of blacks worked (2,160 of 3,775) blacks should be permitted to transfer to any other department where there was a vacancy and carry over their seniority and old rates.

Bethlehem took the position that seniority rights were protected, that remedies under Title VII were prospective, and that retroactive seniority with red-circled rates was unworkable, dangerous, and divisive. The union did not want to shackle Title VII, so its position was more nuanced. It argued that Title VII protected seniority systems, but it suspected that the court might go along with *Quarles*. So, it spent most of its time devising an alternative to the government's remedy, which it called a "'blockbuster,' in no way proportionate to the extent of the problem, which would lead to unmitigated chaos within the Plant."[29]

The facts of *Quarles* were not the facts of Lackawanna. To recall, discriminatory hiring at the Philip Morris plant had been nearly perfect. Until the early 1960s, blacks worked in the prefabrication department, whites in the fabrication department. Nearly all white jobs paid more than the black ones. To compensate for past discriminatory hiring, transferring blacks were permitted to use their plant seniority in manufacturing.

But at Lackawanna, two-thirds of all workers in the eleven departments were white, mainly of Eastern European origin. (The Justice Department acknowledged that there had been ethnic as well as racial assignment, but chose to limit its case to blacks.) Moreover, the blacks in the eleven departments earned slightly more than these whites. The average hourly earnings in the eleven departments were located in the middle of plant remuneration. Black hourly earnings in the eleven departments were 96.8 percent of the average of all employees throughout the plant. Given steadier employment, the average annual earnings of blacks in the eleven departments were above the plant average.

Thus, the union denied that the eleven departments were like the prefabrication department at the tobacco factory. The blacks were not uniquely aggrieved. This "affected class" at Lackawanna did better financially than whites in the eleven departments and thousands of blacks and whites in departments inferior to the eleven. To make matters worse, the penalty for discriminatory placement would fall upon other men guilty of no wrong, including those blacks who had already taken advantage of the transfer rules negotiated in 1962. In many instances those who would be bumped were earning less than those eligible for transfer.

The local unions had tried to effect transfer rights since 1954, but it was not until 1962 that workers were permitted to transfer at all, and they did so without retaining their seniority. Of the 306 applicants for transfer, 47 were black; 23 of 193 who actually transferred were black. The union did not view transfer as the panacea the government believed it to be but argued that if statistical concentration violated the law then changing seniority was not the only way to alter the numbers. The union believed that the 1968 steel contract offered new training and mobility measures that were fairer.[30] Like TCI's managers, Bethlehem's had formerly required transferees to be qualified to perform the top job in a line of promotion. Under the 1968 contract, they would only have to be able to do the job for which they applied. The USWA believed that rate retention was unnecessary and disruptive of worker morale and the union's principle of "equal pay for equal work." Thus, it argued that the seniority system at Lackawanna was bona fide but also claimed that if the judge accepted the *Quarles* interpretation of Title VII, the different history and facts of Lackawanna would mandate a different solution.

While the parties waited for the court decision, racial tensions rose. The trial itself heightened workers' sense of discrimination. It produced a wave of both white and black complaints about promotions and admission to apprenticeship programs.[31] In July 1969, the regional director of EEOC told Lackawanna workers that many allegations of discrimination "had no validity under the law."[32]

George Williamson, the black leader of the civil rights forces at Lackawanna, believed that race relations deteriorated because the company halted work on many of the union grievances as it waited for the court decision. Williamson reported to Attorney General John Mitchell that "[s]ince the litigation suit . . . things have been at a standstill. . . . Bethlehem has discontinued the ten (10) week training school for Negroes to be trained to become Bricklayers, and all Civil Rights have come to a halt. Upgrading and promotions seem to be out and things on the whole are about to become critical again." While the government was preoccupied with transfer, most civil rights issues involved the less grandiose but still important issues involving promotion within units. Bethlehem simply refused to discuss grievances with the union's civil rights committee if they had also been filed as complaints with state and federal agencies. The company's position was rigid, but making the state and courts arbiters encouraged management to work with bodies that had the final authority. The effect was to allow grievances to fester.[33]

Finally, the company's crude efforts to satisfy the Justice Department produced a backlash. John F. Meta, the white president of Local 2604, believed that the company was causing racial tension because it hired not one white in the strip mill in early 1969. All of the hires were blacks; whites who specifically asked to go to the mill were refused. The company claimed that the government was insisting upon a racial mix. Meta said that he welcomed mixed hiring but complained, "This is not mix, this is 100% Negro. . . . All the whites went to the Coke Ovens. This is a serious complaint."[34]

Bethlehem's behavior was a variant of the policies of all large companies under pressure from civil rights activists or the government. Hershel Donald, a union staffman, summed up company policy as "a spirited campaign to keep a step ahead of the Justice Department." The rush to hire blacks and grandstand "offers" to hire disadvantaged youths for summer mill jobs at reduced rates were typical.[35] After a racial disturbance in Buffalo, Bethlehem offered to hire 100 youths for summer jobs at $1.50 an hour. The USWA objected because the regular jobs paid $2.38 and the company was laying off regular workers. Companies were reimbursed for the extra training costs under the JOBS program, but regular workers, black and white, whose incentives depended upon group efforts, were not compensated when their work fell short because of the inefficiencies of the new hires.[36] In addition, international representative Sal Amarante could not get the company to budge from its position that senior black helpers were ineligible for its apprenticeship program in the pipefitting unit because they lacked a high school degree.[37]

Judge John O. Henderson ruled on April 13, 1970. Like the court in *Quarles*, Henderson found the flaw to be in company hiring, not in the seniority system. Unlike the union, he found the eleven departments did contain less desirable jobs, but, unlike the government, he found that ethnics were as disadvantaged as the blacks. "Bethlehem Steel Company's discriminatory employment policies related not alone to Negroes, but also to ethnic minorities," Henderson concluded. Thus, he ruled, "all employees, both Negroes and whites, in the eleven departments as of October 1, 1967, shall have the right to transfer to other departments on the basis of seniority without rate retention or seniority carry-over." The affected workers were to be given preferential access to vacancies in other departments, but they would not take their seniority with them. Seniority retention, Henderson ruled, would be "arbitrary and inequitable to employees guilty of no wrong"; moreover, he wrote, it would have "adverse effects wholly out of proportion to the injustice which it seeks to cure," words that echoed the union brief.[38]

Seeking a blacks-only solution, the government opposed the inclusion of ethnics in the transfer plan and appealed the decision, seeking instead plant seniority with red-circled rates for the blacks in the eleven departments. The decision transformed tension into full-blown racial polarization. Its first effects were seen in union elections on June 23.

Traditionally, union slates had been interracial. In Local 2602, which was about 15 percent black, George Williamson had been vice president. When President Sal Amarante was put on the union's staff, Williamson moved up to the presidency, shortly before the trial. Now, he wanted to run in his own right. There were two other candidates: Vincent Takas, a white liberal; the other, a white rallying those opposed to the Henderson decree. Fearing that the civil rights forces would be split, Amarante asked Williamson to withdraw, support Takas, and instead run again for chairman of the civil rights committee. Williamson refused and stayed in the race. Amarante put together an interracial slate behind Takas.

On the Sunday before the Tuesday election, a leaflet appeared in the lockers. It read in part:

> Vote the Takas-Williamson Ticket. We feel the Negro must have super seniority and rate retention and the right to take white employees jobs. The White Employees have discriminated against the Negros long enough. The Supreme Court will prove this. The Takas ticket is behind Williamson who is the chairman of the Negro movement and who takes orders from the NAACP. A vote for the Takas ticket is a vote for the Williamson ticket. A vote for Williamson is a vote for Takas.

The leaflet did its dirty work. Both Takas and Williamson lost.

In a letter to USWA vice president Joseph Molony, Takas explained what had happened. "[W]ords or phrases such as 'super-seniority,' 'rate retention,' 'the right to be placed on white workers jobs'" were prominent features of the newspaper reports of the trial. Then, "[t]his insidious slinger [the flyer] rekindled the alarm and fear of the white workers." He added, "no stone should be left unturned to find the persons responsible for this foul act, who are devoid of Union Principle and destitute of honor, and should not have the privilege to retain membership in our Union." Williamson agreed, telling Molony that the opposition's false charge that he espoused "super-seniority," was the cause of his defeat.[39]

Neither Williamson nor other blacks active on civil rights issues in the plant at the time were advocating special black rights. Most of the complaints accused the company of failing to accept the bids of senior blacks, a situation we observed in Birmingham. Indeed, this charge transcended race. One case involved the appointment of an outside black to be foreman of a labor gang when black workers thought one of their own should be promoted. "Super-seniority" was espoused by a few blacks, but was primarily a government goal.

Racial divisiveness affected not only Local 2602. Not one black was elected to a major office in any local! In the largest local, Stanley D. Murphy, another black, narrowly lost the presidency by four votes. Murphy had been the elected grievanceman for the bar mill. One of the eleven departments, it was still only 21.8 percent black. Murphy attributed his defeat to similar white fears. He told the USWA's civil rights director Alex Fuller that "many of the white[s] . . . think that it means that the black members will now take the jobs of white members."[40] But African Americans were in a desperate situation. Black representation, Murphy concluded, had assured workers that their grievances would get a hearing. Now that "they are wiped out," as he put it, Murphy prepared to organize a black local at Lackawanna. Yet interracial traditions were too strong and blacks too few at Lackawanna for a "black power" solution. Williamson opposed the idea, and Murphy himself thought better of the idea.[41]

Rumors about plant closure heightened everyone's fears. The impact of Burns Harbor was a constant topic of conversation. There were other immediate problems. In September, three months after the divisive election, thirty men, black and white, spontaneously walked out of the 44-inch mill, one of the eleven departments in the suit. The company planned to combine the soaking pits of this mill with those of the 40-inch mill, without union consultation. (A soaking pit is a furnace used to reheat ingots before rolling.) Bethlehem won a court injunction on the grounds that the wildcat strike violated the contract. The men returned, and the union took up the question of job elimination. Then, on November 30, 1970, Bethlehem announced a cutback in steelmaking capacity from 6.7 to 4.8 million tons, a cut affecting every department. In June 1971, Local 2603 called an unprecedented mass meeting for company officials, supervisors, employees, and union representatives to resolve the soaking pit problem. The union reluctantly lent its support to Bethlehem's efforts to reduce its local tax bill and delay installing pollution-control equipment.[42]

The pot kept boiling. At the end of the month, Judge C. F. Feinberg, speaking for the Second Circuit Court of Appeals, overturned the district court decision in two key areas. First, Feinberg agreed with the government that only blacks could transfer out of the eleven departments. He said that although ethnic whites may have been assigned on a discriminatory basis vis-à-vis other whites, such preference was not proscribed by Title VII. Second, he ruled that blacks could transfer with their old rates and plant seniority. He remanded the case to Judge Henderson to enter a new order consistent with his ruling.[43]

Sixteen hundred blacks in the eleven departments were given 120 days to apply for transfers with "rate retention." Although 430 signed up, only 70 actually changed jobs, and many of them ultimately returned to their former jobs.

"Soaked" (reheated) ingot leaving pit for rolling process. (Courtesy of HCLA, Penn State)

The new right was intended to remedy past discrimination, but blacks made their decisions with an eye on the effects that current cutbacks would have on their future security. By this measure, the eleven departments were more desirable than others to which they might transfer, because they offered more job security. A white, Frank Gombos, who had worked since 1935 in the blast furnace, one of the eleven departments, said, "I was never laid off except for a penalty in 1939 for wearing a union button." The government's single-minded concentration on transfer, as disruptive as it was, was in real terms much ado about nothing. That was why another suit was filed, demanding more.[44]

Six workers, including the embittered George Williamson, filed a private suit seeking more than Feinberg's remedy. They were represented by Russell Specter, who had been deputy general counsel of EEOC but was now a private practitioner of Title VII law. Specter argued that in light of the massive layoffs at the Lackawanna plant, the Court of Appeals remedy would be of little benefit to black employees, since none could transfer until laid-off employees had been recalled. Although a transferring worker could not bump an incumbent, he claimed that workers on layoff were not incumbents. The lawsuit, which also demanded back pay, was supported by EEOC but not Justice.[45]

But at a hearing on the suit, another lawyer dissented, claiming that his black clients would be disadvantaged by it. As the union had argued, many blacks in other departments and on layoff feared that senior blacks from the eleven would use their plant seniority against them. The lawyer planned to sue, too, but only for back pay. Then during lunchtime, a group of fifty white picketers, under the banner of "Equal Rights for Blacks and Whites," entered their criticism of the Feinberg ruling. They had learned the value of publicity. On a cold, snowy day in Buffalo, they stayed around only long enough to be photographed and interviewed by newspaper and television reporters.[46]

Judge Henderson ruled against the additional measures, but the Second Circuit again overturned his decision. Everything necessary for the Second Circuit decision to be implemented had been made ready—procedural questions formulated, lists of eligible workers compiled—when Henderson died. By the time a new judge was assigned to the case and the proceedings resumed, industry-wide consent decrees had been negotiated, which made the decision moot. As we shall see, these agreements rejected the Second Circuit approach.[47]

From the beginning, politics outside of the plant intruded. Donald M. Dade, president of an independent construction union, offered to "join forces" with black steel workers in "a civil rights labor movement." When it was clear that few black workers wanted to transfer out of the eleven departments, the Third World Workers Organizing Committee, a community organization, asked for lists of eligible workers. It assumed that it, not the workers, knew their own interests. James Forman, the former head of SNCC, came to Lackawanna and addressed forty-two black steelworkers a month later, in February 1972.

Forman's best political days were over. After a brief flirtation with the Black Panthers in 1968, he embraced the League of Revolutionary Black Workers, a militant caucus of the UAW in Detroit. Forman wanted to expand the league into a national organization and founded the Black Workers Congress, which was to organize similar groups in other cities. Indicting the "sellout leadership in power," he asserted that the USWA like the state, "should be ours." He declared that "it is not just a question of Black people transferring from this job or that job. . . . [W]e want working class people to run the total society."[48] More interested in power than workers' lives, Forman revealed through his dismissal of the world of work why he, a former Chicago teacher, and others like him were tourists among the working class. The new black left was ambivalent about class. Forman urged working-class power, but his talk was saturated with the experiences of race, not class: "We are tired of 400–500 years of oppression as Black people." The Forman of this period raised the heat of argument, but little else.[49]

The intervention of the government and private lawyers was more significant. Neither the government's agenda nor the private suit's proposals emerged from blacks in the mill. Of course, it was not difficult to convince Williamson and some others that they were entitled to additional remedies, especially as the conflicts polarized the work force.

But the Title VII solutions could not catch up with Bethlehem's cutbacks. The lawsuits were played out against a backdrop of declining operations. General Manager Robert Jordan announced that the limited production was "due to [Lackawanna's] inability to compete with sister plants." He ignored Burns Harbor's new equipment and product mix. Bethlehem's chairman, Stewart S. Cort, remarked in 1972 that he would keep Lackawanna's "employment level as high as can be supported by the business the plant is able to attract in competition with other producers," hardly reassuring given other statements about Lackawanna's inability to compete. From 1969 to 1972, employment fell from 18,500 to 12,000. Thus, at the time that Lackawanna was reducing production and employment, the avenues of "escape" for the blacks in the eleven departments were disappearing. For EEOC and the Second Circuit this meant that more radical changes were needed to facilitate transfer.[50]

The Justice Department and court's separation of black experiences from those of other Lackawanna workers and then from the facts of declining employment were typical of elite formulations of labor issues during this period. They offered black workers little that was concrete and embittered a good many whites. The limits of a civil rights approach to the situation of black workers came early at Lackawanna.

Sparrows Point

In March 1974, black and white workers in the coke plant at the Sparrows Point mill of Bethlehem Steel walked out in a wildcat. One black striker told a reporter, "It's all right for the guys who want to transfer out, but what about the man who wants to stay in this department, especially the older man. All his friends are down here and he knows all the jobs. Most of the guys don't want to transfer." Nevertheless, the Lackawanna solution was ordered at Sparrows Point. The main actors in Sparrows Point were civil rights organizations and government regulators at OFCC, not the courts and the Justice Department. The Congress of Racial Equality (CORE) and the LDF had more influence at Sparrows Point than James Forman enjoyed at Lackawanna.[51]

A barren peninsula jutting into Chesapeake Bay just east of Baltimore, Sparrows Point was the site of the nation's first tideland steel company. When the plant began operations in 1890, managers created a company town, initially without elected officials. Like those at Lackawanna, the skilled workers were primarily Americans of British or German descent, many from Pennsylvania. Although the company hired immigrants from Eastern Europe, unlike Lacka-

Aerial view of the Bethlehem steel plant in Sparrows Point, Maryland, in 1946. (Courtesy of Hagley Museum and Library)

wanna managers, those at Sparrows Points considered the foreigners inferior labor. Axel Sahlin, the superintendent, concluded in 1902 that, "only a moderate percentage [of the immigrants] have the necessary strength and intelligence to fit them for the work." The foreigners were housed in a section aptly named Shantytown. Sahlin could afford to be choosy because he had an alternative supply of cheap labor—southern blacks. He believed that blacks worked well in the hot Maryland summers which "make it difficult for white men to perform such heavy manual labour." [52] Half of Shantytown's single males were black. Another section of town was reserved for black families. [53]

This pattern of recruitment continued over time, making the black presence at Sparrows Point more significant than at Lackawanna. In 1967, the mill employed 12,602 whites and 7,864 blacks. Although the racial statistics at Sparrow's Point were like those at TCI, it followed the northern pattern of concentrating ethnic/racial groups in particular departments. [54]

Civil rights at Sparrows Point was pretty much a local affair until CORE intervened in 1966. CORE's championing of black steelworkers was a by-product of its failing Target City project of 1966. Well-known for its Freedom Rides in the South, CORE, an interracial organization formed in 1942, had organized demonstrations to integrate schools, housing, and jobs during the 1950s and early 1960s, with some success. But the ghetto problems, as Martin Luther King Jr. had discovered in Chicago in 1966, were not so amenable to direct action tactics. A member of CORE's executive board acknowledged that the organization has "a reputation for exposing civil rights problems but not solving them."[55]

The project of organizing the ghettos encouraged black nationalist tendencies, which were rising in all the civil rights organizations in 1965. By 1966, most whites had left CORE, and its new chairman Floyd McKissick was firmly in the Black Power camp. But Black Power was a posture, not a program. CORE retained a certain tactical diversity—black politics, black economic development, black caucuses, and black unions. These tendencies were all present in the African American community. But because each implied different political alliances and visions, CORE discovered that they were not easily housed in one organization.

CORE decided to make Baltimore its Target City in 1966. It planned to concentrate its forces in one city, like King's simultaneous efforts in Chicago. Actually, its prospects in Baltimore were more promising. Unlike SCLC in the Windy City, CORE already had a local chapter and satellite organizations in Baltimore. Its Maryland Freedom Union (MFU) was the major one.

Inspired by Cesar Chavez's Mexican-American Farm Workers Association and the Mississippi Freedom Labor Union, some activists were attracted to unionizing low-paid workers, united by race or ethnicity. The MFU aimed to organize retail and service workers. Many were southern migrants, who no longer found work at the city's shipyards, steel mills, and foundries. Industrial work was shrinking in Baltimore, as elsewhere. Because of the strategic weakness of service workers, consumer boycotts, political pressure, and public relations became surrogates for strikes. But successes were scattershot. CORE discovered that it was not so easy to organize low-paid workers. Those workers who wanted to unionize preferred established unions to CORE.[56]

At the beginning of the Target City initiative, CORE approached workers at the Sparrows Point mills to help the MFU. Staff went out to the gates of the mill on one payday and collected $300 from the workers, white as well as black. But as the difficulties of organizing the unorganized mounted, the complaints of Sparrows Point blacks became a more attractive project. In the fall of 1966, Walter S. Brooks, head of the Target City project, and Baltimore CORE Chairman James M. Griffin embraced the cause of blacks at Sparrows Point.

Although CORE's numbers in the mill were always small, the psychological power that CORE and the new black power organizations possessed was considerable. Elite whites, possessing a potent brew of concern, guilt, and desire to retain control of the social order, accepted the rhetoric of the new organizations as reality. The *New York Times* and *Wall Street Journal* breezily decided that groups like CORE had more relevance to blacks than the traditional black organizations like the NAACP or the National Urban League. Some CORE leaders eyed such certification with satisfaction. The more serious were less impressed. "In the eyes of white folks" the Baltimore project was a success, observed one CORE leader. But Baltimore CORE was simply "an amalgamation of rebellious individuals, lacking any cohesive community class base, and representing Negroes only by proxy." Another concluded: "We have done a beautiful job of being militant and responding to the white folks, but we haven't concentrated enough on the black folks." [57]

Nevertheless, the white folks at Sparrows Point agreed to meet with a CORE delegation on October 20, 1966. Representatives from the Department of Defense (DOD), company officials, and CORE leaders, toured the plant from October 31 through November 4. Neither CORE nor the government had a diagnosis or remedy for Sparrows Point. DOD found technical violations of the executive order and an inadequate affirmative action program. The transportation department lacked black truck drivers and the police department was all white. Few blacks were in supervisory positions. Bethlehem promised to rectify the violations.

To remain in the limelight, CORE widened its criticism. On December 16, it added air pollution and price rises to its bill of complaint. Two months later, CORE urged Labor Secretary Wirtz to impose a comprehensive solution. On April 2, 1967, CORE called for a black union and a black wildcat strike. LDF lawyer Gerald Smith told steelworkers that blacks could take over the union because they made up 60 percent of the workforce.(In fact, blacks composed about one-third.) At a CORE meeting, held on company property on April 27, Lincoln Lynch, national director of CORE, announced a "Freedom Bus Ride" to Washington.[58]

The name revealed that CORE was hoping to organize in the North by invoking the kinds of emotions that had been evoked during civil rights demonstrations in the South. Working with other community groups, CORE did mobilize 500 persons, although most were not steelworkers. The number was considerably smaller than CORE's target of 10,000 but significant enough to obtain an audience with Wirtz, who promised action.[59] CORE had good relations with the Labor Department, which had awarded it a $147,000 grant to train youths to operate a gasoline station in Baltimore.[60] These relationships ensured that CORE continued to be a factor in the deliberations, even though its position in the mill was contested by many new black caucuses representing small groups of younger men in various departments, men who were often contemptuous of both CORE and the union.[61]

The Washington Freedom Ride convinced Labor's Office of Contract Compliance (OFCC) to take over the investigation. OFCC head Edward Sylvester had been meeting with DOD and company personnel during the spring of 1967. In response to government prodding, managers hired blacks as truck drivers, policemen, clerical workers, and supervisors and made other suggested changes in their personnel policies.[62] OFCC had difficulty getting a handle on the plant because unlike other steelworkers, Bethlehem workers had won transfer rights in 1956, not 1962. Fixated on transfer, OFCC negotiators were at a loss. Sylvester concluded that seniority would not be a "major" problem.[63]

Nevertheless, on August 2, with the fires of Detroit barely extinguished, Sylvester replaced the DOD team with one from Labor, headed by Robert Hobson, a black OFCC official. Hobson was impatient, determined, and militant. He demanded new information and acted as if the proceedings were just beginning. He was seeking what was by then a boilerplate solution: transfer with seniority and red-circled rates. His manner, assumptions, and demands hardened the company position.[64]

While the government-company negotiations were at a standstill, the international sent Curtis Strong, a black staffperson, to Sparrows Point to assess the situation. Strong reported that the company was "dragging its feet." Racial and nonracial problems were compounded by the "serious cut-back in the work force at the plant and . . . very few new hires." Adding to white fears, Strong noted, the "newspaper has repeatedly inferred that the government has ordered that Negros be up-graded and at the expense of whites." The June elections in Local 2610 both reflected and contributed to the tension—an essentially white slate defeated a black one.[65]

After talking to black and white union officials and one steelworker active in CORE, Strong reported that Bethlehem was interested only in "visible integration," or "tokenism," meaning the appointment of blacks to the rank of foremen and into all-white departments. The behavior was remarkably similar to the actions of the Lackawanna and TCI managers. In both cases, the institutional mechanisms for promotion went unreformed. Thus, Ivory Dennis, a black grievanceman, charged that the company continued to select junior whites over senior blacks, the same problem as in Birmingham. He vowed to file charges at the NLRB over the company's unwillingness to negotiate.[66] As in Lackawanna, rigid qualifications also were keeping blacks back. Thus, to remain in the plate mill a worker needed to pass a battery of tests and possess a high school diploma. The testing requirements for transfer, established in the 1950s when hiring hurdles rose because of the labor surpluses, continued into current period. The union claimed that the tests were discriminatory. The company had promised to bargain with the union but then backed off.

As in Lackawanna, when managers were negotiating with the government, they stopped talking with the union. USWA leaders also felt frustrated because both the company and the government were more responsive to CORE than to the union itself. Taking a leaf from CORE, the two local unions voted on January 19, 1968, to go to Washington to urge government agencies to force the corporation to bargain in good faith. After the trip was prominently reported in Baltimore newspapers, the company quickly set up a meeting with the union's district director, Al Atallah.[67] On February 14, Ben Fischer, the international's expert on contractual matters, and Dee Gilliam, an able young black technician, came to Sparrows Point to meet with local unionists.[68]

Fischer and Gilliam found four problem areas: refusal to promote blacks to foremen or supervisors, failure to promote or transfer eligible blacks, discrimination in apprenticeship, and refusal to bargain in good faith with black unionists. The intervention had its effect. The company sent Richard Schubert, Bethlehem's assistant manager of industrial relations, to the talks. Schubert was relatively young and less infected with the old Bethlehem culture. For the first time, the company began working with the union on institutional processes, testing, transfers, job posting, and apprenticeships. But progress did not come fast enough.[69]

The *Quarles* and *Crown* decisions in early 1968, amplified by new riots after King's assassination, strengthened OFCC's hand. On May 13, LDF lawyer Gerald Smith pressured Wirtz to act. Ten days later, OFCC sent debarment orders to five companies, including Bethlehem's Sparrows Point division. Bethlehem demanded a hearing, its right under the executive order, and Wirtz set up a panel chaired by Father Dexter L. Hanley, a law professor at Georgetown University, and two labor arbitrators—one white, Peter Seitz; the other black, Lloyd Baylor.[70]

One month later, on June 20, Sylvester in essence instructed the panel. He issued new seniority guidelines, applicable everywhere, which, he wrote, were "not negotiable." Declaring that remedies for past discrimination still operative in seniority systems must "provide for the total elimination of all discriminatory elements," he insisted that "seniority will have to be altered." Companies would come up with the plans, but OFCC would judge them. Thus, the guidelines became hostage to the vagaries of OFCC decision making.[71] Because the OFCC demands included changes in collective bargaining agreements, Bethlehem now asked that the union be allowed to participate in the hearings. The panel heard testimony in September and October of 1968. The session scheduled for February 4, 1969, was postponed, however, because workers were electing a new director for District 8 on February 11. The hearings always raised racial tensions, but in this case, one of the candidates was black, and the government did not want to hurt his chances.[72]

The international had been under pressure to appoint a black to its executive committee, which was made up of the directors of the 38 districts. But in this matter USWA democracy was a barrier. Had district directors been appointed, not elected by the rank and file, Abel could have appointed a black. But he preferred to keep the democratic character of the board. The top USWA leaders believed that the UAW approach of appointing a black to the executive board produced a "coopted" and "captured" individual, because the person did not have an independent political base.[73] It seemed possible to elect an African American in District 8, which possessed a significant black minority. Atallah's decision to retire gave Abel an open position and he threw his weight behind black staffman, Leander Simms.

Simms, a modest but very capable man, had been president of a small can local, which had a white majority. His personal qualities and his ability to attract whites as well as blacks made him a good choice. In an unusual move, Abel came into the district to campaign for him. Simms's opponent Edward E. Plato was a white staffman at Sparrows Point, who was supporting Abel's opponent for union president. Plato was a "rank-and-filer" or an "oppositionist," depending upon one's point of view. He functioned as a rallying point for whites opposed to civil rights in general and others who opposed the particular demands for seniority changes at Sparrows Point.[74]

Unfortunately, the seniority issue was still alive and Plato defeated Simms, 7,549 to 5,668. Even though Simms won more white votes than expected, the large black vote had not materialized, partly because of black divisions. Moreover, he was not very well known by blacks or whites at the steel mill, because he had come out of the small container local. Such things carried weight in elections.[75]

The campaign and election only made racial tensions worse. Strong concluded that "the leaders of both the Blacks and the White seem reluctant to forget the past election and the chasm that was opened between the races." Ivory Dennis was completely demoralized. Dennis and local president Joe Capp tried to maintain some sort of interracial cohesiveness, but in the short run this was difficult.[76] Because of the racial tensions, panelist Peter Seitz suggested that mediation should be substituted for more public hearings. President Nixon's new Secretary of Labor George Shultz agreed in March and appointed Robert Livernash, the author of the government report on the 1959 steel strike, to aid Father Hanley. The talks produced quick agreement on the so-called "minor" issues: testing, training, supervision, and office employees. Seniority was more difficult, but a compact was reached.[77]

The essence of the plan was to merge units. With 62 fewer seniority units, 31 percent of the black workers would be employed in units with higher ranges of job opportunities. Other blacks, approximately 55 percent, would be in larger, broader based units, which would enhance their job promotion opportunities and job security. Transfers to new units continued but without seniority carry-over. The system was universal. Although tailored to enhance black promotion, white workers in the merged unit, in the same situation as blacks, would benefit too.

OFCC was ambivalent about the negotiated plan. Sylvester had left OFCC, and its new head, Ward McCreedy, a holdover from the Johnson administration, accepted the plan, but the new assistant secretary for wages and hours, Arthur Fletcher, a black Republican, held off. Fletcher, who had not been involved in the negotiations, had just announced a new affirmative action plan in construction and was in no mood to compromise. Supported by OFCC staff, lawyers in the solicitor's office, and the civil rights organizations, he decided that complete seniority transfer and rate retention for blacks only would have to be the heart of any solution.

Fletcher ordered more open hearings, which resumed in November. Both the union and the company argued that rate retention would be unworkable, fearing morale problems when a black transferred into a department but retained a prior wage rate that was higher than coworkers doing the same job. Richard L. Rowan of the Wharton School, a government witness, testily responded: "I never said it would be easy, but it could be done." Rowan acknowledged that current system was nondiscriminatory but said that the key issue at Sparrows Point was past discrimination. If their actions were any measure, many blacks disagreed. While Rowan was testifying, over 100 blacks from the blast furnace were conducting a wildcat and threatening to stop production; to them, equal opportunity meant inclusion in a recently announced incentive plan.[78]

In December 1970, the panel came to a split conclusion. Chairman Hanley and Peter Seitz endorsed the company-union remedy; Lloyd Bailer upheld OFCC's position that rate retention and plant seniority carryover for an affected class of blacks was required. Finally, on January 15, 1973, Secretary of Labor James Hodgson reversed the panel and ordered seniority carry-over with rate retention for blacks.

Hodgson relied heavily on the Second Circuit Court's 1971 decision in Lackawanna. He explained that he had delayed the decision until the appeals court ruled in Lackawanna. But the administration waited nearly two years after the Feinberg ruling. The delay reflected the divisions within the Labor Department between the industrial relations people and the lawyers in the solicitor's office and OFCC. The lawyers and OFCC won. They cited the judicial principles at Lackawanna, the *Crown* and *Quarles* decisions. But none asked whether any of these legal victories had helped the black workers in those plants.[79]

The underlying assumption was that transfer was the only route to progress, that if blacks were permitted to move on the basis of plant seniority and given financial incentives they would choose to leave their departments. However, as we saw in the coke plant, most blacks at Sparrows Point preferred to remain where they were. Of the 5,400 blacks in the "affected class," only 130 applied for transfer. The president of Local 2609, David Wilson, told Abel, "we let the tail wag the dog." Parts of the tail were not genuine transferees but participants in a new competition among whites. Because a black bid produced a competition based upon mill seniority, if two whites were competing for a job, the white with longer plant but shorter line seniority would invite, and pay, a black to compete for the job, thereby shifting the competition and allowing him to attain a job over another white. Such were some of the results of abstract assumptions and symbolic solutions.[80]

Beginning in Lackawanna in 1971 and continuing in Sparrows Point in 1973, the courts and the government concluded that in cases where minority groups were identifiable victims of pre–Civil Rights Act hiring discrimination, the vestiges of past discrimination must be removed. But blacks were not the only groups assigned to what the government and court decided were "undesirable" departments. And, desirability is in the eye of the beholder, particularly in a climate of economic and technological change. It goes without saying that gazing at the past blinded them to the present, not to say the future. Regardless of how they were hired, workers often found decent pay, steady employment, and practicing acquired skills with friends in old departments preferable to transferring to new jobs. Even though in practice the policy affected few workers, the contentiousness of the debate, with its complete separation of the black and white experience, produced social conflict wherever it was proposed and effected. The few affected sometimes embraced racist champions. Under the Sparrows Point plan, workers on layoff stemming from production fluctuations were not considered incumbents. There were instances of blacks bumping whites of relatively long service. One group hired a Georgia lawyer, who regularly ran for office on a white supremacy ticket, to plead their case. The president of the local believed that if the bumped workers had obtained their old rates, some of their racial animosity would ebb. He thought that if the Experimental Negotiating Agreement (see Chapter 8) ended the fluctuations that were due to strike fears some of the conflicts stemming from post-layoff bumping would end.[81] Such thinking was not part of government policymaking, which was dominated by abstract universals. It was the blacks and whites in the mill who sought to counter polarizing policies. In 1973, Ivory Dennis, who had a consistent record of fighting discrimination and upholding working-class interests, was elected president of the big local at Sparrows Point. In his acceptance speech, he said, "there are those who contended that a Black man would never again take over the leadership in this great local." They were wrong.[82]

The government's single-minded pursuit of a principle whose symbolism exceeded its practical value was propelled by the riots of 1967 and 1968. By 1968, all parts of the bureaucracy—the Justice Department, OFCC, EEOC, and the courts—filled with concern, guilt, and arrogance, responded to the urban crisis with the powers they possessed. The regulatory bodies could not produce jobs, only distribute them. They created plans that integrated on paper but ignored working-class life and culture. In the current argot, their acts socially constructed racism. Nevertheless, the Justice Department and civil rights litigators continued to seek new interpretations of the law in the South and apply them to the nation. The court strategy was invested with even more significance after 1968, because of President Nixon's opposition to most items on the civil rights agenda.

Litigation Is Everything:

The Nixon Years

Examined in isolation, Secretary of Labor Hodgson's affirmation of OFCC's remedy at Sparrows Point was a civil rights victory. But the decision, based upon court compliance, was in harmony with the minimal civil rights policies of the Nixon administration. President Richard M. Nixon instructed his aides to "only do what the law requires, nothing more." When in doubt, he said, "don't do it, let the court bring it on." As the White House disengaged from black issues, the slowing economy increased black unemployment, and mass action ebbed, civil rights activists inside and outside of government also agreed to "let the court bring it on." It is true that congressional Democrats, freed from the loyalty they had given to presidents of their party, now advocated public employment. But lawyers became the vanguard of the civil rights movement. Nixon's Justice Department, OFCC, and EEOC, populated by activists from the Kennedy-Johnson era, became islands of activity in a quiet sea. In 1970, when the situations at Lackawanna and Sparrows Point seemed to be going against it, the Justice Department decided, in essence, to start anew, by suing U.S. Steel in Birmingham, a prelude to an industrywide suit. The strategy was to win remedies for the "affected class" in a southern case, where past discrimination was easier to document, and then apply them throughout the industry. Birmingham played its historic role, but, as it turned out, the remedy ordered was closer to the union's solution than the government's.[1]

Why Litigation Was Necessary: Nixon's Racial Policies

The zeal of lawyers in the Justice Department and regulators in OFCC and EEOC was partly self-generated, but it stemmed from two sources: the judgment that the White House was hostile to blacks and civil rights in general and the rising black employment of the Nixon years. Actually, the president's racial policies were propelled by political calculations, unsullied by personal animus or interest. Nixon was no bigot, but he was deaf to black voices.[2] The truth was that he was uninterested in domestic policies of any sort but was a weather vane on their political implications. He lived by the maxim that presidential victories went to those who captured the center, which was now moving right as the business community became more adversarial toward labor and conservatives gained control of southern and southwestern Republican parties. Nixon was elected in 1968 because of the divisive Vietnam war and the social conflicts spawned by liberal politics. His positive mandate was less certain. The president understood that his interests were not identical with those of business, the white South, or "Sunbelt" fundamentalists, all of whom he had wooed during the campaign. Keeping the southern GOP united with liberal and moderate Republicans from the North and West required constant tacking. Making the task even more difficult, he had been elected with only 43.4 percent of the vote and was the first president since Zachary Taylor, in 1849, to enter the White House with opposing majorities in both houses of Congress.[3]

Without political commitments or interest, Nixon acted on black matters when congressional initiatives and court decisions forced his hand or when African American goals coincided with his own. His bureaucracy in domestic affairs, staffed by holdovers from the Kennedy-Johnson years and liberal Republican additions, often exercised some independence, which he tolerated, unless it clearly threatened his own political future. Still, he planned to clean house in some of the departments, including Justice, after the 1972 elections. Watergate made that impossible.[4]

It was Nixon's slowing of the economy, more than any single measure going under the name of civil rights, that most affected blacks. The purpose of the wave of new litigation was to compensate for a black unemployment rate that rose from 6.4 percent in 1969 to 10.3 in 1972. The increases now included black adults, not only teenagers, and were still higher in industrial cities. The ratio of black to white unemployment rose above its 2:1 average, first visible in 1955.[5]

This view differs from a common one, often called "ironic," which puts a more positive light on Nixon's black employment record.[6] The argument, reflecting the political consensus of the 1990s rather than the 1970s, assumes that the source of black gains in the civil rights era came from the affirmative action programs begun by Nixon. The first of these was the Philadelphia plan, which mandated employment quotas or goals in the construction industry, an approach that was subsequently required of all federal contractors. There are two problems with this interpretation. First, scholars examining the source of black gains disagree. A few argue that market forces were the source of progress. Most attribute the gains to a combination of economic expansion, superior education, and broad government actions against discrimination during the 1960s, not the 1970s.[7] Second, and more relevant to the argument here, Nixon's contemporaries, civil rights advocates and his own staff, believed his affirmative action plans were impotent.[8]

When he took office, Nixon confirmed the skepticism of his critics by opposing new civil rights legislation and picking a fight with outgoing EEOC chairman Clifford Alexander. At that point, a bipartisan congressional majority concluded that EEOC should be armed with cease-and-desist powers and the various enforcement bodies consolidated. Such a law passed the Senate and enjoyed a majority of the House, but southern Democrats and a GOP minority, covertly backed by the White House, were able to block the bill for three years. Finally, in 1972, Nixon and business lobbyists yielded, accepting an alternative that transferred the right to sue from Justice to EEOC and expanded coverage to employees of state and local governments and educational institutions.[9]

Defensive actions to prevent unwanted legislation were insufficient in 1969, the last year of significant, often violent, street demonstrations, mainly around construction sites. There was no consensus in society about what needed to be done, but everyone agreed that government had some obligation to address black unemployment. Nixon's own solution was black capitalism, a logical program for a Republican president and one that was supported by Whitney Young of the Urban League and some corporate leaders.[10] On March 5, 1969, Nixon created the Office of Minority Business Enterprise (OMBE), a coordinating agency in the Commerce Department that had no budget, no authority, and no set-asides. On the day of the announcement, Nixon met with a group of black officials from various government departments. They were not impressed with the new program, and he was not impressed with them.[11] Even Nixon's friend Don Kendall, head of Pepsi Cola and the National Alliance of Businessmen, shared the skepticism. Kendall told him, "You're spinning wheels on black capitalism. For every one success, there are failures. If you get jobs, on the other hand, they'll get into the mainstream."[12]

But in 1969 such a strategy was difficult to effect. Inflation was at 5 percent. The Federal Reserve Board was tightening the money supply, and the president was slowing the growth of federal expenditures. Nixon battled inflation, but he wanted to avoid a genuine recession, believing that he had lost the 1960 election because the tight fiscal and monetary policy of the Eisenhower administration had kept unemployment high. His advisers fastened upon a solution, which they claimed would help reduce the inflation rate and also help blacks obtain employment.

The White House and the business community believed that the motor of rising prices was high construction costs, pushed up by the wages won by powerful unions. The president's economic counselor Arthur Burns claimed that construction wages in the past year had risen an average of 15 percent, although the Bureau of Labor Statistics reported an increase of only 7.6 percent. CEA head Paul W. McCracken subsequently discovered that union wages in construction had lagged behind rises in nonunion wages and the recent increases were catch-up gains. Secretary of Labor Hodgson also agreed that the unions were "not the major source of the trouble." But Burns's view was amplified by a powerful movement among businessmen. Chamber of Commerce head Winston Blount, a large nonunion contractor from Alabama, convinced executives of the nation's leading companies to create the Construction Users' Anti-Inflation Roundtable in 1969. Its head was Roger Blough, who had retired from U.S. Steel the year before. The group merged with the Labor Law Study Committee to form the Business Roundtable in 1972. The Roundtable would lead the business offensive against unions during the 1970s. The campaign against the building trades was the spring training of the new adversarialism.[13]

The connection between reducing construction wages and hiring blacks was made quickly.[14] On February 18, 1969, Nixon asked Secretary of Labor George P. Shultz to propose measures to eliminate the "restrictive practices of construction unions." A labor economist and head of the University of Chicago's graduate school of business, Shultz had been influenced by the work of his Chicago colleague Milton Friedman. Both believed that labor unions restricted the supply of labor and bid up wages and thus prices. This conclusion triggered the Philadelphia plan, the government's effort to increase black employment in the construction industry.[15]

In May, Henrik S. Houthakker, a member of Nixon's CEA, urged the president to rally "public opinion behind the twin objectives of increasing minority employment in construction and of restraining construction costs." On June 13, Don Kendall called on Nixon to "take on the trade unions." Two weeks later, on June 27, the Labor Department announced the Philadelphia plan, created but not implemented during the Johnson years, to increase the numbers of blacks in selected elite crafts.[16]

Nixon explained to Republican congressmen, who were unhappy with the onus being placed upon contractors, that unions were the cause of "high construction costs and we have to make every possible effort to reduce those costs by increasing the supply of labor, and this [the Philadelphia plan] is one way to do it." Shultz told them that "the Plan expands the potential labor supply. This is among the reasons why many contractors are supporting the Plan and unions are fighting it." [17] In the fall, the president told reporters that "America needs more construction workers." [18]

The origin of the Philadelphia plan was economic, not political, although the president appreciated the possibilities of dividing civil rights groups and labor. But the administration soon discovered that there were superior ways to reduce wages, partly because the Philadelphia plan, even if extended to other cities, was too puny to make much difference. Moreover, it was too puny to help blacks.

The Philadelphia plan required federal contractors to hire specified percentages of minority workers in six elite crafts, crafts that employed 4 percent of the area's construction workers. Thirty-five percent of the city's construction workers were black, but African Americans made up only about 2 percent of those in the mechanical trades, the targets of the plan. Clearly, actions affecting just 4 percent of the construction labor force, even very potent actions, would not do the trick. Nixon, therefore, instituted other measures less friendly to the black 35 percent already working. In August, the administration cut federal construction by 75 percent. One and a half years later, the Office of Management and Budget (OMB), the transformed Bureau of the Budget, acknowledged that the cutback had curtailed "the influx of minority groups into the higher skilled construction trades." The freeze also stalled many of the unions' ongoing affirmative action plans. Joseph T. Jackson, of the Negro American Labor Committee, bitterly observed, "We fought to get into the trades and now he's [Nixon's] cut back model cities funds which were geared toward helping the black worker." [19]

In 1970, CEA chair McCracken proposed repealing the Davis-Bacon law, which required that prevailing, usually union, rates be paid in federally funded construction. He added, "as with the Philadelphia plan, the government can emphasize the benefit to minority workers, thereby partially offsetting the expected strong adverse reaction by craft unions." Davis-Bacon was suspended, not ended, in February 1971. Shultz believed Nixon could get away with it because "the construction industry now is experiencing unemployment, the contractors are hungry, there's lots of non-union help." [20] In the end, Shultz simply used the government manpower programs to train more workers, particularly Vietnam veterans, for the industry. Nixon wanted no publicity on the matter, but the Labor Department expenditures on training programs in construction increased from $45 million in 1970 to $165.6 million in 1971. In 1969, Nixon had proclaimed that "all Americans are entitled to an equal right to be a member of a union." Now, Shultz's aide Arnold Weber told John Ehrlichman that "we will need . . . a large non-union labor pool." [21]

This nonunion labor pool was hardly buoyant water for blacks. Actually, unionized contractors had better racial records than the nonunion ones. [22] Assistant Secretary of Labor Arthur A. Fletcher, the cheerleader for the Philadelphia plan, inadvertently acknowledged this truth. Fletcher told a convention of contractors that "the era of [union] arrogance and discrimination . . . has ended. . . . We are within a year of a great influx of minority workers into the construction trades, as the citadel of labor supply control plus overt discrimination is being destroyed." The savvy Fletcher knew his audience. He warned them not to discard blacks after "they have served the purpose of breaking the union."[23]

The Philadelphia plan neither broke the unions nor helped blacks. Numerical goals were met by the game of musical chairs. Contractors moved blacks from private jobs to federal ones or accepted individuals of whatever competence from community organizations, paid laborers skilled rates, and usually were found to be in compliance, when measured by man-hours of work. This solved everyone's short-term goals but not the long-term problems for blacks: a job on a federal project was temporary employment, not a career.[24]

With this evidence, contemporaries could hardly view the Philadelphia plan as significant. The truth was that the crafts were changing (with a few egregious exceptions, like the Philadelphia group), and the problem was not so much the old restrictions but rising black unemployment. Black leaders now supported public service jobs, which were included in a manpower reform law passed by both houses of the Congress in late 1970. But the president opposed and vetoed the law.[25]

Nixon was in a bind on unemployment. The rate kept rising, and inflation was contained but not ended. Nixon then fastened upon a way to minimize the significance of the numbers. Economist Milton Friedman's ideas were making their way through the profession and into the White House. Friedman provided a rationale for the rising unemployment, one again unfriendly to black interests. He argued that government spending could not reduce unemployment below some natural rate. Although it was not clear what the number was, it was above four percent, the figure the political culture accepted as the norm. Changing that culture was a tricky enterprise. In 1971, Nixon ended the independence of the Bureau of Labor Statistics, which had publicly announced that the current unemployment rate was 6 percent. From then on, the spin would come from the White House.[26]

One way to minimize the impact of numbers was by disaggregating them, for example, by stressing the lower rate for married males. With new vision, black joblessness became evidence that unemployment was a minor problem. Ehrlichman sent Nixon and Shultz a *Reader's Digest* article that argued that unemployment was a statistical rather than a real problem because the "brunt of unemployment is borne by black male and female teenagers, an unemployment rate of 34%." Omitting the racial example, Treasury Secretary John Connally told the Joint Economic Committee in 1972 not "to be carried away by an un-employment figure of say, 6 percent" when the relevant rate for married males was 3 percent. Only as the 1972 election approached, did Nixon change course. He signed a Democratic public employment bill, which the president viewed as a temporary two-year program and the Democrats as the first step toward a permanent policy of public jobs.[27]

Given Nixon's record, those concerned with black employment concluded they had much to do. The Justice Department was staffed by activists hired during the Kennedy and Johnson years. Jerris Leonard, the new head of the civil rights division, was willing to go along. Leonard, a liberal Republican who had lost the governor's race in Wisconsin in 1968, was loyal to Nixon, but he supported a more active civil rights policy and accepted the orientation of the division's lawyers.[28]

The lawyers' ability to litigate employment suits was enhanced when the division was reorganized from geographical to functional sections in late 1969. Under the new setup, the employment section, with a national jurisdiction, could now contemplate industrywide suits. Nixon inadvertently helped. Many of the lawyers from the southeastern and southwestern sections, enraged when the president threw his support behind a delay in the integration of Mississippi schools in 1969, transferred to the new employment unit, bringing with them the same determination, honed by their sense of presidential betrayal. They planned to focus on trucking, textiles, railroads, and steel. The theory was that if the Justice Department could fix big industries, it could fix America. With confidence in themselves and the courts, the lawyers in the civil rights division aimed to tackle U.S. Steel itself, and what better place to make new law than in Birmingham, Alabama.[29]

Litigation at TCI

"We are quite concerned about our inability to have our cases heard in court," wrote Thomas Johnson, head of the Ad Hoc Committee of District 36 on January 22, 1970. Johnson informed the attorney general that "[t]hese cases were filed in 1966." This was not the first time the Birmingham litigants had asked Justice to take over the cases filed but not tried by the LDF. But this time, the reorganized civil rights division was eager to respond, for many reasons.[30]

In 1970, northern successes were not as complete as they would be 1971, when the Second Circuit ordered the southern solutions in Lackawanna. Even in the South, the courts were divided on whether Title VII required retrospective remedies. The lawyers believed they needed a decisive victory on seniority. To obtain industrywide settlements, they would have to first win in a big case and then use the victory as a bargaining chip with the industry. And what better place than Birmingham, with all of its emotional resonance, and what better industry than steel, which was national and fundamental.

But they worried about another Birmingham steel case, *United States v. H. K. Porter*, which they had lost in December 1968. The government had sued the Connors Steel division of Porter in 1967, at the same time Lackawanna was sued, when the Justice department decided to tackle employment matters. But at that time, the division was still organized along geographical lines. Although the filing of both suits marked the determination of the Justice department to address seniority, each emerged independently, was tried poorly, and lost in district courts. The Justice Department lawyer, Robert Moore, had gone into the *Porter* case blind, thinking that all southern industry and unions were the same. But as the USWA had worked on TCI, it had worked throughout the district, including on Porter. And the corporation was open to change. Richard Rowan of the Wharton School, who testified for the government at Sparrows Point, supported the Porter company and the union in Birmingham. Judge Clarence Allgood had declared that blacks were not blocked at Porter, where, after 1962, transfer was possible on the same basis as for whites and numerous reforms had produced many promotions, vertically in departments and horizontally between departments.[31]

The government appealed the ruling to the Fifth Circuit. When the Justice Department approached TCI in June 1970, John Bird, U.S. Steel's regional lawyer, said that the corporation was "ready to do what is right as soon as the court tells us," meaning as soon as the judges ruled on *Porter*. But the appeals court seemed in no hurry to decide it. Like Godot, Porter would be slow in coming.[32]

Robert Moore did not want to wait. A Texan, Moore had graduated from Duke and then the University of Texas law school. He was not a civil rights activist when he applied for a job in the Justice Department in 1961. He had considered joining the FBI. But working in the South in the early 1960s, he embraced the civil rights cause, as did other young white Southerners. *Porter* was Moore's first employment case and he did not want to allow an important issue to rest upon his own poor performance.[33]

Whatever the decision, Porter was still a small steel company and would not fit well into Moore's larger plan for an industrywide settlement. Jerris Leonard, whose goals were less grandiose, thought it was reasonable to wait. Moore, aching to try the case, responded that there were issues other than seniority at TCI which would not be decided by *Porter*. Leonard yielded a bit. He decided to delay the suit, but the government would proceed as though the suit were pending and would negotiate on the issues unaddressed by *Porter*.[34]

The new issues flowed from OFCC's Order No. 4 of November 20, 1969, which generalized the theory of the Philadelphia plan to all contractors. The order required goals and timetables that aimed to "equal the minority ratio of the local applicant population." Contractors would have to propose some kind of numerical commitment related to the local minority population, subject to OFCC approval. The order assumed that absent discrimination, hiring in industries and occupations in a labor market would result in proportionate representation of minority groups, irrespective of skill requirements and labor demand. One of the order's architects, Undersecretary of Labor Laurence H. Silberman, subsequently explained that because "there was no conceptual base" for any figure, "orders were directed towards proportionate minority representation."[35]

Reflecting new coordination between Justice and OFCC, Moore embraced the guidelines to keep his hand in TCI. The new rules affected supervisory and clerical positions.[36] Moore tentatively accepted the corporation's offer to hire one black out of three new hires for clerical work and select one black out of three workers promoted to supervisory positions. TCI pledged that 15 percent of its newly hired college graduates would be black. But a month later, on October 29, realizing he had overestimated the number of openings, Moore changed his mind and proposed one black for every two new hires in clerical and office work and one of two supervisors from the ranks, for a period of five years. As in other cases, when openings were few, more radical measures were proposed. But now U.S. Steel balked and refused to make another offer. On the basis of the company's refusal, Moore converted a reluctant Jerris Leonard, who announced on December 12, 1970, that Justice was suing U.S. Steel.[37]

The corporation responded immediately and publicly. Chairman E. H. Gott denied "any pattern or practice of discrimination" at the Fairfield mill. Gott charged that the hiring demands violated Title VII by requiring preferential treatment. He inadvertently revealed the real motivation when he stated that he had rejected the "grossly outrageous demands" of the government. The 50 percent hiring quota for office and clerical jobs and 40 percent for management exceeded the ratio of blacks to whites in Jefferson County, he said. Gott had not objected to quotas, but to the size of the quotas. U.S. Steel and many corporations raised ideological objections when they disagreed on numbers. They accepted affirmative action, but their first principle was to keep decisions in their own hands.[38]

Howard Strevel responded for the union. "We will stand on our record of having cooperated in every reasonable way with management and with the Federal Government in providing non-discriminatory employment rights for all our members." He charged that Attorney General Mitchell and President Nixon were "trying to divide organized labor for political advantage and weaken the union in coming negotiations with the industry" and vowed that the "strategy won't work. . . . We Steelworkers—all of us, black and white—will remain united." In fact, Strevel welcomed the suit. He believed that only a trial could clear up the uncertainty of the diverse court decisions.[39]

Despite the public posturing, negotiations continued. The government was now fortified by the Second Circuit's reversal at Lackawanna, mandating plant seniority for the affected class. Moore said that he aimed at a "very reasonable" industrywide settlement but would take a tough stance until the industry agreed. Proposals were thus formulated on the basis of his larger purpose, not on what was appropriate or workable at Fairfield.[40] Aiming at that larger goal, the government went beyond its position at Lackawanna and Porter. As in the private suit at Bethlehem, it demanded variations of "leapfrogging." After lay-offs, black workers could use plant seniority to come back to jobs higher than those that they held at the time of the layoff. Members of the affected class could transfer to a new line of progression ahead of laid-off employees with less plant seniority.[41]

While these matters were under discussion, U.S. Steel suddenly broke off discussions again in May 1972 over the issue of back pay. Jerris Leonard had told U.S. Steel in 1970 that the government was not seeking back pay. The rationale was that disputes over seniority, where there had been legal uncertainty, were different from garden-variety discrimination. But the LDF was arguing that back pay was part of any "make whole" remedy, and the government followed.[42] Moore was not so interested in pursuing back pay but embraced it as a bargaining chip for substantive issues. A new man, David L. Norman, now headed the civil rights division and agreed with Moore.[43]

U.S. Steel believed that an agreement had been broken and that back pay implied unmerited wrongdoing. The new demand unloosed its real feelings.[44] Bird told Moore that "if Fairfield never hired any Negroes it would be receiving accolades for numbers of Negroes employed and promoted." USWA lawyer Buddy Cooper detected a hardening at that time, an "adamant refusal to come to terms with the government." Right up until the trial, Cooper, who preferred negotiation to litigation, was convinced that the government and the union could reach agreement "assuming the company can be persuaded to get off its present suicidal course." The company, believing it could win, continued on its course. There would be a trial.[45]

Samuel C. Pointer, the judge assigned to the case, was an unknown quantity. Named to the bench by Richard Nixon in 1970, Pointer was a graduate of Vanderbilt and the University of Alabama Law School. He lived in Mountain Brook, the elite Birmingham suburb, and belonged to a Methodist Church attended by many of the top steel managers. He had been counsel to the state GOP but was not a "new Republican," one created in the Goldwater years in opposition to the civil rights. His father had been an Eisenhower Republican, labor arbitrator, and president of the Birmingham bar.[46]

During the city's integration crisis, the younger Pointer was as timid as the rest of the city's white elite. When fellow lawyer David Vann, a leader in the fight to rid the city of the Bull Connor regime, asked the Birmingham bar to urge the city government to obey the federal court's order to integrate the parks, Pointer, with the rest, refused, arguing that lawyers should not get involved in politics. But by the time he was appointed to the bench Pointer had embraced the new order. Nevertheless, he was untested. The union feared he would be antiunion; the corporation expected to overwhelm a young judge with its high-powered expertise and power. Black plaintiffs were simply grateful they had obtained a judge other than Seybourn Lynne, an unreconstructed southern aristocrat.[47]

The LDF's private suits were languishing in Judge Lynne's chambers. Lynne, unable to function well under the new civil rights law, reassigned school desegregation and Title VII cases to Pointer. On June 17, 1971, Pointer joined the private suits at TCI to the government case. The Justice Department had proceeded independently of the LDF cases because some of the private cases were weak, but also because not much had been done on them. Now, the government and private suits would be decided together.[48]

The Trial

Every trial is a drama. But the 56-day trial beginning in July 1972 was a historical drama. James Forman Jr., the lead lawyer for U.S. Steel, recalled, "we were fighting the social struggles of the 1960s in the law suit." Two hundred seventy witnesses testified, and about 1,000 exhibits were introduced into evidence.[49]

U.S. Steel shouldered the main burden. The corporation began with a slide show demonstrating how steel is made. The manipulation of molten metal and massive steel products is a stunning sight. But the purpose of this fiery spectacle was to buttress the company's point that changing the seniority system would endanger workers and reduce productivity. Its lawyers and witnesses defended TCI's record since Title VII's effective date in 1965, implicitly admitting past discrimination but arguing that the law did not reach that past. They pointed to the facts that from 1965 to 1971 the gap between black and white wages at TCI was reduced from 23 to 14.4 percent and that TCI's black workers earned 50 percent more than the average of all blacks in the United States. If blacks were still concentrated more in low-paying jobs, it was because they refused to bid on jobs open to them and because many were poorly educated. Professor James D. Gwartney, an economist at Florida State University, testified that earning differentials correlated with schooling, a sin of the society, not the corporation.[50]

TCI's major witness was Dennis "Flynt" Hooten Jr., head of labor relations, a fair but typical manager. Hooten took aim at the government's objective, the right to transfer to new lines using plant seniority. He made it clear that he found nothing good in seniority systems. Like managers everywhere, he preferred the narrowest seniority possible. The government proposal, he argued, would remove any link between experience and movement. If you allow a man to enter a new line with his "old age," he could advance much higher than his experience, training, or ability. When reductions came, he cautioned, "he would stay and all your experienced people would roll around him and out." It would not work.[51]

Hooten was open about the partial mergers of 1962 and 1963, which joined, but did not completely merge, lines. He explained that these had been "adopted to prevent complete turnover of experienced employees upon the resumption of operations following shutdowns" in marginal mills. The most important of these was the case of William Hardy and others in the stock house at Ensley. Oscar Adams Jr., Hardy's lawyer, protested, "[W]here there is a depressed employment situation in a particular plant, there is a need to exercise or exert more ingenuity to see that blacks are given equal opportunity." Hooten retorted, "Well, they are just words; you have to have a vacancy. . . . You can write all the rules you want to and do all the good faith negotiations you want but if you don't have a vacancy, no one is going to move."[52]

The union was not originally a defendant, but it was brought in as an indispensable party. Believing it could reach an agreement on the seniority issues, the union hoped to avoid back pay liabilities. Therefore, it simply defended its record. It contrasted its behavior from the 1930s with that of every other institution in the city. It was integrated from its birth in 1936. Before others got into it, the union had attempted to broaden seniority and enforce the contract for blacks. It acknowledged that every grievanceman was not perfect, but the union record was clean, citing the numerous grievances and arbitration cases filed for blacks.

The main union witnesses were Bruce Thrasher and E. B. Rich, the international representatives who had done much of the practical work of integrating the mills. While Thrasher recounted the early history of the union's efforts to broaden seniority, Rich went through the union's recent efforts to facilitate black promotions—the mergers of 1963, the pool, the temporary assignment. Indeed, many of the black witnesses confirmed that they had obtained promotions only after the union had protested the company's award to a younger man. Rich admitted that the union had to educate some whites to accept the task of training blacks. "We tried to make ourselves available to be around people [the blacks in new positions] and talk to them, try to make them feel as comfortable as we could, and to help advise them about the duties of their job and more or less help train them."[53]

The government's aim was to create a record that would justify instituting mill seniority. It argued that differences between employment opportunities for blacks and whites were still considerable and systemic. Company discrimination and an imperfect bidding system, not educational differences, were the causes of differences between black and white wages. Blacks did not bid into new lines because they could not carry their seniority with them. The argument was undercut by much company evidence that many blacks "froze" on their jobs and did not bid up even their regular LOPs. Therefore, Moore pointed to instances where the company chose junior over senior bidders. The implication was that this injustice discouraged other blacks.

The audience to the drama heightened the tension in the courtroom. Most of the men, of course, did not attend the trial but continued working; after all these years, most steelworkers simply wished the issue resolved. Those who attended the trial were whites and blacks committed to a clear-cut victory. Union lawyers and witnesses were subject to the cross-currents. Thrasher recalled that he entered the courtroom each morning running a "gauntlet of blacks saying 'not enough'" and one of whites accusing him of "selling us out." Easing some of this tension was Jerome A. "Buddy" Cooper, the union's lawyer.[54]

Supreme Court Justice Hugo Black's first law clerk, Cooper had worked in the Wages and Hours Division of the Labor Department before he entered the Navy after Pearl Harbor. Returning home to Birmingham after the war, Cooper became the lawyer for the USWA on the recommendation of CIO counsel Lee Pressman. He also had been the lawyer for Operation Dixie, the CIO effort to unionize the South after the war. Cooper's gentle manner covered a deep commitment to workers and civil rights and buffered a sharp mind. As a child he had observed his father, a small merchant in an Alabama coal town, plead in vain with mine owners intent on dispossessing families during the strikes of 1919. Even if his social ideology had been less liberal, this Jewish graduate of Harvard College and Harvard Law School would not have been hired by any of the city's top law firms. Confronted by open anti-Semitism, Cooper found that the ostracism of representing labor unions and blacks added few additional penalties. The only time these loyalties conflicted, Cooper remarked, was when he had to sue one of the railroad brotherhoods on behalf of a group of black railroad workers.[55]

Buddy Cooper's record mattered. One black would not testify for the government because Cooper had helped him obtain his job. He had good currency among black lawyers as well as workers. In 1963, Cooper had petitioned the bar to admit black lawyers. It refused.[56] When the rules did change, black

Jerome "Buddy" Cooper (center) embraces federal judge U. W. Clemon in October 1996, after receiving the Lifetime Achievement Award of the Lawyers' Committee for Civil Rights Under Law. In 1973, Cooper represented the USWA and Clemon was a lawyer for one of the plaintiffs in the seminal trial addressing Title VII of the Civil Rights Act. The third man is Thomas J. Henderson, Deputy Director of the Lawyers' Committee. (Courtesy of Ellen Cooper Erdreich, photograph by Benjamin Erdreich)

lawyers required sponsors for admission, and Cooper was always there to endorse their applications. Demetrius Newton, representing one of the plaintiffs, acknowledged it was difficult to go against Buddy, explaining that he was a personal friend and the "friendliest of lawyers for black causes." As it turned out, the union was "a friendly defendant for the most part," Newton added. The facts often threw the government into the union's arms. At one point when a company lawyer was cross-examining a black worker, trying to show how much money the man was making, Lewis Ferrand, one of the government lawyers, asked, "Wasn't it the union that got you your money?" The man quickly agreed.[57]

Similarly, after Thrasher's lengthy recital of union efforts for black members, Forman asked whether he was "only interested in the testing issue when it affected blacks." Thrasher replied that he got testing complaints only from blacks. Playing to the white side of the gallery, Forman asked whether Thrasher ever represented whites. Thrasher told the court "I have handled arbitration where they are all white, all black, and mixed." Forman yielded.

But the recital of union virtue was too much for Moore. He asked Thrasher, "it is not your opinion, is it, that as of today the union has done everything possible to correct the problems of racial discrimination at Fairfield Works, in that nothing in effect is left to be done?" The union rep replied, "[We did] "the best job that we could do under the circumstances. . . . When we started out there was nobody, nobody available to this Union for assistance. We started out prior to 1952, and we were standing alone." The retort implicitly rebuked the government and lawyers like Moore, newcomers to the fight against discrimination. Moore acknowledged that these were important steps and changed the subject.[58]

Indeed, Moore was impressed. Like many middle-class people politicized by the race issue, he had adopted common assumptions that all southern unions were racist. The black lawyers also were enlightened. Most had cut their teeth on traditional civil rights cases. Although familiar with the experiences of their own clients, they did not have the whole picture. After hearing testimony and interacting with union officials, they restricted their criticism to individual grievancemen, leaving the union's larger record alone.

The director and real audience for the drama was Judge Pointer. All sides acknowledged his scrupulous fairness. U. W. Clemon, who represented plaintiff Luther McKinstry, concluded that Pointer was "brilliant," listened to arguments, and ruled in accordance with the law. Clemon had a wealth of experience in other civil rights cases where that had not been the case. McKinstry recalled that Pointer was "as nice to me as any person could be to anybody." During one cross-examination Pointer chastised a company lawyer for his aggressive questioning of McKinstry: "I don't want you to badger [him]." Pointer's discipline was even-handed. He frequently rebuked Grover Smith, currently working for Herbert Hill at the NAACP, for the audible sneers that greeted the recital of any progress at TCI.[59] Thrasher concluded, "We were lucky we didn't get a racist judge." Union lawyers were impressed with his ability, too. Michael Gottesman, who shared responsibilities with Cooper, found Pointer "sharp," and was relieved to discover that the judge was not routinely antiunion, after Moore told him that Pointer was impressed with the international's efforts over the years.[60]

But Pointer refused to accept high wages, progress, and other company statistics uncritically. After listening to one of the company's comparisons between its own behavior and that of other industries and the federal government, he said: "You cannot in effect establish your innocence for running a stop sign by showing that other people run stop signs." A mathematics major at college, Pointer razored company attempts to correlate earnings with education. Tutored by Hooten and Rich, he mastered the seniority system at TCI as well as regression analysis. He learned to distinguish a hooker from a rigger, determine whether a greaser's job should lead to a millwright's, and understand why, despite its hard work and racist environment, blacks preferred the plate mill.[61]

Although Pointer was skeptical about some of the company's testimony, he was willing to hear Father William Thomas Hogan's assessment of the industry's economic prospects. Father Hogan, a professor at Fordham University in

New York, had written the definitive history of the steel industry and testified frequently before congressional committees and administrative agencies on its behalf. Hogan said that the industry was in crisis and could not afford the inefficiency resulting from seniority changes. If the industry could not compete internationally, he claimed, "we will lose jobs and lose opportunities for all the people of all races." Moore had hoped to strike Hogan's testimony on the grounds of irrelevance. Pointer overruled, explaining that "the question as to the future growth of . . . jobs is of some significance." Such testimony, however, could only limit remedies, so Moore tried to insert an alternative diagnosis when he questioned Hogan: "Isn't the plight of the steel industry also due to management inefficiency . . . ? Don't you have too much rolling capacity for your melting?"[62]

Pointer's most significant role was off the bench. A mediator as well as a judge, he met daily with all the parties, trying to reduce differences and create a consensus. One month after the trial began, on July 25, he told the parties that he was thinking about broadening seniority for everyone, not just the "affected class." He was leaning toward ruling in favor of entry into trade and craft jobs through seniority, not quotas.[63] He urged all sides to settle the cases on this basis.[64] The union and the plaintiffs were ready to settle at this point. But the LDF and the government were now insisting upon back pay for blacks. U.S. Steel was willing only to pay small amounts in a couple of the private suits where it admitted to a wrong. The trial resumed in August and continued through December.[65]

On May 2, 1973, Pointer announced his decision. The law on seniority was clear, he argued, following the judges in *Quarles*, *Crown*, and *Lackawanna* and the ruling of the secretary of labor at Sparrows Point. Although there was no active discrimination at TCI when the Civil Rights Act was passed in 1964, there was a violation of Title VII, he said, because of the perpetuation of the effects of prior discrimination. However, Pointer rejected an "affected class" solution and ordered that mill seniority be applied for all workers.

Pointer concluded that the 1962–63 changes were radical alterations in the employment practices at Fairfield and that some passage of time was needed for this process to begin transforming the statistical profile of the workforce.[66] Recalling the Birmingham of those years and perhaps his own inaction at the time of the city crisis, he asserted that the merging of the lines had predated the city's dramatic changes in education, housing, public accommodations. For their actions, responsible leaders of the company and the union had been "subject to vilification. Ten years later, when the battle-cry has changed such that it typically begins, 'We're not fighting integration, but . . .' there is a tendency to block out the memory of what was said and done in the early '60s."

Pointer found the current management at TCI fair, although there were instances when foreman were not. But the effectiveness of any seniority system, he noted, depended upon the quality of the union leadership. Pointer found that on promotional disputes as well as in other matters the USWA had "fairly pursued such remedies for the employees without regard to their race or color." Since 1962, everyone had started in the pool and then bid to lines of promotion. Vacancies depended upon the vagaries of steel production. Thus, choice and chance governed the promotional system.

Judge Pointer asked why there had been less progress than one might expect. He agreed that the loss of seniority and wages was a factor in workers' decisions about changing lines of promotion. And rules were confusing. Some blacks were rejected because of failure to meet legitimate ability and fitness standards; others were reluctant to bid, judging their likelihood of success on the basis of past experience; some white workers were hostile to the changes; some older blacks were reluctant to leave familiar conditions, assume greater responsibilities, or learn new skills. But the bottom line was that the overall manpower levels at Fairfield had declined during the decade.

Pointer concluded that "it is understandable that black employees, having experienced various forms of direct and indirect racial discrimination in other areas of life, would frequently perceive any disappointments in employment matters from a like perspective. Nevertheless, sometimes they are right." Thus, some of the individual plaintiffs were victims of discrimination; others were not. But, he emphasized, the trial was about the system, not individuals: "When is a seniority system discriminatory? Only when it impacts on blacks; and when the beneficiaries are white? If that was the case, few of the plaintiffs' claims could be sustained." Even for the blacks hired before the 1962–63 merging of lines, the racial results of the seniority system were mixed.

Unlike Judge Butzner in *Quarles* and Judge Feinberg in *Lackawanna*, Pointer weighed declining employment and the arbitrary character of all seniority systems. And, unlike Feinberg, he did not dismiss the burdens of change on whites. Feinberg had asked, "If relief under Title VII is denied merely because the majority of employees, who have not suffered discrimination, will be unhappy about it, there will be little hope of correcting the wrongs which the Act is directed." Judge Pointer disagreed with both the predicate and conclusion.

Because the Pointer rules benefited older whites as well as senior blacks, it slightly slowed black progress. Indeed, the government had convinced the Second Circuit to overturn Judge Henderson's inclusion of ethnics in the Lackawanna remedies on just those grounds. But it was also true that many long-term white employees had also been limited by initial placements. Under the old system, no one could transfer; a person's future had depended on which line had had an opening on the day he applied for a job. Moreover, instituting a uniform system eliminated the complexities and petty manipulations that burdened the Lackawanna and Sparrows Point solutions. Although he did not say so, Pointer probably thought it would be easier to defend relief based upon universality; better race relations in and of themselves would facilitate black promotion.

Twenty years later, Judge Pointer recalled that from the beginning he thought the retrospective interpretation of Title VII on seniority had been established by other courts. By the time the trial began, the Second Circuit had overruled the district court in the Lackawanna case and mandated plant seniority for the affected class. Before it ended, the Labor Department had overruled its own panel and imposed the same solution at Sparrows Point. We see in the next chapter that, as it turned out, the Supreme Court finally reviewed the matter in 1977 and concluded that seniority systems that were not created with racial purposes were bona fide under Title VII, even though they inevitably carried forward pre-Act hiring discrimination. But in 1973, Judge Pointer's reading of the law found ample confirmation. Pointer said he knew that the affected-class remedy had created chaos at Lackawanna and Sparrows Point. His problem was to devise a "workable" solution. He saw himself as a technician, not an architect of the law.[67]

Although Pointer considered his decision a technical one, he had moved beyond the existing paradigm of affected-class thinking and crafted a nuanced solution that incorporated more of the relevant facts of industrial life than earlier decisions had. The four parties—government, company, union, and the plaintiffs—had been locked into the recent case law, attempting to devise remedies within the framework begun with *Quarles* and *Crown*. It was the judge who transcended it.

According to Pointer's ruling, mill seniority would be the basis for all promotions and retentions, as well as recalls after layoffs of more than fifteen days. Pointer responded to the company's production fears by exempting "critical jobs," about 10 percent of the total, from the bumping-up process. In addition, to insure a minimum period for training and experience, a new person would have to wait a year before using his mill age in a new line. Pointer also provided extra relief for blacks hired before 1963. If they transferred to new lines of promotion during the first three years, they would receive red-circled rates during the first year.[68]

Pointer split the difference between the company and government on the hiring quotas. (Because hiring was a management prerogative, the union was not a legal party to this decree.) The judge accepted U.S. Steel's numbers on management training and supervisory personnel—one for three. On craft and clerical jobs, he accepted the government quota of one in two for apprentices, until 25 percent of all apprentices and 20 percent of clerical workers were black.

Pointer created an implementation mechanism to explain and monitor the court order—one person from the company, one from the union, and one representing the plaintiffs. The company initially wanted two, arguing that the union in effect had two, the official union and the black representative. The judge disagreed. Plaintiffs chose wire mill president Thomas Johnson, the union selected E. B. Rich, and the company Flynt Hooten.[69] To facilitate compliance, Cooper urged the judge to bring in the officers and grievancemen of the local unions and explain the decree to them, to prevent the misinformation and rumors that accompanied the Lackawanna and Sparrows Point decisions. Pointer did that. The union, company, and government sent letters to everyone explaining the changes in clear language. Then, for the first six weeks, the implementation committee met every day to answer questions and hear complaints.[70]

The government did not challenge the universal solution at Fairfield, as it had done at Lackawanna. The same argument—that it slowed the movement of blacks to their rightful place—could have been made. But Moore had come around. He told Gottesman that the relief granted "is both more workable and more equitable than the decrees in the *Bethlehem* cases."[71]

However, Moore did challenge the judge on the issue of back pay. Pointer had weighed "the general good faith efforts at compliance" of both parties, but especially those of the union, noting its role in implementation of the executive order and in the passage of Title VII. Pointer added that both parties had every reason to believe that the prospective solution established in *Whitfield* was legal. Even when the court judged that the present effects of past discrimination violated the law, it had not overruled *Whitfield*. Neither the union nor the company gained financially from the system. Moreover, some of the beneficiaries of the old seniority system were black, just as some of those hindered were white. All of these factors led Pointer to deny back pay in the government suit.

Moore argued that Pointer's recital of good intentions and the ambiguity of the courts was irrelevant because back pay was not a penalty but part of a make-whole remedy. Back pay had been transported from the National Labor Relations Act of 1935. In a typical unfair labor practice case when a person was fired for union activity, it was fairly easy to compute a make-whole figure. In a simple discrimination case, it was not difficult either. But in a case involving a seniority system—where money lost depended upon available vacancies, other men's seniority, and countless other variables—it was more difficult.[72]

Pointer awarded back pay in some of the private suits, but lead plaintiff William Hardy obtained nothing. The judge merged his line of progression with a white one, as he had asked, but he and two-thirds of the blacks in his line had actually benefited from the arrangement they had protested. Contrary to the theory of mill seniority, had the system they preferred been in effect, they would have earned less.[73] Hardy and those who received no money now aimed their fire at their own attorney, Oscar Adams Jr., who had received $26,500 in lawyer's fees. To sustain the litigation, the LDF had made extravagant promises about back pay. It now reaped what it had sown. The LDF's Barry Goldstein tried to explain the situation, but some workers believed they merited additional money and sued U.S. Steel for back pay.[74]

Although the parties to the Fairfield agreement were more knowledgeable than others who had attempted to reorganize work, even they misjudged the workers. One of the big battles had been over rate retention in transfer. The government had assumed that because blacks had been assigned to poor lines the best means for progress was transfer, the steel mill's equivalent of integration; the workers did not transfer, so the argument continued, because it would cost workers their seniority and, initially, reduced wages. The union feared the racial tensions that would result when transferring blacks earned more money than whites doing the same job. But in fact there was very little rate retention. As at Lackawanna and Sparrows Point, most workers decided to stay where they were and used mill seniority to move up their regular line of promotion. This produced less integration in the short run, but it was what workers preferred. The debates over transfer, carrying so much symbolic meaning, had ignored workers' actual culture and wishes. And the earlier cases had revealed that demanding instant integration was not only impossible to effect but actually hindered integration in the long run.

In the real world, transfers took place for nonracial reasons. For example, when a man's home unit was down, he was demoted to a pool job. Concluding that he should enter a more promising line, he often transferred to a new line from the pool. If the person was a black hired before 1963, he could qualify for rate retention, but rate retention was computed from current wages. The pool, the most frequent launching pad for transfer, paid less than jobs in lines of promotion. Thus, blacks invariably bid into higher paying jobs and did not qualify for rate retention.[75] One might argue that the base should not have been the pool. But red-circled rates were not a remedy for technological change or economic decline.

The trade and craft quotas were never contentious, because of the insignificant role they played in steel. While the craftsmen were the kings of the auto industry, they were not in steel. The most ambitious blacks did not choose to enter the few training programs offered by the company. The union had wanted apprentices to be chosen from current employees on the basis of seniority, but the company and judge preferred simple quotas, which had become a boilerplate solution in many industries and which permitted management to pick and choose among applicants. From the beginning, the company went outside the plant for apprentices, rather than train blacks and whites already working in the mill. And, as Buddy Cooper accurately feared, the company began to contract the work out rather than train. The company ended its apprentice programs in 1980.[76]

The new system was implemented even before the final order was issued in December. Pointer noted that the process had been implemented "with fewer problems than had been anticipated." Twenty years later, E. B. Rich said that "overall the Pointer decree strengthened the rights of the membership, white and black. We got more out of the consent decree than we would ever have gotten out of negotiations, a tough set of seniority rules." Rich insisted upon placing the consent language into every new contract the union negotiated in District 36. The government finally dissolved the decree in 1989, over the union's objections.[77]

Rich believed that the strength of the decree was paragraph 6, which required the company to "provide all employees with such appropriate training and learning opportunities as are necessary to enable them to take full advantage of the promotional and other advancement opportunities provided for by this Decree." The clause, which the union convinced Pointer to include, gave the seniority system teeth, especially in the late 1970s and 1980s, when the union was weaker. It was a happy exception to most Title VII agreements, which dealt with positioning and rights but not the substance of mobility. In instances where unions were hostile, indifferent, or ignored, the triumph of legal principles often masked ineffective change.[78]

But the changes also produced resentments. Understandably, the vocal opponents were those workers, mainly whites, who ended up being "promoted around." Rich acknowledges that some are still bitter about it, but most whites and blacks recognized its fairness. Ending the conflicts fostered by extravagant proposals and uncertainty improved race relations. Luther McKinstry said simply that it was "better for all of us."[79]

Twenty years after the trial, James Forman Jr. reiterated the argument he had made earlier: "If you saddle American industry, the steel industry, with not being able to put the best man on the job, you will make us more inefficient; for every wrong man you promote, you are less competitive. . . . The court tried to solve social problems by making industry pay." These remarks attribute the subsequent history of the industry to the seniority changes. As we will see, there were more significant reasons for the industry's problems. Nevertheless, Forman and U.S. Steel believed they had won the case because the judge found that there had been no discrimination after 1965. His assessment also reflected the 1977 Supreme Court reversal of the law on seniority.[80]

Nevertheless, Forman's remarks, if not rationale, were accurate barometers of U.S. Steel's unenthusiastic response to the Pointer decision. Robert Moore agreed that the Fairfield decision was superior to the two Bethlehem ones, but because it did not fit into the older paradigm, Moore was thrown off balance. Only the union was enthusiastic. Pointer had crafted a solution that allowed the union to promote civil rights through a universal system that strengthened seniority. With a court-sanctioned solution, the union was now prepared to act after years of indecision.

The Limits of Fair Employment:

The Consent Decrees and the

Economic Crisis of the 1970s

SEVEN

T
he Fairfield settlement became the model for industrywide consent decrees signed on April 15, 1974.[1] Because the decrees were another tripartite agreement among the government, the union, and the industry, they addressed how Title VII would be enforced as well as how seniority would operate in the steel industry. The actors with a stake in the matter exceeded the 350,000 workers, the union, and the steel companies covered by the order. The EEOC, OFCC, LDF, and eventually the National Organization of Women (NOW) had institutional roles to preserve as well as solutions to defend. Thus, the settlement challenged and altered the whole regulatory regime—litigation, standing, and multiple venues—as well as the Bethlehem-affected class solution.

But in 1977 the courts took a 180-degree turn. Addressing the issue for the first time, the Supreme Court ruled in a case involving a trucking company that Title VII did not require seniority changes. The steel settlement had been negotiated under the assumption that the law was clear, but it was not.[2]

The consent decrees continued in the absence of a legal mandate because of the union role in fashioning the decision. Technically, the decrees were now part of the union contract, but initially they had been incorporated because they could be defended as fair as well as required by law. Representing both blacks and whites, the union had been forced to balance interests, unlike the government, industry, and civil rights lawyers, who had other imperatives or single constituencies. Ironically, the union's experience in fashioning solutions for a biracial constituency eventually yielded the most effective argument for affirmative action, a minor issue in the steel industry but a major one in the larger society.[3] Nevertheless, whatever the merits of the issues, the process of determining the meaning of Title VII through adversarial combat and incremental court review had worsened race relations and added to the insecurity of all workers.

The Making of the Consent Decrees

The Fairfield decision broke the logjam of USWA thinking, freeing leaders to act. The burdens of liberal conflict weighed most heavily on the union because it represented both whites and blacks. Government officials and civil rights lawyers went home at night and returned to other cases the next morning. Despite a certain amount of tension, companies still made steel. But the union had to implement and defend court decisions, live with the results, and maintain unity for other purposes.

Initially, the government suit in Fairfield did not mean much to leaders in other union districts. After all, it was Birmingham. Howard Strevel recalled that other district leaders still thought he had the problems with the "Ku Kluxers." But the urgings of Ed Plato, director of the district that included Sparrows Point, could not be dismissed so easily, because Sparrows Point hiring had not been that different from the situation in many plants in the North. Secretary Hodgson's decision in January 1973 had enraged Plato, who feared, correctly, that the disruption at Lackawanna would be visited upon Sparrows Point. Plato lacked Strevel's stature and commitment to civil rights, but black and white staffmen at the mill shared his forebodings. Two weeks after Hodgson's ruling, Plato was in Pittsburgh for the International Executive Board (IEB) meeting on February 15, 1973. He brought with him an animus toward the top union leaders, who had supported his black opponent in the elections in 1969, as well as the Sparrows Point problem. Plato summoned Ben Fischer, Alex Fuller, and the union's lawyers, demanding that they "solve the crisis."[4]

The lawyers and technicians, knowing the substance of Judge Pointer's thinking even though the formal ruling would come down later in May, told Plato that the only solution to Sparrows Point was an industrywide agreement mandating plant seniority for everyone. They convinced him to make the case to the IEB. On the next day, Plato, backed up by Strevel, did just that. The IEB appointed a committee to study the effect of civil rights law on seniority. Chaired by Strevel, the group included Plato and three other district leaders whose members included significant numbers of blacks or Hispanics. The strategy was to agree upon a plan, sell it to industry, and then obtain government sanction.[5]

After Judge Pointer announced the Fairfield decree on May 3, their efforts quickened. "The decision represents a splendid result," lawyer Bernard Kleiman told I. W. Abel, adding that Pointer's decision required "rethinking our approach to seniority," which had followed the courts' affected-class approach. The Strevel committee fashioned a modified version of the Pointer plan, which the IEB accepted on June 26.[6]

The report stressed the "moral obligation to act" now that the law was clear. Any court could apply *Crown* remedies, like those at Lackawanna, Sparrows Point, and Fairfield, wherever a company had discriminated against minority employees at initial assignment and where transfer rules made it difficult to move. Virtually every mill fit these conditions. The chaos produced by various court solutions threatened to escalate as each judge mandated different remedies.

At the same time, the civil rights issues harmonized with the union's efforts since 1962 to give greater weight to plant seniority in decisions about layoffs, manning new facilities, and transfers between units, departments, major operating divisions, and other mills. Noting that the measures taken so far had not kept pace with "galloping technology," the IEB concluded: "Only by establishing plant service dates as virtually the sole measure of seniority for all purposes . . . can true equity be achieved. Thus, the demands of technology and the economic forces that influence steel industry employment point us in the same direction as the civil rights considerations."[7]

The essence of the proposal was that mill seniority would guide movement for all purposes and that all workers would obtain a one-shot transfer with rate retention. Seniority units would be merged and pools combined where possible; wherever craft and maintenance jobs did not reasonably reflect the minority population, entrance into apprenticeships would be filled on the basis of seniority, facilitated by pre-apprentice training where necessary.

The union contacted Vice President Warren Shaver of U.S. Steel, who assembled executives of the other companies. After hearing union and company counsel, they accepted the lawyers' analysis of the law. Five members of industry, headed by George Moore of Bethlehem Steel, joined the union committee to hammer out an agreement. The group met thirteen times during July and August.[8]

The key goal for the union was obtaining changes for all employees, which was fortified by the imprimatur of Judge Pointer. The companies were of two minds. On the one hand, a black-only solution was cheaper, affecting fewer individuals. But the racial conflict produced by such policies at the two Bethlehem plants led them to calculate beyond dollars and cents. Reluctantly, the companies accepted the union solution. The industry, seeking to insulate itself from government regulators, insisted upon using the minority quotas and the recently added gender quotas that OFCC was requiring to fill craft slots. Although the union preferred to fill these jobs on the basis of seniority, it agreed, but insisted that production workers, not outsiders, fill the quotas. Apprentices would be selected through seniority, computed separately for minority and nonminority workers. An audit and review committee, composed of equal numbers of union and industry people, would oversee and evaluate the changes.[9]

The remaining disagreements were over issues that the public did not consider civil rights but which were crucial to blacks. The union wanted a training clause, the equivalent of Section 6 of the Fairfield decree, to make abstract rights concrete, but the industry opposed a provision stating that "[t]he Company will undertake training of employees to implement these provisions [of the consent decree]." Another conflict was that the company men wanted to charge the cost of rate retention to the wage settlement of the 1974 negotiations: all workers would pay for rate retention for some. The union, understandably, disagreed.[10]

But by September 19 the parties had adopted a framework, and the union was prepared to implement it immediately. The companies, whose major purpose was to avoid litigation, were determined to first secure government blessing, which meant bringing in the Departments of Labor and Justice and EEOC. In early October, George Moore informed George Shultz, now head of OMB, that the industry wanted to reach a settlement with the government. Shultz in turn contacted J. Stanley Pottinger, the new head of the civil rights division, Secretary of Labor Peter Brennan, and John H. Powell Jr., soon to become EEOC chairman. They picked Robert Moore to represent the government in the negotiations. Even though the legislation of 1972 had given EEOC the power to litigate in the private sector, the agency had been out of the steel picture since 1969. Moore was the only government official competent enough to bargain with the union and the industry.[11]

Moore had aimed for a carbon copy of Pointer's decree—plant seniority for all, rate retention for blacks only, and goals and timetables for crafts, clerical, technical, and management positions. But he had to convince OFCC, the main architect of the Lackawanna-Sparrows Point approach, which wanted to order the same arrangements at four or five major steel mills. Moore held some aces because OFCC was bogged down in mastering the particulars in each mill. Moreover, OFCC's Leonard Bierman, who was then in charge of the steel project, and others familiar with the industry now agreed that the Fairfield remedy was superior to the Bethlehem solutions, even though some of the staff held on

to the black-only settlement. The OFCC ideas were scrapped, and Moore negotiated on the basis of the union-industry plan, called Consent Decree I. The
main difference between it and Pointer's solution was that rate retention would
be the rule for all workers, not just blacks.[12] Aided by Moore's advocacy, the
union obtained its training clause.[13]

Consent Decree II, to which the union was not legally a party, created the
trade and craft goals based upon OFCC regulations; mill workers ranked on the
basis of seniority would have first crack at these positions. The implementing
ratio would be 50 percent; that is, one of two hires would be a minority or a
woman, until appropriate goals—agreed upon by industry, union, and government—were reached. The Audit and Review Committee would be chaired
by Moore, and other government officials would be added to local implementing committees. The parties chose Judge Pointer to oversee the decree because he knew more about the steel industry than any other judge on the
bench.

At the midnight hour, the agreement nearly came unglued over back pay,
propelled by the tendentious politics of EEOC. President Nixon was in the process of replacing the agency's chairman, William Brown, a black Republican
who had turned out to be too independent and too close to civil rights activists
for his taste. Brown's replacement, John Powell, was currently general counsel
of the Civil Rights Commission. Although Powell would not be confirmed as
EEOC chairman until January 1974, Shultz had asked him, rather than Brown,
to attend the first meeting, held on October 16.

Brown, who had been campaigning to retain his job, bristled; in addition,
some high-level EEOC staffers and lawyers disliked the universal seniority approach. Nixon's hostility to civil rights leaders and the agencies where they
were influential made many in EEOC suspicious of any agreement brokered by
other government officials. Moreover, they had the confidence born of successful intervention. In January 1973 EEOC, with the help of NOW and the LDF,
had altered a consent decree fashioned by the General Services Administration
and American Telephone and Telegraph and obtained a back pay award of
$45 million.[14] Discovering that the steel settlement did not include a financial
award, EEOC staffers threatened to revolt.[15] Thus, Powell demanded back pay
as the price for EEOC acquiescence, necessary because of the agency's new
power to litigate what it did not like.[16] The consent decrees thus distributed
$30.9 million to black and Hispanic steelworkers hired before 1968 and to
women hired before the date of the decree. The sum was allocated to each company on the basis of the numbers of minorities and women in its workforce
and distributed to workers according to a formula that attempted to award the
most money to those whose losses seemed the greatest.[17]

Back pay helped EEOC and civil rights lawyers in two ways. First, it was a tangible measure of victory, which convinced clients that their government or lawyers were succeeding; it built institutional support. Second, it warned others that there was a price to pay for noncompliance, a standard American way of regulating. However, this purpose did not explain the steel agreement. It is often forgotten that a key element of compliance is clarity of the law. It was not the threat of back-pay penalties but the consensus after the Fairfield decision on what Title VII required and the potential chaos of protracted litigation that convinced the union and then the steel companies to negotiate the consent agreement. The demand for back pay nearly destroyed it. Inland Steel withdrew from the agreement over the issue. Union lawyers had to employ their greatest advocacy skills to keep the rest of the companies on board. I. W. Abel, too, was furious about the USWA's $3 million obligation.[18]

Suing for back pay posed other problems. While individuals may enjoy cash awards, such awards did not necessarily further the purpose of Title VII. Financial penalties could become ends in themselves, as lawyers concentrated on back pay to the detriment of systemic issues. However they were computed, financial awards usually caused contention among recipients and jeopardized change. The Supreme Court eventually ruled in 1975 that back pay rarely could be denied if unlawful discrimination was proved.[19] As a result, companies thereafter rarely acknowledged discrimination, which would open them up to back pay lawsuits. Instead, they claimed to compensate for the discrimination existing in society at large. But preferences and affirmative action based upon statistical imbalances were less acceptable to the courts and public opinion than remedies triggered by actual discrimination suffered by individuals. Thus, the demand for back pay in practice undercut systemic change.

Criticism of the substance of the consent decrees of 1974 was inevitable, but thin. Some EEOC officials, committed to black-only solutions, complained that the purpose of the agreement was "to protect incumbent white employees." The NAACP's Herbert Hill claimed that the back pay was inadequate, charged that "transfers would take place only when white workers leave the company," and predicted that the federal courts would disapprove the entire agreement. The Black Panther Party thought that the purpose of the agreement was "to put the fire out from under a fast growing rank and file workers movement, led by Black workers." The left-wing *Guardian* preferred the solutions of "leap-frogging or preferential hiring."[20]

The better-informed LDF, joined by NOW, targeted the process, not the substance. Both organizations had been major players in the AT&T settlement but not the one in steel. The LDF believed it represented all blacks, and NOW likewise all women, and both felt they should therefore have a role in every major agreement. Both were part of a left political culture hostile to big organizations—government (especially the one headed by Richard Nixon), corporations, and unions. As LDF head Jack Greenberg recalled, "we didn't trust them."[21]

Joined by the American Civil Liberties Union and the Center for Constitutional Rights, LDF and NOW appealed the consent decrees to the Fifth Circuit. LDF's Robert Belton said "interested parties should have been invited to the bargaining table prior to the formulation of the decree." Belton feared that if the tripartite agreement became the model for other industries, LDF's own role would be reduced.[22] Thus, he argued that the decrees were "illegal compromises, . . . devices for exempting or limiting company and union liability for illegal acts, and an attempt by business and unions to make a national settlement that will bar individual suits." The complaint was a typical expression of the new public advocacy culture.[23]

But an LDF role was not sanctioned by the law. LDF had to argue that the decrees deprived minority steelworkers of their rights to private and government litigation. Inevitably, this required some rewriting of history. Claiming credit for the Fairfield decision, the LDF implied that its exclusion from the negotiations on the industrywide decrees was tantamount to excluding black workers. Then Greenberg charged that the settlement deprived employees of the right to representation by the government as well as private representation, since EEOC had agreed that it would not sue on issues addressed by the consent decrees and OFCC had made the Audit and Review Committee a surrogate for its monitoring. Finally, he argued that requiring minority workers to release all claims related to discrimination prior to the decrees in return for back pay deprived steelworkers of their rights.

The legal and political issues forced the union to defend the decrees strictly on civil rights grounds, not on the basis of the agreement's superiority, the fact that the plan offered tangible black gains that did not come at the expense of whites. Thus, the union contrasted the concrete black gains with the minimal results of private litigation, arguing that the "desultory" history of "private litigation" in the steel industry made it unlikely that employees who were victims of discrimination would have obtained relief during their working lives. Only eleven private actions had been instituted at the 250 plants covered by the decree; only one, at Fairfield, had yielded a final court order. (The Lackawanna case was tied up in litigation.) Moreover, the government, not the LDF, had tried the Fairfield case. Private suits were still available to the dissatisfied. It was not unreasonable to require, however, that accepting a check ended the matter.

Reproducing every argument that labor and the civil rights organizations had employed during the 1960s, the USWA stated that proceeding with individual suits would entail expense and delay of many years. It was unlikely that courts would award more money than the agreement. The per capita relief awarded in the Fairfield case was less than the individual shares provided by the consent decree.[24] Because no one had the right to have the government sue on his or her own behalf, the USWA claimed that the EEOC agreement "simply constitutes an exercise . . . of its discretion to decide what actions it will leave to private enforcement." Given the 100,000 charges then pending before the agency, the union argued that it "surely was not an abuse of discretion for the EEOC to conclude that it would channel its limited resources to suits in other industries." Similarly, the Department of Labor would misuse public funds if it duplicated the compliance mechanism created by the decrees.[25]

The union argument and language made some political, as well as legal, points. Union lawyers and technicians were liberals. At least one USWA lawyer had been on the LDF board, and many union officials were on its mailing list of contributors. They were offended when they received financial appeals that advertised the LDF's "20-year campaign to eliminate the nation-wide pattern of discrimination in the steel industry." Some of these resentments inevitably filtered into the union brief.[26]

The Fifth Circuit affirmation of the settlement on August 18, 1975, was complete. Applauding the fact that "so many self-interested parties were able to leave so few unresolved remedial issues," the court praised the parties for working "unselfishly toward a settlement keyed to broader public goals." Implicitly rebuking the LDF, NOW, and the other groups, the court concluded that "if a multitude of interveners and representatives of private individuals with conflicting personal interests had participated in the framing of the decrees, then probably no comparable industry-wide agreement could have been reached."[27]

The court characterized the LDF's proposals as "unpredictable, protracted class actions managed by strangers," undercutting its claim to represent black steelworkers. It called the challenge "unrealistic, unsound and ultimately rooted in dogmatism" and warned that the LDF would deprive "the employee of the chance to make a choice that previously was not available, even though the opportunity itself doesn't cost the employee a wink." Settlements, it argued, were essential to enforcement; otherwise, "the courts of the country would be burdened with excessive and needless litigation and champertous practices would be encouraged." Because the LDF failed to show that the back pay awards were inadequate, the court concluded, "it would be plainly irresponsible . . . to assume that the vast majority of affected employees could be persuaded by appellants' [LDF's] gratuitous advice, or that such advice is rendered in those employees' best interests."

The LDF's legal challenge had delayed the back pay awards for a year. The NAACP, too, had urged steelworkers to hold the checks, promising greater remuneration, but by the end of 1976, over 95 percent of eligible workers had cashed the checks.[28] When the LDF yielded, some workers were seduced by private lawyers promising greater awards. Indeed, the litigation over back pay that took place after the consent decrees was a principal reason why other industries did not enter into settlements.[29]

The LDF appeal temporarily heated up the conflict between the NAACP and the USWA. Initially, Roy Wilkins thought the decrees "a good beginning." But one year later, he adopted the critique of Herbert Hill, who made certain that Michael Gottesman was not permitted to speak at the panel on employment at the NAACP convention at the end of June 1975. Hill had the field to himself to attack the decrees. The union succeeded, however, in preventing a formal condemnation.[30]

Consent Decrees in Practice

The consent decrees would remain in effect for a minimum of five years. At the end of 1978, Robert Moore reported that the seniority and transfer reforms were "firmly in place and working well." He was right. Nevertheless, the truth about seniority changes held here: they are not panaceas. This was especially true in plants that had few minority employees. Where changes simply rearranged whites, they lacked the rationale of public policy. For example, Milton Burlison, a white who had chosen to become a millwright in 1968, reported, "Individuals who didn't want this job in the beginning now have the privilege to go around me, on the coattails of this ruling and are not blacks, Spanish-surnamed Americans, or females." Donald Magee had the same experience. In 1964 Magee had yielded his seniority in the open hearth department and transferred to the new BOF department, while others with better paying jobs had remained in the open hearth department. "Years later, when the open hearth was on the decline, they decided to transfer to the BOF. We, the original group to come to the BOF took a chance. If we stayed in the new shop for thirty days we forfeited our floor rights in the open hearth. So I cannot see the fairness of taking a chance and then having it taken away from us after ten years."[31]

Men who worked their way up from the bottom to the top of a line discovered that if the lines were now desirable, a man with longer plant service could bid and rise to the top of the line, without spending long years in the lower ones. Many of the displaced were no youngsters. William Comer had been working in the Fairless plant of U.S. Steel since 1955. He had previously worked in another U.S. Steel plant. Although he had less Fairless "age" than the man who rose above him, he had more company time, which he thought should be the standard.

If some workers were embittered by displacement, corporations wondered why so many of those who transferred returned to their pre-transfer jobs. In a two-year study at its Burns Harbor plant, Bethlehem discovered than nearly one-third returned to their old jobs within 45 days of the transfer. Blacks, whites, Hispanics, and women all did it. In the slab mill, one group of workers left and transferred to new jobs. After the vacancies were posted, men with lengthier seniority were hired to replace the transferrees. When the original group, disappointed in their new jobs, returned, they now were further down the seniority list in their original jobs. The disgruntled workers now left again.[32]

As in Fairfield, however, most people did not transfer. When the plan went into effect, people resumed their old jobs in the old order. But leapfrogging and bumping—the results of plant seniority—came into play in promotions and layoff recalls. Workers were inevitably surprised, and sometimes blamed their local implementation committee for the results.[33]

The Lackawanna facility, suffering from a volley of court orders and on-going economic cutbacks, produced many of the most difficult problems. Mill worker Gregory Fred Wade, saying that he did not "view this issue as a black/white issue or a young/old issue," wrote, "To me the issue is simply that I feel *no one* has any job security left." Wade asked the Audit and Review Committee to write or call him at his home, where, he said, "I should be available nearly twenty-four hours a day, as I just received my Christmas gift from Bethlehem—a lay-off slip." In mills on the decline, the seniority changes and the cutbacks became one.[34]

Some workers of foreign descent objected to the back pay awards made to blacks. William J. Toth wrote that at Republic Steel in Warren, Ohio, "there are cases of Blacks who have had good jobs right along, yet some will get near $1,000.00 while some of us Whites have been discriminated against because we are of foreign decent [*sic*], yet that is supposed to be OK." This problem was inherent in class-action lawsuits. There would have been no way to individualize back pay awards. Inevitably, some blacks who had suffered no discrimination obtained money. Workers who had suffered ethnic discrimination obtained nothing.[35]

Some white steelworkers from the North made much of the fact that Judge Pointer was from Alabama. One argued: "If there is so-called discrimination in Alabama and other southern areas of the United States, is it meant necessarily that there was and is discrimination at Granite City Steel? Have you . . . checked the practices of Granite City Steel?" A group of dissidents reckoned that "the Decree was in large part predicated upon the assumptions that may have been true in Birmingham, Alabama, but not in Youngstown, Ohio."[36] Others believed that they were paying for "big business's discrimination of minority groups." One asked, "Must we pay with our jobs and positions when we are not at fault? Is it *just* for us to pay for the steel industries [*sic*] errors? . . . How sad it will be if I, and hundreds like myself, must suffer and take on the burden of equalizing all of societies [*sic*] injustices in the steel industry, especially when we have not committed those injustices."[37]

As one might expect, opponents wrote more letters than did supporters. Because they obtained back pay awards, blacks as a group were probably more supportive than whites. The few writers who could be identified as black equated the plan with unionism. Walter Thompson, who worked at Armco Steel in Kansas City, Missouri, complained about a proposed lawsuit by some white workers to keep out "more Blacks or older Whites" from bidding into their department. To Thompson, they were "try[ing] to bust the Union or break the by-laws and Constitution of International Union of United Steelworkers of America." He added, "I believe in Unionism and am a Union Brother to my heart, I am not for Black or White, I am for what is best for all."[38]

One anonymous letter was signed simply, "Proud to be an American—People for the Consent Decree." Ignoring the issues of race or age, the signers believed that the old departmental form of seniority originated in "favoritism, nepotism and payola" and that "the Consent decree has been the most significant and just thing to happen to the American working people in 40 years."[39]

The Audit and Review Committee answered each letter and investigated those that presented problems of interpretation. A typical response acknowledged the "dislocations," but went on to say, "the change was one which was required by law, in order to provide a remedy to inequities. . . . We are confident that the long term benefits to all employees which will derive from it will more than outweigh the immediate, short term inconveniences which it has of necessity caused." Many workers did not view the changes as mere "inconveniences" but as matters "affect[ing] our lives and jobs forever."[40] Some wrote directly to Judge Pointer, who explained that seniority rights were contingent and the changes made in good faith. Pointer did not exaggerate his persuasiveness. "I understand that these comments will not improve your position, nor eliminate the bitterness you probably feel," he wrote, " but I hope that they will at least aid in clarifying what the role of the court has been."[41]

In general, the conflicts were between the young and the old and between those who benefited and those who did not. Race percolated up in some instances, but the language of opposition was not racism but an amalgam of democracy, rights, and populism. The decrees fed notions that workers' lives were dominated by distant, impersonal institutions. Many felt that their local union was close to them but that the international was not. One lumped together "the Big 3, courts, International and Companies." Another put it this way: "A Federal Judge from the State of Alabama, which passed the above Civil Rights Decree, sacrificed my position and hundreds of others."[42]

These sentiments spawned new rank-and-file groups that attacked the consent decrees in the name of democracy. The Committee of Concern for the Rights of Steelworkers represented white workers in the Youngstown-Warren area, and eventually linked up with a group from Pittsburgh. The committee filed suits, lobbied legislators, and picketed. Its political orientation was populism—the working man was a victim of "big government, big business, and the big union." The notion that the agreement was reached secretly assumed ominous significance. "I would think what Nixon did at Watergate is nothing compared to what was done to us." That the committee was strongest in the Youngstown-Warren and Pittsburgh areas, where employment was declining, was not coincidental. On the other side of the color line, the National Coalition of Disenfranchised United Steelworkers charged that the decree had deprived minority and women steelworkers of more than $500 million in back pay and was evidence of a union-management conspiracy. That group, however, was more a vehicle for black dissident John Thornton than a significant caucus. These organizational responses to the decree were short-lived.[43]

Predictably, the older rank-and-file groups like the National Ad Hoc Committee (the radicalized remnant of the black dissidents of the 1960s), the District 31 Committee to Defend the Right to Strike, and the Rank and File Team opposed the settlement. But the decrees did not fit neatly into political categories. Jim Balanoff, part of the District 31 group in Chicago (he was elected director in 1977), recalled that when the decrees came down, he and most of the others looked the other way. The truth of the matter was that they were difficult to incorporate into traditional union dissent.[44]

These older caucuses fashioned an opposition based on democracy, rarely discussing specifics. They argued that the consent decrees should have been put to a vote. Yet their appeal to democracy conflicted with their other argument, that the union's interest conflicted with the rights of women and minority workers, which the decrees limited. If this charge was more than standard new-left rhetoric, they must have believed that minorities and women were entitled to more than they had obtained. But how could such a program have won a majority in an election where blacks, Hispanics, and women were a distinct minority? If the consent decrees had been voted upon, they probably would have been rejected. The caucuses' worldview, rank-and-file versus union, was incompatible with the truth that seniority conflicts lay within the ranks of steelworkers and that legal obligations trumped democratic ones.

Because each steelworker judged the agreement on the basis of his own interests, the decrees probably undercut coherent politics. Although I have attempted to tease out some of the ideological currents, most of the letters of complaint protested an individual injustice. Collective action flourishes when the enemy is clear and solutions foster cohesion. Seniority issues lacked both requirements, which is why dissident groups stressed procedure, not substance.

Teamsters

As the machinery of the consent decrees moved into high gear, the wheel turned again. The trucking industry, like steel, had been on the Justice Department's list of targets for seniority reform. But in 1977 the Supreme Court reversed ten years of lower court rulings in *International Brotherhood of Teamsters et al. v. United States*. The court concluded that "an otherwise neutral, legitimate seniority system does not become unlawful under Title VII simply because it may perpetuate pre-Act discrimination. Congress did not intend to make it illegal for employees with vested seniority rights to continue to exercise those rights, even at the expense of pre-Act discriminatees." Or, in the words of an astonished Bethlehem official on the Audit and Review Committee, "the law required none of this [the steel seniority changes]."[45]

Despite the apparent certainty of the law, the Supreme Court had never addressed the seniority issue. Lower courts had interpreted the justices' refusal to hear the union appeal in *Crown* as approval. The USWA had never challenged the principles underlying seniority changes or the interpretation of Title VII. Initially, it did not believe that the law required changes, but after the court rulings, it did not contest the judgment. Its differences with the government and civil rights groups were always about appropriate remedies. The union assumed, too, that the Supreme Court was more, not less, committed to an expansive reading of Title VII. The steel companies had opposed the practice and principle of retroactive seniority until convinced by their lawyers that the law was clear.[46]

The teamsters union and the trucking firm T.I.M.E.-D.C., Inc. (TIME) had adopted a different course. Because trucking lacked steel's tradition of industrial leadership, the possibility of any kind of consent decree was a pipe dream, especially in view of the strong opposition of both the companies and the union. The Justice Department hoped that a victory in one big case would turn the industry around. As it had in all nationwide cases, the government began in the South, challenging TIME's operations in Tennessee and Texas, but then expanded the suit to the company's fifty-one terminals in twenty-six states and three Canadian provinces. It won in the lower courts, but both TIME and the union appealed a Fifth Circuit decision to the Supreme Court, something the steel industry and union had never done.[47]

Before 1965, TIME's "over-the-road" (long-distance) drivers were white. Most city drivers were also white, but nearly all blacks and Hispanics were city drivers. At the time the case was tried in 1972, the court concluded that "minority hiring progress stands as a laudable good faith effort . . . in the area of hiring and initial assignment." That is, TIME was hiring minority workers for over-the-road work. But the Justice Department argued that because of the separate seniority systems, minority city drivers hired under the old system who now transferred to the over-the-road departments would have less opportunity than the incumbent white drivers. Therefore, they should be given credit for their earlier city service and rights to vacancies ahead of laid-off over-the-road drivers. They invoked the standard argument that no seniority system that tends to perpetuate past discrimination can be "bona fide."

But now the Supreme Court spoke. Justice Potter Stewart, an Eisenhower appointee, wrote the opinion. Stewart agreed that there was a pattern of discrimination before 1965. But he argued that blacks who had been hired as city drivers before 1965 should be treated exactly like those not hired before 1965. Just as the second group could not claim retroactive seniority, so the first group could not. "If anything, the latter group [those not hired] is the more disadvantaged." Like Henderson in Lackawanna, Stewart also noted that the overwhelming majority of the city drivers were white and apparently content to retain their city jobs. Even if the transfer rule "locks" employees into city driver jobs, he wrote, "it does so for all," so the system was not rooted in discrimination. The Court had separated pre-1965 hiring discrimination from seniority.

The decision had done more than that. Even on post-1965 violations, the justices altered the morality of Quarles, because the case was not simply about seniority. The lower court had concluded that TIME had not ended discriminatory assignments in 1965. Only in 1969 were significant numbers of minorities hired for the over-the-road jobs. TIME had argued that poor economic conditions explained the record from 1965 through 1969, but a combination of statistical and anecdotal evidence had convinced the district court that discrimination had not ended in 1965.

Who was entitled to relief in this four-year period? The Court did not, as the company had wished, limit relief to those who had actually applied for the over-the-line jobs, reasoning that some potential applicants would have been deterred by past hiring policies. Neither did it accept the government and LDF position that all minority city drivers should be considered discriminatees, because one could not assume that all city drivers had wanted the over-the-road jobs. Most city drivers, after all, were white and like most of the blacks had not applied for these jobs. Long-distance drivers did not always earn more. Moreover, city drivers had regular working hours, were not required to spend extended periods away from home, and did not face the hazards of long-distance driving at high speeds. Thus, one could not assume that every city driver wanted to become a long-distance driver. The differences between the situations of blacks and whites were not stark, and the results of discrimination were somewhat ambiguous.

However, it was clear there were some victims, and the Fifth Circuit court had ruled that they were entitled to a "rightful place" remedy, retroactive seniority. Even so, relief had to be fashioned so to balance the impact on the expectations of innocent parties, particularly those on lay-off. The Fifth Circuit had accepted the government and LDF argument that the class of post-1965 victims (black city drivers) had hiring priority over laid-off, over-the-road drivers. The union challenged that judgment, arguing that whatever the rationale, the court was preferring the man with a job over another one who was unemployed. The Supreme Court did not presume to judge this issue or to determine who was entitled to relief for the 1965–69 period. This it left to the district court. Nevertheless, the Court declared that lower courts must "look to the practical realities and necessities inescapably involved in reconciling competing interests," in order to determine the "special blend of what is necessary, what is fair, and what is workable."

Stewart's vocabulary was different from that of Judges Butzner and Feinberg. Defining the problem in terms of competing interests and blending moral, legal, and practical considerations made the thinking process different from earlier cases, which spoke of rightful place, illegitimate occupants, and merely "unhappy" white workers. Moreover, some of the justices pondered the fairness of penalizing workers for employer's wrongs.

Even though *Teamsters* overturned the legal necessity for the consent decrees, the thinking behind it was not so different. After all, the steel settlement had rejected the affected-class solution for a universal one based upon the more complicated social reality. The year before the Supreme Court decided *Teamsters*, in *Franks v. Bowman Transportation*, Justices Thurgood Marshall and William J. Brennan Jr., the two who stood for the broadest interpretation of Title VII, had accepted a USWA balancing formulation on remedies for hiring discrimination.[48]

The Union's and Civil Rights Organizations' Approaches to Discrimination

From the very beginning, the USWA was forced to balance because it had a biracial constituency. Thus, its reasoning and its remedies differed from those of the NAACP and LDF. Civil rights lawyers represented a portion of the working class. Their interest in general labor practices was always contingent upon its effect on blacks. The intellectual basis for their position was that *any* employment practice that had a "disparate impact" on minority workers violated Title VII unless the practice was sufficiently job-related to be justified by business necessity. The court accepted that reasoning in *Griggs v. Duke Power Co.* (1971), a case involving job testing.[49] Civil rights lawyers attempted to use "disparate impact" analysis to invalidate a whole range of economic activities. Courts did not buy the argument when it came to business freedom; thus, if a plant relocated to a place with fewer minorities, that was not considered a violation of Title VII. But they accepted the analysis in employment matters, like hiring, testing, and promotion.[50]

No union that had both black and white members could embrace disparate-impact reasoning. The USWA had filed a brief supporting Griggs and the other blacks suing Duke Power, but it argued that the testing was not job-related, not that the tests had a disparate impact. The union evaluated employment practices as good, bad, or indifferent on the basis of their impact on workers in general, not simply when they affected blacks adversely. The USWA's civil rights policies were premised upon the assumption that in the overwhelming number of cases, blacks would benefit from the general strengthening of workers' rights, whether it was in regard to testing, training, or seniority.[51]

The differences in the two groups' reasoning did not lead to different results in *Griggs*, but it did in a series of layoff cases. As the economy slowed and unemployment rose in the 1970s, the courts began to hear a series of cases that involved groups of newly hired blacks who were not victims of discrimination but who were being laid off on the basis of having less seniority. The downturn pitted seniority against newly integrated workforces. At this point, the LDF and NAACP reversed themselves and challenged plant seniority.

A Louisiana company that had begun hiring blacks in 1965 came on hard times in 1971 and laid off half of its workforce. All the whites hired after 1952 and all the blacks hired in recent years were dismissed. The LDF claimed that the company had violated Title VII by laying off the newly hired blacks, arguing that maintaining an integrated workforce was a goal of the law. On the basis of disparate-impact analysis, the LDF had supported plant seniority when advocating the interests of older workers but now opposed it to protect younger blacks from layoffs.

The district court agreed with the LDF, but the Fifth Circuit in *Watkins v. United Steelworkers* and other circuits facing similar problems did not. Title VII was clearer when it came to layoffs. The Justice Department's interpretative memo of 1964 stated, "if, for example, a collective bargaining contract provides that in the event of layoffs, those who were hired last must be laid off first, such a provision would not be affected in the least by Title VII. This would be true even in the case where owing to discrimination prior to the effect date of the title, white workers had more seniority than Negroes."[52]

Independent of the statute, the union viewed seniority as an unalloyed good, protecting all workers. Speaking before the American Bar Association in April 1975, Elliot Bredhoff, a Washington lawyer often used by the USWA, said that efforts to maintain an integrated workplace were socially desirable and morally right. But Bredhoff opposed altering seniority, the bedrock protection for workers, even for such a laudable goal.[53]

The arguments were not driven simply by philosophies or the letter of the law. In 1975 the deep recession after the oil crisis produced aggregate unemployment rates of nearly 10 percent. The most significant black response was Congressman Augustus Hawkins's full employment bill, which was supported by other black representatives and by the labor movement. Embodying a different politics but reflecting the same statistics, the National Urban Coalition urged modifying seniority to preserve affirmative action.[54] Herbert Hill convinced the NAACP convention to litigate the issue. "Black workers, women and other minorities will make a sustained attack on contractual seniority systems which have a disparate effect," Hill asserted. After all, he argued, "the courts have not hesitated to order fundamental changes." But they did not order the changes because of Title VII's explicit language on the subject and the courts' conclusion that layoffs were more of an unmerited penalty than slowed promotions. This calculus became firmer when the rationale was affirmative action, a less compelling goal than remedying discrimination.[55]

What do these cases of the mid-1970s mean? E. C. Perkins, a lawyer for Bethlehem Steel, believed that in *Teamsters* the Court was trying to limit litigation. It is also true that the Fifth Circuit lobbed grenades at the challengers of the steel consent decrees. But was the Court also becoming more conservative? It was retreating from the liberalism of the late 1960s and early 1970s. As we have seen, that liberalism had been an improvised response to the urban riots, which elites believed posed immediate danger to the social order. If that brand of liberalism is taken as the standard, then the consent decrees were in fact more conservative than the Bethlehem decisions. But such a conclusion means preferring a decision that did not help blacks and that produced racial turmoil, a decision that arguably posed a greater threat to liberalism than any more moderate court decision. Moreover, a liberalism defined as gains for a some members of the working class at the expense of other members is not only perverse but unsustainable. There was, and remains, a tendency to define liberalism in this way, though surely it is not the only measure.[56]

These Supreme Court decisions, especially *Teamsters*, were a blow to the LDF as an organization. Seniority systems had been at the heart of its litigation. Jack

Greenberg informed the directors of the Rockefeller Fund, which had been financing the LDF's seniority project, that "[w]e at the Legal Defense Fund are confronted by the devastating impact" of the decision [*Teamsters*]. Now, he predicted, the LDF would have to "identify practices and rules other than seniority which have the effect of locking black workers into inferior situations." Another possibility was to "demonstrate that such [seniority] systems had their genesis in discrimination, and have been maintained with that intent and purpose." Most of these alternative paths turned out to be blind alleys.[57]

OFCC and EEOC attempted to preserve as much of the past as possible. OFCC announced that the *Teamsters* case did not apply to it because the executive order lacked the limiting language of Title VII. Yet it was unlikely that OFCC would demand what the court proscribed. OFCC had called for seniority changes only after the judicial blessings granted in *Quarles* and *Crown*. Like the LDF, EEOC announced it would look for direct discriminatory evidence to invalidate seniority systems and would infer intent when jobs had been segregated. It stated that settlements made before *Teamsters* were binding. On this point the USWA agreed.[58]

The union quickly informed local leaders that the ruling did not change the seniority system in steel. It defended the justice of plant seniority, which was "desirable for all members. We will adhere to our policy of broadening seniority at other plants within our jurisdiction whether or not such changes are required by Title VII." *Teamsters* encouraged a few more white challenges, which were duly rejected by Judge Pointer. The EEOC, headed now by Eleanor Holmes Norton, was completely committed to the consent decrees. The decrees had been incorporated into the union contract in 1974, which made it unlikely that the court would overturn them, because they became part of a consensual agreement. On the other hand, the new ruling made it unlikely that the few blacks who had rejected the settlement would obtain more back pay from the courts. But if the *Teamsters* decision had been handed down before the consent decrees were signed, there would have been no changes, because of the inevitable conflicts among workers and corporate opposition.[59]

The Weber Case

Ironically, it was the least controversial part of the consent decrees that became the most controversial in society. Despite its subordination of affirmative action to seniority when it came to layoffs, the union fashioned the winning argument on affirmative action in hiring, guaranteeing that it remained a viable social option.

Brian Weber worked at Kaiser's aluminum plant in Gramercy, Louisiana, during the time that OFCC had been examining the aluminum industry's craft hiring. Kaiser, like most companies in the industry, hired tradesmen from the outside, who were required to have five years of prior experience. Given the composition of the area's trades, only 5 of its 273 craftsmen were black. In 1971, OFCC notified Kaiser that these numbers were inadequate. The USWA, which represented aluminum as well as steelworkers, offered a way to improve the situation. It convinced the aluminum industry, at the same time the steel consent decrees were being negotiated, to institute similar craft procedures. But unlike the steel companies, in 1974 Kaiser agreed to a union plan to allow production workers to train for craft jobs at its Gramercy plant. To the union, providing workers opportunities to obtain craft positions was not simply a racial issue. Most white workers were as excluded from outside craft opportunities as blacks. Craftsmen were often of a distinct ethnic group, but even when they were not, most whites, as well as blacks, were outside the networks of tradesmen. The plan proposed to select apprentices from among Kaiser employees, using ratios of one black to one white until the proportion of black craftsmen at Kaiser reached the black proportion of the labor force in the area. Each person was chosen for the apprenticeships on the basis of seniority, but there were two lists, one for blacks and one for whites. Seven black and six white trainees were selected in 1974. Weber, who was white, unsuccessfully applied for one of them. His seniority was higher than most of the blacks who were chosen but it was not high enough to obtain a white slot.

Weber was an active unionist and had a good record on civil rights. Because of his liberalism, union leaders tried, but failed, to convince him to drop the suit. Weber believed he had been discriminated against because of his color, which was forbidden by Title VII. The law, he claimed, prohibited preferential treatment to remedy racial imbalance.[60] Without money or union support, Weber received a court-appointed lawyer, Michael R. Fontham, a graduate of the University of Virginia law school. Employed in a prestigious New Orleans law firm, Fontham, a young, white Southerner, had defended blacks in numerous cases. He believed that a judge unsympathetic to civil rights had assigned him a white worker as "punishment" for his earlier representation of blacks. Fontham agreed to take the case only after assuring himself that there had been no actual discrimination at Kaiser.[61]

Weber won in the district court, and a panel of the Fifth Circuit confirmed his victory, two to one. Courts had accepted the use of quotas to remedy legally certified discrimination, but this was a quota to remedy the vaguer notions of racial imbalance and statistical distribution. Weber did not raise constitutional questions because the quota was applied in a private company, unlike the *Bakke* case which had rocked the nation the year before.[62]

In 1978, the Supreme Court had rejected a plan that set aside 16 of 100 places for minorities at the medical school of the University of California at Davis.

The school had acted, it said, in an effort to remedy societal discrimination, not its own. Initially, the Carter administration prepared a brief supporting Bakke, using the occasion to state its support for affirmative action but opposition to quotas. The original brief was written by Drew Days III and Wade McCray, both black civil rights lawyers before their appointments to the Justice Department. But as word got out, the reaction of blacks and liberals was ferocious. Typically, EEOC chair Norton warned that "the entry of the United States for the *first* time . . . on the side of an individual claiming reverse discrimination can only accelerate the deterioration" of affirmative action plans. The political reaction caused the administration to retreat and support the medical school plan.[63]

But in a 5–4 decision, the Supreme Court rejected the affirmative action plan, although there was no majority opinion. Four of the five in the majority concluded that the quota was a racial preference, which violated Title VII; they did not raise constitutional issues. The fifth, Justice Lewis Powell, did, concluding that the quota violated the equal protection clause. But Powell also said that benign racial preferences could be one, if not the only, factor in selections. Thus the four in the minority who supported the quotas plus Powell equaled a majority, who concluded that some form of preference, under some circumstances, was constitutional.

Bakke addressed voluntary, government quotas. The issue in *Weber* was whether Title VII prohibited a private employer from voluntarily adopting a racial quota to remedy societal discrimination, "racial imbalance" in its workforce. In other words, could an employer do what a statute and the Constitution prohibited the government from doing? Initially, Lewis Powell's answer was yes. But by early January Powell had changed his mind. Potter Stewart, too, was sympathetic to Brian Weber's argument. Both had opposed the medical school quotas and were having trouble distinguishing the school's plan from the USWA-Kaiser plan. Justice John Paul Stevens, too, had opposed the quotas, but he was ill and not part of the deliberations.

Adding it up, the danger was that the Supreme Court would uphold Weber's victory in the Court of Appeals, 4–4. Powell, Stewart, and the two Nixon appointees, William H. Rehnquist and Warren Burger, backed Weber; the four supporters of the California plan, Marshall, Brennan, Byron R. White, and Harry A. Blackmun were behind the USWA-Kaiser plan. Such a decision on affirmative action would make the Court look foolish, opening up the justices to criticism for taking the case when they knew that Stevens was ill. Given his own leanings and the vote count, Powell considered reexamining the court's decision to hear the case.[64]

The stakes were high because a majority of the court, like the nation's elite, wanted to encourage affirmative action programs, which in one way or another involved black preferences. Burger told his colleagues that he would "much prefer to have employers free to initiate their own private programs to give minorities preferential treatment. However, I can find no principled basis to avoid the explicit language of the relevant statutory provisions which foreclose such programs based on race."[65]

Weber did not create the same political tempest that *Bakke* had because it affected workers, not applicants to professional school and elite colleges. Liberal and academic elites had supported the Philadelphia plan and subsequent expansion of affirmative action to all of industry. Some now drew a line at higher education, because they took university qualifications more seriously than blue-collar ones. But Attorney General Griffin Bell told President Carter that many corporations were waiting for the decision "before going forward with their own plans."[66]

On what basis could the plan pass muster? Kaiser and the Justice Department essentially submitted Judge John Wisdom's Fifth Circuit dissent. To Wisdom, racial statistics created the presumption of discrimination, the first stage of proof for a Title VII violation. He concluded that Kaiser could act on what it believed to be a *prima facie* violation of Title VII, meaning it could act to prevent litigation. Companies often acted in this manner, but it was not a truth the courts were comfortable with. It created a state of quasi-discrimination, "arguable violation" in court language. Michael Gottesman, the union's specialist on Title VII matters, did not believe that such an argument was logical or could win the needed fifth vote (the four dissenters in *Bakke* plus one). Gottesman thought that an argument rooted in voluntarism would win the vote of Potter Stewart. Effective implementation of Title VII presumed a fair amount of voluntarism. He said the law did not require such efforts, but it did not prohibit them either when viewed in the light of the broad purposes of the law. When Section 703(j) stated that nothing in the Title VII should "require" preferential treatment, the Congress could have easily said "require or permit." Thus, voluntary preferential treatment was permitted, although the government could not require a preference without a legal finding of discrimination. Through this verbal sleight of hand, Gottesman distinguished *Weber* from *Bakke*.[67]

The notes of the justices reveal that it was this argument that won over Stewart, who rejected the government/Kaiser argument of prima facie discrimination or preemptive action to avoid litigation.[68] He agreed with Burger and Rehnquist that the statute forbade the government to require affirmative action. But he "sufficiently agreed with [the] USWA brief" to "join 4 others to make a Court. I'd do this without reaching [the] question whether [the] Court, pres[ident] or EEOC" could require it. The oral argument demonstrated how critical the distinction was. N. Thompson Powers, the lawyer for Kaiser, began with the argument that *Weber* was like *Bakke*. Brennan intervened quickly to say it was not. The distinction was vital to retaining Stewart's vote.[69]

The USWA-Kaiser plan was sustained 5–2 by the four *Bakke* dissenters plus Stewart. Stevens and Powell did not vote. Powell, for unknown reasons, decided to take no role in the decision. Although ill at the time of the oral argument, he could have voted. His difficulties with the case must have been a part of his forbearance. Rehnquist's dissent, joined by Burger, read Title VII literally, arguing that its protections applied to whites as well as blacks. Because that reading would have made any affirmative action plan illegal, Rehnquist had ensured that he would not win over Powell or Stewart.[70]

Brennan's opinion, a paean to voluntarism and the "spirit of the law" rather than "the letter of the statute," required a certain amount of historical distortion, which Rehnquist's dissent duly noted, calling it Orwellian. Practically plagiarizing the USWA brief, Brennan argued that the supporters of Title VII did not want undue government interference with management prerogatives. Of course, Dirksen, the main spokesman for business during the negotiations, wished to retain as much autonomy as possible for business, which was why he initially opposed Title VII. The assumption of Title VII's advocates was that business was discriminating against blacks. But the culture of 1963 and 1964 also proscribed preferential treatment. The debates centered upon what government could and could not require because it was assumed that the state would do the requiring. Interpreting the silence on what business could do as acquiescence was a stretch. Dirksen never imagined that management would voluntarily implement such a plan, and he was right. The trigger for the USWA-Kaiser plan was government pressure; the actual genesis of the plan was far less voluntary than its legal form.[71]

It is unlikely the plan would have been sustained without the union's support as well as its argument. The union provided cover because, unlike the California admissions quota, which was the result of a secret administrative process, the Kaiser training program was a product of collective bargaining. Gottesman began his oral argument by informing the justices that the delegates to the 1978 USWA convention had overwhelmingly supported the plan. The union represented whites as well as blacks; that fact alone suggested that it did not "unnecessarily trammel the interests of white employees." The plan, he explained, was temporary, and whites were not excluded. Without the affirmative action plan, he argued, there would have been no worker training program, so the plant's white workers as a group were also net gainers.[72]

The USWA had initially preferred using seniority and pre-apprentice training for selecting workers for the craft training program. It had never opposed quotas on constitutional or even statutory grounds. It accepted the quotas as a vehicle for affirmative action because it believed that the demands were legally supported, that the program affected few workers, and that compromise was the essence of collective bargaining. Only by parsing the literal words of Title VII and 1964 meanings was the plan objectionable, as Justice Rehnquist's dissent expansively detailed. Rehnquist's reasoning lived in a world of abstractions. The USWA usually lacked the luxury of inhabiting regions of pure principle. And it did not do so here.

The Court went no further than concluding that the Kaiser plan did not violate Title VII's prohibitions. It did not set up standards distinguishing permissible from impermissible affirmative action, which would be decided on a case-by-case basis. Most commentators believed the ruling provided employers with a defense against "reverse discrimination" suits. Although liberals celebrated it as a victory over "racists," Weber was no racist. The *Weber* case involved competing moralities. It was in the interest of society to limit the occasions when the two did battle: any policy that consistently transported the Webers of the world into the anti–civil rights camp produced a world hostile to the broader objectives of African Americans.[73]

Despite the tortuous and tortured language, in the end the Court accommodated to the history that had led to the craft quotas. Whether or not the justices approved of them, quotas were part of social reality. After *Weber*, affirmative action plans continued to be executed informally, outside of public scrutiny. In the end, preferential hiring would be determined by management, prodded by political pressures, personal attitudes, and the like. *Bakke* yielded an identical result in university admissions. In the end, a majority of the Court could live with such indeterminacy because it supported the general concept of affirmative action.[74]

In 1980, in *Fullilove vs. Klutznick*, the Supreme Court declared, 6–3, that the 10 percent set-asides for minority contractors, part of the Public Works Act of 1977, was constitutional. As in *Bakke*, there was no majority opinion. Unlike the medical school quota, the numbers were not rigid, and nonminorities who did not obtain a contract were not excluded from their calling. And, in this instance, the Congress of the United States, unlike the Board of Regents of California, was specifically charged with eliminating discrimination.[75]

Chief Justice Burger's opinion, joined by Powell and White, revealed the consensus on affirmative action, if not the rationale. Burger had wanted to permit employers like Kaiser to use racial preference policies in hiring, but he found the Title VII language to be a barrier. However, there were no such prohibitions on government contracting. Similarly, Powell constructed a strict test to determine whether a plan passed muster, but the set-asides came through with flying colors, despite the fact that the close scrutiny the Court imposed on itself was not evidenced by the Congress. The minority set-asides were inserted from the House floor by Congressman Parren Mitchell without debate or hearings. Still, three justices dissented. The failure to enunciate clear principles meant that the courts would be in the business of judging government affirmative action plans. Unlike the private sector, the state could not practice affirmative action with the secrecy permitted private institutions.[76]

Civil Rights and Employment

Despite the controversy on the edges, the acceptance of fair employment completed the distributional project the New Deal had begun. It would be misleading to leave the impression that the conflicts resolved in the consent decrees and *Weber* were the only racial interactions among workers during the 1960s and 1970s. The USWA and civil rights organizations cooperated as well as conflicted. Although it has received less attention from historians, the story of Korf, a German minimill that set up operations in Georgetown, South Carolina, in the late 1960s, was common. Advised by an antiunion law firm and Senator Strom Thurmond, the company tried to operate without the USWA. The mill's wages were low even for southern minimills, and promotions were determined by the whim of supervisors. A white, Charles Parker, president of the Atlantic Steel union, which had civil rights problems of its own during the period, led a successful organizing drive. In April 1970, the majority-white mill voted overwhelmingly for the USWA and elected a black president, but Korf would not negotiate in good faith. The workers struck in 1971, and the company hired "replacement workers," which inevitably provoked violence. The USWA then discovered that the mill was financed partly by a union bank in Germany. Exerting pressure on the German unions helped, but it took a group of internationally prominent black leaders, including Coretta King, the widow of the civil rights leader, to get Korf to negotiate with the union.[77]

On the other hand, black workers discovered, as the *Weber* case was working its way through the courts, that government intervention on behalf of civil rights was insufficient. Until the late 1970s, the company union of the Newport News Shipbuilding and Dry Dock Company, which had launched its first ship in 1890, had managed to survive many organizing drives. Although company presidents had had good relations with southern black leaders, beginning with Booker T. Washington, the company was riddled with discrimination. Black workers had appealed to EEOC and OFCC in 1966. Empowered by the company's complete reliance on federal contracts, the government negotiated and trumpeted a comprehensive affirmative action plan. But the old company union and old labor practices remained; although some blacks had secured new positions, both they and white workers lacked an effective seniority clause and other standard labor protections. First a group of elite white designers in 1976 and then the biracial production and maintenance workers, led by some of

This is not Birmingham in 1963, but the scene of one of the many strikes workers of the Newport News Shipbuilding Company waged between 1977 and 1979 in attempts to convince the conglomerate Tenneco to bargain with the USWA. (Courtesy of HCLA, Penn State)

the blacks who had appealed to the EEOC in 1966, asked the USWA to represent them.

Although the union won elections, the shipyard, owned now by the conglomerate Tenneco, refused to negotiate from 1976 through 1979. Tenneco ran the city and controlled the state police, who beat up the union president and other workers. The USWA effort was led by Bruce Thrasher, formerly a union representative in Birmingham and now the head of District 35, which included Virginia. Thrasher moved to Newport News from district headquarters in Atlanta for a year to direct the strike and negotiations. But Tenneco defied ten decisions of the NLRB. It attempted to appeal to whites by accusing the USWA of racism because it had brought in black congressman Harold Ford of Memphis to speak at a rally in support of the strike; the company used A. Philip Randolph's criticism of the AFL-CIO in the early 1960s to label the USWA a racist union, hoping to convince blacks to cross picket lines. But when Thrasher asked a company vice president how he treated blacks, he replied, "we throw 'em coconuts."[78] The USWA persisted, using every power it possessed, eventually negotiating a contract for the 20,000 workers, unaided by the government. Blacks, remembering the government intervention in 1966, could not understand why it was appropriate to threaten to debar employers from government contracts to enforce civil rights laws but not the national labor laws.[79]

This state of affairs resulted from the way in which black employment had entered the national agenda. Ignored during the 1950s, black employment was initially conceptualized as an aspect of the broader problem of inadequate work in the early 1960s. Instead, Title VII of the Civil Rights Act assimilated work issues into a civil rights framework rather than a labor framework. It addressed discrimination but not the declining number of jobs in northern manufacturing cities, which were the destinations of many southern blacks. After riots in 1967 and 1968 threatened cities, white elites became more color-conscious and acted to secure the social order by hiring more blacks. Federal judges, affected by the same crisis, began to interpret the law to achieve the same purpose. Broader definitions of discrimination were proposed and accepted by courts during the late 1960s until the mid-1970s, when the recession caused some pulling back.

The new regulators in OFCC and EEOC made the process more contentious than it need have been. They ignored unions that were prepared to cooperate. Their opposition to business was ingrained. The rigidity of universal rules, the agencies' distrust of expertise, the proliferation of arenas of decision making, and bureaucratic arrogance often hardened opposition, which was then invoked to justify coercive rules. Many civil rights activists judged government effectiveness on the basis of the number of contracts canceled by OFCC and lawsuits brought by the Justice department. Thus, failure to effect an agreement became the measure of success.

The union, industry, and government transcended this adversarial culture and rejoined the severed racial and employment questions when they negotiated the consent decrees in 1974. The steel industry's seniority changes in 1962 had been driven by the recession and technological changes affecting employment even while they facilitated black mobility. The changes of 1974 were powered by the civil rights imperative, but they completed the union's longstanding goal of broadening seniority and thereby protecting senior workers from rapid technological changes. Nevertheless, the decrees were simply better answers to the question, "What is fair?" They did not, however, address the quantity of work in the steel industry, which in the end was the most critical factor for all workers.

The Supreme Court sustained the USWA-Kaiser plan, but the recession of 1975–76 did not. After one year, Kaiser suspended the program. The court had ruled on a training program that had ended. But it was typical of the legalized culture of U.S. society in the late 1970s that the debates over Weber ignored this salient fact. Aluminum companies, like their steel competitors, found training craftsmen expensive. It was cheaper to hire already trained craftsmen when needed. Eventually, corporations discovered that it was cheapest to contract out work, where possible. Neither seniority reform nor affirmative action addressed the amount of work available.

In the end, the economic conditions of the industry affected steelworkers more than the 1974 decrees. The fair distribution project was overtaken almost immediately by the global steel crisis. The settlement was negotiated in a year of a strong steel market, which turned out to be the last year of the American steel era. In 1976 Robert Moore noted that the declining employment slowed promotions but announced optimistically that "the economic downturn experienced over the last two years must be viewed as a temporary situation which will correct itself." It did not. When they were dissolved in 1988, the decrees affected only about 135,000 workers, not the 350,000 of 1974.[80]

The number of black steelworkers declined steadily after 1974, from 38,096 to 9,958 in 1988. The black presence in the crafts increased, from 5.30 to 8.39 percent in the electrical trades, for instance; however, it would be difficult to call this progress, because the number of black electricians declined from 718 to 431. The most significant changes were among female workers: the percentage rose from 1.69 to 4.92 percent. But even here the number of women declined from 3,543 to 3,209. Only in the crafts did female numbers rise, from 81 to 345. Because of the precipitous decline in employment, Moore was unable to evaluate the effect of the decrees.[81] Other attempts to evaluate the role of specific settlements in the society as a whole falter too, because of the broader factors affecting employment.[82] Viewed in this light, the conflicts over affirmative action may very well be a narcissism of small differences.

The remaining chapters of this book address economic policies that had a huge impact on the supply of jobs in steel and other industries, an issue that had originally been part of the 1963 discussion but which was erased by the advent of the 1964 tax cut, the War on Poverty, and Title VII. As we have seen, the economic situation of the steel industry occasionally entered discussions about fair employment; what was remarkable about these debates, however, was that they took place for the most part in an economic vacuum. The weakness of the liberalism of the 1960s was not its ambitious social goals, as has so often been asserted. It was that liberalism lacked an economic blueprint to match its social agenda. Moreover, liberal foreign economic policy undercut the whole enterprise.

U.S. Foreign and

Domestic Policies in Steel:

The Creation of Conflict,

1945–1974

T he steel consent decrees added the goal of fair distribution of work among whites, minorities, and women to the New Deal goal of fair distribution of rewards between capital and labor. Just as the government attempted to influence steel wages and prices, racial reformers had targeted the steel industry because they thought it was a fundamental industry. The many critics of big business inveighed against its power but assumed the corollary that corporate productiveness was durable. Liberal projects of the 1960s tried to capture the dividends of the growth to produce racial equality, end poverty, enlighten the populace, restore the environment, and promote a more egalitarian social and political order.

But the goal of winning the Cold War increased the number of applicants for the dividends. To secure and sustain strategic alliances, the government resurrected and created steel industries abroad and then encouraged imports into the United States. "Free world" access to the American market was a crucial part of the nation's arsenal. The resulting diminished market for domestic steel raised the cost of modernization and reduced the number of jobs in the U.S. steel industry. The situation was worsened by a domestic policy—monetary, fiscal, antitrust—inherited from the American past. By 1974, both the industry and the union had come to question key elements of the postwar order, although neither was fully aware how public policies had shaped their options.

Building a Cold War Trading System, 1945–1974

Once upon a time the bulk of international trade consisted of raw materials and food. From 1953 to 1973, trade in manufactured goods grew from less than half to more than 60 percent of international commerce. The amount of steel production traded in international markets jumped from 10.7 percent in 1950 to 25 percent in 1980. The new steel trade was an offshoot of the decision to construct a liberal order to stave off the economic nationalism of the interwar period. Key institutions governing currency, development, and trade were put in place during and shortly after World War II—the International Monetary Fund and International Bank for Reconstruction and Development (later known as the World Bank) in 1944 and the General Agreement on Tariffs and Trade (GATT) in 1947.[1]

After World War II, tottering European economies required more than international liberalism. American leaders believed that if the Europeans responded to their problems through regimented regimes of the right or left, the United States would have to follow suit. The Marshall Plan of 1947 and related grants and loans were antidotes to both viruses. While some have argued that the corporate need to invest and sell abroad impelled the policy, most American businesses were oriented to the domestic economy. It was the systemic political dangers that impelled the Marshall Plan.[2]

As the Cold War developed, European recovery took precedence over domestic economic interests. A Bureau of the Budget memorandum of April 1950 announced: "Foreign economic policies should not be formulated in terms primarily of economic objectives; they must be subordinated to our politico-security objectives and the priorities which the latter involve." President Truman's Public Advisory Board for Mutual Security believed that the U.S. economy was so strong that there would be no injury. It urged unilateral removal of "unnecessary" tariffs on manufactured goods because "the country has nothing to fear." Others foresaw that there would be domestic casualties but felt that the price was well worth paying. In 1952, the assistant secretary of state for economic affairs stated privately that "the great question is . . . whether the country is willing to decide, in the broader national self-interest to reduce tariffs and increase United States imports even though some domestic industry may suffer serious injury."[3]

President Eisenhower continued Truman's priorities. One trade negotiator of the 1950s subsequently acknowledged, "we did make some big tariff cuts and didn't get any reciprocity. It was quite deliberate." Eisenhower added non-statist measures to Democratic grants and aid. To promote overseas investment the government deferred taxes on foreign earnings. Thus, affiliates reinvested them to reduce their American obligations. Taxes paid to foreign governments were not simply deductions against income, but credits against American obligations. A dollar earned abroad was taxed less than one earned at home. The growth of transnationals was a product of policy, not the market.[4]

The signing of the Treaty of Rome in 1957, which established the European Economic Community (EEC), was the capstone of this U.S. policy. The result of ten years of American prodding, the six nations of Western Europe erected a common external tariff while the internal tariff was reduced in increments of 10 percent. Fearing they would be unable to sell in a market fortified by high tariffs, U.S. producers rushed to set up new manufacturing plants in Western Europe from 1957 to 1962.[5]

George W. Ball, who headed President Kennedy's task force on foreign economic policy and became under secretary of state for economic affairs, was unconcerned about this American investment in Europe. Ball, a fervent Atlanticist, had represented the EEC in Washington. He admitted in his memoir that he operated on the premise that "we Americans could afford to pay some economic price for a strong Europe."[6] Meanwhile, the slow growth and high unemployment of the early 1960s led others to question whether the United States could pay that price. In 1963, the Joint Economic Committee of the Congress held comprehensive hearings on prices, wages, imports, and shipping rates in the steel industry. Senator William Proxmire of Wisconsin forced a State Department official to admit that "in the case of iron and steel, European rates may be higher than ours." But he quickly added, "on many other commodities our rates are higher than theirs." Another senator asked, skeptically, "you might sacrifice in one instance steel in order to get a more favorable treatment of your exports in other goods?" The official hoped that "'sacrifice' is not the word, but we might make concessions, yes sir, on steel products . . . and in return . . . we got concessions on other products."

Proxmire, no friend of the steel industry, could not believe his ears: "The injustice here is so striking, because this exact period when we were being excluded from part of this market coincided with the period when in Western Europe they were virtually eliminating their internal tariffs between 1957 and 1962, and it looks as if we are being not only excluded but discriminated against. . . . [W]hile none of us are anxious to retaliate against our friends, they are taking advantage of us and our relative low tariff to double their imports into the United States."[7]

Thus, European unity and prosperity posed new problems. British Laborite Harold Wilson told Hubert Humphrey that American foreign economic policies simply "suck in imports and kill exports," producing the unemployment and balance of payment problems that distinguished the American economy from those of Europe.[8] President Kennedy was aware of the problem, although he was more concerned with the impact on foreign policy than with employment. Kennedy asserted that expanding American sales abroad went "to the heart of our ability to keep more than one million Americans in uniform who now are serving the United States outside [its] borders." Lower prices and wages would make U.S. goods more competitive, but Kennedy warned that "if the United States should be denied the [European] market, we will either find a flight of capital from this country to construct factories within that wall, or we will find ourselves in serious economic trouble." [9]

Kennedy's solution was his austere domestic policy of 1961 and 1962 and the Trade Expansion Act in 1962. The trade act empowered the president to cut tariffs by 50 percent and provided a mechanism for across-the-board reductions, instead of item-by-item haggling. Two of Kennedy's friends, Seymour Harris, an economist in the Treasury Department, and John Kenneth Galbraith, questioned whether the president could reduce European tariffs. Harris believed that EEC trade barriers injured the domestic economy by limiting American exports and also diverting the world's exports from Europe to the United States. But he told the president that the Europeans "generally made concessions where the result was not likely to be large increases of United States exports at the expense of their domestic producers." Thus, while European rates on wristwatches, leaders in world sales, were low, the European tariff on automobiles was 22 percent compared to the American duty of only 6.5. Oscar Gass, an economist who had worked in the Roosevelt administration, went further, challenging the root assumptions of the liberal traders. Writing in *The New Republic*, Gass predicted that the trade act would reduce wages and that U.S. losses from imports would exceed its gains from exports. Nevertheless, he added, because it had become the administration's "Holy Cause," "[d]ecent people are prepared to lie for it." [10]

The president seemed unaware that his interest in increasing U.S. exports to Europe conflicted with the strategic priorities of his State Department. Congressional opposition to the diplomats' dealings forced Kennedy to create the Special Trade Representative (STR) to conduct the trade negotiations. But he filled the post with former secretary of state Christian Herter, whose foreign policy priorities were the same as George Ball's. Commerce remained the handmaiden of the "Grand Design." [11]

The talks launched by the new trade law, the Kennedy Round, ended in 1967. Insofar as the United States had an economic strategy, it was to trade manufacturing concessions for opening up the European market to U.S. agricultural exports. The negotiations reduced tariffs on manufactured goods by 35 percent. Perennially one step behind the latest obstacles, the agreement failed to tackle nontariff barriers and export incentives, which were the key issues for the steel industry. [12] Moreover, little was done to open up European markets to American farm products. The key American negotiator, Francis Bator, told

President Johnson that even though the United States would come out on the short end of the economic stick, Johnson should sign it because the failure of the Round would produce "jungle warfare" in trade, "make the EEC into an isolationist, anti-U.S. bloc," and set off "spiraling protectionism" everywhere. Johnson, who had many other things to think about in 1967, agreed.[13]

Europeans knew that the United States was more committed to fortifying the anti-Soviet bloc than to obtaining any item on its domestic agenda. The Europeans refused to budge on agriculture, rebated value-added taxes for exports, and sheltered domestic industries from the manufacturing cuts.[14] In November 1967 the English devalued the pound, followed by similar moves by other nations.[15]

The Japanese were pleased with the results, too. A Cold War agenda had been transported to the Pacific, especially after the victory of the Chinese Communists in 1949. This meant rebuilding the Japanese economy and finding outlets for Japanese goods. American pressure obtained GATT membership for Japan in 1955, but the Europeans excluded Japanese goods. Washington cut American duties on products of interest to third countries in exchange for permitting Japanese access to their markets. Inevitably, Japanese exports found their most secure outlet in the United States. By 1965, Japan enjoyed regular trade surpluses with the United States, and the Kennedy Round promised to increase them.[16]

A Japanese reporter explained that the cuts the United States made "include many heavy industrial and chemical products which this country [Japan] intends to emphasize in the future." Moreover, Japanese negotiators excluded "almost all the strategic industrial goods" from the list of cuts it was prepared to make.[17] William M. Roth, who became STR in 1967 after Christian Herter's death, discovered anew that the Japanese had erected numerous trade barriers, such as quotas on more than 120 product categories, including computers, office machinery, and auto components, as well as numerous nontariff obstacles to imports. Noting the "unjustifiable disparity between [Japan's] aggressive export policy and its restrictive import policy," Roth concluded that Japan should act like other mature economic powers. Tokyo agreed only to study the situation.[18]

When it came to Japan, experts brought in their special knowledge. Former ambassador to Japan and Harvard professor Edwin O. Reischauer thought that Tokyo "was a good customer. Until the last year or two, we have always run a large trade surplus. . . . Our hope for building a stable Southeast Asia depends on friendship with Japan."[19] The State Department agreed, noting Japan's willingness to hold reserves in dollars, accumulated from trade surpluses and American defense outlays, instead of withdrawing gold from the U.S. Treasury. This short-term "help" for the dollar actually aided Japan and also Germany, which was equally forbearing. Because both nations' currencies continued to be undervalued, their exports were advantaged. The United States was beginning to pay a steep price for its military and currency hegemony.

Kennedy had assumed that the tax cut and trade liberalization would end the balance of payments deficit, but in January 1968 the deficit ballooned to $3.6 billion, forcing Johnson to impose mandatory controls on American money going abroad. A lowly assistant secretary in the Commerce Department asked a related question: "Is it in our national interest to encourage the rapid transfer of our new technology to foreign countries through branch plants and subsidies abroad or by licensing arrangements?" The concern even reached a *Wall Street Journal* columnist, who sounded an alarm on runaway shops (businesses that relocate, usually for cheaper labor), declining exports, and increased imports of "unsophisticated electronics" for U.S. teenagers from U.S. companies in Taiwan. These issues were buried, however, because politics pointed to military causes for the deficit, especially spending for the Vietnam war. The year 1968 rained too many crises for the president or the society to focus on long-term issues like trade, foreign investment, or technology.[20]

The Kennedy Round did not slow the movement of capital abroad or reverse trade trends. U.S. exports faced greater difficulties, and imports continued to grow. Between 1962 and 1974, imports rose 311.8 percent, compared to a 51.7 percent growth in GNP. From 1955 to 1965, imports increased 7 percent in the United States and actually fell 5 and 14 percent, respectively, in Europe and Japan. During the next ten years, imports to the United States jumped 104 percent, while they grew only 38 percent in Europe and Japan. U.S. exports did not match these numbers, and in 1971 the nation suffered its first merchandise trade deficit.[21]

Numerous complaints from labor, business, and Congress forced President Nixon's hand. In 1971 Nixon created a White House council, headed by Bell and Howell chairman Peter Peterson, a prominent free trader, to examine American foreign economic policies.[22] Peterson gave the president grim news: The nation's "economic superiority was gone" and "other industrialized nations have been more vigorous in the pursuit of their economic interests." He recommended reversing U.S. priorities: economic interests should take precedence over diplomacy.[23]

Instead, Nixon created a blue-ribbon advisory group, the Commission on International Trade and Investment Policy, chaired by Albert L. Williams of IBM, which ratified current policy. The commission acknowledged that the United States had shouldered the burdens of the international economic system and recommended that Europe and Japan assume some of them. It called for the exchange rate changes which the president would effect in August. But the commission's main recommendation was to continue to "eliminate all bar-

riers to international trade and capital movements within twenty-five years."
At bottom, the report was a brief for transnational corporations, which it
claimed created jobs at home as well as abroad and helped the balance of payments deficit through remittances from their foreign offshoots.

The committee's two labor members, I. W. Abel of the USWA and Floyd E.
Smith of the International Association of Machinists dissented, arguing that
the "sharply rising foreign investments of U.S. companies . . . have caused the
rapid transfer of American technology, production, and employment to foreign operations." In 1969 Nixon had removed the temporary controls Johnson
had placed on overseas investment. The Commerce Department reported that
between 1969 and 1971 American capital abroad increased 31.5 percent compared to 7.4 percent in the United States. Abel concluded that this outflow was
a major reason why labor productivity and growth rates had fallen absolutely
and in comparison to EC countries and Japan.[24]

By 1973, largely due to a two-year campaign by the AFL-CIO, public opinion
favored curbing transnationals by a margin of two to one.[25] The labor federation helped write the Foreign Trade and Investment Act, the Burke-Hartke
law, first introduced in 1971, which would have ended the tax advantages
transnationals enjoyed and empowered the president to regulate international
capital transactions if he determined that they reduced domestic employment.
The bill also proposed to create a tripartite commission with strong powers to
regulate imports and capital flows.[26] Labor, business, and government together had to determine how capital was deployed, not simply because of the
payments balance, which had been President Johnson's concern, but become
of the impact on the American standard of living. Burke-Hartke was labor's
first critique of the institutional arrangements of the affluent society.

Abel was the chief AFL-CIO spokesman for the proposed law, although steelworkers were not directly threatened by transnationals.[27] Unlike the consumer
electronics, textiles, and auto industries, the steel industry could not threaten
to take work offshore.[28] The industry could not defeat or finesse the USWA.[29]
But Abel concluded that the exodus of capital made it difficult for steel companies to raise money. Moreover, the exodus of steel-using industries depressed the domestic demand for steel. The import relief sections of the bill,
which required a rollback of imports to the quantity of goods taken in between
1965 and 1969, would attempt to maintain a relationship between domestic
production and imports, a key problem, as we shall see, in the steel industry.[30]

Nixon repulsed this challenge because the labor-liberal opposition was di-
vided and distracted. The Democratic platform of 1972 made no mention of
Burke-Hartke. The internal division within the party between the AFL-CIO and
McGovern liberals was underscored by another between the AFL-CIO and the
UAW, which had left the federation in 1968. The UAW did not support the legis-

lation because it hoped to create a global automobile union, and auto jobs were not then threatened, as they would be at the end of the decade. UAW support for trade adjustment assistance instead of Burke-Hartke was one reason that liberal Democrats failed to realize that the labor movement was not concerned with compensation but with, in the words of Abel aide Frank Fernbach, "the trade-off itself—namely the loss of jobs—which we can no longer accept." Liberals opposed transnationals mainly because of their presumed negative impact on third-world nations, not their effects on American workers. Liberals had not manned the barricades with the likes of George Meany for many years. Finally, liberal preoccupation with Watergate and Vietnam in 1973 and 1974 delayed coming to grips with the changing U.S. economy.[31]

Nixon's trade and investment policies continued Kennedy's. By the time the Trade Act of 1974 came up for a vote, two devaluations in 1971 and 1973 had brought imports down. The new law reaffirmed presidential authority to reduce barriers, this time with "fast-track" procedures, allowing President Gerald R. Ford to begin new negotiations, the Tokyo Round. Like Kennedy, Nixon had promised to open up foreign markets in the new round of trade talks. The law also empowered the president to give special zero tariffs on imports of products from developing countries. Future exporters of steel to the United States—Brazil, Taiwan, and Mexico—were on the first list.[32] The law did liberalize criteria for awarding trade adjustment assistance for workers and for determining an industry's injury from tariff concessions. (The Kennedy act had set high hurdles on both.) It authorized industry committees to advise the STR, which the AISI hoped would prevent steel concessions being offered "in return for greater U.S. exports of agricultural commodities or other manufactured products," as in the past.[33] The administration judged these measures a cheap price to pay for authority to begin the new round of GATT talks.[34]

Still, it was difficult to harmonize the ideology of free trade with the reality of trade. Corporations discovered that nontariff barriers forced them to manufacture abroad because they could not sell abroad. By 1968, American affiliates were selling two and one half times the value of American exports to the European Community (EC).[35] Even economist Fred Bergsten, who had resigned from the National Security Council because of what he believed were Nixon's "isolationist" currency policies, worried that "foreign direct investment and multinational enterprises have now replaced traditional, arms-length trade as the primary source of economic exchange." Encouraged by the state to help revive European economies, multinationals took on a life of their own. The international companies benefited from the protected markets of nations where they invested, even though U.S. domestic exporters did not. Capital was freer than trade.[36]

It was becoming more difficult for government to manage an overloaded plate. Nixon, unwilling or unable to reduce the nation's strategic commitments, institute capital controls, or press for a genuinely multilateral monetary system, effected several quick fixes—devaluation, wage and price controls, fiscal expansion before the 1972 election, and then the promise of worker assistance and fair trade enforcement in the Trade Act of 1974. The president bought some time, which he squandered in Watergate. His successors would have to go over the same ground.

The Origins of the Global Steel Market

American trade policy made it possible for steel to be exchanged internationally, but U.S. postwar reconstruction policies provided capital and technology to produce the traded steel. From 1947 through 1960, U.S. and U.S.-dominated international agencies loaned over $2.1 billion for the construction of steel mills in foreign countries, including many that never had produced steel. The lion's share went to areas at the Cold War's critical frontiers: Europe, Japan, Turkey, and India. Only Great Powers, with supreme economic confidence, can employ such cavalier policies. The more old-fashioned Eugene Grace, head of Bethlehem Steel, warned in 1949 that "we are industrializing the whole world [and] deindustrializing the United States."[37]

From 1960 to 1973, global steel production doubled from 345 to 697 million tons. With U.S. aid, Europe and Japan were responsible for most of the new capacity. Americans midwifed the European Coal and Steel Community (ECSC) in 1951.[38] Technically, the ECSC violated GATT, which permitted customs unions only when they included all products. With some state ownership, comprehensive planning, and negotiated market shares, the ECSC looked more like a cartel than the free enterprise of American ideology. In 1955, European producers reclaimed their twentieth-century dominance of export markets, capturing 65 percent of world trade. European capacity doubled in the late 1950s, and jumped from 77 to 144 million tons between 1960 and 1973.[39]

With identical purposes, American policy fostered Japanese steel production, which rose even faster, from 25 to 129 million tons from 1960 to 1973. Japanese steel exports grew 17 percent a year, taking 25 percent of the global export market by 1973.[40] The Japanese industry was a troubling case for free trade ideology. Without abundant raw materials, capital, or engineering talent, the Japanese became the world's leading steel producer. Its leaders refused, in the words of one official, to entrust "its future, according to the theory of comparative advantage, to . . . industries characterized by intensive use of labor." The ability to flout trade theory required the help of the American occupation authorities and the outbreak of war in Korea.[41]

By the end of World War II, Japan's steel industry had been partially destroyed and its ties to raw material sources severed, bringing into question the very survival of the industry. The Japanese government and occupation authorities helped steelmen obtain raw materials, subsidized the sale of steel, and financed investment. Nevertheless, whether the Japanese steel industry could become competitive was a subject of intense debate. The Korean War tipped the balance to those advocating the creation of a modern steel industry. The leading historian of the Japanese steel industry, Yoshitaka Suzuki, concluded that "it was nothing more than superb luck . . . that the Korean War broke out" at the key moment. Americans bought steel in Japan for strategic reasons even when it was cheaper to buy in the United States.[42]

Contrary to economic orthodoxy, this success may be attributed to the Japanese state. Tokyo rejected the American view that the state should confine its activities to aggregate management. A vice minister of the Ministry of International Trade and Industry (MITI) said that "[i]t is an utterly self-centered [businessman's] point of view to think that the government should be concerned with providing only a favorable environment for industries without telling them what to do." Until the 1960s, Japan's economic relationships with the world were brokered by state agencies, facilitated by the close relationships between company executives and bureaucrats at MITI, the Ministry of Finance, and the Economic Planning Agency.[43] The state controlled foreign exchange, licenses, and capital, which permitted direct management of economic development. MITI protected the domestic market for Japanese firms, provided cheap capital, facilitated the purchase of technology, coal, and iron, planned investment, and managed excess capacity.[44]

Instead of encouraging competition in the steel industry, the Japanese built up a few large companies. From 1951 to 1956, 72 percent of state funding went to four of Japan's forty-four steel companies. Rapid depreciation laws helped firms accumulate capital by transforming profits to expenses. Cheap, long-term credit was crucial when individual firms lacked internally generated funds and private investors were wary. If companies had had to rely upon their own resources or the stock market, there would have been no Japanese steel industry.[45]

MITI drew up plans in the late 1950s to construct brand new facilities, or "greenfield" mills, each capable of producing from 9 to 16 million tons a year, using the new basic oxygen furnace (BOF) to make the steel. MITI made the construction of huge seaside mills economically feasible by creating the infrastructure, extending loans, and ordering the pace of construction for each company. These technically advanced, integrated mills, sited at modern, deep-water, coastal ports, received cheap raw materials and shipped increasing amounts of low-priced steel.

MITI forced companies to compete for funds on the basis of productivity, but it also freed them from the headaches of imports and immediate profits. Even after modest tariff reduction in the 1960s, the Japanese protected their domestic market through other means. Interlocking ownership discouraged foreign purchases. Distributors, controlled by leading steelmakers, threatened to withhold supplies to trading corporations that handled foreign steel. Protection from cheaper imports combined with price-fixing agreements during downturns sustained investment. Historian Kiyoshi Kawahito concluded that "technically" the monthly industry meeting "may not be a cartel, but undoubtedly it is in substance."[46] When one firm refused to cut production during a recession in late 1965, MITI concluded that persuasion was inadequate and that the only genuine solution to overcapacity and excessive competition was a stable oligopoly. In 1969, MITI effected the merger of the two largest steel companies, the equivalents of U.S. Steel and Bethlehem, forming Nippon Steel, to discipline the industry.[47]

The steel industry was at the core of Japanese strategy of growth through exports. From 1957 to 1976, exports accounted for 40 percent of the growth of the Japanese steel industry. Bureaucrats targeted and concentrated steel exports to the United States but purchased raw materials from diverse sources. By 1967, 52.6 percent of Japanese exports went to the United States. On the other hand, coal supplies came from domestic mines and imports from the United States, Canada, and Australia.[48]

The Japanese steel industry first challenged the Europeans. The EEC easily excluded Japanese steel at home, but the new industry was displacing European steel exports in third markets, especially the United States. Between 1961 and 1971, the European portion of American steel imports fell from 66.6 percent to 47.2 percent; during the same period the Japanese share rose from 21.4 to 39.1 percent. Losing world markets, European utilization rates fell to 78.6 percent in 1966. The resulting deterioration in prices made the European industries the least profitable in the industrialized world.[49]

Although the president of the ECSC complained that there was excess global capacity, due to technological changes and Cold War developmental aid, and suggested some international agreement to moderate production, European nations continued to add to the glut. They nationalized, protected, subsidized, expanded, merged, and cartelized. The EC increased tariffs from 6 to 9 percent, and most countries installed so-called "border taxes." In 1967, the returning Labour government in Britain nationalized and merged fourteen firms to form British Steel. The government provided subsidies for users who bought domestic steel. German companies formed four regional cartels to limit price competition; orders were shared to defend against price cuts. In 1967, the government bailed out Krupp, one of the largest steel producers, when it went bankrupt. The government took over German coal mines and sold coal to the steel companies at the low world price, preserving German mining without penalizing its steel industry, and raised border taxes. In 1966, the French government pledged to supplement the already extensive government aid to two greenfield plants begun in the early 1960s.[50]

Whether governments were successful or not, no steel industry managed the transition from the open hearth to the new BOF technology or confronted the new global market without state aid that included capital and some protection. The American industry was not in so much trouble as the others during the 1960s because it had not expanded so much and was more efficient. But unlike the others, it was expected to execute the transition to the BOF and to confront the new global market without government assistance—relying on its own cash flow and financial markets—and also to keep prices low.

Macroeconomic Policies

At the beginning of the 1960s, American foreign policy did not seem to present obstacles to the American steel industry. A report by economist Robert Livernash, commissioned by Secretary of Labor James P. Mitchell after the 1959 steel strike, concluded that "it does not seem likely that imports will be a much greater factor in United States markets than they were before 1958." Steel imports in 1961 composed only 4.7 percent of the market and these were mainly low-value commodities, like wire.[51]

That government continued to hold that point of view during the 1960s because the U.S. market seemed to be accommodating rising domestic production and rising imports. The mid-decade year, 1965, had been one of record domestic production, 131 million tons. It was also a year of record imports, 10.3 percent. The government viewed the two sets of statistics with some satisfaction. The American market provided space both for domestic growth and for outlets for America's allies. Republican representative Thomas B. Curtis agreed. He acknowledged in 1967 that imports were taking a larger share of the U.S. market, but said he felt confident that "the total pie has increased so much that there is no damage to the industry."[52] But because of the imports, the American steel industry was losing market share even as it increased productivity, which inevitably raised the cost of investment. It was not reaping the full rewards of Keynesian stimulation, an early instance of the way imports would undercut the potency of fiscal policy.

Macroeconomic policy also raised the price of modernization. The CEA's single-minded focus on the dangers of inflation was a classic case of tunnel vision. From the CEA's perspective, steel prices had "a major symbolic importance," they were "a bellwether of inflationary trends." As in the past, labor negotiations were the occasion for action. In the spring of 1965 the CEA prepared a special study on steel prices and wages in order to influence the summer contract talks. The report acknowledged that the industry was not optimistic about its ability to stem rising imports, but the CEA was certain that in the long run the prospect for U.S. steel exports would be brighter. Relevant measures—productivity, costs, and financing—were improving. But the CEA ignored the dynamics of the global industry, the government-sponsored reconstructions, and the role the American market played in the planning of foreign nations.[53]

Armed with CEA forecasts, Johnson brought the union and industry negotiators to Washington and virtually locked them up until they reached an approved settlement. The August wage settlement was close to the guidepost figure of 3.2 percent. Like Kennedy, Johnson thought he had agreement for price stability and was taken aback when Bethlehem raised structural steel prices by 5 percent on December 31, 1965.[54]

The subsequent scenario was not a replay of the Blough-Kennedy confrontation of 1962. On New Year's Day of 1966, Bethlehem officials met with key White House officials in Washington and explained that the rise was necessary to finance a $90 million facility producing lightweight steel. Presidential aide Joseph Califano agreed that "this is perhaps a special case," but added that "[t]he economy is full of 'special cases' which could jeopardize the expansion and impair the war effort." Inland, the maverick company of 1962, and Colorado Fuel and Iron matched the price rise. The government demonstrated its disapproval by ordering federal agencies to buy only lower-priced steel. Five days later, U.S. Steel raised its price half as much as Bethlehem, and balanced it with a $9 reduction on cold rolled steel on the West Coast. U.S. Steel's chief, Roger Blough, who now kept one eye on the market and the other on the government, had come to an unpublicized agreement with Secretary of Defense Robert McNamara. Bethlehem responded by halving its increase, and President Johnson breathed a sigh of relief.[55]

In the labor negotiations of 1968, the CEA again focused on inflation. Though the government now privately acknowledged that steel profit rates had been on the low side in the 1960s, the CEA concluded that "*steel is not a sick industry* with profit rates so low as to threaten its ability to raise capital." Johnson's jawboning was imperfect, but it kept steel prices lower than they would have been without his interventions.[56] In 1968 the union achieved a better package than it had won in 1965; it included a 3.6 percent wage increase, lower than the inflation rate of 5 percent.[57]

The doctrine of steel fundamentalism persisted, but neither steel wages nor steel prices set national patterns during the 1960s, any more than they had in the 1950s. From 1959 to 1972, steel wages increased 16 percent, compared to 21.5 percent in other manufacturing industries. Moreover, the rise in output per man-hour consistently exceeded wage gains, a source of much of the dis-affection among workers in basic steel. At the same time, steel prices rose only 0.45 percent annually, less than rises in the prices of industrial commodities. In the end, Johnson's wage and price policies in steel had little effect on inflation, which was caused by the war spending, excessive stimulation after the various tax cuts of the first half of the decade.[58]

Price restraint did diminish the pool of investment capital, because price in-creases during periods of rising demand was a key source of such funds. The resulting low profit rates, caused also by the modernization program itself, de-pressed stock prices, which in turn made borrowing more costly. The invest-ment tax credit was suspended in 1966 but then restored in 1967 as the econ-omy dipped. Manipulating the tax credit for fiscal purposes was a crude way to practice industrial policy. At a time when European and Japanese governments were restructuring their industries, the American government continued to use the steel industry to regulate the macroeconomy.[59]

Antitrust and Banking

Other nations reduced the costs of modernization through mergers, joint ven-tures, and nationalizations, but the United States continued to pursue compe-tition. Antitrust laws increased the price of modernization and harmed the industry by encouraging conglomerates. The Celler-Kefauver Act of 1950 had raised the hurdles for joint action and outright mergers. Courts were no longer asked to determine whether monopolistic conditions existed but whether a specific merger might in the future create conditions that would weaken com-petition. Judges were asked to be economic forecasters.

In 1962 the Supreme Court followed the legislative script and severely lim-ited the scope for economic rationalization when it ruled that a merger be-tween Kinney Shoe and Brown Shoe Company violated the law. Brown Shoe, the fourth largest manufacturer in the country, held 4 percent of the market; Kinney, the twelfth in manufacturing, had 0.5 percent of the market. Both were also retailers, the third and eighth largest, respectively. Although these figures were not objectionable, the court detected a trend toward vertical inte-gration, which could produce a market dominated by a few big firms. The court voided the marriage, ruling that "[m]ergers were illegal where compe-tition *may* be lessened." It was hard to imagine that any merger could pass that test.

Antitrust law steered courts to the wrong problem. The government and court were convinced that big retailers who also were manufacturers would threaten other producers by keeping their competitors' shoes out of their stores. Alas, the threat to American shoe manufacturers came not from retailers but from cheap, foreign imports; imports produced by American allies in Taiwan and Korea and then by Spain and Brazil decimated American producers.[60]

Brown set antitrust policy for the next twenty years. By prohibiting horizontal and vertical mergers, the government precluded the kind of restructuring going on in Europe and Japan. In the 1960s the steel industry built ten continuous hot strip mills in the United States, none of which operated at full capacity. The overexpansion could have been reduced through joint ventures or some planned growth. Other economies could have been effected by selected mergers to take advantage of the strengths of the new steel-making technologies.[61]

The antitrust tradition, despite its populist rhetoric, was in the end a conservative one. It maintained the illusion that the market and competition would solve industrial questions. It allowed lawyers and courts with narrow agendas and expertise to make economic policy. Moreover, the hard line on traditional mergers led to an unprecedented wave of conglomerate mergers, which harmed the industry. In 1969, Emanuel Celler himself remarked that "the success of the Celler-Kefauver Act, which prevented horizontal and vertical mergers . . . has probably encouraged conglomerates." Historian Alfred Chandler Jr. agreed. The conglomerate, he wrote, did not grow by controlling production or expanding markets. Rather, through acquisition and financial evaluation of diverse and unrelated products—like textiles, toys, and toilets—it managed assets to produce the highest yields. A Nixon-appointed commission, chaired by University of Chicago economist George Stigler, concluded that conglomerate mergers did not have "uncompetitive" consequences. Whether they were good for the economy was an unasked question. Easy disposal of pressed businesses made corporate support for proactive policies less likely.[62]

A record number of conglomerate mergers took place from 1968 to 1972. In 1969, conglomerates accounted for 161 of 192 mergers of firms with assets more than $10 million. Chandler concluded that the new enterprises often appeared in industries faced with international competition. One of the first, Royal Little's Textron abandoned the textile industry, an early victim of imports, and became a conglomerate in 1954.[63] Unlike other countries, where it was not so easy to take over and dismantle corporations, the United States permitted shareholders to seek out the profits of higher-than-market offers and allowed buyers to pay off their debt with tax write-offs. Individual shareholders gained, but long-term corporate planning became more difficult. James Burnham's 1941 classic, *The Managerial Revolution*, was turned on its head; managers proved less powerful than Burnham had predicted. John Kenneth Galbraith's *The New Industrial State*, published in 1967, was more of a swan song to a dying era of production-oriented managers than a description of the future.[64]

Diversification was a minor factor in steel strategies in the 1960s. Companies bought unrelated assets to level the ups and downs of the volatile steel cycle. The conglomerate movement affected steel from the other end. During 1968, five of the top twenty steel companies became targets of conglomerates, attracted by the low market prices and the large cash flow of steel companies.[65]

In 1969, Jones and Laughlin (J&L), the seventh largest steel company, was bought by the conglomerate Ling-Temco-Vought (LTV). Shareholders received $85 for shares whose market value was $50. James J. Ling noted that "the steel industry is the kind of solid operation that we were looking for." Its high cash flow and debt-heavy corporate structure were useful for tax purposes. Like all steel companies, J&L's debt had risen due to heavy investment in the 1960s. Ling thought the purchase was risk-free, saying that the steel industry was "too vital to the national economy for somebody to just let it go down the drain. If nothing else, it would be nationalized—to save it." He admitted that it would have made better economic sense for J&L to merge with another steel company, but antitrust law foreclosed that option.[66]

In the same year, Lykes, a New Orleans–based shipping company, purchased Youngstown Sheet and Tube (YST). The roots of this merger reached back to the Eisenhower years. The low price that attracted Lykes to YST was partly the result of the refusal of the antitrust division to permit YST's merger with Bethlehem in the 1950s. As a result, Bethlehem built its Burns Harbor plant for the midwestern market, and YST built another at Indiana Harbor, which contributed to the overexpansion of the industry in flat-rolled products and to Youngstown's subsequent problems.[67]

Richard McLaren, head of the antitrust division, opposed the Lykes merger. He too believed that the Celler-Kefauver act had fostered conglomerates, which should be subject to the antitrust laws. McLaren had been an antitrust lawyer for old-line corporations, which were often targets of the new acquisition movement. He and his clients looked askance at the new conglomerates. (It must be recalled how novel they seemed in the 1960s.) McLaren concluded that YST would not fare well under Lykes, which had no experience in steel and now had a large debt. His assessment was accurate, but the antitrust laws were about competition, not competence. It would be hard to argue that the purchase would lessen competition in the steel industry. Attorney General John Mitchell overrode his antitrust division and approved the merger. McLaren did sue LTV, perhaps because James Ling was such a big operator, and in 1970 forced the conglomerate to divest itself of two of its units, but not J&L. By then LTV was in trouble, the result of Ling's ambitions, not McLaren's.[68]

The conglomerates were midwifed by an American banking system, divorced from production.[69] The two steel mergers were about one thing only—financial profits. Responding to the chicaneries of an unregulated banking system, the Glass-Steagall Act, passed in 1933, prohibited commercial banks from underwriting securities. This separation, contrasting sharply with foreign practice, effectively limited the stake that banks had in American industry. The divorce also limited the bankers' knowledge of the industries they financed. Decisions were based upon short-term considerations, facilitated by the growth of "price banking," which began to replace the more regulated, relational banking of the past. Shareholder democracy spawned a new industry of acquisition bankers. As more competition entered the investment banking industry, because the law no longer fixed commissions, white-shoe investment banks were forced to hustle for business. Often the only profits were those produced by the transactions themselves. The banks and the current shareholders of YST and J&L benefited from the deal—no one else. Even when the bloom was off the conglomerate rose, the practices infected corporate practice.

The best example of the combined impact of American trade, antitrust laws, and macroeconomic policy during the 1960s was the fate of the western steel industry. In 1972, when imports comprised 17 percent of the American market, they represented 37 percent of western consumption. During the 1960s, U.S. Steel, Bethlehem, Armco, and National Steel had all considered constructing new coastal steelworks in the San Francisco area. Bethlehem purchased an ideal 1,800-acre tract in September 1963. Two months later, its new president, Stewart S. Cort, warned of dumped imports on the West Coast. Neither Bethlehem, nor any of the others made the investment.[70]

The darling of New Dealers, Kaiser Steel, failed to retain this market from its outpost in southern California. Determined to industrialize the West and break Big Steel's domination of the industry, Ernest Kaiser constructed a steel mill in Fontana, California, with a loan from the Reconstruction Finance Corporation during World War II. Kaiser's entrepreneurial imagination always required government backing, and New Deal policy was to foster new entrants in steel. But he failed to break into the auto market after the war precisely because he lacked state help. Now without government support, Kaiser Steel failed to hold the West.

In 1967 Kaiser contemplated expanding its steelmaking capacity, responding to the buoyant western market. But the company was concerned about the flood of imports coming into the region. In the same year, with the rest of the steel industry, it sought a temporary quota on imports. As we shall see later in this chapter, the industry failed to obtain relief. Instead, Kaiser decided to spend $51 million to develop coalfields in British Columbia for the Mitsubishi trading company, which represented seven major Japanese steel companies.

The U.S. government had looked into the Canadian decision in early 1968 when President Johnson was concerned about the U.S. overall balance of payments. Kaiser convinced the Commerce Department that the transaction would involve "no immediate dollar outflow." That ended the matter, because Johnson was uninterested in what the company produced. When Kaiser's finances faltered in 1971, Mitsubishi rushed in with credit for the Canadian mining operations. While Kaiser developed coal, Japanese producers sold steel to western U.S. users. In 1974 Kaiser contracted with Mitsubishi to import the semifinished steel Kaiser could no longer produce. Kaiser abandoned the steel business in 1983.[71]

The ups and downs of Kaiser Steel demonstrate that the incentives to which all companies must respond are constructed by states. After the war, American trade policies, dominated by strategic political considerations, permitted other nations to configure the incentives for U.S. steel production. Japanese trade and industrial policies facilitated imports of the raw materials it needed to make steel, and Kaiser responded. It was not only steel. The United States was providing the inputs for a variety of Japanese industrial sectors. In 1976, raw materials composed more than 60 percent of U.S. exports to Japan.[72]

It was not simply Kaiser that was affected. The West Coast situation affected the entire industry. Bethlehem's Sparrows Point plant and the Fairless Works of U.S. Steel were partially West Coast plants. (They shipped steel via low-cost bottoms through the Panama Canal.) In 1962, Kaiser had tried to meet the import challenge by dropping prices. The move did not help Kaiser, but its first effect was to exclude East Coast plants from western markets. We have seen that U.S. Steel reduced its western prices in 1966, but there were limits to how low they could go. As a result, U.S. Steel and Bethlehem suddenly had excess capacity, which heated up competition in the East and then spilled over to the Midwest.[73] For the industry as a whole, U.S. trade, fiscal, and foreign policies increased the costs of steel modernization at a time when American efficiency was being matched by foreign competitors that were supported by their governments.

Steel Modernization

Many who have written about the American steel industry ignore or downplay state policies and the institutional arrangements of American economic life; instead, they attribute steel's behavior primarily to the industry's oligopolistic structure.[74] The assumption, a corollary of antitrust doctrine, is that structure determines behavior. Those on the right indict oligopoly because they believe that only the whip of competition yields progress. The left attack on oligopoly stems from the left's general opposition to big business and occasional prefer-

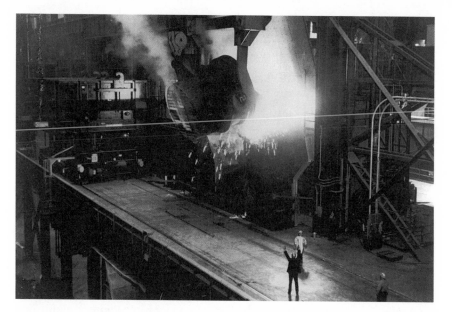

Man with raised hands is signaling the craneman to lift and tilt the hot metal transfer ladle to pour molten iron into the mouth of the basic oxygen furnace. (Courtesy of Hagley Museum and Library)

ence for small enterprise. But the steel industries in all nations were oligopolies when they were not state-owned. Nevertheless, the structural argument cannot be dismissed out of hand, because it is a staple of the American literature. Critics claimed that because the U.S. industry was an oligopoly, it was slow to adopt the basic oxygen furnace (BOF). Unconcerned with improvement, the industry committed itself in the 1950s to expanding open hearth facilities at a time when steelmaking was about to be revolutionized.[75]

The open hearth furnace was used all over the world in the 1950s because it refined a wider range of pig irons for a wider range of steels than alternative furnaces. But the productivity of the open hearth was relatively low, the costs of construction were high, and economical operation depended upon low prices for scrap metal, an essential ingredient. Scientists everywhere attempted to improve the process. The BOF was developed by two, small, government-owned, Austrian firms in the early 1950s. It reduced fuel and labor costs and was cheaper to build than the open hearth. Steelmaking in the new BOF began with a lance of oxygen shot through the top of the furnace. The pure oxygen created a violent chemical reaction that maintained the heat in the furnace, so that additional fuel was unnecessary. The BOF produced a batch of steel in less than one hour; the open hearth required six to twelve hours.

Initially, the BOF was not widely used. It was untested in large-scale operations, emitted large amounts of reddish-brown pollutants, and worked best with the kind of ore used by Austrian firms. Even the few small firms that employed the BOF did not view it as the wave of the future. Other companies, including U.S. Steel, were experimenting with other technologies.[76] At the beginning of 1957, after five years of successful commercial operation, there were still only four BOFs in the world. None was used by a major firm. New open hearths were still being constructed.

Leonard H. Lynn's study of Japanese and American companies concluded that the decision to adopt the BOF technology was unrelated to the industry's structure. Indeed, if the critics are correct, Japan should have been a laggard, because its steel industry was more concentrated than the American. Actually, the concentration helped the Japanese. Because Japanese manufacturers bought raw materials from the same trading firms, they faced the same technical problems with the BOF.[77]

Japan's MITI began advocating the BOF in 1957 at the onset of its steel expansion, at the time that American expansion encouraged by the Korean war was completed. The Japanese decision had little to do with corporate structure but much to do with scrap. Because the BOF required no scrap, companies that had difficulty acquiring scrap—and Japanese companies in general—were eager to pursue the technology. (This also explains why the electric furnace, another economical means of producing steel but one that is completely dependent upon scrap, was slow to come to Japan.) Japan's attempt to free itself from scrap was reinforced by historical memory—the American embargo of scrap exports in 1937.[78]

McLouth Steel, the first American firm to employ the BOF, installed it after a round of scrap price increases in 1954. The Detroit firm was able to use the BOF because its small size matched the technology's current capability and because the company was financed by General Motors, which required more steel for the growing auto market. Jones and Laughlin, one of the oldest and least efficient firms, became the first major American steelmaker to use the BOF in 1957. The most productive firm, Inland, built a BOF only in 1966. There was little relationship between efficiency, structure, and the adoption of BOF.[79]

Lynn concluded that Japanese companies possessed more BOF capacity during the 1960s because they built most of their steelmaking capacity after the BOF was established as the best technology. But once the BOF was established as the state-of-the-art process, Lynn found that the United States adopted it more quickly than the Japanese, Europeans, and Canadians. The recession of the late 1950s and early 1960s depressed steel investment in the United States. But beginning in 1962, the American industry invested rapidly, using funds from the tax credit, the profits from higher operating rates, and new borrowing. Be-

A bin of auto scrap for use in this minimill's electric furnace, seen in background. There are over 300 classifications of scrap, the main ingredient for the furnace, and each must be segregated in different bins. The end product determines what kind of scrap is fed into the furnace. (Courtesy of Hagley Museum and Library)

tween 1960 and 1970, the amount of American steel produced by the BOF increased from 3.4 to 50 percent. If one adds the 15.3 percent produced by another efficient process, the electric furnace, only one-third of American steel was produced by open hearth by decade's end. And contrary to oligopoly theory, U.S. Steel was a leader here. By 1973, U.S. Steel was using efficient methods to produce 85 percent of its steel.[80] Between 1964 and 1968, steel spending on BOFs and other new technology totaled $9 billion, which was more than all the steel plants were worth at the start of 1964. National Steel's president, G. A. Stinson, told stockholders that increasing labor costs and price restraints "will be a continuing way of life." American steelmakers thought that technical advances would be the answer to the cost and price squeeze they all faced.[81]

With the exception of Bethlehem's Burns Harbor plant, none of the BOF investments were part of new, completely modernized plants. Companies upgraded existing plants, which meant that layouts were not optimal. The Europeans also possessed much open hearth capacity, but European companies received large amounts of government capital for building new plants. Stinson noted that foreign steelmakers "don't seem to be concerned about borrowing. They can go to their governments."[82] Because much of Japan's prewar industry had been destroyed by the war, its companies did not have so much capacity to replace. MITI's provision of capital and infrastructure and its allocation of production quotas enabled Japanese companies to build greenfield mills. Still, it was not until 1972 that Japan matched U.S. productivity.[83]

American capital and construction costs were high. The Kennedy-Johnson tax reductions enabled the industry to increase capital expenditures from $1 billion a year in the early 1960s to $2.3 billion in 1968, 25 percent more than during the 1950s. But the cost of adding one ton of integrated steel capacity was $85 in Japan, $399 in the United States. The untargeted investment credit and tax reduction had rapidly accelerated investment in the United States, at a rate double and triple the growth of the GNP. The unusual demand for capital goods bid up the prices. In steel, the increase was burdensome because capacity remained constant and the industry did not capture all of the increased consumption because of imports. Thus, the industry faced increased capital costs per unit.[84]

Other critics of the industry, conceding that American efficiency in the 1960s still was the highest in the world, indict its pricing policies. But foreign steel, despite higher costs, often sold more cheaply than domestic steel in the United States. The sale of foreign steel in the United States was well below costs of production. Obviously, if a firm does not meet fixed costs, it will not be able to stay in business, but foreign firms maintained a two-price system, one for their closed domestic market and another for sales abroad. In 1967 and 1968, Japanese producers sold a ton of sheet steel for $116 dollars at home; in the United States the same ton cost $96 in 1967 and $86 in 1968, despite the additional costs of moving steel across the ocean. Sometimes the purpose was to increase market share; at other times, marginal cost prices aimed to maintain employment at home, fund fixed debts, or achieve other domestic purposes. Fulfilling all of these goals, however, required an open U.S. market. The critics of U.S. companies did not recognize that U.S. steelmakers could not compete with below-cost prices of foreign steel, much less accumulate capital for modernization under these conditions. No other steel-producing nation encouraged price competition in domestic markets.[85]

But the United States was oriented now toward consumer benefits, not the difficulties of producers. The government successfully wooed the big auto and machinery makers, the consumers of steel. This was possible because in the United States, unlike in Japan and Europe, steel companies were not part of industrial empires. Typically, Joseph Califano announced that presidential jawboning in 1968, which had reduced a steel price increase from 7.0 to 2.5 percent, had saved consumers $550 million. If foreign governments wanted to subsidize low prices for their products in the United States, so the argument went, let them. The auto companies, for instance, and the American consumer would benefit. This moral economy formed the basis of a Consumers Union suit challenging a voluntary restraint agreement (VRA), which limited steel imports during the early 1970s. Although the court upheld the government's power, it is impossible to imagine such a suit being filed in Japan or in Europe.[86]

Import Restraints

The Consumers Union suit challenged the one new element in American steel policy—the containment of imports. Johnson and then Nixon negotiated "voluntary" agreements to limit the rate of the increase of imports, not the amount of imports. Thus, the Cold War's open market blueprint remained. Because the temporary measures were designed merely to neutralize opposition to the policy, they did not strengthen the steel industry.

Throughout the 1950s, the AISI saw its main challenge as coming from competing materials—aluminum, plastics, etc. In 1962, the industry began to notice "dumped imported steel products," and in 1963 Blough complained to Kennedy about the problem. The turning point came in late 1964 when the AISI abolished its Committee on Foreign Relations, which arranged tours and training for foreign steelmakers, and created a Committee on International Trade. Just in time. Beginning in 1965, sheet steel, the product of mature Japanese and European finishing facilities, invaded the heart of steel country, the Great Lakes area, via the St. Lawrence seaway. Imports of hot rolled sheet steel, the bread-and-butter of the industry, jumped from 5.3 percent in 1964 to 14.7 percent in 1965. The industry was rightly "pessimistic" about obtaining relief at the current Kennedy Round negotiations. At the end of the talks, the world steel tariff was lowered to 6 percent; it had been 7 percent in the United States and about 9 percent in the EEC. The genuine issues in steel were not these numbers but nontariff barriers that the U.S. government refused to tackle.[87] Even before the talks ended, L. B. Worthington, chairman of the AISI, urged a temporary tariff in February 1966, which was permitted under the GATT for unusual situations. European nations had limited steel imports through various taxes and tariffs as they had restructured.[88]

Although the AISI was not wild about public hearings, Senator Vance Hartke of Indiana held Finance Committee hearings on steel imports in June. Unlike President Kennedy, who had been concerned with the impact of the steel trade on the U.S. balance of payments deficit, Hartke addressed the impact of imports on U.S. employment, even though the jobless rate was falling: "What we have is full employment of skilled personnel. We still have a vast reservoir of unskilled and potentially developing personnel which could be utilized. If those people were trained, and that 30 million tons [imports] were produced here, it would provide an opportunity for 180,000 jobs." Trying to make the War on Poverty more potent, he added: "Without jobs the training led to little."[89]

President Johnson was no more happy about the steel hearings than he had been in January when Hartke sent him a letter signed by fifteen other Democrats urging him to suspend bombing in Vietnam. Fred Smith, general counsel of the Treasury Department, repeated the CEA's belief that "the improvement in the competitive situation of the United States steel industry will be dependent . . . upon the relative success of our efforts to hold down costs and prices in our domestic economy." Smith was confident the U.S. steel industry "can outproduce and outsell producers anywhere else in the world. We always have been able to, and I think we will." Hartke retorted that "this sort of blind faith in the American competitive position is what leads us to some of our troubles. . . . I am not one who thinks that God gave us any special right to live in a prosperous economy without giving some thought and some idea to it."[90]

Dean Peterson of the steel division of the Commerce Department urged the industry "to make more vigorous efforts than heretofore to expand markets abroad" but said he did not know of any efforts that negotiators at the current Kennedy Round negotiations were making to open up European markets. Peterson was unable to explain why the costs of freight, import duty, and transaction tax for a ton of cold rolled sheet coming from France into the United States was $42, while the costs for an identical ton from the United States to France was $82.20. He claimed to know little about the cartelization of the European steel industry, but admitted, "we . . . do have information that the Belgian Government had given the steel industry some low-interest loans in the past." In fact, Belgium had just formed a tripartite industry-labor-government group to devise a general investment program for the steel industry, complete with public funds. Belgium was the third largest importer into the United States, behind Japan and West Germany.[91]

Hartke obtained no support from his colleagues in 1966. Johnson opposed a government study, so the best Hartke could do was get senators to commission one. The 523-page report, prepared by Professor Robert Widenhammer of the University of Pittsburgh, was released in December 1967. It opposed the industry's goal of a temporary levy to raise the price of imports to the domestic level but concluded that "some responsible, short-term measure along these lines may be the prod needed to cause the steel producing nations of the world to join together in an effort to solve the problems of world steel in a manner calculated to serve the best interests of all of them." If European and Japanese planned expansions continued, he concluded, the steel surplus would escalate, and end up in the U.S. market.[92]

The government strongly opposed sectoral negotiations, which undercut its power to trade concessions in steel for export access in other sectors.[93] As we have seen, the U.S. strategy during the Kennedy Round was to reduce U.S. rates on manufactured goods in exchange for reduced European rates in agriculture, even though American negotiators failed to obtain significant access for U.S. exports. It is important to remember that in trade negotiations nations draw up lists of products whose rates they are prepared to reduce at home and lists of other products whose rates they seek to reduce abroad. Thus, a willingness to reduce U.S. steel rates does not ensure that the government would seek to reduce the rates in another country. But a sectoral negotiation would seek to harmonize the behavior of all the major steel exporters. Implicitly it would "manage" trade, which undercut the U.S. government's free trade ideology. In 1967, Johnson condemned both the proposed steel quota bill plus many others offered in the wake of the trade pact, as inflationary: "They're not going to become law as long as I am president." But the government was on the defensive.[94] Reaction to the round was negative. Like Hartke, George Baldanzi of the United Textile Workers worried about the impact of low U.S. textile rates on American workers, particularly blacks entering the industry: "What the hell good are we doing for this country or for world peace by exporting jobs to Taiwan or Hong Kong?" The failure to reduce European agriculture rates provided no political support to counter the industrial sector's opposition to the round. Congressman Odin Langen charged that the U.S. farmer had been "sold out." Hartke said the Kennedy Round amounted to "unilateral disarmament."[95]

The beneficiaries of government policy came to the rescue. With presidential prodding, David Rockefeller assembled the leaders of big banks and transnationals—Lehman Brothers, Chase Manhattan, Bank of America, IBM, Xerox, Time, Texas Instruments, General Motors, Boeing—to form the Emergency Committee for American Trade (ECAT). As it turned out, the emergency persisted, and ECAT remains the American guardian of open trade and investment. But in 1967, ECAT thought it could secure free trade once and for all with an attack on managing the steel trade. On November 17, ECAT placed a full-page advertisement in the *Wall Street Journal* opposing both steel quotas and a global steel agreement, charging that it would jeopardize $30 billion in foreign sales and raise prices for consumers. The government's opposition to international steel talks was amply fortified.[96]

The Europeans were equally uninterested in quotas or a global steel agreement and proposed only a ten-year study by the steel committee of the OECD. They were reconstructing their steel industries and did not want outsiders prying into the ways they limited steel imports, subsidized enterprises, and promoted exports. The combined opposition of the American government, transnational corporations, Europeans, and Japanese—all satisfied with the status quo—guaranteed that global steel problems would not be tackled.[97]

There it stood until the 1968 statistics began registering. Imports reached 18 percent that year. A five-year quota bill, rolling back imports to the 9.6 percent figure of 1964–66, now had thirty-five cosponsors in the Senate. To keep control of trade policy, Assistant Secretary of State Anthony Solomon initiated talks with the Japanese and Europeans, who feared that the proposed restrictions would destroy their expansion plans. They offered to limit the rate of increased imports, not to reduce them or even maintain the status quo. Even so, the U.S. government had dual goals. Solomon put off clinching the deal in August because the CEA and Nicholas Katzenbach, now in the State Department, wanted to use the carrot of a trade agreement to deter domestic price increases. Bethlehem had just raised prices 5 percent and the government wanted to prevent the rest of the industry from following suit. It worked, and price rises were reduced. On January 4, 1969, the administration signed a voluntary restraint agreement with the Japanese and Europeans to limit increases to 5 percent above previous imports for three years. Temporary VRAs put out domestic fires without damaging the trading order that so many American administrations had labored to construct.[98]

The industry thought the VRA was "unsatisfactory." "We can't plan our investments . . . on this basis," said a U.S. Steel official. Philip D. Block, chairman of Inland Steel, added, "I want something I can count on." Moreover, the rate of permissible increase was twice the annual average increase in U.S. steel consumption. The industry went along because the votes for quotas were not there. Having lost the public opinion wars of the early 1960s, steelmen lacked a reservoir of goodwill to draw upon. They had trouble deciding among themselves what measure would work. They did believe that the agreement would add 3 or 4 million more tons to domestic production. With selective price-cutting and a lot of investment, the industry thought it could reverse current trends.[99]

The self-confidence was bolstered by new steel leadership. In December 1968, U.S. Steel replaced chairman Roger Blough with Edwin H. Gott, who had come up through the production route, unlike recent officers, who were recruits from the financial or legal departments. With Gott as chairman and another production man, Edgar Speer, as president, the top men were investment hawks. Other companies made similar personnel choices.[100] Yet new men in other companies viewed the future differently. John Lobb of Crucible Steel said, "if imports keep coming in, the rules of the game have to change." To Lobb, foreign investment, the route taken in other industries, was "not very interesting because you're competing with a nationalized industry." Crucible had tried it in Italy. Lobb still thought his company could improve its margins, but if Crucible could not earn a satisfactory return, he would have to ask, "[h]ow much more should you put in?"[101]

Steel in the Nixon Years

Investment hawks had little to cheer about during the first Nixon administration. The slowing of the economy in 1969 and repeal of the investment tax credit reduced profits.[102] In 1970, net earnings plummeted 43 percent, the worst performance since 1939, and returns on investment shrank to 2.8 percent. Capital spending, the lifeblood of resurrection, dropped to $1.6 billion, the lowest since 1964. By 1972, the year that the Japanese matched U.S. efficiency, investment fell to $1.1 billion. Had the investment levels of the 1960s been sustained, the industry could have invested more rapidly in the crucial continuous caster, which eliminated the reheating and cooling required to transform molten steel to final shapes.[103]

Like his predecessors, Nixon publicly monitored steel prices, at first. But the decision to institute comprehensive wage and price controls in late 1971 made it unnecessary to invoke steel fundamentalism, the symbolic politics of previous presidents. The controls weighed heavily on industry, not on rising raw material and agricultural prices. While steel prices were restrained, the price of scrap rose 153 percent, zinc 250 percent, and fuel 244 percent between early 1973 and 1974. The controls were accompanied by fiscal expansion, which artificially pumped up the economy before the 1972 elections. None of this helped steel investment, nor did it help the economy.[104]

Despite the VRAs, imports rose to 17.9 percent in 1971, the year of the nation's first merchandise trade deficit. Domestic steel production declined by 3.7 million tons while imports increased by more than 5 million. Predictably, the VRAs had permitted Japan and Europe to increase their imports by 5 percent even though domestic steel consumption grew only 2.1 percent. The agreements did not limit the imports of Great Britain and the rest of the world and were evaded easily. Thus, Nixon negotiated new VRAs in 1971, which would last through 1974. They included Britain, limited the increase of imports to 2.5 percent, and plugged some of the holes of the first VRAs.[105]

External factors kept the lid on imports more than the new VRAs. Because the American market was more open than others, it was affected more strongly by the oscillations of the international business cycles. In 1971, a year of recession abroad, steel came to the United States. The next year steel was channeled away by the Nixon price controls, rising prices elsewhere, and the effects of dollar devaluation. The boom in 1973–74 led all producers to concentrate on domestic markets, so the import tide receded. The VRAs lapsed just before the 1975 downturn.

Because the government looked at the import statistics, not the dynamics of the global steel industry, it thought the trade problem was solved. The industry knew better and continued to advocate sectoral negotiations. The steel in-

"Torching" (cutting) a continuously cast slab of steel. The caster eliminates many of the stages of cooling and reheating as molten steel is transformed into the shapes required by different products. (Courtesy of Hagley Museum and Library)

dustry's goals were compromised by its professions of free enterprise but call for action on imports. The AISI opposed capital controls, but it liked the quota provisions of Burke-Hartke. It wanted quotas but, judging them impossible to effect, settled for VRAS. The VRAS won the industry the protectionist label without the benefits of protection.[106]

Containing Imports through Labor Relations

Unable to move the government, the steel industry hoped to limit imports through labor agreements. Through most of the 1960s, the USWA's major concern was the impact of technological change, not imports, on jobs. The union understood that the BOF was the only way the industry could remain competitive. The BOF not only used fewer workers on each furnace but required fewer furnaces. Two BOFS replaced ten open hearths at the J&L plant in Cleveland, Ohio. When U.S. Steel installed a different kind of oxygen furnace, one using the Q-BOF process, in Fairfield, it replaced twelve. The only way that increased productivity could benefit workers was if the steel market grew. Ignoring foreign inroads initially, the union expended most of its political capital supporting fiscal and monetary policies that promoted domestic growth.[107]

The USWA had supported Kennedy's Trade Expansion Act. Only glassware, hat, and leather unions had opposed it.[108] The labor movement had insisted that extra unemployment compensation, "adjustment assistance," be made available to workers who lost their jobs as a result of trade concessions. The idea was David McDonald's.[109]

McDonald had been appointed to a blue-ribbon commission President Eisenhower had appointed in 1953 to consider foreign economic policies. Headed by Clarence B. Randall, chairman of Inland Steel, the group had weighed in for liberal trade. Inland, located in the Chicago heartland, was at that time well insulated from foreign competition. In his minority report, McDonald had suggested financial assistance to workers, firms, and communities injured by tariff reduction. Although the commission rejected what was considered a radical idea at the time, Senators Kennedy, Humphrey, and Douglas endorsed it. In 1962, President Kennedy accepted the provision, over the opposition of the Chamber of Commerce and the National Association of Manufacturers, as the political price to be paid for tariff reduction. His own view was that the increased economic activity coming from trade would absorb any dislocation.[110]

That overall judgment explained why the U.S. Tariff Commission found that no worker in any industry was eligible for assistance until late 1969. We have seen that during the King demonstrations, the USWA had presented the case of Alabama ore miners whose jobs ended in 1962 when U.S. Steel began importing ore from Venezuela. In this instance, the tariff reduction had been negotiated bilaterally in 1952. With assurances that the ore could enter the United States tariff-free, the corporation had developed the mines. The tariff commission, requiring iron-clad proof of cause and effect, disagreed, and it adopted the same philosophy in subsequent cases. In 1967, Meyer Bernstein, the union's international affairs head who tracked global developments, concluded that the "[dislocation] provision turned out to be a dead letter." Congress liberalized criteria and expanded benefits only in 1974.[111]

Bernstein epitomized the union's frustration with internationalism. A graduate of Cornell, he had become a volunteer union organizer in the steel campaign in 1936 and after combat service in World War II became assistant director of research. During the 1950s he had worked with German metal worker unions and cultivated ties with unions all over the world. Bernstein opposed the industry's temporary levy in 1966, but his knowledge of the global industry raised some troubling issues.[112] The reason for increased steel imports was not lower foreign wages. During the 1960s, European wage increases exceeded productivity growth, while in the United States they stayed below the 4.1 percent gains in productivity. Rather, the American users of foreign steel tended to be those with operations abroad, which suggested that tie-ins, not market decisions, were driving import purchases. Moreover, European social policies discouraged layoffs when demand fell. Steel companies had every incentive to produce fully and then "dump abroad." Bernstein knew that the EEC restricted American steel. He warned German unionists, who had seats at the managerial table, to urge German steel companies to limit their exports to the United States.[113]

At a meeting of the International Metalworkers Federation in 1967, Bernstein asked for support for a proposal to harmonize U.S. steel imports with domestic production through international agreement. The UAW's Victor Reuther rushed to the podium and denounced the USWA proposal as "blatant protectionism." Bernstein deflected Reuther but was disturbed that the European metalworkers did not comprehend that their exports were causing or could cause any difficulty in the United States. The German unionists, he concluded, despite their socialist professions, were close to industry and "maintained that they had a God-given right to export to us."[114] However, Bernstein still accepted the role of the American market in stabilizing world steel production. He told a convention of Japanese steelworkers that "imports do not hurt us when they simply share in a growing market." It was when domestic production declined that they were troublesome.[115] That happened in 1967.

The combination of the domestic decline in steel consumption, caused by the economic slowdown in the United States, and the rise in imports from 10.9 percent to 12.2 percent transformed Bernstein. He now warned Abel that it would be "irresponsible for us to wait until the foreseeable crisis is upon us." Though Bernstein still hoped for international solutions, he informed his friend Willi Michels, head of the steel department of the metalworkers union of Germany, that in the "absence of any firm call for an international steel conference, we shall continue to press for passage of the Vanik Bill [steel quota bill]."[116]

Thus, USWA vice president Joseph P. Molony, testifying before the Senate Finance Committee, supported quotas. Molony hoped that reasonable limitation of access to the American market would moderate the growth of world steel capacity, which was increasing rapidly everywhere but in the United States. Still, he was a little defensive. He acknowledged that some might consider the quota "protectionist" but that it was temporary measure "to allow the malady of over-capacity in world production to adjust itself."[117]

As we have seen, Johnson negotiated the VRAS to undercut the support for quotas. When the assistant secretary of state for economic affairs outlined the plan to him, Bernstein was appalled that "diplomats couldn't multiply," pointing out that the 5 percent permissible growth in imports was double the increase in U.S. consumption. If the rate continued, the Japanese and Europeans would have as large a share of the market as U.S. producers. Bernstein foresaw a future where Japan would buy raw materials in the United States and ship steel back in return. The State Department had informed President Johnson of

Meyer Bernstein addresses delegates of Tekkō Rōren, the Japanese steelworkers' union, at their convention in September 1964. The large sign in the background states the union's key demands: that wages be increased to western standards before the industry rationalizes production and that (U.S.) nuclear-powered submarines be banned from Japanese ports. (Courtesy of HCLA, Penn State)

USWA opposition to the VRA, and Johnson made one of his legendary personal appeals to I. W. Abel, who acquiesced. When Bernstein spelled out the implications, Abel, who had not yet fully assimilated trade issues, said "Well, I'll be damned." [118]

Under the VRAS, imports could increase during America recessions, as they did in 1967, and recessions were still the USWA's key concern. They rose, too, during the years of labor negotiations. The memory of the 1959 strike lived on, even though it was the last industrywide stoppage of the century. Imports rose in contract years, as steel users sought protection from a walkout. In order to secure foreign steel, purchasers sometimes had to commit themselves to future orders. The first surge of imports entered during the four-month strike in 1959. The fear of a steel strike in 1965 contributed to the 66 percent import increase from 1964 to 1965 and to the same increase from 1967 to 1968, another contract year. In the contract year 1971, imports rose to an all-time high, 17.9 percent of the U.S. market. [119]

The industry was well aware of this pattern. In 1967 it proposed a no-strike agreement, prodded by the threat that major steel consumers would place massive orders with foreign firms unless they could be assured that there would be no strike in 1968. Abel had agreed in principle, but demanded a price for giving up the right to strike: a minimum 3 percent wage increase in each year of the contract and reinstatement of the cost-of-living clause that had been removed in the 1962 contract. The union's interest in the proposal stemmed from the import problem and the "boom-bust" cycles that surrounded negotiations. As the expiration date of contracts approached, customers would stockpile steel as insurance against a strike. These buildups raised costs, because companies brought marginal facilities into production and paid overtime wages. After each agreement, customers would draw from bloated inventories and steelworkers would be laid off for several months. (We saw in Chapter 5 how these layoffs fostered the racial leapfrogging that plagued Sparrows Point.) The USWA insisted that workers were entitled to share the gains that companies would reap by eliminating these extra costs. The industry refused in 1967 but agreed in 1973, because it was seeking uninterrupted operations during that boomtime. That year production reached 151 million tons, and the industry realized its highest utilization since 1951. Workers accepted the Experimental Negotiating Agreement (ENA), with some notable exceptions, in part because the country was still under a form of wage control and because they had gained the right to strike on local issues.[120]

Thus, the industry and the union were guardedly optimistic at the end of 1974. The consent decrees promised to end civil rights conflicts; the ENA provided some insurance against one source of imports; and steel production had held up in 1974 despite the oil price rises in the fall of 1973. Investment topped $2 billion in 1974, reversing the lull of the early Nixon years. The industry was optimistic about the growth of world steel demand. It believed that the new trade advisory committees created by the Trade Act of 1974 would convince the government to embark upon the sectoral negotiations it had sought for ten years.[121]

The union had added imports to its agenda but also the productivity question, the legacy of the Burke-Hartke effort. In 1971, the year of the negative merchandise trade deficit, Abel's two assistants Bruce Thrasher and James W. Smith began tracking productivity. Thrasher asked, in 1972, "why, after the 16-billion dollar capital spending in the sixties is productivity in the steel industry barely higher than it was in 1965?" Smith and Thrasher continued to worry about the long-range problem of expanding American steel capacity, given existing interest rates. These questions started the USWA down a new road that they had not mapped. However, for the nation as a whole, the boom of 1973–74 buried the productivity questions and the shortcomings of U.S. policies that had taken center stage briefly in 1971.[122]

NINE

The Locomotive Loses Power:

Jimmy Carter's Industrial

and Trade Policies

Industry confidence in 1973 and 1974 was built upon a solid foundation of steel orders. Many businessmen and investors even feared that the nation was short of industrial capacity. In March 1973, U.S. Steel president Edgar Speer assured the nation that the industry possessed sufficient capacity to fill foreseeable demand. The industry, operating at 97 percent of capacity, shipped a record 151 million tons during that year. But after the Israeli-Arab war in October, OPEC nations quadrupled crude oil prices.[1] Steel output declined slightly to 146 million in 1974, but tumbled to 117 million tons, 74.5 percent of capacity, in 1975. Still, *Fortune* crowned the American industry "king among the crippled." The Japanese operated at 68.2 percent and the Europeans 64.0 percent of capacity.[2]

As steel went, so went the nation and most of the world. Expensive oil precipitated an international inflation, which was quickly followed by an international recession. Higher energy costs siphoned wealth from industrial nations to oil-producing nations, causing the severest downturn since the 1930s. In the United States, the GNP fell 7.5 percent in the last quarter of 1974, and a year later unemployment hit 9 percent.

When growth resumed, it was tepid. From 1974 to 1980, GNP in the United States grew 2.8 percent annually; from 1950 to 1973, it had advanced 3.9 percent each year. Germany's growth rate was 2.7, falling from 6.3; Japan's 4.9 percent was much better than the others, but it had dropped from 9.8 percent. The United Kingdom and Italy did even worse. Despite the poor economic performance, prices rose everywhere. The editors of *Business Week* observed that the government was faced with "the necessity of doing something that never has been done before: It must fight inflation and recession simultaneously." Although American inflation rates were lower than those of every industrialized country but Germany, they rose from an average of 2.4 percent in the 1960s to 7.0 percent in the 1970s.[3]

From the perspective of the 1990s, the crisis challenged many of the arrangements of the postwar world and sharpened conflicts between domestic and international economics goals that had been manageable during the years of global growth. But at the time most U.S. policymakers considered the 1974–75 recession a pause, not the end of the era of postwar growth. *Fortune*'s observation about the relative well-being of the U.S. steel industry was applied to the economy as a whole. The growth rate rebounded to 4.4 percent in 1976, and the inflation rate fell to 3 percent. The jobless rate was still 7.8, but it was down from the highs of 1975.

In 1977 President Jimmy Carter feared the fragility of the world, not the U.S. economy. The relatively unknown, southern governor became president in a very close election, due as much to the lingering effects of Watergate as to the unemployment rate. Even when confronted with a domestic steel crisis in the fall of 1977, the Carter administration doctored the world economy, not the domestic one.[4]

The Economic Policies of the Carter Administration

Like the policies of previous presidents, Jimmy Carter's steel policy was a corollary of his macroeconomic and foreign policies. The first aimed to reduce inflation, where steel always had a role; the second, increasing imports, also had a history in steel, but had been revised in the recent past. Carter returned to the early postwar policies of encouraging steel imports.

The president's temper reinforced his policies. Carter possessed the personal frugality that made him a natural inflation-fighter. He acknowledged the popular base of his party with a $31.6 billion stimulus, composed of tax cuts and some public service jobs. But on March 24, before the ink was dry on the package, Carter warned about the inflation danger, even though U.S. rates were lower than those of other industrialized nations. The engines driving this inflation were energy, food, hospital, and housing costs. Nearly 90 percent of the changes in the CPI from 1977 to 1980 can be accounted for by energy and housing items.[5] As Carter struggled to obtain energy legislation, he continued to pursue traditional anti-inflation policies—jawboning and wage and price standards—aimed at industrial America. Like many southerners, Carter believed that inflation was caused by monopolistic structures. Thus, he supported deregulating industries, like airlines and trucking, to lower prices. In the case of telecommunications, deregulation opened the U.S. market to foreign equipment manufacturers, but Carter's negotiators failed to ask for reciprocity.[6] Encouraging competition and encouraging imports were policies cut from the same cloth. The battle against inflation only added another purpose to Carter's trade policy.[7]

Special Trade Representative Robert S. Strauss recalled that Carter was "almost puritanical" in his opposition to "protectionism" and had conjured up "visions of Senate conspiracies to make a protectionist of me, and in turn, out of him." Carter's convictions reinforced the strategic goals of his foreign policy. These were imported from David Rockefeller's Trilateral Commission, a private organization of leading figures from Japan, Europe, and the United States that Carter had joined as he prepared to win the Democratic nomination for president. He chose the commission's director, Zbigniew Brzezinski, to head his National Security Council. Brzezinski believed that Americans had three tasks: repairing relations with Europe and Japan, which had been damaged by the unilateralism of the Nixon-Ford years; integrating third-world nations into the global economy by providing them access to western markets and funds; and reaching some accommodation with the Soviet Union.[8] Even before Carter won the nomination, USWA economist Edmund Ayoub perceived the danger of this blueprint: both free trade and income redistribution from industrial to third-world nations presented "serious challenges" to the interests of American workers.[9]

In line with trilateral thinking, economists at the OECD and Brookings Institution urged the United States, Japan, and Europe to stimulate their domestic economies to become "'locomotives' for global recovery." The big powers, they argued, should run trade deficits to provide markets for the weaker oil importers, third-world nations that "have already exhausted their ability to finance oil related trade deficits." Americans urged Japan and Germany, who, despite oil imports, enjoyed trade surpluses, to follow the American example by increasing domestic consumption and accepting more imports. But at the London economic summit in May 1977 it became clear that Japan and Germany would build their recovery on exports, not on domestic expansion. They would export industrial unemployment as well as goods. Put another way, their priority was the nation, Carter's was the world.[10]

Brzezinski was not deterred: "The United States would have to do more than our allies, unpalatable as this may seem to some sectors of our public. If we could demonstrate fortitude and commitment, if we were prepared to undertake the necessary sacrifices," he wrote, Japan and Europe would "emulate our commitment." The American trade deficit was an example of the necessary sacrifice. It jumped from $9.5 to $31.1 billion between 1976 and 1977. (Japan's surplus, in contrast, rose from $9.8 to $17.2 billion, despite its dependence upon foreign oil.) Still, the White House consensus in April 1977 was that "relatively free access to U.S. markets is a matter of ranking importance for our allies and almost all the developing countries of the world." [11]

Trilateral thinking dominated other branches of the government. Secretary of the Treasury W. Michael Blumenthal, a leading member of the Trilateral Commission, had led the U.S. delegation to the Kennedy Round trade negotiations in Geneva. Now, his department, believing "that the U.S. competitive position remained strong," opposed taking "measures which would attempt to improve our trade balance at the expense of our trading partners," Europe and Japan. Richard Cooper, another trilateral scholar, in charge of international economics at the State Department, feared that any talk of an American balance of payments problem would lead to protectionism. Alan Wm. Wolff, Strauss's deputy, reminded Carter of the broad objectives of opening markets and strengthening the GATT. Like Brzezinski, Wolff warned that "other countries will take the position that the relative strength of the U.S. economy requires a clear exhibition of our self-restraint on trade issues if the U.S. is to take the lead (and no one else is in a position to do so) in avoiding a general resurgence of trade restrictive actions." At the same time, any relief should minimize the impact on the newly industrializing countries (NICs)—South Korea, Mexico, and Brazil. Finally, relief should not disturb the Tokyo Round of the Multilateral Trade Negotiations (MTN) because the Europeans were not anxious to commit themselves to "a major negotiating effort." [12]

The Steel Crisis of 1977

Steel had a role to play in Carter's domestic politics and geopolitics. In a speech in April 1977, Carter announced that "trade can play an important role in the fight against inflation." At his request, Strauss prepared a memorandum, "Trade Measures to Increase Supply of Foreign Steel in the U.S. Market." Strauss told the president that he could review the quota for specialty steel that had been imposed by the Ford administration after a surge of dumped imports. Specialty steel composed only 4 percent of the industry but it was a high-value product. The EC had asked for the end of the restriction. Carter agreed to review it, in a move to warn the basic steel industry to keep prices low as well as to improve relations with the EC. The state of the specialty steel industry was secondary. [13]

CEA head Charles Schultze led a round of jawboning, reviving the tradition of steel fundamentalism. In May, government advocacy had bargained down to 6 percent a planned rise in the price of carbon steel. White House aide Stuart Eizenstat and Schultze acknowledged that the American price increases might be justified on the basis of rising oil, ore, and coal prices. Throughout the world, steel prices rose because of increased material costs. Nippon Steel, the price leader of the Japanese industry, had raised prices 8 percent. But Eizenstat repeated the words of previous American leaders: "[T]he sacrifices which must be made in the fight against inflation must begin somewhere, and price increases such as this in the steel industry will have a ripple effect throughout the economy."[14]

No one in the administration was aware that foreign steelmakers were helping them out on the inflation front. Thus, Schultze and OMB head Bert Lance were pleasantly surprised when rising imports began to register in the middle of the year and informed Carter that this development would keep domestic steel prices down. As it turned out, 1977 was the third highest year in steel consumption in U.S. history, but steel mills were operating at only 78 percent of capacity, and imports had swallowed up 20 percent of the U.S. market.[15]

The import surge was the fruit of European and Japanese miscalculations. Both had begun huge expansions in the early 1970s, anticipating continued world growth. EC capacity grew from 126.6 million tons in 1970 to 169.4 million tons in 1976 and the Japanese from 103 to 151, while American capacity rose from 155 to 159. After the sharp downturn in 1975, European utilization rates plummeted from a comfortable 87 percent in 1974 to a profitless 65 percent for the rest of the decade, falling to 57 percent in 1982. Although the Europeans closed mills after the oil crisis, they did not reduce capacity, which rose from 178 to 203 million tons. (U.S. capacity remained constant.) They shut down older, inefficient facilities and expanded the new ones built on the coast.[16] The EC subsidized closures, extended loans for new plants, financed research and worker retraining, set minimum prices, and negotiated import quotas with nearly every steel exporter in the developed and developing world.[17] Governments of all political complexions in one way or another subsidized steel operations. The EC in effect closed its borders by imposing antidumping levies on Japan, Canada, South Korea, Spain, and East European countries.[18]

Japan was not immune from the crisis. Tokyo established recession cartels and provided credit to firms that closed underused plants and absorbed weaker companies. But, like the European, Japanese capacity expanded, from 138 tons in 1974 to 157 in 1979. When steel imports threatened to take 3 percent of the domestic market in 1979, MITI suspended the preferential tariff that the United States had forced Japan to extend to developing countries. Now, it could no longer afford to help.[19]

As domestic economies contracted in the wake of the oil crisis, foreign markets became even more critical to the Europeans and Japanese. U.S. Steel's Edgar Speer charged foreign steelmakers with engaging in counter-cyclical exporting to compensate for their domestic shortfalls. In 1976, the AISI had filed suit under the 1974 trade act charging that an EC/Japan agreement in 1976, limiting Japanese steel imports to the EC, had diverted steel, sold below home market prices, to the United States.[20] It seemed to be a reasonable conclusion given the fact that in 1976, Japanese imports into the United States, comprising 55.9 percent of all imports, were 37 percent higher than the 1975 figure. Between 1975 and 1976 the price of Japanese exports fell 32 percent, even though companies were losing more than $15 per ton shipped. (European shortfalls were greater. In 1977, the Germans lost $42 and the French $76.)[21]

While the determination of dumping is never scientific, Japanese newspapers documented it. One scholar, sympathetic to Japan, characterized its policy as "the greatest supply-oriented export phenomenon" in Tokyo's history. As domestic demand fell in 1975, MITI forced production cuts, price rises at home, and an export drive abroad. But foreign protests caused Tokyo, which feared retaliation, to pull back. MITI warned steelmakers to cease "offering their products for export at cheaper prices than for domestic customers for whom they have recently raised the price." In 1976, Japan negotiated quota and price agreements with Australia and Canada, as well as the EC. The only outlet for Japanese steel was the United States.[22]

The cacophony of presidential jawboning on price and industry trade suits forced a summit meeting at the White House. Secretary of the Treasury Blumenthal, Barry Bosworth, the executive director of Carter's Council on Wage and Price Stability (CWPS), and officials from Treasury and Commerce met with the heads of the largest companies in August. Speer told them that the industry could compete on everything—quality, service, and costs—but not on price, because foreign producers, aided by their governments, dumped steel.[23]

Barry Bosworth, the inflation czar, was skeptical. Bosworth was no steel expert, but he knew that the biggest problem in the United States was high labor costs and doubted that Japanese export prices were lower than those in their home market. Armco Steel's William Verity insisted that the problem was not only Japan. Verity explained that he had pledged to meet Japanese prices in the Gulf Coast region. Within three months, British Steel, a particularly inefficient producer, came in at $30 below the Japanese price. Next the South Africans undercut the British. Speer said that the only permanent solution was sectoral negotiations at the MTN, but he warned that without government action on dumping some very big plants, even whole companies, would go under.[24]

The meeting convinced some in the government that steel prices were only part of the story, but Brzezinski's view that the United States had to lead, even sacrifice, held. The president was well aware that the Japanese method of ending its recession by increasing its exports was hurting global recovery. Carter knew that the EC had restricted first Japanese and then South Korean, Spanish, and South African steel, all of which would likely end up in the U.S. market. A CIA report had warned that the Japanese imperative to produce at full operation in combination with European protectionism "leaves only the U.S. and possibly Canada as potential major outlets for surplus Japanese steel." Earlier in February, Alan Wolff, STR Strauss's deputy, informed Carter that the EC's allocation of domestic shipments "has a reasonable likelihood of resulting in the dumping of EC steel in the U.S. market." But none of these reports interfered with his analysis of the U.S. industry's difficulties. Carter told steelmakers "I can't single out an industry, even when it is as important as yours, and make a decision . . . that might escalate enormous inflationary pressures." [25]

The government set out to work with its traditional missions unchanged. The CWPS surveyed prices, the FTC examined competitive practices, the Justice Department began a preliminary antitrust investigation, and a White House task force examined trade policy. Marching to its own drummer, the Export-Import Bank approved a $17.9 million loan to South Korea's Pohang Iron and Steel Company to finance equipment for a new mill. Adding up the actions and inaction, the United States continued to promote competition at home and abroad. [26]

Thus, Carter was at a loss when confronted with a wave of mill closings a few weeks later in August and September. More than fourteen major steel mills shut down, and operations were curtailed at many others. After halving its dividend in July, Bethlehem laid off 3,500 workers in Johnstown, Pennsylvania, and an equal number in Lackawanna, New York. On September 19, the Campbell Works of Youngstown Sheet and Tube announced it would take no new orders, threatening the jobs of 5,000 workers. The Alan Wood Steel Company, the oldest producer in the nation, went bankrupt, throwing 2,300 out of work. Kaiser closed three mills on the West Coast, Jones and Laughlin shut down a mill in Michigan, and Armco and National Steel cut back operations in Kentucky and West Virginia. U.S. Steel ceased operations at three mills in the East and one in the West and threatened to close its South Works plant, which employed 8,500 workers in Chicago. At least 20,000 steel jobs were gone. [27]

The Solomon Task Force

The resulting insurgency could not be ignored. George Pino, an operator at the closed Campbell mill of Youngstown Sheet and Tube, felt he had been "stabbed in the back": "We gave him [Carter] our votes, and now he's not helping." Charles A. Vanik of Ohio, chairman of the House Ways and Means Subcommittee on Trade, warned Strauss that legislators would not passively watch the closure of steel mills. Former Kennedy aide Ted Sorensen underscored the political imperative: "[T]he coalition that elected Carter—blacks (disproportionately hurt by steel layoffs because of their higher proportion among recent hirees), urban and industrial areas, labor, ethnics—"demanded some response.[28]

The *Wall Street Journal* captured the president's situation: "Caught off balance without a steel policy, the administration is scrambling to develop one." The government tried to stand aloof from the shutdowns. CEA member William D. Nordhaus announced that "the federal government is not in the business of telling industry not to shut down, when to shut down or where to shut down." Richard Heimlich, Strauss's assistant, stated that the trade office did not approach its work "from the standpoint of what our industry should be like." Both conveyed the message that the elimination of some mills was desirable and that imports still had a role to play in disciplining prices. The president himself told journalists and editors that "the steel question" was "highly complex," but that "large steel imports . . . are legitimate and needed . . . to ensure competition." What he did not say was that resolving the steel question would require modification of his domestic and foreign policy.[29]

Carter invited politicians, steel executives, and labor leaders to a White House Conference on Steel on October 13. He created a Special Task Force on Steel, headed by Undersecretary of the Treasury Anthony Solomon, who had negotiated the VRA agreements for Johnson in 1968. Now, Solomon announced he would address all of the problems facing the industry.[30]

Despite the talk, the White House was seeking a minimal trade solution. The relevant cabinet secretaries were on the committee, but the task force was run from the Treasury Department, which enforced the antidumping law at this time. The decision effectively isolated Commerce Secretary Juanita Kreps and Labor Secretary F. Ray Marshall. It also excluded Robert Strauss by design. Strauss now agreed "that the surge of Japanese exports to us was basically the result of dumping and strong demand conditions here as compared with other markets." (He omitted the fact that those other markets in the EC, Canada, and Australia were now closed.) But Strauss wanted to stay as far away as possible from the steel issue until the MTN negotiations were completed, because he was attempting to promote U.S. agricultural and high technology exports by ending European subsidies, procurement preferences on telecommunications, and other nontariff barriers. Keeping the steel question off the MTN table would help U.S. negotiators achieve the other, apparently more important, objectives.[31]

Most of the dumping suits were against European exporters. There was a debate within the administration about whether the Japanese were dumping steel, but all agreed that the Europeans were. The problem was to devise a solution that preserved a part of the American market for the inefficient Europeans. Unlike in 1967, the Europeans were now prepared to manage the steel

USWA president Lloyd McBride addresses 500 USWA delegates at a rally against unfair trade in Washington, D.C., on October 11, 1977, two days before President Carter's White House Conference on Steel. At the table from left to right are Congressman John Murtha, McBride, USWA legislative representative John Sheehan, Congressman Roy Ledderer, USWA vice president Joseph Odorcich, Congressman Joseph Gaydos, and Senator Richard S. Schweiker. (Courtesy of HCLA, Penn State, photographer Gail S. Rebehan)

trade. Étienne Davignon, the EC Commissioner for Industrial Affairs, acknowledged the dumping, although he observed that after looking the other way for a long time, enforcing the law in effect created new rules. Davignon was prepared to accept a minimum price structure, some rule on capacity expansion, and temporary quantitative measures. American trade negotiator Alan Wolff now agreed and advocated a global steel pact.[32] Carter was dead set against it and would accept only some mechanism on fair prices. Had he agreed to discuss steel capacity and market shares, the subsequent history of the industry would have been different.[33]

Carter had not altered one whit his views on the virtues of competition and the sins of oligopoly. He accepted some trade relief because the mere filing of antidumping suits had the effect of reducing imports. But imports were still crucial to his foreign and domestic policies. Carter continued to believe that fewer imports would simply benefit the steel companies, by producing "greatly increased prices, which would have to be paid for by the American consumers." He opposed the options of another VRA or of government-to-government "orderly marketing arrangements." The Europeans and Japanese, fearing stronger measures, would have accepted either. Japanese officials were amazed that Carter opposed any form of quantitative limits. The president preferred dumping remedies because they conflicted least with free trade and anti-inflation goals, not because of their usefulness to the steel industry.[34]

The Solomon report, completed on December 6, concluded that dumped foreign steel had sharply reduced steel earnings, making it difficult for the industry to raise capital for modernization and antipollution investments. But its puny solution warred with this analysis. Carter acted against runaway dumping, not systematic dumping. The heart of the Solomon plan was a minimum price system, similar to the one used within the EC.[35] The government would no longer wait for petitions for relief but would enforce new minimum prices, based on the costs of the most efficient producer, Japan. Imports selling below the reference price would trigger a "fast track" investigation, which would take two or three months, not the seven to nine months of the typical antidumping suit. It also allowed other foreign producers to sell at the Japanese price, which was below their own costs of production. Evaluating the program ten years later, the Congressional Budget Office concluded that this trigger price mechanism (TPM) "essentially gave less efficient firms in other countries a license to dump." [36]

But the TPM did preserve Carter's inflation, foreign, and trade policies. Eizenstat informed the president that the TPM would "deter the domestic steel industry from excessive price increases." Solomon explained that it "would not require the effective exclusion of the bulk of steel imports from Europe which will probably occur if pending and projected antidumping petitions against European producers continue to be prosecuted." By preserving an American market for the Europeans, the TPM would help stem European social unrest, which the government believed was fueling Eurocommunism. The Japanese were pleased, too. They had accepted quantitative limits imposed by many countries. The TPM did not limit them at all, although there is some evidence that the Japanese government restrained exporters.[37]

Carter had rejected a proactive policy. Labor Secretary Marshall had advocated tax credits for pollution-control equipment, special investment incentives for marginal plants, and rebuilding rail and water networks in coal and steel areas. This kind of a program won some support in the Congress. Representative Charles Vanik admitted that infrastructure expenditures and tax incentives would cost money, but felt it would be better to spend "to modernize the steel industry" than to "sprinkle $20 billion in tax cuts throughout the economy which could only be financed by increased public borrowing and additions to the budget deficit and the public debt." Vanik was referring to the tax cut then making its way through the Congress in 1978. The cut reflected the traditional macroeconomic approach, relying on the market to allocate resources.[38] Vanik was advocating more targeted interventions to make the economy more productive.[39]

The president was deaf to such suggestions. Carter made much of the fact that his "comprehensive program" for steel required "no specific legislative measures and can be implemented quickly." Existing programs would help. The Economic Development Administration (EDA), the legacy of the Area Redevelopment Act of 1961, could make loans for modernization and anti-pollution technology to firms that could not enter the capital market. But the administration accepted this modest measure reluctantly, and only under pressure from the USWA. In February 1978, Congress approved about $550 million of guaranteed loans for the EDA to distribute. The largest steel companies were no more enthusiastic about the loan program than was the administration. Part of the steelmen's opposition was ideological, but part of it was the correct judgment that EDA was incapable of assessing steel questions. Operating at the margins of the economy, EDA was used to evaluating individual projects of $5 million to $10 million, mainly in rural areas; it lacked the expertise to evaluate the steel industry, and its puny funding demonstrated that it was never intended to address the multibillion-dollar modernization projects the steel industry needed.[40]

The Solomon plan did not address the capital needs of the industry as a whole, even though it stated that imports had reduced profits and thus capital for everyone. By authorizing only the loan of small sums to small firms, the government apparently assumed that the industry could generate enough funds for modernization. The White House opposed modification of antitrust laws to permit joint ventures and only reluctantly accepted Solomon's recommendation to shorten depreciation schedules to facilitate modernization. In fact, the Treasury Department had just completed a study that contemplated increasing the guideline for depreciation schedules from eighteen years up to twenty! It took two years, a sign of its low priority, for Treasury to reduce the guideline to fifteen years, still much higher than schedules of foreign nations. (Canada, for example, had a two-year schedule.)[41]

Carter was more assertive on what the Solomon plan would not do than on what it would do: it would have little impact on inflation and the federal budget, it would not violate antitrust laws or pollution standards, and it would not foster industrial concentration. Strauss warned Carter that the report "will be read as insufficient." U.S. Steel's new board chairman David Roderick agreed, concluding that there was "nothing tangible" in the plan. The industry had wanted a temporary quota, which Carter had rejected.[42]

Even though the steelmen were dissatisfied with the Carter package, they remained confident. Speer planned to upgrade equipment at many facilities. He had been the guiding light behind the decision to build a new greenfield plant on the shores of Lake Erie at Conneaut, Ohio, an old dream of Andrew Carnegie. Roderick predicted that once the company got over "the capital punishment" of financing the facility, the Conneaut mill would produce steel using 35 percent less energy and 30 to 50 percent less labor. Financing, he predicted, would be forthcoming because of Wall Street optimism. The U.S. steel industry, unlike those of Japan and Europe, were uniquely dependent upon the stock market for capital. Thus Roderick was pleased when a leading Wall Street "bear" became bullish on the industry, concluding that "the worst is over" and that the industry outlook was "promising" into 1981."[43]

The union was odd man out in 1978, criticizing first Solomon's minimal program for workers and then the entire plan, which simply ended runaway dumping. Initially, the USWA feared that the Solomon plan would resurrect the industry but not workers, "who face the prospect of permanent job losses." No additional money was allocated for displaced workers entitled to trade adjustment assistance (TAA). TAA, first available under Kennedy's Trade Expansion Act of 1962, had been liberalized in the Trade Act of 1974. It guaranteed displaced workers 70 percent of their weekly pay plus expense money to travel outside the area to seek a new job for a year. Every president had viewed TAA as the unwanted but necessary political price to be paid for free trade. Juanita Kreps and Stuart Eizenstat told the president that "the overriding question concerning these initiatives [TAA] is how much spending is actually needed to help blunt moves toward protectionism." Apparently not much in 1977.[44]

Other nations had better means to confront the unemployment stemming from shutdowns. The French, with a significant state sector, built a new auto plant and other enterprises in a region experiencing closures. Japanese steel managers, whose companies were part of industrial empires, shifted workers from steel to other enterprises. Sweden used its excellent retraining programs. The American government, relying in the past upon the migration of workers from old to new regions, simply offered a program of income maintenance.[45]

The USWA had not given up on the mills. It urged Solomon to tie trade relief to modernization at the crisis-stricken mills. The union also suggested relaxing antitrust laws to permit joint ventures, to economize on the costs of modernization. But by March 1978, the union was asking for a full-blown industrial policy.[46] It had questioned U.S. foreign economic policy in the wake of the merchandise trade deficit in 1971 and pondered productivity questions as the rest of the nation enjoyed the 1973–74 boom. But by 1977, the questions had been answered. Jack Sheehan, head of the USWA's Washington office, now realized that the growth of steel capacity since World War II had "come about because of planned programs of the governments involved. These programs have normally involved direct grants, guaranteed loans, or some other form of assistance." Estimating that the steel companies could generate only $48 billion of the $82 billion needed to modernize the industry over the next twelve years, the USWA urged Congress to provide $2.5 to $3 billion a year in guaranteed loans to the industry. J. C. Turner, head of the union of operating engineers, advocated that an agency modeled after the Reconstruction Finance Corporation of the New Deal be established to provide the low-interest loans that steel industries in Western Europe and Japan received. Labor's advocacy of government financing and planning was a direct result of its experience at Youngstown, Ohio.[47]

Youngstown

The center of the 1977 crisis was Youngstown, midway between Cleveland and Pittsburgh, the site of U.S. Steel and Republic mills as well as the doomed Campbell Works of Youngstown Sheet and Tube (YST), which had employed 5,000 workers. Every U.S. mill confronted the new global steel order, but Campbell was in the worst position to survive in it. YST had developed a long-range strategy for modernization in the 1960s. Instead of upgrading its Youngstown facilities, some of World War I vintage, it decided to enter the Chicago market by building a state-of-the-art mill at Indiana Harbor on Lake Michigan. The strategy paralleled Bethlehem's decision to build at Burns Harbor, dooming Lackawanna. But YST, loyal to its home city, planned to use profits from the new mill to modernize Campbell.

Good intentions were derailed by two unforeseen events. Although all new mills required some time to achieve efficient operation, Indiana Harbor had more bugs than most. The profits needed to modernize the Campbell works were not forthcoming. More important, YST's acquisition by Lykes in 1969 had been a bloodletting. Critics of conglomerates had plenty of evidence here. It was not a question of power or concentration, but efficiency. Lykes was a shipbuilding and carrying company, number 144 among the Fortune 500. Flush with cash, partly reaped from the very profitable business of ferrying war materiel to Vietnam, Lykes wanted to diversify. YST was attractive because of its large cash flow, low price, and dispersed stockholdings, which gave Lykes's shares more weight than they normally would have possessed. Even so Lykes borrowed $150 million from a group of New York banks to acquire the necessary shares to exercise its fancy. It issued $191 million in bonds, with a new issue of preferred stock, to finance the takeover itself. A company with $137 million in assets purchased a steel company that was worth $806 million.

A year after the merger, several key steel managers departed, now that Lykes's managers were calling the tune. The modernization plan was ignored, maintenance was deferred, and marketing problems were neglected. As a result, net earnings averaged a third less than those of other steel companies, but its dividends were a third more. Money taken out of YST helped pay for the acquisition of an insurance company, cargo ships, a steamship company, and other assets. *Business Week* subsequently remarked, "the conglomerate's steel acquisitions were seen as cash boxes for corporate growth in other areas." In the steel boom of 1973, when the whole industry was making money, Youngstown ran operating deficits. In the tough times from 1975 through 1977 losses escalated. A former YST manager bitterly told a Senate subcommittee, "it took only seven years for some steamboat captains from New Orleans that didn't know a damned thing about running a steel company to wash down the tubes what it took seventy years to build." A member of the Lykes family explained, "Steel just wasn't something we grew up with."[48]

Lykes had wakened to YST's troubles in 1974 and brought in William R. Roesch, former CEO of Kaiser, to fix things. Roesch convinced the board to authorize $90 million for a BOF. But in 1975, Chemical Bank, Chase Manhattan, and Citibank, the same banks that had financed the merger, radically reduced their lending to YST. The decision, which had the effect of shelving the BOF, was made mainly on the judgment that the steel company's debt of 40 percent was too high. As the three banks were pulling out of YST, however, they were increasing their loans to Japanese steel companies, which operated with 90 percent debt. Between 1975 and 1977, Citibank alone increased its loans to Japanese steelmakers from $270 million to over $1 billion. In 1977 and 1978, American banks, flush with Mideast oil money, loaned nearly $1 billion to steel companies in Latin America and East Asia.[49]

Roesch believed that "lenders may have too much say in which firms survive and which do not." Their decision, he predicted, would "probably be made more on quality of balance sheet than efficiency of facilities." He was right. Campbell's seamless pipe mill was profitable in the oil boom of the mid-1970s. In June 1977, Standard and Poor thought that investment could make YST viable. Campbell's costs were high because it still made open hearth steel, which was why Roesch had ordered a BOF. But in 1976–77, when European and Japanese exporters were slashing prices and underselling efficient American companies, Campbell had difficulty balancing its books. It too cut prices, but it was selling at a loss. Then there were maintenance problems: blast furnaces needed to be relined, and the coke plant needed to be improved simply to be able to keep operating. Finally, on September 16, the Sierra Club won a ruling in federal court that vacated a prior agreement with the Environmental Protection Agency (EPA) that had allowed Campbell to delay the installation of water pollution devices. Two days later, over the objections of its managers, the Lykes board of directors voted to shut down Campbell.[50]

The history of YST reveals several characteristics of key American institutions that explain the difficulties of the steel industry as a whole in the crisis. First, American banks, unlike the Japanese and German, had no permanent interest in and little direct knowledge of the steel industry. The decisions to finance the merger in 1969 and to disinvest in 1975 were made on the basis of short-term financial considerations. But even in those countries where banks had an interest in the steel industry, they stayed in the industry during the crisis primarily because the state underwrote or contributed to the solution. In the case of YST, the state exacerbated the problem when it permitted the merger in 1969. Another uniquely American characteristic of the steel picture was that pollution mandates were determined by the accidents of lawsuits, propelled by private, single-interest parties like the Sierra Club. In the roller-coaster market of the mid-1970s, companies delayed installing pollution technology because they were uncertain about the future of marginal plants. Heated battles with environmentalists were the inevitable result.[51] But what nailed the coffin shut was trade policy. The surge of imports in 1976 and 1977 convinced the banks that the mill in Youngstown was no longer needed.[52]

Fragmentation and inaction in Washington worsened the already abundant local divisions in Youngstown. Several metropolitan planning organizations, fostered by new national bureaucracies dedicated to the environment and urban development, proposed a menu of solutions. The Solomon task force made the key decisions affecting the steel industry, but three local development agencies attached themselves to three other entities—EPA, EDA, and the Department of Housing and Urban Development (HUD)—federal agencies that possessed marginal resources and marginal competence.[53]

The most promising local group, and the one that best anticipated the crisis of 1977, was the Western Reserve Economic Development Agency (WREDA), a coalition of community, labor, and industrial leaders. In 1973, it had negotiated the water pollution schedule with EPA, the agreement that the Sierra Club overturned in the courts. In the course of its pollution studies, WREDA had stumbled upon transportation issues. Railroads were so poor in the Youngstown region that ore was brought in by truck. The cost of shipping a ton of coking coal to Youngstown was $7, compared to $1 to ship by barge to Pittsburgh mills. Had the city been more alert, it would have concluded earlier that YST's decision to build its new plant at Indiana Harbor was a sign that Youngstown's infrastructure required refurbishing.[54] WREDA thought that a "unit train" system to haul iron pellets 65 miles from Lake Erie would overcome the valley's lack of water transportation.[55] It also proposed a feasibility study for a joint venture to build large-scale coke and blast furnaces in Youngstown, which could provide hot metal to each of the steel-making furnaces.

The USWA's Jim Smith, who had worried about sufficient steel capacity during the early 1970s, was enthusiastic about WREDA's proposals and enlisted

Abel's support. In 1976, with unemployment still high in the region, Frank Leseganich, the director of USWA District 26, believed the plan could save the 29,000 basic steel jobs. The fitful decision making of EDA delayed approval in 1976. Then, WREDA's head, Republican William Sullivan, fell out of favor with Washington Democrats after Carter's election. Sullivan, the most knowledgeable and most committed to stabilizing the steel industry, was out of the loop on subsequent planning. Nevertheless, because the Carter administration had also rejected Ray Marshall's plan to refurbish steel infrastructure, it was unlikely that Sullivan's party affiliation was decisive.

Frank Leseganich was marginalized for other reasons. In October 1977, Democratic congressman Charles Carney set up the Mahoning Valley Economic Development Committee, known by another clumsy acronym, MVEDC. Carney was chairman of the bipartisan Congressional Steel Caucus and had been on the staff of 50,000-member District 26 of the USWA. He chose to work with James Griffin, a former USWA district director, not Leseganich, who had defeated Griffin in 1969. MVEDC obtained an EDA grant to study the valley yet again. It became a tool of the Youngstown Chamber of Commerce's diversification strategy. Many local businessmen believed that "steel in the Valley is dead."[56] Some thought that the shutdown would attract new industries and lower their own wage bills. MVEDC obtained a $1 million research grant from EDA and proposed a steel research center.

Competition stemming from political boundaries was another source of division. Believing, correctly, that MVEDC was ignoring them, the satellite cities of Campbell, Struthers, and Lowellville joined together to form another development agency called CASTLO, under the patronage of Republican governor James Rhodes. The mills were located in these surrounding cities, not in Youngstown, and they bore the brunt of the unemployment from the shutdown. CASTLO, too, pursued industrial diversification, not steel resurrection.

The most visible of all the responses was a new church mobilization dedicated to saving Campbell.[57] An ecumenical group of clerics decided that the shutdown produced an urban-industrial crisis that was an issue of conscience, like civil rights during the 1960s. It created the Youngstown Religious Coalition and obtained moral and financial support from the U.S. Catholic Conference, the National Council of Churches, the Synagogue Council of America, and other religious bodies. Staughton Lynd, historian, antiwar activist, and now labor lawyer in Youngstown, put the clergymen in touch with the National Center for Economic Alternatives, a liberal think-tank headed by his friend Gar Alperovitz, a former Harvard economist.

Alperovitz and the National Center represented the evolving position of the New Left on the economy. Rejecting the traditional left preference for nationalization, the center melded the 1960s notion of community control with the older idea of workers' control to formulate a route to socialism based upon the creation of alternative institutions that embodied the ideals and practices of the new society, a kind of Knights of Labor vision. Lynd was particularly attracted to salvaging a steel mill because "employee-community ownership of the Campbell Works would . . . [challenge] the capitalist system on the terrain of the large-scale enterprise in basic industries."[58]

The religious leaders and New Left economists met in Washington on October 6, 1977, to draw up plans to buy and restore the Campbell Works. In December, the coalition and Alperovitz's think-tank obtained a $300,000 planning grant from HUD, after a preliminary study concluded that it could be reopened. In 1977, Congress had given HUD the new Urban Development Action Grant program, which allowed it to move beyond its traditional arena, housing, to economic development. HUD viewed the Campbell proposal as an opportunity to use its new authority.[59]

The report, released on September 14, 1978, proposed to modernize with electric furnaces instead of the more expensive BOF, a solution that had recently been adopted by a Republic mill in nearby Warren. The modernization would cost $345 million, and the total bill to restore Campbell added up to $525 million. (To put that figure in context, the capital expenditures for the entire steel industry in 1978 was $2.5 billion.[60]) The plan required $300 million in federally guaranteed loans from EDA, as well as a variety of local financing. Its economic logic assumed productivity increases that were extrapolated from studies of the few examples where worker ownership was installed. Future sales were calculated on the basis of an optimistic forecast of steel use and government procurement. Based upon most favorable assumptions, Paul Marshall, the only steel expert consulted by Alperovitz, believed that the project was economically feasible—just barely.

But others had plans, too. In early 1978, before the study was completed, the other 1969 conglomerate, Ling-Tempko-Vaught (LTV), which owned J&L, announced its intention to buy Lykes. The marriage was put together by the Lehman Brothers firm, which represented both corporations. It was Lehman who had urged Lykes to close Campbell and concentrate on Indiana Harbor. On the other side of the aisle, Lehman was LTV's investment banker, retained to search for new acquisitions. But the merger idea came from LTV's steel executives, not its bankers.[61] The J&L managers thought that the strengths of each company "fit" together nicely and would make both more efficient.[62]

The merger of the nation's seventh and eighth largest steel companies, of course, brought in the Justice Department.[63] Measured by the antitrust division's concentration standards, the proposal was unacceptable. But under the "dying company rule" of the Celler-Kefauver Act, mergers were permitted to rescue a firm, because the elimination of a company always made a market less competitive. Predicting corporate death, though, was a public policy judgment, not a science. The head of the antitrust division, John Shenefield, believing that competition was the solution to industrial problems, concluded that Lykes's problems were not terminal. Attorney General Griffin Bell, however, who considered his antitrust staff to be "'messianics' whose positions were not to be taken seriously," was swayed by the arguments of William Hogan, the steel industry's expert, and overruled the antitrust division on June 21, 1978.[64]

There was an alternative to the fundamentalism of the antitrust division and the industry-dominated reorganization espoused by Bell and Hogan. The USWA submitted a brief to the Justice Department that concluded that if the financial danger was genuine, the merger should be approved with four conditions. First, it should not increase the debt of LTV. The government would thus serve notice that it would no longer approve the practice of draining a steel company's earnings to pay for its acquisition. Second, LTV should be required to reopen the Campbell Works or cooperate with other groups trying to save it. Third, it should not shut down other units without Justice's approval. Finally, closure should be allowed only after the merged corporation demonstrated severe losses and failure to obtain modernization funds from communities and EDA, as well as the private market.

The union rejected the criterion of simply counting the number of competitive firms in an industry. "Price competition will be promoted by policies which preserve and/or increase the market shares of any producers other than the two biggest companies [USS and Bethlehem]." If YST went under, competition would be reduced because the big two would pick up its orders. But if the new merged company shut down some of its facilities, competition would also be reduced.

LTV had a better record in steel than Lykes, and steel operations would be the major economic activity of the merged corporation. The debts of the two corporations would not grow if shares were swapped. Finally, the merged steel operations would be more efficient than either separately because the raw materials holdings and manufacturing facilities of the two complemented each other. J&L's steel, from its Aliquippa plant about forty miles from Youngstown, could feed YST's finishing facilities. The USWA reminded the Justice Department that it had permitted the two conglomerate mergers and could not rectify these errors by simply prohibiting the merger. The union knew that the antitrust division was not the body to implement industrial policy, but having failed to sway the Solomon task force, it offered a proposal to the only available government body examining the industry.[65]

The approval of the merger, with no strings attached, was only the latest action to weaken the alternative proposals. Paul Marshall, the Youngstown Religious Coalition's consultant, now concluded that the sale of Campbell was unlikely, although his views were not communicated to the coalition. Even if the coalition obtained Campbell, the financial plan had assumed it could regain sales to other parts of YST. But with J&L's facilities in Cleveland, Pittsburgh, and Aliquippa, this prospect was out of the question. The proposal now looked hopeless.[66]

Failing to sway the Justice Department, the USWA reassessed its relationship with the Campbell advocates. Although Leseganich had been working with the religious coalition, top union leaders had maintained some distance from it, as they hoped for White House action. The USWA was inhibited, too, by the divisions in the Youngstown movement. Three different USWA factions worked with three different development bodies. The former district director supported MVEDC; the current one, WREDA. Staughton Lynd and steelworkers who had been active in the campaign of Edward Sadlowski, President Lloyd McBride's opponent in the union elections earlier in 1977, were at the center of the ecumenical coalition.[67] Leseganich, a McBride supporter, had been reelected, but Sadlowski had carried the district, mobilizing the working-class anger in the valley. Before the shutdown, as the financial difficulties at YST increased, the company had tried to intensify work. Jim Smith observed that the company was "reopening the very issues involved in the 1959 Basic Steel strike."[68] And the reasons were the same: labor intensification as opposed to the modernization the bankers would not finance.[69]

The rancorous USWA election in February 1977 left a bitter legacy at this crucial time. Initially, McBride saw the movement to reopen Campbell as the Sadlowski campaign in new clothes. It looked that way because the heart of the movement was not at Campbell, but in Brier Hill, the center of the dissidents. Even without the political rivalry, no single solution and organization spoke for Youngstown, so a wait-and-see attitude seemed reasonable. Nevertheless, the union missed an opportunity to power legislative goals with the grassroots activities.

After the White House offered its inadequate program, the international patched up problems with the coalition. USWA economist Jim Smith and two former YST executives, Frank McGough and John Stone, radically revised the operating plan. First there would be a phased reopening, beginning with the profitable finishing facilities, instead of Alperovitz's all-at-once plan. The trio judged that it would be physically dangerous to operate the old open hearths while the company waited for electric furnaces to be built. Smith thought they could buy the steel in the market. The immediate cash needed to spruce up the rolling mills was much less than the sum required to construct steel-making facilities, and it could be done quickly. In phase two, an electric furnace and caster could be installed. During Campbell's third phase, facilities to make other kinds of steel could be constructed. The project required $17 million from HUD to purchase Campbell from LTV and $245 million in guaranteed loans from EDA, half of the original amount. Now it was up to the coalition and the government.

The coalition's political skills had committed the administration much further than it wanted to go because of the elections in the fall of 1978. Robert Strauss, Anthony Solomon, House Majority Leader James Wright, HUD Secretary Patricia Harris, Senator Edward M. Kennedy, and Vice President Walter Mondale all came to Youngstown. They sounded optimistic, even if no one made any commitment. Carter's staff, led by Jack Watson, had been skeptical about the whole project, which conflicted with the Solomon approach. Although the government went through the motions of studying the proposal, its unpublicized judgment in October 1978, made before the revisions in the plan, was that the "worker-purchase proposal appears infeasible because of the substantial federal loan and procurement guarantees required to make it financially sound."[70]

HUD had funded the study and could finance the purchase, but the necessary loans for modernization would have to come from EDA, which was vying with HUD for control of redevelopment programs. EDA had sent the proposal out to a Harvard Business School expert, who raised valid questions about its financial and marketing assumptions. Although the objections could have been addressed, coalition leaders were still better at producing support than producing steel. The Campbell plan was rejected on March 29, 1979, technically because the request exceeded EDA's $100 million limit on loan guarantees to a single company.[71]

Alperovitz and Lynd, intent on demonstrating a theory of worker ownership, either were blind to these legal and economic facts of life or believed they could be overcome by political mobilization. While they had some success in Washington because their purposes and HUD's coincided, their determination to create an ideological model, as opposed to a viable project, undercut both. Opting for ideology produced more national than local support. The decision to save Campbell, as opposed to saving the region, limited their Youngstown support. At the same time, the religious leaders, imbued by the morality of their cause, were uninterested in the economic issues. Meanwhile, the social crisis had turned out to be less dire than first feared. Other local steel companies were profitable in 1978. The nearby General Motors plant at Lordstown recalled a work shift of 1,600 and hired 1,100 new workers. For the moment, the Campbell workers were getting the various kinds of unemployment assistance the union had negotiated. Youngstown-area unemployment fell from 9.0 percent in March 1978 to 5.9 percent in the fall. Nevertheless, the parade of Democratic luminaries did not prevent the defeat of Congressman Carney, which perhaps was a vote on Carter's steel program. The Campbell Works never re-opened. In the end, the trade solution of the Solomon plan was all the government had to offer, and it was not enough to save Campbell.[72]

The Youngstown story demonstrates that grassroots mobilization is not everything. Much of its power was dissipated by the fragmented national bureaucracy, which channeled popular protest to sympathetic parts of the government that lacked the power to counter presidential steel policy. The USWA would eventually create some viable worker-owned mills during the 1980s, when the wave of steel closings became so unrelated to economic reality that good as well as bad mills were being eliminated. But steel policy was made in Washington, not in the communities.

Marginal government agencies attracted financial moths as well as social dissidents. The hardheadedness EDA displayed in Youngstown disappeared when it was faced with a request from Wisconsin Steel, the first company to apply for a loan under the Solomon plan. The Chicago mill was just the independent sort for which the program had been devised. Or so it seemed. Wisconsin sold about 40 percent of its steel to its former owner, International Harvester. In the early 1960s, Harvester had poured money into the mill; it had two BOFs and a continuous caster. But Harvester's own problems had halted the investments in the late 1960s. The coke ovens and blast furnaces were inefficient, defective, and caused pollution.

Harvester, which was losing money, could not find a buyer, in large part because its pension fund was short $65 million. If it closed Wisconsin, it would incur an additional $20 million in costs due to special shutdown benefits that workers would be entitled to receive. Jim Smith concluded that but for the pensions, the company would have been better off closing Wisconsin, selling its coal, iron ore, and land, and scrapping the mill. Instead, Harvester transferred the steel company in August 1977 to Envirodyne Industries, a small high-technology company ("two yuppies in a garage") with no steel experience.[73]

Chase Manhattan, well practiced in setting up corporate structures dedicated to preventing loss, put together a series of dummy corporations, which permitted Envirodyne to swallow Wisconsin, ten times larger, without having to pay cash.[74] Both Harvester and Envirodyne were well insulated from the pension obligations. In the words of Pretty Boy Floyd, the workers were robbed with a fountain pen. The deal was too much for Harvester's investment bankers, again Lehman Brothers, who objected on simple moral grounds. They were ignored.[75]

Nevertheless, EDA, lobbied by the Chicago Democratic machine, approved a $90 million loan, nearly one-fifth of the agency's money, on November 1, 1979. On the next day, Harvester's main plants were shut down by a strike, forced on the UAW by a new chairman's demand for radical work-rule changes. Everyone but EDA seemed to know the strike was inevitable. The five-month strike doomed prospects for Wisconsin Steel's resurrection. The end came in March 1980 when Harvester and Chase moved to collect their collateral before a declaration of bankruptcy.[76]

The 2,500 workers were not so well protected. The union president, unwittingly, had signed away remaining shutdown benefits due them. Harvester had kept the USWA out of the mill by accepting the industry package negotiated by the international, cultivating union leaders, and overmanning the plant. The workers were members of an independent union and, left to their own devices, were easily hoodwinked. Nearly sixteen years later, after years of litigation, survivors obtained about 7 or 8 percent of Envirodyne stock, the only assets available after the company entered Chapter 11 bankruptcy in 1993.[77]

Having been milked by financial powers, Wisconsin became a target for political experiments. Thomas Fleming, a Philadelphia businessman who had helped broker the original deal between Harvester and Envirodyne, thought a solution lay in the federal "set-aside" program for minority businesses. The Reverends Leon Sullivan and Jesse Jackson believed that the mill could be turned around. Jackson said it would be "an important step in the direction the emancipation of black people must go." It was a road untaken.[78]

EDA became an instrument for social movements, financially strapped corporations, and politicians. Fostering initiatives that were trumped by the main elements of state policy, EDA simply contributed to the notion that government was impotent. Similarly, the Small Business Administration, HUD, HEW, and the Department of Labor scattered various programs to assist economically impacted communities. These agencies succeeded in squelching political insurgencies but did not possess the clout, expertise, or money to address either the dislocation or resurrection in steel.[79]

Missed Opportunities

Two opportunities for revival were missed in 1977 because of President Carter's industrial views, fortified by a generation of Keynesian analysis of industry. Despite the imperatives of foreign policy, a global steel pact could have been negotiated in 1977, because the EC and Japan were willing and the uncontrolled expansion of third-world steel production had not begun. At home, inflation was still moderate, so a combination of infrastructure spending, joint ventures, and tax relief, which could have sustained the industry's modernization program, was politically feasible. The major companies were headed by steelmen like Edgar Speer, eager not only to modernize but to expand.

The trigger price mechanism of 1977 provided a measure of trade relief, which, together with a falling dollar, reduced imports to 15 percent without addressing fundamental steel and industrial policies. The cheap dollar of 1978 was a shallow response to the belated recognition that the United States was the only locomotive pulling the train. Assuming that the other industrial powers would follow suit, the United States had ignored trade deficits in 1977.[80] The rising deficit of 1978 was caused by declining exports as well as increased imports. Treasury Secretary Blumenthal discovered that "adjusted for inflation, U.S. exports have not grown since 1974; the volume of U.S. manufactured goods has actually declined." This could not be the result of the recession, he noted, because "the rest of the world, by contrast, has seen a 12 percent growth in export volume since 1974." CEA head Charles Schultze pointed out that those global exports were coming to the United States.[81]

The government proceeded to work on the export side of the trade ledger. The apparently immutable U.S. deficit with Japan was number one on the list. But Tokyo had promised only to increase its quotas on citrus and beef, which the CIA privately characterized as "peanuts." However, the administration believed these concessions were of "symbolic" importance to the "unsophisticated" and would also satisfy key congressional figures. But a sophisticated California electronics maker wondered if the United States was on the road to becoming a "banana republic": "If we think we are trying to balance our trade imbalance with the Japanese by selling them beef and grapefruit, we'll end up killing our industrial base." Eventually Carter assimilated the news. At a press conference during the Bonn economic summit in July 1978, he told a Japanese reporter that "most of our trade balance now comes from the purchase of manufactured goods, not oil. Of course, the nations like Japan and Germany, who sell a lot of manufactured goods to us, like to talk about our oil imports, but they don't deplore the fact that we also buy larger quantities of manufactured goods from your country and others." He urged Japan and Germany to stimulate their economies so they could buy more American goods, but moral suasion could not alter the consequences of the 1977 decisions. Both nations resisted and continued to register surpluses, even after the second oil shock in 1979. In 1980, when most nations' GNP barely grew, Japan's rose 4.8 percent; 3.3 percent of the growth came from exports, only 1.5 from the domestic economy.[82]

The U.S. recipe for restoring the 5 percent global growth rates of the postwar period had failed. Under conditions in the late 1970s, which had reduced international trade by 13 percent, global commerce was a zero-sum game, and the United States was a loser. The question in 1979 was, would the cheaper dollar—both a sign of the problem and a short-term solution—do the trick, as it had during the Nixon administration. The Carter administration thought it would, believing that the nation and the steel industry had weathered the storms of the 1970s.

An Industrial Policy for Steel?
The Decline of the Democratic Party

On November 27, 1979, less than a month after the EDA plan to save Wisconsin Steel collapsed, U.S. Steel announced that it was closing fifteen mills in eight states. The shutdowns included the Ohio and McDonald Works in Youngstown. Both had been on the chopping block in 1977, but William Kirwan, superintendent for the Youngstown works, had asked for time, and Edgar Speer's sentimental attachment to the place where his career began had saved both mills. There was no room now for decisions based on sentiment. By late 1979, the two facilities, which had opened in 1893, were producing only small orders for about 1,000 customers, all within 150 miles of Youngstown. Then the EPA had decided that the electrostatic precipitators that had been installed on open hearths in 1971 were not good enough. The high cost of transportation still had not been solved. Despite good management and good labor relations, the expenses of an integrated company that generated only the revenues of a minimill had put Ohio and McDonald in the red.[1]

With the fifteen closings, U.S. Steel had eliminated about 3 percent of its raw steel capacity. All the closed mills were ones still making open hearth steel. At the finishing end, it closed the wire and plate mills at Fairfield, Alabama, the rod mill at Pittsburg, California, and a few others that were most affected by imports or located far from markets. All told, 13,000 workers lost their jobs.[2]

The shutdowns were ordered by new leadership. Edgar Speer had left in

April because of poor health. His replacement, David Roderick, an ex-marine and finance man, lacked Speer's attachment to steel. A Wall Street lawyer remarked, "Ed Speer was in love with the hum of the machinery. He thought all you needed to solve any problem was time and money." Roderick viewed time and money through the eyes of an accountant. He had graduated from the University of Pittsburgh with a degree in economics and finance and had begun working for Gulf Oil before he joined U.S. Steel in 1959. Roderick was committed to modernization, but his timeframe would be shorter. One of Roderick's first acts was to cancel plans for Speer's dream plant in Ohio. He chose Youngstown's William Roesch to head U.S. Steel's operations and instructed him to evaluate every mill "with an eye toward paring the hopeless cases."[3]

The government downplayed the significance of the closings and declining steel production. A month before, Roderick had given Stuart Eizenstat an earful of industry woes. After the announcement, Eizenstat met with fifteen members of the congressional steel caucus, now up to 170 legislators, to show an obligatory concern, but offered no new proposals. CEA head Charles Schultze defended Carter's steel policy, attributing the closures to obsolete plants, falling auto sales, and the general "softening of the economy," a euphemism for the recession produced by the policies of the new Federal Reserve chief, Paul A. Volcker. Carter had appointed Volcker in July to wage an all-out war against inflation.[4]

The steel crisis in 1977 had occurred in a recovering economy with moderate inflation. The 1980 crisis was taking place in a weakening economy with rising inflation. Because fighting inflation was Carter's principal interest, the president stood by in the first half of 1980, as the recession and a rush of imports brought steel operations to a low of 50 percent. But as the fall presidential election approached and the economy showed little sign of improvement, the administration opened to new approaches dubbed "industrial policy," a left-tilting, supply-side approach to the steel industry and the economy. The resulting policy clash was a microcosm of two postwar divisions in the Democratic party: one between foreign and domestic policy, the other between Keynesian and structural interventions in the economy. Choosing foreign and Keynesian policies cost Carter and the Democrats a good part of their working-class constituencies in 1980 and the years to come.

Inflation, Trade, and Steel

Carter had appointed Volcker in hopes that he could improve the administration's poor record on fighting inflation. Like the Nixon controls, Carter's had targeted the industrial sector, when the problem lay elsewhere. The rise in prices—led by food (especially meat), energy, mortgage rates, and medical care—began in late 1978. A bill deregulating natural gas passed in October 1978, which eventually increased supplies by removing archaic price regulations, but in the short run it contributed to rising prices. At the same time, Congress did not pass a bill to reduce hospital costs, which were rising at an annual rate of 15 to 16 percent.

Carter could have continued to labor in the troublesome vineyards that were causing inflation. Instead, he addressed the effects of these price rises on the industrial economy. His new inflation-reduction program, announced on October 24, 1978, called for more competition, deficit reduction, and voluntary wage and price standards for major industries. He vowed to examine the balance sheets of the nation's 400 largest corporations. Carter focused public attention on government, big business, and labor, not on the sectors causing the problem. For example, from 1977 to 1979 the costs of materials, including energy, rose 21 percent in the steel industry, while employment costs rose only 12 percent and prices about 7 percent.[5]

The president opined that "government has been spending too great a portion of what our Nation produces." Actually, the deficit fell from $66 billion in 1976 to $27.7 billion in 1979. Carter's words only fed the growing attacks on government, and thus undercut alternative policies. His TV address promised to hold the budget deficit to $30 billion "or less," even though he also promised NATO allies in May to increase defense expenditures by 3 percent and had signed a tax cut of about $20 billion on November 6.[6]

This arithmetic meant $15 billion of cuts in domestic programs. A rise in social security taxes and the tax cut, which gave the lower half of the income spectrum 21 percent of the cuts, were regressive and nonproductive. The tax bill reduced the capital gains tax, which aided the finance industry and wealthy individuals, but refused more generous allowances for asset depreciation, a targeted incentive for capital investment. Carter signed the bill, which he had lost control of, because his advisers, fearing a recession, thought some stimulus was necessary.

In an earlier period, the 1978 tax reduction would have aided American industry. Now, liberal congressman Charles Vanik concluded that "these tax cuts have had a diminishing effect." Conservative Democrat Joe Waggoner Jr. agreed: "It does not appear to me that we are getting the same rate of return for each dollar of tax reduction as far as dollars returned to the economy are concerned." Imports, necessary to secure foreign objectives, trumped Keynesian techniques at home. If the increased purchasing power resulting from government deficits was used to buy foreign goods—clothes, electronics, or steel—the multiplier was weakened, imparting an inflationary tilt to a given level of government spending.[7]

The president's incomes policy did not counter the tilt. It moved from wage and price "deceleration" to "standards"—a 7 percent limit on wages and an economywide 5¾ percent ceiling on prices.[8] Like the steel fundamentalism of the 1950s and 1960s, the plan targeted the industrial sector. Carter's sense of himself as being above special interests precluded bargaining with business and labor.[9] He simply announced the standards and threatened to withdraw government contracts, subsidies, protection from foreign competition, and other "economic privileges" from violators.

Carter acknowledged that his program "will not end inflation," that it would only improve "our chances of making it better rather than worse." It did neither. In the fall of 1979, Alfred Kahn, head of the effort, acknowledged as much. Kahn told Carter (but not the nation) that the 13 percent inflation was caused by rises in sectors not susceptible to wage-price guidelines—fuel, housing, and medical care.[10] In 1979, for the first time in history, the inflation rate in the United States was higher than the average of all industrialized countries.[11]

Carter's failure to control inflation through neo-Keynesian restraint led to Volcker's appointment to the Fed. He began his chairmanship by raising interest rates. Schultze, already tracking a slowdown in the economy, feared that the policy might produce a genuine recession. Then in October 1979, the Fed did more, slowing the growth of the money supply. Volcker had just returned from a meeting with foreign central bankers in Europe, who had told him that the weakness of the dollar required the United States to do more to check inflation. Carter distanced himself from the Fed chief's statement that Americans must accept a lower standard of living if the inflation rate was to be controlled. But the president's *Economic Report* in January 1980 named inflation as the number-one economic problem, and it was to determine his steel policy through the middle of the year.[12]

Given this single-minded focus, the government did nothing about a new flood of imports caused now by the depreciation of the yen. Although Japanese production costs rose during this period, trigger or minimum prices fell in 1979 because of the new dollar/yen relationship. The 1977 agreement had allowed the Europeans to sell below their costs as long as they were not below the TPM. The lower trigger increased that margin considerably. Although the U.S. industry believed that Japanese steelmakers and others were also dumping, their strongest case was against the Europeans, as it had been in 1977.[13]

In January 1980, U.S. Steel and Republic announced plans to file dumping suits against European steelmakers, which in theory would end the TPM, which was a substitute for the suits. The threat, unlike the mill closures, attracted attention because of its international implications. Bob Ginsburg, Eizenstat's assistant on steel questions, warned that "the filing of dumping suits against our

European allies would come at a time when the nation gravely needs European cooperation on Afghanistan and Iran." After the Soviet invasion of Afghanistan and the taking of American hostages in Iran, Carter needed to marshal European support behind American countermoves. A White House aide worried that the suits came at the worst time, just "when we are pressing them . . . to confront the Soviets, urging them to restrict trade with the USSR and advocating a boycott of the Olympic games." In February, the *Wall Street Journal* asked, "Can you imagine Secretary of State Vance going over to Europe and telling them that they can't export more steel to the United States . . . and then tell them that they shouldn't export to Russia either? He'd be thrown off the Continent."[14]

Eizenstat told the president that it was possible to preserve TPM, stop the suits, and avoid a confrontation with the Europeans if he was willing to change investment, regulatory, inflation, and trade policy. The choice was to promote steel investment or exclude imports. The Solomon plan—in deeds, if not words—had been premised on the false assumption that the industry had sufficient capital. Now, Eizenstat warned that "[p]rojected capital needs for the steel industry are of such magnitude that only substantial measures to aid investment or tough import restrictions are likely to generate the revenues the industry will need. If you are not willing to consider changes in policies that affect investment, the burden will fall on trade policies with potentially serious international and inflationary repercussions. We would not recommend that you approve this review unless you are willing to consider such tradeoffs."[15]

Eizenstat wrongly perceived the problem to be either a new trade policy or a new investment policy, when in fact both were needed. Modernization or the introduction of new technology cannot be separated from trade issues. The "rush" to modernize, with its accompanying technological unemployment, was impelled by rising imports. But Eizenstat's greater error was to assume that the president was interested in a new steel policy. Carter made it clear in January that he rejected both the trade and investment options. The CEA and his wage-price board told him if the suits were filed and the TPM ended it would "*help us* on the inflation front," because of the resulting increase of imports.[16]

When February's import figures approached 21 percent of the market and domestic shipments continued to fall, the industry went ahead and filed the dumping suits on March 10. The crisis escalated, and the president had to decide whether he should suspend the TPM. Carter told his cabinet that his decision would turn on which course would be the least inflationary, not on the state of the industry. The new secretary of commerce, Philip Klutznick, and the new STR, Reubin O. Askew, were in favor of retaining TPM and reaching some agreement with the Europeans, even though they played to the president's priorities, arguing that such a policy would be less inflationary than dropping the TPM. But the economic heavies were unsympathetic to the industry's situation and wielded the inflation argument more effectively.[17]

Schultze told Carter that "the steel TPM is our first test" of "the effectiveness of our anti-inflation program." The new Secretary of the Treasury, G. William Miller, agreed. During the first half of the year, Carter's key advisers judged that any attempt to limit the imports "could contribute by mid or late summer to the collapse of the credibility of the President's anti-inflation program. If that happens, the President will be headed into a general election without any economic policy." Making inflation his only economic policy did not stem from objective statistics. Prices rose everywhere in 1980, and they were now even higher in Europe than in the United States. But European governments distinguished between long-run steel policies and short-term energy shortages. By going to the mat on inflation, Carter lost the initiative, allowed the situation to deteriorate, and precipitated a confrontation with the industry and the EC.[18]

The Europeans were prepared to accept a rise in the TPM because they knew that the complaints were justified. Thus, Secretary of State Cyrus Vance, like Askew and Klutznick, was for retaining the TPM. Singing the president's song, they argued that antidumping suits would dry up imports and allow the steel companies to raise prices, thereby increasing inflation.[19]

But Carter followed Miller and Schultze, refused to increase the trigger prices, and suspended the whole system on March 21. The industry then filed additional dumping suits covering 26 percent of all steel imports. On May 5, the U.S. International Trade Commission (ITC) found that EC producers had dumped steel and began determining whether an injury had occurred. (Both were required for action.) Carter tried to put a positive spin on the situation and told a group of journalists on May 13 that "the very difficult transition phase to a more modern plant and one that can comply with environmental standards is substantially over." CEOs of steel companies began questioning his competence. By July, the steel industry, affected by sharp declines in automobile production and housing starts, was operating at 50 percent of capacity. Foreign tonnage declined, but the import share of the market rose.[20]

The EC, ironically, seemed to be more concerned with the deteriorating situation than the president. European companies informed American officials that they were ready to accept voluntary quotas because they feared that they would lose the suits and would be shut out of the American market. The EC had created an informal cartel in October 1976 that followed mandatory production quotas to keep up prices while the industry restructured. It had allocated 10 to 12 percent of its output for export, mostly to the United States. But the cartel had broken down in the summer of 1980 as domestic demand plummeted. Capacity utilization fell from 70 percent to 58 percent; a wave of price cutting combined with rising production costs threatened the entire industry, which was losing $20 million a day. Assigning the reduced tonnage was difficult enough; losing the American market would make it impossible to hold things together. EC Commissioner Davignon acknowledged that without the TPM, the "EC would not be able to compete with prices charged by the domestic [American] steel companies." To keep it, Davignon was prepared to accept a small rise.[21]

The administration had no choice but to accept a minimum increase, recognizing that Davignon "does have somewhat of a community of interest with us in desiring a very modest settlement." A deal was struck in September on terms first suggested by Davignon in July. New trigger prices would be about 12 percent higher than they had been when TPM was suspended in March. If the Europeans dumped heavily when the U.S. industry was pressed, the government would examine the situation.[22] The system would continue for three and possibly five years.[23]

Like the original TPM, the new one aimed to protect European steelmakers as well as the Americans. The revised agreement still allowed them to sell steel below their costs of production. Carter had decided not to look too closely at European steel subsidies or trade diversions, like the EC-Japan agreement of 1976. If these GATT violations had been pursued, the American government could have imposed countervailing duties on European steel. But the Europeans explained that the subsidies and agreements, although illegal, were temporary and would result in less capacity. American foreign policy imperatives in Iran and Afghanistan guaranteed that this rationale remained unquestioned.[24]

Alan Wolff, in a private letter to Lloyd McBride in 1979, had acknowledged that during the 1977 crisis the government had lacked "information," "interest," and the tools "to monitor economic trends and trade measures." Two years later, Wolff believed that the government was better equipped, but it turned out he was speaking only for himself. Richard Heimlich, deputy to the STR, told representatives of U.S. Steel, Armco, and Bethlehem that neither the Japanese nor European governments fostered their steel industries and that the subsidy provisions of the new trade act would be enforced loosely.[25] Industry leaders had wanted quantitative limits, which Carter opposed. They did not trust government enforcement of the TPM; the process was tedious, involving product-by-product, country-by-country examination. Even when one country was penalized for dumping, the imports of other countries simply stepped forward to fill the space. The steel industry's second choice was to establish a special TPM for the EC, better reflecting European costs of production. Nevertheless, the new TPM eliminated the distortions of changing yen/

dollar exchange rates. Carter was forced to acknowledge that it was not in the nation's interest to import a price war, even to fight inflation. But his inflation priority contrasted with the sectoral concerns of the EC.[26]

Industrial Policy

If the war against inflation made Carter complacent about 50 percent operating rates in steel, others inside and outside of his administration were not. As Carter's reelection prospects dimmed, some of his advisers convinced the president to consider alternatives to neo-Keynesianism. Macroeconomic policy was not working, and space opened for new solutions to make the economy more productive. The government had already put together an "industrial policy" to save Chrysler from bankruptcy in 1979, think-tanks around the nation were studying industrial innovation, and coalitions of businessmen, mayors, governors, and labor in the hard-hit Northeast and Midwest added political weight to the idea that the nation required a recipe for growth.[27]

According to the new thinking, the government's task was no longer to assure that the growing pie reached all at the table, but rather to bake a larger pie. Ezra Vogel's book *Japan as Number One*, which attributed Japanese business potency to its coordinated national strategy, had been a best-seller in 1979. In the same year, Bethlehem Steel chairman Lewis Foy had advocated a new "business strategy." By 1980, the National Association of Manufacturers (NAM) agreed, the *New York Times* ran a five-part series on industrial policy, a congressional committee held hearings on the subject, and *Business Week* published a special issue on "The Reindustrialization of America." Democratic representative Henry Reuss believed Americans "must undertake the most fundamental reassessment of our economic structure since 1932, or perhaps of all time."[28]

The talk was propelled by sober statistics. Workers' after-tax income, which rose 34 percent in the 1960s, increased only 7 percent in the 1970s, and actually declined 5.5 percent in 1980. Only 5 percent of the new jobs produced in the 1970s were in manufacturing. Manufacturing workers composed 38 percent of the workforce in 1960 but only 28 percent in 1981. This decline could not now be attributed to automation, because the rate of increase in productivity had slowed from an annual rate of over 3 percent in the 1950s and early 1960s to only 1.6 percent in the 1966–75 period. In 1979 it was −2.0 percent.[29]

The decline of manufacturing had been observed earlier but had been deemed natural, even desirable. In 1966, Harvard economist Raymond Vernon updated the theory of comparative advantage with the idea of the "product cycle." One nation pioneered a process, which then became internationalized, produced by low-wage labor. The initiator went on to newer industries.[30] The state could ameliorate resulting domestic distress through redistributive programs such as unemployment insurance and retraining, but it could and should not alter the process. Vernon had sanitized Joseph Schumpeter's portrait of capitalism's "gales of creative destruction" releasing capital and labor to create new enterprises. Change was painful, Vernon argued, but it assured progress and affluence in the long run.[31]

In 1973, Daniel Bell, writing in a more popular vein, announced that the United States was now a "post-industrial society." Adopting an organic metaphor, Bell argued that mature nations naturally moved to a postindustrial phase in which new service industries replaced traditional means of employment. The various "green" movements added environmental arguments to the economic and biological ones. The demise of polluting industries, such as steel, was a social gain.[32]

Others, like the mayor of Sioux City, Iowa, dissented. In 1977 he informed Carter of the "shocking announcement by Zenith Radio Corporation that some 5,600 Americans will soon be permanently laid-off and their jobs transferred to other countries such as Mexico and Taiwan where wages are considerably below American standards." The president sympathized, but had no answer.[33]

Vernon, Bell, and their followers had assumed that the United States would prosper in a postmanufacturing regime, though there was little evidence to support this claim in the 1970s. GNP fell from a 4 percent annual growth rate in the 1960s to 2.5 in the 1970s.[34] The U.S. standard of living slipped to fifth from its number-one rank of 1972. Apparently the nation faced economic as well as industrial decline. The complacent could find specific reasons for problems in textiles, shoes, electronics, autos, steel, and other industries. Together, the record suggested more basic problems. Many explanations were offered: oil was too expensive, the workers were lazy and received too much money, the rate of savings had declined, managers were complacent, equity financing produced the myopia of the short-term, the baby boomers diluted the stock of experienced workers, and the government spent and taxed too much.[35]

While all agreed that more investment was needed to increase productivity, there were many ways to skin that cat. Business was united around lowering taxes on the rich and corporations and reducing regulation and government spending. But the advocates of industrial policy—academics, business and labor leaders, and politicians—generally favored targeted rather than aggregate tax relief. They believed that the manufacturing decline was neither inevitable nor desirable and could be reversed. Although their ideas were diverse, they concluded that the new global economy required microeconomic interventions in specific sectors. *Business Week* observed that "industrial policy overseas is becoming a contest among advanced countries in which the government attempts to pick the winners . . . and push their development as hard as possible."[36] Although they were skeptical, the editors of the *Wall Street Journal* acknowledged that the talk about "sectoral solutions reflects an explicit claim that the problems of U.S. industry cannot be solved solely by macroeconomic policy."[37] Thus, many Americans were coming around to the European view that macroeconomic tools could deal with inflation but stagnation could be met only with industrial policy.

Trade issues were usually a part of the discussion. James Fallows, writing in the *Atlantic Monthly*, believed that Japanese targeting and domestic protection produced the Japan–U.S. trade deficit and also the terms of that trade: the United States imported manufactured goods but exported low-value raw materials to Tokyo.[38] Global trade was now dominated by items that reflected not national differences in resources but national decisions to promote sectors that produced high returns, had positive spillover effects, and thus promoted the general welfare.[39] What if the public benefit of a sector exceeded its private benefit, the judgment most of the world had made about the steel industry? Unlike U.S. policy elites of the 1990s, the proponents of industrial policy during the Carter years did not accept the job loss of globalization as a law of economics. The third world had not yet entered the picture.

Agreeing that sectoral policies were needed did not answer all questions. Advocates disagreed on how additional resources would be obtained. *Business Week*, along with the larger business community, seemed to think that consumption would have to be suppressed. Others believed that inefficient subsidies in housing, agriculture, small business, and what was often called "urban policy" could be transferred to bona fide economic reconstruction.[40] Still others believed a public-private industrial bank, modeled on the Reconstruction Finance Corporation, could provide funds. The criterion for assistance would be whether a loan would create conditions under which the firm would become competitive tomorrow. However, unlike the tax reducers and the Keynesians, most urging change advocated some form of planning and coordination among government, business, and labor.

The idea of sectoral policies divided intellectuals, regions, and classes. In the academy, institutional economists, who usually had labor sympathies, were for it. Orthodox Keynesians and monetarists, the mainstream of the economics profession, fashioned the arguments for the opposition. Most politicians from the Sunbelt opposed industrial policy, but those who supported it usually excluded older industries, which were often outside their districts. Thus, Senator Lloyd Bentsen of Texas believed the error in U.S. policy was "that we try to bolster our failing industries, rather than pay attention to the ones that are growing."[41] Representatives from the Frostbelt disagreed with Bentsen's judgment. But even in the North, the middle-class segment of the baby-boom generation were suspicious of such New Deal–type solutions. They may have started out antibusiness in the 1960s, but in the economic crisis they muted their critique and often became anti-labor.[42] Meanwhile, the New Left—still dominated by foreign policy and racial, gender, and environmental issues—had little to contribute initially. Thus, Gar Alperovitz and Jeff Faux were suspicious of the talk of reindustrialization, asking for more discussion and more explicit use of the term "economic planning."[43]

Most of the supporters of industrial policy were Democrats, and the conflict divided them more than Republicans. Within the Carter administration, Keynesian inflation-fighters held the key economic positions on the CEA and in OMB and Treasury, while supporters of industrial policy could be found in Commerce and Labor, bodies with less clout on economic matters. Thus, Secretary of Labor Ray Marshall was excluded from the steering committee of the White House's key Economic Policy Group in the fall of 1977, at the same time he had been marginalized in the resolution of the steel crisis. Arnold Packer, assistant secretary for policy at the Department of Labor, advocated policies that would "choose winners and enhance US capacity to produce and sell . . . through increased federal financial, technological and market support." Packer was not optimistic about converting White House economists, who, in his words, "believe the market, high interest rates and investment tax credits will solve all our problems." He was right. The CEA thought "the potential for a successful massive program is low, for a large embarrassment, high." Peter Solomon at Treasury scoffed at the notion of "a plan to pick or fund winners" or, he added, "supporting losers."[44]

But as rising unemployment rates and forecasts of a deeper recession made the president's reelection uncertain, some of his advisers embraced industrial policy as a means of political revitalization. Fed chief Volcker's monetary stringency had produced a recession, without significantly reducing inflation. The GNP fell in 1980 and the unemployment rate rose to 7.2 percent, but the inflation rate remained at 12.5 percent.[45]

In May 1980, Eizenstat informed Carter, "we are now in a balanced budget box." By making anti-inflation and a balanced budget the linchpin of his economic policy, the president was vulnerable to Republican candidate Ronald Reagan's promised across-the-board tax cut and the traditional Democratic promises of Senator Edward Kennedy, who challenged Carter in the presidential primaries. Eizenstat told Carter that his economic policy was "viewed solely as one of austerity, pain and sacrifice, with few positive aspects." He should have added that for all the pain, it was not working. Eizenstat suggested distinguishing the short-term measures in place from "long-term structural solutions to inflation," which, he pointed out, would also help reduce unemployment. The new program, he advised, would concentrate on "productivity, industrial policy, and savings." A plan to reindustrialize "would excite workers disillusioned with the administration and offer the Nation hope that our basic industries will remain competitive." Finally, he concluded, "if we are to continue to champion free trade and avoid import restrictions, a positive thrust to our troubled industries is necessary." [46]

Eizenstat had been talking with the AFL-CIO's Lane Kirkland and Felix Rohatyn, the investment banker who had been instrumental in resolving the New York City fiscal crisis of 1975. Both advocated the creation of a Reconstruction Finance Corporation–type bank, with private and public funds and authority to make loans to and purchase equity in companies. The plan had already been embraced by Kennedy and the Senate Democratic caucus. The president drew closer to the labor movement as the election approached and Lane Kirkland assumed more of the functions of the aging George Meany. The AFL-CIO proposed putting $600 billion of employee pension funds in the bank, a financial contribution ensuring that "the labor movement" was "a partner, not a special interest." By creating a consensual instrument with capital resources, the government role in growth would be direct. Carter was unmoved. He rejected the plan for a bank and proposed instead to give more money, $1.5 billion, to EDA. [47]

On August 28, the president presented his program to a diverse group of cabinet officers and government, business, and labor leaders. He promised to create a tripartite advisory board, called the Economic Revitalization Board, to mobilize public and private resources to restore industrial development and create jobs in areas affected by economic dislocation. The board would be chaired by Irving Shapiro, head of the Du Pont Corporation, and Lane Kirkland. Kirkland had agreed to serve even though he thought that the penniless board "only guarantees inaction." [48]

The rest of the program Carter announced was equally conventional, although it was larded with the lingo of industrial policy—structural, long-term, partnership. The president located the initiative, properly, outside of traditional macroeconomic policies, calling it "neither a traditional stimulus program nor a general tax cut proposal." To clear the deck, he declared victory over inflation and recession. He advocated no new institutions, and his proposals amounted only to a series of tax cuts for business and individuals. Carter promised public investment "in crucial areas like energy, technology, transportation, and exports." He pointed to other initiatives already signed into law. Carter had already opted for an industrial policy for energy, which included a plan to fund "winners": synthetic fuels and liquid and gaseous fuels made from coal. The government had created a new corporation, provided loans, loan guarantees, and price and market guarantees to private firms building the plants. The synthetic fuels example was apt in theory although, as it turned out, not in practice.

But Carter's speech also included a proud recital of the industries he had deregulated—airline, trucking, rail, banking, and communications—which together covered a much greater swath of the economy than did the new energy industry. Deregulatory policies like these dissolved the promised partnership between government and business in favor of competition. Carter did not even mention the steel and auto industries.[49]

Eizenstat pressed on, urging the development of a comprehensive industrial policy, but neither Carter nor his top economic advisers were interested. The infinitive verb used in OMB's question—how far do "we want the government to intrude in . . . specific industrial sectors?"—presaged the office's answer. It was better, OMB concluded, to rely upon "market forces to encourage the mobility of labor and capital to their more productive uses." Schultze concurred. Only the president could have overcome this opposition. But Carter's interest, even his understanding, was minimal.[50]

Industrial Policy for Steel

Carter's rejection of an industrial bank tells us what he did not want, not what the consequences of that rejection were. The Steel Tripartite Advisory Committee (STAC), created on July 26, 1978, as part of the Solomon plan, had been discussing an industrial policy for steel. Ray Marshall had suggested creating the committee, which Carter initially opposed. Chaired by the Secretaries of Commerce and Labor, STAC included top union and industry leaders and the more sympathetic members of the administration but not the key figures from Treasury, CEA, and OMB who determined Carter's policies. The president ignored the committee until faced with the 1980 crisis. Government members of STAC simply transmitted policies made in the White House. Thus, STAC lacked a presidential mandate to forge an industrial policy for steel. Only the union representatives urged a steel policy with "objectives, some goals in terms of size, market share, and everything." Roger Altman from Treasury told USWA president Lloyd McBride and U.S. Steel chief David Roderick that Carter would not pursue "special packages," only general policies like changing taxes and perhaps deregulation.[51]

If the government rejected specific measures, how would the steel industry fare under the president's "economic renewal" plans? Everyone agreed that the industry required more capital. But the amount needed was determined by the projected size of the industry. At the first STAC meeting, David Roderick predicted that there would be a steel shortage in the mid-1980s. He thought that increasing steel's capacity from the 158 million tons of 1978 to 168 in 1988 was a reasonable goal. The government aimed to reduce capacity, but because it rejected a sectoral policy it lacked carrots or sticks. The matter was compromised by assuming constant tonnage. But the discussion was not informed by analysis of domestic and international markets, particular products, or specific firms.

Capital requirements were computed by assuming a 4 percent replacement rate for current capacity, which added up to $6.1 billion annually. Projected industry resources for the next four years were estimated at between $4.1 and $4.4 billion a year. Carter's balanced budget pledge meant that he would support no tax relief before the election. Roderick made it very clear that even had the government been willing to fund them, the industry did not want loan guarantees to close the investment gap. The industry continued down the path it had laid out during the first steel crisis in 1977. In December 1979, the AISI had declared that "[m]any of the actions they [the Europeans] have taken— such as government takeover, subsidization, and cartelization of the industry—are not appropriate in the United States." Instead, the industry sought tax and regulatory changes. To obtain capital for investment, the industry wanted faster capital recovery, a refundable investment tax credit, higher prices to improve earnings, and more flexible environmental regulations. Roderick aimed to "maintain this industry in a free enterprise posture, rather than a government owned or government guaranteed posture."[52]

Despite his mistrust of big business, Carter agreed with U.S. Steel on the desirability of free enterprise, if not on the specifics of its tax, price, and environmental wish list. On September 30, Carter announced his steel program along the lines previewed by government representatives on STAC. He said his program was an example of his "economic revitalization program" for modernizing basic industries. However, the revised TPM, announced as part of the package, was the only specific measure in the plan. Carter explained that he had imposed no quantitative restrictions and guaranteed no market share, underscoring his rejection of an EC-type plan. The resulting contradictions followed logically. Although the plan specified that "the size of the industry should be determined by market forces," at the same time it referred to steel as "perhaps the most crucial [industry] of all [for] national defense." Asserting that "the comprehensive steel agreement that we've reached is proof that the proper role of government is to be a partner in economic change, not an impediment and also not an uninterested or indifferent spectator," it nevertheless concluded that "the challenge of revitalizing this essential industry must be met primarily by the industry itself." Acknowledging that "the industry has exceptional capital needs," Carter noted that the steel industry would have to convince "the financial community and the public" to provide capital. On the other hand, he offered assurances that the general tax proposals contained in his August revitalization speech would be sufficient to provide the necessary capital. He promised, after the election, to shorten depreciation schedules and make the investment tax credit partially refundable, offering industries like steel help in a world of meager profits.[53]

The industry believed that the president's package, which would yield about $165 million in relief, was inadequate. All the parties on STAC had agreed that the industry would suffer a $2.1 billion investment shortfall. Carter apparently did too and stated that further funds would come from a laundry list of tax benefits gained from profitable nonsteel assets, wage reductions, reduced dividends, and plant closures, which would counter the shortfall.

Carter supported amendments to environmental laws that would extend compliance deadlines when a commitment to modernization was made. Although environmentalists played a big role in his administration, many Carterites were critical of EPA policy in steel. CEA member George Eads concluded that EPA viewed the industry as "the 'enemy' and [believed] every opportunity should be sought to push them back." Schultze discovered that some of the EPA regulations had the paradoxical result of slowing modernization, closing otherwise viable facilities, and at times producing higher emissions. Even Eizenstat, an avid environmentalist, inveighed against EPA regulators in steel. Particularly at lower levels of the agency, EPA was rigid and inflexible. Hard-line regulators entered into a common-law marriage with the opponents of industrial policy. William Drayton Jr., in charge of EPA planning and management, told EPA head Douglas Costle that the steel industry should be left to decline.[54]

Although the government shared some of the steel industry's criticisms of EPA, it would modify EPA rules only on a case-by-case basis, not grant blanket exemptions, which was the industry's goal. Many environmentalists were unhappy with this more flexible policy, partly because they had not been part of the negotiations. But they were given enough assurances to guarantee their silence, if not their endorsement. And Carter promised to modify the charter of STAC so representatives of public advocacy groups could be included.[55]

Assistance to laid-off steelworkers, the trade adjustment assistance (TAA) program, was limited to the standard income maintenance for thirteen weeks beyond the standard twenty-six and the promise of a few pilot training programs planned for 1981. Steelworker petitions for TAA relief in late 1979 and 1980 were uniformly rejected. Given the heavy use by auto workers, TAA costs rose to $1.6 billion in fiscal year 1980. Nearly 350,000, about one-third, of all autoworkers were unemployed. At the same time, the cutback of public employment under the Concentrated Employment and Training Act (CETA) and the introduction of means testing ensured that CETA jobs would be reserved for those who were poor as well as unemployed.[56]

This meager provisioning was the result of the government retreat on public employment and training after the disappointments with CETA, which had originally been forced upon a reluctant Richard Nixon. Carter's stimulus package in 1977 had included an expansion of CETA. However, lacking technical capability and adequate staffing, the Labor Department could not prevent CETA workers from simply replacing others who would have been hired and could not veto employment projects of questionable value. Thus, the economic logic of CETA disappeared, and the media served up numerous examples of CETA corruption, fraud, and mismanagement to lampoon. Politicians abandoned the program in droves. The nation's failure to reform the U.S. Employment Service (USES) in the 1960s was paid for by the unemployed in the 1970s. Institutional links needed to connect USES with training and jobs did not exist. One study of the aftermath of the Youngstown closings demonstrated that the Ohio service could not provide workers information about work or training.[57]

Was this an industrial policy for steel? At the White House news conference announcing the Carter steel program, Eizenstat called it "the nation's first sectoral policy for a particular industry." But talking about a sector is not a sectoral policy. Carter offered only vague proposals for the future. From 1977 on, an unwilling Carter had to be literally forced to address steel issues. At each point, he did as little as he could get away with. The tripartite STAC never enjoyed his support. It was resurrected during the political crisis of 1980 when the administration, groping for an economic policy and a strategy for reelection, embraced some of the language of industrial policy.

In the end, the administration denied that there was a problem in manufacturing. Schultze told Carter in August that "with two exceptions [steel and auto] individual American industries had not suddenly turned into problem children." Minimizing the significance of two of America's leading industries, and ignoring many smaller ones, was a triumph of ideology over common sense.[58] Renaming the problem to downplay it, Schultze now concluded that the problem of steel was "*world* overcapacity," noting that up until the recession "this problem in Europe was *worse* than in the U.S."[59]

The Europeans had approached the matter differently. They decided in 1980 that by 1985, 23 percent of their steel capacity would be eliminated. To gain industry acceptance of this plan, the EC provided and permitted subsidies for investment, closure costs, and operating deficits and import quotas. There was some echo of such a program coming from the Congress. A report by the GAO in 1980 urged a national policy on steel that would set production goals. The government would help develop and test new technologies, tax policies would encourage environmentally sound and technologically advanced equipment, and trade and worker adjustment policies would be coordinated. As in the Chrysler package, both industry and labor would have to contribute to the solution. The report was rejected in the last days of the Carter administration. Schultze again denied that the industry required government assistance to meet the new situation.[60]

Schultze's Keynesianism, still the leading economic approach of the party, became a doctrine of government passivity. Democrats lacked the intellectual muscle to power their historical promises. This weakness extended to Edward Kennedy, who had challenged but failed to defeat the president in the primaries. Kennedy was all over the map, supporting industrial policy, deregulation, and antitrust vigilance. He forced Carter to accept a platform plank that promised a $12 billion jobs program. A favorite among the labor and black contingents of the Democratic convention, the pledge floated above politics and the nation's economic woes. Ignoring the private sector and putting people on the public payroll was no policy at all. In an emotional, crowd-pleasing speech, the senator said, "programs may sometimes become obsolete, but the ideal of fairness always endures."[61] That ideal had been adequate for a growing economy, but Kennedy failed to place the ideal of fairness into a viable economic program that would restore growth. His words were merely sentimental.

The president's acceptance speech, contrasting a Reagan future of "risk" based upon "fantasy" and a Carter future of "security, justice, and peace," made it clear that he was counting on the electorate's fear of a Reagan presidency, not the appeal of his own future plans, to win the campaign for him. Carter mentioned his "economic renewal program," but it was overshadowed by what he called his proudest achievement, ending government regulations in order to "put free enterprise back into the airlines, the trucking and the financial system of our country." He called his deregulation of these industries "the greatest change in the relationship between Government and business since the New Deal." A man who held up those trophies was not about to plan the steel industry. It was hard to see what was new about Carter's economic renewal.[62]

The USWA had initially welcomed the formation of STAC. But in June 1980, when the limits of Carter's policy became clear, Jim Smith expressed his forebodings to Jack Sheehan:

When we consider what the Japanese government has accomplished with guaranteed loan programs for steel and other target industries, . . . [one wonders] if the United States government can compete in the modern world. The U.S. industry will not be able to modernize itself, with its own cash flow, and fulfill its pollution control obligations. Therefore, we see U.S. Steel and others shifting capital out of the industry as fast as possible. . . . Either we obtain a massive program of loan guarantees to the competent steel managements that want them or worker investment in the industry.

If neither took place, he warned, "we might as well prepare to lose 150,000 jobs and half our domestic capacity during the 1980's." [63]

The USWA supported loans instead of tax relief because a loan program would require industrial planning. The union still felt uncomfortable supporting such items as liberalized depreciation allowances and the investment tax credit. Like the rest of the liberal community, the union had evaluated taxation on the basis of its distribution of yields between rich and poor. It did not endorse but merely "lent a sympathetic ear to such [tax] proposals." And it was not accustomed to advocating the need for greater profits. To industry, profits meant capital needed for modernization. To the union and liberals, profits signified exploitation, inequality, and capital exports. But basically tax relief, as opposed to loans, kept decision making in the hands of industry alone. And the union was determined to have some say in these matters. But without government support, the loan option disappeared. There were few others. [64]

Although top union officials knew that some mills would have to close, they could not simply promote the retiring of marginal plants without obtaining genuine retraining and placement policies. No union leader could have asked workers to forgo the proposed wage increase and COLA when inflation was over 12 percent. The COLA had been agreed to in 1973, in a world of growing steel demand. By the late 1970s, a worldwide recession, combined with foreign expansion of steel production, had produced a glut. The government's failure to control inflation made the COLA an instrument of wage increases, even though energy and material costs were rising even more. [65]

Carter had told the USWA convention in 1978 that "as both business and labor try to catch up with past inflation and protect themselves against future inflation, prices and wages keep mounting. . . . And in the end, no one wins." But he could not get the USWA or other unions to practice wage restraint before inflation had ebbed. Workers will sacrifice, but only if they see a light at the end of the tunnel. Ray Marshall and Robert Strauss cited a Harris poll demonstrating that "workers would rather take a pay increase smaller than the comparable price rise if they were sure that the cost of living would be brought under control rather than a pay raise that is more than the rising costs of living without that assurance." They viewed that statement as evidence that workers were behind the president's program, missing the obvious point that most workers had no faith in the president's ability to reduce the rate. [66]

Carter, and a growing school of academics, attributed the political stalemate of the 1970s to special interest groups that were unwilling to compromise for the common good. They mistook cause for effect. Carter had passed up many opportunities to end self-interested behavior in steel. He preferred the market to a global steel pact and to the tripartite steel committee. Carter's moral injunctions failed to persuade because they were asserted, not negotiated, and were unconnected to any long-term payoff for either workers or industry.

As in the past, the inaction of the state transported the problem to collective bargaining. To reestablish the link between short- and long-term goals, Jim Smith proposed to convert the COLA to stock ownership. Workers would forgo immediate income but gain a measure of security and future income from modernization. Lloyd McBride got the companies to insert the stock option in the 1980 contract. A modest measure, it embodied an approach that would eventually move the union beyond the parameters of postwar collective bargaining.[67]

In 1980 the steel industry believed it had a superior alternative in Republican presidential candidate Ronald Reagan. Reagan's steel program, announced just before Carter's, had consisted of the specific tax relief the industry wanted, strong enforcement of antidumping laws, and relaxation of the environmental laws. Reagan would "allow the steel industry to earn a reasonable profit on investment and sales," implying that the industry would have freedom to set its prices. The industry tried to get what it could from Carter, bought time with the union, but put its money on Reagan.[68]

Carter captured only 41 percent of the vote in 1980. A rejection so mammoth cannot be attributed to a single cause. But Carter's economic policy, the glue keeping the Democratic party's diverse constituencies together, was at the core of it. By failing to protect industrial workers, he sent some shopping for other candidates and programs. Others simply stopped voting.[69] Carter had ignored repeated warnings during his term in office. He had deluded himself and others into believing that the U.S. economy was healthy and had set about to solve the world's problems, not the nation's. Carter had little to draw upon from his own experience. As governor, he had helped integrate blacks into the body politic and brought Georgia's state government into the twentieth century. These experiences did not prepare him for the industrial crisis he faced. So he turned to the mandarins of the Democratic party, the Keynesians, who offered austerity. The party relinquished both New Deal legacies: modernization and social reform.[70] It would not get another chance soon. Ronald Reagan had alternative ideas and understood, as Carter did not, that a marriage had to take place between political ideas and constituencies.

Steel Is Not So Fundamental:
The Reagan Reconstruction
and Contemporary America

I n July 1982, the U.S. member of the OECD Steel Committee explained President Ronald Reagan's industrial policy to the representatives of the other nations: "It is simpler than some of the policies you have adopted. It requires no major public expenditure, no planning, and no direction by government. Key decisions are left to those closest to the market—the firms themselves. But our policy which relies on the free play of market forces to ensure that structural change and adaptation take place regularly, is a true industrial policy." [1]

The result of that policy was that the steel industry lost $12 billion dollars from 1982 to 1986. Over twenty-five companies, including some big ones, filed for bankruptcy. In 1984, imports increased to a record 26 percent of the market, and American companies lost $18 for every ton shipped. The next year, STR Clayton Yeutter told the Senate Finance Committee that some industries, "like steel, textiles, and footwear," would have to be phased out. "Not everyone can survive," Yeutter decreed. He should have said survive in the United States. Germany and Japan continued to enjoy trade surpluses in steel, textiles, and footwear. Previous administrations had facilitated imports of these products to cement strategic alliances. Reagan's transformed these policies plus some new ones into economic laws of nature. [2]

Reagan's industrial policy—tax, monetary, trade, and antitrust measures—channeled resources into real estate, finance, defense, and high technology. Propping up the nontrading sectors and hobbling the manufacturing ones smoothed relationships with Cold War allies but also produced the highest trade deficits in U.S. history. The president's actions and inactions effected a structural transformation of the U.S. economy that also enhanced the power of capital and diminished the power of labor. The industrial policy debates of the late 1970s had assumed that the social compact between labor and capital still held. During the Reagan years, the New Deal's marriage between efficiency and working-class progress was severed in fact and in theory.

Reagan's Economic Policies

The sectoral changes were a far cry from Republican intentions when the president took office. Reagan's economic program and specific pledges to the steel industry—tax cuts and less regulation—promised a strong industry. Even before the Economic Recovery Tax Act passed in August 1981, the AISI announced a $7 billion dollar investment program, which became the poster child of Reagonomics. Like a proud father, Reagan told Democratic House members on June 23 that "all of this [steel investment] was planned and decided upon . . . with the expectation that the economic package is going to be passed." In the afternoon he repeated the same good news to Republican lawmakers. He informed a group of taxpayer associations in California on June 25, an Illinois gathering on September 2, and probably many others. The president added that "when they [the tax cuts] actually begin to be implemented," steel investment would be even greater.[3]

Reagan articulated the expectations of the entire business community, which acted with remarkable unity in 1981 to promote capital formation. Corporate leaders rallied around the accelerated depreciation schedules for fixed assets and the investment tax credit. The value of write-offs, based upon the original cost of investment, had eroded because of inflation and technological change. Thus, for U.S. steel plants the write-off for equipment was fourteen years, compared with two years in Canada. The Accelerated Recovery Capital System (ARCS) would speed up the process to provide capital for new investment. Carter had considered the change too costly, but Reagan embraced ARCS and also vowed to make the 10 percent investment credit refundable, a move essential to the low-profit steel industry.[4] The tax bill Congress enacted in August 1981 contained the kernel of both measures, a traditional accumulation strategy beneficial to capital-intensive industries such as steel.

But Reagan's GOP was a broad tent. His candidacy was a product of a more radical movement, one less deferential to elite opinion than traditional Republicans. A new breed of Republicans, dubbed supply-siders, rallied around the Kemp-Roth 30 percent income tax cut, first introduced in Congress in 1978. Like the proponents of industrial policy, supply-siders were dissatisfied with the rate of growth. But they believed that lower tax rates would stimulate more savings, and thus capital, and more work, and thus labor from Americans. Lowering taxes across the board, not simply reducing levies on capital, they argued, would yield higher rates of growth and thereby tax revenues to offset initial losses. The poor would benefit from the economic activity unleashed by the tax reduction, not from social programs. Entrepreneurship would render government superfluous.

Reagan was attracted to supply-side wisdom, heresy to conventional economists on the right and the left, because it avoided the pinched austerity of traditional Republican economics. It did not order wage reduction, lower consumption, and the other bitter medicine the GOP usually prescribed for hard times. Business elites were not enamored of the broad tax reduction advocated by the supply-siders, but Reagan added the income tax reduction, scaled down to 23 percent over three years, to the tax cuts on capital. His political genius was to unite the GOP factions, even though the editors of the *Wall Street Journal* suspected that the various "tax cutters, tight-money advocates, and budget balancers" could not all succeed.[5]

During the spring of 1981, Wall Street viewed the Reagan tax program, regulatory reform, and investment plans as signs of a steel revival. Value Line, the investment advisory service, predicted in March that the steel industry would experience a major profit surge in the next three to five years. For the first time since 1974, it predicted that U.S. Steel would outperform the market. Merrill Lynch agreed. The head of the steel section of MITI, Kunio Ogawa, judged: "The American industry is one of the few still capable of catching up with the Japanese industry. They are making an effort to obtain technology, and there still is something of an independent spirit among them."[6]

Industry leaders were eager and planned to complete the modernization of steelmaking facilities, like installing the continuous caster, an innovation that had been delayed due to the tightfisted investment budgets of the 1970s. The caster permitted molten steel to be poured directly into semifinished shapes instead of into ingots that had to be reheated and rerolled. The savings in labor and energy costs were considerable, $30 a ton. Other projects, such as new pipe mills for the oil industry, reflected the changing demand for steel products.[7]

Unfortunately, desire and low taxes are not everything. By the fall of 1981, expensive dollars and high interest rates produced a nasty recession. In January 1982, the Commerce Department predicted that steel investment would be down for the year. Reagan retained his optimism about steel: "We're just seeing a little caution," he remarked. He was wrong. Capital spending was cut back radically from the $3.4 billion of 1981 to $2.1 billion in 1982, and even less in 1983.[8]

The exchange rate did its work first. If yen changes had wrecked the TPM in

1980, the rising dollar destroyed it in 1981. Steep interest rates kept the dollar high during the first Reagan term. The dollar appreciated 72 percent from the summer of 1980 to the fall of 1984, but the rise was particularly dramatic in 1981.[9] The costly dollar produced an avalanche of steel imports, reaching 26.3 percent by the end of the year. European exporters admitted that they were taking advantage of the situation and selling below the trigger price, which suddenly exceeded their costs when computed in dollars. Put another way, exchange rate changes lowered the price of imports by 40 percent while raising the price of U.S. exports by 70 percent. Typically, the cost of making a ton of steel in Germany rose, but the price of that ton in the U.S. market fell from $528, higher than what American producers were charging, to $397, about 30 percent below domestic offerings. "The U.S. steel market is under assault," concluded an economist for Chase Manhattan.[10]

Reeling from the currency distortions, the steel industry was nearly knocked out by the 1982 recession. The Federal Reserve Board's restriction of the money supply reduced inflation but also the GNP, which actually fell 2.1 percent in 1982, yielding an unemployment rate approaching 11 percent. In June, Chairman Volcker announced that he was staying the course. Volcker told the Joint Economic Committee that "the challenge is to make this recession not another wasted, painful episode, but a transition to a sustained improvement in the economic environment."[11]

U.S. Steel's David Roderick saw it differently. "This is not a recession," he told a congressional committee. "[W]e are back into the 1930s." In August, the AISI reported the lowest number of employed workers since it began collecting statistics in 1933. Between 1981 and 1982 over 100,000 steelworkers, almost 25 percent, lost their jobs. Steel mills operated at below 40 percent capacity in September. Companies lost about $53 for every ton of steel sold. Inland sustained losses for the first time in fifty years. Wheeling-Pittsburgh and McLouth Steel were close to bankruptcy.[12] Bethlehem's president Donald H. Trautlein appreciated the tax benefits from the 1981 act, but said that "because of the tremendous economic depression in the steel industry, we have not been able to utilize them."[13] Then, a reluctant Reagan, pressured by Wall Street's fear of the mounting deficits, accepted the 1982 tax law, which raised business taxes by $24 billion, removing provisions useful to the steel industry.[14]

Reagan's original tax bill was less helpful than it had first seemed. Some 40 percent of the investment incentives went to industries like oil, gas, timber, and coal, which did not need them. Ideology undercut the provisions that remained. Thus, Treasury had opposed the refundable investment credit because the government would be writing the checks. Instead, it supported "safe-harbor leasing," which allowed profitless firms, like steel companies, to sell new assets to profitable firms capable of using the tax credit and then lease them back. The virtue of the scheme was that the market, not government, made the decision. The market did not help Bethlehem Steel, which ended 1982 with unused credits of $230 million. But the provision produced a carnival of bizarre deals, permitting highly profitable firms to escape taxation. The inevitable public outcry forced Congress to repeal safe harbor leasing in 1982. In 1984, the steel industry's unused credits were nearly $4 billion.[15]

The recession created fault lines among different sectors of the economy—manufacturing, finance, high-tech, small business, and real estate. During the recession, the united businessmen of 1981 went their separate ways, and the steel industry ended up losing. A harbinger of change, Secretary of the Treasury Donald T. Regan hinted in October 1984: "We have to decide whether we want our corporate tax policy to be an industrial policy. Accelerated depreciation and the investment tax credit have definitely favored manufacturing over services." One of his aides indicted "tax-code socialism," arguing that taxes should not be used as an "industrial policy." The government would not promote a manufacturing revival.[16]

Under the banner of tax neutrality and rate reduction, still another law was passed in 1986, which lowered individual and corporate rates but also eliminated selective tax incentives, both the shameful and the useful. The constants in American tax policy—subsidies for oil, gas, real estate, and multinational corporations—remained. The first anti-industrial tax bill in U.S. history, the law raised the cost of capital for manufacturers and provided more resources for the service sector. The effective rate for equipment rose from 4 to 42 percent.[17] Thus, the tax code exacted an additional toll on long-term investment, already fettered by the currency changes, imports, and recession.[18]

The law reflected the new political power of leaders from the high-tech, financial, and service sectors, who concluded they had more to gain from the lower rates. A shrewd reporter at Fortune characterized the bill as "proconsumption and anti–capital investment, one destined to accelerate the nation's already powerful shift from a manufacturing to a service economy."[19] Despite the support of groups like Common Cause, Citizens for Tax Justice, and the Children's Defense Fund, tax neutrality was a Trojan Horse in the city of liberalism. While these reform groups believed that they were limiting the power of business to escape taxes, they were actually shackling the ability of the government to steer the economy. Tax policy was the primary lever the nation possessed to induce private businesses to produce socially desirable goods. Combined with the budget restraints, passed the year before, the meager scope of American macroeconomic policy narrowed even further.[20]

Reducing tax rates gave individuals and corporations more spending choices, but there was no guarantee that the funds would be invested. The personal savings rate fell from 9.1 percent of disposable income in 1980 to 5.1 percent in 1987. Investment during the 1980s was lower than in the period from 1974 to 1980. Given the redistribution of income upwards, the wealthy apparently consumed more than they invested. When they invested, they acquired and speculated more than they expanded productive capacities. The instability of economic life and the annual alterations of government policy in the early 1980s made short-term calculations rational for the individual and the firm but not necessarily for the nation. For investors, the incentives created by Reaganomics, combined with the industrial recession, made luxury consumption, real estate, shopping malls, financial services, and speculation more attractive than steel mills.[21]

Because of rising imports, less investment was needed. In 1988, William A. Niskanen, a member of Reagan's CEA, admitted that initially the government had given "little thought" to where the resources for increased defense spending and investment would come from. Only afterwards was it clear, he said, that the funds would come from "an increase in imports, permitting diversions from the domestic trade-affected sectors." Reagan told a radio audience in 1983 that "a strong dollar makes our purchases from abroad less expensive, and that's good." Consumers seemed to agree. Between 1980 and 1985 the American trade deficit rose from $25 billion to $122 billion. But like Yeutter's death sentence on the steel industry, a ballooning deficit had not been the goal in 1980, when Niskanen and the supply-siders had predicted that broad tax reduction would unleash the American enterprising spirit, which would "enhance our ability to compete with other countries in world markets, easing protectionist pressures at home."[22]

"Free Trade" and Trade Restraint

Traditional Republicans and supply-siders were free traders, but the administration lacked a trade policy because it believed that domestic resurrection would solve the import problem. Early on, Secretary of Transportation Drew Lewis argued that some protection from the flood of Japanese imports would enable the auto industry to attract the capital needed to convert to the manufacture of small cars. Secretary of State Alexander Haig countered with the diplomat's argument that the United States needed to maintain the international trading system. Regan argued that tax cuts would provide enough capital for the industry. But half a million unemployed auto workers, a nineteen-year low in production, $4 billion losses, and congressional threats possessed logic, too. The government acted, but allowed the Japanese to determine the extent of auto restraint.[23]

No one doubted Japanese auto efficiency. Steel followed a different script, because the imports were contaminated by subsidies and dumping. In December 1981, the EC announced a new aid package for European steel companies, $35 billion through 1985. The money would finance plant-closing costs, modernization, severance and pension benefits to laid-off workers, and R&D. This came at a time when European imports were flooding the American market, a source of the "material injury" required by the law. Another basis for steel industry complaint was the Tokyo Round's new code on subsidies, which allowed penalties in the form of countervailing duties. In January 1982, U.S. steel companies deposited 494 boxes, documenting 132 cases of unfair competition, on the steps of the International Trade Commission (ITC).[24]

Jan Tumlir, chief economist for the GATT in Geneva, thought the U.S. industry had "a strong case." In June 1982, the Commerce Department calculated the British subsidy to be 40 percent; the French, Italian, and Belgian, from 20 to 30 percent; and the German and Dutch insignificant. Most, including the Germans and Dutch, were dumping, too. Then the ITC ruled that the European exports injured the industry, a necessary part of the brief. EC Commissioner Étienne Davignon complained of "massive harassment" and threatened to retaliate against American exports. Davignon argued that the U.S.-EC agreements in 1977 and 1980 had permitted subsidies to revamp the industry, but he yielded a bit when he said that any penalty "should take into account customary patterns of trade." European steelmakers were as pressed as the Americans although their continuing expansion through 1979 made them the architects of their own fate. They lost $6 billion in 1982 alone. Even the German government, religiously opposed to state aid, was forced to help.[25]

Independent of its merits, the dispute posed some ideological problems for Reagan. He opposed "protectionism," but he also opposed European industrial policies. Economist Milton Friedman discovered a way out of the dilemma: If foreign states made cheap items for Americans, so be it. Friedman believed that when the foreigners discovered their errors and stopped subsidizing, American industries would spring up again.[26] Unlike the Canadian government, which initiated a series of unfair trade cases on steel imports, the White House followed Friedman's advice and stepped aside as the private suits took their cumbersome course. But it began to dawn on the president, as it had on his predecessor, that the results would exclude a good portion of the European imports. U.S.-EC relations were already frayed by Reagan's decision in June of 1982 to embargo use of American licenses by European firms working on the Urengoi gas pipeline, a project that would make Soviet fuel available to Western Europe. Added to conflicts over European farm policy and American monetary policy, transatlantic trade relations were at a danger point.[27]

No one on either side of the Atlantic wanted to compute another TPM. Countervailing duties, the legal penalties for subsidies, would dry up European imports. The U.S. industry was determined to obtain quantitative limits, which were common all over the world. It sought quotas on each product line so there could be no diversions. Most Europeans now agreed, and a deal was struck allotting 5.5 percent of the American market to the EC. The industry agreed to not file any new suits until the agreement expired in January 1986.[28]

Unrestrained imports from Brazil, Korea, Spain, Taiwan, and South Africa now flooded the U.S. market. Lynn Williams, the USWA's new president, protested, "it's unreasonable to have developed stability in European and Japanese steel imports but to see the effects of these restraints dissipated by the extraordinary surges from Third World countries." From the beginning, the industry and the union had wanted global quotas, which Reagan opposed.[29]

The newly industrializing countries (NICS) were now significant steel traders, even though only Taiwan and South Korea produced steel efficiently. In March 1977, under the auspices of the United Nations, executives from steel industries in developing countries agreed to aim for at least 30 percent of the world's supply. They had been encouraged by the U.S. Trade Act of 1974, which granted developing nations duty-free access for a range of products, including steel. The NICS obtained funds to construct mills from American banks that recycled petrodollars. Between 1975 and 1980, NIC steel production increased from 44 to 76 million tons. By 1981, third-world steel imports to the United States reached 29 percent of the total.[30]

South Korea was a major source of the new imports. Just as Japanese growth had taken off with the Korean War, Korea's was sparked by the Vietnam War. Following Tokyo's example, Korea made steel the priority of its development plan, but used a heavier hand. In 1968, it created the state-owned Pohang Iron and Steel Company (Posco), which today is the second largest steel producer in the world.[31] Posco set wages low and discouraged unions. In 1985, labor rates were 10 percent of the U.S. figure. The Korean government provided cheap loans and subsidies, attracted foreign capital, and encouraged a countercyclical export policy to take up the slack when its economy slowed. Posco exported 30 percent of its steel in 1982. If Reagan's currency policy hurt the U.S. steel industry, the Bank of Korea's decision to depreciate the Korean won facilitated its steel exports. Despite the world glut, Koreans pressed ahead, and U.S. agencies helped. In January 1984, the U.S. Export-Import Bank approved a $100 million loan guarantee to help Posco finance a new greenfield mill.[32]

Third-world imports posed as many political problems as did European imports. Brazil was in the midst of a debt crisis, caused in part by Fed stringency. One-third of Brazil's debt was owed to U.S. banks, which had lavished loans in the mid-1970s at a time when they were flush with funds from oil-producing nations. When domestic demand plummeted in the early 1980s, Brazil's debt-heavy steel industry had to "export or die." The U.S. Commerce Department determined that Brazilian plate was dumped at a margin of over 100 percent and hot-rolled sheet at nearly 90 percent.[33]

Pennsylvania's senators sprang into action. John Heintz threatened to oppose the American IMF contribution to bail out Brazil. Arlen Specter asked Treasury Secretary Regan why he was asking Congress to bail out a government whose policies were eliminating American jobs. Regan explained that "if we were to stop that practice [unfair trade] for Brazil, it would throw thousands of Brazilians out of work." But "we are throwing thousands of American steelworkers out of work," Specter protested. "Yes, Senator," Regan replied, "but that is not the sole problem; there are other problems." Indeed. Brazil's Commerce and Industry minister had warned that if the United States did not buy enough steel, Brazil would be unable to pay its debts.[34]

The durability of the international trading system required separating these transactions. The Brazilian crisis spotlighted the different interests of American banks and American industries, which threatened to bring down the house of cards. A compromise was fashioned. Brazil agreed to limit finished steel exports to the United States, U.S. Steel withdrew its unfair trade suits, and Heintz withdrew his opposition to the bailout. The Brazilians discovered a way around the limits and began building a new mill to make semifinished steel for export. No longer was it necessary for international agencies or American banks to pick up the bill. The Brazilian government, Kawasaki Steel of Japan, and Finsider of Italy financed the new mill.[35]

Despite the agreement with the Europeans, Japanese, and Brazilians, imports continued to rise, reaching 26.4 percent of the market in 1984. U.S. consumption rose 16 million tons, but American producers supplied only 6 million of the increase. Desperate times produced desperate measures. On January 24, 1984, the USWA joined with Bethlehem, Inland, and several others, but not U.S. Steel, to petition the ITC for relief under Section 201 of the Trade Act of 1974. Under this provision one did not have to prove that steel was being traded unfairly, only that imports were seriously injuring the industry. The ITC hearings, covered by thirteen separate television teams, including crews from foreign nations, received unusual attention. On July 14, by a vote of 3–2, the ITC accepted the industry-union brief, urging the president to impose a combination of tariffs and quotas on five of nine products investigated.[36]

The judgment placed the administration in a bind. Under Section 201, nations whose shipments were restricted were entitled to compensation via measures against U.S. exports. Some Reaganites worried about retaliation against American soybeans. The government was divided, and in familiar ways. Commerce Secretary Malcolm Baldrige and Labor Secretary Ray Donovan supported restriction, while Regan, Secretary of State George Shultz, Defense Secretary Casper Weinberger, and the CEA opposed. However, after the ITC found injury, it would have been difficult to refuse to act in an election year. Even so, White House chief of staff James A. Baker III, gazing at the president's 22 percent lead over his Democratic rival, Walter F. Mondale, calculated that an outright rejection of aid would hurt the president only in Pennsylvania.[37]

One day after Mondale presented his own industrial policy for steel, the president acted to protect free trade ideology and his chances in Pennsylvania. STR William E. Brock highlighted the president's rejection of the tariffs and quotas recommended by the ITC. "Protectionism is not in the national interest," he asserted; the nation needed "to liberalize world trade." Only then did Brock inform the nation that he would "negotiate voluntary restraint agreements" with other countries even where "there was no injury determination." The negotiations produced voluntary restraint agreements (VRAs) that limited imports to 20 percent of the market for five years. The industry and the union had wanted 15 percent—5 for the EC, 5 for Japan, and 5 for the NICs. Still, the VRAs stabilized the industry. Imports were at 26 percent in 1986, but by 1989 they were down to 18 percent.[38]

Bringing in Industrial Policy through the Back Door

Trade relief was not enough for steelworkers and other industrial workers. In 1982, 79 percent of the new jobless were blue-collar workers. The unemployment rate for professional and technical workers was less than 4 percent, for workers in primary metals over 28 percent, for auto workers 23 percent. In 1983, the economy recovered from the deep recession, helped by the tax cuts and defense spending and by temporary relaxation of monetary policy. The GNP rose 3.5 percent in 1983 and 7 percent in 1984. But job growth in retailing and restaurants did not extend to manufacturing. When a reporter asked David Roderick about a turnaround, he said it existed only for sellers of "tennis shoes and shirts." There was a boom in tennis, but one in steel was difficult to see. And the budget deficit reached record heights, rising from 2.7 to 5.2 percent of GNP from 1981 to 1984. Was this a durable recovery, or were Americans going on a spending binge, financed by debt? For steelworkers the answer was clear: the number of jobs fell from 512,000 to 334,000 from 1980 to 1984, and would fall to 237,500 in 1985.[39]

The hemorrhaging of industrial America brought Democrats twenty-six new House seats in the 1982 elections. Most Democratic liberals attempted to shelter safety nets from the Reagan assaults. But many congressional committees held hearings on industrial policy in 1983 and 1984, which yielded seventeen bills establishing industrial councils and banks. The president's opposition and the Republican control of the Senate made action in 1983 and 1984 unlikely, but a few Democratic legislators readied themselves for a Democratic president after 1984. Representatives Timothy Worth of Colorado and Richard Gephardt of Missouri proposed an Economic Cooperation Council. Stanley Lundine of New York and David Bonior of Michigan offered a National Industrial Bank. George Eads, who had been on Carter's CEA, complained that Washington was again suffering from "industrial policy fever," which had subsided after Reagan's election.[40]

Representative John J. LaFalce's proposal typified the thinking. LaFalce, a Democrat from the Buffalo-Lackawanna area, which was experiencing a blizzard of plant closures in steel and auto, proposed an industrial bank. His banking subcommittee had shepherded the New York City and Chrysler financial reconstructions. LaFalce aimed to overcome the adversarial and ad hoc character of U.S. decision making. The bank would be advised by a council representing industry, banking, labor, and government. Funded at $8.5 billion, the sum the United States had just given to the IMF, the bank could leverage money to yield about $141 billion.[41]

LaFalce argued that his proposal was not a radical departure from past policy. Each year existing government credit programs awarded $47 billion directly and $84 billion more in guaranteed loans. Added to $115 billion disbursed via tax incentives, government policies already allocated 13.9 percent of the GNP. The bulk of credit and tax benefits went to housing, petroleum, coal, and timber; procurement policies aided aviation, maritime, petroleum, and semiconductors. Even after the ending of the Reconstruction Finance Corporation, the nation was awash in special banks for housing, agriculture, and exports. This targeting reflected nineteenth-century goals of resource development, New Deal promotion of housing and farming, and Cold War purposes. LaFalce suggested a new goal—industrial competitiveness. If the United States for the first time in its history was faced with imports from "developmental" states, ones that funded industries, the government would have to foster competitive industries.

LaFalce and other industrial policy advocates were buoyed by the publication of Chalmers Johnson's *MITI and the Japanese Miracle* in 1982. Johnson's subtitle "The Growth of Industrial Policy" contained his thesis that the miracle was produced by the Japanese state's pursuing market effectiveness and results, not the market efficiency and rules that characterized U.S. policy. Debate over Japan became the prologue to a debate about the United States. Manuel H. Johnson, assistant secretary for economic policy at Treasury, told LaFalce's committee that MITI was not the source of Japanese economic prowess, though he admitted that the best example of MITI's success was steel. "Incentives," which had reduced the cost of capital, "produced remarkable results in terms of new, highly efficient steel plants." Navigating an Orwellian turn, Johnson concluded, "[T]hese results may have been failure in disguise. It now appears that Japanese steel industry is overexpanded." This was too much for one legislator, who marveled at the implication that "ours [the American steel industry] is a model because we don't have overcapacity."[42]

Under LaFalce's questioning, Johnson stated that the United States possessed the Export-Import Bank to finance exports only because other nations had one. Without missing a beat, LaFalce asked why he opposed an industrial bank, which most nations also possessed. Johnson said that the United States had trade laws to deal with the subject. The distinction between export and industrial credit was a policy, not a theoretical distinction. In 1974, advocates of Burke-Hartke had attempted to return investment from overseas to the United States. Now, some legislators attempted to provide funds by creating a bank.[43]

Reagan was on the defensive. An entire chapter of the *President's Economic Report* of 1984 explained why the United States did not need an industrial policy. The administration preferred to see Japanese success as a result of its high saving rate and transfer of labor from agriculture to industry. The report tallied Japan's failures as well as successes and indicted European industrial policies as being even worse than Japan's. But Reagan could not simply fight on foreign soil. He argued that if an American steel industry was truly vital to other industries, "the profit motive will ensure that this demand will be filled. If the demand can be met more cheaply by producers abroad, then it makes good economic sense for the firms that use the input to buy it abroad." The logic for tolerating imports was stated clearly, uncontaminated by the politics that had forced Reagan to offer some protection later in the year. Reagan had gone one step beyond Carter. The Democratic president had welcomed steel imports to discipline steel prices. Reagan severed linkages between steel and other economic activities. Steel was no longer fundamental, but just another "input"— for some Reaganites, less valuable than soybeans.[44]

Holding fast to the Keynesian consensus, Democratic elites were no more sympathetic. Carter's CEA head Charles Schultze had not altered his opposition to industrial policy. Japan "does not owe its industrial success to its industrial policy," Schultze told the Joint Economic Committee. Insisting that "America is not deindustrializing" he warned that the government's selecting winners would simply end up as "pork" or "monopoly." Other reputedly more liberal Keynesians agreed. Robert Eisner stuck with monetary and fiscal policy, arguing, "If the basic industries are to decline, perhaps they should." James Tobin believed the United States "did not need an industrial policy, but better macroeconomic policy: Looser money and a tighter budget."[45]

Although some business leaders had been tempted to support industrial policy in 1980, they too now opposed it. Jerry Janowski, chief economist of NAM, scoffed at the notion that the United States could exist as a postindustrial society but urged better fiscal and monetary policy. The vice chairman of Intel, Robert Noyce, representing the "sunrise" semiconductor industry, believed the nation needed more engineers and investment capital, but not a bank. Noyce did worry, however, about Japanese targeting. The Reagan administration had totaled the amount of government funds going directly into Japanese industry and found the sums paltry, compared with the size of its economy. Noyce stated that it was not the size of the contribution to semiconductors but the message it sent to financial decision makers that investment in this industry carried little risk because the government was preferring it. Reducing the risk while protecting the home market as companies develop products can yield enduring competitive advantages. Two years later, as we shall see, the entrepreneurs of Silicon Valley came to the government and received both trade protection and research money. But in 1983 the high-technology industry still weighed in with opponents of industrial policy.[46]

Many corporate leaders nonetheless concluded that American institutions and policies were defective. In June, the president responded by creating the Commission on Industrial Competitiveness, without labor representation, to study the matter. Even before the group assembled, Reagan laid out the parameters for its work. He rejected "detailed plans or solutions to problems for particular companies or industries." Documenting Chalmers Johnson's depiction of U.S. political economy, Reagan said, "government serves us best by protecting and maintaining the marketplace, by ensuring that the rules of free and fair trade, both at home and abroad, are properly observed and by safeguarding the freedoms of individual participants." Proper monetary and fiscal policy "will facilitate the movement of capital toward promising economic activities," providing jobs "for workers displaced by changes." Although the commission was to study "how to meet international competition at home and abroad," Reagan stressed the utopias of high technology and appointed John A. Young of Hewlett-Packard to chair the commission. Cataloguing a businessperson's wish list of more investment, education, cooperation, etc., the report, submitted after the 1984 elections, stayed true to its charge and offered no specific advice.[47]

Congressional and presidential inaction catapulted politics to the top of the USWA agenda in 1984. The union attempted to alter politics in the long run by inserting elements of an industrial policy for steel into the new trade legislation in 1984. President Lloyd McBride died in late 1983, literally of heartbreak. His successor, Lynn Williams, was more comfortable with political action than his predecessor. Williams, a native of Canada accustomed to social democratic politics, was the first genuine intellectual to head the USWA.[48] He was soft-spoken but demonstrated a strategic and tactical virtuosity that got the union through the most difficult period of its history.

Williams concluded that only a president could overcome the Democratic divisions on industrial policy. He convinced presidential candidate Walter Mondale to support a comprehensive industrial policy for steel. Although Mondale waged his campaign on macroeconomic issues, he promised to revitalize steel and other sectors "along the Chrysler model." He advocated a council similar to the one proposed by LaFalce to analyze the effects of federal government policies on competitiveness, but not a bank.[49]

The USWA did not wait for November. Trade legislation was the most practical vehicle for enacting industrial policy. The Steel Caucus had introduced two quota bills in 1984, the threat that had forced the president to agree to the VRAs in September. The union's version required "a verifiable modernization plan"; the industry's did not. In response, the CEA's William Niskanen intoned the old mantra: "[W]e are not here to plan the future of the United States steel industry. . . . I think it is inappropriate and possibly illegal for us to require firms to make public their long-range plans." STR William Brock told Congressman Don J. Pease of Ohio, "it is my view that the individual company concerned should be solely responsible for deciding how modernization should proceed." When the president chose to negotiate VRAs, both bills were dropped, but investment requirements entered through another door.[50]

VRAs were policed by the exporting nation. They were unenforceable under U.S. laws unless Congress granted authority to the Customs Office, which is what Senator Heintz's steel trade bill enacted. The day after Reagan's decision to restrain imports, Lynn Williams convinced the House steel caucus to condition American enforcement upon modernization and to aim for imports of 17 percent, instead of the president's 20 percent. Both proposals won the support of Ways and Means chairman Dan Rostenkowski, who insisted upon it in the House-Senate conference committee.[51]

Title VIII of the Trade and Tariff Act of 1984 was the closest the United States came to creating, in the words of the Act, a "national policy for the steel industry." Concluding that the high value of the dollar, mounting deficits, and burgeoning imports had damaged the industry, the Act stated that trade relief would be ineffective without modernization. Thus, "substantially all" of the "net cash flow" of the major producers should be devoted to modernization, and 1 percent should be spent on training and worker adjustment programs. The ITC was to monitor the industry's spending and report annually to Congress, which could end enforcement if the results were inadequate. The administration and its congressional allies opposed this section, but Reagan's desire for other parts of the law forced him to go along.[52] The steel industry was not pleased, though subsequent ITC reports demonstrated that the industry complied fully with the provision.[53]

Title VIII still did not provide resources or shape policy. But ideologically it challenged Reagan's conception of pure markets. Representative Lundine thought "this dose of specific 'industrial policy' . . . very refreshing." LaFalce added, "if we do not . . . condition trade relief on specific efforts to improve this industry's competitiveness, we risk simply repeating the mistakes of the past." But the future of the steel industry had already been determined by that past.

Steel in an Era of Laissez-Faire

Most of the decade's $27 billion investment was undertaken after the market was stabilized by import restraint and the dollar devaluation of 1985. But these sums modernized an industry that had shrunk radically in the preceding four years. Toyoo Gyohten, a vice minister of international affairs at the Japanese Ministry of Finance at the time, concluded that "fundamental changes in the import patterns affecting U.S. industry" would not easily be reversed by dollar devaluation.[54] During this laissez-faire period, American steel production fell 40 percent, in contrast to drops of 12 and 21 percent in Japan and Europe. Companies cut back investment, imported semifinished steel, merged, diversified, dediversified, and went out of business. No company pursued a consistent strategy.

U.S. Steel has often been associated with the strategy of diversification; its purchase of Marathon Oil in 1983 and then Texas Oil and Gas in 1984 meant that over half of its revenues came from energy. In 1986 it renamed itself USX and made its oil and steel companies separate subsidiaries. Still there was no grand design. Chairman David Roderick acted like a cornered bull, determined that the corporation would survive but uncertain how to proceed. Roderick traveled down two roads when he announced his intention to file suits against subsidized European steel producers and also to purchase Marathon in November 1981. Even the Marathon purchase was not an escape route but a revenue maker, assuring income in the down portion of the steel cycle, a perennial problem that was then assuming crisis proportions. The money for the Marathon purchase was not taken from steel. U.S. Steel sold nonsteel assets worth $2.2 billion and used a portion of that, $1.4 billion, plus a $4.7 billion loan to buy Marathon. Roderick correctly stated that such a loan would not have been available for steel investment but admitted that the debt incurred "has certainly impinged upon our desire to further borrow." University of Pennsylvania economist F. Gerard Adams pointed out: "If we had a rational industrial policy . . . if we had told United States Steel you cannot buy Marathon Oil with $6 billion, and instead said, if you take that $6 billion [and put it in steel,] then we'll give you $3 billion for 20 years at 9 percent, that might have been a constructive way to finally begin modernizing the steel industry."[55]

Instead, the corporation eliminated a fifth of its steelmaking capacity in 1983 and announced it planned to import steel slabs from British Steel Company's (BSC) mill at Ravenscraig, Scotland. This was to take the place of modernizing the hot end of its Fairless Works, which still made open hearth steel. The British slabs cost from $20 to $50 per ton less than those produced at Fairless, and Roderick claimed that the $2 billion price of modernizing the mill could not be recovered. The package was sweetened by a $600 million BSC investment in U.S. Steel.[56]

A CEO from a competing firm reckoned that the deal was "a brilliant move if you just look at the economics, but from the public relations standpoint, it's the dumbest thing U.S. Steel has ever done." To traffic with the most subsidized company in Europe after winning trade relief because of those subsidies threw ideological consistency to the winds. Bethlehem and the USWA believed that the proposed sale circumvented the EC quota, computed on the basis of finished products. Moreover, the deal rubbed salt in the very raw wounds of labor relations. U.S. Steel had just won wage reductions at Fairless, and the workers believed that their concessions would be used for modernizing the mill. The USWA feared that the practice of importing semifinished steel would spread through the industry.[57]

Although the USWA waged a vigorous campaign against the venture, the British ended up pulling out because of a similar combination of smart economics and stupid politics. A decade before, during the boom years, government-owned BSC had begun a vast expansion to double its capacity to 30 million tons. When the steel market contracted after 1974, it was difficult to halt the construction of new plants or close older plants. The company existed on subsidies, which did not stop the losses ($4 million a day in the summer of 1980). The sale of Ravenscraig slabs might have saved the mill, but British taxpayers were incensed at the price—investing government money in U.S. Steel.[58]

The politics of the deal doomed it, but importing semifinished steel, which had been deliberately exempted from trade restraint, and concentrating on the finishing end became common. Throughout the industrialized world, but especially in the investment-short United States, construction of BOF furnaces declined. U.S. Steel not only refused to build one at Fairless, it shut down others already operating in Chicago and Duquesne, Pennsylvania. Kaiser planned to import 500,000 tons of semifinished steel, phase out its BOFS, and concentrate on finishing. Wheeling-Pittsburgh was negotiating with Brazil to obtain cheap steel. The USWA tried to hold the line. When Armco Steel asked its Houston workers whether they would roll foreign billets, they said no. Armco closed the mill.[59]

Plans for new finishing mills were also shelved. In 1983, despite concessions from workers and local and state governments, U.S. Steel canceled plans to build a $225 million rail mill in Chicago. The company claimed that it had not obtained the wage rates obtained by competitors, but in fact it bowed out because of the recession. Wheeling-Pittsburgh's new rail mill was running at only 25 percent of capacity. Determined to lower wages, U.S. Steel could not resist an occasion to bolster its case.[60]

Though plummeting revenues pulled the corporation toward diversifying, importing cheap slabs, retiring facilities, and scaling back investment, it had no intention of leaving the steel business. Roderick hired Thomas C. Graham, president of LTV's Jones and Laughlin, to run U.S. Steel. Graham was determined to increase the company's market share, a goal it had renounced since its creation in 1901. He closed facilities supplying the capital goods industry, the weakest part of the current market. But he spent $290 million for two continuous slab casters at the Gary and Fairfield Works. Graham planned to expand capacity in steel for consumer goods, autos, and appliances, where the corporation was weak. The high cost of capital made buying a strong company that produced light sheet an attractive alternative to constructing a new facility; National Steel was an obvious choice. The deal would have made U.S. Steel the world's second largest steel company behind Japan's Nippon Steel.

Even though National Steel was part of a highly diversified company, it possessed modern, efficient mills. In 1983, National operated at 81 percent of capacity, the highest in the industry, and was the only integrated producer to end the year in the black. But because steel profits were still low and the government made it clear that it would tolerate imports, National Steel decided to leave the industry. It sold its Weirton Steel Works to its workers and in 1984 proposed to sell its entire steel operations. Standing Darwin on his head, often the fittest left the industry. U.S. Steel was willing to buy the National mills for $575 million. It had recently sold nearly a billion dollars of nonsteel assets, so it had the cash. The corporation would be paying about $170 for each ton of new capacity, in contrast to $450, the price for modernizing Fairless.[61]

If the Marathon purchase led to charges that U.S. Steel was abandoning steel, now it was accused of stifling competition. Although it supplied only 16 percent of the market, the merger of the number one and number seven steelmakers had to pass the antitrust test. But U.S. Steel was second in line, behind LTV and Republic, who had earlier announced plans to merge. If U.S. Steel's purpose was to strengthen weak product lines, LTV aimed to rationalize two firms that made the same kinds of steel. The enlarged LTV could shut down the least efficient mills and still retain markets and revenues.

Although the 1980s was an era of frenetic merger activity, they were of the conglomerate type. Celler-Kefauver's prohibitions against sectoral concentration lived on. Reagan's first antitrust chief, William Baxter, had obtained a law permitting joint ventures for research and development and had liberalized the concentration rules, but Baxter continued to exclude imports when he computed the size of the U.S. steel market. That calculation made the steel sector appear more concentrated than it actually was. Thus, the antitrust division rejected the LTV-Republic merger. Paul McGrath, who headed the division in 1984, told a congressional committee that "the best way for the integrated steel industry to become more efficient and productive is to preserve and promote an industry structure that maximizes competition."[62]

One steel executive from another firm was dumbstruck. "[B]y killing this merger, the government is effectively telling troubled companies, 'forget any restructuring' . . . From an industrial-policy point of view, it's confusing." USWA head Lynn Williams mused, "whether we like it or not, there is no free market in steel. . . . The absence of any defined national policies regarding steel and our major industries is highlighted in the confusion from the president, who was saying that he was unopposed to steel mergers." Reflecting the division within the government, Secretary of Commerce Malcolm Baldrige called it "a world-class mistake."[63]

Steel customers were appalled, too. The president of a hardware concern in Cleveland, home to plants of both companies, said, "This has got to be the stupidest thing the government has ever done. I'm not worried about price. I'm concerned about the availability of domestic supplies." The heads of Maytag and Caterpillar Tractor agreed. Unlike Reagan, manufacturers believed that there were industrial cultures, linking steel and the fabricating companies.[64]

Using similar logic, McGrath rejected the U.S. Steel–National merger in March. One month later he okayed the purchase of half of National Steel's stock by Nippon Kokan (NKK), Japan's number-two producer and the fifth largest in the world. In the U.S. market, however, Nippon was a small player. Foreign firms could purchase American companies more easily than domestic ones could. How this affected the goal of revitalizing American industry was an unasked question. If U.S. Steel's merger with National had gone through, its subsequent history might have taken a different path. By the end of the decade, USX had closed seven integrated facilities, maintaining only three—in Fairfield, Alabama, Lorain, Ohio, and Gary, Indiana; it became the leading American importer of semifinished steel, an offshore solution.[65]

Mergers were no silver bullet. McGrath reconsidered and accepted the LTV-Republic plan, with some divestment. The new LTV reduced costs, but the collapse of prices in 1985 threw it into bankruptcy, where it remained until 1993. During the Carter years, the USWA had accepted mergers as a means of reducing the costs of modernization, but it now opposed liberalizing antitrust rules because mergers were being used to eliminate mills and workers. The USWA believed that the industry was shedding too much capacity. As it turned out, the USWA was right.[66]

Dennis Carney, CEO of Wheeling-Pittsburgh, also opposed mergers, because they did not add needed capital and "power to defend against foreign government financing." Carney, who had obtained an EDA loan for his rail mill, advocated an assortment of government financing, including an industrial bank, to equalize capital costs in the United States and Japan. If the government refused, he said, "the steel industry in this country will be very similar to the television industry. . . . There are no televisions made in the United States." Without capital, "it is just a matter of time until they [steel companies] are going to have to join the foreigners." He spoke from experience. Wheeling-Pittsburgh was the first major American steel company to obtain Japanese equity capital, 10 percent, in 1983. Such solutions became common after the steel market stabilized in 1985.[67]

Post-Darwinian Reconstruction

During the 1980s, the steel industry realized annual returns of −2.5 percent. Financing modernization from retained earnings, borrowing, and stock issues was out of the question. Companies raised capital by selling nonsteel assets and employing novel financing, but most entered into arrangements with foreign steel companies, suppliers, and governments, who had more interest in American steel than did the Reagan administration or U.S. banks.

In 1983, when capital was literally unavailable, Bethlehem leased two continuous casters from their Austrian builders, who obtained financing from foreign bankers and the Austrian government. U.S. Steel executed a similar arrangement with other banks at its Gary works. But after 1985, direct foreign investment became common. By 1991, fifty-six joint foreign ventures brought in new investment of more than $3 billion. U.S. steel companies became transnational in their own fashion.[68]

Importing slab steel, mainly from NICs like Brazil and Korea, for finishing mills became a permanent feature of the industry, because the shutdowns had eliminated capacity. U.S. Steel joined South Korea's Posco to make sheet steel on the West Coast. Posco supplied hot-rolled, semifinished steel coils to U.S. Steel's Pittsburg Works in California, allowing it to close its plant in Geneva, Utah, which still produced open hearth steel. Kaiser sold its Fontana mill to a group of California, Brazilian and Japanese companies. The younger Kaiser was more interested in the Denver Broncos than the steel industry. The new owner, California Steel, imported Brazilian slab to make sheets and plates.[69] The motives of NICs were defensive. State-owned Korean and Brazilian steelmakers with large plants were efficient only when producing at full capacity. Joint ventures guaranteed a stable outlet. Brazil became the world's largest exporter of slabs. The disaggregation of steel production was a partial return to nineteenth-century models, but with an international twist.

Japan's purposes were also defensive. Fearing it would be shut out of the U.S. market, Tokyo acted to strengthen Japanese companies by investing in American industry.[70] Rejecting the notion that steel was a sunset industry, President Minoru Kanao of Nippon Kokan told a reporter, "[W]e are looking at the long term. America is the largest market for steel products." He meant large in the sense of openness, not simply size. In the midst of the recession in 1982, the head of Nippon Steel said that the U.S. economy was "the key" to recovery of the critical Japanese export market. After Reagan announced the steel quotas in September 1984, Japan feared that third-world steelmakers would be accommodated at the expense of Japan's 6.5 percent share. Thus, the Japanese invested in American companies to ensure access to the American market over and above the VRAS. MITI sometimes provided low-interest government loans for these purchases. The U.S. opposition to steel imports had produced an industrial policy of sorts—foreign investment in the United States.[71]

The first Japanese firms to invest in the United States were the steel suppliers of the Japanese automakers, who were also producing in the United States because they too feared being shut out of the American market. Japanese auto firms transplanted to the United States preferred to purchase steel from their traditional Japanese providers, who joined American steelmakers to continue these relationships in the United States. The marriage between Armco and Kawasaki Steel was typical. Armco spun off its steel operation in 1989 to form AK Steel, in partnership with Kawasaki Steel. Kawasaki invested $375 million and eventually owned 50 percent of the company. AK Steel supplied Nissan, Toyota, and other Japanese transplants.[72]

The Japanese government often subsidized these investments. When NKK bought into National Steel in 1984, the Japanese firm was losing money and deeply in debt. Nevertheless, its bankers and the Japanese government supplied the funds. In 1987, Nippon Steel joined Inland to build a cold-reduction rolling mill. Inland and Nippon each contributed $60 million, and three Japanese trading companies added $250 million. A second venture was financed with a $330 million loan from the government's Industrial Bank of Japan. Nippon now owns a sizable share (14 percent) of the voting rights in Inland Steel. Other Japanese companies, Kobe Steel and Sumitomo Metals, shared the cost and ownership of particular lines at U.S. Steel and LTV, though not of the companies themselves. By the end of the 1980s, the Commerce Department estimated that foreign, mainly Japanese, steelmakers held substantial positions in nearly 25 percent of the integrated mills. In 1995, the president of NKK characterized the relationship as "competition through cooperation."[73]

The minimill was another new element in the industrial structure. As their name suggests, minimills produced steel without using coke ovens and blast furnaces, instead melting scrap in electric furnaces, which had first been used in the United States in 1906. Using a continuous caster, minimills then directly cast the molten steel into semifinished billets or blooms, bypassing the reheating required before the primary rolling. Saving capital, minimills also saved labor. They benefited from low prices for scrap and electric power in the United States and from the perversities of trade policy in the 1970s. Import controls calculated on the basis of tonnage had caused foreign producers to shift to higher value products, leaving a free field for the cheaper ones that minimills produced.[74]

Because the typical electric furnace was small, minimills tailored their capacities to meet local and regional demand, thereby minimizing transportation costs as well. Because they used scrap, they were free to locate away from the major waterways in low-wage areas. Villages and towns staged competitions (prohibited in most other countries) to obtain them. Only half were unionized. Nonetheless, wages at minimills were usually similar to union scale, although they were often achieved through performance-based bonuses. Labor costs were lower at minimills because they had no legacy of retirees and thus lacked the pension and health expenses of the integrated firms.

A national phenomenon today, minimills began in the South and Southwest. In the late 1960s, Georgetown, South Carolina, put together an attractive package to lure the German minimill Korf, whose labor policy was discussed in Chapter 7. The town issued low-interest, tax-free bonds and gave Korf a ten-year property tax holiday, a highly favorable power contract with the state-owned utility, and state-sponsored job training. South Carolina built a $2 million deepwater dock to serve the mill. Its German equipment was financed with an export loan from Bonn. Minimills enjoyed a price flexibility that Big Steel could not afford. The president of the mill explained, "If they [U.S. Steel] reduce the price, everybody goes down with them—they won't sell a ton more steel. But with our infinitesimal market share, we are assured of selling all we can produce. All we have to do is ship it farther or cut the price."[75]

In addition to making steel, minimills shored up ideology on both the right and left. To Donald F. Barnett and Louis Schorsch, they were proof that competition, not industrial policy, was the fuel that powered steel resurrection. But minimills did not obtain a dispensation from the effects of downward spiraling prices in the 1980s. Costs at the integrated mills declined, foreign producers enjoyed the benefit of overvalued dollars, rising scrap prices eliminated cost advantages, and overexpansion created gluts. Five minimills failed and shut down in 1985. Korf joined the campaign to limit steel imports and filed for bankruptcy. Robert Garvey, the head of the minimill North Star Steel acknowledged in 1990 that "minimills today are confronted by the same problem that the integrated mills have faced throughout the 1980s—excess capacity in their basic product lines."[76]

On the left, Michael Piore and Charles Sabel viewed minimills as the vanguard of a future regime of flexible, democratic, small-scale manufacturing, typical of post-Fordist production. But minimills functioned best when they concentrated on a small number of uniform products. They opened new product lines in new mills precisely because they were not inherently flexible. As Christoph Scherrer put it, "[the] mills are not run by artisans and the mill equipment is not all-purpose machinery."

When its product niches filled, Nucor, the leading minimill, attempted to move up into the profitable sheet steel market. However, obtaining high enough quality for this market is not assured, because steel scrap is not the purest raw material.[77]

Operating at the margins, as most minimills do, left little surplus for science. Nucor has a reputation for cutting corners on engineering and research. In 1988, Nucor obtained technology from the Japanese steel company Yamato Kogyo. The Industrial Bank of Japan, acting to enhance Tokyo's place in the U.S. market, proposed and financed the venture, which is located in Blytheville, Arkansas. In 1995, Nucor teamed up with U.S. Steel to develop a type of purified iron which, when combined with scrap, could produce a superior sheet steel, currently out of its reach. Nucor's president, John Correnti, explained, "We bring construction expertise on how to build these types of plant. USX has great physicists." There is no free lunch in the steel industry.[78]

Still, minimills retain their strength. They currently produce over one-third of U.S. steel output. Nucor, the largest, operating seven plants, was the number-six U.S. steel producer in 1996. Minimills, constructed by independents and traditional steelmakers alike, often with foreign capital, are the only new additions to U.S. steel capacity since the 1960s.[79] They have not, however, made a dent in the import market, and their own markets are glutted. Instead of aiming to export its products, Nucor has just announced a plan to build a $700 million minimill in Brazil, counting on receiving favorable tax considerations and low-priced electricity from the state. Other minimills facing identical conditions are also going abroad.[80]

However, the new diversity reflected by the minimills is less significant than the overall reduction in U.S. steel capacity, which exceeded the losses in every other steel-producing nation. The U.S. industry absorbed the lion's share of the

European and Japanese overexpansion of the 1970s. Between 1960 and 1986, European production declined from 29 to 18 percent of the global share. Over the same period, the U.S. share fell from 26 to 10 percent. Between 1982 and 1988, the industry retired over 42 million tons of capacity, representing more than 25 percent of the total. In 1975, twenty integrated companies operated forty-seven plants in the United States; by the end of the 1980s, there were only fourteen companies, operating twenty-three plants. Production, at 105 million tons in 1997, has not returned to the 1981 level of 120.8 million tons. Capacity is smaller than that of the mid-1950s. Steel imports have permanently taken up the slack. In 1994, when the industry was competitive, the dollar cheap, and interest rates low, imports took 24.9 percent of the market. The United States is the only major industrial nation that is not self-sufficient in steel.[81]

Labor Relations

Imports, price wars, red ink, and shutdowns inevitably shattered the collective bargaining system created after World War II. Some writers, like John P. Hoerr, not content to simply describe the unraveling, attribute the industry's ills to "the American system of organizing and managing work." With exquisite impartiality, Hoerr blamed both the USWA and corporations for the adversarial labor relations, the principal cause of the industry's situation.[82] But across the Atlantic, European restructuring was accompanied by strikes and violence exceeding those in the United States. In May 1982, police in Belgium clubbed and teargassed thousands of protesting steelworkers when layoffs were announced.[83]

Bad labor relations are not the original sin of the steel industry. A BOF, a continuous caster, and favorable public policy are more important than the warm feelings of labor-management cooperation. Conditions in the mills worsened because, as in so many other areas of American life, collective bargaining was forced to carry too much weight. Unlike the Belgian government, the U.S. government stepped aside in the steel crises of the 1980s, and the union and companies fought it out among themselves. The period of conflict was protracted and still remains unresolved. The laissez-faire period produced managers bent on wage reduction and altering work rules. When pressed to the wall, some companies went after the pensions and health benefits of retirees. Poisoned labor relations were the result, not the cause, of steel industry woes.

High steel wages is a related, common diagnosis of what went wrong. But during the 1960s, when productivity rose at an annual rate of 2.6 percent, real employment costs rose only 1.3 percent. It is true that the COLA ballooned because of the inflation. From 1973 to 1980, the COLA accounted for 70 percent of wage increases. But even though inflation raised employment costs from $136 to $159 per ton between 1979 and 1980, wages were a smaller proportion of costs in 1980 than they had been in 1965.[84]

The 1980 USWA contract had been modest, but the industry refused to renew the Experimental Negotiating Agreement (ENA) for future negotiations, signaling its withdrawal from consensual relations. The crisis of 1982 led the companies to ask for a reopener. In late July the industry, led by U.S. Steel, demanded givebacks amounting to $6 billion. Employment costs had shot up again in 1982 to $195 per ton for reasons unrelated to wage rates. As production fell, the massive layoffs spread fixed costs for pensions, supplementary unemployment benefits (SUBs), and insurance over a smaller number of workers. Provisions that once had stabilized an industry and a society now became millstones. But even while employment costs rose 23 percent from 1980 to 1982, energy costs rose 53 percent and interest rates 86 percent.

Top union leaders understood that the industry was pressed, but the $6 billion giveback demand was out of the question. The USWA countered with a package of $2 billion in wage concessions and tried to soften the impact by diverting scheduled raises to SUBs, investment in steel facilities, and employee stock ownership. Union economist Jim Smith reminded workers that John L. Lewis's policy of "no backward steps" only destroyed the United Mine Workers during the 1925 coal slump. But applying that historical lesson was more difficult than stating it.[85]

Twice in 1982 the industry and union failed to agree. The second time, in November, company and union leaders reached an understanding, but it was rejected by the Basic Steel Industry Conference, composed of local presidents. The reasons were diverse, but Thomas Cervola, president of the big local in Lackawanna, expressed a common sentiment: "I can't see voting for concessions without some kind of guarantee that what we give up will be put back into the operation here." Few guarantees could be offered in 1982. The industry had shipped only 61.6 million tons of steel, it smallest output since the recession year of 1958. Nearly 40 percent of the 1981 workforce was laid off. Reagan was silent.[86]

The union presidents changed their minds in March 1983. Roger B. Smith, head of General Motors, warned that before placing steel orders for the 1984 models he required a firm commitment that there would be no strike. The current impasse made it likely one would take place when the contract expired in the summer of 1983. GM's threat was a catalyst to an agreement. Wages were reduced by 7 to 9 percent, less than what the industry had demanded, and were scheduled to be restored over the life of the three-year contract. The companies agreed in writing that the savings, $2.5 billion, would be used for steel investment.

Not only were wages reduced, but industrywide bargaining ended. Wheeling-Pittsburgh, National, and Allegheny-Ludlum were already bargaining on their own at the time of the formal dissolution in 1985. The change reflected the new diversity of the steel industry. The situation of each company was unique, depending upon its technology, product mix, and corporate milieu. Some were conglomerates, others were partly owned by foreign steel companies. Inland and Bethlehem produced steel only. U.S. Steel, with large revenues from its oil interests, could withstand a long strike, which others could not afford. Firms with large numbers of retirees had high labor costs; those with a young workforce, lower ones. To equalize labor costs and prevent wages from becoming a factor in competition, the union adopted a new policy of accepting different wage rates at different companies. The process was contentious everywhere, but neither the union nor workers were unreasonable. They were prepared to sacrifice. They simply asked others to do the same.

The travails at Wheeling-Pittsburgh demonstrate the inadequacy of the view that high wages were at the root of the steel industry's problems. In the late 1970s the company initiated a major modernization of its mills in Pennsylvania, West Virginia, and Ohio. At that time, 70 percent of its steel was continuously cast. Increasing the efficiency of the mills came at a steep price—high-interest private loans as well as low-interest EDA loans. When the market collapsed in 1982, default was likely. That year Wheeling twice turned to its workforce for concessions, and twice the union extended temporary wage and benefit cuts. But just as taxes are not everything, costs are not everything. The recession and imports kept revenues down. In 1985, Wheeling again came to the union for concessions.

This time the union hired the investment bankers Lazard, Frères to assess the company's prospects. The consultants predicted that even if wage relief was granted, Wheeling would fail unless it could reduce and restructure its debt. The union agreed to another round of concessions, but only if Wheeling's lenders contributed, a principle employed at Chrysler in 1979. The bankers refused and would only extend the loans, extracting a lien on assets valued at $300 million. If the company went under, the banks would be protected and the workers would be out in the cold. The union refused, and on April 16, 1985, Wheeling-Pittsburgh filed for Chapter 11 bankruptcy, asking the court to cancel the labor contract so it could unilaterally effect what the union had refused. The use of the bankruptcy law to void labor contracts and restructure companies had become common. Bankruptcy courts performed the role of governments in other countries.[87]

The judge hearing the Wheeling case permitted a wage reduction of over $3.00 an hour, down to $15.20, lower than what the USWA had been willing to consider. The union challenged the ruling, and a federal appeals court overturned the decision. Then the company appealed. Employing a risky strategy, the union decided to strike the company rather than accept the company/court package. It was the first authorized steel strike since 1959. The USWA aimed to remove the company's autocratic CEO, Dennis Carney. After two months, Carney was forced to resign when it became clear that the union was united. At the bargaining table, not at the bar, a new contract was negotiated. It provided the company some cash relief, eliminated 600 jobs, and tied wages to prices, but it gave the union a significant voice in managing the company.

USWA president Williams was flexible on temporary wage concessions and manning, but Carney's attempt to supplant the union with the court threatened to destroy the USWA. The strike convinced other steel companies that the union would not simply agree to any proposal to save jobs. After many bad experiences in the early 1980s, the USWA concluded that wage concessions were acceptable only if they were part of a viable plan to turn a company around, the first significant instance of its new determination to have some say in management decisions.

LTV had also tried to use bankruptcy to stay afloat. In this case, too, the union had given considerable wage relief. But when prices fell in 1986, bankers called in their loans, and the company could not make cash payments. Filing for bankruptcy, the Dallas-based CEOs, not the steel managers, announced that they would ignore the contract and cease paying health benefits for retirees. It took only a six-day strike to convince LTV that unilateralism would not work.

Bankrupt LTV tried but failed to take advantage of another marginal government agency to lower its costs. Largely as a result of pressure from the USWA, the Pension Benefit Guarantee Commission (PBGC) had been created in 1974 to protect workers' pensions when companies went under. It was funded by fees levied on all pension plans. But now PBGC was being used for a new purpose—to save companies technically in bankruptcy. Whether PBGC assumed the pension liabilities of a bankrupt company, and the extent of its commitment, could mean life or death for a company, not to say for the retirees.

The key roles played by bankruptcy courts and the PBGC fostered reconstruction on the basis of low wages, not efficiency. Survivors were not necessarily the companies with the most modern plants but rather those who could convince judges and bureaucrats to relieve them of wage or pension liabilities. The litigious process prolonged the restructurings, consumed resources, and hindered long-range planning. Moreover, the American way was not cost-free; in 1987, Congress raised the fees on all pension plans from $8.50 to $16 per employee. The European approach of offering direct aid to finance reconstruction and closure was superior.[88]

In 1985, new labor contracts had been signed with the bulk of the industry, providing for temporary wage reductions, some form of profit-sharing, and manning reductions. The exception was U.S. Steel. David Roderick, with the oil business shoring up his hard-nosed attitudes, wanted to obtain the lowest labor costs in the industry, which fit his determination to increase the company's market share. But if Roderick seemed to be returning to the Carnegie era, the ensuing battle was no Homestead. After a six-month strike, technically a lockout, U.S. Steel failed to win a significantly better contract. By striking at a most unfavorable economic moment, the USWA made it clear that the rumors of its death were premature. Most steel firms subsequently chose some form of productivity bargaining, not an assault on the union.

Williams had insisted that companies "open their books" in bargaining sessions, which strained the union's slimmed-down staff. The USWA could not afford Lazard, Frères as permanent advisers. Instead, it hired Locker/Abrecht Associates to provide regular economic analysis. The heads of the consulting firm had been activists in the 1960s. Mike Locker, whose parents were teachers in New York City, had been active in Students for a Democratic Society at the University of Michigan and had worked with the North American Congress on Latin America during the 1970s. Labor-oriented, Locker nevertheless invested his time on third world projects, typical of members of the New Left of the 1970s. Some of the divisions that had developed between the New Left and the labor movement during the 1960s dissolved in the late 1970s during the campaign to unionize textile giant J. P. Stevens and another defending workers at Eastern Airlines, both of which Locker worked on. The union's Jim Smith, realizing that the USWA would have to manage industry, convinced Lynn Williams to commission Locker to make a comprehensive study of the industry.[89]

Locker's report, completed in 1985, underscored the political origins of the industry's current problems. From 1982 to 1985, combined wage reductions and productivity increases reduced employment costs 35 percent, but the macroeconomy canceled the efficiencies. Direct and indirect imports drove down prices, aided by the high dollar, which lowered the price of imports 40 percent and raised the price of American exports 70 percent. Lax enforcement of the VRAS meant domestic production fell by 4 million tons. Probably the most surprising conclusion of Locker's report was that U.S. steel consumption had not declined significantly. Locker argued that the traditional means of measuring steel use did not include the steel content of imported manufacturing goods, which had increased 136 percent from 1977 to 1985. If these 13.7 million tons of steel were added to the direct amount used, steel consumption in 1985 was only slightly less than that in 1977. The industry had been hurt not simply by foreign steel imports but by imports of autos, machinery, and other items.[90]

Locker concluded that the industry needed better public policy with regard to trade, interest rates, and currency. Collective bargaining could not do it alone. The control of direct and indirect steel imports and the initiation of a public investment program to rebuild deteriorating infrastructure would increase steel consumption. (In the 1960s, public investment was 3 percent; in the 1980s, it was 1 percent.)[91]

These findings reinforced Lynn Williams's social democratic proclivities. In urging that a mixture of macroeconomic and sectoral policies was needed to support steel and other industries, the report provided the economic underpinnings for his own broad social and political agenda. Typically, Williams supported the founding in 1988 of the AFL-CIO Organizing Institute, a new entity charged with restoring labor's diminished numbers and clout. John Sweeney, the other union president who backed the initiative, was elected president of the labor federation in 1995.[92] In the short run, Williams searched in vain for a political vehicle to fulfill his purposes. After its 1984 loss, the Democratic Party turned right. The centrist Democratic Leadership Council, created in 1985, and new "Atari" Democrats like Senator Gary Hart and 1988 presidential candidate Michael Dukakis disengaged from traditional Democratic constituencies. The party's leaders ignored industrial decline and chased high-tech miracles.

Contemporary Steel and Contemporary America

The new rules that produced industrial decline were generic, not specific. The high-tech industries, once scornful of what they called the whines of old industries like steel, were in trouble too. In 1986–87, the manufacturing trade deficit reached a record $170 billion even though the Plaza agreement of September 1985 produced a radical decline in the value of the dollar, especially relative to the yen. But despite orthodox theory, U.S. exports to Japan increased only 5.5 percent while Japan's exports to the United States climbed 21 percent in 1986. (Japanese producers absorbed the yen rise, helped along by aid from the finance ministry, especially easy money, and by MITI; they "gobbled up," in the words of historian Walter LaFeber, choice pieces of manufacturing, often in the United States.) The ballooning trade deficit of 1986 included the United States' first deficit in high-technology products. The sunrise semiconductor industry was on its way to becoming a sunset one, without ever having experienced high noon. In 1984 Reagan had explicitly rejected an industrial policy for semiconductors as well as for steel, preferring "market" solutions. But in 1986 Reagan altered the rules for this high-tech industry. The contrast between government policy in semiconductors and in steel illuminate the politics and economics of the Reagan resurrection.[93]

In 1975, the American semiconductor industry had supplied 60 percent of world markets, but by 1985 its share had dropped to 43 percent, behind Japan, whose dominance was growing. That year the industry lost $2 billion and laid off 25,000 workers. The individualists of Silicon Valley sought and obtained government help—an agreement to open the closed Japanese market so that foreign chips reached 20 percent and to end dumping in American and third markets. When the Japanese government winked at enforcement, the United States imposed tariffs of up to 300 percent on a range of Japanese electronic imports; this convinced Tokyo. The U.S. government also threw in an annual contribution of $100 million to a research consortium for semiconductors. The interventions constituted an industrial policy that violated every stated norm of the administration.[94]

The interventions had not gone unopposed. The State Department had not wanted to offend Tokyo, and the National Security Council worried about Japanese participation in the Strategic Defense Initiative, Star Wars. All in the administration feared that they were picking winners and indulging in the other deadly sins of industrial policy. These various arguments might have been as potent as they had been in defeating an industrial policy for steel but for the fact that Reagan was convinced that semiconductors were vital to American defense. Moreover, the semiconductor industry did not carry the negative baggage that had weakened the steel industry's case. Thus, Sam Gibbons, chair of the Ways and Means subcommittee on trade, could still argue that steel's troubles were caused by poor investment decisions and high wages.[95] The glamorous industry of relatively small producers was a different story: the "little guys" were up against the Japanese government and its conglomerates. Because the government stressed the opening of Japan's market, not the antidumping provisions, the package was sold as a free trade measure. Coming at a time of huge manufacturing trade deficits, the semiconductor industry capitalized on the growing popular view that Japan was an unfair trader. It also enjoyed the benefit of new expertise, the strategic trade school of economics.[96] But Reagan made it clear that his decision was an exception, not a precedent. Free trade and laissez-faire idols remained in the temple.[97]

For the less ideological, the semiconductor experience challenged conventional explanations for the manufacturing declines. To the economist Lester Thurow, who had welcomed the phase-out of industrial sectors like steel, the troubles of the high-technology industry violated every tenet of orthodox economic theory and convinced him that industrial policies might be needed after all. Another young economist, John Zysman, underwent a similar transformation. As late as 1983, observing Japan's industrial policy in semiconductors, Zysman concluded that "threats to the long-run development of the U.S. industry and economy are no more than possibilities, and U.S. policy should not be formulated to confront them." His Berkeley colleague, Michael Borrus, agreed and ignored the potential lessons of the earlier but identical cycle of Japanese targeting in steel. Borrus attributed the difficulties of the steel industry to the errors of corporate leaders.[98]

But in 1987, after the near-collapse of the semiconductor industry, Zysman diagnosed a broader American problem and ordered new medicine. In *Manufacturing Matters*, he and Stephen Cohen critiqued Daniel Bell's and the president's rosy portrait of the postindustrial economy. In 1985, Reagan had asserted that "the progression of an economy such as America's from agriculture to manufacturing to services is a natural change." Zysman and Cohen pointed out that although labor had been transferred out of farming, the nation had not given up agriculture, and this was the main reason why the United States led in the manufacture of agricultural products, machinery, and chemicals. Using similar logic, they argued that manufacturing anchored high-paying service jobs, which would depart if production left U.S. shores. The term "service" may describe a new sociology of work, they argued, but the discrete categories of manufacturing and service embodied neither a theory nor the realities of economic organization. Services cluster about productive activity: design and engineering, legal and financial, waste disposal and janitorial services are all linked to production. By abandoning the production of TVs, the U.S. industry lost the ability to design as well as make the next product, the VCR. Despite American inventiveness, manufacturing weakness threatened the high-tech future.[99]

Banker Peter G. Peterson, who had sounded the alarm on manufacturing trade deficits in the Nixon administration, came to a similar conclusion in an *Atlantic Monthly* article published in October 1987. Peterson pointed out that the United States was importing $3 of goods for every $2 of exports, a ratio that was a sure route to dollar depreciation and reduced wages—a lower standard of living. His pessimism, followed by the Black Monday stock market crash of 1987 and a spate of gloomy books on America's future, generated a new cycle of concern. Reagan's successor, George Bush, was forced to create a Council on Competitiveness, but Bush too opposed an explicit industrial policy, which led many businessmen from Silicon Valley to support Democrat Bill Clinton for president in 1992.[100]

The women and men advising President Clinton were more savvy than their predecessors. Representing the Berkeley school, John Zysman's colleague and collaborator Laura D'Andrea Tyson was made head of the CEA. Clinton's actual program was not so different from Bush's: deficit reduction and extension of free trade and investment. In 1995, as Clinton announced that U.S. industry was competitive and profitable and the Dow Jones averaged over 5,000, the nation discovered that Intel was saved but that 80 percent of the workforce was not. The steel industry's resurrection explained some of the characteristics of the new order.

By 1989, the U.S. industry produced a ton of steel in 5.7 hours, less time than it took in Japan and Europe.[101] Today, publicists celebrate steel's "renaissance." [102] Productivity has doubled, exceeding wage rises, thus reducing the labor cost of a ton of steel from $262 in 1982 to $159 in 1995, compared to $162 for the Europeans and $195 for the Japanese. Employment once averaged 35 percent of steel costs; it now accounts for only 28 percent. U.S. labor costs are less than Japan's and the same as Germany's.[103]

Despite the views of many pundits and economists, the history of the postwar steel industry demonstrates that efficiency and low wages have never been decisive factors in the global steel trade. The diminished American share of the global industry created during the Reagan years remains. When steel imports reached nearly 25 percent in 1994, there was no hue and cry as there had been in the 1980s, because the industry was operating at capacity. The scaled-down industry could not supply domestic consumption, which has been growing by more than 2 percent annually over the past ten years.[104] By downsizing to adjust for global overcapacity in the 1980s, the United States served the global trading system but not its own workers.

Although the American steel industry is probably the most efficient in the world, exports are not a viable option for steelmakers. Despite the ideology of free trade, the international steel trade is managed by the "East of Burma Agreement," which in essence divides the export market between European and Asian producers.[105] The many foreign owners of U.S. integrated mills have little incentive to compete with their own mills at home. The celebrated Nucor is building a mill in Brazil, not exporting steel from its American mills, and U.S. Steel has just announced a joint venture with the leading steel company in Slovakia.[106]

The USWA is not relying upon the industry to figure ways out of the corset of steel trade barriers. Its current president, George Becker, told the steel executives and analysts at the ninth annual Steel Survival Strategies conference in 1994 that "management was too important to leave to managers." Mike Locker and another consultant, Ronald Bloom, an investment banker, now work with companies and the USWA to figure out ways to remain profitable through new market strategies. LTV, USX, and Inland are moving into higher value coated steels and downstream into fabrication, which sells by the unit rather than by the ton, which is falling in price. All of this may be insufficient, however. The announced purchase of Inland by the London-based transnational Ispat of the Netherlands may be the beginning of a new round of consolidation in the U.S. industry.[107]

The prophets of American economic decline might have overstated their case, but the steel industry may be a better mirror of U.S. economic life than the global corporations whose profits dominate the headlines. The American competitiveness crisis of the 1980s was resolved by reducing production and accepting stagnant or falling wage rates in the United States. Although the menu of international production was created by bipartisan U.S. foreign policy, during the critical Reagan years domestic steel manufacturing and workers did not matter. State-created incentives encouraged the steel industry to reduce its capacity and fill the gap with imports from abroad, which explains why the negotiated import quotas of 1985 have been allowed to lapse. Other manufacturers shifted production offshore, and they continue to do so. American transnational corporations produce twice as much outside their borders as do their European and Japanese equivalents. Thus, the United States is a net importer of autos and auto parts, as well as steel.[108] Moreover, General Motors does not use U.S. steel in its plants in Europe while it imports Japanese steel for its Pacific coast plants.[109] Between 1982 and 1991, American global companies reduced employment in the United States by 37 percent at the same time they increased offshore by nearly one-third.[110] For the first time in U.S. history, it is small businesses rather than large that are celebrated for their job-creating qualities.

U.S. transnationals face pressures from local host governments but little from their own. Trade is based not on the theology of comparative advantage but on tolls, paid in the coin of jobs and technology, prerequisites for commercial sales in China and other Southeast Asian nations. In a glutted market, these buyers have an advantage. Still, not all nations are willing to substitute short-term corporate gains for long-term national welfare. A Malaysian high official complains that the Japanese are "very, very difficult," explaining, "[They allow] no technology transfers, no locals hired for management, no research centers. The Americans are very different."[111] U.S. policy has been laissez-faire on the location of production, permitting the policies of foreign states to govern this issue. On the other hand, American laws require little from foreign investors in the United States. Because the major strategic investors in manufacturing have been government-aided, Japanese industrial conglomerates operating from a protected home base, it is short-sighted to argue, as former Secretary of Labor Robert B. Reich did, that the nationality of a firm is unimportant. Japanese investment has given U.S. steel firms access to technology, but steel is atypical in this instance; overall the United States exports five times more technology than it imports. Moreover, the bulk of Tokyo's investment in the United States is not in new technology but in wholesaling, whose purpose is to facilitate Japanese imports.[112]

Imports of manufactured goods rose from 14 percent of domestic consumption in 1977 to 36 percent in 1993. The manufacturing sector's trade deficit accounts for the nation's.[113] Over time, each of the economists' explanations for this state of affairs has proved wrong: neither high wages and inefficiency in the early 1980s nor budgetary deficits later in the decade proved to be the culprits behind the growing trade deficit. It is not only American workers who lost out. Although the balance sheets of global corporations look good, the exporting of jobs may be bad for the global trading system. Motorola may be getting low-wage workers in Malaysia and China, but the system as a whole is generating less purchasing power. Declining wages may help a company, but they also reduce consumption. We may be facing a system like the one preceding the Great Depression, when production outstripped purchasing power. There is now a global surplus in aircraft, autos, steel, consumer electronics, and other manufacturing products, which is at the root of recent economic woes in East Asia. The future is more uncertain than public oratory makes it out to be.

In the United States, a by-product of the structural changes produced by public policy was the "disappearing middle." That middle contained 600,000 steelworkers in 1973 but only 169,000 in 1995. From 1981 to 1987, contracting industries, like steel, paid 47 percent more than expanding ones. Put another way, the share of the workforce in the higher paying industries declined nearly 8 percent. The resulting pressure on wages (abetted by Reagan's various policies weakening unions) made the United States the only industrialized nation where the hourly compensation of production workers in manufacturing fell.[114]

As employment in manufacturing has declined, work has grown in the low-wage service sector, despite the talk of the "information society." Microsoft is at the top of the charts in profits, but it employs only 15,000 people, fewer than a shrunken Bethlehem Steel.[115] The growth in the number of new computer programmers, analysts and operators, economists, paralegals, and other white-collar workers does not equal the increase in fast-food workers in the new economy. The growth of low-wage work in retailing, health, and "services to buildings," which include janitors and security guards, is one reason why the Service Employees International Union has been one of the few growing unions in the recent past. Still, the FIRE group—finance, insurance, and real estate—is mainly a low-wage, nonunion sector.[116]

Because workers in the shrinking, manufacturing sector were heavily unionized, the decline has had a social and political significance that transcends numbers. The USWA survived the 1980s, but today only 11 percent of the private sector is organized, and the antiunion culture threatens the union's cooperative relationships with the industry. Bethlehem was the first major firm to embrace labor-management collaboration. Even U.S. Steel has accepted a labor member on its board of directors. Labor-management teamwork has become a faddish panacea, but it works best when workers have unions. The USWA helped save LTV in the 1980s and obtained a contractual promise to remain neutral in union contests. Nevertheless, taking its cue from its surroundings, the company has joined with Sumitomo and British Steel to build a non-union minimill in Decatur, Alabama. If LTV and others persist, the new labor-management relations may vanish.[117]

Declining union density explains much about contemporary America. The recurrent concern about the "disappearing black male" loses some of its mystery when we realize that unionized black men earn 54.1 percent more than their unorganized brothers. From 1967 to 1990, both the number of blacks earning more than $50,000 and those earning less than $5,000 grew at the expense of those in the middle. The black steelworker was in that middle.[118]

Without organization, workers have less political clout than at any other point after World War II. The proliferation of business lobbyists and corporate financing of political campaigns—80 percent of the contributions to national candidates in 1992 came from businesses or business PACs—is lamented across the political spectrum. But lobbyists on the liberal side of the aisle, the Children's Defense Fund or Ralph Nader's public interest empire, are middle-class professionals or college students. People weakly represented fare poorly. So it is with workers. The 1995 census reported that only those in the top 20 percent of the population in terms of income have returned to their incomes of 1989, the last year of growth before the 1990 recession. Even in a cyclical recovery, lost income has not been recovered. The decline in the wages of males working full time began after 1973; then, household incomes were sustained by working wives. By 1990, the family strategy faltered, and household income took the same downward path as male wages.[119]

The leading ideas of the nation reflect this new balance of power: Low inflation is the most important goal of monetary policy, balancing the budget the aim of fiscal policy, and 2.0–2.5 percent growth and, until very recently, 6 percent unemployment the best the nation could achieve.[120] Because global growth is constrained by the same ideas, Europeans have traded higher unemployment for a higher wage rate and Japanese workers face underemployment. Although the structure of trade with Europe and Japan that was created during the postwar years remains, most American policymakers now recognize that the U.S. market is not infinite. It is harder for Europe and Japan to export their way out of difficulties as they have in the past. Foreign investment in the United States is a sign of the change. But the U.S. trade deficit with Japan has been rising since the United States agreed in 1995 to raise the value of the dollar, which allowed Japan to continue to use its export strategy to address its economic problems. U.S. relations with China and other East Asian nations are reruns of earlier U.S. policies toward Japan. Although Bill Clinton began his presidency promising to reverse traditional international economic strategy, he quickly began privileging security matters, marking a return to Cold War policies of subordinating economic concerns to strategic goals. The president attempted to get around the trade laws to permit imports of Russian, Ukrainian, South African, and Chinese carbon plate, which totaled 20 percent of the U.S. market in 1996.[121] The 1997 collapse of East Asian economies may encourage the administration to tolerate more imports from that region. Once again, U.S. manufacturing may be asked to pay the price for overexpansion abroad. Such policies threaten to perpetuate the United States' status as the world's leading debtor. At the end of 1996, America's external debt totaled $871 billion. By contrast, years of surpluses have given Japan the world's largest net foreign assets, $891 billion.[122]

In his second inaugural address, President Bill Clinton asserted that "our economy is the strongest on earth" and promised "the tools to solve our problems for ourselves." Government," he insisted, "would be smaller, live within its means and do more with less." [123] This political passivity rests upon a sunny view of the ongoing global transformations. If not government, then the market will shape the opportunities he seeks for Americans. To repeat the words of Reagan's representative to the OECD steel committee in 1982: American policy "requires no major public expenditure, no planning, and no direction by government." That recipe was not good for the steel industry and it is unlikely that it will be good for the nation.

Steel and

the History

of Postwar

America

The story of the steel industry can be an input for another
industry, that of explaining postwar American history. The
liberal tradition and the power of classes, usually labor and
capital, are the two favorite paradigms of modern American
history. The two frameworks come together around the idea
of the weak state, a staple of the academy, if not of contemporary politicians.[1]

The idea of the weak state propels some of the explanations of the decline of
New Deal liberalism. I have assumed that the state and political culture were
sufficiently potent to maintain liberalism during the postwar era. Others have
argued that the flaws of the New Deal settlement overwhelmed its virtues and
that by the end of World War II the future was determined. Alan Brinkley's
analysis of New Deal economic liberalism, *The End of Reform*, is an excellent
synthesis of this view. Brinkley argues that by the end of World War II the state
was shorn of all policies but fiscal management and of all purposes but enhancing consumption. Liberals and the labor movement no longer aimed to
reform capitalism, which had been the primary goal of the New Dealers.[2]

The argument raises two questions. Is Brinkley's reading of the 1930s and
1940s correct? Second, if it is, did the state of the reform movement in 1945
determine subsequent history? Brinkley believes that the authentic New Deal
goal was to "reshape . . . the structure of capitalism" by attacking "the extor-
tionate methods of monopoly."[3] This judgment rests upon the thinking of selected New Deal bureaucrats, like Thurman Arnold, Adolph A. Berle, and Leon

Henderson. It is true that much New Deal thinking attributed the Great Depression to overly concentrated economic power, but Brinkley accepts the accuracy of the judgment uncritically.[4] Even if one adopts this definition of reform, the history of the postwar steel industry reveals that this New Deal tradition lived on after the war.

But there is more to the Brinkley thesis than the changing ideas of bureaucrats.[5] Recent scholars have demonstrated that although the state is more than the sum of the interest groups making up society, it is not so autonomous than it can act alone.[6] Brinkley powers his conclusion with an interpretation of the labor movement. The new CIO, he argues, was the prime candidate to link the reformers in the state to society. Strangely, Brinkley first indicts the CIO for attempting to forge links to the state, preferring the syndicalism of John L. Lewis to the "accommodation" of Sidney Hillman, who had taken a government post.[7] But judging labor's position precarious, he concludes that Hillman's course was inevitable. Then, Brinkley assumes that the labor politics practiced while the nation was at war were the essence of labor relations.[8] The unmentioned, huge strike wave in 1945 and 1946 undermines this depiction. Nevertheless, the taming of the labor movement along with the eclipse of the true New Dealers propels his judgment that it was all downhill after 1945, leading to the current crisis of the welfare state.[9]

Many social scientists share Brinkley's view of the postwar period. After the economic crises of the 1970s, they ceased writing about the United States as a unique nation, steered by liberals and monopolists or various interest groups, and compared its state and societal institutions with those of other industrial nations. They discovered capitalisms, not capitalism. Their portrait of the United States, nonetheless, was not that different from the one produced by historians. In most accounts, the state became the agent of a strong business class, which overwhelmed a weak labor movement. These judgments projected the balance of power in the 1980s backwards in time, inserting another essentialism into U.S. history and skirting crucial questions.[10]

Why do Japanese workers, who are much weaker than their American equivalents and employed by a more powerful business class, enjoy the job security that U.S. workers lack? If businessmen are all-powerful in the United States, why did they not succeed in forming cartels like their counterparts in Japan and Europe? Why were American corporations unable to prevent the tough consumer, environmental, health, and safety laws during the early 1970s? Why did the steel industry lose the capacity to supply its own market during the Reagan years, the most openly pro-business administration in the postwar era? Each answer challenges the consensus.[11]

The year 1945 was not the end of history, or even the end of reform. But after the war, Americans lived in a nation objectively different from the one of the 1930s: the popular abandonment of the land, when New Dealers had aimed to revive rural America; a reinvigorated capitalism, which had seemed to be in its death throes; and a strong labor movement, replacing a group of craft unions operating on the outskirts of big industry. It was inconceivable that the recipes of the 1930s could be transported easily to the postwar world. Moreover, it is an error to consider the retention of a planning agency or of specific measures like price controls as litmus tests of a reform regime.[12] David Plotke's formulation of the New Deal project as one that combined modernization and democracy is more accurate, distinguishing the broad goal from specific techniques.[13] The New Deal had devised an economic strategy compatible with mass interests and participation. It empowered social groups, particularly the labor movement, to maintain this vision. It fostered the development of the West and South.

It was not that capital was strong and labor and the state weak after the war.[14] American business, unlike its equivalents in Europe and Japan, emerged from the war self-confident and free of the scabs of fascist accommodation, however, labor was also at the peak of its power in the shops, and the state accepted responsibility for maintaining high levels of employment. The self-interest of labor was linked to the well-being of society by John Maynard Keynes's new economics. Collective bargaining ensured that wages were linked to productivity, maintaining the demand essential to keep the economy buoyant and making it more difficult for corporations to employ low-wage strategies, which were viewed as being harmful to the entire economy.[15] The British social scientist Andrew Shonfield called the system "modern capitalism" in 1965.[16]

Still, those who posit an end to reform in the postwar era have detected something, even if they have fingered the wrong culprit. After the war, from right to left, the nation assumed that the marriage between efficiency and working-class progress was unproblematic and permanent. The country's unique economic strength during the first years after the war, more than the power of capital, made it appear that new institutional arrangements for maintaining New Deal traditions—economic prosperity and democracy—were unnecessary. The general economic collapse of the 1930s, the war-propelled resurrection, and then the strong consumer demand afterwards yielded a Democratic legacy that stressed aggregate demand measures. The economic dynamism, measured by the recent past, allowed the Cold War to be waged with little regard for its effects on the domestic economy.

As David Vogel has demonstrated, American state policy toward business was more complicated than the "free enterprise" themes voiced in political rhetoric.[17] The key question after the war was not state intervention per se but rather the goals and targets of policy. Decisions about making autos and TVs were left to businessmen, but a plentiful supply of cheap steel was considered to be a legitimate government goal.

When the state and the steel industry disagreed, government breathed new life into the antimonopoly tradition, which indicted corporate power and prescribed competition as the cure. The government assumed that productivity was a given, not a problem, and that reluctance to add steel capacity reflected the caution of an oligopoly. Industry leaders rejected both judgments, and they were right. The subsequent dispute lived on until the Korean War, when more tonnage was obtained through tax incentives, rationalized on the basis of defense needs. The route to cheap and ample steel reflected the antimonopolist tradition as well as the newer state fiscal policy and Cold War objectives. Monies were dispersed among the regions and among old and new companies according to historic competitive principles. Liberals and conservatives secured a tough new antitrust law in 1950, and the courts proved to be willing allies. Business would produce and invest, but government ensured that all regions developed and that large firms had competitors. The Japanese and Europeans, seeking high productivity, proceeded differently. Possessing little of the American faith in competition, they allocated resources to the large companies and fostered cartel-like structures, employing other means to keep business harnessed to the national interest.

Another tenet of the New Deal settlement was that business efficiency was not to be obtained at the expense of labor and the consumer. The many steel strikes during the 1950s demonstrated that the formula for reconciling the interests of labor and capital had not been found. The many disputes between the steel industry and the government on prices revealed that the question of how to finance increased efficiency, how to modernize, was also unresolved.

From the vantage point of the 1990s, the regional pattern of unionism and the excessive burdens placed on collective bargaining were critical. Strikes in 1945 and 1946 secured the union role in industry without producing a state-sanctioned incomes policy. Without such a policy, labor militancy fed antiunionism, which was strengthened by the labor movement's regional weakness in the South and West and led to the Taft-Hartley Act of 1947, which made organizing more difficult. Then, facing a political roadblock in Congress, the USWA and other unions obtained a package of social welfare measures—pensions and health insurance—from the corporations, not the state.

Thus, collective bargaining carried too much of the weight of social welfare and eventually of technological change and economic restructuring as well. These obligations would burden the steel industry over time, but they immediately gave unorganized industries additional incentives to oppose unions. Where social welfare was provided by the state, unionization met less opposition. But this was not so apparent at the time. Guarding and expanding the social security state, unions acted to represent all workers and helped maintain purchasing power and secure distributional equities, which gave the economy a moral legitimacy in the eyes of most Americans.

The new arrangements were barely visible in the South, however, where the power of the planter class had weakened, if not completely effaced, unions and had deprived Southerners of much of the social security system. The modernization of the South produced as much dislocation as democracy. Industrialization, the mechanization of cotton growing, and urbanization undermined the power of the planter class and its distinctive signatures—racial segregation and black disfranchisement. The demise of labor-intensive agriculture permitted a civil rights movement to dismantle legal segregation and guarantee African American voting rights. By so doing, it transferred power to the South's urban and corporate elites but without the input of the unions that their northern equivalents had been forced to accept earlier.

The South's structural transformation shaped the emergence of the "race question" of the 1950s and 1960s. Barely recognized at the time, thirty years of agricultural policy had sent blacks and whites with minimal skills in droves to the cities, producing a new unemployment in places that had once easily absorbed refugees from the nation's farms—Gary, Indiana, as well as Birmingham, Alabama. Agricultural mechanization was matched by automation in steel, mining, automobiles, meatpacking, paper, and tobacco, an inevitable result of the rising wages produced by unionization. Black unemployment was double that of whites, but both were concentrated in the same sector, manufacturing, and in the same location, the industrial cities. Those who found work labored more in poorly paid service industries and the secondary labor markets than in manufacturing.

Adding to the labor market transformations, from late 1957 through 1962 the economy was either sluggish or in recession. This state of affairs heated up conflicts between labor and capital, producing the steel strike of 1959 and the Kennedy-U.S. Steel dispute over steel prices in 1962. It also threatened to break up the alliance between the labor and the growing civil rights movement.

In 1964, the state reinvigorated New Deal political economy by utilizing tax cuts to address modernization and equity conflicts. By increasing the funds available for investment and consumption, the tax cuts of the early 1960s reconciled labor, capital, and public interests in practice, if not in theory. The resulting economic growth and state commitment to nondiscrimination also moderated conflicts between the civil rights and labor movement.

Others believed that the structural changes in the South and in the manufacturing sector required more targeted interventions. Senators Humphrey and Clark led a group of legislators, academics, unionists, and civil rights activists to the conclusion that the economy was not employing or training enough of the labor force. They were the first to notice the impact of agricultural mechanization and automation on blacks and other workers with meager education. They proposed to overhaul the nation's manpower machinery to upgrade skills, link workers (especially blacks) to growing work sectors, provide appropriate training, and offer public works jobs to the unemployed. Their efforts bore no fruit. The Keynesian consensus that the American economy, braced with the 1964 tax cut, could provide jobs for all trumped their call for structural interventions.

Given the assumption that the economy had been fixed, racial policy assumed that the causes of black unemployment were extra-economic. In 1964, the government acquired two new tools, Title VII of the Civil Rights Act, which banned employment discrimination, and the War on Poverty, which consisted of various youth training programs. Both reshaped the political culture by separating the causes of black unemployment and poverty from the economy. Title VII conceptualized the black situation as unique and caused by prejudice; the War on Poverty assumed the poor were poor because they were unmotivated or unorganized, not because of the diminished supply and changing character of work in the cities. Both flowed inevitably from an economic policy that addressed aggregates, not industrial sectors and specific labor markets.

Still, the economic stimulus did help blacks, just as it helped the steel industry. The 1964 tax cut and the Vietnam War produced a booming economy, even though they masked the structural changes in sectors and labor markets. The high growth rates, the war-induced expansion of industrial jobs, and the assault on racial barriers were potent stimuli. From 1966 to 1970, the income of black males and their earnings relative to whites both grew. The greatest gains were made by the educated young, but the unemployment rate for all black males twenty and older fell to 3.7 percent in early 1969. While these numbers were real, at the time other statistics seemed more relevant.[18]

In 1967, unemployment had not come down as far as government economists had predicted. Despite the falling aggregate rates, black unemployment remained in the double digits in manufacturing cities of the North, which had been losing jobs for two decades. White House advisers now concluded that there was a structural problem, but the government's new fear of inflation, caused by the increased war spending on top of the tax cut, muted concern until after big riots in Newark and Detroit in the summer. Unemployment and relations with police became combustible items in the heated political climate of the late 1960s. Events drove responses. The elite consensus, certified by the Kerner report, was that American institutions worked for all except blacks.

Although blacks and whites in the aggregate occupied different economic positions, there were many blacks and whites who shared similar life and work experiences. That was not so apparent because the political culture compared white with black, affluence with poverty, the suburbs with slums. With race as their sole critical category, riot-impelled solutions left the supply of work to the market and simply redistributed jobs within the working class by increasing the demand for black workers. The government subsidized the employment of the "hard-core," who were untouched by the expansion. Corporate elites—possessing equal measures of guilt, concern, and self-interest—began hiring more blacks, even though corporate strategies like globalization and automation continued. Policies attending to demand and ignoring supply set off quiet and noisy conflicts within the working class.

The same urgencies affected both judges interpreting Title VII and government regulators enforcing an executive order forbidding discrimination among government contractors. Neither could create more jobs for blacks, but they could create new rules to effect the desired results. Rectifying the past became the rationale for various forms of preferences because there was no acknowledgment of the concurrent changes taking place in the labor market.

The new rules worked best when supported by the strong labor demands of growing industries. But in the world of the contracting steel industry they became solutions for declining employment. Title VII was enforced by private individuals through lawsuits, an example of the new citizen enforcement. The technicalities of the law, not the potential for employment, determined court calendars. Although civil rights lawyers assumed that victories meant more jobs, the knottiest questions, those most likely to end up in court, involved zero-sum situations, where gains were meager. The legal process was protracted and offered few incentives for compromise. Courts operate according to broad, universal principles. The outcome of a particular case became a precedent for future ones. Thus, civil rights lawyers often rejected reasonable solutions, fearing they might become precedents elsewhere. In a lawsuit, there was an individual wrong, a victim, a perpetrator, and a remedy. Except for cases of garden-variety discrimination, this corset did not fit the typical employment situation. The concept of racial discrimination expanded because the government had not tackled the supply of work in specific sectors and locations, assuming that declining aggregate unemployment rates meant that job opportunities were abundant.

Although courts accepted broader definitions of discrimination after the riots, applying the definitions in two Bethlehem steel mills worsened race relations, because the experiences of African Americans demonstrated statistical rather than systemic differences and because workers would not move about like chess pieces to create preferred patterns. Steelworkers made decisions on the basis of their present prospects, which were determined by the technological and economic changes that were ignored by courts and lawyers.

Finally, in 1974, the government, union, and industry fashioned an agreement. Its key provision, plant seniority for all, departed from recent court remedies. Addressing the economic changes affecting the steel industry as well as civil rights, the agreement more closely approximated the working-class world of steel than the landscape painted by the Kerner Commission. By the mid-1970s the procedures of fair employment had become regularized in state and society, as well as in the steel industry.

Looking back at this era, some have viewed the racial conflicts as pivotal.[19] There is a tendency among historians to highlight conflicts but not their resolutions. The effect of such history is to make racial conflicts more essential than they were. Moreover, merely recording strife does not explain or assess its causes. It is true that there were racists and that integration was effected unevenly, but government, labor, and business policies were antiracist and potent. Also, racial policies of whatever sort are always attached to other policies. By conceptualizing black unemployment as a problem external to the economy, elites preserved their ideology, their consciences, and the social order, but the policies stemming from this assumption meant that solutions to racial discrimination often came at the expense of other workers, as happened in the two Bethlehem mills. Such solutions fostered racial conflict, which in turn reinforced the assumption that blacks faced prejudice, not declining work opportunities. Nevertheless, the consent decrees, not the Bethlehem remedies, were the final acts of enforcement.

The consent decrees, like any fair employment agreement, did not produce any more steel jobs. Almost as soon as the ink was dry on the settlement, the question of sufficient work—treated as a racial question during the 1960s—returned to the nation's agenda. But now it was married to the viability of American corporations, not simply to the unemployment statistics. African Americans were disproportionately concentrated in industries like steel, industries that were automating and adversely affected by foreign trade.[20] But because the majority of workers in these industries were not black, civil rights leaders lacked the appropriate ideology or clear interest to tackle them. During the late 1970s, activists moved on to other issues like higher education, public employment, or black business. Black steelworkers were not so fortunate.

The global recession and inflation of the mid-1970s made it clear that the productivity question had not been solved by the aggregate measures of the 1960s and had in fact been worsened by other government policies. Postwar presidents, as well as civil rights activists and regulators, intervened in steel matters with extrasectoral purposes. In the aftermath of the Korean war, the nation had financed steel expansion for defense purposes. In the 1970s, government planners sought low steel prices because it was assumed that high prices were the cause of inflation. It was never considered whether cheap steel was compatible with the industry's huge modernization project in the 1960s, with worker's claims to wages, or with the new fair employment mandate. As the regulatory arms of government pressed the industry to hire and promote more blacks, those in charge of economic and foreign policy pursued policies that hampered the industry's ability to meet these goals.

The New Deal's Keynesian insight that aggregate demand was the crucial variable was an understandable conclusion in the 1930s, but it was an incomplete understanding of growth. American Keynesians concluded that markets may not always work in the aggregate, but they accepted their role in the microeconomy. Continuing the antimonopoly ideal, they believed that competition would allocate resources to their optimal uses based on supply and demand. They never considered that markets might not reliably price innovation, that competition might be ruinous, that technological advance might be promoted by government, and that financial markets and other nations structure incentives. In short, their model of the economy ignored the role of institutions, culture, and other states. The 1964 tax cut had ignited a huge investment boom, but the law increased the supply of available funds indiscriminately; it was untargeted. According to Keynesians, the market would make correct decisions, however U.S. foreign policy was shaping the choices investors would make.

American manufacturing superiority after the war allowed diplomats to wage a Cold War with little concern about costs and to pursue a trade policy geared to strategic rather than domestic interests. The investment bankers and corporate lawyers who designed Cold War strategy were by and large generalists with "panindustrial" interests.[21] Restoring European, Japanese, and then developing third-world economies meant fostering steel industries abroad. Trade policy opened the U.S. market to the imports of allies and ignored other nations' restrictions on American exports. As a result, steel imports became significant beginning in 1965.

The tax cuts of the early 1960s bought the steel industry some time, but the rise of conglomerates and transnationals in the 1960s was a sign that the market and trade incentives created by American diplomats and foreign developmental nations determined how banks and corporations deployed resources and used the capital unleashed by the tax cut. State-created incentives steered capital away from domestic manufacturing, which was facilitated by the separation of financial and industrial institutions in the United States.

The steel industry modernized on a terrain of quicksand. Costly investment and eroding domestic markets were a fatal combination. It was not Vietnam that was the sign of imperial overreach. As traumatic as the war was for Americans, not to say for the Vietnamese, it ended. The arrogance of U.S. policy was the notion that one could develop the industrial capacities of allies and the rest of the world and promote imports without damaging the nation's industrial base. Still, throughout the 1960s the U.S. steel industry was the most efficient in the world. It was only with the slowing of the economy during the first Nixon administration that there began the rationing of investment that reflected the new incentives. Steel investment followed in the path of plummeting steel profits.

The merchandise trade deficit of 1971 demonstrated that steel was not the only industry affected by public policy. Devaluation of the dollar and the continuing worldwide boom in 1973 and 1974, reduced the deficit, which allowed the nation to continue to live complacently with postwar assumptions. Even after the quadrupling of oil prices in the fall of 1973 produced crises throughout the developed and developing worlds, the society immunized itself from the results. The strategic need to anchor Cold War alliances via access to U.S. markets gave the government a strong incentive to downplay the problem. Intellectuals adopted organic models—cycles of young, mature, and aging industries, or sunset and sunrise sectors—which made the changes seem natural. Economists discovered that corporate managers were slow to modernize and that workers were overpaid. "Green" sensibilities anesthetized the middle class to industrial decline. The new consumer movement and transnationals stressed the advantages to buyers in the wide-open American market. These cultural values and interests were enhanced by the growing political weight of the nonindustrial Sunbelt.

President Jimmy Carter's economic stimulus in 1977 produced steel imports, not steel investment. Attempting to stabilize the world economy, Carter was complacent about the domestic situation until faced with a series of plant closures in the fall. But as global growth slowed, the conflict between foreign and domestic goals became more pronounced. The domestic question for Democrats was, could one encourage more investment without reducing the standard of living of workers. Keynesian policies did not ensure that pressed industries received the investment they needed to remain viable. In the past, the nation had met challenges in energy, housing, agriculture, and health care with sectoral policies—by shaping the market, not surrendering to it. Some of these ideas, going under the name of "industrial policy," were resurrected during the late 1970s as an alternative to the Keynesianism of the recent past.

Carter had opportunities to implement an industrial policy during the steel crises of 1977 and 1980, but he traveled down a different road. Instead of reshaping the market that U.S. policy had created, he reinforced it with policies that promoted competition, deregulation, and imports. Trade policy remained an arm of the National Security Council and State Department, required to work overtime because the crisis of the mid-1970s threatened Cold War alliances, which were cemented by access to the U.S. market as well as the more visible defense pacts. Carter's refusal to alter American industrial and trade policies destroyed his own political prospects in 1980 and separated industrial workers from the Democratic party. The party failed to foster a modernization that was compatible with working-class interests.

Ronald Reagan better understood the necessary union among his constituencies, policies, and ideology. On the surface, Reagan's program seemed to be a traditional accumulation strategy, redistributing income upwards and privileging profits over wages. But by examining the full record—who won and lost, the fiscal and trade deficits, high interest rates, and the deep recession of 1982—it becomes clear that the new Republicanism discriminated among sectors as well as among classes. The government privileged the energy, real estate, high technology, defense, and financial service industries—all mainly nontrading enterprises. Imported steel and manufactured goods made up for the investment shortfall in those U.S. industries, liberating capital for preferred sectors and preserving Cold War strategic policies.

Allowing the global market to resolve steel matters while other nations protected domestic markets, adopted export strategies, and subsidized restructuring produced predictable results. U.S. industry paid a disproportionate price for reducing the global steel surplus. Four years of conflict between labor and capital, whipsawed by Darwinian international competition, was the American road to reduced U.S. steel capacity and restructuring. Eventually, in 1984, Reagan, who had watched from the sidelines, negotiated comprehensive quotas that prevented additional losses. The decision elicited an industrial policy of sorts. Foreign steel companies, with the support and aid of their governments, either bought into American companies, entered joint ventures, or leased equipment and technology to secure a place in what was still the world's largest open market for steel. Today the U.S. industry is the most efficient in the world, but the nation is no longer self-sufficient in steel. The shrinkage was a variant of a low-wage solution to the new global competition. Large steel imports, which have grown to 25 percent of the domestic market, are a permanent part of that solution. Some American industries took production offshore. Others responded by installing labor-displacing new technology. (Technological displacement and trade displacement are related, not separate, phenomena.) The results were similar. Manufacturing work has declined in the United States.

The shrinkage of the steel industry was more than a series of mill closings or a gradual shift from manufacturing to service. To effect these results, the Reagan administration had to propose a new blueprint. Policies promoting free trade, deregulating industry and financial markets, discouraging unions, and reducing safety nets assumed that if capital is freed from government and social obligations, the whole society will benefit. The menu of production was taken to be less important than the alleged efficiency of capital allocations. The assumption that business success would eventually produce labor well-being replaced the New Deal article of faith that capital and labor would prosper together.

This outcome was not simply the result of the power of business, although corporations organized mightily during the 1970s. The oppositional heritage of the 1960s offered little to counter the offensive. Liberals, the New Left, and an array of new advocacy groups had cut their teeth on foreign policy, civil rights, and the environment. They too had believed that American affluence was permanent. Academics on the left assumed that if change were to occur at all, it would come from an exploited third world, revolting against American economic domination. This worldview bred a generation that had never grappled with American economic questions. Civil rights law addressed the injustices of the past, not the economic realities of the present. The EPA was enjoined from taking costs into consideration in the Clean Air Act amendments of 1970.[22] When confronted with a steel crisis in Youngstown, Ohio, in 1977, New Left economists attempted to finesse it and the market by creating a community-owned steel plant. Suspicious of the state, industry, and unions, they attacked social democracy, which they called corporate liberalism, and interpreted agreements like the consent decrees as accommodations. These attacks on the state sounded very similar to the growing criticism from the right.

Preferring the tactic of direct action, 1960s activists discovered that militancy can be a perishable commodity. They were disarmed when the political and economic climate dampened popular action. Litigation was no substitute. The new public interest law firms, funded by foundations like Ford and Rockefeller and inspired by the guerrilla warfare of Ralph Nader, had assumed that the power of business was not only antisocial but permanent. As that power vanished, the activists' own credibility weakened. The reform movements of the 1960s had very little to say about the crisis of the late 1970s. They offered more of a moral critique than an economic alternative to Reagan's supply-side measures. By defining Reaganomics simply as an attack on the poor and seeking welfare solutions to compensate for the decline of industry, they yielded the economic terrain and thus themselves offered little to the working class and the poor.[23]

The liberal middle class, centered in the professions and sectors that benefited from the reconstructions of the 1980s, lacked the incentive to do more than protect the environment, defend the idea of affirmative action, and guard secular culture from the assaults of social conservatives. These politics sometimes buffered the harsh edges of market solutions, but they did not challenge them. The sensibility proved too puny to shield many safety nets.[24] With their assumptions challenged, some intellectuals embraced poststructural analyses of the world and celebrated the resistances, but not the victories, of the past, assuming that a "culture of opposition" was the best that history offered the present.[25]

Still, it was not so easy to alter the New Deal legacy of state activism. Conservative intellectuals lubricated the transition. Schools of monetarism, "rational expectations," and "public choice" assaulted Keynesianism as well as industrial policy and challenged the notion that government could act wisely.[26] Although they have new names, the ideas are identical to those hegemonic before the Great Depression. At a more popular level, George Gilder's *Wealth and Poverty* offered an intellectual defense of capitalism in its pure form, not the "modern capitalism" described by Andrew Shonfield in 1965.[27] Social scientists and journalists, housed in new think tanks, targeted social policy, magnifying every flaw, concluding that each failure demonstrated that government was incapable or culpable.[28]

Racial ideology played a role in the transition. During the 1960s, the nation attributed black unemployment to racism; during the 1980s, black unemployment came to be seen as a preference for idleness—whether caused by welfare, lifestyle, or family structure. In both eras, racial ideology mystified the sources of black unemployment and shored up the legitimacy of institutional arrangements. But race now was only a way station on the road to a broader goal. Reagan indicted welfare abusers, usually those with dark faces, but the newest Republicans, triumphant in 1994, indicted the welfare system as a whole. The next year a "Million-Man March" of African Americans in support of family values and self-help came to the same conclusion. In 1996 a Democratic president signed a bill ending the federal government's commitment, made in 1935, to poor mothers and children. The decision was a symbol of a new bipartisan consensus. After the deed was done, inflammatory racial rhetoric moderated, although the fifteen-year assault on welfare has surely left a residue of racialism in popular thinking.

The stable growth rates of the past few years demonstrate that it is possible, at least in the short run, to restrain wages and social benefits and raise corporate profits. As *Fortune* had gushed in the 1950s, it claimed in the summer of 1997 that the U.S. economy is "stronger than it's ever been."[29] The stock market ascended, elites celebrated their management skills, and the president boasted that the U.S. economy was number one. But in 1996, Japan, beset with economic problems, still managed to produce a 3.6 percent growth rate, while the U.S. figure was 2.4. The United States did better in 1997, but the CEA forecast of 2.3 percent growth through the year 2000 is not a number to cheer about.[30] For all the romance with computers, U.S. productivity growth is both less than comparable rates in Germany and Japan and less than U.S. rates during the 1950s and 1960s. If U.S. industry has achieved such strides in efficiency, why is it that the United States currently suffers a trade deficit of nearly $200 billion a year?[31]

Even if we include 1997, the "good" year, the domestic economy is not growing as fast as it did before the mid-1970s. This is partly because the Federal Reserve Board, like generals fighting the last war, has set policy to combat inflation while the economy has in fact been undergoing disinflation. Fed policies were fine for global corporations, but they were not for the 60 to 80 percent of the population who have not benefited from current growth rates. Thus, Barry Bluestone and Bennett Harrison suggested that the government may not be "forecasting" growth rates but "setting" and limiting them. Although economists argue about whether "we can grow faster," if the future in any way resembles the past on these matters, the question is ultimately a political one.[32]

Thus, the balance of political power is crucial. There is no reason to believe that the current balance will hold, any more than earlier ones did. Unlike elites "trapped in their comfort zones," Stephen Roach, chief economist and director of global economics at Morgan Stanley, sees signs that "the politics of austerity are on their way out" all over the world.[33] Responding to domestic challenges to the new order, the Institute for International Economics, a bastion of free trade orthodoxy, published Dani Rodrik's *Has Globalization Gone Too Far?* Rodrik acknowledged the popular brief against the new global order by demonstrating that U.S. trade with rich as well as poor countries has reduced U.S. wages, redistributed surpluses toward employers rather than enlarging that surplus, and destabilized U.S. society. Although Rodrik continues to believe in free trade, he is honest enough to admit that the dogma that expanding trade was very important in postwar growth is an article of faith among economists but unproved. Rodrik's purpose is to humanize globalization without altering the shift of income or the behavior of transnational business and finance. His indictment, however, overwhelms his solutions, which are essentially bromides like better welfare provisions.[34]

The defeat in November 1997 of legislation that would have given President Clinton "fast track" authority to negotiate new trade agreements demonstrated more fundamental questions about U.S. international economic policies. It was not a vote for "protectionism" but a critique of past dealings, which have protected capital more than labor or trade. Contemporary defenders of globalization inadvertently admit this past. Jagdish Bhagwati, a professor of economics at Columbia and GATT trade adviser, argued that despite Clinton's defeat, "Japan and Europe have no option but to follow the U.S. example, belatedly but surely, in opening their own markets. . . . Other countries will see our success, and seek to emulate it."[35] But American presidents and the academic community for the past twenty-five years have told the nation that as a result of a series of GATT negotiations, these markets had already been opened. The seeds of contemporary skepticism have been well watered.

That skepticism will deepen in the wake of the East Asian economic crisis, which is just beginning at the time I am writing. Even if Asian troubles do not trigger a deep economic contraction, in the short run they can only depress U.S. economic growth by reducing exports and encouraging imports in tradable goods—autos, appliances, semiconductors, machine tools, and, of course, steel. Like foreign steel producers in the 1970s and 1980s, Asian industrialists desperate for cash will have every incentive to dump, aided by currency devaluation. That U.S. transnationals with plants abroad may be better able to weather the storm is irrelevant to the domestic situation. Producers in the United States may be asked to "pay" for the global overcapacity effected by the East Asian nations and U.S. banks. As in the late 1970s and 1980s, U.S. banks and investment houses, in an effort to protect their loans, will urge the president to fight "protectionism" by accepting more imports in order to preserve the international economic system and control American inflation. U.S. producers will offer different advice, and they will be right. But if the debate is only about the geography of production, resolutions will not address the genuine problem: anemic demand caused by depressed or cheap labor rates. If global austerity is to be avoided in Asia and the United States, the labor movement will have much to do.

To be effective, unions must address inequality in the United States with economic as well as moral ideas and will need to seek state as well as collective bargaining solutions. During the 1980s, the USWA retained a good part of its past achievements for its remaining members because it addressed the production questions that it had ignored after World War II.[36] It proved that wage reduction, closures, and imports were not the only routes to modernization, but it could not counter unfavorable state policies. The United States will probably never have industrial banks, but the state has other ways of steering capital, encouraging unions, and fostering domestic production. The nation is awash with specific solutions for making trade fairer, capital more patient, foreign affiliates more job-creating, growth more robust, incomes more equal, and workers more employable.[37] There are plenty of ideas, but they are not powered by social and political movements.

Just as the postwar order was created by the rise of the CIO, a new compact will require a stronger labor movement, because organized workers are the only group that has a collective interest in marrying efficiency with labor progress. Lacking the weight to lead, the USWA will be dependent upon what others do. Its decision to join with autoworkers and machinists to form a union of metalworkers may be fifty years too late, but then it may not be. Men and women can make history, even in an era of globalization.

Abbreviations

This book draws upon records of presidents, executive agencies, courts, state and local governments, labor and civil rights organizations, and individuals. The papers of presidents Kennedy, Johnson, Nixon, and Carter are uniformly abbreviated by each president's initials (JFK, LBJ, RN, JC). Unlike those of the other presidents, the records of President Nixon (RN) are housed not in his presidential library but at the National Archives. Citations of the White House Central Files (WHCF) all refer to the executive section of these files; collections of documents from other White House staff and administrative structures are specified. The abbreviation OHI refers to the Oral History Interviews that are part of each presidential collection. Citations from the series *Public Papers of the Presidents of the United States* (Washington, D.C.: GPO, various years) use the abbreviated style shown in this example: Kennedy, *Public Papers, 1962.*

Most of the records of the United Steelworkers of America are at Pennsylvania State University; however, I also used USWA records in Birmingham and Fairfield, Alabama. The records of the USWA Legislation Department, which I used in the Washington, D.C., office, are now deposited at Pennsylvania State University. The records of the union's legal department are stored in Pittsburgh.

Container and file numbers appear in that order, separated by a slash. Thus "1/5" indicates container 1, file 5; "1/Civil Rights" indicates container 1, subject file on civil rights.

Depositories

BPL	Manuscript Division, Birmingham Public Library, Birmingham, Ala.
Catholic	Manuscript Division, Catholic University of America, Washington, D.C.
Georgia St.	Southern Labor Archives, Georgia State University, Atlanta
JFK	John F. Kennedy Presidential Library, Boston, Mass.

JC	Jimmy Carter Presidential Library, Atlanta, Ga.
LBJ	Lyndon Baines Johnson Presidential Library, Austin, Tex.
LC	Manuscript Division, Library of Congress, Washington, D.C.
Meany	George Meany Memorial Archives, Silver Spring, Md.
Minn.	Minnesota Historical Society, St. Paul, Minn.
NA	National Archives, College Park, Md.
NA-Ga.	National Archives, East Pointe, Ga.
Penn St.	Historical Collections and Labor Archives, Pennsylvania State University, University Park, Pa.
Schomburg	Schomburg Center for Research in Black Culture, New York, N.Y.
USWA-Birm	District 36 office, USWA, Birmingham, Ala.
USWA-FF	Subdistrict office, USWA, Fairfield, Ala.
Wayne St.	Archives of Labor and Urban Affairs, Wayne State University, Detroit, Mich.

Collections

A&R	Audit and Review Committee, Penn St.
Abel/USWA	I. W. Abel, Penn St.
ACHR	Alabama Council on Human Relations, BPL
APR	A. Philip Randolph, LC
Bernstein	Meyer Bernstein, Penn St.
Boutwell	Albert Boutwell, BPL
Brennan	William J. Brennan Jr., LC
BSCP	Brotherhood of Sleeping Car Porters, LC
Burke/USWA	Walter J. Burke, Penn St.
Carey	James B. Carey, Wayne St.
Celler	Emanuel Celler, LC
CIO-EB	Executive Board, Congress of Industrial Organizations, Meany
Clark	Joseph S. Clark, Historical Society of Pennsylvania, Philadelphia (unprocessed)
Connor	Eugene T. Connor, BPL
CORE	Congress of Racial Equality, Schomburg (microfilm)
CR/AFL-CIO	Civil Rights Department, AFL-CIO, Meany
CR/USWA	Civil Rights Department, USWA, Penn St.
Dist. 35	District 35, USWA, Georgia St.
Dist. 36/Ala.	Subdistrict Office, District 36, USWA, USWA-Birm and USWA-FF
Dist. 36/Penn St.	District 36, USWA, Penn St.
Duncan	Clarence Duncan (in possession of James Seay, Gary, Ind.)
EEOC	RG 404, Records of the Equal Employment Opportunity Commission, NA, Suitland, Md. (unprocessed)
Eizenstat	Stuart Eizenstat, JC
Goldberg, LC	Arthur J. Goldberg, LC
Goldberg, NA	RG 174, Records of Secretary of Labor Arthur J. Goldberg, NA
Haldeman	H. R. Haldeman, RN
Hamilton	William Hamilton, BPL
Hanes	Arthur Hanes, BPL
HHH	Hubert H. Humphrey, Minneapolis, Minn.
Hodgson	RG 174, Records of the Secretary of Labor James D. Hodgson, NA
IEB	Minutes of the International Executive Board, USWA, Penn St.

IA	International Affairs Department, USWA, Penn St.
IRRA	Industrial Relations Research Association
Justice	Records of Justice Department, Department of Justice, Washington, D.C.
LDF	NAACP Legal and Educational Defense Fund, Rockefeller Brothers Fund papers, Rockefeller Archives, North Tarrytown, N.Y.
Leg/AFL-CIO	Legislation Department, AFL-CIO, Meany
Leg/USWA	Legislation Department, USWA, Penn St.
Legal/Pittsburgh	Legal Department, USWA, Pittsburgh, Pa.
Leg-DC/USWA	Legislation Department, USWA, Washington, D.C. (unprocessed; now housed at Penn St.)
Marshall	Thurgood Marshall, LC
McDonald/USWA	David J. McDonald, Penn St.
Miller/USWA	Marvin Miller, Penn St.
Molony/USWA	Joseph P. Molony, Penn St.
Murray	Philip Murray, Catholic
NAACP	National Association for the Advancement of Colored People, LC
NALC	Negro American Labor Council, Schomburg
NUL	National Urban League, LC
ONB	Operation New Birmingham, BPL
Randolph	A. Philip Randolph, LC
Rauh	Joseph L. Rauh Jr., LC
Research/USWA	Research Department, USWA, Penn St.
RG 228	Records of the Fair Employment Practices Committee, NA
RG 51	Records of the Bureau of the Budget, after 1968, Office of Management and Budget, NA
RN	Richard M. Nixon presidential papers, NA
Rustin	Bayard Rustin, LC
Seibels	George Seibels Jr., BPL
Shultz	RG 174, Records of the Secretary of Labor George P. Shultz, NA
SRC	Southern Regional Council, copies in BPL
Trial	51-volume transcript, United States v. U.S. Steel, et al., 371 F. Supp. 1045 (N.D. Ala., 1973), Records of the Federal Courts, NA-Ga.
Waggoner	James T. Waggoner, BPL
WHCF	White House Central Files
Wirtz	RG 174, Records of Secretary of Labor W. Willard Wirtz, NA

Introduction

1. The latest study of Johnson's tenure, Irving Bernstein's *Guns or Butter: The Presidency of Lyndon Johnson* (New York: Oxford University Press, 1996), is mute on the subject.

2. David Plotke has recently used the term "Democratic order" in his *Building a Democratic Political Order: Reshaping American Liberalism in the 1930s and 1940s* (Cambridge: Cambridge University Press, 1996). It is a very smart book, which revises many views about New Deal liberalism. Plotke promises to narrate the decline, which he dates from 1968 to 1972, in a forthcoming study.

3. Alan Brinkley, *The End of Reform: New Deal Liberalism in Recession and War* (New York: Alfred A. Knopf, 1995).

4. Fred Siegel, *Troubled Journey: From Pearl Harbor to Ronald Reagan* (New York: Hill and Wang, 1984); William O'Neill, *Coming Apart: An Informal History of America in the 1960s*

(Chicago: University of Chicago Press, 1971); Thomas Byrne Edsall and Mary D. Edsall, *Chain Reaction: The Impact of Race, Rights, and Taxes on American Politics* (New York: W. W. Norton, 1992); Jonathan Rieder, *Canarsie: The Jews and Italians of Brooklyn Against Liberalism* (Cambridge: Harvard University Press, 1985).

5. Thomas J. Sugrue, *The Origins of the Urban Crisis: Race and Inequality in Postwar Detroit* (Princeton: Princeton University Press, 1996); Leonard J. Moore, "Good Old-Fashioned New Social History and the Twentieth-Century American Right," *Reviews in American History* 24 (1996): 555–73. The growing interest in the history of popular or working-class "conservatism" stems from this analysis of the decline of liberalism.

6. David Vogel, *Fluctuating Fortunes: The Political Power of Business in America* (New York: Basic, 1989); William C. Berman, *America's Right Turn: From Nixon to Bush* (Baltimore: Johns Hopkins University Press, 1994).

7. Walter Russell Mead, *Mortal Splendor: The American Empire in Transition* (Boston: Houghton Mifflin, 1987); Robert Kuttner, *The End of Laissez-Faire: National Purpose and the Global Economy After the Cold War* (New York: Alfred A. Knopf, 1991). Others simply make the Vietnam war the culprit. See, e.g., Kevin Boyle, *The UAW and the Heyday of American Liberalism, 1945–1968* (Ithaca, N.Y.: Cornell University Press, 1995).

8. A thoughtful example of eclecticism is James T. Patterson's *Grand Expectations: The United States, 1945–1974* (New York: Oxford University Press, 1996). Patterson spends the bulk of his time discussing affluence, social movements, and Vietnam. When he gets to the very end, he tells us that people were feeling anxious and that there were a host of economic problems facing the nation, which had been developing over the years. One wonders why he had not told us about them earlier. He solves the problem by concluding that America's expectations were too grand. His solution fulfills thematic requirements, but raises more questions than it answers.

9. Ira Katznelson and Bruce Pietrykowski, "Rebuilding the American State: Evidence from the 1940s," *Studies in American Political Development* 5 (Fall 1991): 301–39; Brinkley, *End of Reform.*

10. Paul A. Volcker and Toyoo Gyohten, *Changing Fortunes: The World's Money and the Threat to American Leadership* (New York: Times Books, 1992), 11.

Chapter One

1. Donald F. Barnett and Louis Schorsch, *Steel: Upheaval in a Basic Industry* (Cambridge, Mass: Ballinger, 1983), 13, 21.

2. G. G. Schroeder, *The Growth of Major Steel Companies, 1900–1950* (Baltimore: Johns Hopkins University Press, 1953), 404. The standard history of steel technology, companies, and markets is William T. Hogan, *Economic History of the Iron and Steel Industry in the United States,* 5 vols., (Lexington, Mass.: Lexington Books, 1971).

3. Hogan, *Economic History,* 5:1665.

4. Gilbert Burck, "American Genius for Productivity," *Fortune,* July 1955, 87.

5. Mark McColloch, "Consolidating Industrial Citizenship: The USWA at War and Peace, 1939–46," in *Forging a Union of Steel: Philip Murray, SWOC, and the United Steelworkers,* ed. Paul F. Clark, Peter Gottlieb, and Donald Kennedy (Ithaca, N.Y.: ILR Press, 1987), 63.

6. Simon Kuznets, *Share of Upper Income Groups in Income and Savings* (New York: National Bureau of Economic Research, 1953); Joint Economic Committee (JEC), *Productivity, Prices, and Incomes,* 89th Cong., 2d sess. (Washington, D.C.: GPO, 1967).

7. Editors of *Fortune, Markets of the Sixties* (New York: Harper and Brothers, 1960), chap. 6; Kenneth T. Jackson, *Crabgrass Frontier: The Suburbanization of the United States* (New York: Oxford University Press, 1985), chaps. 11, 13.

8. Steven M. Gillon, *Politics and Vision: The ADA and American Liberalism, 1947–1985* (New York: Oxford University Press, 1987), 83–89.

9. James Wechsler, *Reflections of an Angry Middle-Aged Editor* (New York: Random House, 1960), 65; Daniel Bell to Otis Brubaker, Nov. 21, 1956, 67/13, Research/USWA.

10. Paule Marshall, Eleanor Leacock, David Walker to A. Philip Randolph, Nov. 6, 1961, 2/7, NALC. They hoped that by working with Randolph's NALC they would be "fighting for the liberation of black people and hence the liberation of all people," including themselves.

11. John Kenneth Galbraith, *The Affluent Society* (Boston: Houghton Mifflin, 1958), 325–26.

12. Herbert Marcuse, *Eros and Civilization* (Boston: Beacon Press, 1955). In *One-Dimensional Man: Studies in the Ideology of Advanced Industrial Society* (Boston: Beacon Press, 1964), Marcuse argued that the manipulated contentment of the masses was so complete that rebellion was unlikely. This judgment was one source of the ideological and political "third-worldism" among western intellectuals.

13. Martin J. Sklar, *The Corporate Reconstruction of American Capitalism, 1890–1916* (Cambridge: Cambridge University Press, 1988), 154–56; Thomas Goebel, "The Political Economy of American Populism from Jackson to the New Deal," *Studies in American Political Development* 11 (Spring 1997): 134–41

14. George Bittlingmayer offers a slightly different interpretation in his article "Did Antitrust Policy Cause the Great Merger Wave?" *Journal of Law and Economics* 28 (1985): 77–111. Bittlingmayer answers yes, arguing that the antitrust tradition harmed economic development.

15. The most recent work finds that legislators were more concerned with the welfare of small producers hurt by trusts than with the interests of consumers. Christopher Grandy, "Original Intent and the Sherman Antitrust Act: A Re-examination of the Consumer Welfare Hypothesis," *Journal of Economic History* 53 (1993): 359–76.

16. *United States v. United States Steel Corporation et al.*, 251 U.S. 417 (1920).

17. Tom Freyer, *Regulating Big Business: Antitrust in Great Britain and America, 1880–1990* (Cambridge, Eng.: Cambridge University Press, 1992), 189; Neil Fligstein, *The Transformation of Corporate Control* (Cambridge, Mass.: Harvard University Press, 1990), 75–105. Fear of prosecution also may have accounted for the company's caution, which critics attributed to oligopoly. For a parallel with IBM, see James Fallows, "The Computer Wars," *New York Review of Books*, Mar. 24, 1994, 34–41.

18. Robert R. Brooks, *As Steel Goes: Unionism in a Basic Industry* (New Haven: Yale University Press, 1940); Irving Bernstein, *The Turbulent Years: A History of American Workers, 1933–1941* (Boston: Houghton-Mifflin, 1969).

19. Nelson Lichtenstein, *Labor's War at Home: The CIO in World War II* (Cambridge: Cambridge University Press, 1982), chap. 5; CIO-EB, Jan. 24, 1942. During the war, private investment plummeted to between 3 and 6 percent of GNP. The federal government funded 7.9 of the 15.2 million tons of new steel capacity. JEC, *Productivity, Prices, and Incomes*, 89; Paul A. Tiffany, *The Decline of American Steel: How Management, Labor, and Government Went Wrong*, (New York: Oxford University Press, 1988), 197, n. 59; Paul A. C. Koistinen, *The Hammer and the Sword: Labor, the Military and Industrial Mobilization, 1940–1945* (1959; reprint, New York: Arno, 1975), 586–97.

20. Ira Katznelson and Bruce Pietrykowski, "Rebuilding the American State: Evidence from the 1940s," *Studies in American Political Development* 5 (Fall 1991): 301–39; Margaret Weir, *Politics and Jobs: The Boundaries of Employment Policy in the United States* (Princeton: Princeton University Press, 1992), chap. 2. The definitive account of the passage of the law is Stephen Kemp Bailey, *Congress Makes a Law* (New York: Vintage, 1950).

21. Tiffany, *Decline of American Steel*, 61. For the industry's point of view, see *New York Times*, May 3, 1949; Henry W. Broude, *Steel Decisions and the National Economy* (New

Haven: Yale University Press, 1963), 213; William Odell Wagnon Jr. "The Politics of Economic Growth: The Truman Administration and the Recession of 1949" (Ph.D. diss., University of Missouri, 1970), 85.

22. Broude, *Steel Decisions and the National Economy*, 25, 31.

23. Tiffany, *Decline of American Steel*, 29–31, 96.

24. JEC, Hearings, *Steel Prices, Unit Costs, Profits, and Foreign Competition*, 79th Cong., 1st sess. (Washington, D.C.: GPO, 1963), 187; Theodore Philip Kovaleff, *Business and Government during the Eisenhower Administration: A Study of the Antitrust Policy of the Antitrust Division of the Justice Department* (Athens: Ohio University Press, 1980), 78–83.

25. Barnett and Schorsch, *Steel*, 23.

26. The best history of steelworkers and the labor relations of the industry before the Great Depression is David Brody, *Steelworkers in America: The Nonunion Era* (Cambridge: Harvard University Press, 1960).

27. See Melvyn Dubofsky and Warren Van Tine, *John L. Lewis: A Biography* (New York: Quadrangle, 1977). Unfortunately, there is no modern biography of Philip Murray.

28. IEB, Apr. 2, 1946.

29. IEB, May 19, 1943, Feb. 16–17, 1961. Economist Otto Eckstein concluded that from 1939 to 1947, steel wages rose 71.7 percent, while the wages of all manufacturing workers rose 95.4 percent. Otto Eckstein, *Steel and the Postwar Inflation* (Washington, D.C.: GPO, 1959), 17.

30. Tiffany, *The Decline of American Steel*, 148.

31. IEB, Mar. 21, 1947. The 1950 Congress did improve pensions. But Edward Berkowitz has shown that until the mid-1950s, the elderly were supported more by the dole than by social insurance. Edward Berkowitz, *America's Welfare State: From Roosevelt to Reagan* (Baltimore: Johns Hopkins University Press, 1991); see also Alan Derickson, "Health Security for All? Social Unionism and Universal Health Insurance, 1935–1958," *Journal of American History* 80 (Mar. 1994): 1333–56.

32. IEB, June 29, 1946.

33. IEB, Dec. 10, 1945.

34. David Plotke, *Building a Democratic Political Order: Reshaping American Liberalism in the 1930s and 1940s* (Cambridge, Eng.: Cambridge University Press, 1996), 247; IEB, Oct. 1, 1946; Barbara S. Griffith, *The Crisis of American Labor: Operation Dixie and the Defeat of the CIO* (Philadelphia: Temple University Press, 1988).

35. For assessments that conclude that the impact of Taft-Hartley was less significant than I have made it out to be, see Melvyn Dubofsky, *The State and Labor in Modern America* (Chapel Hill: University of North Carolina Press, 1994), 201–8 and Plotke, *Building a Democratic Political Order*, 255–61.

36. Weaver to James B. Carey, Sept. 18, 1953, 188/Carey-Weaver, James B. Carey Papers, Wayne St.; Robert H. Zieger, *The CIO, 1935–1955* (Chapel Hill: University of North Carolina Press, 1995), 312.

37. Mary Sperling McAuliffe, *Crisis on the Left: Cold War Politics and American Liberals, 1947–1954* (Amherst: University of Massachusetts Press, 1978); Steven Rosswurm, "Introduction," in *The CIO's Left-Led Unions*, ed. Steven Rosswurm (New Brunswick: Rutgers University Press, 1992), 1–18.

38. See David L. Stebenne's excellent biography, *Arthur J. Goldberg: New Deal Liberal* (New York: Oxford University Press, 1996).

39. David J. McDonald, *Union Man* (New York: Dutton, 1969), 139; John Herling, *Right to Challenge: People and Power in the Steelworkers Union* (New York: Harper and Row, 1972), 16.

40. JEC, *Employment and Unemployment* (Washington, D.C.: GPO, 1962.), 9.

41. Cited in Tiffany, *Decline of American Steel*, 103.

42. Charles S. Maier, "Inflation and Stagnation in Politics and History," in *The Politics of Inflation and Economic Stagnation: Theoretical Approaches and International Case Studies*, ed. Leon N. Lindberg and Charles S. Maier (Washington, D.C.: Brookings Institution, 1985), 10–11, 55. Flanders, a Vermont industrialist, was cofounder of the Committee for Economic Development, an elite business think tank.

43. Ruggles in U.S. Congress, Senate Subcommittee on Antitrust and Monopoly of the Judiciary Committee, Hearings, *Administered Prices*, pt. 1, 85th Cong., 1st sess. (Washington, D.C.: GPO, 1957), 134. Similarly, from 1952 to 1959 steel prices rose 47 percent, while the prices of machinery and equipment rose only 29 percent and other metal-using products 19 percent. JEC, *Steel Prices*, 250; Robert Lekachman, *The Age of Keynes* (New York: Vintage, 1968), 249.

44. JEC, *Steel Prices*, 136.

45. Harold G. Vatter, *The United States Economy in the 1950s* (New York: W. W. Norton, 1963), 125; John W. Sloan, *Eisenhower and the Management of Prosperity* (Lawrence: University Press of Kansas, 1991), 124–25, 143–44; Karen Orren, "Union Politics and Postwar Liberalism in the United States, 1946–1979," *Studies in American Political Development* 1 (1986): 235; Tiffany, *Decline of American Steel*, 150–51.

46. Kefauver to Lorne H. Nelles, Apr. 7, 1959, 49/District 35, McDonald/USWA.

47. Rufus Tucker, cited in Ellis W. Hawley, *The New Deal and the Problem of Monopoly* (Princeton: Princeton University Press, 1966), 467–68.

48. Senate, Hearings, *Administered Prices*, pt. 1, 119.

49. JEC, *Steel Prices*.

50. Tiffany, *Decline of American Steel*, 157.

51. Ibid., 40–41, 179.

52. Ibid., 160–61; JEC, *Steel Prices*, 29, 279. Senate, Hearings, *Administered Prices*, pt. 11, (Washington, D.C.: GPO, 1959), 5394.

53. Eugene B. Germany, OHI, LBJ, 27–29; author's telephone interview with Jim Smith, May 6, 1993; IEB, May 14, 1958, 15–18.

54. Brubaker to Carey McWilliams, May, 12, 1959, 67/13, Research/USWA; Senate, Hearings, *Administered Prices*, pt. 11, 5201.

55. JEC, *Report on Employment, Growth, and Price Levels* (Washington, D.C.: GPO, 1960), 13.

56. Senate, Hearings, *Administered Prices*, pt. 1, xxv, 27, chap. 3; Tiffany, *Decline of American Steel*, Table 2.1, 27.

57. Lekachman, *Age of Keynes*, 209–10; James L. Sundquist, *Politics and Policy: The Eisenhower, Kennedy, and Johnson Years* (Washington, D.C.: Brookings Institution, 1968), 16–28; Robert M. Collins, *The Business Response to Keynes, 1929–1941* (New York: Columbia University Press, 1981), 176–77; Iwan W. Morgan, *Eisenhower versus "The Spenders": The Eisenhower Administration, the Democrats and the Budget, 1953–60* (New York: St. Martin's, 1990), 119.

58. Ronald F. King, *Money, Time, and Politics: Investment Tax Subsidies and American Democracy* (New Haven: Yale University Press, 1993), 144.

59. R. Alton Lee, *Eisenhower and Landrum-Griffin: A Study in Labor-Management Politics* (Lexington: University of Kentucky Press, 1990).

60. IEB, Aug. 11–12, 1958.

61. IEB, Jan. 6–7, Aug. 11–12, 1958.

62. IEB, July 13, 1959; Brubaker to Carl Zirbal, Nov. 9, 1961, 85/13, Research/USWA; Jack Stieber, "Work Rules and Practices in Mass Production Industries," in Industrial Relations Research Association (hereafter IRRA), *Annual Proceedings, 1961* (Madison, Wisc.: IRRA, 1962), 401–5. The steel industry had insisted upon "the right to manage" investment and

technology, but the USWA succeeded in limiting managerial discretion on promotions, lay-offs, transfers, rehiring, job content, and work practices. In theory, there was a line between personnel matters and management prerogatives. In practice, as the 2B battle revealed, the two were connected. Howell John Harris, *The Right to Manage: Industrial Relations Policies of American Business in the 1940s* (Madison: University of Wisconsin Press, 1982); David Brody, *Workers in Industrial America: Essays on the Twentieth Century Struggle* (New York: Oxford University Press, 1980), 179; Jack W. Stieber, *The Steel Industry Wage Structure: A Study of the Joint Union-Management Job Evaluation Program in the Basic Steel Industry* (Cambridge: Harvard University Press, 1959).

63. Smith interview, May 6, 1993. In his otherwise excellent book, *The Decline of American Steel*, Paul Tiffany attributes the strike and concerns for modernization to the trade issue, claiming that the industry's actions of the late 1950s "could only have been developed in the context of heightened global competition" (168). As his words suggest, his formulation is advanced rhetorically, but it is not supported by the evidence. Tiffany does not acknowledge the role of competing products and labor costs in the postwar industry. Moreover, he wrote his book before the AISI opened the minutes of the meetings of its board of directors, which reveal that the international trade issue became important only in 1964. See Chapter 8 below.

64. Erwin C. Hargrove and Samuel A. Morley, eds., *The President and the Council of Economic Advisers: Interviews with CEA Chairmen* (Boulder, Colo.: Westview, 1984), 153; IEB, Oct. 4, 1949. Only Justice William Douglas agreed that the government offered insufficient evidence of the danger of a continuing steel strike.

65. McDonald at IEB, Mar. 15, 1960; Roy Stevens, "Off the Record Remarks of R. Conrad Cooper at Harvard University on December 7, 1960," 155/5, McDonald/USWA.

66. JEC, *Employment and Unemployment*, 19; Gilbert Bruck, "Armco: Precocious at Sixty," *Fortune*, Nov. 1959, 129; Otis Brubaker, "Long-Term Employment Trends in the Basic Steel Industry," Mar. 3, 1961, 59/16, Research/USWA.

67. "Steelworker Employment Surveys—Aug 1960 and May 1960," Sept. 15, 1960, 51/8, Research/USWA; IEB, May 18, 1961; Margaret S. Gordon, "U.S. Manpower and Employment Policy," *Monthly Labor Review* 87 (Nov. 1964): 1314–19.

68. Meyer Bernstein, analysis of monograph, "Capital Expenditures by Steel Producers for Cost-Reducing Improvements," July 15, 1949, Research/USWA; Bernstein to Brubaker, Aug. 9, 1949, 63/1, ibid.; Frank Pollera to Economic Guidelines Subcommittee, Nov. 17, 1961, 80/11, ibid.; Barnett and Schorsch, *Steel*, 28.

69. Tiffany, *Decline of American Steel*, 135; Vatter, *U.S. Economy in the 1950s*, 53; JEC, *Steel Prices*, 181; Brubaker to James M. Cobb, Jan. 19, 1961, 67/14, Research/USWA.

70. Lekachman, *Age of Keynes*, 208–9, 236–38; Arthur M. Okun, OHI, Mar. 20, 1979, LBJ; Charles C. Killingsworth, "The Fall and Rise of the Idea of Structural Unemployment," in IRRA, *Annual Proceedings, 1978*, (Madison, Wisc.: IRRA, 1979), 1–13.

71. Walt W. Rostow, OHI, Apr. 11, 1964, 149, JFK; Morgan, *Eisenhower versus "The Spenders"*, 175.

72. In 1958, Democrats increased their numbers from 49 to 64 in the Senate and from 183 to 234 in the House.

73. Sundquist, *Politics and Policy*, 57–83. The senators held hearings in twelve states, produced nine volumes of testimony, and painted a collective portrait of the structurally unemployed—persons living in depressed areas, young school dropouts, older workers, and minorities.

74. IEB, May 17–18, 1961; Meyer Bernstein to McDonald et al., Dec. 12, 1960, 79/19, IA. Brubaker to editor, *Reporter*, Mar. 1, 1961; Sar Levitan to Brubaker, Mar. 24, 1961,

and Brubaker to Levitan, Mar. 29, 1961, 67/5, Research/USWA; Charles L. Schultze, OHI, Mar. 28, 1969, LBJ; Sundquist, *Politics and Policy*, 85, 106; IEB, Oct. 23, 1963.

75. David E. Beller, OHI, July 11, 1964, 46–47; Joseph S. Clark, OHI, Dec. 16, 1965, 69, JFK; Sundquist, *Politics and Policy*, 93; Goldberg, "Memo for the President," Oct. 17, 1961, Goldberg, LC. The Bureau of the Budget and the CEA argued that the public would not accept it, that it would unbalance the budget, and that it was unnecessary because business was improved. Various drafts may be found in ser. 61.1a, C-49, RG 51, NA.

76. R. F. King, *Money, Time, and Politics*, 305–6; Bernstein, *Promises Kept*, 160–91; Gordon, "U.S. Manpower and Employment Policies," 1314–19.

77. Bernstein to McDonald et al., Dec. 12, 1960, 79/19, IA.

78. Sar A. Levitan, *Vocational Education and Federal Policy* (Kalamazoo, Mich.: W. E. Upjohn Institute for Employment Research, 1963), 5; Thomas Janoski, *The Political Economy of Unemployment: Active Labor Market Policy in West Germany and the United States* (Berkeley: University of California Press, 1990), 199–201; David Brian Robertson, "Politics and Labor Markets: Toward an Explanation of the Formation and Adoption of U.S. Labor Market Policy" (Ph.D. diss., University of Indiana, 1981), chap. 5.

79. Desmond King, *Actively Seeking Work?: The Politics of Unemployment and Welfare Policy in the United States and Great Britain* (Chicago: University of Chicago Press, 1995).

80. "Training of War Workers under Various Programs," *Monthly Labor Review* 59 (Dec. 1944): 1237–38; "The Hard Realities of Retraining," *Fortune*, July 1961, 242.

81. Walter Heller, Kermit Gordon, James Tobin, Gardner Ackley, Paul Samuelson (henceforth CEA), OHI, Aug. 1, 1964, 60. Tobin agreed with Samuelson: "I don't think economic issues were very prominent in the campaign at all except for the general notion of accelerating the rate of growth and getting the country moving." Ibid., 84.

82. R. F. King, *Money, Time, and Politics*, 160; Richard Reeves, *President Kennedy: Profile of Power* (New York: Simon and Schuster, 1993), 295.

83. Bernstein's *Promises Kept* represents the view that Kennedy was confronted with political barriers; Allen J. Matusow's *The Unraveling of America: A History of Liberalism in the 1960s* (New York: Harper and Row, 1984) claims that Kennedy was pro-business.

84. R. F. King, *Money, Time, and Politics*, 159. Samuelson admitted that he tried, but failed, to save Kennedy from "universal geniuses like Walt Rostow" (CEA, OHI, Aug. 1, 1964, 51).

85. Cited in Bernstein, *Promises Kept*, 135. The recommendation was simply a repetition of the ideas Rostow presented in *The Stages of Economic Growth: A Non-Communist Manifesto* (Cambridge: Cambridge University Press, 1960), 104–5.

86. Rostow, *Stages of Economic Growth*, 105. The equation of the steel and auto industries was possible only on the basis of the theory of oligopoly. The auto industries lived in a world of expanding markets and high profits, the steel industry did not. This situation was finally recognized in 1989 by President George Bush. However, in a classic example of Catch-22, Bush used the long-term low profits of the steel industry as an argument for government inaction. Bush, "Memorandum for the United States Trade Representative," July 25, 1989, copy in Leg-DC/USWA.

87. Kennedy, *Public Papers, 1961*, 89.

88. Arthur K. Okun, OHI, Mar. 20, 1969, 18–25, LBJ; Neil H. Jacoby, "Wage-Price Guideposts as an Instrument to Attain U.S. Economic Goals," in *Government Wage-Price Guideposts in the American Economy*, Charles C. Moskowitz Lectures, no. 7 (New York: School of Commerce, New York University, 1967), 55; Heller, CEA, OHI, 284, JFK; Herbert S. Parmet, *JFK: The Presidency of John F. Kennedy* (New York: Dial, 1983), 92.

89. Kennedy, *Public Papers, 1961*, 57–58; JEC, *Productivity, Prices, and Incomes*, 190–91; Theodore C. Sorensen, *Kennedy* (New York: Harper and Row, 1965), 405–6, 444.

90. JEC, *The United States Balance of Payments: Report* (Washington, D.C.: GPO, 1964); JEC, Hearings, *The United States Balance of Payments*, 88th Cong., 1st sess. (Washington, D.C.: GPO, 1963), 47–48.

91. Arthur M. Okun, OHI, Mar. 20, 1969, 12–15, Apr. 15, 1969, 1–5, LBJ.

92. Parmet, *JFK*, 92. The AFL-CIO, as well as the USWA, bitterly opposed the implication that high wages hurt U.S. exports. "Suggested Points that May Be Discussed with CEA at Meeting Nov. 8, 1961," 15/13, Leg/AFL-CIO; Rostow, OHI, 119–20, JFK.

93. Reeves, *President Kennedy*, 294.

94. Heller to Goldberg, Dec. 29, 1961, 79/Steel, 1962, Goldberg, NA; Grant McConnell, *Steel and the Presidency* (New York: W. W. Norton, 1963), 65; Frank Hoffmann to McDonald, June 2, 1961, 79/17, IA.

95. *Economic Report of the President, 1962* (Washington: D.C.: GPO, 1962), 16, 185–90.

96. JEC, *Productivity, Prices, and Incomes*, 193. I am not arguing that workers should have obtained all the gain. One could argue that the costs of modernization required a lower wage bill. But the administration's policy was not dedicated to the health of the steel industry but to the health of the macroeconomy. That productivity in steel from 1958 to 1962 was higher than that of other nonfarm industries and that the industry's rise in employment costs per unit was lower were irrelevant. JEC, *Steel Prices*, 84–85.

97. Heller to Goldberg, Dec. 29, 1961; Steel Working Party to Council [of Economic Advisers], May 7, 1963, 194/1963 Steel, Wirtz. With pride unbecoming to a Democrat, Sorensen bragged that "average wage rate increases during Kennedy's tenure were this nation's lowest for any comparable period since the Second World War." Sorensen, *Kennedy*, 438.

98. During the same period, steel productivity was slightly higher. Thus, the employment cost per unit of output, a measure that combines productivity and wages, was lower in steel than in the rest of the economy.

99. JEC, *Steel Prices*, 61–113; U.S. Department of Labor [E. Robert Livernash], *Collective Bargaining in the Basic Steel Industry: A Study of the Public Interest and the Role of Government* (Washington, D.C.: U.S. Department of Labor, 1961).

100. Heller to Goldberg, Dec. 29, 1961.

101. McConnell, *Steel and the Presidency*, 65; Frank Hoffmann to McDonald, June 2, 1961, 79/17, IA; Edmund Ayoub to Russell H. Cook Jr., Feb. 17, 1965, 85/1, Research/USWA; *Wall Street Journal*, Dec. 11, 1961; *Pittsburgh Post-Gazette*, Feb. 14, 1966.

102. Cited in Reeves, *President Kennedy*, 295.

103. As it turned out, the percentage was probably lower. Gardner Ackley, Heller's successor, used the figure of 1.8 percent. "Memorandum for the President," Feb. 3, 1963, WHCF, BE4/Steel, C-12, LBJ.

104. Richard Manger, "The Determinants of Steel Prices in the U.S.: 1947–65," *Journal of Industrial Economics* 16 (Apr. 1968): 156–57; IEB, Feb. 16–17, 1961, Feb. 5–6, 1962, May 14, June 18, 20, 1963. Union lawyer David Feller, who had replaced Goldberg, concluded that the USWA had little leverage in 1962. David Feller, telephone interview with author, May 16, 1994.

105. Heller to Goldberg, Dec. 29, 1961; Herling, *Right to Challenge*, 98, 100; *Wall Street Journal*, Dec. 11, 1961; McConnell, *Steel and the Presidency*, 75; *Iron Age*, Apr. 8, 1962.

106. JEC, *Productivity, Prices, and Incomes*, 191.

107. Goldberg, "Memorandum for the President," Apr. 10, 1962, 79/Steel 1962, Goldberg, NA; Kennedy, *Public Papers, 1962*, 316.

108. In 1974, five years after he left U.S. Steel, Blough reaffirmed what his position had been: "wage negotiations and prices were separate matters. . . . I did not wish to talk about prices with the union." *The Washington Embrace of Business* (New York: Columbia University Press, 1975), 39–41.

109. Broude, *Steel Decisions and the National Economy*, 265. David Stebenne concluded that the Blough-Kennedy confrontation "doomed both the effort to strike a new social contract in steel and the postwar order [New Deal settlement]." Stebenne, *Arthur J. Goldberg*, 299. On the one hand, this is another example of a scholar ending an era when his subject exits the historical stage. Shortly afterward, Kennedy appointed Goldberg to the Supreme Court. On the substance of the matter, I view the incident as the showiest example of steel-government conflicts. Stebenne stresses the industry's rejection of the process but ignores the substance and purpose of White House policy, which Goldberg either shared or was ignorant of. Kennedy's purposes had little to do with the steel industry but much to do with his deflationary economic policy of 1961 and 1962. The incident was not an example of tripartite management but an assertion of presidential authority. The government had not addressed the capital needs of the industry, which of course was in the forefront of industry concerns. Conflict was inevitable.

110. Cited in Arthur Schlesinger Jr., *A Thousand Days: John F. Kennedy in the White House* (Boston: Houghton Mifflin, 1965), 638, 640.

111. Kennedy, *Public Papers, 1962*, 332, 338–39, 348–52; Kennedy, *Public Papers, 1963*, 300; Heller, "Memorandum for the President," Apr. 14, 1962, 79/Steel 1962, Goldberg, NA.

112. Heller, "Memorandum for the President," Apr. 14, 1962; Heller, OHI, Feb. 20, 1970, LBJ.

113. *Iron Age*, Mar. 7, 1963, 101.

114. JEC, Hearings, *State of the Economy and Policies for Full Employment*, 87th Cong., 2d sess. (Washington, D.C.: GPO, 1962), 215; "Suggested Points that May Be Discussed with CEA at Meeting November 8, 1961," 15/13, Leg/AFL-CIO; Kennedy, *Public Papers, 1962*, 713. Paul Samuelson recalled that the president "began to seriously contemplate the possibility that there would be a recession blamed on him and that he ought to do something about it." Samuelson, CEA, OHI, 431, 602–4, JFK.

115. Heller, CEA, OHI, 434; Kennedy, *Public Papers, 1962*, 456–57.

116. Hargrove and Morley, *President and the CEA*, 205; R. F. King, *Money, Time, and Politics*, chap. 8, 493–94, n. 47.

117. Kennedy, *Public Papers, 1962*, 553–54.

118. Ibid., 616, 547–50; Sorensen, *Kennedy*, 429–30; Kennedy, *Economic Report of the President, 1963*, 89.

119. Herbert Stein, *The Fiscal Revolution in America* (1968; reprint, Washington, D.C.: AEI Press, 1990), 407–21.

120. Heller, "Memorandum for the President," Oct. 18, 1964, WHCF, BE 4/Steel, C-12, LBJ; JEC, *Twentieth Anniversary of the Employment Act of 1946: An Economic Symposium* (Washington, D.C.: GPO, 1966).

121. JEC, Hearings, *Fiscal Policy Issues of the Coming Decade*, 89th Cong., 1st sess. (Washington, D.C.: GPO, 1965), 31.

122. *Iron Age*, Mar. 7, 1963, 101.

123. R. F. King, *Money, Time, and Politics*, 296; JEC, *State of the Economy and Policies for Full Employment*, 690; Nelson Lichtenstein, *The Most Dangerous Man in Detroit: Walter Reuther and the Fate of American Labor* (New York: Basic, 1995), 368; *Iron Age*, Nov. 5, 1964, 29.

124. JEC, *Productivity, Prices, and Incomes*, 23.

125. *Iron Age*, Aug. 9, 1962, 44.

126. Barnett and Schorsch, *Steel*, 52–53; JEC, *Productivity, Prices, and Income*, 194; Heller, "Memorandum for the President," Oct. 18, 1964, WHCF, CF BE5/N.Econ, C-2, LBJ. Sometimes expansion was a by-product of modernization, because the new furnaces and mills were larger, but the industry's primary purpose was modernization.

127. IEB, Sept. 3, 1964; R. F. King, *Money, Time, and Politics*, 204–5. The technological unemployment was not erased. In 1957, 600,000 workers produced 117 million tons; in 1965, 541,000 workers produced 131.2 million.

128. Heller, "Memorandum for the President," Aug. 1, 1964, WHCF, BE 4/Steel, C-12; George E. Reedy, "For the President," WHCF, CF LA6/Work Stoppage, C61; Blough, OHI, July 29, 1971, 3, all in LBJ.

Chapter Two

1. The USWA's Birmingham lawyer, Jerome Cooper, had made the arrangements to provide the bail money with UAW lawyer Joseph L. Rauh Jr., who had initiated the project. Howard Strevel, interview with author, July 12, 1988.

2. In 1947, the unemployment rate for nonwhites was 64 percent higher than that for whites; in 1952, it was 92 percent higher; in 1957, it was 105 percent higher; in 1962, it was 124 percent higher. Nat Goldfinger to Don Slaiman, Sept. 15, 1965, CR/AFL-CIO.

3. Bruce J. Schulman, *From Cotton Belt to Sunbelt: Federal Policy, Economic Development, and the Transformation of the South, 1938–1980* (New York: Oxford University Press, 1991), 152, 160.

4. Ibid., 172, chap. 5.

5. Daniel M. Johnson and Rex R. Campbell, *Black Migration in America: A Social Demographic History* (Durham, N.C.: Duke University Press, 1981), 141, 145; Gavin Wright, *New South, Old South: Revolutions in the Southern Economy Since the Civil War* (New York: Basic, 1986), 245; Gilbert C. Fite, *Cotton Fields No More: Southern Agriculture, 1965–1980* (Lexington: University Press of Kentucky), 209, 233; Virgil L. Christian Jr. and Adamantios Pepelasis, "Rural Problems," in *Employment of Blacks in the South: A Perspective on the 1960s*, ed. Ray Marshall and Virgil L. Christian Sr. (Austin: University of Texas Press, 1978), 23.

6. Gavin Wright, *Old South, New South*, 255; Schulman, *From Cotton Belt to Sunbelt*, 171–72.

7. IEB, Oct. 4–5, 1961, 149; *Wall Street Journal*, Oct. 24, 1957.

8. Wright, *Old South, New South*, 253; *Alabama Business* 37 (Dec. 1966), 15; Christian and Pepelasis, "Rural Problems," 31.

9. Schulman, *From Cotton Belt to Sunbelt*, 148, 159.

10. Alan L. Sorkin, "Education, Migration, and Negro Unemployment," *Social Forces* 47 (1969): 272.

11. Fite, *Cotton Fields No More*, 233; Brian S. Rungeling and George Ignatin, "Black Employment Patterns in the Birmingham SMSA," 39, Aug. 1971, 7/58, ONB. W. David Lewis, *Sloss Furnaces and the Rise of the Birmingham District: An Industrial Epic* (Tuscaloosa: University of Alabama Press, 1994), 448.

12. Dorothy Newman, "The Negro's Journey to the City—Part I," *Monthly Labor Review* 88 (May 1965), 502–7; Paul F. Schultz Jr. "Labor Force Participation and Employment Changes in Alabama's Transitional Economy," *Alabama Business* 41 (Dec. 1970), 23; U.S. Bureau of Census, *Census of Population, 1960*, Vol. 1, *Characteristics of the Population*, Pt. 2: *Alabama* (Washington, D.C.: GPO, 1963), 15; *Census of Population, 1970*, Vol. 1, *Characteristics of the Population*, Pt. 2: *Alabama* (Washington, D.C.: GPO, 1973), Table 23, 2-60.

13. Sheldon Schaffer, "Economic Change in the Birmingham Area," *Alabama Business* 33 (Dec. 1962), 1–5; Arthur A. Thompson, "Manufacturing Expansion in Alabama, 1960–1971," *Alabama Business* 43 (Sept. 1972), 1–7; Director of Public Relations, City of Birmingham, "Information," n.d. [1965], 16/16, Boutwell. By 1985, manufacturing accounted for 27 percent of the jobs in the rural South but only 18 percent in southern cities (Schulman, *From Cotton Belt to Sunbelt*, 159).

14. Virginia Foster Durr, *Outside the Magic Circle: The Autobiography of Virginia Foster Durr*, ed. Hollinger F. Barnard (University: University of Alabama Press, 1985), 25; Geraldine Moore, *Behind the Ebony Mask* (Birmingham: Southern University Press, 1961).

15. Bruce Thrasher, interview with author, July 10, 1988.

16. Herman Taylor, interview, in "Working Lives," W. S. Hoole Special Collections Library, University of Alabama, Tuscaloosa.

17. Thrasher interview; Charles Morgan Jr., *A Time to Speak* (New York: Harper and Row, 1964), 2.

18. *Reynolds v. Sims* 377 U.S. (1964).

19. Judith Stein, "Southern Workers in National Unions: Birmingham Steelworkers, 1936–1951," in *Organized Labor in the Twentieth-Century South*, ed. Robert H. Zieger (Knoxville: University of Tennessee Press, 1991), 183–222. One result of the UAW's late start was the abandonment of its southern, mainly white, locals. See Kevin Boyle, *The UAW and the Heyday of American Liberalism, 1945–1968* (Ithaca: Cornell University Press, 1995), 119–21.

20. For a theoretical analysis of this point, see F. Ray Marshall, "Civil Rights and Social Equity: Beyond Neoclassical Theory," in *New Directions in Civil Rights Studies*, ed. Armstead L. Robinson and Patricia Sullivan (Charlottesville: University Press of Virginia, 1991), 164.

21. Herbert Hill, "Confidential Memorandum to Walter White," May 8–17, 1953, A4-15, Murray; John W. Brown to Mr. Murry [Murray], Aug. 26, 1945; Farr to Murray, Sept. 19, 1946, Dist. 36/Penn St.; Elmer J. Maloy, USWA, OHI, Mar. 25, 1968, 17, Penn St.

22. Grievance 153-890, Arbitration proceeding T-218, Dec. 13, 1951, Dist. 36/Ala.

23. Cited in E. Q. Hawk, "Defense Training for Negroes, Birmingham, Ala.," Jan. 27, 1942, C-470, RG 228, NA.

24. Cited in Richard L. Rowan, "Negro Employment in Birmingham: Three Cases," in *Employment, Race, and Poverty*, ed. A. M. Ross and H. Hill (New York: Harcourt Brace and World, 1967), 315.

25. Trial, June 22, 1972, 3:1.

26. W. Willard Wirtz, "Memorandum for the President," June 21, 1963, 66/President's Committee, June 19–30, 1963, Wirtz.

27. Peter B. Doeringer and Michael J. Piore, *Internal Labor Markets and Manpower Analysis* (Armonk, N.Y.: M. E. Sharpe, 1971), 136–37.

28. Unlike the steel mills, some of the USWA fabricating plants had plant seniority. See John W. Grazciar to Meyer Bernstein, Jan. 26, 1949, 46/7, Burke/USWA. The narrow seniority was industry-specific. Seniority for operators in all auto companies was plantwide, but the seniority system at the steel mill at the Ford Motor company, the only auto company that produced its own steel and whose workers were also represented by the UAW, was based on job seniority instead of plant seniority. "Automobile Industry Seniority Systems," Appendix A, 1–3, Seniority Subcommittee, Dec. 16, 1961, 9/Seniority 1962–63, Miller/USWA.

29. Trial, June 22, 1972, 3:727.

30. Thrasher interview; Donner to John A. Stephens, June 18, 1945, 12/9, Dist. 36/Penn St.

31. Stein, "Southern Workers in National Unions," 203–4.

32. Strevel interview.

33. Cooper to Goldberg, Mar. 29, 1952, Dist. 36/Ala., USWA-Birm; "Statement of Arthur Goldberg," 82, Case No. D-18-C, Union Exhibits, I, U.S. Wage Stabilization Board, copy at Uris Library, Columbia University, New York.

34. Strevel interview; Trial, Aug. 29, 1972, 25:203–8.

35. Grievance 154-190, Sept. 3, Mar. 20, 1946; Grievance 154-234, Jan. 10, 1949, Dist. 36/Ala., USWA-FF.

36. Thrasher interview; Willie George Phillips, interview with author, July 25, 1989.

37. Grievance 154-328, Sept. 3, 1954, Feb. 28, 1955, Dist. 36/Ala., USWA-FF; Strevel interview.

38. Woodward Iron Company, "Leaflet," n.d. [1950s], Dist. 36/Ala., USWA-FF.

39. Cited in Jervis Anderson, *Bayard Rustin: Troubles I've Seen: A Biography* (New York: HarperCollins, 1997), 189. King reported that their contribution saved the boycott.

40. George E. Sims, *The Little Man's Big Friend: James E. Folsom in Alabama Politics, 1946–1958* (Tuscaloosa: University of Alabama Press, 1985), 163–66.

41. O. L. Garrison to David McDonald, Apr. 16, 1956, 140/3, and "Report District 36" [Apr. 1956], 140/2, both in McDonald/USWA; Alan Draper, *Conflict of Interests: Organized Labor and the Civil Rights Movement in the South, 1954–1968* (Ithaca, N.Y.: Industrial Labor Relations Press, 1994).

42. Philip J. Clowes to McDonald, July 18, 1957, 9/7, CR/USWA.

43. Otis Brubaker and Edmund Ayoub, "Basic Steel Industry Employment Survey," Dec. 7, 1965, 63/19, Research/USWA; John E. Lewis Jr., "Recession and Recovery in Alabama," *Alabama Business* 32 (Feb. 15, 1962), 4–5.

44. *Alabama Business* 38 (Feb. 15, 1967), 2–4; *Alabama Business* 41 (Feb. 15, 1971), 4; Trial, Nov. 8, 1972, 44:119.

45. "Seniority Subcommittee Study," Dec. 15, 1961, 9/Seniority 1962–63, Miller/USWA.

46. Ibid.; "Interim Report of the Seniority Subcommittee," Feb. 9, 1962, Miller/USWA; Ben Fischer to David McDonald, June 7, 1961, Miller/USWA; IEB, Jan. 6, 1959.

47. W. A. Lavett to I. W. Abel, Easter Sunday, 1966, 16/9, Abel/USWA.

48. "Seniority Subcommittee Study," Dec. 15, 1961, 9/Seniority 1962–63, Miller/USWA.

49. Ibid.

50. Walter Davis to Boris Shishkin, Dec. 28, 1961, CR/AFL-CIO.

51. Francis Shane to McDonald, Nov. 9, 1961, 12/CR, Shane 1961–65, Miller/USWA; Francis Shane, "Chronology of Civil Rights Actions, 1961–65," ibid.; IEB, Oct. 4, 1961, 133–40; McDonald to officers and staff, June 27, 1961, 44/PCEEO 1961, Goldberg, NA

52. *Pittsburgh Post-Gazette*, Nov. 28, 1961.

53. "Statement of David J. McDonald," Subcommittee on Labor of the House Education and Labor Committee," Jan. 18, 1962, copy in 40/2, Burke/USWA.

54. Shane to Hill, June 1, 1962, III, A-195/Labor, USW, 1956–1965, NAACP; Trial, Aug. 19, 1972, 25:189.

55. James Swindle, interview with author, July 15, 1988.

56. Ibid; Jimmie Lee Williams, interview with author, July 22, 1988.

57. Clarence Duncan to R. E. Farr, Sept. 16, 1961; James Seay to David J. McDonald, Oct. 16, 1961; Duncan to Lyndon B. Johnson, Mar. 23, 1962; Duncan to NLRB, Atlanta, May 9, 1962; Clarence Duncan papers, in possession of James Seay.

58. Author's interview Virgil Pearson, July 12, 1988.

59. Author's interview Freddie Rogers, July 15, 1989

60. Pearson interview.

61. Trial, Aug. 29, 1972, 25:41; Thrasher interview.

62. Percy H. Williams to John G. Feild, July 31, 1962, 39/Committees, July–Aug, 1962, Goldberg, NA.

63. Ibid.; Trial, July 20, 1972, 23:99; Manual for staff, n.d. [Dec. 1962], 15/Pres. Comm., Goldberg, NA.

64. Trial, exhibit 702. The PCEEO pressure had altered some areas.

65. *Birmingham World*, July 21, 1963.

66. Duncan to Francis C. Shane, Oct. 28, 1962, 49/Dist. 36, 1961–63, McDonald/USWA; Shane to Duncan, Nov. 16, 1962, ibid.; Buddy Cooper to Louis Lipsitz, Mar. 29, 1963, Dist. 36/Ala., USWA-FF; Pearson to Shane, Jan. 16, 1963, Duncan.

67. Ben Fischer, "Birmingham Visit," Nov. 27, 1962, 49/Dist. 36, McDonald/USWA; Trial,

June 20, 1972, 2:26–27; Emile Bourg Jr. "Report of Labor Liaison Section," May 29, 1963, 65/1963 Committee, Goldberg, NA; Farr to McDonald, June 4, 1963, 49/Dist. 36, McDonald/USWA.

68. Trial, July 20, 1972, 2:99; Strevel and Pearson interviews.

69. Winn Newman to Bernard Kleiman, Mar. 30, 1967, Legal/Pittsburgh; Trial, Oct. 9, 1972, 29:84, and Nov. 8, 1972, 44:97; Fred Jackson to John W. Nixon, Nov. 2, 1965, Duncan; James Seay, telephone interview, June 3, 1993.

70. *New York Times*, Oct. 21, 1964.

71. Judge U. W. Clemon, interview with author, Oct. 1, 1991; Phillips and Williams interviews; "Petition by the United Steelworkers of America," May 1, 1963, copy in 79/13, Research/USWA.

72. "Housing Sub-Committee Meeting, Jan. 31, 1955," 1/26; "Minutes of Executive Committee, Joint Community Chest—Red Cross," Apr. 2, 1956, 1/19; "Statement," Mar. 1, 1956, 1/20, all in ACHR.

73. William A. Nunnelley, *Bull Connor* (Tuscaloosa: University of Alabama Press, 1991).

74. "Birmingham Downtown Improvement Association," n.d., 9/8, ONB; Morgan, *A Time to Speak*, 2.

75. John E. Steger and R. A. Puryear Jr., "Resolution, Mar. 6, 1962," 2/13, ONB.

76. Norman C. Jimerson to Benjamin Muse, Nov. 14, 1961; Jimerson to Paul Rilling, Dec. 11, 1961, 1/23; Jimerson to Leslie W. Dunbar, Oct. 26, 1961, 1/23, all in ACHR. Peggy Crosswhite, "Birmingham's Problems, Causes, and Suggested Solutions," 2/39, Hanes.

77. "Quarterly Report, Dec. 1962–Feb. 6, 1963," 1/35, ACHR.

78. PR [Paul Rilling] to LWD [Leslie W. Dunbar], Mar. 5, 1962, 1/24, ACHR; David Garrow, *Bearing the Cross: Martin Luther King, Jr., and the Southern Christian Leadership Conference* (New York: William Morrow, 1986), 237–38.

79. See J. E. Lambert to Jamie Moore, "Re: Meeting of the Alabama Christian Movement for Human Rights," Mar. 31, 1961, 9/24, Connor.

80. These events are described in a series of quarterly reports that the ACHR sent to the Southern Regional Council: "Quarterly Report," Dec. 1962–Feb. 6, 1963, March, Apr., May, 1963, 1/35, ACHR.

81. Report of Southern Regional Council, May 4, 1963, 2/14, SRC; *Birmingham World*, Apr. 10, 1963; Burke Marshall, OHI, June 13, 1964, 95, JFK.

82. Cited in Taylor Branch, *Parting the Waters: America in the King Years, 1954–63* (New York: Simon and Schuster, 1988), 737.

83. Adam Fairclough, *To Redeem the Soul of America: The Southern Christian Leadership Conference and Martin Luther King Jr.* (Athens: University of Georgia Press, 1987), 126–33; *Birmingham World*, Mar. 15, 1963; Dan T. Carter, *The Politics of Rage: George Wallace, the Origins of the New Conservatism, and the Transformation of American Politics* (New York: Simon and Schuster, 1995), 126; Donald R. Matthews and James W. Prothro, *Negroes and the New Southern Politics* (New York: Harcourt, Brace, and World, 1966), 240.

84. Thrasher and Cooper interviews.

85. *Birmingham World*, Apr. 6, 13, 1963.

86. Farr to McDonald, June 5, 1961; McDonald to Farr, June 9, 1961; McDonald to Clarence Duncan, Sept. 25, 1963, 49/Dist. 36, 1961–63, all in McDonald/USWA.

87. E. B. Rich, interview with author, Sept. 30, 1991.

88. Virginia Durr to Lyndon [Johnson], June 26, 1962, Vice Presidential Papers, Civil Rights section, 3/CR, 1962, LBJ; Williams interview.

89. Williams, Thrasher, and Rich interviews.

90. Cooper interview.

91. Stephan Lesher, *George Wallace: American Populist* (Reading, Mass.: Addison-Wesley, 1994), 196; Potomac Institute, "Economic Impact of Racial Unrest," 1963, 2/26, Southern Regional Council, BPL.

92. Carter, *Politics of Rage*, 165–74.

93. Edward Shannon LaMonte, *Politics and Welfare in Birmingham, 1900–1975* (Tuscaloosa: University of Alabama Press, 1995), 194–99, 230–34.

94. Robert F. Kennedy, "Memorandum Re: University of Alabama, May, 1962"; Kennedy to Wirtz, June 17, 1963, 66/June 11–18, Wirtz; John Martin to Burke Marshall, Dec. 2, 1963, 18/Alabama, Burke Marshall papers, JFK.

95. Hobart Taylor Jr. to Marshall, Oct. 9, 1963, 64/Pres. Comm. EEO, Wirtz.

96. Taylor to Marshall, Attachment B, Oct. 9, 1963, 64/Pres. Comm. EEO, Wirtz; A. C. Burtramm, interview with author, July 7, 1988.

97. Rev. Maple L. Copeland to Marshall, Apr. 10, 1963; Marshall to Taylor, Apr. 29, 1963, 64/Pres. Comm. EEO; "Summary of Pending Cases," July 11, 1963–Dec. 31, 1963," 2–3, all in CR/AFL-CIO.

98. Paul Bowron, interview with author, July 8, 1989.

99. Thrasher and Cooper interviews; *New York Times*, Oct. 25, 1963.

100. Taylor to Marshall, n.d. [Oct. 1963]; Ward McCreedy to Taylor, Aug. 13, 1963; McCreedy to Thompson Powers, Sept. 6, 1963, all in 64/President's Committee, Wirtz.

101. "Attachment A," McCreedy to Thompson Powers, Sept. 6, 1963, 3, 64/President's Committee, Wirtz.

102. *New York Times*, Oct. 25, 1963.

103. Fischer, "Memorandum, Birmingham Visit," Nov. 27, 1962, 49/Dist. 36, McDonald/USWA.

104. "Radio and Television Report to the American People on Civil Rights," June 11, 1963, in Kennedy, *Public Papers, 1963* (Washington, D.C.: GPO, 1964), 469.

Chapter Three

1. For the president's minimal plans before Birmingham, see Kennedy, *Public Papers, 1963*, 14, 160, 229. Even minimal plans required some criticism of race relations. Other commentators preferred to note black progress. See *Wall Street Journal*, Mar. 1, 1963.

2. Kennedy, "Special Message to the Congress on Civil Rights and Job Opportunities," in Kennedy, *Public Papers, 1963*, 487, 493; Stephen C. Halpern, *On the Limits of the Law: The Ironic Legacy of Title VI of the 1964 Civil Rights Act* (Baltimore: Johns Hopkins University Press, 1995), 23–24.

3. W. Willard Wirtz to President, June 10, 21, 1963, 66/PCEEO, Wirtz.

4. Kennedy, "Special Message to the Congress," 448; Director [Kermit Gordon] to Mr. [Theodore] Sorensen, June 17, 1963, 110/EEOC-1, ser. 60.26, RG 51, NA.

5. Adam Yarmolinsky, in "Poverty and Urban Policy" (discussion held at Brandeis University, 1973), OHI, 286, JFK; "Should There Be an FEPC?," Jan. 22, 1962 (internal memo), ser. 60.26, RG 51, NA; A. A. Coppotelli to Philip S. Hughes, Jan. 15, 1962, 110/EEOC-3, ser. 60.26, RG 51, NA; William S. Taylor to John G. Stewart, Jan. 9, 1963, Clark; "Minutes of Civil Rights Committee, AFL-CIO," Mar. 19, 1963, CR/AFL-CIO; Lee White to President, June 13, 1963, 66/PCEEO, June 11–18, 1963, Wirtz.

6. *Wall Street Journal*, Aug. 12, 1963; Wirtz to President, June 8, 10, 1963, 66/PCEEO, June 1–10, Wirtz.

7. HKS [Harry K. Schwartz] to JSC [Joseph S. Clark], May 23, 1963, Clark.

8. *Congressional Record* 110:7204; Garth L. Mangum, ed., *The Manpower Revolution: Its Policy Consequences* (Garden City, N.Y.: Doubleday, 1965).

9. Reuther, "Implications for Manpower Policy," in Mangum, *Manpower Revolution*, 78; Biemiller, in U.S. Congress, Senate, Subcommittee on Employment and Manpower of the Senate Committee on Labor and Public Welfare, Hearings, *Nation's Manpower Revolution*, June 19, 1963, copy in 59/18, Leg/USWA; Garth L. Mangum, *MDTA: Foundation of Federal Manpower Policy* (Baltimore: Johns Hopkins University Press, 1968), 23.

10. Walter Heller, Memorandum for the President, Nov. 20, 1963, WHCF, LA2, C-6, LBJ; Walter Heller, "The Case for Aggregate Demand," in Mangum, *Manpower Revolution*, 143; Carl M. Brauer, "Kennedy, Johnson, and the War on Poverty," *Journal of American History* 69 (June 1982): 98–119.

11. U.S. Congress, Senate, Subcommittee on Employment and Manpower, *Toward Full Employment: Proposals for a Comprehensive Employment and Manpower Policy in the United States*, 88th Cong., 2d sess., 1964.

12. Thus Gardner Ackley, the new chairman of the CEA, welcomed increased spending for Vietnam in July 1965. Gareth Davies, *From Opportunity to Entitlement: The Transformation and Decline of Great Society Liberalism* (Lawrence: University Press of Kansas, 1996), 106.

13. Ibid.; Yarmolinsky, in "Poverty and Urban Policy." From 1964 through 1969, half of the blue-collar jobs created in the economy were in the defense sector. The Vietnam War had removed many young men from the labor force and had induced others to enroll as full-time students in colleges. After 1965, enrollees in War on Poverty programs were excluded from the unemployment count, unlike the practice followed during the 1930s, when those working on Works Progress Administration (WPA) projects were considered unemployed. Thus, most of the decrease in unemployment after the 1964 tax cut, roughly three-quarters, may be attributed to war-related factors, not to fiscal policy. Charles C. Killingsworth, "The Fall and Rise of the Idea of Structural Unemployment," in IRRA, *Annual Proceedings, 1978* (Madison, Wisc.: IRRA, 1979), 1–13.

14. Howard M. Wachtel, "Hard-Core Unemployment in Detroit: Causes and Remedies," in IRRA, *Annual Proceedings, 1965* (Madison, Wisc.: IRRA, 1966), 236–67; Herbert Northrup, *The Negro in the Automobile Industry* (Philadelphia: Wharton School of Finance and Commerce, 1968), 29.

15. Joseph Clark, "Clark Introduces Job Discrimination Bill" (press release), July 2, 1963, 75/56, Leg/AFL-CIO. The Ad Hoc Committee on the Triple Revolution—a group of intellectuals led by British economist Robert Theobald and including Michael Harrington, Walter Reuther, and Bayard Rustin—sometimes responded to the automation problem by proposing a policy of guaranteed income, thereby implying a future of joblessness. Clark's thinking, although overlapping with the Ad Hoc group in some ways, considered automation a labor market problem that could be addressed through government planning.

16. Biemiller, in Senate, Hearings, *Nation's Manpower Revolution*, June 19, 1963.

17. Mangum, *Manpower Revolution*, 552; National Committee for Children and Youth, *Social Dynamite* (Washington, D.C.: Committee, 1963).

18. Garth L. Mangum, *The Emergence of Manpower Policy* (New York: Holt, Rinehart and Winston, 1969), 40.

19. Clark, press release, July 2, 1963; Clark, diary, Dec. 10, 1963, Clark; Margaret Weir, *Politics and Jobs: The Boundaries of Employment Policy in the United States* (Princeton: Princeton University Press, 1992), 71–73; Johnson, *Public Papers, 1963–64*, 357.

20. Michael Harrington, *The Other America* (New York: Macmillan, 1962); *Economic Report of the President, 1964*, 55.

21. James L. Sundquist, OHI, Apr. 7, 1969, LBJ.

22. L. A. Nikoloric to Humphrey, Mar. 20, 1963, Legislative Files, L, 1961–1964, in Senatorial Files, 1948–1964, HHH.

23. John Dittmer, *Local People: The Struggle for Civil Rights in Mississippi* (Urbana: University of Illinois Press, 1995), 366, 382.

24. Wirtz to President, Mar. 11, 1964, WHCF, LA2, C-6, LBJ.

25. Shriver to the President, Feb. 2, 1968, WHCF, LA2, C-9, LBJ; Lawrence C. Sullivan to Biemiller, 15/14, Leg/AFL-CIO.

26. Leon H. Keyserling, *Progress or Poverty: The U.S. at the Crossroads* (Washington, D.C.: Conference on Economic Progress, 1964), 36, 87.

27. Johnson, *Public Papers, 1963–64*, 1147–51.

28. Lyndon B. Johnson, Diary Backup, Sept. 22, 1964, C-9, LBJ.

29. This demography would be potent even after the tax cut of 1964. From 1961 to 1965, unemployment for black males aged 20–64 was reduced from 11 to 6.8 percent. The rate for black teenagers fell only from 24.7 to 23.2 percent. Nat Goldfinger to Don Slaiman, Sept. 15, 1965, CR/AFL-CIO.

30. Joseph P. Lyford, "The Negro in the Manpower Revolution," in Mangum, *Manpower Revolution*, 210–11.

31. Statements of Whitney Young, A. Philip Randolph, and Eli Ginzburg, U.S. Congress, Senate Subcommittee on Employment and Manpower, Hearings, *Equal Employment Opportunity Act*, 178, 170–75, 312–13.

32. Clark, diary, June 19, 1963; Humphrey to Joe [Clark], July 17, 1963, both in Clark. Statement of Hubert Humphrey, in Senate, Hearings, *Equal Employment Opportunity Act*, 136, 142.

33. Humphrey ate up discussions with Willy Brandt, Harold Wilson, and the others about technological unemployment, the rise of the white-collar economy, and the underdeveloped world. Carl Solberg, *Hubert Humphrey: A Biography* (New York: W. W. Norton, 1984), 219–20; Trip Files, Senatorial Files, HHH.

34. Hobart Taylor Jr. OHI, Jan. 6, 1969, 18, LBJ.

35. See statements of A. Philip Randolph, Whitney Young, Roy Wilkins, and James Farmers, Senate Subcommittee, *Equal Employment Opportunity Act*, 170–80, 196–212, 217–26.

36. Humphrey to Joe [Clark], July 17, 1963; "Administration and Enforcement [of S. 1937]," n.d., Clark.

37. U.S. Congress, Senate, Committee on Labor and Public Welfare, *Equal Employment Opportunity Act: Report to Accompany S. 1937*, 88th Cong., 2d sess., Feb. 4, 1964, S. Rept. 867, 12; statement of Erwin N. Griswold, Senate Subcommittee, *Equal Employment Opportunity Act*, 495. This provision was similar to the one used to enforce the Fair Labor Standards Act.

38. James R. Watson, "Unemployment Rates of Negroes in States Having Fair Employment Practice Commission Laws," in Senate, Hearings, *Economic Opportunity Act*, 108–9; Andrew J. Biemiller to Kenneth O'Donnell, "Labor Views on Administration Civil Rights Package," June 10, 1963, 9/10, Leg/AFL-CIO; Peter B. Doeringer and Michael J. Piore, *Internal Labor Markets and Manpower Analysis* (1971; reprint, Armonk, N.Y.: M. E. Sharpe, 1985), 135–36.

39. Doeringer and Piore, *Internal Labor Markets and Manpower Analysis*, 135–36.

40. Griswold, Senate Subcommittee, *Equal Employment Opportunity Act*, 489.

41. "Additional Views of Senator Jacob K. Javits," S. Rept. 867, 37–38.

42. Young, Senate Subcommittee, *Equal Employment Opportunity Act*, 177; [George Reedy] to Vice President, n.d. [July, 1963], 7/PCEEO, July 1–15, 1963, Civil Rights File, Vice-Presidential Papers, LBJ; Clark, diary, Oct. 29, 1963, Clark; John Feild to Senator [HHH], Oct. 28, Dec. 2, 1963, Civil and Human Rights file, Vice-Presidential Papers, HHH.

43. Archie Robinson, *George Meany and His Times* (New York: Simon and Schuster, 1981), 319; statements by Meany and McDonald, Senate Subcommittee, *Equal Employment Opportunity Act*, 165–66, 295.

44. McDonald to Emanuel Celler, Sept. 11, 1963, 468/CR corresp. 1963, Celler, LC.

45. "Notes on Conversation with Clarence Mitchell," July 29, 1963, III, Washington Bureau, A-332, NAACP.

46. David Garrow, *Bearing the Cross: Martin Luther King, Jr., and the Southern Christian Leadership Conference* (New York: William Morrow, 1986), 266; A. Philip Randolph, "Proposed Plans for the March," 26/MOWM, Randolph.

47. Clarence Mitchell, OHI, Feb. 9, 1967, 37, JFK; Garrow, *Bearing the Cross*, 281–82.

48. Jervis Anderson, *Bayard Rustin: Troubles I've Seen* (New York: HarperCollins, 1997), 239–64.

49. Tom Kahn to Bayard Rustin, Aug. 23, 1963, 473, Reel 8, Rustin, LC.

50. Katzenbach to Celler, Aug. 13, 1963, 465/HR 7152 (1), Celler, LC; O. Jack Buchanek to Hughes, Aug. 15, 1963, EEOC, ser. 60.26, RG 51, NA; *Congressional Quarterly*, Aug. 2, 1963, 1374.

51. Irving Bernstein, *Promises Kept: John F. Kennedy's New Frontier*, (New York: Oxford University Press, 1991), 110–13.

52. Walter Davis to Shishkin, Jan. 16, 1964, CR/AFL-CIO; Wirtz, "Memorandum," n.d. [Dec. 1963], 23/Labor-Wirtz memos, George Reedy papers, LBJ. Katzenbach recalled that Johnson "felt the employment section impossible." Nicholas Katzenbach, OHI, Nov. 16, 1964, 128, JFK.

53. Rauh, "Unpublished history," 16, Rauh.

54. Doris Kearns, *Lyndon Johnson and the American Dream*, (New York: Harper and Row, 1976), 191.

55. Clark to Mannie [Celler], Jan. 14, 1964; Celler to Joe [Clark], Jan. 24, 1964, 483/H.R. 7152 (88th), both in Celler, LC; Clark, diary, Jan. 16, 1964.

56. Charles Whalen and Barbara Whalen, *The Longest Debate: A Legislative History of the 1964 Civil Rights Act* (Cabin John, Md.: Seven Locks Press, 1985), 153.

57. Alexander P. Lamis, *The Two-Party South* (New York: Oxford University Press, 1988), 77; Virginia Van der Veer Hamilton, *Lister Hill: Statesman from the South* (Chapel Hill: University of North Carolina Press, 1987), chap. 13.

58. *Congressional Record* (Apr. 8, 1964) 110:7205–7, 7212–15; "Minutes of the AFL-CIO Civil Rights Comm.," Feb. 4, 1964, and "Comments on Senator Lister Hill's Criticism of Civil Rights Bill," Jan. 31, 1964, both in 9/13, CR/AFL-CIO.

59. John G. Stewart, "Independence and Control: The Challenge of Senatorial Party Leadership," (Ph.D. diss., University of Chicago, 1968), 248.

60. Cited in Hugh Davis Graham, *The Civil Rights Era: Origins and Development of National Policy, 1960–1972* (New York: Oxford, 1990), 149–50.

61. Ibid.

62. *Labor Relations Reporter* 57 (1964): 264; Michael Sovern, *Legal Restraints on Racial Discrimination in Employment* (New York: Twentieth Century Fund, 1966), 18, n. 36; *Labor Cases* 53 (1966): 6553–60; *Wall Street Journal*, Mar. 28, 1966.

63. Graham, *Civil Rights Era*, 144–51.

64. Harris to Biemiller, Apr. 9, 1964, 85/46, Leg/AFL-CIO.

65. Title VII, sec. 707(a); Stewart, "Independence and Control," 249.

66. John H. Beidler to Biemiller, May 15, 1964, copy in Clark; McDonald to Robert F. Kennedy, May 8, 1964, 56/3, McDonald/USWA; Clark in Whalen and Whalen, *The Longest Debate*, 171. Because the NLRB was open now to the view that discrimination was an unfair labor practice, unions, in effect, would have greater obligations than corporations. David Feller, "Memo for McDonald," Oct. 17, 1963, 27/Civil Rights 1961–62, McDonald/USWA.

67. *Congressional Quarterly*, Feb. 3, 1964, 383.

68. Katzenbach, OHI, 132; Clarence Mitchell, OHI, Feb. 9, 1967, 43, JFK; Neil MacNeil, *Dirksen: Portrait of a Public Man* (New York: World, 1970), chap. 10.

69. Clark, diary, Sept. 16, 1966.

70. Clark, diary, Feb. 2, 1967.

71. Ibid., 209; Joseph S. Clark, OHI, Dec. 16, 1965, 74, JFK; *Congressional Record* (Feb. 11, 1964), 110:7295.

72. *Congressional Record* (June 17, 1964), 110:13694.

73. Cited in *Labor Relations Reporter* 57 (1964): 39.

74. LeRoy Collins, "Analysis of Civil Rights Functions of the Federal Government and Recommendations for Their Consolidation in a Single Agency," Dec. 7, 1964, 20, C-91; CEA and BOB, "Task Force in 1965 on the Legislative Programs," June 17, 1964, 4, C-94, both in Bill Moyers papers, LBJ.

75. Charles E. Clark to Ward McCreedy, Sept. 27, 1965, 247/PCEEO 1965, Bill Moyers papers, LBJ; John Roche to John Stewart, Dec. 17, 1964; minutes of Potomac Institute meeting, Dec. 20, 1964; "Employment Task Force Agenda," June 2, 1965; Vice President to President, June 17, 1965, Equal Opportunity, 1965–67, Civil and Human Rights, Vice Presidential Files, all in HHH. OFCC's reorganization was announced in Executive Order 11246.

76. *Labor Relations Reporter* 57 (1964), 41; Graham, *Civil Rights Era*, 180–86; Kenneth O'Donnell, OHI, July 23, 1969, LBJ; Solberg, *Hubert Humphrey*, 269–73; Girard P. Clark to Wiley Branton, Sept. 1, 1965, 250/EEOC-3, Wirtz.

77. Vice President to President, Sept. 17, 1965, WHCF, HU2-1, C-43, LBJ.

78. Vice President to Secretary of Labor et al., Sept. 17, 1965, 247/PCEEO 1965, Wirtz; "Should the Execution of the Executive Orders be Assigned to the Equal Employment Opportunities Commission rather than the President's Committee?," n.d. [1965], 106/EEOC, ser. 60.26, RG 51, NA.

79. Clark, OHI, Dec. 16, 1965, 74, JFK; Solberg, *Hubert Humphrey*, 221; Rauh to Clark, May 26, 1967; HKS [Harry K. Schwartz] to JSC [Joseph S. Clark], July 15, Sept. 16, 1967, all in Clark.

80. Gary Mucciaroni, *Political Failure of Public Employment Policy, 1945–1982* (Pittsburgh: University of Pittsburgh Press, 1990), 53–59; Weir, *Politics and Jobs*, chap. 3.

81. Although most of the NAACP attacks were against the former AFL unions, in 1962 Robert C. Carter and Herbert Hill of the NAACP asked the NLRB to decertify a USWA local at Atlantic Steel in Atlanta, Georgia. Although the board disagreed, the political significance of charging the USWA with discrimination was profound. The case reflected the new managerial offensive, the effect of the recession on African Americans, the new black assertion, and the state of the law, which allowed proceedings only against unions. Although he acknowledged the weakness of the case, the NAACP's Gloster Current told Roy Wilkins that the vigorous championing of the black workers was "received with wide acclaims by our own rank and file. . . . We must find additional ways of pushing harder against all obstacles, even if we do overstate our case from time to time." Current to Wilkins, memorandum, Jan. 3, 1963, III, A-317/Wilkins Memos, NAACP.

82. Wilkins statement, Senate Subcommittee, *Equal Employment Opportunity Act*, 199; "Minutes of AFL-CIO Civil Rights Comm.," Feb. 4, 1964, 4; Shishkin to Meany, Jan. 20, 1964, CR/AFL-CIO.

Chapter Four

1. David McDonald to Jack Greenberg, June 23, 1964, 55/64, McDonald/USWA. For a list of activities from passage to the end of 1965, see J. Edward White to Alex Fuller, Jan. 7, 1966, 11/32, CR/USWA; *Labor Relations Reporter*, Aug. 10, 1964.

2. Randolph to King, Apr. 7, 1964, 2/B-W, 1964; "Invitation to a Conference of Negro Leaders from A. Philip Randolph," 17/Conference of Negro Leaders, APR; Adam Fair-

clough, *To Redeem the Soul of America: The Southern Christian Leadership Conference and Martin Luther King, Jr.* (Athens: University of Georgia Press, 1987), 196–97.

3. Nick Kotz and Mary Lynn Kotz, *A Passion for Equality: George A. Wiley and the Movement* (New York: W. W. Norton and Co., 1977), 136–37; Whitney H. Young Jr., "Help Wanted: New Jobs for Negroes," 17/Conference of Negro Leaders, APR.

4. Randolph held the honorary title president emeritus of the NALC from 1964 to 1969. 1/4, NALC papers.

5. James R. Ralph Jr., *Northern Protest: Martin Luther King, Jr., Chicago, and the Civil Rights Movement* (Cambridge: Harvard University Press, 1993).

6. NAACP, press release, Feb. 5, 1965, C-31, APR; press release, Jan. 12, 1966, 11/4, NALC.

7. Rustin, "The Influence of the Right and Left in the Civil Rights Movement," 17/Conference of Negro Leaders, APR; John D'Emilio, "Homophobia and the Trajectory of Postwar American Radicalism: The Career of Bayard Rustin," *Radical History Review* 62 (1995): 95; John Stewart to Humphrey, Nov. 1, 1965, John G. Stewart files, Vice Presidential Files, HHH.

8. McDonald to Greenberg, June 23, 1964.

9. Jack Greenberg, *Crusaders in the Courts: How a Dedicated Band of Lawyers Fought for the Civil Rights Revolution* (New York: Basic, 1994), 413–14.

10. John Herling, *Right to Challenge: People and Power in the Steelworkers Union* (New York: Harper and Row, 1972), 101; Walter J. Burke interview with John Herling, July 1, 1966, 3/19, Burke/USWA.

11. *Business Week*, May 28, 1966, 57.

12. *National Journal*, Mar. 25, 1989. For Sheehan's activism on civil rights, see Sheehan to Roy Stevens, Mar. 8, 1966, 53/10; Sheehan to Molony, Dec. 28, 1966, 53/4, McDonald/USWA.

13. Abel to Randolph, May 23, 1960, 3/7, NALC.

14. *Business Week*, May 28, 1966, 57–58, 60, 62; Herling, *Right to Challenge*, 310.

15. Herling, *Right to Challenge*, 226; Joseph P. Molony to Curtis Strong, Jan. 13, 1966, 11/32, CR/USWA.

16. Herling, *Right to Challenge*, 226; Bernard Kleiman, interview with author, Aug. 20, 1991.

17. Molony to Strong, Jan. 13, 1966; Raymond Moody to Molony, Jan. 26, 1966, 11/32, CR/USWA; Ruth Needleman, "'Oh That Kimbley: He's Union Crazy': Early African-American Leadership in the USWA," unpublished paper in possession of author.

18. J. E. White to Alex Fuller and Richard Moss, June 15, 1966, 16/6, CR/USWA.

19. Herling, *Right to Challenge*, 398.

20. Ibid., 221–23; E. B. Rich, interview with author, Sept. 30, 1991.

21. Kleiman interview.

22. Kleiman and Rich interviews.

23. Bruce Thrasher, interview with author, July 10, 1989; Donald D. Stafford to "All AFL-CIO Members," Mar. 27, 1963, 4/6, Boutwell.

24. Rich interview.

25. Bureau of National Affairs, *The Civil Rights Act of 1964* (Washington, D.C.: BNA, 1964), 73; *Iron Age*, July 2, 1964, 15.

26. "Meeting with Human Relations Committee," Subcommittee on Seniority, Aug. 17, 1964, 9/Seniority 1964, Miller/USWA.

27. On January 1, 1964, U.S. Steel consolidated its independent operating divisions, including TCI. Although motivated by economics, the reorganization gave Pittsburgh more to say on civil rights matters as well as on sales, marketing, and operations (*Iron Age*, Sept. 26, 1963, 105–6).

28. Hugh Brimm, "Report of Equal Employment Opportunity Compliance Status of USS Corp," Sept. 2, 1965, Dist. 36/Ala., USWA-FF.

29. Only Eddins's last name appears in the record.

30. Measured by company seniority (number of years with the company), Eddins was more senior. At the time of the consent decree in 1974, when plant seniority became the rule, some former ore miners argued for company seniority. The point is that all seniority systems have arbitrary elements. While all are rooted in age, the calculation of that age involves specific complexities that are unique to industrial situations.

31. Trial, Dec. 4, 1972, 51:96; Grievance SFS-64-248, Mar. 12, 1965, Dist. 3/Ala., USWA-FF; USS Corp. and USWA, Local 1013, case no. USS-5228-S, Dec. 30, 1965; Trial, July 20, 1972, 17:132.

32. Trial, exhibit 633; United States Steel Corporation and United Steelworkers of America, Case No. USS-5223-S, 17/US Steel, Misc., CR/USWA; Trial, Dec. 4, 1972, 51:96, and July 20, 1972, 17:158; IEB, Nov. 16, 1964.

33. The union failed to get companies to agree to limit testing in hiring for trade and craft jobs and filling of apprenticeships. Ben Fischer to Hugh C. Murphy, Apr. 1, 1969, 18/23, Contract Department/USWA.

34. Trial, July 21, 1972, 18:99, exhibit 674.

35. Trial, June 20, 1972, 17:153.

36. The Phillips incident reveals concretely that the behavior of white steelworkers cannot be explained by the concept of "whiteness." Whatever their ideological beliefs about race, steelworkers possessed other ideas and interests that explain their behavior. The sheer diversity of response demonstrates that the ideological approach to studying white workers begun by David Roediger in his *Wages of Whiteness: Race and the Making of the American Working Class* (London: Verso, 1991) cannot account for the behavior revealed here, much less for the history of the American working class.

37. Howard Strevel, interview with the author, July 12, 1988, Fred Shepherd, July 11, 1989; Trial, exhibit 638.

38. Thrasher interview; William Hardy to Strevel, Oct. 19, 1965, Dist. 36/Ala., USWA-FF.

39. See "Charges of Discrimination," [1965], Dist. 36/Ala., USWA-Birm; Luther McKinstry, interview with author, June 2, 1990.

40. Strevel interview.

41. Trial, Aug. 25, 1972, 23:64. Bob Jones denied the statement (ibid., 23:51).

42. John Macy, "Memorandum," Mar. 1, 1965, 774/EEOC, John Macy papers, LBJ.

43. "Biographies of the Members of the Equal Opportunity Commission," May 10, 1965, 237/EEOC, Jan.–July, 1965, Wirtz; Herman Edelsberg, *Not for Myself Alone: Memoir of a Lawyer Who Fought for Human Rights* (Berkeley: Interstellar Media, 1988), 174.

44. EEOC minutes, Jan. 13, 1966, EEOC.

45. O. Jack Buchanek to William Carey, Oct. 20, 1965, ser. 60.26, RG 51, NA; Minutes, Sept. 22, 1965, EEOC.

46. EEOC minutes, Oct. 20, 1965, Feb. 24, 1966, EEOC.

47. Former USWA counsel, David Feller, after failing to obtain EEOC help to force a cottonseed and soybean processing plant in Clarksdale, Mississippi, to pay blacks wages equal to those of whites, concluded that the EEOC's refusal to allow unions to play any role but that of defendant was encouraging divisions that need not exist. David Feller to Charles Duncan, Mar. 1, 1966, 28/Corresp EEOC, Wash., 3/66–12/66, EEOC files, CR/AFL-CIO; EEOC minutes, Apr. 26, 1966, EEOC; Feller to Roy Wilkins, May 24, 1966, IV, A-29/EEOC 1966–69, NAACP; *Labor Relations Yearbook, 1966*, 352; David Feller, telephone interview with author, Sept. 13, 1993; *Labor Relations Yearbook, 1967*, 449.

48. Alfred W. Blumrosen and Albert Pergan, "Birmingham," in "Report on Six Cities, Oct. 4, 1965," comp. Ben D. Segal, Equal Opportunity, Civil and Human Rights, Vice Presidential Papers, HHH; EEOC minutes, Sept. 2, 1965, EEOC.

49. Gottesman to Cooper, Oct. 1, 1965, Legal/Pittsburgh.

50. EEOC minutes, Oct. 6, 14, 18, 1965, EEOC; Nixon to Franklin Roosevelt Jr., Mar. 14, 1966, IV, A-29/EEOC 1966–69, NAACP. See Chapter 7 for the results of EEOC efforts.

51. Girard P. Clark, "Memorandum to Mr. Wiley Branton," Sept. 1, 1965, 251/EEO-3, Wirtz.

52. Sylvester to Secretary, Mar. 24, 1967, 61/EEO-2, Wirtz; J. Warren Shaver to Jack Moskowitz, July 28, 1966, 16/9, CR/USWA.

53. Shaver to Moskowitz, July 28, 1966.

54. Leo Teplos to Steven Shulman, Dec. 5, 1966, EEOC.

55. "Comments on a Report Distributed by Birmingham Branch NAACP," May 3, 1966, 3/34, Hamilton.

56. Roger M. Blough, "Industrial Compass Points South," May 4, 1966, copy in 24/5, Boutwell.

57. Nixon to Alex Fuller, Sept. 27, 1966, 16/9, CR/USWA; Hill to John W. Nixon, May 13, 1966; Hill to Wilkins, May 16, 1966, A36/Labor, Alabama, NAACP; "Notes," June 7, 1966, 3/34, Hamilton; *Atlanta Journal*, June 6, 1966; *Birmingham Post-Herald*, June 7, 1966.

58. *Wall Street Journal*, June 1, 7, 1966.

59. Jerome "Buddy" Cooper, telephone interview with author, July 18, 1992; Virgil Pearson, interview with author, July 12, 1988; Grover Smith Jr. to John W. Nixon, Jan. 3, 1966, A36/Labor, Ala., NAACP; Fuller to Kleiman, Jan. 6, 1970, and Cooper to Kleiman, Dec. 18, 1969, 24/15, CR/USWA. Alfred Blumrosen had recommended Smith to Cooper, but Blumrosen either told Smith that the deed was done or Smith interpreted it that way.

60. Gloster Current to Walter White and Wilkins, Feb. 6, 1952, II, A-582; Hill to Bruce M. West, Apr. 13, 1953; Hill to White, "Confidential Memorandum," May 17, 1953; "Memorandum to Mr. Walter White from Herbert Hill," Nov. 23, 1953, II, A-346; Hill to Charles S. Zimmerman, Feb. 10, 1959, III, A-195/Labor Unions, 1956–1965; "Memorandum to Mr. Wilkins from Herbert Hill: Re: Meeting of AFL-Civil Rights Committee, Jan. 29, 1959," Feb. 2, 1959, III, A-195; Wilkins to Hill, Nov. 30, Dec. 10, 1962, Jan. 28, 1963, Sept. 9, 1965, III, A-309/AFL-CIO; Current to Wilkins, Jan. 3, 1963, III, A-317/Wilkins Memos 1961–65; Morsell to David E. Feller, Oct. 1, 1965, III, A-187/Labor-ICWU, 1965, all in NAACP; Hill to U. S. Tate, Dec. 8, 1953, copy, 7/4, CR/AFL-CIO; Stuart Rothman to Robert Carter, Apr. 8, 1963, 2888/2, Dist. 35.

61. Pearson to I. W. Abel, June 17, 1966, Duncan.

62. Gottesman to Blumrosen, Feb. 21, 1966, 12/23, CR/USWA.

63. *Southern Courier*, June 11–12, 1966.

64. Nixon to Alex Fuller, Sept. 27, 1966, 40/11, CR/USWA.

65. Pearson interview.

66. Jackson to Director of Compliance, May 2, 1966, Compliance Department, EEOC; EEOC minutes, May 4, 11, 1966, EEOC.

67. EEOC minutes, May 13, 1966, EEOC.

68. Notes, meeting of officials of TCI, USS, USWA, EEOC, May 13, 1966, Legal/Pittsburgh.

69. *Wall Street Journal*, Sept. 16, 1966; *Iron Age*, Oct. 18, 1962, Dec. 2, 1965; Trial, exhibit 702; Thrasher to Strevel, Jan. 18, 1971, and William Hardy to Leon Lynch, Aug. 30, 1977, Legal/Pittsburgh.

70. Cooper to Ben Segal, Sept. 21, 1965, Legal/Pittsburgh; Cooper interview.

71. *Southern Courier*, June 11–12, 1966; Hill to Roy Wilkins, Sept. 13, 1965, III, A195/Labor USW 1956–65," NAACP; Winn Newman to Kleiman, Jan. 19, 1967, 16/9, CR/USWA.

72. The legal requirement to charge unions rather than employers, regardless of the facts, communicated a message that unions were the principal cause of discrimination. One of the reasons the unions were so insistent upon passing a bill to establish a national fair employ-

ment practices commission was to make corporations as well as unions liable for discrimination. The situation arose first in the railroad unions. The Railway Labor Act of 1926 had given the railroad unions exclusive bargaining rights. In 1944, based upon the fear of "monopoly power," the Supreme Court required the unions to treat everyone, members and nonmembers, fairly (*Steele v. Louisville & N.R.R.*, 323 U.S. 192 [1944]). Twelve years later this imprecise obligation was imported into the National Labor Relations Act of 1956. Archibald Cox, "The Duty of Fair Representation," *Villanova Law Review* 2 (Jan. 1957): 154–55.

73. EEOC minutes, June 7, 1966, EEOC.

74. Fischer to Kleiman, Dec. 17, 1969, 18/12, CR/USWA.

75. Ibid.

76. *Birmingham Post-Herald*, July 8, 1966; Cooper to Elliot Bredhoff, July 8, 1966, 16/9, CR/USWA; Jack Greenberg to Nicholas deB. Katzenbach, July 13, 1966, IV, A-53/NAACP Leg. Defense-USS, 1966, NAACP.

77. Blumrosen to Executive Director Powers, Sept. 23, 1965, 237/EEOC, 1965, Wirtz; Blumrosen, "Report of the Office of Conciliations, 1965–1967," 41–41a, EEOC; Newman to Edelsberg, Nov. 2, 1966, 5, EEOC.

78. Most EEOC complaints were not about seniority. During the first six months of its existence, the EEOC logged a total of 2,169 complaints alleging discrimination— 773 involving hiring, 480 promotion, 396 seniority, 227 layoffs, 152 training, and 141 firing— and received 215 complaints about segregated facilities. Employers were charged with violations in 86.3 percent of the complaints, unions in 22.1 percent. (The totals, which exceed 100 percent, reflect the fact that in some instances both employers and unions were named.). These same proportions continued during the early years of the commission. *Labor Relations Yearbook, 1966,* 342–43; *Labor Relations Yearbook, 1969,* 546.

79. The AFL-CIO wanted an off-the-record conference. EEOC minutes, May 4, 1966, EEOC. My recounting of the union position is based upon the recorded informal meeting that took place on May 4, the day before the meeting with EEOC officials. "Informal Meeting, re possible Seniority Guidelines under Title VII of Civil Rights Act," May 12, 1966, 28/ International Union Meetings, Mar. 1966–May, 1966, EEOC files, CR/AFL-CIO.

80. EEOC, Seniority Conference, June 10, 1966, copy in 17/19, CR/USWA.

81. Ibid., 12, 14, 18.

82. Doeringer, "Promotion Systems and Equal Employment Opportunity," Sept. 5, 1966; Newman to Edelsberg, "Doeringer Report," Nov. 2, 1966; Blumrosen to Executive Director, "Comments on Doeringer's Report on Seniority," Oct. 26, 1966, all in EEOC.

83. Blumrosen to Executive Director Powers and General Counsel Duncan, Sept. 23, 1965, 237/1965, Wirtz; Blumrosen, review of *Legal Restraints on Racial Discrimination in Employment* by Michael Sovern, n.d. [Nov. 1966], 13/29, CR/USWA; O. Jack Buchanek to William B. Cannon, Aug. 4, 1966, ser. 60.26, C-106, RG 51, NA; Newman to Edelsberg, Nov. 21, Dec. 6, 1966, EEOC.

84. Aileen C. Hernandez, "Addendum to Decisions," Oct. 3, 1966, EEOC Steel files, EEOC; Newman to Edelsberg, Oct. 12, 1966, 13/8, CR/USWA.

85. The skip car operator transported the raw material from the stockhouse to the top of the blast furnace and weighed and assembled the load. These tasks were now done automatically, and the material was transported on conveyer belts.

86. Trial, June 11, 1972, 11:67; June 20, 1972, 15:52; Aug. 28, 1972, 24:197–205. In 1968, the company agreed to merge the lines for promotion; that is, blacks from 1B would be allowed to use their combined seniority to qualify for promotion. However, in the event of force reduction or recall after layoff, a worker's LOP1-A service would be controlling. The company feared losing experienced workers more than the risk of occasionally promoting an inexpe-

rienced one. U. W. Clemon, interview with author, Sept. 29, 1991; Cooper to Gottesman, Dec. 6, 1966, Legal/Pittsburgh.

87. Cooper to Bernard Kleiman, Sept. 14, 1966, Legal/Pittsburgh; Demetrius Newton, interview with author, July 21, 1989; Herbert R. Northrup, *The Negro in the Tobacco Industry* (Philadelphia: Wharton School of Finance and Commerce, 1970); *The Negro in the Paper Industry* (Philadelphia: Wharton School of Finance and Commerce, 1969).

88. Note, "Title VII, Seniority Discrimination, and the Incumbent Negro," *Harvard Law Review* 80 (1967): 1266–68.

89. Newman to Edelsberg, Nov. 2, 1966, EEOC; Note, "Title VII, Seniority Discrimination, and the Incumbent Negro," 1268–69.

90. Note, "Title VII, Seniority Discrimination, and the Incumbent Negro," 1277, 1275.

91. *Quarles v. Philip Morris, Inc.*, 279 F. Supp. 505 (E.D. Va. 1968); Patricia Eames to EEOC, n.d. [Sept. 1965], 26/66E-1 (no. 1), Case Files, CR/AFL-CIO.

92. There were alternatives to the *Quarles* approach. In December 1964 a black arbitrator named Ronald W. Haughton was appointed by PCEEO (OFCC's predecessor) to resolve a situation at Liggett & Myers that was similar to the one at Philip Morris. The essence of his solution, arrived at through discussions with all parties, was that plant seniority—open to all workers, not simply blacks—would be the rule for most of the jobs. However, vacancies in the machine lines would be filled by plant seniority within that line. Although the plan would benefit blacks especially, it helped all who were in the same situation. Moreover, those who would be hurt financially by being "bumped" in a layoff because of the new plant seniority—and these were mostly whites—retained their old rate. Thus, no worker would lose money as a result of the new system. Although the agreement was reached in April 1966, only in May 1967 did OFCC accept it and then did so reluctantly, even though Haughton concluded that a by-product of the agreement had been "the establishment of increasingly good relationships and better understandings between white and Negro employees of Liggett & Myers." From OFCC's perspective, the plan was too ambiguous about black rights. Inevitably, the Haughton plan could not be a vehicle for the expression of the new morality of the Harvard note, amplified by Judge Butzner's rhetoric. Ronald W. Haughton, "In the Matter of Local 208 of the Tobacco Workers International Union and Locals 167 and 177 of the Tobacco Workers International Union and Liggett & Myers Company," Apr. 8, 1966; Ward McCreedy to William W. Sturges, Oct. 30, 1964; Haughton to Edward C. Sylvester Jr., Feb. 20, 1967; James Carroll to Sylvester, May 9, 1967, all in 25/62–50, Case Files CR/AFL-CIO; William W. Sturges to Wirtz, Mar. 30, 1967, 62/EEO-3, Wirtz; Northrup, *Negro in the Tobacco Industry*, 72–73.

93. Greenberg to Rauh, Jan. 16, 1968, C-82, Rauh.

94. *United States v. Local 189*, 301 F. Supp. 906 (E.D. La. 1969), affirmed 416 F.2d 980 (5th Cir. 1969), cert. denied 397 U.S. 919 (1970).

95. Vera Rony, "Bogalusa: The Economics of Tragedy," *Dissent* (1966): 235. On the civil rights struggle, see Adam Fairclough, *Race and Democracy: The Civil Rights Struggle in Louisiana, 1915–1972* (Athens: University of Georgia Press, 1955), chap. 12. Fairclough's discussion of the work issues is minimal.

96. EEOC minutes, Nov. 4, 1965, EEOC; Lawson B. Knotts Jr. to Franklin D. Roosevelt Jr., July 23, 1965; Roosevelt to Knotts, Aug. 30. 1965, all in 237/EEOC, Jan.–July, 1965, Wirtz; Leonard Bierman, interview with author, July 23, 1993; Ward McCreedy to Crown Zellerbach, Mar. 19, 1967; Jack Greenberg to Sylvester, Apr. 12, 1967, both in 61/EEO-3, Wirtz.

97. Louis F. Oberdorfer to Secretary [Wirtz], June 16, 1967; McCreedy to Crown Zellerbach Corp., Jan. 3, 1968; James E. Jones Jr. to Charles Donahue, Jan. 4, 1968; O. S. "Buck"

Day and W. S. "Jack" Gentry to Harry D. Sayre, Jan. 17, 1968; Day to T. I. Meehan, Jan. 17, 1968, all in 54/EEOC 1968, Wirtz; Northrup, *Negro in the Paper Industry*, 101–2.

98. The court also ordered the segregated locals merged and required that there be a black vice president and other representational guarantees for several years. *United States v. Local 189*, 301 F. Supp. 906 (E.D. La. 1969).

99. A second decree on June 26, 1969, revamped the system more extensively. It permitted job skipping, advanced entry into higher positions in lines of promotion, and red-circling of black rates. *Labor Relations Yearbook, 1970*, 118–19; Richard L. Rowan and Herbert R. Northrup, *Educating the Employed Disadvantaged for Upgrading: A Report on Remedial Education Programs in the Paper Industry* (Philadelphia: Wharton School, 1972), 12–29.

100. Bierman interview.

101. 416 F.2d 980 (5th Cir. 1969).

102. The court revamped the testing system in November 1970, and ordered the substance of the paper mill settlement applied to the box and bag plants in January 1971. *Daily Labor Report*, Jan. 19, 1971.

103. *Wall Street Journal*, Aug. 6, 1965, July 10, 1963.

104. "Conciliation Agreement," attachment to Springer to United Steelworkers, June 9, 1967; Springer to Jerome Cooper, May 23, 1967, 16/9; Newman to Kleiman et al., May 25, 1967, 13/11; Newman to Molony, June 3, 1967; Springer to United Steelworkers of America, June 9, 1967; Andrew Muse to Newman, June 16, 1967; Cooper to Newman, June 21, 1967, 13/11; "United States Steel Corporation Memorandum Regarding Equal Employment Opportunity Commission Proposed Conciliation Agreement," June 26, 1967, 16/9, all in CR/USWA.

105. Shulman to President, Apr. 22, 1967; McPherson to President, June 22, 1967, 7/EEOC, Harry McPherson papers; Macy to President, May 11, 1967, 774/EEOC, John Macy papers, all in LBJ.

106. Sylvester to Contract Compliance Officers, June 20, 1968, 17/25, CR/USWA; Samuel Jackson, "Addendum to Decision, Local 189A v. Crown Zellerbach," Aug. 1969, 67E-174, 17/Paper, EEOC files, CR/AFL-CIO.

107. Benjamin Erdreich to Donald Muse, Apr. 17, 1968, Dist. 36/Ala., USWA-FF; *FEP Cases* 1: 284–86.

108. Jerome Cooper, interview with author, July 13, 1989.

109. Fischer to Abel, Aug. 18, 1969, 18/23, CR/USWA.

110. Jack Greenberg, speech in *Labor Relations Yearbook, 1968*, 97–98; Ben Fischer, interview with author, Aug. 21, 1991.

Chapter Five

1. The report should be read as part of the liberal attempt to shock the nation into action and to combat growing congressional and popular resistance to the Great Society programs. Although the report was weak analytically, it demonstrated commitment to racial equality and a fear that the society was coming apart. The words "our nation is moving toward two societies: one black, one white—separate and unequal" appears in the "Summary Report," penned principally by commission member Mayor John. V. Lindsay of New York, not in the text. Although commentators then and now have attributed the racial situation to white racism, in the report itself racism often took a back seat to other explanations. Thus, the report attributed black poverty to three conditions, the first and most important being the fact that "the Negro migrant, unlike the immigrant, found little opportunity in the city; he had arrived too late and the unskilled labor he had to offer was no longer needed." Racial discrimination, according to the report, was "undoubtedly the second major reason." The

third was the decline of the political machine. National Advisory Commission on Civil Disorders, *Kerner Report*, 20th anniv. ed. (New York: Pantheon, 1988), 10, 278–79.

2. James T. Patterson, *Grand Expectations: The United States, 1945–1974* (New York: Oxford University Press, 1996), 451.

3. Charles J. Zwick, "Memorandum for the President," June 21, 1968, T2-2, ser. 61.1a, RG 51, NA.

4. Arnold M. Ross to the Secretary [Wirtz]. Feb. 9, 1966, WHCF, LA2, C-7, LBJ.

5. CEA chair Gardner Ackley's views reported in Frank L. Lewis to Director, Dec. 31, 1966, T-2, ser. 61.1, RG 51, NA; "A Program to Insure Stable Prosperity" (memorandum for President), Aug. 29, 1966, WHCF, CF BE5, C-3, LBJ; Charles C. Killingsworth, "Jobs and Incomes for Negroes," 68, 86, 9/29, Leg/AFL-CIO.

6. For an intelligent discussion of some of these issues, see Nat Goldfinger to David Sullivan, Aug. 14, 1967, 29/49, Leg/AFL-CIO.

7. One example of this approach was the St. Louis Model City agency's grant to subsidize a bus line from the "inner city" to the McDonnell-Douglas plant in North St. Louis County. "Field Community Tension Factors Report, St. Louis," Oct. 23, 1967, "CRS Field Tension," C-65, both in Ramsay C. Clark papers, LBJ.

8. Califano to the President, Nov. 24, 1967; Charles J. Zwick, "Memorandum for the President," June 21, 1968, WHCF, LA2, C-8, LBJ; Ted Curtis to Edward C. Sylvester Jr., Apr. 30, 1966, 361/EEO-4, Wirtz (emphasis in original).

9. Todd Swanstrom, *The Crisis of Growth Politics: Cleveland, Kucinich, and the Challenge of Urban Populism* (Philadelphia: Temple University Press, 1985), 98–100.

10. Wirtz, "Memorandum for the President," Nov. 3, 1967, WHCF, LA2, C-8; Califano to President, Sept. 12, 1967, and Ernest Goldstein to President, Sept. 7, 1967, WHCF, LA2, C-7; Sargent Shriver, "Memorandum for the President," Feb. 2, 1968, WHCF, LA2, C-9, all in LBJ; Thomas Janoski, *The Political Economy of Unemployment: Active Labor Market Policy in West Germany and the United States* (Berkeley: University of California Press, 1990), 207.

11. Califano, "For the President," Sept. 20, 1967; Johnson to Secretary of Defense, Commerce, et al, Oct. 2, 1967, WHCF, LA2, C-8, LBJ; Steven M. Gelber, *Black Men and Businessmen: The Growing Awareness of a Social Responsibility* (Port Washington, N.Y.: Kennikat Press, 1974), 157, 210.

12. *Iron Age*, May 20, 1965, 38.

13. Arthur M. Ross to Secretary [Wirtz], Dec. 30, 1965, WHCF, LA2, C-7, LBJ; Ted Curtis Jr. to Edward C. Sylvester Jr., Apr. 30, 1966, 361/EEO-4, Wirtz; John David Skrentny, *The Ironies of Affirmative Action: Politics, Culture, and Justice in America* (Chicago: University of Chicago Press, 1996), 90; *Wall Street Journal*, June 11, 1968.

14. Robert Conot, *American Odyssey* (New York: Bantam, 1974), 790.

15. Ibid., 157; Swanstrom, *Crisis of Growth Politics*, 72–73.

16. "Statement of Secretary of Labor George Shultz Before the Subcommittee on Employment, Manpower and Poverty," U.S. Senate, May 11, 1970, C-72, Shultz; Robert B. Reich and John D. Donahue, *New Deals: The Chrysler Revival and the American System* (New York: Times Books, 1985), 24–25.

17. Gelber, *Black Men and Businessmen*, 168, 172; *Iron Age*, July 24, 1969, 39. Daryl Michael Scott in *Contempt and Pity: Social Policy and the Image of the Damaged Black Psyche* (Chapel Hill: University of North Carolina Press, 1997) traces the ups and downs of the notion of the "damaged black" from 1880 to the present. Scott discusses social science thinking, not policy. Paying less attention to political and business actions, his argument that conservatives successfully co-opted damage imagery from liberals in the late 1960s is simply wrong. Like any work that traces one theme, the book ignores the diversity of the arguments put forward—justice, self-interest, fear—which are revealed in the words of the businessmen cited

in the text. Nevertheless, Scott correctly notes the instrumental character of the damage argument and the truth that whatever its short-term gains, damage ideology is not a durable basis for black politics.

18. Hugh Graham, *The Civil Rights Era: Origins and Development of National Policy, 1960–1972* (New York: Oxford University Press, 1990), 190–97, 468–70.

19. Sylvester, a black civil engineer who had formerly worked for the city of Detroit, had been assistant secretary for international affairs in the Labor Department before moving over to OFCC.

20. Califano, "Memorandum for Ramsey Clark," Sept. 25, 1967, C-41, Joseph A. Califano Jr. papers, LBJ; Sylvester to Secretary, Feb. 8, 1967, 61/EEO-4, Wirtz.

21. "Employment," n.d. [late 1966], 74/Civil Rights Division; "Title VII Cases and Investigations," C-76, Ramsay C. Clark papers, LBJ.

22. Hirst Sutton to the Director [Bureau of Budget], Apr. 24, 1967, E6-2, ser. 61.1; Boylen to Mr. Kummerfeld, Aug. 21, 1967, 4/CR Activities, ser. 60.5, both in RG 51, NA; John Doar, "Memorandum for the Attorney General," July 14, 1967, 76/Title VII, Ramsay C. Clark papers; Stephen J. Pollak, OHI, Jan. 27, 30, 1969; Ramsay C. Clark, OHI, Oct. 30, 1968, Mar. 21, 1969, Apr. 16, 1969, all in LBJ; NA, "Points with Respect to Section 707," June 3, 1968; Pollak, "The Role of the Department of Justice in Securing Equal Employment Opportunity," speech before Labor Relations Section of the American Bar Association, summer 1968, IV, C-27, CR/AFL-CIO.

23. Thomas E. Leary, *From Fire to Rust: Business, Technology and Work at the Lackawanna Steel Plant, 1899–1983* (Buffalo, N.Y.: Buffalo and Erie County Historical Society, 1987).

24. David Brody, *Steelworkers in America: The Nonunion Era* (New York: Harper and Row, 1960), 242.

25. *Fortune*, Apr. 14, 1941, 62; John Strohmeyer, *Crisis in Bethlehem: Big Steel's Struggle to Survive* (Bethesda, Md.: Adler and Adler, 1986), 89–92.

26. R. K. Branscom to David McDonald, Dec. 7, 1961, 3/1, Burke/USWA.

27. Strohmeyer, *Crisis in Bethlehem*, 93; Strong to Alex Fuller, Jan. 26, 1968, 12/64, CR/USWA.

28. Michael Gottesman to Bernard Kleiman, May 20, 1968, 18/16, CR/USWA.

29. Gottesman to Kleiman, July 26, 1968, 20/28, Burke/USWA.

30. First, companies were required to post vacancies prominently and throughout the plant. Second, the contractual provision stemming from the Walker case in Birmingham limited company use of the ability clause in selection. Third, a worker could transfer after only one year rather than having to wait two years. Fourth, the new agreement gave transferring employees thirty-day "bump-back" rights, that is, the right to transfer back to their previous jobs within that timeframe and still retain their seniority in the old LOP. Finally, the union proposed reducing the number of pools, a change first made in the Republic steel plant in Chicago, which even the government acknowledged had effected a "tremendous amount of mobility."

31. For a sampling of complaints, see "Civil Rights Complaints from Dept. 6, 1968–Apr. 29, 1971," 26/10, CR/USWA.

32. "Civil Rights Committee Meetings with Director of EEOC," July 17, 1969, 18/16, CR/USWA.

33. Williamson to John Mitchell, Feb. 20, 1969; "Civil Rights Committee Meeting with Company," May 20, 1969, both in 18/16, CR/USWA.

34. "Civil Rights Committee Meeting with Company," May 20, 1969, 18/16, CR/USWA.

35. Frank Evans, of the Negro American Labor Council of Cleveland, made a similar critique of the rush to employ the unemployed. Evans claimed that the government was simply "placing the one on the job on the streets and the other [unemployed] in the jobs."

Notes from NALC executive board meeting, Apr. 8, 1967, 1/2, Richard Parrish papers, Schomburg.

36. "Draft Statement," July 14, 1967, 12/64; Hershel B. Donald to Alex Fuller, Apr. 28, 1969, 18/15, both in CR/USWA; *American Metal Market*, July 3, 1967.

37. Gottesman to Fischer, Jan. 9, 1969, 17/16, CR/USWA. Fischer followed up the issue and discovered that the Bureau of Apprentice Training did not require high school diplomas and allowed labor and management to determine qualifications. Hugh C. Murphy to Ben Fischer, Apr. 15, 1969, 18/236, CR/USWA.

38. *U.S. v. Bethlehem Steel Corp. et al.*, (W.D.-N.Y. 1970), 2EPD, 823–49.

39. Takas to Molony, July 3, 1970, 24/22, Molony/USWA; "Report of Mr. Alex Fuller and Mr. D. M. Storey Concerning Charges of Discrimination," July 10, 1970, 25/21, CR/USWA.

40. "Report of Mr. Alex Fuller."

41. *Buffalo Evening News*, July 14, 17, 1970; Leaflet, 24/22, Molony/USWA.

42. Strohmeyer, *Crisis in Bethlehem*, 128.

43. *U.S. v. Bethlehem Steel Corp.*, 312 F. Supp. 977 (W.D.- N.Y. 1970), mod. 446 F.2d 652 (2d Cir. 1971).

44. *Buffalo Courier Express*, Dec. 6, 1968.

45. Gottesman to Kleiman, Nov. 23, 1971, 15/6, Abel/USWA.

46. Ibid.; Gottesman to Hon. John Curtin, Apr. 12, 1974, 15/6, Abel/USWA.

47. Gottesman to Curtin, Apr. 12, 1974; A. F. Barbieri to Mitchel Mazuca, June 23, 1975, 54/20, Burke/USWA.

48. Strong to Fuller, Feb. 19, 1972, 23/District 4, CR/USWA; David A. Collins to H. Evenden, Jan. 12, 1972, 3/26, Abel/USWA.

49. Strong to Fuller, Feb. 19, 1972.

50. Strohmeyer, *Crisis in Bethlehem*, 129–30.

51. *Baltimore Afro-American*, Mar. 14, 1974.

52. It was not uncommon at the time for the foreign-born to be called "foreigners" in most contexts but "whites" when African Americans entered the picture.

53. Cited in Mark Reutter, *Sparrows Point: Making Steel—The Rise and Ruin of American Industrial Might* (New York: Summit Books, 1988), 65.

54. Ibid.

55. National Action Council (NAC), Meeting, Dec. 31, 1965–Jan. 2, 1966, Addendum, Reel 9, CORE.

56. See the article by one of the union's founders, Michael Flug, "Organized Labor and the Civil Rights Movement of the 1960s: The Case of the Maryland Freedom Union," *Labor History*, 31 (Summer 1990): 322–46. Also, Louis C. Goldberg, "CORE in Trouble: A Social History of the Organizational Dilemmas of the Congress of Racial Equality Target City Project in Baltimore, 1965–1967," (Ph.D. diss., Johns Hopkins University, 1970).

57. Board of Directors Meeting, Core Target City, Aug. 9, 1967, Addendum, Reel 2; NAC meeting, Oct. 23, 1967, Addendum, Reel 9, both in CORE; Strong to Fuller, Nov. 4, 1966, 13/2, CR/USWA.

58. Walter S. Brooks and James M. Griffin to Stewart Cort, Dec. 16, 1966; "Field Reports Maryland," Reel 24, both in CORE; Brooks and Griffin to Willard Wirtz, Feb. 3, 1967; Edward C. Sylvester Jr. to Brooks and Griffin, Mar. 10, 1967, 61/J-M, 1967, both in Wirtz; Brooks et al. to A. Philip Randolph, May 5, 1967, 8/CORE, BSCP; *Baltimore Sun*, May 6, 1967.

59. *Washington Post*, May 27, 1967; *Baltimore Sun*, May 29, 1967; Strong to Fuller, May, 23, 1967, 12/67, CR/USWA; Sylvester to B. C. Boylston, June 6, 1967; Boylston to Sylvester, July 3, 1967; Sylvester to Secretary [Wirtz], June 1, 1967, all in 12/64, CR/USWA.

60. George Gelston to Floyd McKissick, Sept. 26, 1966, A-II-95, Reel 2, CORE; *New York*

Times, Apr. 16, 1967; Milton Holmes to Bill Welch, Feb. 7, Mar. 28, 1968, Civil and Human Rights, Bus. and Ind. Corresp, Jan.–Apr. 1968, Vice Presidential Files, HHH.

61. Strong to Fuller, July 9, 1968, and attached leaflet, 18/18, CR/USWA; Maryland Commission on Human Relations, "Systematic Discrimination," Oct. 18, 1968, 18/18; Raymond W. Pasnick to Fuller, Nov. 1, 1968, 17/28, CR/USWA. CORE's links to the White House, however, were severed. See Harry McPherson Jr., "For the President," Sept. 12, 1966, "Civil Rights (2)," C-22, Harry McPherson papers, LBJ.

62. B. C. Boylston to Edward C. Sylvester Jr., July 3, 1967, 12/64, CR/USWA.

63. *Baltimore Sun*, May 3, 1967; Strong to Fuller, Mar. 24, 1967, 12/2, and Apr. 11, 1967; L. D. Sweier to Walter Wynn, Apr. 6, 1967; Ben Fischer to Fuller, Apr. 11, 1967; B. C. Boylston to Fuller, Aug. 2, 1967; Hobson to Sylvester, Aug. 15, 1967, 12/64; "Eighth District Meeting on Civil Rights," Apr. 14, 1967; Strong to Fuller, May 4, 1967, 13/2, all in CR/USWA; Walter Brooks, James Griffin, Gerald A. Smith to Wirtz, Apr. 26, 1967; Wirtz to Brooks, Griffin, Smith, May 11, 1967; Sylvester to Secretary [Wirtz], June 1, 1967, 62/EEOC-3, all in Wirtz.

64. Boylston to Fuller, Aug. 2, 1967, 12/64, CR/USWA.

65. Strong to Fuller, June 15, 1967, 13/2, Aug. 18, 1966, 12/64, CR/USWA.

66. *Baltimore News*, Feb. 2, 1968.

67. Minutes, "Joint Civil Rights Committee Meeting with the Company," Jan. 17, 1968; Strong, "Minutes of Meeting, District #8," Oct. 12, 1967; Strong to Fuller, Feb. 5, 26, 1968, all in 12/64, CR/USWA.

68. Strong to Fuller, Oct. 3, 1967, 12/64.

69. Strong to Fuller, Mar. 15, 1968, 12/64.

70. Sylvester to Secretary [Wirtz], May 24, 1968; Gerald A. Smith to Wirtz, May 13, 1968, both in 54/EEO-3, Wirtz.

71. Sylvester to Contract Compliance Officers, June 20, 1968, 17/25; Elliot Bredhoff to Ben Fischer, May 24, 1968, 20/28, both in CR/USWA.

72. Ralph L. McAfee to Father [Dexter] Hanley, Aug. 28, 1968, 20/28, Burke/USWA.

73. Meyer Bernstein, "The Steelworkers Election," 172, 9/10, Bernstein.

74. Ben Fischer, interview with author, Aug. 21, 1991; David Taylor to the Secretary [Shultz], Feb. 4, 1969, 68/EEOC-3, Shultz.

75. Meyer Bernstein, "Trade Union Democracy," 7–9, 9/19, Bernstein. In 1976, a USWA convention created a new office of vice president for human affairs and filled it with Mississippi-born Leon Lynch, an African American steelworker from Gary, Indiana. Until that time Lynch had been a staff representative in Memphis, Tennessee.

76. John Herling, *Right to Challenge: People and Power in the Steelworkers Union* (New York: Harper and Row, 1972), 379; Strong to Fuller, Mar. 14, 1969, 18/18, CR/USWA.

77. Peter Seitz to Secretary of Labor, marked Confidential and Personal, Mar. 15, 1969; Lew Douglas to Shultz, Apr. 18, May 5, 14, 19, 1969; Shultz to Douglas, May 14, 1969; [Arthur Fletcher], "Notes Taken During Bethlehem Steel Meeting," May 28, 1969, 68/EEO-3, all in Shultz; *Baltimore Sun*, Apr. 28, 1969.

78. Father Hanley, "Statement Concerning Conciliation," Aug. 8, 1969; Fletcher to Hanley, Aug. 7, 1969, 68/EEO-3; Fischer to Abel, Apr. 8, 1969, 18/23; George Cohen to Kleiman, Aug. 8, 1969, 18/27, all in CR/USWA; *Baltimore Sun*, Oct. 24, Nov. 19, 20, 21, 1969; Elliot Bredhoff to Edward Plato, Nov. 19, 1969; Bredhoff to Kleiman, Nov. 26, 1969, 25/6, both in Burke/USWA.

79. *Baltimore Sun*, June 7, 1971; Charles C. Robinson to James D. Hodgson, July 13, 1972, 18/EEOC 1972, Hodgson; Richard Schubert, telephone interview with author, Sept. 14, 1994; Laurence Silberman, telephone interview with author, Sept. 16, 1994; *Wall Street Journal*, Aug. 8, 1973. Hodgson turned the task of implementation over to George Hildebrand, a Cor-

nell University professor of industrial and labor relations, who was given the power to translate the principles of the decision into specific actions.

80. Fischer interview.

81. David Wilson to I. W. Abel, Jan. 22, 1974, 13/34, Abel/USWA.

82. Ivory Dennis, acceptance speech, n.d., copy in 8/4, Abel/USWA.

Chapter Six

1. H. R. Haldeman notes, Aug. 4, 1970, C-42, H. R. Haldeman papers, RN; A. James Reichley, *Conservatives in an Age of Change: The Nixon and Ford Administrations* (Washington, D.C.: Brookings Institution, 1981), 179–86.

2. Haldeman notes, Apr. 28, 1969, C-40; Feb. 21, 1970, C-41; Aug. 4, Nov. 7, 1970, C-42; John C. Whitaker, "Memorandum for Members of the Cabinet," June 24, 1969, WHCF, CF HU2, C-2; Leonard Garment, "Memorandum for the President," Feb. 19, 1971, WHCF, HU2, C-3, all in RN. John Ehrlichman, *Witness to Power: The Nixon Years* (New York: Simon and Schuster, 1982), 229.

3. The Democrats enjoyed a 58–42 majority in the Senate and a 243–192 majority in the House. Stephen E. Ambrose, *Nixon: The Triumph of a Politician, 1962–1972* (New York: Simon and Schuster, 1989), 220.

4. H. R. Haldeman, *The Haldeman Diaries: Inside the Nixon White House* (New York: G. P. Putnam's Sons, 1994), 507.

5. Margaret Weir, *Politics and Jobs: The Boundaries of Employment Policy in the United States* (Princeton: Princeton University Press, 1992), 122; William J. Wilson, *Declining Significance of Race: Blacks and Changing American Institutions* (Chicago: University of Chicago Press, 1978), 90.

6. The word "ironic" was first used by Hugh Graham in his *The Civil Rights Era: Origins and Development of National Policy, 1960–1972* (New York: Oxford University Press, 1990), 278. It has been picked up in John David Skrentny's *The Ironies of Affirmative Action: Politics, Culture, and Justice in America* (Chicago: University of Chicago Press, 1996) and in James T. Patterson's synthesis, *Grand Expectations: The United States, 1945–1974* (Oxford: Oxford University Press, 1996), 725.

7. James P. Smith and Finis R. Welch, "Black Economic Progress after Myrdal," *Journal of Economic Literature* 27 (1989): 519–64.

8. Thus, John David Skrentny's puzzlement over the civil rights organizations' lukewarm response to the affirmative action of the Philadelphia plan is misplaced. He assumes that they should have supported it; they judged it ineffective. Skrentny, *Ironies of Affirmative Action*, chap. 7.

9. Ken Cole to Ehrlichman, Oct. 1, 1970; Laurence Silberman to Cole, Apr. 6, 1971, both in WHCF, FG 109, C-1, RN; Cole, "Memorandum for the File," Nov. 9, 1970; Gif, "Memorandum for the Director," Dec. 8, 1970, both in T2-10/1, ser. 69.1, RG 51, NA; *New York Times*, Sept. 16, 17, 1971. The law also extended Title VII to state and local governments, but the Justice Department obtained the power to regulate this area. EEOC was strengthened, but the purposes of the reformers—to end excessive litigation and fragmentation, to create an agency with expertise, and to construct uniform government policies—were not achieved. Joan Hoff's revisionist book *Nixon Reconsidered* (New York: Basic, 1994) counts the enactment of the 1972 law as a Nixon achievement, ignoring his three-year opposition to it. Yet perhaps she is hinting at recognition of his recalcitrance when she states that the president "was not always on the cutting edge of this controversial issue" (94).

10. *Iron Age*, Oct. 17, 1968, 54.

11. The symbolic and political nature of the program was revealed in July 1971, when the president rejected a set-aside plan to foster minority construction firms despite its backing by most of the relevant agencies, including OMB. Leonard Garment, "Memorandum for the President," July 20, 1971; Charles Colson, "Memorandum for Staff Secretary," July 26, 1971, both in WHCF, HU2, C-3, RN.

12. Haldeman notes, Mar. 5, 1969, C-40, Haldeman papers; Presidential Meeting, June 13, 1969, President's Office Files (hereafter POF), C-79; Alexander P. Butterfield, "Memorandum for Maurice Stans and Dr. D. P. Moynihan," Aug. 7, 1969, WHCF, HU2, C-2; Caspar W. Weinberger, "Memorandum for Honorable George P. Shultz," June 29, 1971, WHCF, HU2, C-3, all in RN. The White House obtained contracts for businessmen associated with Rev. Leon Sullivan and Floyd McKissick; this was not a program, but traditional political patronage. Herbert Long to Paul Lavrakas, Mar. 10, 1972; Lavrakas to James E. Johnson, Mar. 15, 1972; Robert J. Brown to Peter G. Peterson, June 30, 1972, all in WHCF, CF PQ2, C-50, RN.

13. McCracken, "Memorandum for the President," Aug. 20, 1969, 29/Cabinet Committee on Economic Policy, 55/1969 CEA, Shultz; Cabinet Meeting on Economic Policy, Sept. 19, 1969, POF, C-79; Shultz to the President, July 30, 1969, WHCF, FG22, C-1; Haldeman notes, Jan. 15, 1971, C-4, all in RN. Clinton C. Bourdon and Raymond E. Lefitt, *Union and Open-Shop Construction: Compensation, Work Practices, and Labor Markets* (Lexington, Mass.: Lexington Books, 1980), 7, 99–100, 108–9.

14. Some believe that Nixon sought to break up the coalition between blacks and labor. At the time, the NAACP's Clarence Mitchell charged the plan was "a calculated attempt . . . to break up the coalition between Negroes and labor unions." *Congressional Quarterly Weekly Report* (Nov. 27, 1970) 28:2859–61. While that dividend was attractive, it was still a dividend. There is no evidence that the plan originated from politics. Hugh Graham, believing that the "quotas" were implemented by an aggressive bureaucracy, ignores the economic purposes undergirding the plan and the supporting elite culture. While the plan, like many, did emerge from the bureaucracy, it became policy only because Nixon and Shultz were interested in reducing construction wages. See Graham, *Civil Rights Era*, chaps. 11, 13, esp. 475.

15. Shultz, "Memorandum for Under Secretary Hodgson and Assistant Secretary Weber," Mar. 6, 1969, 29/EEO, Shultz.

16. Presidential Meetings, POF, June 13, 1969, C-79; Shultz to the President, July 30, 1969, WHCF, FG22, C-1, both in RN; H. S. Houthakker, "Memorandum for the Cabinet Committee on Economic Policy," May 15, 1969, C-29, Shultz. Announced by OFCC, it was put together by Solicitor of Labor Laurence H. Silberman and lawyers in the Justice department. Arthur A. Fletcher to Secretary and Under Secretary, July 15, 1969, 67/EEO-1, Shultz.

17. "Memo to President," PJB meeting, July 9, 1969, POF, C-78, RN; Shultz, "Why Vote to Recommit?," 67/EEO, Shultz.

18. Cited in Skrentny, *Ironies of Affirmative Action*, 197.

19. "Minutes of Joint Meeting of Cabinet Committee on Economic Policy and Cabinet Committee on Construction," Nov. 13, 1969, 55/1969-CEA, Shultz; William A. Boleyn to Arthur Weber, Dec. 17, 1970, T1-1, ser. 69.1, RG 51, NA; NALC, executive board minutes, Mar. 14, 1970, 10, 1/2, Richard Parrish papers, Schomburg.

20. McCracken, "Memorandum for the Cabinet Committee on Construction," Nov. 13, 1970, T2-2, ser. 69.1, RG 51, NA; James Hodgson, "Memorandum for the President's file," Jan. 18, 1971, C- 83; Shultz, "Memorandum for the President's File," Jan. 28, 1972, C-87, both in Charles W. Colson papers, RN.

21. Haldeman notes, Jan. 15, 1971, C-2, RN; Weber to Ehrlichman, Feb. 10, 1971, T1-11, Ser. 69.1, C-37, RG 51, NA.

22. In 1976, the Department of Labor found that minority workers constituted 21 percent

of the apprentices in union programs but only 10 percent in nonunion programs. At the same time, the drop-out rates in the open-shop programs were six times as high as those in the union sector. In both sectors, blacks predominated in the same trades, those in which blacks had historic roots, such as cement masons, painters, and roofers. Peter B. Doeringer and Michael J. Piore, *Internal Labor Markets and Manpower Analysis* (Lexington, Mass.: Heath, 1971), 71–73. Others confirm that blacks enjoyed much greater participation and opportunities in union programs as opposed to nonunion ones. See Richard L. Rowan and Lester Rubin, *Opening the Skilled Construction Trades to Blacks: A Study of the Washington and Indianapolis Plans for Minority Employment* (Philadelphia: University of Pennsylvania Press, 1972), 93; and Bourdon and Lefitt, *Union and Open-Shop Construction*, 69–73.

23. Shultz, "Memorandum for Paul W. McCracken," Dec. 3, 1970, T2-2, RG 51, NA; *Labor Relations Yearbook, 1971*, 102–3.

24. Evaluation Division, OMB, report, May 1972, 11, 21; Weber to Mr. Shultz, May 25, 1971, T1-11, ser 69.1, RG 51, NA.

25. "Report of the Civil Rights Department to the Executive Council [AFL-CIO], Feb. 19, 1971, 26/7, Abel/USWA; Lamar Alexander to Bryce Harlow, June 17, 1970, WHCF, HU2 FG1, C-2, RN; Haldeman notes, July 18, 1970, C-42, Haldeman, RN; Weir, *Politics and Jobs*, 110.

26. Shultz, "Memorandum for the President's File," June 8, 1971, C-85, Colson papers, RN; Weir, *Politics and Jobs*, 113.

27. George [Shultz], "Memorandum for Mr. William Safire," Dec. 16, 1970; Arthur B. Laffer, "Unemployment—What If?," n.d. [Feb. 1972], T2-11; Ehrlichman to Shultz, May 3, 1972, T2-11, all in ser. 69.1, RG 51, NA; Weir, *Politics and Jobs*, 116–18.

28. "Notes for Equal Opportunity Conference," May 27, 1969; "Equal Opportunity Conference," ser. V, C-28, CR/AFL-CIO; Elliot Bredhoff to Jacob Clayman, May 29, 1969, 18/10, CR/USWA.; Jerris Leonard, "Developments in the Interpretation and Implementation of Title VII," Aug. 10, 1970, *Labor Relations Yearbook, 1970*, 106–11.

29. Leonard to Don Slaiman, Mar. 9, 1970, ser. IV, 27/Department of Justice Corresp., CR/AFL-CIO; Robert Moore, interview with author, May 15, 1993.

30. Thomas Johnson to Attorney-General, Jan. 22, 1970, DJ 170-1-15, Justice.

31. Rowan had studied the Connors Steel company in 1964, as part of a Ford Foundation study of black employment in Birmingham. He testified that the company's efforts were genuine. To this day, Jerome "Buddy" Cooper, the USWA's lawyer, cannot not understand why the government brought the case. Buddy Cooper, interview with author, July 13, 1989; *United States v. H. K. Porter*, Judgment and Order, No. Dist. Ala., Civil No. 67–363, Dec. 30, 1968.

32. John Bird, "Memorandum of Meeting of June 4," June 8, 1970; Benjamin Erdreich to Gottesman, June 4, 1970; Cooper to Gottesman, June 15, 1970, Legal/Pittsburgh.

33. Moore interview.

34. Ibid.; Cooper to Leonard, Sept. 29, 1970; Cooper to Kleiman, Aug. 28, Oct. 6, 1970, Legal/Pittsburgh.

35. Graham, *Civil Rights Era*, 342–44; Harry J. Waisglass, "'Toward Fair Employment and the EEOC'—the Adams Papers," IRRA, *Annual Proceedings, 1972* (Madison, Wisc.: IRRA, 1973), 372–73; *Wall Street Journal*, Aug. 11, 1977.

36. Cooper to Leonard, Sept. 29, 1970, Legal/Pittsburgh.

37. Leonard, "Memorandum for the Attorney General," Dec. 15, 1970, DJ 170-1-15, Justice. This explanation succeeded the announcement. The decision was made by Leonard, not the attorney general.

38. *New York Times*, Dec. 15, 1970.

39. Strevel, "Statement," Dec. 12, 1970, 23/37, CR/USWA; Howard Strevel, interview with author, July 15, 1990.

40. Gottesman to Kleiman, Apr. 27, 1972, 4/23, Abel/USWA.

41. Ibid.

42. *Albermarle Paper Co. v. Moody* 422 U.S. 405 (1975).

43. Cooper to Kleiman, Aug. 28, 1970; Kleiman, "Notes on Conversation with Mike Gottesman," June 7, 1972, Legal/Pittsburgh. In 1971, Leonard became head of the new Law Enforcement Assistance Administration (LEAA).

44. The available records do not disclose the specific reason for the decision, because U.S. Steel records are unavailable. The Justice Department records do not discuss the reasons for the turnabout. The only hint is a note penned by Bernard Kleiman on Cooper's October 12, 1971 letter to him: "I explained Shaver's turnabout." Warren Shaver was U.S. Steel's vice president for personnel. Kleiman does not recall the reason for Shaver's change of mind. Jared Meyer, currently legal counsel of USX, speculated that U.S. Steel "thought they could win the case." That conclusion was reinforced by John Bird, at the time the regional attorney for the corporation in Birmingham. He too said that "the law was not that clear." Over time, he was proved right. Jared Meyer, telephone interview with author, Oct. 14, 1991; John Bird, interview with author, Nov. 1, 1991.

45. Kleiman, "Notes," May 15, 16, 26, 1972; John Bird, "Memorandum of Meeting of June 4," June 8, 1970; Cooper to Kleiman, Oct. 1, 12, 1971, Apr. 27, 1972; Cooper to Gottesman, Oct. 25, 1971; Gottesman to Kleiman, Dec. 9, 1971, Apr. 19, 1972, all in Legal/Pittsburgh.

46. Samuel C. Pointer, interview with author, Sept. 25, 1991.

47. U. W. Clemon, interview with author, Sept. 29, 1991; Gottesman to Kleiman, Apr. 19, 1972, Legal/Pittsburgh; James Forman Jr., interview with author, Oct. 28, 1991; Bird interview.

48. No. 66-423-S; Pointer and Clemon interviews; Cooper to Gottesman, June 15, 1971, Legal/Pittsburgh.

49. Forman interview.

50. Trial, June 20, 1972, 1:64; Nov. 30, 1972, 49:2–25, 66–85.

51. Trial, Aug. 29, 1972, 25:60–61.

52. Trial, Aug. 28, 1972, 24:167–205.

53. Trial, June 20, 1972, 1:20–26; June 22, 1972, 3:601–53; July 21, 1972, 18:64–69.

54. Bruce Thrasher, interview with author, July 10, 1989.

55. Cooper, interview with author, July 13, 1989; Demetrius Newton, interview with author, July 21, 1989; Bird interview.

56. Cooper interview. On page 133 of *To Redeem the Soul of America: The Southern Christian Leadership Conference and Martin Luther King, Jr.* (Athens: University of Georgia Press, 1987), Adam Fairclough cited Cooper's petition, mistakenly believing Cooper to be black— a small but revealing error. Much movement history suffers from inadequate analysis of local histories.

57. Newton interview; Trial, July 21, 1972, 18:25.

58. Trial, July 21, 1972, 18:96.

59. Luther McKinstry, interview with author, June 2, 1990; Thrasher interview.

60. Thrasher and Clemon interviews; Gottesman to Kleiman, June 20, July 7, 1972, Legal/Pittsburgh.

61. Trial, Nov. 9, 1972, 45:49.

62. Trial, Nov. 28, 1972, 47:131–74.

63. Pointer's inclination to fill trade and crafts jobs on the basis of seniority was probably based upon the record at TCI. Prior to 1963, apprenticeships at Fairfield were unavailable to blacks. This changed in 1963, but from 1964 to 1968, when the company had a wide measure of discretion, less than 10 percent of apprenticeships were held by blacks. After 1968, when seniority was the determining factor, black participation rose to 21 percent.

64. Cooper to Gottesman, July 26, 1972; Gottesman to Kleiman, July 27, 1972, Legal/Pittsburgh.

65. Cooper to Kleiman, Aug. 28, Sept. 29, 1972; Flint Hooten to Thrasher, Sept. 11, 1972; Cooper to Gottesman, Sept. 29, 1972, ibid.

66. Pointer, "Memorandum of Opinion" Dec. 11, 1973, 371 F.Supp. 1045.

67. Pointer interview.

68. Cooper to Gottesman, Apr. 9, 1973, Legal/Pittsburgh.

69. "Proceedings, Oct. 3, 1974," *United States v. Allegheny-Ludlam Industries, Inc.*, Civil Action No. 74-P-339, 34–36, Justice.

70. Moore to Rich, July 27, 1973, DJ 170-1-15, and attached letter, Justice.

71. Gottesman to Kleiman, May 17, 1973, 10/10, Abel/USWA.

72. J. Stanley Pottinger, "Memorandum for the Solicitor General," 170-1-15, Justice.

73. Barry Goldstein to Jack Greenberg et al., Aug. 9, 1973, 170-1-15, Justice; The Fifth Circuit ordered the back pay after the Supreme Court decision, *Albermarle Paper Co. v. Moody* 422 U.S. 405 (1975). See *John S. Ford, et al. v. US Steel Corp., et al.*, 525 F.2d 1043 (5th Cir. 1975).

74. Goldstein to William Hardy, Nov. 2, 1973, 170-1-15, Justice; Cooper to Kleiman, Aug. 7, Nov. 1, 1973, 10/9, Abel/USWA. When I interviewed Sylvester Wright, who sued for back pay, he initially thought that I was a lawyer from the Justice Department informing him that he obtained more back pay. Sylvester Wright, interview with author, July 18, 1989.

75. E. B. Rich, interview with author, Sept. 30, 1991; Cooper interview; *EEOC v. US Steel, et al.*, 28, CA No. 70-906, Dec. 16, 1974.

76. Rich interview.

77. Robert Moore, telephone interview with author, July 24, 1997.

78. Rich to Moore, Feb. 5, 1981, Civil Rights Division, Justice; Winn Newman, interview with author, July 20, 1991.

79. McKinstry interview.

80. Forman interview.

Chapter Seven

1. *United States of America v. Allegheny-Ludlum Industries, Inc., et al.* The most accessible record of the main provisions and the decree itself appears in the *Daily Labor Report*, Apr. 15, 1974.

2. *International Brotherhood of Teamsters v. United States*, 431 U.S. 324 (1977).

3. *United Steelworkers v. Weber* 443 U.S. 193 (1979).

4. Ben Fischer, interview with author, Aug. 21, 1991; Howard Strevel, interview with author, July 15, 1990.

5. Ben Fischer, telephone interview with author, Sept. 16, 1994; Joe Molony to Strevel, Bussa, Mazuca, Plato, Ward, Apr. 11, 1973, Legal/Pittsburgh.

6. Bernard Kleiman to I. W. Abel (labeled "Confidential"), May 3, 1973, 10/9; Kleiman to Members of the International Executive Board (also "Confidential"), June 5, 1973, both in 7/17, Abel/USWA; Kleiman, notes, May, 15, 1973, Legal/Pittsburgh.

7. "Statement of Policy on Seniority Adopted by the International Executive Board, USWA" ("Confidential"), June 26–27, 1973, 7/17, Abel/USWA.

8. J. Warren Shaver to John Johns, Ben Fischer, J. J. O'Connell, July 6, 1973; *The Joint Study Committee of the Coordinating Committee Steel Companies*, July 6, 1973, both in 7/17, Abel/USWA.

9. *The Joint Study Committee of the Coordinating Committee Steel Companies*, July 6, 1973, 7/17, Abel/USWA.

10. *Joint Report of the Seniority Study Committee*, Sept. 19, 1973, 7/17, Abel/USWA.

11. Fischer interview, Aug. 21, 1991; William Kilberg, telephone interview with author, Sept. 15, 1994.

12. The only exception was in the calculation of rate retention for black and female workers. The government discovered that a transferee coming from an incentive job could move to an entry-level job with a higher hourly rate but without an incentive, thereby producing a lower total rate. Industry accepted the government's position that these workers should obtain incentive pay as well as rate retention as long as these benefits were limited to blacks and females, thus limiting industry's costs. Although the union wanted all employees to have the same benefits, it yielded on this issue. Fischer to Abel, Dec. 6, 1973, 10/9, Abel/USWA; Consent Decree I, Section 8c.

13. David L. Rose to J. Stanley Pottinger, Apr. 25, 1973; Robert T. Moore to William O'Connor, May 15, 1973, both in DJ 170-1-15, Justice; *Daily Labor Report*, Apr. 15, 1974; Robert Moore, interviews with author, July 12, 1990, and May 15, 1993.

14. Kilberg interview; William J. Kilberg, "Current Civil Rights Problems in the Collective Bargaining Process: The Bethlehem & AT&T Experiences," *Vanderbilt Law Review* 27 (1974): 81–113; Herbert R. Northrup and John A. Larson, *Impact of AT&T-EEOC Consent Decree* (Philadelphia: Wharton School, 1979), 1–18. The $45 million was the final cost estimated in 1974.

15. Brown had tangled with the administration from the beginning. He had supported cease-and-desist powers for EEOC when Nixon opposed it. Then, he had refused to campaign for the president in 1972. However, most people concluded that Brown was not a good manager. Other commissioners could not work with him, and various government monitors concluded that EEOC was poorly run. On the other hand, Brown was popular with black groups and had the support of Republican senator Hugh Scott. As late as December, Clarence Mitchell, who also supported Brown, held up hearings on Powell's confirmation. Jerry H. Jones to Al Haig, n.d. [May 1973], WHCF, CF FG 109, C-23; Leonard Garment to President, Dec. 7, 1973, WHCF CF FG 109/A, both in RN.

16. Under the law, EEOC and Justice had concurrent jurisdiction until March 1974.

17. Inevitably, the results were approximations. See Consent Decree I, para. 18; Kilberg and Moore interviews.

18. Fischer interviews; *New York Times*, Dec. 4, 1973; *Daily Labor Report*, Apr. 15, May 29, June 26, 1974; Jonathan Maslow, *Jurisdictor Magazine for the New Lawyer* 4 (Sept. 1974): 9–11; Bernard Kleiman, interview with author, Aug. 20, 1991.

19. *Albermarle Paper Company v. Moody*, 422 U.S. 405 (1975). Justice Stewart, writing for the majority, concluded that after a finding of unlawful discrimination, "necessary relief," "complete justice," and the "make whole" purpose of Title VII created a presumption that back pay would be awarded.

20. *New York Times*, Dec. 4, 1973 (EEOC official quote); *New York Age*, Apr. 20, 1974 (Hill quote); *Black Panther*, Apr. 27, 1974; *The Guardian*, n.d. [Apr. 1974]. Hill continued his attack. Writing to Roy Wilkins, Ben Fischer concluded that "any actions taken to further equal employment opportunity are 'back-door' deals and denial of rights to blacks unless Mr. Hill is involved, consulted, and given the ultimate power of decision." Fischer to Wilkins, July 18, 1975, 77/1, Research/USWA.

21. Jack Greenberg, interview with author, May 8, 1993.

22. Belton cited in *Labor Relations Yearbook, 1975*, 138.

23. LDF, "Memorandum on Pending Steel Consent Decree Litigation," Feb. 10, 1975, NAACP Inc. Fund, 1974–75, LDF.

24. The Fifth Circuit, following subsequent court decisions, overturned Pointer's decision denying back pay.

25. USWA brief, *United States et al. v. Allegheny-Ludlum Industries, et al.*, No. 74-3056, 36.

NOW, claiming to represent women who had been discharged in the 1940s and women who had been discriminated against in hiring, intervened and urged that the decree be set aside because it did not provide transfer rights and back pay to females in plant, clerical, and security jobs. The union argued that it was difficult to prove such a claim and that even if one could, the option of a private suit was not foreclosed. Unlike AT&T, the steel industry lacked significant numbers of women making the claim. The consent decrees required hiring goals of 20 percent for women.

26. David Feller, the USWA's general counsel in the McDonald regime, was on the LDF board. Ben Fischer, and other union officials were on the "liberal" mailing lists that received LDF financial appeals. Fischer interview, Aug. 21, 1991.

27. *United States v. Allegheny-Ludlum Industries, Inc.*, 517 F.2d 826 (CA5 1975); Gottesman to Kleiman, Aug. 23, 1975, Legal/Pittsburgh.

28. Where there was ongoing litigation, the percentages were lower. Thus, at Lackawanna 78.7 percent accepted their settlement checks, at Sparrows Point 88.7 percent. E. C. Perkins to Ben Fischer, Nov. 15, 1976, 59/11, Burke/USWA.

29. Robert T. Moore, "Record of Communication with John Moody," Mar. 23, 1976, A&R.

30. *Detroit News* (Wilkins quote), May 23, 1974; Alex Fuller to Abel, July 29, 1975; Curtis Strong to Fuller, July 24, 1975, both in 21/17, CR/USWA; Fischer to Roy Wilkins, July 18, 1975, 77/1, Research/USWA; Wilkins to Fischer, Sept. 2, 1975, 21/22, Abel/USWA; Fischer to Wilkins, Sept. 24, 1975, 55/16, Burke/USWA.

31. Drew Days III and Robert Moore to James W. Sico, Nov. 8, 1978, C-31; Milton Edward Burlison to Sam C. Pointer, Aug. 14, 1974, C-27; Donald G. Magee to Sir, Aug. 12, 1974, C-27, all in A&R.

32. E. P. Gillett to R. C. Ricker, Sept. 9, 1976, A&R Docket No. 66-5, A&R.

33. William E. Comer to Sam Pointer, Sept. 10, 1974; Hollie W. Neal to Gregory Wade, Jan. 3, 1975, ibid.

34. Gregory Fred Ware to Sir, Dec. 20, 1974, ibid.

35. William J. Toth to I. W. Abel, Sept. 1974, ibid.

36. Burlison to Pointer, Aug. 14, 1974; *Committee of Concern Journal*, Oct. 6, 1975, 2, ibid.

37. Magee to Sir, Aug. 21, 1974, ibid.

38. Walter Thompson to Abel, Aug. 26, 1974, ibid.

39. To Miss Kearney, n.d. [Feb. 1976], 30/6, ibid.

40. Robert T. Moore, G. A. Moore Jr., and Ben Fischer to William Comer, Nov. 11, 1974; Richard F. Beam to Abel, Aug. 11, 1974, 27/6, ibid.

41. Sam C. Pointer Jr. to Warren E. Erickson, Mar. 24, 1976, ibid.

42. Magee to Sir, Aug. 21, 1974.

43. *Committee of Concern Journal*, Oct. 6, 1975; Strong to Fuller, Aug. 31, 1975, 21/17, CR/USWA; *Labor Relations Yearbook, 1975*, 199.

44. Jim Balanoff, telephone interview with author, Sept. 9, 1984.

45. *International Brotherhood of Teamsters v. United States*, 431 U.S. 324 (1977), 27; E. C. Perkins to Mr. Barnette, June 1, 1977, 31/9, A&R.

46. Gottesman to Kleiman, July 26, 1968, June 24, 1971, Legal/Pittsburgh.

47. Moore interview, May 15, 1993.

48. *Franks v. Bowman Transportation Co.* 424 U.S. 747 (1976).

49. 401 U.S. 424 (1971). Michael Evan Gold discusses the practical difficulties of determining "disparate impact" in his essay "*Griggs'* Folly: An Essay on the Theory, Problems, and Origin of the Adverse Impact Definition of Employment Discrimination and a Recommendation for Reform," *Industrial Relations Law Journal* 7 (1985): 432–66.

50. See, for instance, Stanley P. Hebert et al. to William H. Brown III, July 7, 1971; Dapray

Muir to John Dean, Sept. 28, 1971; John Dean to Leonard Garment, Sept. 28, 1971, C-33, John W. Dean III files, all in RN; Richard A. Epstein, *Forbidden Grounds: The Case Against Employment Discrimination Laws* (Cambridge: Harvard University Press, 1992), 262–63.

51. The company required a passing score of 20 on the Wonderlic Personnel Test, a general intelligence test commonly used in industries, although the publisher's manual recommended a passing score of 18 for skilled mechanics and subforemen. Thus, the company was demanding higher scores to qualify for manufacturing jobs that were less demanding than that of a skilled mechanic. The union argued, too, that the test discriminated against any worker who attempted to move from laboring work to manufacturing. *Willie S. Griggs, et al., v. Duke Power Company*, "Motion of United Steelworkers of America, AFL-CIO for Leave to File Brief Amicus Curiae and Brief for United Steelworkers of America, AFL-CIO, Amicus Curiae," October Term, 1969; Kleiman to Jack Greenberg, Feb. 12, 1970, 24/15; David Feller to Winn Newman, Jan. 12, 1966, 15/36, both in CR/USWA.

52. *Congressional Record* (Feb. 8, 1964), 110: 7206.

53. Bredhoff, "Affirmative Action in a Declining Economy: Seniority and the Incumbent Majority," Aug. 13, 1975, 21/12, Abel/USWA.

54. Fischer to Abel, Mar. 11, 1975, 21/22, Abel/USWA.

55. "Black Unemployment," n.d. [Sept. 1977], 230/Labor O/A 63/9, Eizenstat; Hill cited in *Labor Relations Yearbook, 1975*, 396–97.

56. Perkins to Barnette, June 10, 1977, 31/9, A&R.

57. Jack Greenberg to Robert Scrivner, June 17, 1977; "Memorandum," June 17, 1977; both in NAACP Inc. Fund, 1977, Rockefeller Brothers Fund.

58. *Labor Relations Yearbook, 1977*, 312–14.

59. Lloyd McBride et al. to All Directors, staff representatives, June 14, 1977, 75/42, Leg/USWA; Eleanor Holmes Norton to Leon Lynch, n.d. [Sept. 1977]; Abner W. Sibal to Norton, Sept. 13, 1977; Preston David to Steel Coordinators, Sept. 21, 1977; S. G. Clark Jr. to Company Counsel, Dec. 14, 1977; Walter P. DeForest to All Company Counsel, May 30, 1978; Frederick S. Mittleman to Charlotte Frank, July 5, 1978; David W. Zugschwerdt to Charlotte Frank, July 5, 1978, all in 31/6, A&R.

60. Kleiman interview.

61. Michael R. Fontham, telephone interview with author, Sept. 10, 1994.

62. *University of California Regents v. Bakke*, 438 U.S. 265 (1978).

63. Norton to President Jimmy Carter, Sept. 9, 1977, WHCF, FG 123, C-183 (Norton quote); Stu Eizenstat and Bob Lipshutz to the President, with JC comments, Sept. 6, 1977; Eizenstat to Hamilton Jordan, Sept. 6, 1977; Eizenstat and Lipshutz to President and Vice President, Sept. 10, 16, 1977; Jordan to Carter, n.d. [Sept. 1977], 33/Bakke, all in Hamilton Jordan papers, JC.

64. Powell, "Memorandum to the Conference," Jan. 2, 1979, 220/Weber, Marshall.

65. Burger, "Memorandum to the Conference," Apr. 1, 1979, ibid.

66. Griffin B. Bell to President, with Carter comments, n.d., 115/1/15/79 [1], Staff Secretary files; Vice President et al. to President, Jan. 13, 1979, CFO/A44, 50/Weber, Robert Lipshutz papers, both in JC.

67. Michael Gottesman, interview with author, July 10, 1994.

68. In a concurrence, Justice Blackmun accepted the Wisdom argument that "employers and unions who had committed 'arguable violations' of Title VII should be free" to institute such plans.

69. The union brief also appealed to White, Blackmun, and Marshall. Notes, *United Steelworkers & Kaiser Aluminum v. Weber*, n.d., Brennan; Gottesman interview.

70. N. Thompson Powers, telephone interview with author, Sept. 16, 1994; Byron White to Bill [Brennan], May 7, 1979, Marshall.

71. This conclusion is a major reason why Richard A. Epstein strongly opposed the decision. See his *Forbidden Grounds: The Case Against Employment Discrimination Laws* (Cambridge, Mass.: Harvard University Press, 1992), 401.

72. Gottesman interview; *USWA and Kaiser v. Weber*, 443 U.S. (1979), 208.

73. Burt Neuborne, who helped write the ACLU's amicus curiae brief in support of the USWA-Kaiser plan, subsequently acknowledged some of these moral conflicts. Neuborne observed that the Brian Webers of the world bore the burden of affirmative action and preferred to shift it elsewhere. He did not acknowledge that Title VII enforcement and remedies as a whole, not just this plan, had contributed to the dilemma. The conflict was visible in *Weber* precisely because the racism surrounding *Crown* was absent. Neuborne, "Observations on Weber," *New York University Law Review* 54 (1979): 546–59.

74. Big business agreed. Most corporate managers believed that the government compliance machinery was inefficient, chaotic, and punitive. The Business Roundtable, which heavily influenced Carter's reorganization of EEOC and OFCC, preferred voluntarism, to which the *Weber* ruling lent strong support. Donald S. MacNaughton, "Discussion of Problems and Suggested Solutions in Connection with Federal Equal Employment Opportunity Programs," May 7, 1977, WHCF, HU 1–2, C-HU-9, JC; Bob Malson to Eizenstat, Nov. 1, 1977, O/A 233, 164/Civil Rights, Eizenstat; Anne B. Fisher, "Businessmen Like to Hire by the Numbers," *Fortune*, Sept. 16, 1985, 26–30.

75. *Fullilove v. Klutznick*, 448 U.S. 448 (1980).

76. Drew S. Days III, "Fullilove," *Yale Law Journal* 96 (1987): 463–70. In 1995, the Court began to demand the "strict scrutiny" test when it remanded a set-aside back to the lower court to determine whether it passed muster. See *Adarand Constructors, Inc. v. Pena*, 515 U.S. 200 (1995). In June 1997, the district court threw out the plan, arguing it was not "narrowly tailored" to meet the government's "compelling interest" [965 F. Supp. 1556 (D. Colo. 1997)]. I would like to thank Armand Derfner for alerting me to the district court's decision.

77. Meyer Bernstein, "Georgetown Steel Strike, 1971," 9/16, Bernstein.

78. The early negotiations in 1966 are documented in 360/EEO-3, Wirtz; EEOC minutes, Mar. 30, 1966, EEOC. The USWA unionization drive at Newport News is summarized in Lloyd M. McBride to the President [Carter], Jan. 9, 1979, WHCF, LA5-10. JC; Leon Lynch to A. Philip Randolph, Nov. 2, 1977, 24/Labor. Corresp. 1962–77, Randolph; Bruce Thrasher, telephone interview with author, July 19, 1997.

79. Carter did try mediation, but he could not get the company to meet with the union and would not threaten sanctions. Bruce Thrasher, telephone interview with author, July 19, 1997.

80. Audit and Review Committee, "Report on Rate Retention and Transfer Experience," 15, in 6/Docket 7-3, A&R.

81. Moore interviews. Elaine Bloomfield, a lawyer at EEOC who took over government supervision of the consent decrees when Robert Moore retired, kindly made the figures available to me.

82. For a thoughtful attempt to assess the matter, see James P. Smith and Finis R. Welch, "Black Economic Progress After Myrdal," *Journal of Economic Literature*, 27 (June 1989): 519–64.

Chapter Eight

1. Stephen D. Krasner, "United States Commercial and Monetary Policy: Unraveling the Paradox of External Strength and Internal Weakness," in *Between Power and Plenty*, ed. Peter J. Katzenstein (Madison: University of Wisconsin Press, 1978), 51–87.

2. Melvyn P. Leffler, *A Preponderance of Power: National Security, the Truman Adminis-*

tration, and the Cold War (Stanford: Stanford University Press, 1992), 160–61; Alfred E. Eckes, "Trading American Interests," *Foreign Affairs* (Fall 1992): 133–54.

3. Stephen D. Krasner, "The Tokyo Round: Particularistic Interests and Prospects for Stability in the Global Trading System," *International Studies Quarterly* 23 (Dec. 1979): 495–98; Leffler, *Preponderance of Power*, 317 (Bureau of Budget memo); Alfred E. Eckes, *Opening America's Market: U.S. Foreign Policy since 1776* (Chapel Hill: University of North Carolina Press, 1995), 158 (Commission quote), 166 (assistant secretary of state quote). A New York Republican congressman told a British diplomat that most legislators "viewed the Marshall Plan from the strategic rather than the economic standpoint." Diane B. Kunz, *Butter and Guns: America's Cold War Economic Diplomacy* (New York: Free Press, 1997), 39.

4. Steve Dryden, *Trade Warriors: USTR and the American Crusade for Free Trade* (New York: Oxford University Press, 1995), 38; Eckes, "Trading American Interests," 133–54.

5. Robert O. Keohane, "The World Political Economy and the Crisis of Embedded Liberalism," in *Studies in the Political Economy of Western European Nations*, ed. John H. Goldthorpe (Oxford: Oxford University Press, 1984), 20–21; I. M. Destler, *American Trade Politics*, 2d ed., (Washington, D.C.: Institute for International Economics, 1992), 7.

6. George W. Ball, *The Past Has Another Pattern: Memoirs* (New York: W. W. Norton, 1982), 209, 212.

7. JEC, Hearings, *Steel Prices, Unit Costs, Profits, and Foreign Competition*, 88th Cong., 1st sess., (Washington, D.C.: GPO, 1963), 572–77.

8. Notes taken at residence of Prime Minister Erlander of Sweden, July 13, 14, 15, 1963, 4, Trip files, Senatorial files, 1949–64, HHH.

9. "Address and Question and Answer Period at the Economic Club of New York," Dec. 14, 1962, in Kennedy, *Public Papers, 1962*, 881–82; "President's News Conference," Nov. 8, 1961, in Kennedy, *Public Papers, 1961*, 771; G. M. Taber, *John F. Kennedy and a Uniting Europe* (Bruges, Belg.: College of Europe, 1969), 59–62; Thomas W. Zeiler, *American Trade and Power in the 1960s* (New York: Columbia University Press, 1992), 163; John W. Evans, *The Kennedy Round in American Trade Policy* (Cambridge: Harvard University Press, 1971), 140; Judith Goldstein, *Ideas, Interests, and American Trade Policy* (Ithaca: Cornell University Press, 1993), 159–62; Gerard Curzon and Victoria Curzon, "The Management of Trade Relations in the GATT," in *International Economic Relations of the Western World, 1959–1971*, vol. 1, *Politics and Trade*, ed. Andrew Shonfield (London: Oxford University Press, 1976), 149; Richard Reeves, *President Kennedy: Profile of Power* (New York: Simon and Schuster, 1993), 331; Arthur Schlesinger Jr. *A Thousand Days: John F. Kennedy in the White House* (Boston: Houghton Mifflin, 1965), 844–48; Ernest H. Preeg, *Traders and Diplomats* (Washington, D.C.: Brookings Institution, 1970), 45.

10. Dryden, *Trade Warriors*, 49 (Harris quote), 50 (Gass quote), 53; Schlesinger, *A Thousand Days*, 651–55, 847; Kunz, *Butter and Guns*, 107. See also Seymour E. Harris, June 16, 17, 1965, 53–54, 60–62, OHI, JFK.

11. Dryden, *Trade Warriors*, 53; Ball, *Past Has Another Pattern*, 212.

12. The U.S. industry objected to rebated "value-added" taxes, rebated transportation costs from mill to port, subsidized interest rates, special accelerated depreciation allowances for producers who exported, and subsidies that reduced the cost of export credit and insurance. *Iron Age*, Oct. 17, 1968, 54.

13. David Coombs, *Politics and Bureaucracy in the European Community: A Portrait of the Commission of the E.E.C.* (London: George Allen and Unwin, 1970), 172, 181–82; Eckes, *Opening America's Market*, 195 (Bator quote); Otis L. Graham Jr. *Losing Time: The Industrial Policy Debate* (Cambridge: Harvard University Press, 1992), 9–10; Robert S. Walters, *The Politics of Global Economic Relations*, 2d ed., (Englewood Cliffs, N.J.: Prentice-Hall, 1983), 14; T. K. Warley, "Agriculture in the Kennedy Round," in Shonfield, *International Economic Re-*

lations, vol. 1, *Politics and Trade*, 377; Dryden, *Trade Warriors*, 107; *Iron Age*, June 15, 1967, 59, July 13, 1967, 43.

14. An American producer paid taxes on profits, including those derived from exports. In most foreign countries, however, exports were exempt from value-added taxes, which were a larger source of revenue than direct taxation. Existing GATT rules did not consider reimbursement of indirect taxes to be an unfair trade practice. The U.S. steel industry wanted the rules changed.

15. Mira Wilkins, *The Maturing of Multinational Enterprise: American Business Abroad from 1914 to 1970* (Cambridge: Harvard University Press, 1974), 335.

16. Warren I. Cohen, "China in Japanese-American Relations," in *The United States and Japan in the Postwar World*, ed. Akira Iriye and Warren I. Cohen (Lexington: University Press of Kentucky, 1989), 37; Curzon and Curzon, "The Management of Trade Relations in the GATT," 253–70; Eckes, "Trading American Interests," 139; Eckes, *Opening America's Market*, 174.

17. As this example reveals, trade negotiations were not conducted on a sectoral basis. Thus, if nation A reduced its steel tariff, nation B could retain its levy. Theoretically, nation B would reduce a levy on some other product or make some other trade concession. There were other provisions allowing "exceptions" to tariff reductions on account of their particular importance to the importing nation.

18. Eckes, *Opening America's Market*, 200; Dryden, *Trade Warriors*, 122; Nancy Bernkopf Tucker, "Threats, Opportunities, and Frustrations in East Asia," in *Lyndon Johnson Confronts the World: American Foreign Policy, 1963–1968*, ed. Warren I. Cohen and Nancy Bernkopf Tucker (Cambridge: Cambridge University Press, 1994), 122–25; Walter LaFeber, "Decline of Relations During the Vietnam War," in Iriye and Cohen, *U.S. and Japan in Postwar World*, 98; Wilkins, *Maturing of Multinational Enterprise*, 335.

19. *Iron Age*, Mar. 23, 1967, 49.

20. *Wall Street Journal*, Sept. 26 (assistant secretary quote), Nov. 11 ("unsophisticated electronics"), 1968.

21. The figures, compiled by the IMF, are from Goldstein, *Ideals, Interests, and American Trade Policy*, 163, 168.

22. Peterson's transformation was a significant one because he had been a member of the Emergency Committee for American Trade (ECAT), a new free trade organization, active in opposing a steel quota bill in 1967. See "Import Restraints," later in this chapter.

23. Paul McCracken, "Memorandum for John Campbell," July 7, 1970, WHCF, FG22, C-2, RN; Dryden, *Trade Warriors*, 146–47 (Peterson quote); Robert A. Pastor, *Congress and the Politics of Foreign Economic Policies, 1929–1976* (Berkeley: University of California Press, 1980), 128–29.

24. Pastor, *Congress and the Politics of Foreign Economic Policies*, 132; U.S. Congress, House Committee on Ways and Means, Hearings, *Trade Reform Act*, 93rd Cong., 1st sess., 1973, 1257; Thomas K. McCraw, "From Partners to Competitors: An Overview of the Period since World War II", in *America versus Japan*, ed. Thomas K. McCraw (Boston: Harvard Business School Press, 1986), 29.

25. For a summary of the debate on transnationals, see Robert Gilpin, *U.S. Power and the Multinational Corporations* (New York: Basic, 1975). The proper word is "transnationals," but the public often used the term "multinationals."

26. Pastor, *Congress and the Politics of Foreign Economic Policy*, 134; *Wall Street Journal*, Oct. 3, 1968.

27. Abel statement, May 17, 1973, in House, Hearings, *Trade Reform Act*, 1209–90. When the UAW left the AFL-CIO, Abel replaced Walter Reuther as chairman of the labor federation's economic policy committee.

28. There had been a brief flurry of talk about foreign joint ventures in steel in the wake of the signing of the Treaty of Rome in 1957, as other manufacturers attempted to enter a European market that they feared would be closed to U.S. imports. It was a brief period of exploration, and most ventures did not materialize. Raw materials were the steel industry's primary foreign investment, a fact to which the union objected bitterly. See, for instance, Bernstein to McDonald, 29/34, McDonald/USWA.

29. Christoph Scherrer, "Mini-Mills: A New Growth Path for the U.S. Steel Industry?" *Journal of Economic Issues* 22 (Dec. 1988): 1187.

30. *National Journal*, Jan. 15, 1972; Jack J. Sheehan to I. W. Abel, Feb. 2, 1972, 5/10, and June 19, 1973, 10/24, both in Abel/USWA.

31. Leonard Woodcock statement in House, Hearings, *Trade Reform Act*, 849–94; Frank Fernback to Dean Clowes, July 5, 1972, 5/3; Sheehan to Abel, June 19, 1973, 10/21, both in Abel/USWA.

32. Sheehan to Abel, Mar. 26, 1975, 18/5, Abel/USWA.

33. AISI, Board of Directors meeting, May 27, 1965, vol. 10, C-159, AISI, Eleutherian Mills–Hagley Foundation Historical Library, Wilmington, Del. (hereafter Hagley); AISI, "Key Provisions of the Trade Reform Act," n.d. [1974], 13/20, Abel/USWA.

34. *National Journal*, Nov. 24, 1973.

35. In 1967, the European Economic Community (EEC) became the European Community (EC).

36. *Iron Age*, Feb. 16, 1967, 82–83; Pastor, *Congress and the Politics of Foreign Economic Policy*, 207; C. Fred Bergsten, "Coming Investment Wars?" *Foreign Affairs* 53 (Oct. 1974): 149 (Bergsten quote).

37. Paul A. Tiffany, *Decline of American Steel: How Management, Labor, and Government Went Wrong* (New York: Oxford University Press, 1988), 77 (Grace quote), 118–19, 232, n. 71; Paul A. Tiffany, "The American Steel Industry in the Postwar Era: Dominance and Decline," in *Changing Patterns of International Rivalry: Some Lessons from the Steel Industry*, ed. Etsuo Abe and Yoshitaka Suzuku (Tokyo: University of Tokyo Press, 1991), 253–54.

38. The ECSC was incorporated into the EEC, which had been created in 1957.

39. Bernard Keeling, *World Steel: A New Assessment of Trends and Prospects* (London: Economist Intelligence Unit, 1988), 36.

40. Donald F. Barnett and Louis Schorsch, *Steel: Upheaval in a Basic Industry* (Cambridge, Mass.: Ballinger, 1983), 44; Takashi Hiraishi, *Japan's Trade Policies: 1945 to the Present Day* (London: Athlone Press, 1989), 170.

41. McCraw, "From Partners to Competitors," 9.

42. Yoshitaka Suzuku, "The Postwar Japanese Iron and Steel Industry: Continuity and Discontinuity," in Abe and Suzuku, *Changing Patterns of International Rivalry*, 211; Leonard H. Lynn, *How Japan Innovates: A Comparison with the U.S. in the Case of Oxygen Steelmaking* (Boulder, Colo.: Westview Press, 1982), 43–48. Walter LaFeber argues that what was true for the steel industry was true for the entire Japanese economy. *The Claim: U.S.-Japanese Relations Throughout History* (New York: W. W. Norton, 1997), 293–94.

43. Chalmers Johnson, *MITI and the Japanese Miracle: The Growth of Industrial Policy, 1925–1975* (Stanford: Stanford University Press, 1982), 9–10; Lynn, *How Japan Innovates*, 53. MITI has received the most attention, but Eamonn Fingleton argues that the Ministry of Finance is the linchpin of Japanese mercantilism. Fingleton, "Japan's Invisible Leviathan," *Foreign Affairs* 74 (Mar.–Apr. 1995): 69–85.

44. Johnson, *MITI and the Japanese Miracle*, 266–67; David B. Audretsch, *The Market and the State: Government Policy Towards Business in Europe, Japan, and the United States* (New York: New York University Press, 1989), 197; Kiyoshi Kawahito, *The Japanese Steel Industry* (New York: Praeger, 1972), 41.

45. Thomas K. McCraw and Patricia A. O'Brien, "Production and Distribution: Competition Policy and Industry Structure," in McCraw, *America versus Japan*, 96; Lynn, *How Japan Innovates*, 89–97.

46. The Kokai Hanbai Seido, joint open sales program, was begun in the 1950s to avoid "excessive price competition." All members met monthly with their wholesalers and announced prices and quantity on the same day. The decisions were negotiated by producers, representatives of dealers and users, and MITI. Kawahito, *Japanese Steel Industry*, 104.

47. Mark Mason, *American Multinationals and Japan: The Political Economy of Japanese Capital Controls, 1899–1980* (Cambridge: Council on East Asian Studies, Harvard University, 1992); *Wall Street Journal*, Dec. 4, 1995; Clyde Prestowitz Jr., *Trading Places: How We Are Giving Our Future to Japan and How to Reclaim It* (New York: Basic, 1989), 300; Johnson, *MITI and the Japanese Miracle*, 278; Thomas R. Howell, William A. Noellert, Jesse G. Kreier, and Alan Wm. Wolff, *Steel and the State: Government Intervention and Steel's Structural Crisis* (Boulder, Colo.: Westview Press, 1988), chap. 4, 215–21; Tsutomu Kawasaki, *Japan's Steel Industry* (Tokyo: Tekko Shimbun Sha, 1985).

48. Putnam, Hayes and Bartlett, Inc., *Economics of International Steel Trade* (Washington, D.C.: American Iron and Steel Institute, 1977), 18; Robert W. Crandall, *The U.S. Steel Industry in Recurrent Crisis: Policy Options in a Competitive World* (Washington, D.C.: Brookings Institution, 1981), 199; Hiraishi, *Japan's Trade Policies*, 154–58; U.S. Congress, Senate Committee on Finance, Hearings, *Steel Imports*, 89th Cong., 2d sess., 1966, 84; Kawahito, *Japanese Steel Industry*, 67.

49. Destler, *American Trade Politics*, 51; Barnett and Schorch, *Steel*, 49; Howell, Noellert, Kreier, and Wolff, *Steel and the State*, chap. 3.

50. *Iron Age*, Oct. 20, 1966, 44–45; Howell, Noellert, Kreier, and Wolff, *Steel and the State*, 177–79, 128–31.

51. U.S. Department of Labor [E. Robert Livernash], *Collective Bargaining in the Basic Steel Industry: A Study of the Public Interest and the Role of Government* (Washington, D.C.: U.S. Department of Labor, 1961), 174; Crandall, *U.S. Steel Industry in Recurrent Crisis*, 165.

52. *Iron Age*, May 11, 1967, 58.

53. Okun, "Memorandum for Joseph A. Califano, Jr." July 31, 1968, WHCF, BE4/Steel, C-14; Walter W. Heller to President, Aug. 1, 4, 1964; Douglas Dillon to President, Aug. 5, 1964; Gardner Ackley to President, Dec. 30, 1964, WHCF, BE4/Steel, C-12; Heller to President, Oct. 18, 1964, WHCF, CF BE5-4, C-2, all in LBJ; Council of Economic Advisers, *Report to the President on Steel Prices*, Apr. 1965, copy in Uris Library, Columbia University, New York.

54. Otto Eckstein, "Memorandum for the President," Aug. 19, 1965, WHCF, LA6/Steel, C-29; Gardner Ackley, "Memorandum for the President," Aug. 25, 27, 30, 1965, WHCF, BE4/Steel, C-13, LBJ.

55. "Notes on Meeting with Bethlehem Steel Executives, Jan. 1, 1966," WHCF, CF BE4/Steel, C-2; Roger Blough, OHI, July 29, 1971, 19–21, LBJ.

56. Throughout the twentieth century, U.S. Steel had been the leader on price changes. No more. Bethlehem in 1965 and Inland in 1966 took the lead and raised prices on sheet and strip metal by 2.1 percent. Despite Johnson's hope that the industry would not get behind Inland, because it was Inland that had spiked the 1962 increase, everyone followed. Gardner Ackley, "Memorandum for the President," Aug. 3, 1966, WHCF, BE4/Steel, C-14, LBJ.

57. Dennis S. Ippolito, *Uncertain Legacies: Federal Budget Policy from Roosevelt through Reagan* (Charlottesville: University Press of Virginia, 1990), 43–46; Ackley to Roger [Blough], Dec. 5, 1967; Okun, "Memorandum for Joseph A. Califano, Jr.," July 31, 1968; Morton J. Peck, "Memorandum for Mr. Joseph A. Califano, Jr.," July 31, 1968, WHCF, BE4/Steel,

C-14; Fred Panzer, "Memorandum for the President," Feb. 13, 1968, 36/Labor Bloc, Marvin Watson papers, all in LBJ.

58. AISI, *Annual Statistical Report, 1981*, 21, 29; William Scheuerman, *The Steel Crisis: The Economics and Politics of a Declining Industry* (New York: Praeger, 1986), 70.

59. Ronald F. King, *Money, Time, and Politics: Investment Tax Subsidies and American Democracy* (New Haven: Yale University Press, 1993), 308–12. Wirtz believed that in place of the investment tax credit, some corporate profits should be permitted to enter a tax-free escrow fund to be taken out and used for investment when things slowed up, another example of the influence of the Swedish system on American social democrats. Wirtz to President, Mar. 17, 1966, WHCF, CF BE5, C-2, LBJ.

60. Dryden, *Trade Warriors*, 199; Neil Fligstein, *The Transformation of Corporate Control* (Cambridge: Harvard University Press, 1990), 201–2; Andrew Shonfield, *Modern Capitalism: The Changing Balance of Public and Private Power* (London: Oxford University Press, 1965), 327–28; Pastor, *Congress and the Politics of Foreign Economic Policies*, 152–54.

61. *Iron Age*, Jan. 10, 1963, 35; Tony Freyer, *Regulating Big Business: Antitrust in Great Britain and America, 1880–1990* (Cambridge: Cambridge University Press, 1992), 305.

62. James R. Williamson, *Federal Antitrust Policy During the Kennedy-Johnson Years* (Westport, Conn.: Greenwood Press, 1995), 17, 36; Alfred Chandler Jr., "The Competitive Performance of U.S. Industrial Enterprises Since the Second World War," *Business History Review* 68 (Spring 1994): 10, 17; Freyer, *Regulating Big Business*, 316–19.

63. Robert Sobel, *Rise and Fall of the Conglomerate Kings* (New York: Stein and Day, 1984), 23–46, 156. Even when a company did not leave a sector, antitrust law altered investment strategies. After the FTC prohibited Burlington Industries from acquiring another textile company, it began to buy furniture, lighting, and other unrelated companies, and put more money into overseas operations. Richard Paul Olsen, *The Textile Industry: An Industry Analysis Approach to Operations Management* (Lexington, Mass.: D. C. Heath, 1978), 116–17.

64. James Burnham, *The Managerial Revolution* (New York: John Day, 1941); John Kenneth Galbraith, *The New Industrial State* (Boston: Houghton Mifflin, 1967).

65. William T. Hogan, *The 1970s: Critical Years for Steel* (Lexington, Mass.: D. C. Heath, 1972), 11–17. *Iron Age*, Feb. 13, 1969, 11.

66. Sobel, *Rise and Fall of the Conglomerate Kings*, 99; "Some Candid Answers from James J. Ling, Part I," *Fortune*, Aug. 1, 1969, 95.

67. Barry Bluestone and Bennett Harrison, *The Deindustrialization of America: Plant Closings, Community Abandonment, and the Dismantling of Basic Industry* (New York: Basic, 1982), 152–53; Fligstein, *The Transformation of Corporate Control*, 207–11; Sobel, *The Rise and Fall of the Conglomerate Kings*, 158–61; Hogan, *The 1970s: Critical Years for Steel*, 32.

68. Fligstein, *Transformation of Corporate Control*, 206–7; Sobel, *Rise and Fall of the Conglomerate Kings*, 180–81. The Lykes family enjoyed the patronage of two powerful Louisiana lawmakers: Russell Long, chairman of the Senate Finance Committee, and Representative Hale Boggs, second-ranking Democrat on the House Ways and Means Committee. *Wall Street Journal*, Mar. 18, 1969.

69. John Zysman makes this point in his *Government, Markets and Growth: Financial Systems and the Politics of Industrial Change* (Ithaca: Cornell University Press, 1983).

70. *Iron Age*, Nov. 28, 1963, 58; statement by Jack J. Carlson, president of Kaiser Steel, in House, Hearings, *Trade Reform Act*, 4064; William T. Hogan, *World Steel in the 1980s: A Case of Survival* (Lexington, Mass.: D. C. Heath and Co., 1983), 95.

71. *Wall Street Journal*, May 15, Nov. 7, 1967, Feb. 1, 1968, Sept. 25, 1974. The coal investment turned out to be a poor one from Kaiser's perspective, though not from the Japanese. *Wall Street Journal*, June 14, Aug. 10, 1971.

72. Krasner, "The Tokyo Round," 506.

73. *Iron Age*, Nov. 14, 1963, 146–47.

74. The leading works of this school are Donald F. Barnett and Louis Schorsch, *Steel: Upheaval in a Basic Industry*; Robert W. Crandall, *The U.S. Steel Industry in Recurrent Crisis*; and Michael Borrus, "The Politics of Competitive Erosion in the U.S. Steel Industry," in *American Industry in International Competition: Government Policies and Corporate Strategies*, ed. John Zysman and Laura Tyson (Ithaca: Cornell University Press, 1983), 60–105.

75. At the time, commentators interpreted the growing use of the BOF as a sign of the innovativeness of the industry. See Henry Broude, *Steel Decisions and the National Economy* (New Haven: Yale University Press, 1963), 257–59. The first critical commentary was Walter Adams and Joel Dirlam, "Big Steel, Invention, and Innovation," *Quarterly Journal of Economics* 80 (1966): 167–89. But most criticism of the industry began as explanations of the steel crisis of the late 1970s and was always embedded in an ideological frame that ignored the political economy of the U.S. and foreign industries. The fact that only Japan produced, as opposed to sold, at lower costs was ignored in the late 1970s and early 1980s.

76. The U.S. Steel experiments, developed in its South Chicago research laboratory, resulted in the Q-BOF process, which injected oxygen in a different manner. *Wall Street Journal*, Dec. 17, 1971.

77. Lynn, *How Japan Innovates*, 169.

78. Suzuku, "Postwar Japanese Iron and Steel Industry," 223. Even today, when the mini-mill, which uses the electric furnace, is significant all over the world, Japan's Nippon Steel does not use it. "Why Japan Is Losing Its Metal," *Economist*, July 20–26, 1996, 57.

79. Lynn, *How Japan Innovates*, 152–57, 164.

80. Lynn, *How Japan Innovates*, 26; *Iron Age*, May 12, 1966, 23; Barnett and Schorsch, *Steel*, 53–56; *Wall Street Journal*, Mar. 22, 1973.

81. *Wall Street Journal*, May 12, 1966, Sept. 14, 1967.

82. Stinson was referring to Japan's new Nagoya Works, half financed by cheap government loans, and Britain's Spencer Works, which obtained nearly all of its money from government agencies. *Iron Age*, Sept. 14, 1967, 109.

83. Garth L. Mangum, Sae-Young Kim, and Stephen B. Tallman, *Transnational Marriages in the Steel Industry: Experience and Lessons for Global Business* (Westport, Conn.: Quorum Books, 1996), 32.

84. Christoph Scherrer, "Governance in Steel," in *Governance of the American Economy*, ed. John L. Campbell, J. Roger Hollingsworth, and Leon N. Lindberg (Cambridge, Eng.: Cambridge University Press, 1991), 191; Bela Gold, Gerhard Rosegger, and Myles G. Boylan Jr., *Evaluating Technological Innovations: Methods, Expectations, and Findings* (Lexington, Mass.: Lexington Books, 1980), 285; Edmund Ayoub to Louis Kohnke, July 10, 1969, 85/18, Research/USWA. The situation did not improve. Robert Crandall estimated that in 1978 a new greenfield mill would save $60 a ton, but capital charges would increase by $131. Crandall, *U.S. Steel Industry in Recurrent Crisis*, 84.

85. Kawahito, *Japanese Steel Industry*, 164; Howell, Noellert, Kreier, and Wolff, *Steel and the State*, 498–500.

86. *New York Times*, Sept. 24, 1968; *Consumers Union of the United States v. Kissinger*, 506 F.2d (D.C. Cir. 1974). The USWA submitted an amicus curiae brief in support of the VRA. The lawyers for Consumers Union were from the Center for Law and Social Policy, a New Left advocacy group. This division was one of many between the unions and the new social activists of the 1960s. Eliot Bredhoff to Abel, Oct. 25, 1972, 4/23, Abel/USWA.

87. AISI Board of Directors, minutes of meetings, July 11, Dec. 12, 1962, Nov. 11, 1964, May 27, 1965, AISI, Hagley; *Iron Age*, May 25, 1967, 71.

88. AISI Board of Directors, minutes of meetings, Apr. 6, May 26, 1966.

89. Senate, Hearings, *Steel Imports*, 284–85.

90. Ibid., 116–17, 267.

91. Ibid., 277; Howell, Noellert, Kreier, and Wolff, *Steel and the State*, 111.

92. *Iron Age*, June 9, 1966, 23–25, Feb. 16, 1967, 77–79, Dec. 28, 1967, 65; Thomas B. Curtis and John Robert Vastine Jr., *The Kennedy Round and the Future of American Trade* (New York: Praeger, 1971), 144; *Wall Street Journal*, May 2, 1967; Meyer Bernstein to I. W. Abel et al., May 22, 1967, 79/14, IA.

93. The government even opposed continuing the OECD steel committee. AISI, minutes of meeting, Aug. 5, 1965, AISI.

94. Representative John Dent's bill giving the government power to limit imports that damaged industries and workers passed the House 340–29 on September 29, 1967. *Iron Age*, Oct. 12, 1967, 51–52.

95. Curtis and Vastine, *The Kennedy Round*, 238, 240; *New York Times*, Nov. 3, 1967; Eckes, *Opening America's Market*, 202.

96. The AISI switched from advocating a levy to lobbying for a quota, believing that the former was impossible to effect. Hard-hit Kaiser unsuccessfully pushed for a regional quota for the West. AISI, minutes of meeting, Sept. 14, Oct. 3, 1967, AISI; Pastor, *Congress and the Politics of Foreign Economic Policy*, 122; Hogan, *The 1970s: Critical Years for Steel*, 52–54.

97. AISI, minutes of meeting, Jan. 16, 1968, AISI.

98. United States–Japan Trade Council, "Report No. 32," Apr. 5, 1968, 80/2; Bernstein to Abel, Apr. 16, 1968, 79/14, both in IA; Curtis and Vastine, *The Kennedy Round*, 138–43; Jim Gaither to Califano, July 31, 1968; Califano to the President, Aug. 1, 1968; Gaither to President, Aug. 2, 1968; Arthur M. Okun, "Memorandum for the President," Aug. 5, 1968; Larry Levinson to President, Aug. 6, 1968, WHCF, BE4/Steel, C-14, all in LBJ; *Business Week*, Nov. 16, 1968, 62–63. The Japanese had originally offered a 7 percent rise, which was bargained down to 5 percent. *Washington Post*, Dec. 2, 1968.

99. AISI, minutes of meeting, Oct. 31, 1968, AISI; *Iron Age*, Oct. 31, 1968, 53–55.

100. *Wall Street Journal*, Dec. 18, 19, 1968; William T. Hogan, *Economic History of the Iron and Steel Industry in the United States*, 5 vols. (Lexington, Mass.: Lexington Books, 1971), 5:1682.

101. *Iron Age*, Jan. 18, 1968, 46.

102. For Nixon's policies, see Herbert Stein, *Presidential Economics: The Making of Economic Policy from Roosevelt to Reagan and Beyond*, 2d rev. ed. (Washington, D.C.: American Enterprise Institute, 1988), 133–208.

103. *Business Week*, May 15, 1971, 94; *Wall Street Journal*, June 4, 1971. Responding to the boom of 1973–74 and the widely anticipated increased demand for steel, investment rose to $2.6 billion in 1975. U.S. Congress, Office of Technology Assessment, *Technology and Steel Industry Competitiveness* (Washington, D.C.: GPO, 1980), 123.

104. Paul W. McCracken, "Memorandum for the President," Aug. 3, 1969, 29/Cabinet Comm on Economic Policy, Shultz; Peter M. Flanigan, "Memorandum for the President," Apr. 30, 1970; McCracken, "Memorandum for the President," Apr. 30, 1970, WHCF, BE4/ Steel; R. Heath Larry to Hendrik S. Houthakker, Mar. 23, 1970; Saul Nelson to Houthakker, Mar. 26, 1970, C-118, Charles Colson papers; "Meetings with the President," Jan. 15, 1971, C-4, John Ehrlichman papers, all in RN; Heath Larry to George P. Shultz, June 14, 1973, 7/22, Abel/USWA; AISI, minutes of meeting, Feb. 5, 1974, AISI.

105. John J. Sheehan to Abel, Jan. 27, 1969, 64/6, Leg/USWA; Bernstein to Abel, Mar. 9, 1972, 5/6, Abel/USWA; Kent Albert Jones, *Politics vs. Economics in World Steel Trade* (London: Allen and Unwin, 1986), 100–102. The EC and Japan abandoned export restraint because they believed the 10 percent surcharge on imports, which Nixon imposed to counter the domestic effects of devaluation, ended the bargain they had made with the administration. Hogan, *The 1970s: Critical Years for Steel*, 49.

106. AISI Board of Directors, Minutes, May 10, 1973, Jan. 22, 1974, AISI; Hans van der Ven and Thomas Grunert, "The Politics of Transatlantic Steel Trade," in *The Politics of Steel: Western Europe and the Steel Industry in the Crisis Years, 1974–1984*, ed. Yves Meny and Vincent Wright (Berlin: Walter de Gruyter, 1987), 140–43.

107. Stuart Cort statement, in House, Hearings, *Trade Reform Act*, June 7, 1973, 4019; Edmund Ayoub to Russell H. Cook Jr., Feb. 17, 1965, 85/13, Research/USWA; "Ruttenberg Report," July 1971, attached to Bernard Kleiman to Walter J. Burke, Oct. 20, 1972, 4/22, Abel/USWA.

108. The Teamsters' opposition stemmed from conflict between James Hoffa and the Kennedys, not from economic issues.

109. Bernstein to John Rooney, Dec. 20, 1961, 54/2, IA.

110. Daniel J. B. Mitchell, *Labor Issues of American International Trade and Investment* (Baltimore: Johns Hopkins University Press, 1976), 33; Bernstein to Rooney, Dec. 20, 1961, 54/2, IA.

111. Bernstein to Rooney, Dec. 20, 1961, 54/2; Bernstein to R. E. Farr, May 2, 1963 (a copy of the petition, under Sec. 301a of the Trade Expansion Act of 1962, submitted to the U.S. Tariff Commission on May 1, is attached to the letter), 54/4, IA; David J. McDonald, "Statement on Trade and Tariffs," Mar. 16, 1964, 58/5, Leg/USWA; Bernstein to Abel, Burke, Molony, Sept. 12, 1967, 79/13, Research/USWA; Krasner, "United States Commercial and Monetary Policy," 78–79; Destler, *American Trade Politics*, 152.

112. Meyer Bernstein, testifying for the USWA, was unconvinced of the need for the levy. A copy of his testimony on Apr. 6 and Sept. 12, 1966 may be found in 62/10, Research/USWA.

113. Senate, Hearings, *Steel Imports*, June 2, 1966, 239; Melvin Rothbaum, "Wage-Price Policy and Alternatives," in *Challenges to Collective Bargaining*, ed. Lloyd Ulman (Englewood Cliffs, N.J.: Prentice-Hall, 1967), 138; Bernstein to Abel, Burke, Molony, Jan. 14, 1966, 19/16, IA.

114. Bernstein, "The Steelworkers Election," 141–60, 9/10, Bernstein; Bernstein to Abel, Burke, Molony, Oct. 13, 1967, 79/13, Research/USWA.

115. Bernstein, "Speech before Special Convention of Tekko Roren," Feb. 20, 1968, 3/18, Bernstein.

116. Bernstein to Abel, Burke, Molony, May 22, 1967, 14/16, Burke/USWA; Bernstein to Willi Michels, Dec. 30, 1968, 80/2, IA; Borrus, "Politics of Competitive Erosion," 84–85.

117. Molony, "Testimony before the Senate Finance Committee in behalf of the Steel Quota Import Bill, S. 2537," Oct. 20, 1967, 11/33, Burke/USWA; Edmund Ayoub to Russell H. Cook Jr., Feb. 17, 1965, 85/13, Research/USWA.

118. NA, "Memorandum for the File," Aug. 6, 1968, WHCF, BE4/Steel, C-14, LBJ; Bernstein, "Steelworkers Election," 158.

119. Bernstein to Abel, Aug. 15, 1968 (labeled "Confidential"), Dec. 5, 1968, Jan. 16, 1969, 80/2, IA.

120. Roger Blough, OHI, July 29, 1971, 32, LBJ; Califano, "For the President," Nov. 28, 1967, WHCF, Diary Backup, C-83, LBJ; Elliot Bredhoff, "A Better Way than Crisis Bargaining—The Steel Agreement," Aug. 7, 1973, 10/10, Abel/USWA.

121. AISI, minutes of meeting, Feb. 12, 1975, AISI.

122. Thrasher to Abel, Feb. 23, 1972, 5/5; June 18, 1973, 7/7; Smith to Abel, Feb. 2, 1974, 16/13, all in Abel/USWA; Graham, *Losing Time*, 17.

Chapter Nine

1. The prices of oil, other raw materials, and food had been rising before the bold move. Japan's inflation rate was 14.6 percent before the big oil price increase. Takashi Hiraishi, *Japan's Trade Politics, 1945 to the Present Day* (London: Athlone Press, 1989), 186.

2. Jeff Madrick, *Taking America: How We Got from the First Hostile Takeover to Megamergers, Corporate Raiding, and Scandal* (New York: Bantam, 1987), 81; *Wall Street Journal*, Mar. 22, 1973; *Fortune*, Feb. 13, 1978, 122 (quote); Carol J. Loomis, "Steel's Not So Solid Expansion Plans," *Fortune*, Jan. 1976, 107.

3. Charles S. Maier, "Inflation and Stagnation as Politics and History," in *The Politics of Inflation and Economic Stagnation: Theoretical Approaches and International Case Studies*, ed. Leon N. Lindberg and Charles S. Maier (Washington, D.C.: Brookings Institution, 1985), 10–12; John Zysman, "Inflation and the Politics of Supply," in ibid., 144; *Business Week*, Dec. 7, 1974, 84.

4. W. Carl Biven, "Economic Advice in the Carter Administration," in *The Presidency and Domestic Policies of Jimmy Carter*, ed. Herbert D. Rosenbaum and Alexej Ugrinsky (Westport, Conn.: Greenwood Press, 1994), 620–22; *Fortune*, Apr. 14, 1977, 116; *Fortune*, Feb. 12, 1979, 79; Helen Ginsburg, *Full Employment and Public Policy: The United States and Sweden* (Lexington, Mass.: D. C. Heath, 1983), 71.

5. Anthony S. Campagna, *Economic Policy in the Carter Administration* (Westport, Conn.: Greenwood Press, 1995), 112.

6. Foreign markets remained closed, and when the nation woke up to that fact, it had lost the carrot of its own market. Stephen S. Cohen and John Zysman, *Manufacturing Matters: The Myth of the Post-Industrial Economy* (New York: Basic, 1987), 47.

7. David P. Calleo, *The Imperious Economy* (Cambridge: Harvard University Press, 1982), 142; Stu Eizenstat and Bob Ginsburg, "Memorandum for the President," Aug. 12, 1977, O/A 242, C-227, Eizenstat; Erwin C. Hargrove, *Jimmy Carter as President: Leadership and the Politics of the Public Good* (Baton Rouge: Louisiana State University, 1988), 96.

8. Steve Dryden, *Trade Warriors: USTR and the American Crusade for Free Trade* (New York: Oxford University Press, 1995), 220; Lloyd Cutler interview, Oct. 23, 1982, Miller Center Interviews, Carter Presidency Project, 34–35, JC. On the origins and significance of the Trilateral Commission, see John B. Judis, "Twilight of the Gods," *Wilson Quarterly* 15 (Autumn 1991): 43–55.

9. Ed Ayoub to I. W. Abel, Apr. 26, 1976, 23/25, Abel/USWA.

10. I. M. Destler and Hisao Mitsuyu, "Locomotives on Different Tracks: Macroeconomic Diplomacy, 1977–1979," in *Coping with U.S.-Japanese Economic Conflicts*, ed. I. M. Destler and Hideo Sato (Lexington, Mass.: D. C. Heath, 1982), 246–47 (quote); Ambassador Frederick B. Dent, "Memorandum to the President," Jan. 18, 1977, WHCF, FG260, C-FG208, JC; Eizenstat and Ginsburg, "Memorandum for the President," Aug. 12, 1977. Japan's trade surplus rose from $2.5 billion in 1976 to $9.7 billion in 1977; Germany's from $13.8 billion to $16.6 billion. Richard C. Thornton, *The Carter Years: Toward a New Global Order* (New York: Paragon, 1991), 47–50.

11. Zbigniew Brzezinski, *Power and Principle: Memoirs of the National Security Adviser, 1977–1981* (New York: Farrar, Straus, Giroux, 1981), 314–315; Bob Ginsburg, "Memorandum for White House Staff," Apr. 22, 1977, O/A 6237 [7], C-226, JC (White House consensus); Diane B. Kunz, *Butter and Guns: America's Cold War Economic Diplomacy* (New York: Free Press, 1997), 309.

12. Eizenstat and Ginsburg, "Memorandum for President," Aug. 12, 1977, 5 (Treasury opinion); Richard Cooper to Brzezinski, n.d. [Oct. 1–Dec. 31, 1977], WHCF, TA, C-TA-1, JC; Alan Wm. Wolff, "U.S. International Trade Policy," Mar. 21, 1977, International Trade, CF O/A 243, C-227, Eizenstat; I. M. Destler, *American Trade Politics*, 2d rev. ed. (Washington, D.C.: Institute for International Economics, 1992), 45; Stephen Woolcock, "Economic Policies of the Carter Administration," in *The Carter Years: The President and Policy Making*, ed. M. Glenn Abernathy, Dilys M. Hill, and Phil Williams (New York: St. Martin's, 1984), 41.

13. *Wall Street Journal*, May 3, 1977; STR, "Specialty Steel Options: Background Paper,"

Feb. 10, 1977; Eizenstat and Ginsburg, "Memorandum for the President," May 17, 1977, Steel CF, O/A 24 [4], C-284, Eizenstat; W. Michael Blumenthal, "Memorandum for the President," May 11, 1977, WHCF, TA4-8, C-TA19, all in JC. The Ford administration acted under the 1974 trade legislation, which permitted remedies to those who could establish that imports were "a substantial cause of serious injury, or the threat thereof." Under the law of 1962, industry had been required to show that the injury was serious and that the "major cause" was the volume of imports resulting from specific U.S. tariff concessions. Destler, *American Trade Politics*, 114.

14. *Wall Street Journal*, Apr. 28, Aug. 8, 1977; Eizenstat to the President, May 14, 1977, WHCF, CM8, C-CM6, JC.

15. *Wall Street Journal*, May 3, 1977; Charles L. Schultze, "Memorandum for the President," May 12, 1977; Robert S. Strauss, "Memorandum for the President," May 13, 1977, attached to Henry Owen to Zbigniew Brzezinski, Nov. 21, 1977, WHCF, CM8, C-CM6; White House press release, Aug. 5, 1977, CF O/A 24 [3]; Schultze, "Memorandum for the President," July 27, 1977; Bert Lance, "Memorandum for the President," July 30, 1977; Eizenstat and Ginsburg, "Memorandum to the President," July 30, 1977, O/A 6343, C-284, Eizenstat, all in JC.

16. Steelworkers were less willing than political and economic leaders to accept the verdict of the market. The crisis provoked regional struggles between the Flemish and Waloons in Belgium, between the North and South in Italy, between England and Scotland in Great Britain. The protests in France were the most extreme, involving plant seizures, riots, and civil disorder in Lorraine and the Nord. Yves Meny and Vincent Wright, "State and Steel in Western Europe," in *The Politics of Steel: Western Europe and the Steel Industry in the Crisis Years, 1974–1984*, ed. Yves Meny and Vincent Wright (Berlin: Walter de Gruyter, 1987), 30–31; Ray Hudson and David Sadler, *The International Steel Industry: Restructuring, State Policies, and Localities* (London: Routledge, 1989), 83–94.

17. These included Japan, Brazil, South Africa, South Korea, Australia, and all European nations outside of the EC—in short, everyone.

18. Ray Hudson and David Sadler, *International Steel Industry*, 32–33; *Wall Street Journal*, Jan. 24, Sept. 18, 19, 1978; Zysman, "Inflation and the Politics of Supply," 142.

19. Jeffrey A. Hart, *Rival Capitalists: International Competitiveness in the United States, Japan, and Western Europe* (Ithaca: Cornell University Press, 1992), 54–55; Clyde V. Prestowitz Jr., *Trading Places: How We Are Giving Our Future to Japan and How to Reclaim It* (New York: Basic, 1989), 273–74.

20. An identical agreement the year before, limiting Japanese specialty steel in the EC, had contributed to the surge of specialty steel in the U.S. market. Jack Sheehan to I. W. Abel, Aug. 8, 1975, 21/25; Nat Goldfinger to Abel, Apr. 1, 1976, 23/3, both in Abel/USWA.

21. Thomas R. Howell, William A. Noellert, Jesse G. Kreier, and Alan Wm. Wolff, *Steel and the State: Government Intervention and Steel's Structural Crisis* (Boulder, Colo.: Westview Press, 1988), 104, 228.

22. Leon Hollerman, "Locomotive Strategy and United States Protectionism: A Japanese View," *Pacific Affairs* 52 (1979): 196 ("export phenomenon"); *Wall Street Journal*, Aug. 11, 1977; [Eizenstat], "Memorandum of Conversation," Aug. 8, 1977, Steel CF O/A24 [3], C-286, Eizenstat; *Japan Metal Bulletin*, Sept. 20, 1975; *Nihon Keizai*, Nov. 23, 1975 (MITI warning), cited in Howell, Noellert, Kreier, and Wolff, *Steel and the State*, 227–29.

23. [Eizenstat], "Memorandum of Conversation," Aug. 8, 1977.

24. Ibid.

25. [Eizenstat], "Memorandum of Conversation," Aug. 16, 1977 (CIA quote); Wolff, "Memorandum for the Economic Policy Group," Feb. 11, 1977, both in Steel CF O/A 24 [4], C-284, Eizenstat; *Wall Street Journal*, Oct. 14, 1977 (Carter quote).

26. *Wall Street Journal*, May 13, Aug. 16, 1977; Curt Hessler, "Memorandum for the EPG Steering Committee," Steel CF O/A24 [3], C-284, Eizenstat.

27. *Wall Street Journal*, July 27, 1977; Lee Smith, "Hard Times Come to Steeltown," *Fortune*, Dec. 1977, 87–93.

28. *Fortune*, Dec. 1977, 92 (Pino); Ted Sorensen to Eizenstat and Strauss, Oct. 12, 1977, Steel CF O/A 24 [3], C-284, Eizenstat.

29. *Wall Street Journal*, Oct. 12, 1977; *Youngstown Vindicator*, Sept. 11, 22, 25 (Nordhaus and Heimlich quotes), 1977; President's News Conference, Sept. 29, 1977; "Session with a Group of Editors and News Directors," Oct. 14, 1977, in Carter, *Public Papers, 1977*, 1690, 1801 (Carter quote).

30. Blumenthal, "Memorandum for the President," Sept. 29, 1977, O/A 6343, C-284, Eizenstat.

31. Strauss, "Memorandum for the President," Dec. 27, 1977, Staff Secretary files, C-67, JC. Throughout the postwar period, agricultural exports were a priority of the government because of the political weight of agribusiness and farmers. Carter used the agriculture and high technology industries to channel discontent over the trade imbalance from "protection" to export promotion at the Tokyo Round. The results were marginal. Destler, *American Trade Politics*, 111–13.

32. Richard Rivers, Strauss's general counsel, said, "President Carter would have never stood for it." Dryden, *Trade Warriors*, 249.

33. American Embassy, Brussels, to Secretary of State, Oct. 31, 1977, attached to WHCF, CF TA4-8, JC.

34. Jack Sheehan to Lloyd McBride, Oct. 28, Dec. 29, 1977, 75/33, Leg/USWA, Penn St.; "President's News Conference," Oct. 13, 1977, in Carter, *Public Papers, 1977*, 1789; Sato and Hodin, "The U.S.-Japanese Steel Issue of 1977," 45; Charles Vanik to Jimmy Carter, Oct. 11, 1977, WHCF, CF TA4-8; Blumenthal, "Memorandum for the President," Nov. 23, 1977, C-61, Staff Secretary files, JC; Hugh Patrick and Hideo Sato, "The Political Economy of United States Japan Trade in Steel," *Policy and Trade Issues of the Japanese Economy: American and Japanese Perspectives*, ed. Kozo Yamamura (Seattle: University of Washington Press, 1982), 222–23.

35. Jack Sheehan, interview with author, May 18, 1993.

36. Eizenstat and Ginsburg, "Memorandum for the President," Nov. 30, 1977, CF O/A24 [1], C-284, Eizenstat; Congressional Budget Office, *How Federal Policies Affect the Steel Industry*, Feb. 1987, 34.

37. Eizenstat and Ginsburg, "Memorandum for the President," Nov. 30, 1977; Solomon to the President, Nov. 23, 1977, 2, WHCF, CF CM8; Alfred E. Kahn, "Memorandum for Interested Parties," Dec. 4, 1979, Steel CF O/A 731 [3], Eizenstat, all in JC; Michael Borrus, "The Politics of Competitive Erosion in the Steel Industry," *American Industry in International Competition: Government Policies and Corporate Strategies*, ed. John Zysman and Laura Tyson, (Ithaca: Cornell University Press, 1983), 95.

38. The investment provisions lowered capital gains taxes and the minimum tax on individuals claiming high deductions and exclusions. *Congressional Quarterly Almanac, 1978* 34 (1979): 233.

39. Secretary of Labor [Marshall], "Memorandum for Anthony Solomon," Nov. 14, 1977, CF O/A 24 [2], C-286, Eizenstat; Charles A. Vanik to Jimmy Carter, Sept. 30, 1977, WHCF, TA4-8, C-TA19, JC.

40. Anthony Solomon, "Report to the President: A Comprehensive Program for the Steel Industry," Dec. 1977, 9 (Carter's penned comments); Jim Smith to Sheehan, June 2, 1980, 79/27, both in Leg/USWA.

41. Ginsburg to Eizenstat, Nov. 8, 1977, CF O/A24 [3], C-286, Eizenstat.

42. See Carter's comments written on Eizenstat, "Memorandum for the President," Dec. 1, 1977; Strauss, "Memorandum for the President," Nov. 29, 1977, CF O/A 24 [2], C-284, both in Eizenstat; *Wall Street Journal*, Oct. 18, Dec. 9 (Roderick quote), 1977; Sheehan to McBride, Oct. 28, 1977, 75/22, Leg/USWA; Hans Mueller, *Steel Industry Economics: A Comparative Analysis of Structure, Conduct, and Performance* (New York: International Public Relations Co., 1978), 10; U.S. Congress, House Committee on Ways and Means, Subcommittee on Trade, *The Comprehensive Program for the Steel Industry*, 95th Cong, 2d sess., Jan. 25, 26, 1978 (Washington, D.C.: GPO, 1979), 86.

43. *Wall Street Journal*, July 19, 1978 ("capital punishment"); *Fortune*, Feb. 13, 1978, 130 ("worst is over").

44. Jack Sheehan to Lloyd McBride, Dec. 29, 1977, 75/33, Leg/USWA; Juanita Kreps and Stu Eizenstat, "Memorandum for the President," Nov. 3, 1977, O/A 6237[1]; Eizenstat, "Memorandum for the President," Dec. 14, 1977, C-291, both in Eizenstat; Margaret Weir, *Politics and Jobs: The Boundaries of Employment Policy in the United States* (Princeton: Princeton University Press, 1992), 142–43.

45. *Wall Street Journal*, Dec. 7, 1977.

46. Sheehan to McBride, Oct. 4, 1977, 75/33, Leg/USWA; Thomas G. Fuechtmann, *Steeples and Stacks: Religion and Steel Crisis in Youngstown* (Cambridge: Cambridge University Press, 1989), 32–33.

47. AISI, *Steel at the Crossroads: The American Steel Industry in the 1980s* (Washington, D.C.: American Iron and Steel Institute, Jan. 1980), 90; USWA, press release, Mar. 10, 1978, attached to James W. Smith to Charles J. Carney, Apr. 4, 1978, 77/31, Leg/USWA; Robert M. Immerman to The Ambassador [Robert Strauss], Mar. 6, 1978, WHCF, CO78, C-CO-33, JC.

48. James Smith, "Analysis of Lykes and LTV," n.d., attached to Sheehan to Howard M. Metzenbaum, July 27, 1979, 79/41, Leg/USWA; *Youngstown (Ohio) Vindicator*, Mar. 24, 1979 (YST manager); *Fortune*, July 17, 1978, 56 (Lykes family member); *Business Week*, Oct. 3, 1977, 83, 86.

49. Fuechtmann, *Steeples and Stacks*, 48–52.

50. *Wall Street Journal*, Nov. 8, 1977 (Roesch quote); *Standard NYSE Reports*, June 22, 1977; Fuechtmann, *Steeples and Stacks*, 48.

51. J. Bruce Johnston to Abel, June 17, 1976, 25/6, Abel/USWA.

52. Yves Meny and Vincent Wright, "State and Steel in Western Europe," 79; Katzenstein, *Between Power and Plenty*, 3.

53. Nixon's OMB had encouraged the creation of such regional development bodies as vehicles to receive federal funds, part of his New Federalism.

54. Edgar Speer bluntly stated "you can pump as much money . . . as you want to pump into Youngstown, Ohio. . . . With the cost of transportation there is no way [that putting money into Youngstown makes] any sense for steel." *Fortune*, Feb. 13, 1978, 128.

55. Such one-customer, one-product goods haulers were used by Inland, Granite City Steel, Kaiser, and other steel companies that were not located on water. *Iron Age*, Dec. 22, 1966, 30–31.

56. Fuechtmann, *Steeples and Stacks*, 76.

57. Terry F. Buss and F. Steven Redburn, *Shutdown at Youngstown: Public Policy for Mass Unemployment* (Albany: State University of New York Press, 1983), 182–89.

58. Staughton Lynd, *The Fight Against Shutdowns: Youngstown's Steel Mill Closings* (San Pedro, Calif.: Singlejack Books, 1982), 42.

59. *Wall Street Journal*, Dec. 16, 1977.

60. AISI, *Steel at the Crossroads*, 90.

61. James Ling lost his chairmanship in 1970 as his wizardry fell victim to the stock market descent the year before.

62. Fuechtmann, *Steeples and Stacks*, 216–17.

63. According to the 1970 consent decree, LTV could not acquire any company worth more than $100 million without Justice's permission.

64. Bruce Kirschenbaum, "Memorandum for Jack Watson," Mar. 13, 1978, WHCF, BE1, C-BE2, JC; *Wall Street Journal*, June 22, 1978; Fuechtmann, *Steeples and Stacks*, 219 (Bell quote).

65. Brief of the United Steelworkers of America, AFL-CIO to the Department of Justice with Respect to the Proposed Merger of LTV Corporation and Lykes Corporation, [1978], copy in 76/34, Leg/USWA; Jim Smith, telephone interview with author, May 6, 1993.

66. Paul W. Marshall to Robert Brandwin, June 23, 1978, 76/34, Leg/USWA; Jack H. Watson Jr. to the Most Reverend James W. Malone et al., Oct. 18, 1978, WHCF, BE4-4, C-BE23.

67. Abel and Secretary-Treasurer Walter Burke were forced to retire because of age. They supported the director of District 34, Lloyd McBride, who beat the insurgent Edward Sadlowski, the director of District 31, which included Chicago and Gary.

68. Smith to Abel, Feb. 22, 1975, 57/3, Burke/USWA.

69. *Fortune*, Feb. 13, 1978, 128; House Subcommittee, *Comprehensive Program for the Steel Industry*, 97; Frank Leseganich to Wilmer D. Mizell, May 6, 1976, 25/25; James W. Smith to Abel, May 17, 1976; Abel to Mizell, May 17, 1976; William A. Sullivan Jr. to Smith, 27/13; Leseganich to John Eden, July, 1976, 25/25, all in Abel/USWA.

70. Gene Eidenberg, "Memorandum for the Vice President," Oct. 10, 1978, WHCF, BE4-4, C-BE23, JC.

71. Watson to Gentlemen [James W. Malone and John H. Burt], May 9, 1979, WHCF, BE4-4, C-BE24, JC.

72. Smith interview; Fuechtmann, *Steeples and Stacks*, 238–39.

73. Smith to Sheehan, June 2, 1980, 79/47, Leg/USWA; Thomas Geoghegan, *Which Side Are You On?: Trying to Be for Labor When It's Flat on Its Back* (New York: Farrar, Straus and Giroux, 1991), 93 ("two yuppies").

74. On Wisconsin Steel, see David Bensman and Roberta Lynch, *Rusted Dreams: Hard Times in a Steel Community* (New York: McGraw-Hill, 1987), 39–70.

75. Geoghegan, *Which Side Are You On?*, 94.

76. Carol J. Loomis, "The Strike that Rained on Archie McCardell's Parade," *Fortune*, May 19, 1980, 91–99.

77. Smith interview; *American Metal Market*, Jan. 12, 1996.

78. *Wall Street Journal*, Sept. 23, 1980.

79. EDA provided Youngstown with a loan guarantee for a small aircraft firm, money for a sewer line, and another loan guarantee to convert former J&L property into an industrial park.

80. U.S. imports rose 120 percent from 1975 to 1979. Gail Garfield Schwartz and Pat Choate, *Being Number One: Rebuilding the U.S. Economy* (Lexington, Mass.: D. C. Heath, 1980), 38.

81. Dryden, *Trade Warriors*, 238 (Blumenthal quote); Charlie Schultze, "Memorandum for the President," July 11, 1978, C-94, Staff Secretary files, JC.

82. "United States–Japan Trade Talks," Jan. 18, 1978, Steering Committee, 1/19/78, C/A 665, C-190, Eizenstat (CIA); electronics maker cited in Walter LaFeber, *The Clash: U.S.-Japanese Relations Throughout History* (New York: W. W. Norton, 1997), 369; "Interview with the President," July 11, 1978, in Carter, *Public Papers, 1978*, 1254–55; Paul A. Volcker and Toyoo Gyohten, *Changing Fortunes: The World's Money and the Threat to American Leadership* (New York: Times Books, 1992), 368; Business Week, *The Reindustrialization of America* (New York: McGraw-Hill, 1982), 26.

Chapter Ten

1. *Wall Street Journal*, Mar. 21, 1980, June 1, 1979.
2. Ibid., Nov. 5, 18, 1979.
3. Ibid., July 22, 1980. Thus Roderick became CEO as well as chairman of the board.
4. Roderick to Eizenstat, Oct. 25, 1979, WHCF, BE3-10, C-BE39, JC; Charles Schultze, "Memorandum for the President," Nov. 28, 1979, 11/29/79 [1], C-157, Staff Secretary, JC; Ralph Schlosstein and Myles Lynk, Dec. 6, 1979, CF O/A 731 [3], C-283; Schultze to Eizenstat and Tony Solomon, 11/29/79, Steel CF O/A 731 [2], C-284, both in Eizenstat.
5. "Anti-Inflation Program," Oct. 24, 1978, in Carter, *Public Papers, 1978*, 1839–48; Locker/Abrecht Associates, "Confronting the Crisis: The Challenge for Labor," Dec. 16, 1985, 16–17, copy in possession of author.
6. Carter, *Public Papers, 1978*, 1841.
7. Ronald F. King, *Time, Money, and Politics: Investment Tax Subsidies and American Democracy* (New Haven: Yale University Press, 1993), 408.
8. Businesses were to restrain their average price increase to 0.5 percentage points below their average annual rate of increase during 1976–77.
9. George Meany concluded that the wage standard was more rigid than the one governing prices, which he did not believe would be enforced. A year later there was some agreement. Carter created a Pay Advisory Board, signing a "National Accord" with labor. Landon Butler, "Memorandum to the President," Dec. 7, 1978, WHCF, Backup Diary, Jan. 12, 1979, C-PD46; G. William Miller, "Memorandum for the President," Sept. 25, 1979, WHCF, Sept. 27, 1979, C-148, Staff Secretary, both in JC.
10. Alfred E. Kahn, "Memorandum for the President," Oct. 24, 1979, WHCF, PD-64, JC.
11. *Business Week*. June 30, 1980, 57.
12. Schultze, "Memorandum for the President," Sept. 25, 1979, 9/26/79 [2], C-148, Staff Secretary, JC; Carter, *Public Papers, 1979*, 1992; Herbert Stein, *Presidential Economics: The Making of Economic Policy from Roosevelt to Reagan and Beyond*, 2d rev. ed., (Washington, D.C.: American Enterprise Institute, 1988), 229–31.
13. Michael K. Levine, *Inside International Trade Policy Formulation: A History of the 1982 US-EC Steel Arrangements* (New York: Praeger, 1985), 14.
14. Ginsburg to Eizenstat, Jan. 13, 1980; Al McDonald to Eizenstat, Feb. 12, 1980, both in Steel CF O/A 731, C-283, Eizenstat; *Wall Street Journal*, Feb. 2, 1980.
15. Eizenstat to the President, n.d. [Jan. 1980], CF O/A 731, C-283, Eizenstat.
16. Klutznick and Askew, "Memorandum for President," n.d. [Jan. 1980]; Bob Ginsburg, "Memorandum for Stu Eizenstat," Jan. 25, 1980, both in CF O/A 731, C-283, Eizenstat. The quid pro quo for the TPM was that the industry would not file trade suits. The president believed that the removal of the TPM would bring in more steel imports, which he thought would help his anti-inflation efforts.
17. Klutznick and Askew, "Memorandum for the President," Mar. 13, 1980, 3/18/80 [1], C-176, Staff Secretary, JC.
18. Schultze, "Memorandum for the President," Mar. 17, 1980; G. William Miller, "Memorandum for the President," n.d. [Mar. 1980], both in C-176, Staff Secretary; Ginsburg to Eizenstat, Mar. 12, 1980, CF O/A 731, C-283, Eizenstat, all in JC; Leon N. Lindberg, "Models of the Inflation-Disinflation Process," in Lindberg and Maier, *Politics of Inflation and Economic Stagnation*, 36.
19. Ginsburg to Eizenstat, Mar. 12, 1980, CF O/A 731, C-283, Eizenstat; Vance, Klutznick and Askew to President, Confidential, Mar. 8, 1980; Klutznick and Askew, "What to do with the TPM," Mar. 13, 1980, 3/18/80 [1], both in C-176, Staff Secretary, JC.

20. Miller, "Memorandum for the President," with options, Mar. 14, 1980, C-176, Staff Secretary, JC; "Remarks with Editors and Broadcasters," May 13, 1980, in Carter, *Public Papers, 1980–81*, 902 (Carter quote); Askew, "Memorandum for the President," June 18, 1980, CF O/A 731 [2], C-283, Eizenstat. Steel output fell from 100 million tons in 1979 to 84 million tons in 1980. During that same time period, blue-collar employment fell from 342,000 to 291,000. Locker, "Confronting the Crisis," 19.

21. Askew, "Memorandum for the President," June 16, 1980, CF O/A 731 [2], C-283, Eizenstat (Davignon quote); *Economist*, July 12, 1980; Thomas R. Howell, William A. Noellert, Jesse G. Kreier, and Alan Wm. Wolff, *Steel and the State: Government Intervention and Steel's Structural Crisis* (Boulder, Colo: Westview Press, 1988), 81; Thomas Grunert, "Decision-Making Processes in the Steel Crisis Policy of the EEC: NeoCorporatist or Integrationist Tendencies?," in *The Politics of Steel: Western Europe and the Steel Industry in the Crisis Years (1974–1984)*, ed. Yves Meny and Vincent Wright (Berlin: Walter de Gruyter, 1987), 235.

22. If there was a surge when imports exceeded 15.2 percent and domestic producers were operating at below 86 percent of capacity, Commerce would investigate and companies would be free to file dumping suits without the threat of TPM withdrawal. The 1979 Trade Act had removed antidumping enforcement from the Treasury to a more friendly home in Commerce.

23. Ginsburg, "Memorandum for Stu Eizenstat," July 31, 1980, O/A 731 [1], C-283, Eizenstat.

24. Étienne Davignon to Reubin O. Askew, Sept. 30, 1980, WHCF, TA4-8 "8/1/80–12/31/80," C-TA-22.

25. Alan Wolff to Lloyd McBride, May 9, 1979; [Steel] Tripartite Committee Working Group on Trade, meeting, July 16, 1980, 76–77, Leg-DC/USWA.

26. Ginsburg, "Memorandum for Stu Eizenstat," July 31, 1980.

27. Carter accepted the Chrysler plan only after he was convinced that it would pass the Congress. Robert B. Reich and John D. Donahue, *New Deals: The Chrysler Revival and the American System* (New York: Times Books, 1985), 105, 129.

28. *Business Week*, June 30, 1980, 56–142; *Iron Age*, July 7, 1980, 25, 28 (Foy quote), 29 (Reuss quote); Otis L. Graham Jr., *Losing Time: The Industrial Policy Debate* (Cambridge: Harvard University Press, 1992), 46–51.

29. Graham, *Losing Time*, 17–18; OECD, *Economic Outlook Historical Statistics, 1960–1980* (Paris: OECD, 1982), table 3.7.

30. Raymond Vernon, "International Investment and International Trade in the Product Cycle," *Quarterly Journal of Economics* 80 (May 1966): 190–207. Even if the theory was valid for industries like textiles, where cheap labor is often decisive, it does not apply to steel, an industry that requires large amounts of capital and in which cheap labor is not the decisive factor. For example, despite higher labor costs, U.S steel was produced more efficiently than Japanese steel in the 1960s. This was no longer true in the 1970s, when capital became the decisive factor.

31. Ibid.; Howell, Noellert, Kreier, and Wolff, *Steel and the State*, 394–419.

32. Daniel Bell, *The Coming of Post-Industrial Society: A Century in Social Forecasting* (New York: Basic, 1973).

33. Richard B. Freeman and Lawrence F. Katz, "Rising Wage Inequality: The United States vs. Other Advanced Countries," in *Working Under Different Rules*, ed. Richard B. Freeman (New York: Russell Sage Foundation, 1994), 29–62; George Wm. Gross to Carter, Dec. 4, 1977; Jack H. Watson Jr. to Mr. Gross, Dec. 27, 1977, WHCF, LA2, C-LA2, JC.

34. OECD, *Economic Outlook Historical Statistics, 1960–1980* (Paris: OECD, 1982), table 3.7.

35. Graham, *Losing Time*, 16.

36. *Business Week*, June 30, 1980, 120.

37. *Wall Street Journal*, July 10, 1980.

38. James Fallows, "American Industry: What Ails It, How to Save It," *Atlantic Monthly*, Sept. 1980, 36, 40.

39. Steve Merrill to Chairman Cannon, May 24, 1978, Industrial Innovation DPR [Memos 2/14/78–7/19/79], C-32, Al Stern papers, JC.

40. Gail Garfield Schwartz and Pat Choate, *Being Number One: Rebuilding the U.S. Economy* (Lexington, Mass.: D. C. Heath, 1980), 65–87. Schwartz and Choate believed that policies addressing people or places were misplaced. Often, they argued, urban problems were due to the economic problems of a city's leading industries. Fixing industry problems would help people and places more than "urban development" or individual assistance.

41. "The Reindustrialization of America," *Business Week*, June 30, 1980, 134.

42. David Vogel, *Fluctuating Fortunes: The Political Power of Business in America* (New York: Basic, 1989), 231–33.

43. Gar Alperovitz and Jeff Faux, "Who Is to Take Which Bitter Pill?," *New York Times*, Aug. 4, 1980. Four years later, Alperovitz and Faux published *Rebuilding America* (New York: Pantheon, 1984). Its strength was its focus on the energy, food, health care, and housing sources of the inflation of the 1970s. But it evaded manufacturing problems and embodied an abstract notion of planning. While putting in a good word for consensual relations in other nations, they resisted encouraging such relations in the United States, a telltale sign of lingering New Left sensibilities and distrust of unions. Thus, they had no social base for their ideas. Ronald E. Müller's *Revitalizing America* (New York: Simon and Schuster, 1980) likewise stressed process. Although Müller recognized the domestic economic problems, he stressed the impact of OPEC oil price rises on third world countries, not on the U.S. The first major statement from the generation of the 1960s was Barry Bluestone and Bennett Harrison's *The Deindustrialization of America: Plant Closings, Community Abandonment and the Dismantling of Basic Industry* (New York: Basic, 1982).

44. Arnie Packer, "Memorandum for Stuart Eizenstat," Oct. 12, 1979, WHCF, LA, C-LA2, JC; Graham, *Losing Time*, 39 (CEA and Solomon quotes); Margaret Weir, *Politics and Jobs: The Boundaries of Employment Policy in the United States* (Princeton: Princeton University Press, 1992), 126.

45. Herbert Stein, *Presidential Economics: The Making of Economic Policy from Roosevelt to Reagan and Beyond*, 2d rev. ed., (Washington, D.C.: American Enterprise Institute, 1988), 229–31; OMB review, attached to Josh Gotbaum to Eizenstat, June 2, 1980, CF O/A 728, C-224, Eizenstat.

46. Eizenstat, "Memorandum for the President," May 24, 1980, WHCF, CF BE4, C-BE13, JC.

47. "Statement by the AFL-CIO Executive Council on Reindustrialization," Aug. 1980, ibid; White House press release, "Economic Program for the Eighties," Aug. 28, 1980, 8/28/80 [1], C-201, Staff Secretary, JC.

48. Carter, *Public Papers, 1980–81*, 1585–91; Landon Butler, "Memorandum to the President," Aug. 24, 1980, 8/25/80 [1], C-201, Staff Secretary, JC (Kirkland quote).

49. Carter, *Public Papers, 1980–81*, 1585–91.

50. OMB, "Review of Industrial Policy", attached to Gotbaum to Eizenstat, June 2, 1980, CF O/A 728, C-224, Eizenstat.

51. Ed Ayoub statement, "Working Group on Modernization," June 18, 1980, 47, STAC, Leg-DC/USWA.

52. AISI, "A New Policy for Steel," Dec. 7, 1979, "Steel 12/79–2/81, C-112, Lloyd C. Cutler papers, JC; STAC, "To the President," Sept. 25, 1980, CF O/A 731 [4], C-283, Eizenstat.

53. "American Steel Industry," Sept. 30, 1980, in Carter, *Public Papers, 1980–81*, 1959–69.

54. George Eads, "Memo for Charlie Schultze and Stu Eizenstat," Aug. 8, 1980, CF O/A731, C-283, Eizenstat; Schultze, "Memorandum for Stu Eizenstat," July 30, 1980, WHCF, BE3-10, C-BE9, JC; Lloyd Cutler, "Memorandum for the President," Aug. 26, 1980, 8/25/80 [1], C-201, Staff Secretary, JC; New York Times, Sept. 29, 1980; David Vogel, National Styles of Regulation: Environmental Policy in Great Britain and the United States (Ithaca: Cornell University Press, 1986).

55. Eizenstat and Gotbaum, "Memorandum for the President," Sept. 26, 1980, copy in "Steel," C-112, Lloyd C. Cutler papers, JC.

56. Only 6.5 percent of CETA's training money was available without means testing. C. Michael Aho and Thomas O. Bayard, "Costs and Benefits of Trade Adjustment Assistance," in The Structure and Evolution of Recent U.S. Trade Policy, ed. Robert E. Baldwin and Anne O. Krueger, (Chicago: University of Chicago Press, 1984), 184.

57. Weir, Politics and Jobs, 124–25; Trevor Bain, Banking the Furnace: Restructuring of the Steel Industry in Eight Countries (Kalamazoo, Mich.: W. E. Upjohn Institute, 1992), 128.

58. The same logic propelled Carter's auto policy. His auto task force told him that if imports were restrained, 100,000 unemployed workers might find jobs. However, he was more convinced by a prediction that such restraints would add $1 billion to consumer costs, worsening inflation. Dryden, Trade Warriors, 262.

59. Schultze, "Memorandum for the President," Aug. 24, 1980, 8/28/80 [4], C-202, Staff Secretary, JC.

60. Schultze to Peace, Oct. 15, 1980, 3/18/80 [1], C-176, Staff Secretary, JC.

61. Elizabeth Drew, Portrait of an Election: The 1980 Presidential Campaign (New York: Simon and Schuster, 1981), 250.

62. Ibid., 259; Burton I. Kaufman, The Presidency of James Earl Carter Jr. (Lawrence: University Press of Kansas, 1993), 194–95; Carter, Public Papers, 1980–81, 1537.

63. Smith to Sheehan, June 2, 1980, 69/47, Leg/USWA. Smith's predictions were in the right direction, although he overestimated the decline in capacity and underestimated the size of the employment losses. See Chapter 11 below and Bernard Keeling, World Steel: A New Assessment of Trends and Prospects (London: Economic Intelligent Unit, 1988), 42, 67.

64. Smith and Ed Ayoub to McBride, Feb. 11, 1981, 80/29, Leg/USWA.

65. Sheehan to McBride, Sept. 25, 1981, 80/18, Leg/USWA.

66. Carter, Public Papers, 1978, 1550; Marshall and Strauss, "Memorandum for the President," May 8, 1978, O/A 6245, C-231, Eizenstat.

67. Jim Smith, interview with author, Feb. 12, 1995.

68. Wall Street Journal, Sept. 18, 1980.

69. Thomas Byrne Edsall, The New Politics of Inequality (New York: W. W. Norton, 1984), 184, 187.

70. For a parallel formulation of the alternatives facing the British Labour party, see David Coates, "New Labour or Old," New Left Review 219 (1996): 62–88.

Chapter Eleven

1. Cited in Thomas R. Howell, William A. Noellert, Jesse G. Kreier, Alan Wm. Wolff, Steel and the State: Government Intervention and Steel's Structural Crisis (Boulder, Colo.: Westview Press, 1988), 493.

2. Economic Strategy Institute (ESI), Can the Phoenix Survive? The Fall and Rise of the American Steel Industry (Washington, D.C.: ESI, 1994), 61–62; American Metal Market, Nov. 19, 1985 (Yeutter quote); Stephen C. Cohen and John Zysman, Manufacturing Matters: The Myth of the Post-Industrial Society (New York: Basic, 1987), 74–75.

3. Reagan, Public Papers, 1981, 549–50, 554, 565–66, 746. On July 17, Reagan staged a Rose

Garden signing of a law giving the industry extra time to comply with the Clean Air Act, another move designed to free more industry capital for investment. Ibid., 632.

4. The steel industry's profit rate in 1980 was 1.8 percent. Thus, for the investment tax credit to be of any use it would have to be refundable.

5. *Wall Street Journal*, Oct. 27, 1981; *Journal of Commerce*, May 28, 1981.

6. David Roderick statement, U.S. Senate, Committee on the Judiciary, Hearings, *The Domestic Steel Industry and the Antitrust Laws*, 98th Cong., 1st sess. (Washington, D.C.: GPO, 1983), 27; *Wall Street Journal*, Mar. 3, 12, Apr. 19 (Ogawa quote), 1981; *American Metal Market*, Mar. 13, 1981.

7. In 1981, 60 percent of Japanese steel was continuously cast, compared with 22 percent in the United States. Donald F. Barnett and Louis Schorsch, *Steel: Upheaval in a Basic Industry* (Cambridge, Mass.: Ballinger, 1983), 126; *Wall Street Journal*, Apr. 2, 1981.

8. "President's News Conference," Jan. 19, 1982, in Reagan, *Public Papers, 1982*, 41–42; *Wall Street Journal*, Oct. 21, 1982.

9. The strong dollar, which persisted despite the trade deficits, accompanied by an expansive fiscal policy, which ballooned the federal debt. Foreign-held dollars were pulled in by the high real interest rates created by the Fed's tight monetary policy.

10. Ingo Walter, "Structural Adjustment and Trade Policy in the International Steel Industry," in *Trade Policy in the 1980s*, ed. William R. Cline (Washington, D.C.: Institute for International Economics, 1983), 512; Garth L. Mangum and R. Scott McNabb, *The Rise, Fall, and Replacement of Industrywide Bargaining in the Basic Steel Industry* (Armonk, N.Y.: M. E. Sharpe, 1997), 64; *Wall Street Journal*, Oct. 2, 1981, Mar. 1, 1982; *American Metal Market*, July 23, 1981.

11. *American Metal Market*, June 18, 1982. Volcker yielded a bit in the summer, but in late 1983 and 1984 he tightened the money supply again, causing interest rates to rise.

12. *Wall Street Journal*, Apr. 27, 1982; *American Metal Market*, Oct. 15, 1982.

13. Senate Committee, *Domestic Steel Industry and the Antitrust Laws*, 50.

14. About 38 percent of the relief of the 1981 law was removed in 1982. Congressional Budget Office, *How Federal Policies Affect the Steel Industry* (Washington, D.C.: GPO, 1987), 16, 21–23; Charls E. Walker, "The Treasury Tax Reform Plan," in *Technology and Economic Policy*, ed. Ralph Landau and Dale W. Jorgenson (Cambridge, Mass: Ballinger, 1986), 319.

15. Cathie J. Martin, *Shifting the Burden* (Chicago: University of Chicago Press, 1991), 127; Donald Trautlein statement, Senate, Hearings, *Domestic Steel Industry and the Antitrust Laws*, 68; *American Metal Market*, May 24, 1984.

16. Jeffrey H. Birnbaum and Alan S. Murray, *Showdown at Gucci Gulch: Lawmakers, Lobbyists, and the Unlikely Triumph of Tax Reform* (New York: Random House, 1987), 61 (Regan quote), 47 (aide quote).

17. Cathie Martin bases this figure on the government study written by Don Fullerton, Yolanda Henderson, and James Mackie, "Investment Allocation and Growth under the Tax Reform Act of 1986," in *Compendium of Tax Research 1987* (Washington, D.C.: GPO, 1987). The law ended the investment tax credit but provided a transition rule for steel, which yielded a $500 million refund in unused investment tax credits. Birnbaum and Murray, *Showdown at Gucci Gulch*, 242.

18. Otis L. Graham Jr., *Losing Time: The Industrial Policy Debate* (Cambridge: Harvard University Press, 1992), 167; Martin, *Shifting the Burden*, 163–67. William Greider made the same point in *Secrets of the Temple: How the Federal Reserve Runs the Country* (New York: Simon and Schuster, 1987), 597–98.

19. Ann Reilly, "A Tax Bill That Hits Investment," *Fortune*, Dec. 23, 1985, 106.

20. Birnbaum and Murray, *Showdown at Gucci Gulch*, 239.

21. Paul Krugman, *Peddling Prosperity: Economic Sense and Nonsense in the Age of Dimin-*

ished Expectations (New York: W. W. Norton, 1994), 126, 157–58; Robert A. Blecker, *Beyond the Twin Deficits: A Trade Strategy for the 1990s* (Armonk, N.Y.: M. E. Sharpe, 1992), 52–53.

22. William A. Niskanen, *Reaganomics: An Insider's Account of the Policies and the People* (New York: Oxford University Press, 1988), 137–38; Reagan, *Public Papers, 1983,* 1135; I. M. Destler, *American Trade Politics: System Under Stress* (Washington, D.C.: Institute for International Economics, 1986), 200.

23. Steve Dryden, *Trade Warriors: USTR and the American Crusade for Free Trade* (New York: Oxford University Press, 1995), 270; Destler, *American Trade Politics,* 71–72.

24. *American Metal Market,* Jan. 8, 1982; Howell, Noellert, Kreier, and Wolff, *Steel and the State,* 69; Richard I. Korkland Jr., "Steel's Subtle Grab for Quotas," *Fortune,* Feb. 8, 1982, 26–48; Destler, *American Trade Politics,* 128.

25. Korkland, "Steel's Subtle Grab for Quotas," 46 (Tumlir and Davignon quotes); *American Metal Market,* Aug. 5, Nov. 9, 1981, Aug. 24, 1984; *Wall Street Journal,* Dec. 29, 1983.

26. Graham, *Losing Time,* 217.

27. Stephen Woolcock, "US-European Trade Relations," *International Affairs* 58 (Autumn 1982): 610–11; Gary N. Norlick, "American Trade Law and the Steel Pact Between Brussels and Washington," *World Economy* 6 (Sept. 1983): 357–62; Destler, "The Evolution of Reagan Foreign Policy," in *The Reagan Presidency: An Early Assessment,* ed. Fred I. Greenstein (Baltimore: Johns Hopkins University Press, 1983), 145–50.

28. *American Metal Market,* Oct. 20, 1982; "Letter to the Secretary of the Treasury on the European Communities Steel Export Arrangement," Oct. 21, 1982, in Reagan, *Public Papers, 1982,* 1362; *Wall Street Journal,* Oct. 22, 1982.

29. Lynn Williams, "Statement to Steel Advisory Committee," Dec. 6, 1983, Leg-DC/USWA; *Wall Street Journal,* May 18, 1982.

30. Barnett and Schorsch, *Steel,* 49.

31. Three U.S. companies—Westinghouse, Koppers, and Blaw Knox—supplied and financed the machinery for Posco. *Iron Age,* June 15, 1967, 23; *Financial Times,* Nov. 27, 1997.

32. Nancy Bernkopf Tucker, "Threats, Opportunities, and Frustrations in East Asia," *Lyndon Johnson Confronts the World: American Foreign Policy, 1963–1968* (Cambridge: Cambridge University Press, 1994), 131; Blecker, *Beyond the Twin Deficits,* 102–3; Howell, Noellert, Kreier, and Wolff, *Steel and the State,* 286–307; *American Metal Market,* Jan. 5, Mar. 1, 1984.

33. Between 1973 and 1987, Brazil's annual steel output more than tripled, rising from 7.1 to 22.2 million tons. Howell, Noellert, Kreier, and Wolff, *Steel and the State,* 527. Steel was the key industry reflecting Brazil's shift from import substitution to exporting.

34. Senate Committee, *Domestic Steel Industry and the Antitrust Laws,* 6 (Specter/Regan exchange); *Wall Street Journal,* July 6, 1983, May 14, 1984 (Brazilian minister).

35. *American Metal Market,* May 9, 1984; *Wall Street Journal,* Dec. 20, 1983.

36. *American Metal Market,* Feb. 1, 1985; Locker/Abrecht Associates, "Confronting the Crisis: The Challenge for Labor," Dec. 16, 1985, 19, copy in possession of author. Presidents make escape clause decisions, which inevitably bring in broader interests. In contrast, antidumping and countervailing duty proceedings are made on a case-by-case basis by the U.S. International Trade Commission and the Commerce Department, which are both more insulated from politics and less comprehensive.

37. *American Metal Market,* Sept. 13, 1984.

38. Office of USTR, press release, Sept. 1984, Leg-DC/USWA; Niskanen, *Reaganomics,* 141–44.

39. *Wall Street Journal,* May 25, 1982.

40. U.S. Congress, JEC, Hearings, *Industrial Policy,* 98th Cong., 1st sess. (Washington, D.C.: GPO, 1983), pt. 1: 103 (hereafter JEC, *Industrial Policy*).

41. "National Industrial Strategy Act," n.d. [1983], 82/1, Leg/USWA; *Congressional Quarterly*, Aug. 20, 1983, 1679–87.

42. JEC, *Industrial Policy*, 229–30, 250.

43. Ibid., 246.

44. *Economic Report of the President, 1984*, 87–111 (quote on 106).

45. JEC, *Industrial Policy*, pt. 3: 2, 4, 7, 96 (Schultze quote); pt. 1: 176 (Eisner); *Fortune*, Oct. 31, 1983, 56 (Tobin).

46. JEC, *Industrial Policy*, pt. 1: 277, 312, 327, 334.

47. Reagan, *Public Papers, 1983*, 1125–26, 926–27; *American Metal Market*, Aug. 6, 1984.

48. He was the only union leader ever to head the Industrial Relations Research Association, which he did in 1994.

49. Lynn Williams to Local Union Presidents, Oct. 24, 1984, 2883/3, District 35.

50. Sheehan to McBride, Sept. 12, 1983, Leg-DC/USWA; *American Metal Market*, Jan. 18, 1984 (Niskanen quote); William Brock to Don J. Pease, Jan. 11, 1985, Leg-DC/USWA.

51. Don Pease to Sam Gibbons, Mar. 29, 1985; Skip Hartquist to David Hartquist, Mar. 7, 1985, Leg-DC/USWA; Destler, *American Trade Politics*, 86–87.

52. One item the Reagan administration wanted was the renewal of the preferences for NICs established in the 1974 trade act. While most legislators supported the preferences, some wanted South Korea, Taiwan, and Hong Kong excluded because they were already developed. In the end, the three retained their status as NICs. Destler, *American Trade Politics*, 223–37.

53. *Trade and Tariff Act of 1984*, 98th Cong., 2d sess., 95–96; Brock to Pease, Jan. 11, 1985, Leg-DC/USWA; *Wall Street Journal*, Aug. 21, 1984.

54. Paul A. Volcker and Toyoo Gyohten, *Changing Fortunes: The World's Money and the Threat to American Leadership* (New York: Times Books, 1992), 270.

55. Senate, Hearings, *Domestic Steel Industry and the Antitrust Laws*, 28–29 (Roderick); JEC, *Industrial Policy*, 20 (Adams). Adams had worked with Carter's Labor Department on identifying targets for industrial development. Such initiatives were off the table during the 1980s. *Business Week*, June 30, 1980, 121.

56. Senate, Hearings, *Domestic Steel Industry and the Antitrust Laws*, 36–48.

57. *Wall Street Journal*, May 27, 1983.

58. Jeffrey A. Hart, *Rival Capitalists: International Competitiveness in the United States, Japan, and Western Europe* (Ithaca: Cornell University Press, 1992), 152–55.

59. *American Metal Market*, July 12, 1984; *Wall Street Journal*, Feb. 18, 1982, July 28, 1983; Jim Smith, interview with author, Feb. 12, 1995; Edgar Ball, interview with author, Feb. 13, 1995.

60. *Wall Street Journal*, July 28, 1983.

61. William T. Hogan, *Global Steel in the 1990s: Growth or Decline* (Lexington, Mass.: Lexington Books, 1991), 19–20; *American Metal Market*, Feb. 3, Mar. 15, 1984.

62. *Wall Street Journal*, Feb. 16, 1984.

63. Ibid., Feb. 17 (steel executives), Mar. 19 (Baldrige), 1984; *American Metal Market*, Mar. 12, 1984 (Williams).

64. *Wall Street Journal*, Feb. 21, 1984.

65. Ibid., June 13, 1984; U.S. Congress, Office of Technology Assessment, *Multinationals and the National Interest: Playing By Different Rules* (Washington, D.C.: GPO, 1993), 128.

66. *London Financial Times*, Feb. 1, 1995; Sheehan to Niskanen, July 30, 1984, Leg-DC/USWA.

67. Hogan, *Global Steel in the 1990s*, 48.

68. *Wall Street Journal*, July 3, 1983.

69. "Interview with Thomas J. Usher," Locker Associates, *Steel Industry Update/Special*

Report No. 1, 1 (in possession of author); Congressional Budget Office, *How Federal Policies Affect the Steel Industry*, 39.

70. Robert Gilpin argued that Japanese foreign investment increased Japanese exports while U.S. foreign investment replaced U.S. exports, by establishing production abroad. This explained why the U.S. trade deficit with Japan increased even as Japanese investment in the U.S. rose. "Where Does Japan Fit In?" *Millennium: Journal of International Studies* 18 (1989): 337.

71. *American Metal Market*, Oct. 8, 1982, Aug. 29, Apr. 26, Oct. 11, 1984.

72. Hogan, *Global Steel in the 1990s*, 17–18; *American Metal Market*, Dec. 6, 1995, Feb. 7, 1996; John Holusha, "Having Done it All in Steel, He's on Top at Last," *New York Times*, Feb. 12, 1995.

73. OTA, *Multinationals and the National Interest*, 82; *American Metal Market*, Jan. 20, 1995 (NKK president quote).

74. Barnett and Schorsch, *Steel*, 52–53.

75. *Iron Age*, Nov. 23, 1967; "Steel: Recasting an Industry Under Stress," *Fortune*, Mar. 1971, 74–77 (quote on 77).

76. Barnett and Schorsch, *Steel*, 286; *American Metal Market*, Oct. 22, 1984; *Wall Street Journal*, Oct. 22, 1982; Hogan, *Global Steel in the 1990s*, 34 (Garvey quote).

77. Seth Lubove, "When Success Breeds Problems," *Forbes*, Apr. 12, 1993, 84–85; Michael Piore and Charles Sabel, *The Second Industrial Divide* (New York: Basic, 1984); Christoph Scherrer, "Mini-Mills: A New Growth Path for the U.S. Steel Industry?," *Journal of Economic Issues* 22 (Dec. 1988): 1191.

78. Robert S. Ahlbrandt, Richard J. Fruehan, Frank Giarratani, *The Renaissance of American Steel: Lesson for Managers in Competitive Industries* (New York: Oxford University Press, 1996), 50–51; *American Metal Market*, May 25, 1995; *Wall Street Journal*, Nov. 1, 1995.

79. Locker Associates, *Steel Industry Update/103*, Feb. 1996; *American Metal Market*, July 9, 1996.

80. *Business Week*, June 2, 1997, 39.

81. Trevor Bain, *Banking the Furnace: Restructuring of the Steel Industry in Eight Countries* (Kalamazoo, Mich.: W. E. Upjohn Institute, 1992), 20; Bernard Keeling, *World Steel: A New Assessment of Trends and Prospects* (London: Economic Intelligence Unit, 1988), 37–38, 66–67; AMM Online, Weekly Steel Analysis, Mar. 20, 1998.

82. John Hoerr, *And The Wolf Finally Came: The Decline of the American Steel Industry* (Pittsburgh: University of Pittsburgh Press, 1988), 14. Hoerr was one of the *Business Week* writers who put together the magazine's influential "reindustrialization" issue in June 1980. His view that USWA labor relations were adversarial conflicts with the consensus among labor historians, who generally have characterized the relations as bureaucratized and accommodating. See, for example, Nelson Lichtenstein, *Labor's War at Home: The CIO in World War II* (Cambridge: Cambridge University Press, 1982), 233–45. Neither Hoerr nor Lichtenstein analyzes the way the state shapes labor relations either in general or through its policies affecting the sector.

83. *Wall Street Journal*, Mar. 17, 1982.

84. *American Metal Market*, Oct. 26, 1982.

85. *Wall Street Journal*, July 30, 1982.

86. Ibid., Jan. 27, 1983.

87. In addition to Wheeling, McLouth, Weirton, Newport, LTV, Geneva, California, and Gulf States were all restructured by bankruptcy courts.

88. By 1987, PBGC was in financial trouble because of the steel crisis; 75 percent of its $4 billion deficit was attributed to underfunded steel pension liabilities. Health plans were also in jeopardy. *Wall Street Journal*, Aug. 20, 1987.

89. Mike Locker, interview with author, Feb. 23, 1996.

90. Locker/Abrecht Associates, "Confronting the Crisis," 51.

91. Krugman, *Peddling Prosperity*, 127.

92. *(Chicago) In These Times*, Oct. 30–Nov. 12, 1995.

93. Walter LaFeber, *The Clash: U.S.-Japanese Relations Throughout History* (New York: W. W. Norton, 1997), 376–79; *Economic Report of the President, 1984*, 106.

94. Douglas A. Irwin, "Trade Politics and the Semiconductor Industry," in *The Political Economy of American Trade Policy*, ed. Anne O. Krueger (Chicago: University of Chicago Press, 1996), 11–66.

95. *Congressional Quarterly*, June 23, 1984, 1489.

96. Andrew R. Dick observed that a 1984 conference in Washington, D.C., on strategic trade policy presented government officials with new views about industrial linkages, learning curves, and other ideas that altered somewhat traditional free trade theory. "Comment" in Irwin, "Trade Politics and the Semiconductor Industry," 68.

97. Graham, *Losing Time*, 224–27.

98. Lester Thurow, *The Case for Industrial Policies* (Washington, D.C.: Center for National Policy, 1984), 6; Michael Borrus, James E. Millstein, and John Zysman, "Trade and Development in the Semiconductor Industry: Japanese Challenge and American Response," in *American Industry in International Competition: Government Policies and Corporate Strategies*, ed. John Zysman and Laura Tyson (Ithaca: Cornell University Press, 1983), 239; Borrus, "The Politics of Competitive Erosion in the U.S. Steel Industry," in Zysman and Tyson, *American Industry in International Competition*, 60–105.

99. Cohen and Zysman, *Manufacturing Matters*, 5, 13–14. More recently, James K. Galbraith and Paulo Du Pin Calmon have questioned the separation of the manufacturing and service sectors on the basis of wages. They point out that wage rates in services correlate with those of their manufacturing partners. Thus, wages at auto dealerships move with those in auto manufacturing. Service workers in communication make good wages because those who manufacture equipment do. On the other hand, both garment workers and garment sellers make low wages. Galbraith and Calmon, "Industries, Trade, and Wages," in *Understanding American Economic Decline*, ed. Michael A. Bernstein and David E. Adler (Cambridge: Cambridge University Press, 1994), 161–98.

100. Peter Peterson, "The Morning After," *Atlantic Monthly*, Oct. 1987, 43–50ff. The most popular jeremiad was Paul Kennedy's *The Rise and Fall of the Great Powers* (New York: Random House, 1987).

101. By 1995, it was down to 4.2 man-hours. *American Metal Market*, May 19, 1995.

102. The latest version is Robert S. Ahlbrandt, Richard J. Fruehan, and Frank Giarratani, *The Renaissance of American Steel: Lessons for Managers in Competitive Industries* (New York: Oxford University Press, 1996).

103. Mangum and McNabb, *Industrywide Bargaining in the Steel Industry*, 176; ESI, *Can the Phoenix Survive?*, 86–89, 258.

104. *Wall Street Journal*, Feb. 10, 1995; *New York Times*, Mar. 13, 1996; *American Metal Market*, July 9, 1996. In 1997, U.S. steel consumption was about 122 million tons, compared to 88 million in 1991 and 100 million in 1994. Still, imported steel has kept pace, accounting for 25 percent of this buoyant domestic market (AMM Online, Weekly Steel Analysis, Mar. 20, 1998).

105. ESI, *Can the Phoenix Survive?*, 121–22; *American Metal Market*, July 27, 1993.

106. *American Metal Market*, Apr. 14, 1997; *Financial Times*, Nov. 13, 1997.

107. Ibid., May 5, July 1, 1997; Mar. 18, 1998.

108. *Wall Street Journal*, Nov. 22, 1995; *Economist*, Dec. 20, 1997, 153.

109. *American Metal Market*, Apr. 11, 1997.

110. William Greider, *One World, Ready or Not: The Manic Logic of Global Capitalism* (New York: Simon and Schuster, 1997), 91.

111. Ibid., 101.

112. OTA, *Multinationals and the National Interest*, 30; Robert B. Reich, *The Work of Nations: Preparing Ourselves for 21st Century Capitalism* (New York: A. A. Knopf, 1991); OTA, *Multinationals and the U.S. Technology Base: Summary of the Multinationals Final Report* (Washington, D.C.: GPO, 1994), 2.

113. Greider, *One World, Ready or Not*, 206–7.

114. Lawrence Mishel and David M. Frankel, *The State of Working America* (New York: M. E. Sharpe, 1991), 105, 111.

115. Greider, *One World, Ready or Not*, 218.

116. Cohen and Zysman, *Manufacturing Matters*, 56.

117. *American Metal Market*, Dec. 6, 27, 1995.

118. Mishel and Frankel, *State of Working America*, 113; *New York Times*, Sept. 25, 1992.

119. John Judis, "The Contract with K Street," *New Republic*, Dec. 4, 1995, 22; Lester Thurow, "Why Their World Might Crumble," *New York Times Magazine*, Nov. 19, 1995, 78. There is some evidence that family income by 1997 is reaching the 1989 level. Jeff Madrick, "In the Shadows of Prosperity," *New York Review of Books*, Aug. 14, 1997, 40.

120. In 1994 the Federal Reserve Bank in Kansas City published a study claiming that a jobless rate below 6 percent would accelerate wage and price inflation. From 1994 to 1996 the rate hovered about 5.5 percent, which has become the new consensus. As I write in 1997, the rate is about 4.8 percent with no inflation. Despite these errors, the prestige of the Federal Reserve has never been higher.

121. Unfortunately for the president, the ITC found that all four nations were dumping. Nevertheless, Clinton negotiated quotas instead of imposing antidumping penalties, so that the four nations could keep a toehold in the U.S. market. *American Metal Market*, Dec. 4, 1997.

122. *Economist*, Nov. 22, 1997, 119.

123. *New York Times*, Jan. 21, 1997.

Conclusion

1. On liberalism, see Louis Hartz, *The Liberal Tradition in America* (New York: Harcourt, Brace and World, 1955); on the power of classes, Peter Gourevitch, *Politics in Hard Times: Comparative Responses to International Economic Crises* (Ithaca: Cornell University Press, 1986). Jeffrey A. Hart, *Rival Capitalists: International Competitiveness in the United States, Japan, and Western Europe* (Ithaca: Cornell University Press, 1992) addresses state-class relationships.

2. Alan Brinkley, *The End of Reform: New Deal Liberalism in Recession and War* (New York: Alfred A. Knopf, 1995).

3. Ibid., 269.

4. The "monopoly" indictment is a polemical formulation of oligopoly and administrative price analysis. For a critique of this view, see Chapter 1 and Michael A. Bernstein, "Why the Great Depression Was Great: Toward a New Understanding of the Interwar Economic Crisis in the United States," in *The Rise and Fall of the New Deal Order, 1930–1980*, ed. Steve Fraser and Gary Gerstle (Princeton: Princeton University Press, 1989), 32–54. Thomas Goebel challenges the primacy of antimonopolism in the New Deal by noting that "[Thurman] Arnold's crusade was also without much popular support." Goebel, "The Political Economy of Populism from Jackson to the New Deal," *Studies in American Political Development* 11 (Spring 1997): 145.

5. For example, after the war Thurman Arnold set up a Washington law firm that represented "the business interests he had attacked during wartime." Laura Kalman, *Abe Fortas: A Biography* (New Haven: Yale University Press, 1990), 126.

6. Peter B. Evans, Dietrich Rueschemeyer, and Theda Skocpol, eds., *Bringing the State Back In* (Cambridge: Cambridge University Press, 1985).

7. Brinkley relies heavily on Steve Fraser's biography *Labor Will Rule: Sidney Hillman and the Rise of American Labor* (New York: Free Press, 1991) and Nelson Lichtenstein's *Labor's War At Home: The CIO in World War II* (Cambridge: Cambridge University Press, 1982). For a critique of this common view that labor simply accommodated to state and corporate power, see David Plotke's *Building a Democratic Political Order: Reshaping American Liberalism in the 1930s and 1940s* (Cambridge: Cambridge University Press, 1996).

8. Brinkley, *End of Reform*, 234.

9. Brinkley's thesis, too, suffers from the tendency of many authors to argue that "their" subject or period is decisive. The book addresses the period of the 1930s and 1940s but not the subsequent decades.

10. Jeffrey A. Hart's title *Rival Capitalists* reveals this position. Michel Albert's *Capitalism vs. Capitalism* (New York: Four Wall Eight Windows, 1993) is a French businessman's version of these ideas.

11. Colin Gordon has made a brave effort to preserve the consensus by acknowledging business's failure to obtain its objectives but attributing it to disorganization and short-sightedness. "The ruling class rules, but not very well," he concludes. Then, he erects a new test and asks whether the challenges to "business privilege" have ever "over the long haul, really contested business power." His first conclusion is wordplay, the second merely a rhetorical question. Colin Gordon, "Does the Ruling Class Rule?," *Reviews in American History* 25 (June 1997): 288–93.

12. Thus, Nelson Lichtenstein makes too much of the failure of the UAW to control auto prices in his magnificent biography *The Most Dangerous Man in Detroit: Walter Reuther and the Fate of American Labor* (New York: Basic, 1995). Although Lichtenstein argues on the one hand that such failures, and the failures of collective bargaining in general, doomed reform, he ultimately concludes that it was the economics and politics of the 1970s, not Reuther's policies, that doomed labor and liberalism.

13. Plotke, *Building a Democratic Political Order*, 188–89.

14. For a critique of the notion that the strength of one class necessarily means the weakness of another, see Goran Therborn, "Why Some Classes Are More Successful than Others," *New Left Review* 138 (Mar.–Apr. 1983): 37–55.

15. Karen Orren, "Union Politics and Postwar Liberalism in the United States, 1946–1979," *Studies in American Political Development* 1 (1986): 215–52.

16. Andrew Shonfield, *Modern Capitalism* (London: Oxford University Press, 1965).

17. David Vogel, *Kindred Strangers: The Uneasy Relationship Between Business and Politics in America* (Princeton: Princeton University Press, 1996.)

18. James P. Smith and Finis R. Welch, "Black Economic Progress after Myrdal," *Journal of Economic Literature* 27 (1989): 519–64; *Daily Labor Report*, Feb. 11, 1974, B1–B6.

19. Thomas Byrne Edsall and Mary D. Edsall, *Chain Reaction: The Impact of Race, Rights, and Taxes on American Politics* (New York: Norton, 1991); Jonathan Reider, *Canarsie: The Jews and Italians of Brooklyn Against Liberalism* (Cambridge: Harvard University Press, 1985); Allen Matusow, *The Unraveling of America: A History of Liberalism in the 1960s* (New York: Harper, 1984); Dan T. Carter, *The Politics of Rage: George Wallace, the Origins of the New Conservatism, and the Transformation of American Politics* (New York: Simon and Schuster, 1995).

20. William Julius Wilson, *The Truly Disadvantaged: The Inner City, the Underclass, and Public Policy* (Chicago: University of Chicago Press, 1987), 135.

21. Kim McQuaid, *Uneasy Partners: Big Business in American Politics, 1945–1990* (Baltimore: Johns Hopkins University Press, 1994), 42.

22. David Vogel, *Fluctuating Fortunes: The Political Power of Business in America* (New York: Basic, 1989), 162; George Eads, "Memorandum for Charlie Schultze and Stu Eizenstat," CF O/A731, C-293, Eizenstat, JC.

23. Vogel, *Fluctuating Fortunes*, 93–112.

24. Robert Kuttner, *Everything for Sale: The Virtues and Limits of Markets* (New York: Alfred A. Knopf, 1997), 89.

25. See George Lipsitz, *A Life in the Struggle: Ivory Perry and the Culture of Opposition* (Philadelphia: Temple University Press, 1988).

26. Kuttner's *Everything For Sale* contains a good discussion and critique of the intellectual buttress to contemporary economic practice.

27. George Gilder, *Wealth and Poverty* (New York: Basic, 1981).

28. The best example was Charles Murray's *Losing Ground: American Social Policy, 1950–1980* (New York: Basic, 1984).

29. Kim Clark, "These *Are* the Good Old Days," *Fortune*, June 9, 1997, 74.

30. *New York Times*, June 29, 1997.

31. *Economist*, Oct. 25–31, 1997, 115.

32. Lawrence Mishel, "Capital's Gain," *American Prospect*, July–Aug. 1997, 71–73; Andrew Hacker, *Money: Who Has How Much and Why* (New York: Scribner, 1997); Barry Bluestone and Bennett Harrison, "Why We Can Grow Faster," *American Prospect*, Sept.–Oct. 1997, 64.

33. Stephen Roach, "Angst in Global Village," *Financial Times*, July 3, 1997.

34. Dani Rodrik, *Has Globalization Gone Too Far?* (Washington, D.C.: Institute for International Economics, 1997).

35. Jagdish Bhagwati, "Free Trade without Treaties," *Wall Street Journal*, Nov. 24, 1997.

36. See "Rubber Workers with Nerves of Steel," *Business Week*, Dec. 18, 1995, 44.

37. OTA, *Competing Economies: America, Europe, and the Pacific Rim* (Washington, D.C.: GPO, 1991).

Amarante, Sal, 131, 132
American Federation of Labor (AFL): growth of, 16–17; membership of, 17; merger with CIO, 18; NAACP attacks against, 344 (n. 81)
American Federation of Labor–Congress of Industrial Organizations (AFL-CIO), 84, 348 (n. 79); AFL-CIO Organizing Institute, 300; Burke-Hartke law and, 203–4; criticisms of, 106; formation of, 18; on growth rate, 33; on high wages and exports, 334 (n. 92); on tax cuts, 34; Title VII and, 88
American Iron and Steel Institute (AISI), 125, 219; Committee on Foreign Relations, 219; Committee on International Trade, 219; on European steel measures, 266; 1976 suit on Japan and, 233–34; on quotas, 224, 370 (n. 96); on Reagan investment program, 274; on steel concessions, 204; on unemployment, 276
Antitrust laws: Celler-Kefauver Act of 1950, 210, 312; investment strategies and, 368 (n. 63); Kennedy support for, 32; Sherman Anti-Trust Act of 1890, 11; small producers vs. consumers and, 329 (n. 15); Supreme Court ruling on merger of Kinney Shoe and Brown Shoe (1962), 210–11; tradition of, 329 (n. 14); U.S. Department of Justice and, 235. *See also* Monopoly, steel industry
Apprentice programs, 167, 172, 356–57 (n. 22), 358 (n. 63)
Area Redevelopment Act (ARA), 71, 239
Armco Steel, 12, 32, 213, 235, 288, 292
Arnold, Thurman, 309, 386 (n. 4), 387 (n. 5)
Asia: economic crisis in, 307, 323
Askew, Reubin O., 257
Atallah, Al, 141
Atlantic Monthly, 262, 302
Atlantic Steel, 192, 344 (n. 81)
American Telephone and Telegraph (AT&T), 173
Audit and Review Committee, 173, 175, 179, 181
Auto industry: Carter on, 380 (n. 58); imports and, 218; Japan and, 278; labor contracts of, 30; layoffs in, 125, 278. *See also* United Autoworkers of America

Automation. *See* Mechanization
Ayoub, Edmund, 231

Baby boomer generation: politics of, 262–63
Back pay issues, 156, 158, 162, 165–66, 173–74, 359 (nn. 73, 74), 361 (n. 28)
Bailer, Lloyd, 143
Baker, James A., III, 282
Bakke case. *See Regents of the University of California v. Bakke*
Balance of payments deficit, 202
Balanoff, Jim, 180
Baldanzi, George, 221
Baldrige, Malcolm, 281, 290
Ball, George W., 199, 200
Baltimore: as CORE target city, 138
Banking industry: role in conglomerate movement, 213, 242, 249–50
Bank of America, 221
Bankruptcy petitions, 297–98, 384 (n. 87)
Barnett, Donald F., 293
Basic Steel Industry Conference, 296
Bator, Francis, 200–201
Baxter, William, 289–90
Baylor, Lloyd, 141
Bean, Louis H., 13–14
Becker, George, 303
Bell, Daniel, 9, 261, 302
Bell, Griffin, 189, 246
Belton, Robert, 113, 175
Bentsen, Lloyd, 262–63
Berg, Richard, 102
Bergsten, Fred, 204
Berkowitz, Edward, 330 (n. 31)
Berle, Adolph A., 309
Bernstein, Meyer, 27, 92, 225–26, 227, 354 (n. 75), 371 (n. 112)
Bethlehem Steel: affirmative action and, 128–29, 139; courts and, 316; expansion of, 14; foreign steel companies and, 291; grievance processes of, 129–30; growth of, 12; Justice Department and, 131; labor-management teamwork and, 305–6; layoffs of, 235; litigation and, 121; product line of, 297; under Reagan, 277; relief petition to ITC by, 281–82; on seniority rights, 129; steel price increases and, 32, 209, 367 (n. 56); transfer rights at, 140, 142–44; on USX and EC quotas,

288; western expansion of, 213. *See also* Burns Harbor; Lackawanna; Sparrows Point

Bhagwati, Jagdish, 322

Biemiller, Andrew J., 82

Bierman, Leonard, 116, 117, 172

Bigotry: in Birmingham, 67; black unemployment and, 4, 38, 88. *See also* Discrimination

Bird, John, 154

Birmingham: bigotry in, 67; children's march, 37–38, 61; desegregation process in, 59–66; effect of bombing in, 81; 1963 city council elections in, 62. *See also* Tennessee Coal, Iron, and Railroad Company (TCI)

Birmingham Downtown Improvement Association, 59, 66

Birmingham Labor Council, 60, 62

Birmingham World, 57, 61

Bittner, Van, 16, 17

Blackmun, Harry A., 188, 362 (n. 68)

Black Panther Party, 174

Black Power, 138

Blacks: benefits of transfer/seniority litigation to, 142–44; on consent decrees, 179; on CORE, 139; promotion of as cranemen, 99–100; damage ideology and, 351–52 (n. 17); educational levels of, 45; as grievancemen, 44, 55, 100, 140; grievances of, 105; hiring of, 104, 107, 118, 119, 155, 315; labor testing and, 160; LOP and, 99, 100–101, 348 (n. 86); mechanization and, 77; as millwrights, 99; seniority systems and, 100, 105, 118–19, 132–33; unionized vs. nonunionized contractors and, 151–52, 356–57 (n. 22). *See also* Mechanization; Seniority systems; Steelworkers

Black unemployment: in postwar U.S., 313; bigotry and, 4, 38, 88; causes of, 67, 69, 76, 87, 316; Heller on, 70; increase in, 38; under Nixon, 148–49; rates of, 27, 336, 342 (n. 29); S. 1937 on, 78; urban crisis and, 123–24. *See also* Unemployment, U.S.

Black Workers Congress, 135

Block, Philip D., 222

Bloom, Ronald, 303

Blough, Roger M., 20–21, 97, 105; as chair-man of U.S. Steel, 23, 67; Construction Users' Anti-Inflation Roundtable and, 150; on investment tax credit, 33; price increases and, 209; on profits, 36; on urban crisis, 125; on U.S. Steel and steel price increases, 31, 32; on wages and prices, 334 (n. 108)

Blount, Winston, 150

Bluestone, Barry, 322

Blumenthal, W. Michael, 232, 234, 251

Blumrosen, Alfred, 103, 106, 109, 111, 113, 347 (n. 59)

Boeing, 221

BOF (basic oxygen furnace), 215–16, 288. *See also* Steel industry, U.S.: modernization of

Boggs, Hale, 368 (n. 68)

Bonior, David, 283

"Border taxes," 207

Borrus, Michael, 302

Bosworth, Barry, 234

Bourg, Emile, 56

Boutwell, Albert, 61, 62

Bowron, Paul, Jr., 48, 67

Brandt, Willy, 342 (n. 33)

Branscom, Russell, 128

Brazil: steel exports of, 281, 294, 382 (n. 33)

Bredhoff, Elliot, 185

Brennan, Peter, 172

Brennan, William J., 183, 190

Brinkley, Alan, 309–10, 387 (n. 9)

British Steel Company, 207, 234, 288, 306

Brock, William E., 282, 286

Brooks, Walter S., 138

Brown, William, 173, 360 (n. 15)

Brown Shoe Company, 210

Brubaker, Otis, 21, 24–25, 92

Bryant, Leo, 100

Brzezinski, Zbigniew, 231, 234

Bullard, Hiram, 97, 98, 106–7

"Bump-back" rights, 111, 352 (n. 30)

Bumping-up process, 164, 178, 349 (n. 92)

Bundy, McGeorge, 28

Bureau of Labor Statistics, 150, 152

Bureau of National Affairs (BNA), 95–96

Bureau of the Budget, 86, 333 (n. 75). *See also* Office of Management and Budget

Burger, Warren, 188, 189, 190, 191

Burke, Walter, 376 (n. 67)

332 (n. 72); and elections of 1968, 355 (n. 3); and elections of 1982, 282–83; influence on steel industry of, 3–4, 21, 22; labor influence in, 16–17; price rigidity and, 20; on public employment, 147; support for industrial policy, 263; turn to right by, 300; War on Poverty and, 75

Dennis, Ivory, 140, 142, 144

Depreciation schedules, 14, 19, 33, 239. *See also* Taxation

Deregulation, 230–31, 265

Dick, Andrew R., 385 (n. 96)

Dillon, C. Douglas, 29, 34

Dirksen, Everett, 82–83, 84, 85, 86, 190

Discrimination: as cause of black unemployment, 67, 69, 76; civil rights organizations on, 183–86; courts on, 315; inadequacy as explanation for black unemployment, 87; issue of past, 110–14, 143, 144, 157, 162–63; nondiscrimination clauses and, 50, 52, 96; race relations and, 340 (n. 1); racial statistics and, 189; reverse, 188; testing as, 83, 362 (n. 51); as unfair labor practice, 343 (n. 66); unions on, 160, 183–86, 343 (n. 66), 347–48 (n. 72); USWA on, 96, 183–86. See also *Regents of the University of California v. Bakke*; *United Steelworkers v. Weber*

Disparate impact: theory of, 184–85

District 31 Committee to Defend the Right to Strike, 180

Diversification. *See* Steel industry, U.S.: diversification in

Doeringer, Peter B., 112, 113, 115

Dollar, U.S.: impact of value of, 29, 201–2, 204, 205, 251, 256, 276, 318, 381 (n. 9)

Donald, Hershel, 131

Donovan, Ray, 281

Douglas, Paul, 22, 27, 225

Douglas, William O., 332 (n. 64)

Drayton, William, Jr., 267

Dukakis, Michael, 300

Dumping, 236–37, 256–58, 279, 378 (n. 22), 386 (n. 121). *See also* Imports

Duncan, Charles, 102

Duncan, Clarence, 54, 56, 57, 58

Du Pin Calmon, Paulo, 385 (n. 99)

Durr, Virginia, 41, 64

Eads, George, 267, 283

Eastern Airlines, 299

Eastern European immigrants, 123, 127, 129, 136–37

Eastland, James, 82

Eclecticism: in historical analysis, 328 (n. 8)

Economic Development Administration (EDA), 239, 248, 249–50, 376 (n. 79)

Economic Employment Opportunity Commission (EEOC), 69, 79, 86, 87; cease-and-desist powers and, 149, 360 (n. 15); complaints filed with, 348 (n. 78); Crown Zellerbach and, 116–17; endorsement of LDF-TCI suit by, 112; formulation of seniority guidelines by, 111; holding action by, 110; inertia of, 107–8; limitations of, 102–3, 108; members of, 101–2; Nixon appointments to, 173; retrospective remedies and, 113–14; role of unions and, 346 (n. 47); on seniority systems, 186; service industries and, 118; Title VII compliance and, 194, 355 (n. 9); U.S. Steel negotiations with, 117–18

Economic Policy Group, 263

Economic Recovery Tax Act, 274

Economic Report of the President: for 1957, 20; for 1980, 256

Economic Revitalization Board, 264

Eggert, Bob, 31

Ehrlichman, John, 151, 152

Eisenhower, Dwight David: economy policies of, 19–20, 22, 198–99; 1959 steel strike and, 23–24

Eisner, Robert, 284

Eizenstat, Stuart: on balanced budget, 263–64; congressional steel caucus and, 254; on industrial policy, 265, 268; on inflation, 232–33; on TAA, 240; on TPM, 238, 257

Electric furnace, 293–94, 369 (n. 78)

Emergency Committee for American Trade (ECAT), 221, 365 (n. 22)

Emergency Employment Act of 1967, 124

Employment: civil rights and, 70–71, 79–80, 126, 192–95; full, 12–13; future of steel industry and, 1–2, 108–9; impact of imports on, 219–20; Justice Department and, 126; Keynesian economics on distribution of, 38; public, 27, 71, 147, 153;

Fortune, 8, 127, 229, 321
Foy, Lewis, 260
France: steel production in, 208
Franks v. Bowman Transportation, 183
"Freedom Bus Ride" (CORE), 139–40
Friedman, Milton, 150, 152, 279
Fuller, Alex, 94, 111, 133
Fullilove v. Klutznick, 191–92

Galbraith, James K., 385 (n. 99)
Galbraith, John Kenneth, 10, 38, 200, 212
Garrett, R. E., 66
Garrett, Sylvester, 98
Garvey, Robert, 294
Gary Works, 58. See also U.S. Steel
    Corporation
Gass, Oscar, 200
Gaston, A. G., 61
General Agreement on Tariffs and Trade
    (GATT), 198, 259, 365 (n. 14)
General Motors, 35, 216, 221, 248; black
    workers of, 39; Japanese steel imports of,
    304; on steel labor contract, 296
General Services Administration, 173
Gephardt, Richard, 283
Germany, Eugene B., 21
Germany: steel production in, 207–8
Ghettos: organizing in black, 138
Gibbons, Sam, 301
Gilder, George, 321
Gilliam, Dee, 141
Gilpin, Robert, 384 (n. 70)
Ginsburg, Bob, 256–57
Ginzburg, Eli, 79
Glass-Steagall Act of 1933, 213
Global steel industry, 205–8, 218
Goebel, Thomas, 386 (n. 4)
Goldberg, Arthur J.: as lawyer for USWA,
    18; on 1962 steel agreement, 32; as secre-
    tary of labor, 26, 27, 30, 31; as Supreme
    Court justice, 71, 335 (n. 109)
Goldstein, Barry, 166
Gombos, Frank, 134
Gordon, Colin, 387 (n. 10)
Gott, Edwin H., 155, 222
Gottesman, Michael: EEOC and, 103, 106,
    111; Fairfield and, 165; Hill and, 177;
    Lackawanna and, 129; on Pointer, 161; as
    USWA attorney, 103, 129; on Weber case,
    189, 190

Grace, Eugene, 205
Graham, Hugh, 125, 356 (n. 14)
Graham, Richard A., 102, 103
Graham, Thomas C., 289
Great Society programs, 75–76. See also
    War on Poverty
Green, William, 17
Greenberg, Jack, 113; on EEOC, 102; on
    EEOC seniority guidelines, 112; as LDF
    director, 91; on LDF exclusion from con-
    sent decrees, 175; on litigation, 119–20;
    on plant seniority, 116; rejects union
    cooperation, 116; on seniority cases, 186;
    on U.S. Steel lawsuit, 110
Grievancemen: blacks as, 44, 55, 100, 140;
    TCI trial and, 161
Grievance process, 52, 118; in TCI, 55–57,
    58, 97–99, 161; USWA and, 94, 97–99
Griffin, James M., 138, 244
Griggs v. Duke Power Co., 184
Griswold, Erwin, 78, 79
Gross national product: decline of, 251,
    276, 329 (n. 19); growth of, 25, 34, 229–30
Guardian, 174
Gurley, Ralph, 58
Gwartney, James D., 157–58
Gyohten, Toyoo, 287

Haig, Alexander, 278
Hanes, Arthur, 60
Hanley, Dexter L., 141, 142, 143
Hardy, William, 113–14, 119, 158, 165–66
Harrington, Michael, 73, 341 (n. 15)
Harris, Patricia, 248
Harris, Seymour, 200
Harris, Thomas, 84, 85
Harrison, Bennett, 322
Hart, Gary, 300
Hartke, Vance, 219–20
Harvard Law Review, 114–15
Has Globalization Gone Too Far? (Rodrik),
    322
Haughton, Ronald W., 349 (n. 92)
Hawkins, Augustus, 185
Hayes International Corporation, 66
Head Start, 74
Heimlich, Richard, 236, 259
Heintz, John, 281, 286
Heller, Walter: on potential steel strike,
    30; on steel industry modernization, 35;

purchase by, 245–46, 247; minimills and, 306; purchase of J&L by, 212; Republic merger with, 289–90

Lucy, Autherine, 49

Lundine, Stanley, 283

Lyford, Joseph P., 76

Lykes, 212, 241–42, 245–46, 247, 368 (n. 68)

Lynch, Leon, 354 (n. 75)

Lynd, Staughton, 244, 245, 247, 248

Lynn, Leonard H., 216

Lynne, Seybourn, 157

McBride, Lloyd, 247, 259, 265, 271, 285, 376 (n. 67)

McCarthy, Eugene, 26–27

McClellan Committee, 22–23

McCracken, Paul W., 150, 151

McCray, Wade, 188

McCreedy, Ward, 143

McDonald, David J., 18; adjustment assistance and, 225; on black grievances, 56; Blough and, 23; election defeat and, 92; Heller and, 35; on hiring system, 58; Kefauver committee and, 21; 1962 negotiations, 31; nondiscrimination clause and, 52; support for FEPC, 79; on Title VII compromises, 85; on Title VII implementation, 89; on use of union funds as bail money, 63

McGrath, Paul, 290

McKinstry, Luther, 100, 161, 167

McKissick, Floyd, 138, 356 (n. 12)

McLaren, Richard, 212

McLin, Ernest, 48, 55–56

McLouth Steel, 216, 276, 384 (n. 87)

McNamara, Robert, 209

Mallick, Earl W., 97

Maloy, Elmer, 43

The Managerial Revolution (Burnham), 211–12

Manpower Development and Training Act of 1962 (MDTA), 27–28, 71

Manpower programs, 72–73, 74, 87, 125

The Manpower Revolution, 71

Manufacturing: decline of, 40, 260–61, 268, 301, 319, 336 (n. 13)

Manufacturing Matters (Zysman and Cohen), 302

Marathon Oil, 287

March on Washington, 79–80

Marcuse, Herbert, 10, 329 (n. 12)

Marshall, Burke, 61, 84, 85, 109

Marshall, F. Ray, 236, 244, 263, 265, 270

Marshall, Paul, 245, 246–47

Marshall, Paule, 10

Marshall, Thurgood, 183

Marshall Plan, 198, 364 (n. 3)

Martin, Cathie, 381 (n. 15)

Martin, James, 82

Martin, William, 33

Maryland Freedom Union (MFU), 138

Means, Gardiner, 20, 21, 29

Means testing, 268

Meany, George, 79, 204, 264, 377 (n. 9)

Mechanization, 108–10, 313–14, 341 (n. 15), 342 (n. 33); blacks and, 77; BOF and, 224; displaced workers and, 28, 54, 108–9, 127, 224–25, 336 (n. 127); impact of wages on, 25, 50; labor migration and, 39–40, 314; paper industry and, 116; skip car operators and, 348 (n. 85); societal impacts of, 122; tobacco industry and, 114, 115–16; trade and, 319; unions and, 25

Mergers: banks and, 213, 249; conglomerate, 211–12, 241–42, 245–46, 247, 289–91; regulatory traditions resulting from, 11, 14, 210–11

Merrill Lynch, 275

Meta, John F., 131

Meyer, Jared, 358 (n. 44)

Michels, Willi, 226

Miller, G. William, 258

Millwright helper, case study of, 99

Minimills, 2, 293–94, 303, 369 (n. 78), 369 (n. 84)

Mining industry: Alabama, 40–41, 49; U.S., 25

Ministry of International Trade and Industry, Japan (MITI), 206–7, 216, 217, 233, 292, 366 (n. 43). *See also* Japan

Minority set-asides, 191–92, 250

Mintz, Benjamin, 126

Mitch, William, Jr., 56

Mitchell, Clarence, 79, 81; on EEOC commissioners, 102; on Katzenbach and Marshall, 85; as NAACP lobbyist, 51; reaction to Philadelphia plan, 356 (n. 14); support for Brown, 360 (n. 15)

Mitchell, James P., 208

Mitchell, John, 130, 155, 212

Newton, Demetrius, 113, 160
New York Times, 67, 139
Nicholls, William H., 40
Nichols, Johnny, 94
Newly industrializing countries (NICs), 232, 280, 291–92, 383 (n. 52)
Nippon Kokan (NKK), 290
Nippon Steel, 207, 233, 292
Niskanen, William A., 278, 286
Nixon, John, 105, 107, 109
Nixon, Richard Milhous, 147; CETA and, 268; economic policies of, 202–3, 204, 356 (n. 14), 370 (n. 105); EEOC appointments of, 173; on inflation, 149–50; racial policies of, 148–53; steel industry under, 223–24
Nixon Reconsidered (Hoff), 355 (n. 9)
Nordhaus, William D., 236
Norman, David L., 156
Northrup, Herbert R., 104, 124–25
Norton, Eleanor Holmes, 186
Noyce, Robert, 285
Nucor, 294, 303

Office of Contract Compliance (OFCC), 86, 103–4, 116, 139–40, 143, 344 (n. 75); consent decrees and, 172–73; on craft procedures, 187; Order No. 4 of, 154–55; quota requirements of, 172–73, 187; on *Teamsters*, 186; Title VII compliance and, 194. *See also* President's Committee on Equal Employment Opportunity (PCEEO)
Office of Economic Opportunity (OEO), 73–74
Office of Management and Budget (OMB), 151, 375 (n. 53)
Office of Minority Business Enterprise (OMBE), 149, 356 (nn. 11, 12); black capitalism and, 149
Office of Price Administration, 12
Offshore production: consequences of, 304–5
Ogawa, Kunio, 275
Oliver, Bill, 51
O'Mahoney, Joseph, 20, 21
Open hearth furnace, 215
Operation Dixie, 17, 159
Operation New Birmingham, 66
Organization for Economic Cooperation and Development (OECD): on importance of 1962 labor negotiations, 30; steel committee of, 370 (n. 93); on tax cuts, 34
Organization of Petroleum Exporting Countries (OPEC), 5, 379 (n. 43)
The Other America (Harrington), 73

Packer, Arnold, 263
Paper industry, 116–17
Parker, Charles, 192
Patman, Wright, 13, 21
Patterson, James T., 122, 328 (n. 8)
Patterson, John, 49, 64
Pay Advisory Board, 377 (n. 9)
Pearson, Virgil L., 54–55, 58, 105, 107
Pease, Don J., 286
Pension Benefit Guarantee Commission (PBGC), 298, 384 (n. 88)
Pension plans, 298, 330 (n. 31)
Perkins, E. C., 185
Peterson, Dean, 220
Peterson, Peter G., 202, 302, 365 (n. 22)
Philadelphia plan. *See* Affirmative action: Philadelphia plan for
Phillips, Willie George, 48, 100, 346 (n. 36)
Piore, Michael, 294
Pitts, Lucius, 61
Plant closings, 235, 253
Plato, Edward E., 142, 170
Plotke, David, 311, 327 (n. 2)
Pointer, Samuel C., 156–57, 161–65, 173, 179, 186, 358 (n. 63)
Pointer decree, 162–68
Pollak, Stephen, 126, 129
Pollution mandates, 243, 261. *See also* Environmental issues
Posco (Pohang Iron and Steel Company), 235, 280, 291, 382 (n. 31)
Pottinger, J. Stanley, 172
Poverty: automation and, 109; economics of, 75–76
Powell, Adam Clayton, Jr., 79
Powell, John H., Jr., 172, 173
Powell, Lewis, 188, 190, 191, 360 (n. 15)
Powers, N. Thompson ("Tom"), 67, 189–90
President's Advisory Committee on Labor-Management Policy, 26
President's Committee on Equal Employment Opportunity (PCEEO): compliance with Executive Order 10925 and,

Silicon Valley, 285, 301
Simms, Leander, 142
Skip car operators, 348 (n. 85)
Skrentny, John David, 355 (n. 8)
Sloss-Sheffield, 40–41, 66
Small Business Administration (SBA), 250
Smith, Fred, 220
Smith, Gerald, 139, 141
Smith, Grover, Jr., 106, 161, 347 (n. 59)
Smith, Howard, 81
Smith, James W.: on COLA vs. stock-ownership, 271; on International Harvester shutdown, 249; on steel industry future, 269–70, 380 (n. 63); on steel productivity, 228; on WREDA, 243–44; on Youngstown issues, 247
Smith, Roger B., 296
Smyer, Sidney W., 60, 65
Social welfare: collective bargaining and, 16, 312–13; unions and, 28
Solomon, Anthony, 222, 248
Solomon, Peter, 263
Solomon plan, 239–40, 257, 265
Solomon Task Force (Special Task Force on Steel), 235–41, 243
Sorensen, Ted, 235–36, 334 (n. 97)
The South: development and conditions of, 39–41, 313; manufacturing in, 336 (n. 13); unionization in, 17
Southern Christian Leadership Conference (SCLC), 38, 61, 89–90
South Works plant, 235. See also U.S. Steel Corporation
Sparkman, John, 40
Sparrows Point, 5, 136–45; DOD monitoring of violations at, 139; hiring system at, 137, 170; seniority and transfer issues at, 142–43; strike at, 136; transfer rights at, 140–41; worker diversity at, 136–37. See also Bethlehem Steel
Special Committee on Unemployment, U.S. Senate (1959), 26–27, 332 (n. 73)
Special Task Force on Steel (Solomon Task Force), 235–41
Special Trade Representative (STR), 200, 204, 282
Specialty steel, 373 (n. 20)
Specter, Arlen, 281
Specter, Russell, 134
Speer, Edgar: on foreign counter-cyclical

exporting, 233–34; as president of U.S. Steel, 222; retirement of, 253–54; on steel industry expansion, 222, 239–40, 251; on steel industry status, 229; on transportation issues, 375 (n. 54)
Spencer Works, 369 (n. 82)
Spivey, C. Thomas, 37, 56, 57, 67
The Stages of Economic Growth: A Non-Communist Manifesto (Rostow), 28–29
Star Wars, 301
State Department. See U.S. Department of State
"State of the Race" conference (1965), 89–90
Stebenne, David, 335 (n. 109)
Steele v. Louisville & N.R.R., 348 (n. 72)
Steel fundamentalism, 18–22, 30–36, 232–33
Steel industry, U.S.: acceptance of consent decrees, 171–72; antidiscrimination clause and, 50, 52; antitrust policy and, 210–13, 245–47, 289–91; ARA loans to, 27; BOF and, 215–17, 288; capital needs of, 239, 241, 266–67, 270; capital/output ratios, 21; case study of millwright helper in, 99; crisis of 1977, 232–35; critics of monopoly of, 11–12, 21, 218; decline in capacity of, 31, 33, 228, 258, 276, 294–95, 378 (n. 20); diversification in, 212, 287–88, 291–94, 303; employment cost per unit of output, 334 (n. 98); expansion of capacity of, 8, 13–14, 22, 216–17, 335 (n. 126); exports and, 29, 303; foreign steel companies and, 291–94; global, 205–8, 218; growth of, 12, 49; impact of recessions on, 22, 229–30, 271, 275–76; industrial policy for, 265–71, 273; labor contracts of, 24, 31, 209, 228, 296–99; labor relations under Reagan and, 295–300; laissez-faire policies and, 287–91; layoffs, 235; leadership changes in, 222; LOP in, 45–46; macroeconomic policy and, 208–10; modernization of, 214–19; national policy for, 286–87; oligopolies in, 20, 214–15; operations of, 7–8, 45; plant closings, 235, 253; price controls in, 20–21, 209–10; product cycle theory, 378 (n. 30); profits, 20, 31–32, 36, 270, 291; profits for 1980 in, 381 (n. 4); reaction to Solomon plan, 239–40; reasons for resurrection of, 303–4; reconstruction

under Reagan, 291–95; socialization of costs in foreign, 21; government relations, 11–15; support for Reagan, 271; tax cuts and, 35–36, 218; on TPMs, 259–60; transportation issues, 243–44; U.S. foreign policy and, 4, 5, 6, 29, 35; unemployment and, 31, 35; unionization of, 12; on VRAs, 222; wage control by government, 12; western, 213–14; work culture changes in, 99–101; working-class progress and, 9. *See also* Seniority systems; Strikes; *names of individual companies*

Steel Survival Strategies conference of 1994, 303

Steel Tripartite Advisory Committee (STAC), 265, 268, 269–70

Steelworkers: on consent decrees, 178–79; decline in numbers of, 195, 305; "whiteness" and, 346 (n. 36); female, 195; living conditions of, 42, 62; profile of average, 8–9; racial differences in educational levels of, 45; unemployment of, 25

Steel Workers Organizing Committee, 12. *See also* United Steelworkers of America

Stevens, John Paul, 188, 190

Stewart, John G., 83

Stewart, Potter, 182, 183, 188, 189–90, 360 (n. 19)

Stigler, George, 211

Stinson, G. A., 217, 369 (n. 82)

Strategic Defense Initiative, 301

Strauss, Robert S., 231, 232, 236, 248, 270

Strevel, Howard, 37; appointment to Birmingham, 46; consent decrees and, 170; on millwright cases, 99; 1962 contract and, 53; on Fairfield litigation, 155–56; role in racial changes, 47–49; support for McDonald, 94; threats against, 58; on union-endorsed political candidates, 63; on Wallace, 64

Strict-scrutiny test, for set-asides, 363 (n. 76)

Strikes: impact of threats of, 227–28, 332 (n. 64); industry demands in 1959, 23; at Korf, 192; at Lackawanna, 133; quarry miners, 49; 1959, 22–26; at Sparrows Point, 136; at TCI, 46; against Tenneco, 193; USWA against USX, 298–99; postwar wave of, 16

Strohmeyer, John, 127

Strong, Curtis, 94, 140

Student Non-Violent Coordinating Committee (SNCC), 80–81, 90

Sullivan, Leon, 250, 356 (n. 12)

Sullivan, William, 244

Sumitomo Metals, 292, 306

Summer, Clyde, 112

Supplementary unemployment benefits (SUBs), 16, 296

Supply-side economics, 274–75

Supreme Court, 348 (n. 72), 359 (n. 73); "affected class" issue and, 119; on back pay, 174; *Bakke* case and, 187–88; on mergers, 210–11; on price fixing, 11; on quotas, 188–89; on seniority, 169, 181–83; and Taft-Hartley injunction in 1959 strike, 24; Teamsters appeal to, 181–83; on Title VII and seniority, 169, 181–83; on *Weber*, 188–91

Sweeney, John, 300

Swindle, James, 46, 53

Sylvester, Edward C., Jr., 116, 126, 140, 352 (n. 19)

Taft-Hartley Act of 1947, 17, 24, 312

Takas, Vincent, 132

Target City project (CORE), 137–39

Tariffs, impact of, 199–200, 204, 207, 225, 233

Taxation: accelerated depreciation and, 14, 19, 33, 239; "border taxes," 207; capital gains, 374 (n. 38); foreign nationals and, 203; profits and, 365 (n. 14); Reagan tax bill and, 274, 276–78; TCI and, 42–43; value-added, 364 (n. 12). *See also* Investment tax credit; Tax cuts

Tax-code socialism, 277

Tax cuts, 22, 32–34, 35–36, 70, 72, 201, 218, 238–39, 255, 314, 317; business community on, 34, 278; Kemp-Roth cut, 274

Taylor, George, 26

TCI. *See* Tennessee Coal, Iron, and Railroad Company

Teamsters, 181–83, 185, 186, 371 (n. 108)

Technological change. *See* Mechanization

Temper mill, 53–54

Tenneco, 193. *See also* Newport News Shipbuilding and Dry Dock Company

Tennessee Coal, Iron, and Railroad Company (TCI): black hiring at, 104, 107, 118,

119, 155; EEOC and, 112; employment peaks at, 50; Executive Order 10925 and, 52, 66–67; grievances policy of, 55–57, 58, 97–99, 161; litigation and, 153–57, 157–68; location of, 41; monitoring of compliance of, 56, 67, 101–8; NAACP protests against, 105–7; product lines of, 41; on quotas, 155; reorganization of, 345 (n. 27); strikes against, 46, 47–49; taxation and, 42–43; temper mill of, 53–54; unions and, 43; USWA and, 96–99, 158; *Whitfield* and, 109–10. *See also* U.S. Steel Corporation

Tennessee Valley Authority (TVA), 56, 67

Testing, labor: cultural bias and, 98–99; Motorola and, 83; USWA and, 98, 160, 362 (n. 51); *Griggs* and, 184; companies and, 140

Texas Instruments, 221

Texas Oil and Gas, 287

Textron, 211

Theobald, Robert, 341 (n. 15)

Third World Workers Organizing Committee, 135

Thompson, Walter, 179

Thornton, John, 180

Thrasher, Bruce, 48, 57, 106; on Birmingham demonstrations, 62; on discrimination in workplace, 99; on expansion of steel capacity, 228; on LOP, 100; Tenneco and, 193; threats against, 58; as union witness in TCI litigation, 158–59, 160–61; in USWA, 95; Wallace and, 64; on Wiebel, 67

Thurmond, Strom, 192

Thurow, Lester, 301

Tiffany, Paul, 332 (n. 63)

TIME (T.I.M.E.-D.C., Inc.), 181–82, 221

Tin mill, 53, 55–57, 58

Title VII, Civil Rights Act of 1964, 79–88, 314; AFL-CIO and, 88; CEA on, 86; civil rights vs. labor framework in, 194; courts on, 114, 315; employers and, 104–5, 124; enforcers of, 86–87, 101–8, 125–26, 194, 363 (n. 74); impact of notion of affluence on, 4–5; implementation of, 69–70, 89, 91–96; industrial data for, 104; Johnson on, 81; Keynesian economics impact on, 86; opponents of, 82, 83–84, 85, 86; past discrimination and, 110–13, 143, 144,

157, 162–63; provisions of, 111; quotas and, 187; retrospective remedies and, 112–13, 153; S. 1937 alternative, 76–78; scope of, 355 (n. 9); seniority and, 82, 117–18, 129; supporters of, 78, 79, 81; Supreme Court on, 169, 181–83, 188–90; voluntarism and, 189, 363 (n. 74). *See also* Economic Employment Opportunity Commission (EEOC); Office of Contract Compliance (OFCC)

Tobacco industry: mechanization and, 114, 115–16

Tobin, James, 284, 333 (n. 81)

Tokyo Round, 204, 232, 279. *See also* Multilateral trade negotiations

Tower, John, 84

Trade Act of 1974, 204–5, 228, 240, 280, 372–73 (n. 13); Section 201 of, 281–82

Trade adjustment assistance (TAA), 224–25, 240, 267–68

Trade Agreements Act of 1979. *See* Multilateral trade negotiations

Trade and Tariff Act of 1984, 286; Title VIII of, 286–87

Trade deficit: U.S., 231–32, 251, 278, 306, 385 (n. 104)

Trade Expansion Act of 1962, 59, 224, 240; criticism of, 200; results of, 202; domestic economy and, 203, 220–21

Trade liberalization: Cold War and, 198; Nixon and, 204; Carter and, 231; Reagan and, 279, 282

"Trade Measures to Increase Supply of Foreign Steel in the U.S. Market" (Strauss), 232

Training programs, 73–74, 190–91, 314. *See also* Manpower programs

Transfers: Bethlehem Steel and, 140, 142–44; in LOP, 45–46; seniority and, 130–31, 133–35, 142–43, 166; workers' reaction to consent decrees and, 177–79

Transnationals. *See* Multinational corporations

Transportation issues, 243–44, 253, 375 (nn. 54, 55)

Trautlein, Donald H., 276

Treaty of Rome, 199, 366 (n. 28)

Trico, 2

Trigger-price mechanism (TPM): computation of, 279–80; effect of, 238, 251;

Europe and, 238, 259; government enforcement of, 238, 256; imports and, 377 (n. 16); industry opposition to, 259–60; proposed expansion of, 257–58

Trilateral Commission, 231

Trucking industry, 181–83. *See also* Teamsters

Truman, Harry S.: CIO and, 17; economic policies of, 198; on steel shortages, 13; USWA and, 17

Tumlir, Jan, 279

Tyson, Laura D'Andrea, 302

Unemployment: European, 240, 306; Japanese, 240, 306; Swedish, 240

Unemployment, U.S.: AISI on, 276; CEA on, 122; Clark on, 26–27; computation of, 341 (n. 13); of ethnic stockyard workers, 123; Nixon on, 152–53; of nonwhites, 336 (n. 2); rates of, 22, 27, 34, 40, 73, 122, 142–43, 230, 276, 282, 314; Special Committee on Unemployment, 26–27; in steel industry, 31, 35, 276, 282; of unskilled population, 72; in Youngstown, 248–49. *See also* Black unemployment

Unions, 15–18; antimonopolists and, 21; antiunion culture and, 305; Communist Party and, 18; expulsion of Communist-led, 18; future tasks of, 323; government interventions and, 12; growth of, 16–17; ideological divisions in, 16–17; Jim Crow, 43; loss of, 306; mechanization and, 25; membership of, 17; mobilization against, 150–51; Nixon on construction, 150–51; organization of, 15, 49–50; organized crime in, 22–23; political weakness of, 17; social welfare and, 28; Taft-Hartley Act and, 17; TCI opposition to, 43; wage classification schedules of, 43, 44. *See also* Discrimination: unions on

United Autoworkers of America (UAW), 16, 66, 93, 203–4, 337 (nn. 19, 28)

United Mineworkers of America (UMW), 15

United States Steel v. H. K. Porter, 154

United States v. Local 189, 350 (n. 98)

United Steelworkers of America (USWA), 17, 95; Ad Hoc Committee of, 94, 105; on affirmative action, 186; on American foreign investment, 203; antidiscrimina-tion clauses of, 50, 96; attorneys for, 56, 103, 129; back pay issues of, 156, 158, 162, 165, 174, 359 (n. 73), 361 (n. 28); on black promotion, 119; blacks on executive committee of, 141–42; on black unemployment, 89; Civil Rights Department of, 93; consent decrees and, 170, 175–76; on craft procedures, 187; on discrimina-tion, 96, 183–86; elections in, 92–93, 94–95, 132, 142, 247; on exports, 334 (n. 92); formation of, 12; givebacks and, 296; grievance process and, 94, 97–99; on high wages and exports, 334 (n. 92); Human Relations Research Committee, 92; impact on southern mills, 43–44; International Executive Board (IEB) of, 170, 171; labor relations of, 384 (n. 82); layoffs and, 16; leverage of, 334 (n. 104); loans and, 270; on Lykes-LTV merger, 246; managerial discretion and, 332 (n. 62); membership of, 15; on mergers, 290–91; NAACP protests against, 105–6, 344 (n. 81); politics and, 285–86; racial quotas and, 190–91; relief petition to ITC by, 281–82; on seniority, 97–99, 142, 349 (n. 92); on Solomon plan, 240–41; on STAC, 269–70; and Sparrows Point problem areas, 140–41; support for Executive Order 10925, 52; support for liberal candidates, 62; support for Trade Expansion Act of 1962, 224; on tax cuts, 35, 270; TCI and, 96–99, 158; on *Team-sters*, 186; Title VII implementation and, 91–96; UAW and, 93; on use of union funds as bail money, 62–63; on U.S. Steel imports, 288; VRA and, 369 (n. 86); Wage Policy Committee of, 92; on wage reductions, 297–98. *See also* Strikes

United Steelworkers v. Weber, 186–92, 363 (n. 73)

Urban crisis, 122–24

Urban liberals, in Congress, 26

U.S. Department of Commerce, 203, 214, 275, 280–81, 292, 378 (n. 22), 382 (n. 36)

U.S. Department of Defense (DOD), 126, 139

U.S. Department of Health, Education, and Welfare (HEW), 74, 250

U.S. Department of Housing and Urban Development (HUD), 248, 250

U.S. Department of Justice, 153; antitrust investigations of, 235; Bethlehem Steel and, 131; civil rights and employment focus of, 126; Lackawanna disputes and, 128; lawsuit against U.S. Steel, 147; LTV and, 376 (n. 63); Lykes-LTV merger and, 245–46, 247; rejection of EEOC steel cases, 113; shift to focus on employment and the North, 126; Teamsters and, 181; on Title VII and layoffs, 184–85

U.S. Department of Labor, 70–71, 74, 139, 250, 356 (n. 22)

U.S. Department of State, 201, 226–27

The U.S. Economy in the 1950s (Vatter), 38

U.S. Employment Service (USES), 27, 73, 268

U.S. International Trade Commission (ITC), 258, 279, 281–82, 286, 382 (n. 36), 386 (n. 121)

U.S. Pipe and Foundry, 66

U.S. Steel Corporation, 1; acquisition of interest in Gunning Housing Corporation, 8; antitrust law and, 11; apprentice programs of, 167; BOF and, 217; Carter and, 363 (n. 79); diversification of, 287–88; Fairfield works of, 41–50; Fairless on, 7; foreign steel companies and, 291, 292, 303; formation of, 11; investments of, 217; labor-management teamwork of, 305; litigation against, 110, 147, 157–68; march against, 105–7; mergers, 290; mining operations of, 40; negotiations with EEOC, 118; 1986–87 lockout by, 299; plant closings and layoffs, 235, 253; price increases and, 31, 32, 209, 367 (n. 56); Q-BOF process and, 369 (n. 76); renaming of, 287; reorganization of, 345 (n. 27); strikes and, 23–24, 297; western plans of, 213; Wilkins on, 105. *See also* Blough, Roger M.; Roderick, David; Tennessee Coal, Iron, and Railroad Company; USX

U.S. Steel–National merger, 289–90

U.S. Tariff Commission, 59, 225

U.S. Trade Act of 1974, 204, 205, 228, 240, 280, 373 (n. 13); Section 201 of, 281–82

USX, 1, 287. *See also* U.S. Steel Corporation

Utilization rates, 233, 259

Value Line, 275

Vance, Cyrus, 257, 258

Vanik, Charles A., 235, 238–39, 255

Vanik Bill (steel quota bill), 226

Vann, David, 157

Vatter, Harold, 38

Verity, William, 234

Vernon, Raymond, 260

Vietnam War, 314, 341 (n. 13)

Vogel, David, 311–12

Vogel, Ezra, 260

Volcker, Paul A., 254; as chairman of Federal Reserve Board, 256, 263, 276, 381 (n. 11); on steel industry and foreign policy, 4

Voluntarism, 189, 363 (n. 74)

Voluntary restraint agreement (VRA), 218–19, 222, 223, 224, 226–27, 282, 286, 369 (n. 86), 370 (n. 105)

Voting Rights Act, 90

Wages: COLA effect on, 270–71, 295–96; construction industry, 150; decline in low-wage work and, 39; decreases in, 16, 289, 297–98; exports and, 334 (n. 92); freezes on, 23, 30; government controls on, 12; impact on mechanization, 25, 50; increases in steel compared to other industries, 30–31, 35, 209–10, 270, 334 (n. 97); under Kennedy, 334 (n. 97); Kennedy on, 30; labor relations and, 295–96; after 1959 strike, 24; "red-circled" rates, 111, 166; service sector, 305, 385 (n. 99); southern, 43; standard for, 377 (n. 9); during World War II, 15

Waggoner, James, 60

Waggoner, Joe, Jr., 255

Wagner, Robert F., 12

Walker, A. F., 97–98, 352 (n. 30)

Wallace, George C., 64–65, 110

Wall Street Journal: on Carter's steel policy, 236, 257; on CORE, 139; on Reagan's economic policies, 275; on sectoral solutions, 262

Ward, Ed, 94

Ware, J. L., 61

War Manpower Commission, 12

War on Poverty, 4, 71–76, 123, 314, 341 (n. 13)

Washington, Booker T., 192